THE BREAD LOVER'S

Bread Machine

COOKBOOK

BETH HENSPERGER

Illustrations by Kristin Hurlin

THE BREAD LOVER'S Bread Machine COOKBOOK

A Master Baker's

300 Favorite Recipes for

Perfect-Every-Time Bread—

From Every Kind of Machine

THE HARVARD COMMON PRESS, BOSTON, MASSACHUSETTS

The Harvard Common Press
535 Albany Street
Boston, Massachusetts 02118

www.harvardcommonpress.com

Printed in the United States of America
Printed on acid-free paper

Library of Congress Cataloging-in-Publication Data
Hensperger, Beth.
   The bread lover's bread machine cookbook : a master baker's 300
favorite recipes for perfect-every-time bread, from every kind of
machine / Beth Hensperger; illustrations by Kristin Hurlin.
      p. cm.
   Includes bibliographical references and index.
   ISBN 1-55832-155-1 (cloth : alk. paper) — ISBN 1-55832-156-X
(pbk. : alk. paper)
   1. Bread. 2. Automatic bread machines. I. Title.
TX769 .H4435 2000
641.8'15—dc21
                                                            99-087358

ISBN: 978-1-55832-156-4

Special bulk-order discounts are available on this and other Harvard
Common Press books. Companies and organizations may purchase
books for premiums or for resale, or may arrange a custom edition, by
contacting the Marketing Director at the address above.

Cover photographs by Eric Roth
Text illustrations by Kristin Hurlin
Cover and book design by Night & Day Design

30 29 28 27 26

ACKNOWLEDGMENTS

My thanks to editors Dan Rosenberg and Laura Rosenberg. Their interest, intelligent comments, commitment, and hard work have made this book a reality. Laura skillfully and patiently worked with me—assisting on every step of editing the multiple manuscript drafts—with friendly encouragement and sensitive advice. Thank you to the publicists and staff at Harvard Common Press who assisted in the preparation, presentation, and publicizing of this cookbook. And thanks to our project manager, Julie Stillman, wielding her red pen, for her expertise in editing and time spent on overall organization.

To my peerless agent, Martha Casselman, my admiration and sincere gratitude for her counsel every step of the way, from proposal to galley and beyond. Her knowledge and talent are invaluable. Thanks to her assistant, Judith Armenta, for her enthusiastic encouragement and, well, just being there.

Thank you to the following contributors; some provided information, others equipment and ingredients, furthering the information available on this new dimension of baking: Susan Anderson of the Regal Corporation; Lisa Brugellis, Welbilt and Appliance Company of America; Jenny Collier, Sunbeam Consumer Affairs; Jeff Hamano, Zojirushi Corporation of America; Dave Oestreicher and Hope Yingst of Hodgson Mill, Inc.; Jim Rogers, Panasonic Corporation; Brinna Sands and P. J. Hamel of King Arthur Flour; Don Stinchcomb of Purity Foods, Inc.; Barbara Westfield of Breadman/Salton; Chuck Williams of Williams-Sonoma; and Randy Watts, President of SAF Consumer Affairs, who donated *cases* of yeast for this project (I used it all!).

I wish to express my appreciation to the following recipe testers and contributors for their helpful suggestions, comments, and encouragement: food writer Lynn Alley; Mary Cech of the Culinary Institute of America at Greystone; Andi Compton; food writer Marcy Goldman; Erin Kovacs; Jaqueline Higuera McMahan; Gayle and Joe Ortiz; Lou Pappas; M. Quento, who donated the first test machine; Meg Rohacek; Suzanne Rosenblum; Helena Rutkowski; Margery Schneider; Barbara and Jerry Smith; David SooHoo and Elaine Corn; Judith Taylor; Chef Greg Topham, East Meets West Catering Company.

And to Bobbe Torgerson, my recipe tester extraordinaire for many years now, who skillfully and consistently tests myriad recipes with a fine mind to detail and a good heart. I owe her more than I can say or than she would admit.

I wish to add a special note on the contributions of the late Mary Anne McCready, whose generous involvement on this project evolved quickly from recipe tester to co-worker. She was the source of inspiration for many of these recipes and kept me turning out the work on a daily basis; the two of us along with the machines lined up on her kitchen counter, sorting through the initial pile of hundreds of recipe ideas. Her husband, George, ate a *lot* of bread. Her spirit resides within.

CONTENTS

AMERICA'S NEW BREAD BOX

The bread machine. Words that strike terror into the hearts of artisan bakers and advocates of hands-on home baking, while conjuring up visions of delight to the ever-growing hordes of baking enthusiasts who claim they would never bake bread without a machine. An all-in-one appliance that is certainly an innovation in a time-honored craft, a bread machine creates fresh, satisfying, full-flavored yeast breads with no compromise of standards. A large part of the reason that people get so much joy from bread machine baking has little to do with the appliance itself, but comes from the deep emotional value of making bread. Bread machine baking brings the same rewards as any other type of baking. Whether you went out and bought a new machine, inherited one from a friend who never used it, or picked one up at a church rummage sale, whether you embrace this method of baking immediately or retain some skepticism, you will be thrilled with the results if you give this appliance a fair run. Bread machine baking boasts a fast-growing number of advocates, and seekers of gastronomic truth certainly now have to include the bread machine next to pasta makers, cappuccino machines, heavy-duty electric mixers, and food processors on their list of innovations in food preparation that are here to stay. Quite simply, bread machines make fantastic bread.

If, like me, you tried years ago to use a bread machine and were disappointed with the quality of the loaves, take heed: There is a new generation of machines that are nothing short of remarkable. Along with improvements to the hardware, a solid batch of knowledge has accumulated about how to work effectively with the medium. The common denominator in the new and growing world of bread machine baking is the same enthusiasm, friendliness, and spirit of generosity that generally mark the baker's realm. With some of its activity newly housed in a plastic body, the old-fashioned skill of baking must add a whole new vocabulary to its jargon.

Bread machines are made now by a dozen manufacturers and come in many more dozens of models, with a variety of features and sizes to choose from. They are not only easy to use, but inspire you to customize your own baking cycles and end up turning out breads that rival supermarket loaves and even some bakeries, with their thin, crisp crusts and even, soft-textured crumb. Bread machine baking requires so little of your time that you can enjoy the luxury of fresh bread every day, the way things ought to be. When all the hassle of baking is removed, you can enjoy the entire process—from shopping for ingredients to hearing the cries of delight from appreciative eaters. With its impressive repertoire of recipes, bread machines can produce bread for everyone and every lifestyle. The bread machine has found a market in many who would otherwise never bake, but enjoy good bread: those with the busiest schedules, like on-the-go moms with little children, bakers who have physical disabilities that might prevent them from preparing bread by hand, and lots of folks, especially men, who love the fact that baking good bread now includes the chance to program digital commands similar to their VCRs. The bread machine has won over many people already skilled at baking by hand, but it has also reached many who were not inspired to learn to bake bread by an older method. Through the bread machine they were introduced to, and are now hooked on, the evocative aroma, taste, and texture of homemade bread.

As someone who was professionally trained as a baker and worked in the field for twenty-five years, naturally I always encouraged fledgling bakers to make bread by hand, using their senses to become familiar with yeast doughs. Once, while teaching a class in this manner, I was approached by a student who was older. "Are you telling me that I can't make bread?" she inquired as I proselytized on the hand-

crafted technique. "I have crippling arthritis and I love to bake. I use either the food processor or the bread machine, and I love the bread I make." She gave me pause to think. Then and there I adapted my opinions and decided that whatever tool could enable a person to make good bread was fine. I began making doughs with an electric mixer, a food processor, and ultimately the bread machine. I found that the practical, mystical, and spiritual elements that make baking satisfying remain the same no matter how you get to the finished loaf.

I have found that bread machine baking is a type of baking unto itself. When you bake with a machine, the technical part of the process is taken out of your hands, which may cause experienced bakers to be concerned about the quality of the loaf that will be produced. But I found, once I began to allow bread machine baking to stand on its own merits and ceased comparing the process to making bread by hand, that the bread machine gave me the freedom to endlessly create and improvise on a few fundamentals. I began to really enjoy the results, too—the wonderful bread! The loaves are different, perhaps, than handmade loaves, but they are beautiful and delicious in their own right. And so, once you've armed yourself with a bit of knowledge, some fresh ingredients, and your beloved machine, I hope you, too, will approach this wonderful new realm of baking with an open mind.

Often described as looking like a leftover robot from *Star Wars*, the maid in a futuristic Jetsons' cartoon, or even a gem tumbler, the bread machine was originally invented to go in small Japanese kitchens, which typically have no room for Western-style baking ovens. Contained in this machine that is the size of an old-fashioned bread box are an internal motor that turns a kneading blade, a nonstick mixing and baking canister, an electric coil to bake the loaf, and a microcomputer that tells the machine how to take your loaf right through the traditionally hands-on procedure. Sophisticated electronics control the motor, temperature, humidity, all of the timing, and can even store a recipe file in the bread machine's memory bank. The machine can weigh anywhere from fifteen to twenty pounds, and definitely commands your visual attention as it sits on the kitchen counter. Once you get used to how different it is from the method of preparing bread by hand—in which you have to be watching, waiting, and noting times, and your constant presence is needed—you will see how convenient this method's minimal handling of the dough is, and how the fixed timing of the rising and baking cycles eliminates guesswork. The machine truly does the work, leaving you free to do something else while your bread is being prepared. The process is nothing short of magical.

I feel compelled to warn you that this type of baking is very addictive. Once I got rid of my anxieties about blowing fuses in my tiny kitchen, and set aside my disgruntled attitude about making bread MY way, I couldn't leave the machine alone. This appliance begged me to use it. When each loaf turned out better than the last, I was glad to have hundreds of recipes to test. The amount of actual hands-on baking time, after deciding which bread to make and assembling the ingredients, is just minutes. And then, aside from putting away the ingredients and wiping up a bit of flour on the counter, there is no cleanup, which is remarkable for a craft that is known for being messy.

To set the process in motion, all you do is assemble, measure, and pour the ingredients into the bread pan that serves as the mixing canister, then push a button to specify a setting and another to program the timer, if you wish. The machine mixes, kneads, deflates, allows for the proper rising time, bakes, and often cools the loaf, all automatically. The machine does it all—you don't need to know how to bake bread to use it.

With a bread machine, a light, high loaf is the result of using a precise, carefully measured liquid-to-flour ratio in conjunction with the machine's perfectly controlled series of risings. The controls may also be set to "Dough Only," so that the machine can be used just for the mixing-kneading-rising process, after which you can shape the loaf yourself and bake it in your home oven for bread that looks more like the loaves you're used to. Most bread machine models now have a specific setting to produce the crisp crust and airy texture characteristic of bakery-style baguettes and artisan breads, although bread machine loaves will differ in shape from their authentic relatives. You may wish to shape these kinds of doughs by hand into whimsically formed dinner rolls or round country-style loaves and then bake them in a conventional oven. You can almost hear the old French baker sighing, *"c'est un scandale!"* at the mere thought of automating his revered techniques.

A loaf of bread made in the machine is, just like handmade bread, superior in nutrition, texture, and taste to its commercially produced, store-bought cousin. Homemade bread is free of additives, colorants, preservatives, and chemical fixatives. Whenever you have such control over what you put in your bread, you are almost guaranteed quality. While hand-wrought loaves boast an appealing visual charm, each loaf baked in the machine is the same shape as its baking pan. Even so, I find that the loaves fresh from the machine have their own special beauty, eliciting oohs and ahhs from the most stalwart bakers. The aroma and sight of homemade bread are powerfully good—just try to resist tearing off the end of one of these still-warm loaves. These sensory experiences are part of baking's pleasure.

In baking, breads are traditionally defined by the kind of flour used, whether they have yeast or not, their shape, and their added flavorings, all of which give each bread its intrinsic char-acter. Within this book, the recipes vary in each of these regards, with something designed for every type of baker—an impressive variety of breads, from the simple and familiar to the in-novative and challenging. There are breads for the health fanatic, breads for those with a sweet tooth, and even breads for those who cannot eat gluten. There are breads loaded with famil-iar and not-so-familiar ingredients, inventive flat breads, and even artisan breads using the old techniques, adapted here for the bread machine. You will recognize the better-known breads, such as egg breads, yeasted white and whole grain breads, pumpernickel and other ryes, and French bread. The rich and evocative sweet holiday breads, breakfast breads, flatbreads and focaccia, and some of the quick breads may be new areas for you to discover. There is a section on baking with commercial bread mixes and one devoted to pizza, a distinct favorite of home bread machine bakers. You

will learn to make them all if you choose. This collection is composed largely of recipes that are made from start to finish in the machine. They are based on classic formulas that never go out of style because they are the prescribed universal laws of baking. Each simple ingredient reveals undertones of flavor created by the time-honored, ageless principles of harmony and balance in baking. Good, fresh ingredients need little to unlock their natural flavors.

When you have made just a few loaves in the bread machine, you will already have acquired the confidence that you are a good baker, and you will happily find that your loaves are suitable for accompanying meals, making sandwiches or toast, or using in other recipes. Whether you bake for daily consump-tion or for the festive holiday, baking with the bread machine is an opportunity to showcase your well-cultivated or newly awakened talents as a baker. If you like ultimate flavor merged with ultimate convenience in homemade bread, this appliance is for you. Baking bread in a bread machine is an easy, satisfying task, and more fun than you can imagine. In the chapter that follows, Orientation, I guide you into the machine's workings and features and through the pantry so you can set your reservations aside and start right now to enjoy baking in your bread machine as much as I do. I wish I could incorporate into these pages the sen-suous aromas of these breads as they are going through their cycles and being baked, but they are for you to discover. So go ahead, push the button, bake bread, enjoy the delectable results, and stand back to collect the compliments.

ORIENTATION

BATTERIE DE CUISINE: KNOW YOUR BREAD MACHINE

T he three sections that follow will help you become familiar with your machine. They demystify the hardware, offer criteria for how to choose a machine, provide customer service telephone numbers for bread machine manufacturers, and help you figure out what types of bread can be made in your machine. There is a lot of practical information here; you will refer to it often.

Taking Stock of Your Machine

Whether you are acquiring a new machine, looking to begin using one that you purchased or received as a gift, or wanting to better utilize the one you've owned for a while, begin with this guide to understanding the components of a bread machine. There are many manufacturers and models of bread machines to choose from. They range from the simple, offering just a few basic cycles, to the more complex, with many cycles and features, and the ideal machine for you depends on what kind of baking you do. This is a place for experimentation. The section on cycles and settings (pages 6 to 11) will help you understand those functions better. Whether simple or complex, it is important for you to know that all bread machines make bread exactly the same way, using the same progression of steps within the cycles. There is a machine for every pocketbook. Prices range from $49 to $249 (sales and discounts are frequently offered), with plenty of models priced in between the economy machines and the sophisticated "luxury" models. Prices generally reflect the number of features the machine has; the more features, the more the machine costs. The prices for the most elaborate and highest

quality machines are now $150 to $249, which is remarkable, since just a few years ago you could pay double that amount for a similar machine. There is no one perfect machine; which machine you use is a very personal decision, and you, the baker, will adapt to your machine quickly. All the machines make great bread.

Before we proceed to the basics given here, I should tell you that there are a few not-so-pleasant characteristics common to all bread machine models. All machines operate at a high noise level during the kneading (how high depends on the action of the motor, and an intense action is desirable). But this is only during the kneading phase, and you will quickly get used to your machine's pings, pangs, bangs, creaks, and bumps. Sometimes the baking is uneven, leaving you with a loaf that is shaped, cooked, or browned differently in different parts. Caution must be used in handling the machine or any parts of it during the baking cycle while the machine body radiates heat. The baked bread may occasionally stick in the baking pan (this generally occurs only with the thinner-walled baking pans). The loaves are oddly shaped as compared to traditional hand-shaped ones, and sometimes a slight depression occurs in the top of the loaf caused by over-rising in the warm machine (this doesn't hurt the loaf, which is still delicious). The bread machine is not total perfection, and some models may be easier to use than others. But you should know that though all machines have their quirks, none of which prevent them from producing good bread, you will quickly learn to work around them. While automatic bread-bakers produce bread the "painless" or "no work" way, they are by no means no-brainers. Be prepared to familiarize yourself with the idiosyncrasies of your machine.

Understanding the following basic components will help acquaint you with your machine, or narrow down the choices to fit your needs.

What are the bread machine's dimensions?

Bread machines are all countertop appliances, but they have a wide variety of dimensions. Consider your counter space; a machine should fit in a safe place with minimal activity around it, as the body is very warm or even hot while functioning. It should rest about 4 inches away from all walls and cupboards. Make sure there is room above to open the lid; most machines are taller than they are wide. Some machines are quite compact and space-efficient, under 14 inches high and 14 inches wide, while others are much larger, like the Zo V20, one of the largest at 17 inches wide, 11½ inches high, and 8½ inches deep. American Harvest makes an even larger side-by-side bucket unit that allows two loaves to bake at the same time.

What size loaf does the machine make?

Although machines are categorized by pound size, the volume of the loaves is really what differs in different size machines. (A loaf that contains nuts and dried fruit, for example, may be the same size as a loaf that is made with just the basic ingredients, but it will weigh more.) Still, it has become the convention of bread machine manufacturers to designate the volume of a machine in terms of a loaf weight, so that is the terminology used throughout this book. A 1-pounder is a small loaf, a 1½-pounder is a medium loaf, and a 2- or 2½-pounder is large. A machine can always make a smaller loaf, but not a loaf larger, than the capacity of its pan. Figure out what your needs are based on how many people will be eating the bread you make. A single person or a couple would consume the 1- or 1½-pound sizes. A medium family would eat the 1½-pound loaf, and for more than four people, a 2-pound loaf is popular (at this writing, it is the top-selling size). There are also a few 2½-pound-loaf machines on the market.

What shape is the loaf? The unconventional loaves that come out of a bread machine take their shape from their baking pans, and each loaf bears the distinctive mark of the automatic bakery—the hole in the bottom created by the kneading paddle. There are three loaf shapes: round or tall cylindrical (this cube shape is popular since it slices perfectly on the horizontal to fit in a toaster or sandwich bag), vertical rectangle (the most common, and similar to a commercial loaf shape but with fuller sides), and long horizontal (the most similar to a large, standard bread pan and considered by some to be the most attractive loaf—these need two blades to mix the entire dough properly). The vertical rectangle is taller than it is wide, and the long horizontal is oblong. (See page 354 for illustrations of the bread pans and the loaves they make.) Though this has nothing to do with the shape, I would also note that some brands have heavier aluminum baking pans than others. Bread bakes most evenly in thicker pans.

Does the lid have a viewing window? Most machines have a small viewing window. While it tends to fog up during the kneading, it does clear again. The window is really good for seeing if the dough has over-risen up to the window and threatens to push open the lid, or for peering in during the baking, when you can't lift the lid. Many veteran bread machine bakers like to be able to completely remove the lid for easy cleaning.

Is the machine a basic or a multifunctional model? There are basic cycles that mix, knead, and bake white bread, fruit and nut breads, and light whole wheats. The newer machines have lots of extras: Jam cycle, Whole Wheat cycle, French Bread cycle, Pizza Dough cycle, and Quick Bread/Cake cycle. If you are into heavier whole wheat and whole grain breads, you will be glad to have a model with a Whole Wheat cycle; it will have the power necessary to drive the blade through heavy doughs. The kneading and rising in this cycle are also geared toward heavier doughs. There is a multipurpose model by Oster that is known for being a great pasta dough maker. Aroma Bread Chef is a rice cooker and yogurt maker, and there is even a model that churns butter! Older models tend to have only the basic features, and some economically priced newer models are rather basic, too. What type of machine you have probably depends on what type of bread you make most.

Basic models may meet all the needs of most home bakers, although extra features can be fun to experiment with. Along with more functions comes the need for more digital programming.

Many of the older machines and a few of the newer machines do not have built-in timers, although they have become quite standard. The timer enables you to delay the start of the cycle so that the bread will be ready when you want it, up to twenty-four hours after you load and program the machine. Some old models don't have a removable kneading blade; I consider it a must to be able to remove and wash it properly. A handful of machines stop when you open the lid; some people prefer this and others dislike it. Some models have an extra crisping or cool-down phase (which sucks the hot air out of the machine, different than Keep Warm), which could be important if you are not around to remove the bread when it is done.

Does the machine have an audible alert to remind you when to add extra ingredients? It is convenient for the basic cycle to beep as a reminder to add embellishments such as raisins or nuts midway through the kneading, so that they are not pulverized during the mixing. A machine can have this feature built into one or many of its cycles. If your machine does not offer this signal, it is easy enough to set your own kitchen timer to add the extras on your own. See page 430 for more information.

Does your machine's digital screen tell you what phase of the cycle it is in? My testers all seemed to like this indicator feature. You don't have to peek, listen, or write down times to gauge where you are. For those who are used to baking by hand, this indicator allows them to orient themselves to what part of the process the machine is in. I tend to use the cycle indicator more often than the timer to judge how close the bread is to being done.

Does your machine have a power saver memory? The power saver lets the machine restart where it left off in the event of a brief blackout or if the plug is accidentally pulled out mid-cycle. If the machine does not have the power saver feature, you would have to start the machine from the beginning of the cycle again instead of resuming the process where it left off. No matter what machine you are using, if a power outage happens during the baking part of a cycle, you won't be able to retrieve the loaf at all. (However, dough could be removed and baked in a conventional oven.) The standard time limit of the power saver memory is 60 minutes.

What information does the owner's manual provide? Look at the manual provided by the manufacturer. A complete and easy-to-understand owner's manual is a real help. This book offers a great deal of information regarding all aspects of bread machine baking, from descriptions of various features, to troubleshooting, to tips for cleanup. Read your owner's manual and become familiar with its contents. It will tell you the important specifics about your machine, such as the order in which ingredients should be added, and how to program the various cycles and the Delay Timer.

Is service support offered for the machine? Most bread machine manufacturers offer a toll-free customer support line to assist you with any

Customer Service Numbers

This list of customer service telephone numbers for the various manufacturers of bread machines is important to keep on hand for any questions that may come up during the operation of your machine, or for repair information.

Aroma: 800-276-6286

Betty Crocker: 800-446-1898

Black & Decker: 800-231-9786

Breadman/Salton: 888-889-0899

DAK: Out of business; no customer service line available.

Franklin Chef: No customer service line available.

GoldStar LG: 800-243-0000

Hitachi: 800-448-2244

Oster/Sunbeam: 800-526-2832

Panasonic/National: 800-211-7262

Pillsbury (MK Seiko): 800-775-4777

Regal: 262-626-2121

Sanyo: 800-421-5013

Toastmaster: 800-947-3744

Welbilt: No customer service line available.

West Bend: 800-367-0111

Williams-Sonoma (MK Seiko): 877-812-6235

Zojirushi: 800-733-6270

troubles that arise in your use of the machine (see page 5 for a list of these numbers). The people who staff these phone lines are generally very knowledgeable. Know the number for your machine's manufacturer, and don't be afraid to use it. While the failure rate of this complex appliance is very low, you should also hold on to your receipt, and be sure you can take the machine back to where you bought it. Again, a good help line can help you assess whether a problem is caused by the baking method or a faulty machine. A bread machine does have some replaceable parts, such as the drive belt for the blade and a thermal sensor fuse, which can easily be repaired at an authorized service center. Don't attempt home repairs. Finally, be kind to your nonstick pan and paddle; they cost $40 to $60 to replace. If you should need to order replacements, call your customer support line.

Features: Cycles and Settings

In the owner's manual, after acquainting you with the parts of the machine, the basic steps to remove and replace the bread pan, and the order in which to place the ingredients in the pan, each manufacturer will list the features, also referred to as the modes of operation or cycles, of the machine. This list of cycles lets you know what types of breads you can make with your machine, and the amount of time it takes to make a loaf on each of these settings. Most booklets tell you in a chart how long each cycle, and even each part of a cycle, takes; the times are a bit different for each brand of machine. All machines have at least four of the following cycles:

BASIC

This setting is also known as Basic Bread, Basic Mode, Basic Wheat, Standard, or White. This is the all-purpose setting you'll probably use most often. The cycle takes three to four hours, depending on your machine. It is the cycle for white breads and whole wheat or whole-grain breads that contain more than 50 percent bread flour. This cycle can also be used for country breads if you don't have a French Bread cycle. Within this cycle there is sometimes the further choice of "Quick" or "Rapid." (Some machines have you program for this separately. See information about the Quick Yeast Bread cycle, page 8). On many of the newer machines, there will be a beep during the Basic cycle to identify when to add any extra ingredients, like raisins or nuts.

SWEET BREAD

The Sweet Bread cycle allows doughs with a higher fat and sugar content to rise more slowly. This cycle has a longer rise and a lower baking temperature, about 250°F, since the crust of a sweet bread will brown quicker. There is usually a beep in this cycle for the addition of extra ingredients, like chopped glacéed fruit or nuts. Many sweet breads are also mixed on the Dough cycle, shaped, and baked in the home oven.

FRUIT AND NUT

Also known as the Raisin Mode or Mix Bread cycle, the Fruit and Nut setting is used for recipes that require the addition of nuts, seeds, chocolate chips, or dried fruit to the dough. This way the extras are not overmixed or pulverized during the vigorous blade action of the kneading phase of the cycle. Many of the newer machines have this audible alert built into the Basic and Whole Wheat cycles, rather than in a separate cycle. When the beep sounds, simply open the lid and pour in the extras. If your machine does not have this cycle, use the Basic cycle for breads made with these ingredients. The audible alert is not a necessity; see page 439 for information on adding extra ingredients. Sometimes, if I want to vary the color or taste of a bread, I do add the extras, such as onions and nuts, at the beginning of the cycle so that the kneading action smooshes them and they more or less disintegrate into the dough.

VARIETY

This was a common feature on the older machines. The Variety cycle runs about the same length of time as the Basic cycle, and has a beep and displays a signal to "shape" so that you can remove the dough after the second rise, fill and shape it by hand, and then return it to the baking canister for a final rise and the baking. You could use this cycle for a cinnamon swirl or monkey bread. This is a fun feature. If your machine does not have it, you can program for the Basic cycle, press Pause to interrupt it after Rise 2, remove the dough and shape it, and then return it to the pan and press Start to resume the cycle and bake the bread.

DOUGH

This setting may also be known as the Rise or Manual cycle. This is the setting to use when you want to mix and rise a dough in the machine, then remove the dough, shape it by hand, and bake it in your oven. Toastmaster has the shortest Dough cycle at 1 hour and 3 minutes, 1 hour and 30 minutes is the average, and Panasonic's is the longest at 2 hours and 30

minutes (this includes Preheat). Doughs prepared on this setting are intended to be shaped into traditional loaves or in special ways, such as cloverleaf dinner rolls, egg twists, pizza, croissants, bread sticks, or bagels, and baked in the oven. You can adapt your favorite recipes for this cycle, with respect to using quantities that will fit in your machine (see page 321 for information about maximum capacities). Remove the dough at the beep and proceed to shape as directed in the recipe. Within this cycle is sometimes the further choice of Basic Dough or Quick Dough.

WHOLE WHEAT

This cycle is also known as the Whole Grain or Basic Wheat mode. This setting allows heavy whole grain flours a nice long kneading time and an extra, and slightly longer, rising time as compared to the Basic cycle, producing a lighter, higher loaf. This is really nice for all sorts of whole wheat breads made with more than 50 percent whole grain flour. It should definitely be used for 100 percent whole wheat or whole-grain breads, and for breads containing specialty flours, such as barley or spelt. Within this cycle is sometimes a further choice of Basic or Quick. On many of the newer machines, there will be a beep during this cycle to identify when to add any extra ingredients, like raisins or nuts. Models that preheat at the beginning of some, but not all, of their cycles generally do preheat in the Whole Wheat cycle.

FRENCH BREAD

There is often a European, Crisp, or Homemade setting for the same purpose. This cycle has become the new rage in bread machine baking. Use this setting for crusty country breads with no fat or sugar that need longer rising times, giving the yeast a good long while to do its work. (Older National machines have this cycle lasting seven hours, which would bring a smile to the face of a traditional baker from France.) This is also the setting to use for sourdough breads made with yeast. The baking temperature is at the high end, about 325°F. The breads baked on this cycle are crisp crusted with a fine-textured, chewy inner crumb. Some bakers like a dark crust on their country breads.

QUICK YEAST BREAD

While the newer models have this cycle as an option within the Basic, Whole Wheat, and Dough cycles, some older models have it as a separate cycle. Also known as Bake (Rapid), Turbo, Quick Bake, or just Quick, this program is specifically designed for use with fast-acting (instant) or quick rise yeast. This cycle skips the second rise, shortening the entire cycle time by forty-five minutes to one hour. You can make virtually any yeast bread recipe on this cycle. See your manufacturer's manual to find out how to adjust the yeast. When using this cycle, *it is very important that the ingredients be at room temperature when you put them in the machine.* The time the yeast has to work is already shortened; having the ingredients slightly warm at the start ensures that the yeast will get activated right away. In general, this shortened cycle does still give you a very nice loaf of bread. This cycle, or the One Hour cycle, is the one to use for gluten-free yeast breads (pages 170 to 178), since these doughs require less rising time. Note that this cycle is *not* the same as the Quick Bread cycle.

ONE HOUR

The One Hour cycle is a second type of abbreviated cycle that, as its name implies, produces

bread in one hour. Even faster than the Quick Yeast Bread (or Rapid) cycle, the One Hour cycle cuts out more than one rise. It, too, requires the use of fast-acting (instant) or quick-rise yeast. Your manufacturer's manual will tell you how to adjust the yeast in a recipe for this cycle. I find that there is a loss in flavor and keeping quality to breads made on this cycle, so I don't recommend using it. The One Hour cycle can be used in place of the Quick Yeast cycle though when making gluten-free yeast breads (pages 170 to 178).

BAKE ONLY

In newer machines there is sometimes a Bake Only cycle so that a dough that has been prepared on the Dough cycle can be shaped and then returned to the bread machine for baking. You could use Bake Only for a cinnamon swirl bread, or for baking a hand-mixed or a commercial dough. This is the setting to use if you made a dough and planned to bake it in a regular oven, and, well, changed your mind. The Bake Only cycle is invaluable when a cycle ends and a loaf is not quite done baking. You can program Bake Only to continue baking in increments for up to two hours. If you are doing lots of different types of baking, you will use this cycle.

QUICK BREAD

This setting, also known as Cake, is for non-yeast batters leavened with baking powder or baking soda, such as quick breads and loaf cakes. This cycle mixes the ingredients (although older machines require that the mixing be done by hand and the batter poured into the pan without the kneading blade installed) and bakes without any rise time. There is an option for further baking at one-minute intervals. This cycle works well with packaged commercial mixes for cornbread, quick bread, and pound cake. On some models you have to program the bake time for this cycle; with others it is automatically built into the cycle.

PROGRAM

Some machines have a function that lets you manually change the cycle times to whatever you want them to be, letting you increase a kneading, rising, or baking time as needed. You can also create your own recipes and program in all the times for them, and the machine will keep the instructions in its memory. This is a feature that I find people use only when they have become very proficient with the basic baking cycles. (Also called Personal Baker.)

JAM

Some of the new machines have a setting for small-batch fresh fruit refrigerator jams (not jellies), with or without pectin. This cycle can also make chutneys and fruit butters. To prevent leakage and overspills, make jam only in a machine that is designed to do so. Be sure to read the chapter on jams in this book (pages 562 to 583) and the guidelines it provides; there are strict proportions to respect. Skeptical? This is a *great* feature, so give it a try. It makes wonderful jam.

OTHER CYCLES

Some machines have Sandwich or Tender cycles for breads with a finer texture than those baked on the Basic cycle. Use these cycles for recipes that contain more fat and eggs, ingredients that make a softer bread. The Batter Bread setting, a new addition to Breadman machines, is for making especially moist yeasted breads that don't form a traditional dough ball. As machines become more sophisticated, continue to expect more features. Some machines now offer a Pizza Dough cycle, a Bagel Dough cycle, and a cycle specifically for gluten-free breads (which can also be made on the Quick Yeast Bread or One Hour cycles in other machines). Pasta Dough has its own cycle, a subcycle of the Dough cycle, in some Oster machines (but can easily be made on the Dough cycle in any machine designed to handle heavier doughs).

In addition to their baking cycles, bread machines have some or all of the following features:

DELAY FEATURE

Almost all machines have a Delay Timer, which allows you to place the ingredients in the bread pan, choose the baking cycle, and program the machine to begin the process of mixing and baking your dough 3½ to 24 hours later. This is a popular feature, since it enables you to program the machine at night and wake up to fresh bread in the morning, or have fresh bread ready when you get home from work. I have noted throughout the book which recipes are not suitable for this cycle, but please remember that whenever you program the machine for a delay of even a few hours, you should not make a bread that calls for any fresh ingredients, such as milk, eggs, or cheese (including cottage cheese, sour cream, or yogurt), bacon, or fresh vegetables. Ingredients such as these can grow harmful bacteria at room temperature that can result in food poisoning. Many bread machine recipes call for dry milk and powdered eggs, which are safe to use with the Delay Timer.

In order to get optimum results using the Delay Timer, it is important that the yeast not come in contact with the salt (which would inhibit its rising power) nor with any liquid (which would activate it before the mixing began) when the ingredients are standing in the bread pan. Add the liquid ingredients first, then the salt, then all the dry ingredients, and finally the yeast at the end (or switch this order around if your machine so requires). Many bread machine books stipulate this precaution for all their recipes, but it is only really necessary when using the Delay Timer.

PREHEAT

Some machines have a Preheat or Rest period, which was created so that you could put ingredients at cold and warm temperatures into the machine and have them at a uniform temperature by the time the mixing starts. (Perhaps a throwback to the days of warming the flour on the oven door to take off the chill and encourage the best rising?) This allows the yeast to perform at optimum capacity. This phase lasts from 15 to 30 minutes. Remember that there is no blade action, so the machine will be quiet during this phase. In some of the more sophisticated machines you can bypass this step, in others you cannot. Some machines have it built into every baking cycle; others, like Breadman machines, just have it on the Whole Wheat cycle. Some people like this feature, believing it produces better bread, and some don't, since it adds time to the whole process. You can use the Program setting (see page 9), if your machine has it, to bypass the Preheat cycle.

CRUST CONTROL

In addition to choosing the cycle for your loaf, most models offer a setting that, by varying the baking temperature or timing slightly, gives you the choice of a light, medium, or dark crust. You are choosing how your loaf will look when it is finished baking. Some models have just two crust choices, Bake (Light) or Bake (Normal), which are built into their Basic cycle. The crust setting, because it does change the baking time and often the temperature, also affects the doneness of a loaf. I usually use the medium or normal crust setting for basic and whole-grain breads, but I almost always check the loaf to make sure the bread has baked all the way through. (See page 379 for information on how to check for doneness.)

If the crust on your bread is too light and the loaf is underdone, next time set the crust setting for dark; if the crust is too dark and the bread is overbaked, set it for light. Some people like light crusts on whole wheat breads and dark crusts on their French breads. I set the crust on medium or dark for artisan and country breads, and on light for sweet breads, which brown more quickly due to their higher sugar content. Since the specific ingredients in loaves often have a lot to do with how their crusts brown, it is a good idea to experiment with the crust settings.

LOAF SIZE

This setting asks you to choose the size loaf you will be making in the machine—1, 1½, or 2 pound. With this feature, each size loaf has slightly different cycle times and bake times.

PAUSE

The Pause button allows you to interrupt a cycle at any point and resume again where it left off. This is different from pushing Stop/Reset, which cancels the entire cycle. Most of the machines now have a Pause button, but some of the older or less expensive models do not. If your machine does not have this feature, you may wish to skim some of the more complex recipes in this book before making them—there are a few recipes that require this feature in order to manipulate the cycles.

COOL DOWN OR KEEP WARM
Bread recipes always state that the loaf needs to be removed from the pan immediately after baking to prevent it from getting soggy. The Cool Down or Keep Warm feature allows the loaf to stay in the baking chamber as some heat or a fan evaporates the excess moisture and pushes it out of the machine. This is not a separately programmable cycle, but, like Preheat, is a feature preset within one or more of the bread cycles on many machines. If you do not remove your loaf from the machine when the baking has finished and press Stop, a machine that has this feature will automatically go into a Cool Down or Keep Warm mode. The bread will be very moist if it stays in the machine on this mode. Without this feature, expect bread that stays in the machine after baking to be wet and soggy. I advise you not to leave a loaf in the machine on this mode unless it is absolutely necessary, when you have used the Delay Timer, for example, or if you are off taking a nap while the machine is running. Surprisingly, I found that country breads benefited from this Cool Down/Keep Warm phase, as it thickened the crust. Whole wheat breads, rather than getting soggier, dry out too much if left in the machine through this part of a cycle.

Bread Machine Cycle Names

Cycle as referred to in *The Bread Lover's Bread Machine Cookbook*	Alternate cycle names
Basic	Basic Bread Basic Mode Basic Wheat Standard White
Sweet Bread	
Fruit and Nut	Raisin Mode Mix Bread
Variety	
Dough	Rise Manual Basic Dough Quick Dough (a sub-cycle within the Dough cycle)
Whole Wheat	Whole Grain Basic Wheat
French Bread	European Crisp Homemade
Quick Yeast Bread	Bake (Rapid) Turbo Quick Bake Quick (do not confuse with Quick Bread cycle) Rapid (a sub-cycle within the Basic cycle) Quick Wheat (a sub-cycle within the Whole Wheat cycle)
One Hour	
Bake Only	
Quick Bread/Cake	
Jam	

MAKING BREAD

T *his section is very important to understanding baking in your bread machine. It would be worthwhile to familiarize yourself with this information before baking from this book.*

The Ingredients

All loaves are a combination of flour, leavening, salt, and liquids. The equation is so simple that each loaf is only as good as the ingredients that you use to make it. Additional ingredients such as sweetening, eggs, fat, or other flavor enhancers like cheese and herbs, produce loaves of different flavors and with individual characters. I include vital wheat gluten in the following list of basic ingredients, since it is an essential ingredient in every recipe that is baked in a machine.

FLOUR

Grains are milled into a powder called flour. This is the foundation of all of the bread we make. Milling is a complex process we take for granted when we buy our 5-pound sacks of flour. Professionals in the flour industry evaluate each crop of grain for protein levels, gluten strength, water absorption, and mixing tolerances. Flours are carefully blended by each mill to give you consistently good bread from scratch.

Wheat makes the flour most commonly used for breads because of its high absorption ability. There are various types and qualities of wheat, and many different flours are milled from it. Bread machine loaves work best with bread flour. Bread flour can also be labeled "high gluten flour" or "best for bread." Bread machine bakers usually have a favorite brand, sometimes labeled "For the Bread Machine" on the package. These blends have a high gluten content that develops well with machine mixing. All bread flour makes a tall, springy loaf. You can also use all-purpose flour in the bread machine if you add enough vital wheat gluten to boost its protein content. All-purpose flour with gluten added can be used in place of bread flour in any recipe in this book. Some recipes here do call for standard all-purpose flour because they are baked outside the machine.

As you grow familiar with your machine, you can use combinations of wheat germ, cracked wheat, rolled grains, whole wheat flour, all-purpose flour, and other flours to create loaves in an infinite variety of flavors, textures, and muted earth tones. Every flour absorbs a different amount of moisture and does so at a different rate. Remember that the more non-wheat flour you use in proportion to wheat, the denser the loaf and the slower the rising time. Also, remember that proper measurements make a good loaf. If you don't add enough flour, no matter what the type, you will have a collapsed loaf (collapsing from the top or in from the sides) that is often uncooked in the center. If you add too much flour, you will have a dough that strains during the kneading process and bakes into a hard, dense, heavy ball.

VITAL WHEAT GLUTEN

Although vital wheat gluten is not a core ingredient when making bread by hand (the gluten contained in the flour is enough to produce a high loaf when mixing and kneading by hand), I single out gluten here as a main ingredient for bread machine baking because all my testing has shown that it yields a better loaf when added to the dry ingredients. Gluten is called for in most of the recipes in this book. It helps make loaves rise higher and gives them more volume. Vital wheat gluten—also known as just plain gluten—is made by washing the starch from the endosperm in wheat, leaving pure plant protein that is dried, ground, and marketed as a powdered extract. It is *not* a flour. Gluten becomes stretchy during mixing and kneading, and is a premium dough conditioner because it helps trap the rising CO_2 in its strong meshwork, making a puffier loaf. If you are experimenting with your own recipes, I recommend using 1 to 2 teaspoons of gluten per cup of white bread flour and 1½ to 3 teaspoons gluten per cup of whole grain flour for an exquisite texture. Sometimes I add double that if I have a stiff all–whole wheat dough or am using a recipe calling for a non-gluten flour. If you add gluten to one of your existing bread recipes, note that doughs containing gluten can absorb a tablespoon or two more of liquid.

Store gluten in an airtight container in the refrigerator for up to one year, but if you use gluten regularly, it can be kept in the cupboard for up to two months.

Please note: If you encounter vital wheat gluten *flour*, this is a different product than vital wheat gluten, which is much more concentrated. Do not confuse these two items.

YEAST

Yeast is a microscopic plant. The word "yeast" comes from the French word *levant*, meaning "to rise." In France, the same word is applied to the eastern part of the world and to the rising sun. Perhaps this interesting etymology has something to do with the fact that there has always been a degree of mystery and discovery in observing yeast activate and multiply.

Yeast is sold to the consumer in five different forms: active dry yeast, compressed fresh cake yeast, fast-acting or instant dried yeast, bread machine yeast, and quick-rise yeast. (Nutritional yeasts, such as brewer's and torula, are not leavening agents.) Fast-acting yeast and bread machine yeast both work well in the bread machine; quick-rise yeast can also be used.

The most readily available fast-acting or instant yeast comes from the S.I. Lasaffre Company (a French company operating in Belgium and elsewhere), which has been producing commercial yeast since Louis Pasteur figured out how to isolate and cultivate single strains. This yeast, labeled "SAF Perfect Rise" or "SAF Instant" yeast, is very popular among bread machine bakers. My testers and I nicknamed it the "industrial strength yeast" for its incredible and reliable rising power. Composed of a different strain of yeast than our domestic brands, SAF yeast is dried to a very low percentage of moisture and coated with ascorbic acid and a form of sugar, enabling it to activate immediately on contact with warm liquid. This type of yeast needs no initial dissolving in liquid, which makes it perfect for the bread machine. It has free-flowing rod-shaped granules that were developed with easy measuring in mind. SAF yeast contains three times as many yeast cells per volume as other granular yeasts, so the amount used in a recipe should be cut back by about 25 percent from the amount of yeast called for. (You will see that this is taken into account in the recipes in this book.) SAF yeast comes in a two-pack strip or in a resealable 3-ounce bag. The yeast should be stored in the freezer (for up to one year), as the outer coating of dried yeast cells is sensitive to oxidation.

Other brands of instant or fast-acting-style yeast that work well in the bread machine include Fermipan Instant Yeast, a yeast that is well known and loved by Italian-style bakers. This yeast is known for producing great focaccia, old-world-style breads, and hard rolls. Fleischmann's Yeast now offers an ascorbic-acid-coated instant domestic yeast, and Red Star has entered the instant yeast market with Red Star Instant Active Dry Yeast, which has a smaller granule size than traditional active dry yeast so

that it will perform like SAF. These three yeasts are not yet as widely distributed as SAF.

Bread machine yeast was developed, as its name would suggest, with bread machine baking in mind. Both Fleischmann's and Red Star also produce bread machine yeast, a finely granulated yeast that is coated with a layer of ascorbic acid (vitamin C) and a flour buffer. It, too, is able to be mixed into a dough along with the dry ingredients, requiring no previous activation in a warm liquid. Bread machine yeast is not as sensitive to temperature as regular active dry yeast; it can grow and multiply at lower temperatures in the machine's bread pan. Bread machine yeast is sold in 4-ounce jars, and is readily available at supermarkets.

Quick-rise yeast was developed in 1984 in response to the large amount of home baking done using powerful electric mixers. Both Red Star and Fleischmann's (patented as RapidRise)

have quick-rise yeasts on the market. Quick-rise yeast is another strain of very fine, low-moisture yeast that is able to be activated in a dough without first being rehydrated in a warm liquid. It raises dough about twice as fast as regular yeast. This strain is fed with phosphorus to increase enzyme activity, and RapidRise yeast is coated with emulsifiers and antioxidants that boost activity. You can use quick-rise yeast in place of bread machine yeast for the recipes in this book. Replace the given quantity of SAF yeast with the quick-rise yeast.

Whatever type of yeast you are using, always check the expiration date stamped on the package. Fresh yeast works best, and outdated yeast may not work at all. If you question whether a yeast is viable, test it by filling a measuring cup with 1 cup of lukewarm water. Sprinkle in 1 tablespoon of the yeast in question and 1 teaspoon of sugar. Mix the three together and, if the yeast is active, it will bubble immediately. If it does nothing, or if there are only a few bubbles, the yeast is dead and should be discarded.

SALT

Salt is very important in bread not only as a flavor enhancer, but in controlling the rate of yeast fermentation. In the presence of salt, the dough rises at a slower rate and the salt strengthens the gluten. Loaves with no salt collapse easily. The addition of salt results in a good crumb, better keeping qualities, and more flavor. When using the Delay Timer, avoid having the salt come in contact with the yeast, which would slow its action; in these cases add the salt with the liquid. When you are going to mix and make the bread immediately, it really doesn't matter what ingredients come in contact with what others, and I actually prefer to add the salt close to the end, near the yeast, as I think it gets distributed better that way.

LIQUID

To make bread, you must have some type of liquid to moisten the flour, activate the gluten, and begin the action of the yeast. Liquid transforms the ingredients into a pliable dough ball

Bread Machine Baker's Hint: Measuring Your Ingredients

The bread machine, unlike traditional bread recipes that deal in approximates, must have accurately measured ingredients or else the recipes will not work properly or taste balanced. The baking pan has a limited capacity, so ingredients must also be measured precisely to keep them from spilling over onto the heating element. This is extremely important for producing good loaves from the machine. For dry ingredients, use the nested set of plastic or metal cups and use only for dry measuring. Use the old "dip and sweep" method of dipping the cup or spoon into the dry ingredients (do not pack unless it is called for, as in packed brown sugar), such as sugar and flour, and using the back of a knife or spoon handle to scrape across the flat rim.

Dry and wet measuring cups are not interchangeable. For wet ingredients, like honey and all liquids, use a 1- or 2-cup clear glass measuring cup with a pour spout and with increments clearly marked. Set the cup on the counter for it to level itself, and look at the increment lines at eye level; then pour the contents into the machine without spilling them. I don't use the metric measuring gadgets that sometimes come with machines; they are hard to decipher. Just throw them away (or use them in the laundry room).

that will bake into a loaf of bread. Pure water, milk, buttermilk, fruit juice, yogurt, sour cream, beer, or coffee all work, but each gives a different crumb. Nonfat dry milk powder and dry buttermilk powder can be used in conjunction with water to replace their fresh counterparts. Some bakers don't like the flavor of the dried milk powders and always use fresh milk, but for bread machine baking using a delayed cycle, the use of powdered milk eliminates concern over spoilage. Sometimes you will see the addition of baking soda when acidic liquids like buttermilk and sour cream are called for; the baking soda neutralizes the acid. *If you have a Welbilt machine, please note that it usually requires an additional 2 tablespoons of liquid in every recipe; you will need to add these 2 tablespoons to the quantity of liquid in the recipes in this book.*

FAT

Fat is a dirty word in today's food world, but in reality it is an essential element of a healthy diet when consumed in moderation. Generally it is not the type of fat you use, but the proportions, that matter in baking bread. Fat adds lots of flavor, pliability, and tenderness to a loaf of bread, and helps keep it from staling within a few hours. Use unsalted butter (which has an unparalleled flavor), margarine, lard (which is, surprisingly, more flavorful and less saturated than butter), or various olive, vegetable, or nut oils. Add butter by cutting it into pieces and putting it in with the other ingredients; it will mix right in during the kneading. Fats will be included with the liquids in the recipes in this book.

SWEETENING

Sugar provides food for the developing yeast and helps retain moisture in the finished baked loaf. It also enhances flavor, texture, and crust color. Use granulated sugar, superfine sugar, raw sugar, Demerara sugar, light or dark brown sugar, or thick syrups like maple syrup, molasses, corn syrup, barley malt syrup, and honey. You will be adding a bit more liquid if you are using a syrup instead of a granulated sugar.

EGGS

Eggs are a favorite addition to bread. They add flavor, color, a cakelike texture, leavening power, and liquid to a dough. Use only eggs graded large. Never use fresh eggs when baking using the Delay Timer.

CHEMICAL LEAVENER

Chemical leaveners, such as baking powder, baking soda, and cream of tartar, are essential in making quick breads. These leaveners create air bubbles when they come in contact with liquid. This is why quick breads need to bake immediately, so that the bubbles have not dissipated before the loaf has set. I like Rumford brand non-aluminum baking powder. For more information on chemical leaveners, see page 555.

Loading the Ingredients into the Bread Machine

One of the big deals in making bread in the bread machine is how the ingredients are loaded into the bread pan. Most of the models call for the wet ingredients to go into the machine first, followed by the dry ingredients. But a few differ in the order that the ingredients are layered into the bread pan. This chart is for easy reference. This book is written with directions for wet, then dry ingredients to be layered into the pan, since this is the prevalent manner of adding the ingredients. If your machine differs, just switch the order around to fit the pattern outlined in your manufacturer's booklet. As a note, if you are making the dough immediately, it really doesn't matter in what order the ingredients are placed in the pan. This pattern becomes important when you are using the Delay Timer, so that the yeast does not become activated before the dough is being made.

The Process of Baking Bread in the Bread Machine

To make bread, whether by machine, by hand, or by any method, you follow a set of basic sequential steps that are exactly the same as they were when bread was invented thousands of years ago. The process is as follows: You make the dough, you let it rest as the yeast does its work, and then you bake it, killing the yeast and setting the texture, which makes it edible. There may be shortcuts to this process, but the sequence never varies, even when technology is incorporated. The bread machine's contribution to this process has been to take all the guesswork out of baking. In the past, the duration, intensity, and environment of each step had to be calculated by the baker. Using a machine, you don't have to calculate preparation, kneading, rising, or baking times. You don't have to turn the dough out of the machine and shape it, unless you want to. Because of the sheer ease of this baking medium, people who never had the desire to tackle the work involved with hand baking and those who can't find the time to bake by hand, produce wonderful breads using a bread machine. The steps involved in creating a loaf of bread in the machine, which is called "baking in a controlled atmosphere," are

Manufacturer	Order of Loading Ingredients in Pan		
	wet dry yeast	yeast dry wet	dry wet yeast dispenser
Aroma BreadChef	•		
Betty Crocker	•		
Black & Decker	•		
Breadman/Salton	•		
Franklin Chef	•		
GoldStar	•		
Hitachi	•		
Oster/Sunbeam	•		
Panasonic/National			•
Regal	•		
Sanyo		•	
Toastmaster	•		
Welbilt*			•
West Bend		•	
Williams-Sonoma	•		
Zojirushi		•	

*If you are using a Welbilt machine, you will need to add 2 more tablespoons to the amount of liquid called for in every recipe.

Bread Machine Baker's Hint: Measurement Equivalents

Bread machine recipes call for some unusual volume measurements, such as ⅛ or ⅞ cup. The little plastic measuring cup that comes with some machines is divided into eighths, but it is awkward to use; I like my old glass measuring cup and Tupperware dry measures. Once you become familiar with the measuring language associated with bread machines, you won't find it difficult. Use this chart to familiarize yourself with some less common measures and their equivalents; use it for an aid when you are halving a 2-pound-loaf recipe to make a 1-pound loaf, or find out how much of an ingredient to buy when shopping from the bulk aisle of your grocery store.

⅛ cup = 2 tablespoons = 1 ounce
⅜ cup = ¼ cup plus 2 tablespoons = 3 ounces
⅝ cup = ½ cup plus 2 tablespoons = 5 ounces
⅞ cup = ¾ cup plus 2 tablespoons = 7 ounces
1⅛ cups = 1 cup plus 2 tablespoons = 9 ounces
1¼ cups = 1 cup plus 4 tablespoons = 10 ounces
1½ cups = 12 ounces

1½ teaspoons = ½ tablespoon
3 teaspoons = 1 tablespoon = ½ ounce
4 teaspoons = 1⅓ tablespoons
4 tablespoons = ¼ cup = 2 ounces
5⅓ tablespoons = 5 tablespoons plus
   1 teaspoon = ⅓ cup
8 tablespoons = ½ cup
16 tablespoons = 1 cup = 8 ounces

Butter
½ cup = 4 ounces = 1 stick
¼ cup = 2 ounces = ½ stick
2 tablespoons = 1 ounce = ¼ stick
1 tablespoon = ½ ounce = ⅛ stick
   (each stick is divided into 8
   sections on the wrapper)

Grade A Large White or Brown Eggs
1 whole egg = ¼ cup liquid
   measure
1 egg white = 3 tablespoons
1 yolk = 1 tablespoon
1 whole large egg = 3 tablespoons
   commercial liquid egg substitute
1 large fresh egg white = 1 tablespoon egg-white powder and
   2 tablespoons cold water
   beaten together until foamy

Unbleached All-Purpose Flour
1 cup = 4¾ ounces
3½ cups = 1 pound
18 cups = 5 pounds

Bread Flour and Whole Wheat Flour
1 cup = 5 ounces

Granulated Sugar
1 cup = 8 ounces
½ cup = 4 ounces
¼ cup = 2 ounces
1 tablespoon = ½ ounce

Brown Sugar
1 cup = 6 ounces
½ cup = 3 ounces
¼ cup = 1½ ounces
1 tablespoon = ⅓ ounce

Nutmeats (chopped)
1 cup = 4 ounces

Raisins
¾ cup = 4 ounces
1 cup = 5¼ ounces
2¾ cups = 1 pound

Chocolate Chips or Chopped Chocolate
½ cup = 3 ounces

Nonfat Dry Milk or Dry Buttermilk Powder
3 tablespoons dry milk powder +
   1 cup water = 1 cup fresh milk
   or buttermilk. For a richer flavor,
   use 4 to 5 tablespoons per cup.

Firm Cheeses
3 ounces of a firm, moist grated
   cheese = 2 tablespoons liquid
   measurement

described here in detail, in the context of this unchanging sequence of steps that constitute baking. Throughout this book, when the terms Preheat, Mix, Knead 1, Knead 2, Punch Down, Rise 1, Rise 2, Rise 3, Cool Down, and Keep Warm appear beginning with capital letters, they refer to standard segments of all bread machine cycles. The manual for your bread machine will use these terms or very similar ones.

THE RIGHT TEMPERATURE/ PREHEAT

Temperature is an important consideration throughout the entire process of mixing, kneading, rising, and baking bread. Someone baking by hand attempts to control the temperature of the environs for every step, adding water of a certain temperature, mixing the dough in one area of the kitchen, moving it to another spot to rise, perhaps moving it again, and, finally, setting the oven at just the right temperature for baking. The bread machine has been designed to create just the right environment for each step in the process. The first step, an important one, is to properly activate the yeast, which is the primary leavener in most breads.

Yeast is a living organism and very sensitive to temperature. When it has been properly activated, it remains alive through the process of constructing the dough and is killed in the heat of baking. Yeast needs moisture, food, and an environment between 75° and 100°F to become active. Under ideal conditions, the liquid and the dry ingredients are at the same temperature before they are mixed together. This is what the Preheat portion of the cycle, a feature of many bread machines, accomplishes.

Since the bread machine has been carefully programmed to control the conditions inside of

it, you should not have to do any adjusting to the dough or environs. But the machine is not sealed off from its surroundings, so extreme temperatures or humidity can affect the contents of, and effectiveness of, the bread machine. You may find yourself sympathetic to the hand baker's plight. Pay attention to the weather. Since dough is more active when it is warm and humid, add cooler liquid to slow the yeast action; I often use cool water on very hot baking days. Just as many bakers do not bake in extremely high temperatures, it is probably best not to bake in your bread machine under such conditions either. For the best results from your machine, begin with room temperature ingredients. Make sure

The Basic Steps of Bread Machine Baking

What you, the baker, must do:
- Select a recipe
- Assemble the equipment and ingredients on your workspace
- Measure the raw ingredients into the bread pan
- Program the control panel and press Start to begin the process in the machine
- Check the dough consistency and adjust if necessary

What occurs inside the machine:
- Mixing of the dough
- Kneading
- First rise
- Deflation of the dough/Punch Down
- Second rise
- Deflation of the dough/Shape
- Third rise
- Baking
- Bread is kept warm or cooled

any extra ingredients, like sautéed onions or toasted nuts, are cooled to room temperature before they are added. Beginning with all the ingredients at room temperature contributes to the proper consistency of the dough ball and to optimum rising.

MIXING THE INGREDIENTS/ MIX AND KNEAD 1

When baking without the use of a bread machine, the mixing—the combining of liquid and dry ingredients—may be done by hand, using the dough hook of an electric mixer, or by a food processor. The bread machine has a slow clockwise rhythm that blends the dough properly, turning for about three minutes (if the blade was turning more vigorously at this point, flour would be flying up against the lid and over the sides onto the heating element). The yeast gets distributed and moistened during this mixing. The gluten in the flour begins to be moistened by the liquids, and all the ingredients become evenly distributed. The

dough can look anywhere from batterlike to dry and crumbly at this point, depending on the recipe, and there may be lots of lumpy, un-incorporated bits of flour in the corners of the pan; this is okay. In the center of the mass, around the blade, there will be the beginnings of a dough ball coming together. I often look in at the dough during this step and scrape down the sides if there is a lot of flour in the corners of the pan. The mixing and kneading mechanism of the machine is very carefully engineered. There seems to me to be no great difference in the texture or flavor of loaf-style breads made in the bread machine from breads made by other appliance-aided means. In bread machine baking, the initial knead, Knead 1, is more or less an extension of Mix. It is not until Knead 2 that the kneading blade begins to rotate very fast.

This step in the machine is also part of the process used for constructing starters for country-style breads.

KNEADING THE DOUGH/ KNEAD 2

Kneading, in the machine or by hand, is the step of the baking process that thoroughly mixes the ingredients, distributes the yeast, and strengthens the moistened gluten strands to a springy elasticity. It is a continuation of the mixing process. Kneading incorporates fresh oxygen into the dough, which is important to the rising and to the finished shape of the loaf. Hand kneading is a set of pressing, pushing, and folding physical motions that transform a dough from a rough, shaggy mass to a soft and smoothly pliable dough. The kneading paddle in the bottom of the baking pan has an action that simulates hand kneading. But bread

machine doughs do call for high-gluten bread flour, which is especially suited to machine mixing. The action of the mechanical kneading produces more friction than kneading by hand, very slightly warming the dough.

During kneading, the proteins in wheat flour, called gluten, become a meshwork of stretchy strands as they are worked, creating the structure that is strong enough and absolutely necessary to contain the expanding gases that are the by-products of the yeast's reproduction. After rising these strong gluten fibers will create a soft, firm, honeycomb pattern in cut slices of baked bread. The mechanical action of the blade accomplishes this gluten development automatically. The blade moves faster in Knead 2 than in Knead 1, and alternates clockwise and counterclockwise directions. With a slow rhythm it turns the dough and allows the dough ball to pick up the extra dry bits accumulated in the pan. This action is excellent for forming a dough since it accurately simulates mixing by hand. During this knead, the dough will slowly evolve into a smooth ball with tiny blisters forming just under the skin.

As the dough is worked, liquid is absorbed by the flour particles, and the dough becomes more compact. If you look inside the machine, the dough ball will clear the sides of the pan and look small in comparison to the volume of the pan. The top surface will be smooth.

Five to seven minutes into Knead 2, the dough will be far enough along to be able to tell whether it is too dry or too wet. Those baking by hand feel the consistency of the dough under their fingers and make allowances, adding more liquid or more flour, as they go along. You will need to open the lid of the machine in order to assess the dough. (You can set a kitchen timer to remind you when to check.) Open the lid, and, taking care to avoid the moving kneading blade, poke the dough ball with your finger to feel the consistency. Look for a springy, soft feel in white doughs and a very soft, almost loose feel in country bread doughs. Whole wheat and rye doughs tend to be denser, wetter, and tackier to the touch than white doughs. The level of humidity, the amount of moisture in the flour, and the amount of initial beating are all variables that may have affected the dough by this time. Every batch of dough is unique in the exact amount of flour used. Individual recipes will specify the proper consistency of the dough ball when necessary.

Now adjust the dough consistency, if necessary, by adding more flour or more liquid. Remember that a little goes a long way in this medium. Sprinkle the flour down the sides of the pan and let the dough ball pick it up, or dribble liquid, only 1 teaspoon at a time, onto the top of the dough ball. If an adjustment is necessary (most of the time it shouldn't be) the amount of flour or liquid to be incorporated at this point will vary. It is important not to add too much of either, and to give any additions time to be kneaded in before reassessing the consistency of the dough. Remember, too, that more flour will be absorbed into the body of the dough during the rising process. Just as is necessary when kneading by hand, this is also the time to make sure the dough is uniformly moist throughout. If there are dry bits collected on the bottom of the pan and wet dough on the top of the dough ball, I use my plastic spatula to push the bits into the center so the dough ball can pick them up as it journeys around the pan with the action of the blade.

The dough ball changes a lot during the kneading cycle. What it looks like in the first ten minutes of being worked is not at all what it will look like when it is almost done. When baked, a standard loaf will smooth out and be springy. Be patient and let the machine do its work. I find a dough ball can change as many as three or four times during Knead 2. You will now have a dough ready to be "fermented," or "proofed," during the rises.

RISING THE DOUGH/ RISE 1 AND RISE 2

Rising, also known as proofing, is a period of rest that allows the gluten to become smooth and elastic through a process of fermentation. During this stage, an amazing transformation takes place—a firm, heavy dough ball changes into a puffy mass that increases in size. To carry out this step, bakers working by hand would grease their dough and its bowl at this point, cover it loosely with plastic wrap or with a damp cloth, set it in a warm place, and leave it alone to rest. The nonstick coating of the bread pan eliminates the need for greasing, and the closed, warm environment keeps the surface of the dough from drying out.

It is difficult to predict how high a dough will rise during the rising phases, as it will depend on the temperature of the dough after Knead 2, the amount of yeast used, and general atmospheric conditions. Usually on Rise 1, the dough ball will expand only slightly. In Rise 2, it can increase as much as two to three times in bulk. As the dough rises, the gluten mesh network is trapping the expanding gases. Whole grain breads and sweet doughs high in fat, sugar, or fruit take longer than lean white-flour doughs to rise. Generally, a dough will take one

to two hours to rise to the classic "doubled in bulk" stage, filling the pan half to two-thirds full, and this rising occurs in stages. The temperature inside the machine is about 82°F during the rising phases, known as Rise 1 and Rise 2. Rise 1 and Rise 2 are separated by a Punch Down (see following).

The enclosed environment of the bread machine, which has accumulated warmth from the action of the machine and holds the moisture from the dough, is, at this point, a perfect medium for rising. The environment is cozy and warm, and free from the drafts that can cause a dough outside the machine to rise slowly and unevenly. The bread machine is its own miniature proofing box, achieving the very important conditions professional bakers must create. Nonetheless, it is okay to open the lid and peek! The dough will look more moist during this rising period than it did during the kneading. Often it is sticky, but it absorbs this extra moisture during Rise 2.

Don't even consider rushing your bread through the rising phases. Be patient. (This is, by the way, where time is cut for the Quick Yeast Bread and One Hour cycles.) A longer rise always makes for a tastier loaf. For dense whole-grain doughs, bakers often will reset their machines for one more rise.

PUNCH DOWN

Bakers baking by hand use volume, rather than time, as a measure for when to deflate the dough. They deflate the dough for the first time when it has doubled in bulk. The machine, with its more controlled and predictable rising environment, punches down the dough using time, rather than bulk, as its cue. Because the Punch Down phase is timed, different doughs will be in various stages of rising when punch downs occur. The first deflation happens halfway through the composite of all the rising periods, separating Rise 1 from Rise 2, and the second deflation occurs 80 percent through the total rising time, separating Rise 2 and Rise 3 (the dough will reach its full rising capacity in Rise 3). Punch downs are necessary to release the trapped carbon dioxide from the dough. The action of the machine's blade, a few turns lasting less than ten seconds, is all that is needed to deflate the dough. (This time varies by machine—for example, Regal's Punch Down is just three spins in five seconds at the same speed as Knead 1.) I don't really like the term "punch down," since it has a violent connotation and the dough really is deflated gently. No more kneading is required at this point, as it would reactivate the gluten strands and give the dough an undesirable tight tension. A relaxed dough is able to rise smoothly and easily.

If the dough is sitting off to one side of the pan after the Punch Down, I pull it into the middle and center it over the blade to avoid a lopsided baked loaf later.

SHAPE/RISE 3

After the second punch down, which lasts a few seconds longer than the first one, is a third and last rise, after which the loaf is baked. At the end of this rise, the risen dough usually fills the bread pan to its capacity. If the bread were being made by hand, the second punch down would occur as the dough was removed from the container in which it had been rising and pulled or twisted into a loaf shape. It would then be placed in a bread pan, where it would remain, rising, until time for baking. As the dough rises, it takes the shape of the bread pan, which is why this step is called Shape. You will see this happening to your bread as it rises inside the machine.

Usually during this phase, the dough gradually and magically fills the entire pan to just under the rim. Don't worry if the dough is still somewhat low in the pan as this rise nears its end, unless it is like a soft rock. It will rise considerably during baking. If your dough rises higher than the edge of the pan during this phase, or is puffed over the rim of the pan when Rise 3 is nearing the end, open the lid and pierce the top gently with a toothpick or use your fingers to gently deflate it. It will lower slightly, and this should prevent it from possibly baking over the top of the pan, collapsing, or spilling onto the heating element. The temperature during this rise is about 100°F.

BAKE

The proper temperature provides the heat necessary for the best oven spring, or the final push of the dough when it increases in size and the gluten strands stretch to contain the last of the yeast's gases. As the dough bakes, it can increase in volume by as much as a full third. Because of the warm environment during the rising, the bread machine is basically preheated. Each model bakes its cycles at different temperatures, lower than a home oven, but hot enough to bake the bread efficiently and evenly. The temperatures range from 254° to 300°F, with the Sweet Bread cycle the lowest, the Basic cycle in the middle range, and the French Bread cycle the highest. Baking times vary according to the loaf size and choice of cycle.

There is a lot happening during baking. Evaporation of moisture occurs; you will see steam coming out of the top vent. One pound of raw dough loses about 1½ to 2 ounces of

Bread Machine Baker's Hint: Tips for Keeping Bread Fresh

Ideally, you will eat your bread the day it is made. Once you break the crust, the inner crumb is exposed to air and begins to stale. You want to keep the crust crisp and the inside soft for as long as possible. Starter and sourdough breads keep the longest. Any added fat will help bread stay fresh a day longer. Breads that include dairy products need to be refrigerated.

- Eat a freshly made loaf within a few hours of baking. It will taste best within 24 hours.

- Slice the bread as you eat it, rather than slicing the entire loaf as soon as it is cool.

- Store bread in a bread box, bread drawer, brown paper bag, or perforated plastic bag to allow air to circulate. Plastic is best for breads with lots of fat and a soft crust. Storing bread in the refrigerator makes it stale quicker.

- Leave the loaf unwrapped and place it cut side down on a bread board.

- Cut the loaf in half. Eat one half and freeze the other half.

- Slice the entire loaf, then store it in the freezer. Remove as many slices as you need at one time and either thaw them in the microwave or toast them.

moisture during baking. The starch begins to swell at 130°F, transferring moisture. The heat stops the yeast from reproducing at 140°F and coagulates the proteins in the gluten at 165°F. Forming the structure of the loaf by setting the starches, a process called gelatinization, begins at about 150°F. The alcohol by-products of the yeast evaporate at 175°F, creating steam and trapping some of the by-products in the baked dough. There is the smell of evaporating alcohol. Fats melt into the dough and the starch changes into dextrins to create a brown crust. Moisture evaporates from the surface and the heat changes the chemical components of the starches, milk, and eggs. Sugar in the dough will make for a darker crust as it caramelizes in the heat.

If the loaves are too heavy and dense before baking, the baked loaf will be small and compact. If there is too much liquid or yeast in the dough, the bread will collapse when the gluten strands break during baking. A beautiful baked loaf of bread has a golden color to its crust and sounds hollow when it is tapped. Breads are thoroughly baked at 190° to 200°F on an instant read thermometer. You can check the temperature at the end of baking if you are not sure by sight whether the loaf is done. A loaf has not completely finished baking until it is completely cool and all of the internal moisture has evaporated.

COOLING/COOL DOWN

Most bread machine models enter into a Cool Down period to remove the warm, moist air at the end of baking; some even have a steam-injected hour-long Keep Warm period. To avoid a gummy, soggy interior, remove a loaf as soon as the timer sounds that the baking is done. In some models, the kneading blade sticks in the bottom of the loaf; in others it stays in the pan due to its position. Sometimes a shake will dislodge the blade; other times it is lodged in the loaf rather tightly. (See step 12 of the Homestyle White Bread recipe, page 29, for information on dislodging the kneading blade.)

If you are having trouble getting a loaf out of the pan, or if you know you have an exceptionally delicate loaf, turn off the machine, unplug it, and open the lid. Let the loaf sit in the machine with the lid open for five to ten minutes. It will shrink from the sides of the pan as it cools, and should become easy to turn out.

The delicate texture and rich flavor of bread is at its best when it has had a chance to cool completely. Technically, bread has not finished baking until it is cool and the excess moisture has evaporated from the inside out. The crust of your bread will soften as it cools. Cool a loaf on a rack so that air can circulate all around it, before slicing it. You will ruin a loaf if you cut into it too soon. To slice bread, use a serrated bread knife, designed to slice without squashing or tearing the loaf. French breads and rolls are best eaten cooled to room temperature; richer whole-grain and cakelike breads should be cooled completely and then reheated.

Learning Recipes

While all the recipes in this book are written with clear directions, there are a lot of little details to making an electronic bread machine do what it does best—operate properly at the touch of a button and make a good loaf of bread by mixing, kneading, and baking within the machine. I have developed these first three recipes with expanded instructions as a guide to using the machine, and to familiarize you with three common techniques. The Home-style White Bread is a standard—also called simple or straight—dough that uses the most basic bread machine procedure. Shepherd's Bread is an overnight sponge bread in which a small portion of flour and liquid are mixed and left to sit overnight and ferment (forming the sponge) before the rest of the ingredients

Technique: *Mise en Place*

A professional culinary technique known as *mise en place*, simply "everything in its place," is important for excellent, efficient baking. It is one of the first disciplines an apprentice learns in a French-style kitchen. This means that all the basic ingredients and equipment necessary for preparing your loaf of bread are assembled and within easy access on your workstation. The initial preparation of ingredients, like toasting nuts or chopping fruit, is done, and all you have left to do is combine the ingredients in the bread pan. Because bread machine baking is an exact art, the practice of *mise en place* ensures that you are organized and focused, in order to make the best possible loaf of bread.

are added to make a dough. (You will become more familiar with this type of baking in the Country Breads section of the Traditional Loaves chapter.) Whole Wheat Cuban Bread, made overnight using the Delay Timer, will be ever-so-slightly more coarse and chewy than the Homestyle White Bread because it is made entirely with water rather than milk.

The straight dough and sponge dough are the basic techniques that will be used throughout this book, but each recipe will have specific instructions. These recipes produce loaves that are perfect for, but not exclusively for, beginners. Though the ingredients are basic, picture-perfect loaves will emerge from the pan: deep brown hairline crusts, domed tops, evenly browned sides. Once you become familiar with these recipes, the whole process of loading and baking in your bread machine will become as easy as popping the lid to check your dough.

Your First Loaf:

HOMESTYLE WHITE BREAD

T*his style of constructing a dough is known as the plain, direct, or straight dough method. The majority of the loaves in this book are made in this manner. All of the raw ingredients are combined at the same time to make a malleable dough ball. Since bread machine recipes call for a type of yeast that is able to be incorporated into the dry ingredients without being dissolved first in water, it is a variation of the rapid-mix method that became popular with electric mixing. This recipe produces a bread that has an attractive crust, a medium-textured crumb with an appealing cream color, and a rich flavor and aroma.*

1 Place the bread machine on a counter that is outside of main kitchen activity, with plenty of room above to open the lid. Make sure there is room around the machine to use as a work area, and so that steam can freely evaporate from the machine's vents.

2 Read the recipe, choose the size of loaf you will make, and assemble your ingredients on the work area. For this recipe, this would mean your measuring cups and spoons, butter which you have cut into pieces, bread flour, nonfat dry milk, sugar, gluten, salt, and bread machine yeast. Measure out the water. Let the ingredients, including the liquids, come to room temperature. Fluff your flour to aerate it by stirring it with the handle of a large spoon.

1½-POUND LOAF	2-POUND LOAF
1⅛ cups water	1½ cups water
1 tablespoon honey	1½ tablespoons honey
2 tablespoons unsalted butter, cut into pieces	2½ tablespoons unsalted butter, cut into pieces
3 cups bread flour	4 cups bread flour
2 tablespoons nonfat dry milk	3 tablespoons nonfat dry milk
1 tablespoon toasted wheat germ, optional	2 tablespoons toasted wheat germ, optional
1 tablespoon sugar	1½ tablespoons sugar
1 tablespoon gluten	1 tablespoon plus 1 teaspoon gluten
1½ teaspoons salt	2 teaspoons salt
2 teaspoons SAF yeast or 2½ teaspoons bread machine yeast	2½ teaspoons SAF yeast or 1 tablespoon bread machine yeast

(If your recipe called for extras, such as nuts or raisins, you would want to toss them with a bit of flour and have them ready too.)

❸ Take the bread pan out of the oven area of the machine and place it on the counter. Mount the kneading blade(s) on the clean shaft and be sure it is in place correctly.

❹ Check your manufacturer's manual or see the chart on page 17 to be certain of the sequence for adding ingredients to your machine. Most machines require the liquids to be added first, then the dry ingredients, and then the yeast, so that is the order in which the ingredients are given for the recipes in this book. (The ingredients are also grouped according to liquid, dry, and yeast, so it is easy to change the order if your machine calls for the dry ingredients first. Simply switch around the categories.) Once you have determined the proper order for your machine, follow steps 5, 6, and 7 according to it.

❺ Pour the water you have measured into the pan. *If you are using a Welbilt machine, add 2 additional tablespoons of liquid.* Add the honey and room-temperature butter pieces (the size of the pieces is not important), dropping them right into the water; they will be distributed into the dough with the action of the kneading blade.

❻ Measure and add the dry ingredients, in the order they are given, adding the exact amount of flour, powdered dry milk, wheat germ if you are using it, sugar, gluten, (seasonings, if they had been in this recipe), and salt. Do not add the yeast yet. Don't worry about mixing anything; just pour the ingredients in.

❼ Measure and add the yeast on top of the other ingredients (or into the yeast dispenser after you close the lid in Step 8, if your machine so requires). While machine manuals usually make the point that you don't want the yeast and salt to touch (salt inhibits the action of the yeast), if you will not be setting the Delay Timer, it doesn't matter what touches what; it will all be mixing in a matter of minutes anyway. Wipe clean the edge of the pan around the rim.

❽ Replace the bread pan in the machine and click it into place on the bottom of the oven floor. Fold down the handle, close the lid, and plug in the machine. The display surface will light up and there will be a beep.

❾ Program the bread machine for the cycle appropriate to the type of bread you are making. In this case, the desired cycle is Basic. With some machines, choosing the cycle is as simple as pressing the button labeled with the name of the cycle you want; consult your owner's manual for the clearest instructions for programming your machine.

If applicable, press the loaf control button and select the size loaf. Press the setting for the desired crust color. Use the medium setting the first time you make this loaf. You can adjust this setting the next time you make it, if need be. (If you were using a recipe that called for extras, and if your machine has a dispenser, you would place the extras in there, and then press the Extras button as you were programming the machine.)

🔟 Push the On or Start button to begin the cycle, which starts with Mix and Knead 1. Clean up the work area, leaving on hand the measuring spoons, some flour, and some water. Place a long, narrow plastic spatula at the ready for testing the dough.

⓫ During the first 5 to 10 minutes of Knead 2, open the lid and check the consistency of the dough, even if this is not stated in the manufacturer's manual. Every loaf is different and you need to adjust and repair the dough as

needed. (Some bakers regularly withhold 2 to 3 tablespoons of the total amount of flour so they can add it slowly into the dough ball, so they have better control of the consistency.) Pop open the lid and, using the spatula, push the dough around, checking in the corners to make sure all the ingredients are incorporated into the dough ball. Some machines stop when you open the lid, others keep running. If the machine is running, you need to exercise caution to avoid the moving kneading blade, but you will become comfortable with this. Use your fingers to touch and press the dough. If the dough is wet and sticks to the sides and bottom of the pan, sprinkle in some flour, 1 tablespoon at a time, while the machine is kneading (be careful not to splash flour over the sides of the baking pan rim and onto the element because you will smell it burning later during the baking) until the dough forms a ball that is smooth and firm, yet soft and springy to the touch. If it looks like a batter, you can add up to $\frac{1}{4}$ cup of extra flour. If the dough is very firm and dry looking, perhaps lumpy and not holding together, or even if it is a dry ball rolling around in the pan, add water 1 teaspoon at a time until the dough softens up a bit. The humidity of the climate where you live will affect the amount of additional flour or water you need. This is a very important step!

Just before or during Knead 2, your machine may beep. This is to alert you to add any extra ingredients. This recipe doesn't call for any, but if you were adding nuts and raisins you would open the lid and sprinkle them in. (Some machines don't beep to signal for extras; if yours does not, you could just open the lid and add them during the Knead 2 part of the cycle.) The extras would get incorporated as the dough was kneaded.

12 Set a cooling rack on the counter. When the baking cycle ends, you will hear the beep. Press Stop even if your machine has automatically gone into the Cool Down/Keep Warm phase. Unplug the machine, carefully open the lid, and, using heavy oven mitts to hold the handle, carefully remove the pan by pulling up and out of the hot machine. If your bread pan is thin, set it on the cooling rack and let it stand for 5 minutes to allow the bread to contract slightly from the sides of the pan before turning it out. Otherwise remove the bread from the pan immediately by turning the pan upside down and shaking it a few times to release the loaf. Make sure the handle is out of the way so the

loaf is not damaged by hitting it as it comes out of the pan. If it does not slide right out, run your rubber spatula around the edges and shake the pan again to dislodge the loaf.

Check to see if the blade has come off the shaft and is still embedded in the bottom of the loaf. If so, remove it by prying it loose with a bamboo chopstick or the handle of a heat-resistant plastic spatula while holding the loaf upside down in your oven-mitt-protected other hand. Don't use any metal utensils that could scratch this nonstick piece. You can also just let the loaf cool and remove the blade later. (If you have problems getting the blade out of the bread, next time you make bread, spray the kneading blade with a vegetable cooking spray before adding the ingredients to the bread pan.)

13 Place the loaf upright on the rack to cool to room temperature before slicing. If you wish, you can brush the crust all over with melted butter, which will soak in while the bread cools. (Remember that bread technically does not finish baking until it has cooled and the excess moisture created during baking is evaporated, so it will slice and taste different when warm than when cool.)

The Next Step—Using a Starter:
SHEPHERD'S BREAD

T he way of constructing a dough for this Shepherd's Bread is known as the sponge dough method. It is an old-fashioned technique used to create a bread with a more rustic texture and crumb, more irregular holes, a slightly more acidic flavor from developed fermentation, and a slightly thicker crust than bread made by the plain dough method. While this takes a bit more time, this bread is really loved for its exceptional flavor.

A semi-liquid sponge starter, usually made from about a third of the flour and water called for in the recipe along with some yeast, can double in volume in thirty to forty-five minutes, but different recipes call for the sponge to sit for anywhere from two to twelve hours before adding the rest of the dough ingredients and kneading. This waiting step is comparable to the first kneading of a plain dough, since the gluten begins to soften and become more supple. The traditional method for creating full-flavored, long-rising, lean country loaves uses such yeast starters, prepared the same way as this sponge, but referred to as a biga in Italian bread recipes and as a poolish in French ones. The longer the starters ferment, the more the flavor develops and the more irregular the inner crumb will be. Some sponges are allowed to just rise; others to rise and fall back upon themselves. Salt is never added to a sponge starter, as it inhibits the growth of the yeast. Breads made by this method also have an increased shelf life, and a starter is able to give a boost to low-gluten flours, producing light, high loaves.

1½-POUND LOAF	2-POUND LOAF
For the sponge starter:	*For the sponge starter:*
⅔ cup water 1 cup bread flour	⅔ cup water 1 cup bread flour
¼ teaspoon SAF or bread machine yeast	¼ teaspoon SAF or bread machine yeast
For the dough:	*For the dough:*
½ cup water 1 tablespoon sugar 1 tablespoon unsalted butter or margarine, cut into pieces	⅞ cup water 1½ tablespoons sugar 1½ tablespoons unsalted butter or margarine, cut into pieces
2 cups bread flour 1 tablespoon gluten 1½ teaspoons salt	3 cups bread flour 1 tablespoon plus 1 teaspoon gluten 2 teaspoons salt
1½ teaspoons SAF yeast or 2 teaspoons bread machine yeast	1¾ teaspoons SAF yeast or 2¼ teaspoons bread machine yeast

❶ Place the bread machine on a counter that is outside of main kitchen activity, with plenty of room above to open the lid. Make sure there is room around the machine to use as a work area, and so that steam can evaporate freely from the machine's vents.

❷ Read the recipe, choose the size of loaf you will make, and assemble your ingredients on the work area. For this recipe, this would mean bread flour and bread machine yeast to start. Measure out the ⅔ cup water you will need for the starter, and let it, as well as the other ingredients, come to room temperature. Fluff your flour to aerate it by stirring it with the handle of a large spoon. Also, place a long, narrow plastic spatula within reach.

❸ Take the bread pan out of the oven area of the machine and place it on the counter. Mount the kneading blade(s) on the clean shaft and be sure it is correctly in place.

❹ Check your manufacturer's manual or see the chart on page 17 to be certain of the sequence for adding ingredients to your machine. (Once you have determined the proper order for your machine, follow steps 5, 9, and 10 according to it.)

❺ To make the starter, pour the ⅔ cup of water you have measured into the pan. Sprinkle with the bread flour and then with the yeast called for in the starter ingredients. You will fill only a small portion of the baking pan.

❻ Replace the pan in the machine and click it into place on the bottom of the oven floor; fold down the handle, close the lid, and plug in the machine. The display surface will light up. Program for the Dough setting (see your owner's manual for specifics on programming your machine). As the machine starts to mix (this will occur after the preheat time if your machine has this feature), set a kitchen timer for 10 minutes. After 5 minutes, open the lid and scrape down the accumulated bits of flour with your plastic spatula. When the timer rings, press Stop/Reset. Unplug the machine and let the sponge starter sit in the bread machine, with the lid closed, for 4 hours.

❼ About half an hour before the time is complete for the sponge, assemble the dough ingredients on your work area. This would include sugar, un-salted butter or margarine cut into pieces, bread flour, gluten, salt, and bread machine yeast. Measure out the amount of water called for in the recipe, and let all the ingredients sit to come to room temperature.

8 When 4 hours are up, open the bread machine lid; the sponge starter will have swollen and be bubbly, and will have a pleasant fermented smell that will waft up to your nose. You don't need to do anything to the sponge. Remove the pan from the machine.

9 To make the dough, add the ingredients as listed for the dough. Place the exact amount of water (reserving 2 tablespoons if your environment is very humid), the sugar, and the butter pieces in the pan on top of the sponge (here the sugar is added with the liquid ingredients). *If you are using a Welbilt machine, add 2 additional tablespoons of liquid to this recipe.* Then add the dry ingredients: the flour (reserving 2 tablespoons), gluten, and salt, in that order.

10 Measure and add the yeast on top of the dry ingredients (or into the yeast dispenser after you close the lid in Step 11, if your machine so requires). Wipe the edge of the pan around the rim clean.

11 Replace the bread pan in the machine, and click it into place on the bottom of the oven floor. Fold down the handle, close the lid, and plug in the machine. The display surface will light up and there will be a beep.

12 Program for the Basic cycle. If applicable, press the loaf control button and select the size loaf. Press the setting for the desired crust color. Use the medium setting the first time you make this loaf. (You can adjust it the next time you make it, if need be.)

13 Push the On or Start button to begin the mixing and kneading process. Clean up the work area, leaving the measuring spoons and the reserved 2 tablespoons of water and of flour. Place a plastic spatula on the counter for testing the dough.

14 During the first 5 to 10 minutes into kneading, open the lid and check the consistency of the dough. Using the spatula, push the dough around, checking in the corners to make sure all the ingredients are incorporated into the dough ball. Feel the dough ball with your fingers. Some machines stop when you open the lid; others keep running. If the machine is running, you need to exercise caution to avoid the moving kneading blade, but you will become comfortable with this. Use your fingers to touch and press the dough. It should form a smooth, elastic dough ball. If the dough is sticking to the sides and bottom of the pan, sprinkle in more flour, 1 tablespoon at a time, while the machine is kneading. If it is lumpy and not hold-ing together, add more water, 1 tea-spoon at a time. This is a very important step!

15 The machine will do the rest of the work. It is okay to lift the lid and look inside during the entire kneading and initial rising phases (even if you have a viewing window, it may fog up), just leave the machine alone during Rise 3 and Bake. You will notice that this dough has a stronger yeasty aroma than a straight dough.

16 Set a cooling rack on the counter. When the baking cycle ends, you will hear the beep. Press Stop/Reset if your machine has automatically gone into a Cool Down/Keep Warm mode, unplug the machine, and, using heavy oven mitts to hold the handle, care-fully remove the pan by pulling it up and out of the hot machine. If your bread pan is thin, set it on the cooling rack and let it stand for 5 minutes to allow the bread to contract slightly from the sides of the pan. Otherwise, remove the bread from the pan im-mediately by turning the pan upside down and shaking it a few times to release the loaf. Make sure the handle is out of the way so the loaf is not damaged by hitting it as it comes out of the pan. If it does not slide right

out, run your rubber spatula around the edges and shake the pan again to dislodge the loaf. If the blade comes off the shaft with the loaf and is still embedded in the bottom of it, remove it by prying it loose with a bamboo chopstick or the handle of a heat-resistant plastic spatula.

17 Place the loaf upright on the rack to cool to room temperature before slicing. (Remember that bread tech-nically does not finish baking until it has cooled and the excess moisture created during baking is evaporated, so it will slice and taste different when warm than when cool.)

Delay Timer:

WHOLE WHEAT CUBAN BREAD

1½-POUND LOAF

1¼ cups water

1½ teaspoons salt
1¾ cups bread flour
1½ cups whole wheat flour
1½ tablespoons gluten
1 tablespoon sugar

2¼ teaspoons SAF yeast or
2¾ teaspoons bread
machine yeast

2-POUND LOAF

1½ cups water

2 teaspoons salt
2 cups bread flour
2⅓ cups whole wheat flour
2 tablespoons gluten
1 tablespoon plus
1 teaspoon sugar

2½ teaspoons SAF yeast or
1 tablespoon bread
machine yeast

W*hole Wheat Cuban Bread is a simple straight dough, made here using the Delay Timer, which means that you set the machine's timer to begin the bread-making process fifteen to twenty-four hours (it varies by manufacturer) before you want to have a fresh-baked loaf. You can have fresh bread ready when you wake up in the morning or when you get home from work in the evening. This is convenience at its best. Although the machine can be programmed to bake as long as twenty-four hours after the ingredients are loaded, it is important to note that the shorter the amount of time the ingredients sit in the pan before mixing, the better the bread. The ingredients do interact on a slow basis while they sit in the pan, so a loaf made this way may not have as much volume as the same recipe made on the Basic cycle immediately after loading.*

It is important to add the salt right after the liquid ingredients when using the Delay Timer, a precaution that keeps the salt and yeast separated from each other, as the salt can inhibit the action of the yeast.

This adaptation of Cuban Bread, made with part whole wheat flour, is easy and delicious.

❶ Place the machine on a counter that is outside of main kitchen activity, with plenty of room above to open the lid. Make sure there is room around the machine to use as a work area, and so that steam can evaporate from the machine's vents.

❷ When using the Delay Timer, I usually choose a recipe I have made successfully before so that I don't have to worry about making any adjustments to the dough ball during kneading. Do not use a recipe that calls for any fresh ingredients, such as eggs, milk, butter, cottage cheese, or meats (raw or cooked), including fish. Read the recipe, choose the size of loaf you will make, and assemble your ingredients on the work area. Measure out the water. Fluff your flour to aerate it by stirring it with the handle of a large spoon.

❸ Take the bread pan out of the oven area of the machine and place it on the counter. Mount the kneading blade(s) on the clean shaft and be sure it is correctly in place.

❹ Check your manufacturer's manual or the chart on page 17 to be certain of the sequence necessary for adding the ingredients to your machine. (Once you have determined the proper order for your machine, follow steps 5 and 6 according to it.)

❺ Pour the water you have measured into the pan. *If you are using a Welbilt machine, add 2 additional tablespoons of water.* Add the salt. Measure and add the rest of the dry ingredients to the liquid. Don't worry about mixing anything, just add the ingredients one at a time: bread flour, whole wheat flour, gluten, and sugar.

❻ Make a small indentation in the top of the dry ingredients. Measure the yeast and add it to the pan, dropping it into the depression (or place it in the yeast dispenser after you close the lid in step 7, if your machine requires it), taking care not to let the yeast touch any of

the liquid. The salt and yeast should not come in contact when using the Delayed Timer (this type of layering will prevent that). Wipe clean the edge of the pan around the rim.

❼ Replace the bread pan in the machine and click it into place in the bottom of the oven floor. Fold down the handle, close the lid, and plug in the machine. The display surface will light up and there will be a beep.

❽ Program the bread machine for the cycle appropriate to the type of bread you are making. In this case, the desired cycles are Basic or French Bread. Consult your owner's manual for the clearest instructions for programming your machine.

If applicable, press the loaf control button and select the size loaf. Press the setting for the desired crust color. Choose medium for this loaf.

❾ The total time for the cycle you have chosen—Basic or French Bread, about 3½ to 4 hours—will come up on the display. Check your manufacturer's manual to see how far ahead you can program the Delay Timer. Figure out what time you want to have the finished bread. For example, say you want fresh bread ready at 5:00 P.M. to eat for dinner. You are setting up the machine at 8:00 A.M. before you leave for work. You must do some math here. It is 9 hours until you want the bread to be finished baking.

10 There are two Timer buttons, one ascending and one descending. Each push of the button will increase or decrease the amount of time programmed by a certain interval, 10 minutes or 20 minutes, for example. Continue pressing the ascending Timer button until you see the amount of time you want displayed on the screen, 9 hours. (Continually pressing a button will cause the increments to register very quickly, like when you set your bedside digital clock.) If you press the ascending button too many times, you can correct the time by pressing the descending Timer button, which will subtract time. When you finish, the display should read 9:00, or 9 hours, which includes the time for mixing, rising, and baking the bread.

11 Press the On or Start button to begin the Timer. The colon (:) on the screen will flash to indicate that the Delay Timer is in progress. You can look at the display any time of the day and see the countdown. Clean up the work area. If you have made a mistake or decide to bake the bread at a different time, press and hold Stop/Reset. This will clear everything that you have programmed, and you can start all over again.

12 Set a cooling rack on the counter. When the baking cycle ends, the machine will automatically go into a Keep Warm/Cool Down phase in case you can't remove the bread from the pan immediately.

When you are ready to remove the bread from the pan, press Stop and unplug the machine. Carefully open the lid. Using heavy oven mitts to hold the handle, remove the pan by pulling it up and out of the hot machine. If your bread pan is thin, set it on the cooling rack and let it stand for 5 minutes to allow the bread to contract slightly from the sides of the pan before turning out the bread. Otherwise, remove the bread from the pan immediately by turning the pan upside down and shaking it a few times to release the loaf. Make sure the handle is out of the way so the loaf is not damaged by hitting it as it comes out of the pan. Check to see whether the kneading blade has come off the shaft and is still embedded in the loaf.

13 Place the loaf upright on the rack to cool to room temperature before slicing.

High-Altitude Baking

If you have tried to bake with a bread machine at altitudes over 3,000 feet above sea level, you will know that it can either go just as planned, or you can experience a lot of frustration making adjustments to try to get a nice loaf of bread from the bread machine. The higher you go, the more compressed the air is, so flour tends to dry out and will absorb more liquid. Store your flour in airtight plastic containers, in the refrigerator if possible. You will probably have to add a tablespoon or two more liquid when you check the dough ball. Consider adding on a third or even a fourth rising period

if you are still having problems with the texture and your machine is capable of this type of programming.

Dough will usually rise more rapidly at higher altitudes. The higher you go, the faster the fermentation is. Leavening carbon dioxide gases are able to expand faster due to the thinner air, and rising time will decrease up to half. Compensate for this by reducing the sugar and yeast to slow the action of the yeast. This prevents over-rising and possible collapse of the dough, and gives the dough more time to develop the proper texture and flavor. Some people add a bit more salt, 10 to 25 percent, to control the yeast, rather than cutting back

Adjustment	Altitude		
	3,000 feet	**5,000 feet**	**7,000–8,000 feet**
Increase liquid. For each cup liquid, increase by	1–2 tablespoons	2–3 tablespoons	3–4 tablespoons
Increase gluten. For each cup flour, increase by	1–2 teaspoons	2–3 teaspoons	3–4 teaspoons
Reduce yeast. For each teaspoon yeast, decrease by	⅛ teaspoon	⅛–¼ teaspoon	¼–⅓ teaspoon
Reduce sugar. For each cup sugar, decrease by	1–3 teaspoons	1–2 tablespoons	2–3 tablespoons
Reduce baking powder. For each teaspoon baking powder, decrease by	⅛ teaspoon	⅛–¼ teaspoon	¼–⅓ teaspoon

Increase oven temperature by 25°F.

on the yeast. No temperature adjustment of liquids is necessary. Also, add some more gluten; it will give strength to the dough. If you are baking in the oven, temperatures should be increased by 25°F to compensate for faster rising in the oven and slower heating. Usually some combination of all these measures is necessary for producing a good loaf of bread.

The chart on page 37 will serve as a guideline for these adjustments when making yeast, sourdough, or quick breads. Be sure to make notes on your recipes about the adjustments you make, for future reference.

What Can Go Wrong and How to Fix It

Knowing how to fix problems that arise is part of becoming a good baker. While every manufacturer's pamphlet has an in-depth section devoted to the problems that are specific to their machine, there are a few problems that every bread machine baker will run into from time to time. I find it helpful to have a short list to quickly refer to when a loaf comes out looking different than expected and I want to find out why. This is when you get to play with the chemistry of baking. Remember that these problems are seldom caused by machine malfunctions. Usually simple adjustments can be made to fix them. Here is a list of the most common problems I have encountered, with a number of possible causes and solutions listed for each. If I encounter the problem with a certain recipe, I often note the adjustment that solved it right on the recipe for future reference.

Shaggy, unmanageable dough ball: Too much flour.

- *This dough has too much flour, but you may be able to save it.* Add liquid in increments until the dough ball is the right consistency.
- *This dough may not be worth saving.* Press Stop to cancel the program and discard the dough. Make the recipe over again from the beginning.
- *This dough had too much flour.* Next time you make it, hold back 2 to 3 tablespoons of the flour called for and add it slowly, only as needed, during the kneading.

Wet, slick dough: Too much liquid or the dough was made on a humid day.

- *The bread had too much liquid.* Cut back the liquid in the recipe by 2 tablespoons.
- *The bread was baked in hot, humid weather.* Wait until a cooler, drier day to bake again.

Loaf is too dense: Insufficient leavening for the mass of dough.

- *Used all-purpose flour instead of high-gluten bread flour.* Try using bread flour next time.
- *Used too much of a dark spice, such as ground cinnamon, that inhibits the yeast.* Next time cut back on the amount of dark spices used. See page 441 for more information.
- *Flour was packed too densely during measuring.* Next time aerate your flour before measuring by stirring it with the handle of a wooden spoon or pouring it from a large spoon into the measuring cup.
- *Loaf had a high percentage of whole grain flour.* Next time add more gluten or use some bread flour.

- *Too many added ingredients, such as nuts, dried fruit, or cheese.* Next time cut back on the amount of these ingredients.
- *Ingredients were too cold when they were mixed.* Allow ingredients to come to room temperature before putting them in the bread pan.
- *If you are not sure what caused the dense loaf:* Add 1 to 2 teaspoons more gluten *or* add ½ to 1 teaspoon more yeast *or* add 2 tablespoons more liquid next time you bake the bread.

Pale loaf: The bread is underbaked.
- *The loaf needs more baking time.* Clear the cycle and program for the Bake Only cycle. Select a temperature between 325° and 350°F, and select the amount of extra time, 5 to 15 minutes. Or, remove the loaf from the bread pan and place it in the oven, preheated to 325° or 350°F, until the bread is finished baking.

Sunken top: Known as crater bread, this happens when there is too much liquid in the recipe, making the dough overly heavy for the amount of leavening.
- *The loaf needed more flour.* Increase the flour in increments from 2 to 6 tablespoons next time you make this bread.
- *There was too much sugar in the loaf.* Next time cut back.
- *You are baking at a high altitude.* You will need to reduce the sugar and yeast a bit, add a bit more salt, add some more gluten, *or* try a combination of these measures. See pages 37 to 38 for more information about high altitude baking.
- *You forgot to add the salt.* This important ingredient regulates the yeast; try the recipe again, adding the amount of salt called for.
- *Loaf is over-risen.* Next time use the Quick Yeast Bread cycle.

- *The loaf needed more gluten.* Next time add more gluten to help the loaf hold its shape.
- *The loaf was left in the machine too long on the Keep Warm part of the cycle.* Next time remove the loaf from the machine as soon as the beep sounds that the baking has ended.
- *The loaf had too much yeast.* Next time decrease the yeast by ½ teaspoon.

Collapsed top and sides: Too much yeast working too fast, and too much liquid.
- *You can try one of the following solutions:* Decrease the liquid by 1 tablespoon the next time you bake, *or* decrease the yeast by a quarter of the amount called for, *or* decrease the fat *or* the sugar in the recipe by half.

Gnarled loaves or the machine sounds like it is straining during kneading: Too much flour; the blade cannot knead effectively.
- *Too much flour was used for the loaf.* Reduce the amount of flour by 2 tablespoons next time.

Squat, domed loaf: Too much flour.
- *There was too much flour in the loaf.* Reduce the flour by ½ cup the next time you make the recipe and add the flour in increments of 1 tablespoon until the dough ball is the right consistency.
- *Loaf needed more liquid.* Next time add liquid in increments of 1 tablespoon until the dough ball is the right consistency.
- *Loaf needed more yeast.* Increase the yeast by a quarter of the amount called for.

Lopsided loaf: The dough was on one side of the pan during the rises.
- *The dough ball was not in the center of the pan.* Next time check the dough ball during

rising. If you see it sitting to one side, pick it up (carefully, so as not to remove the blade with it) and set it in the center on the blade.

Loaf balloons up over the rim of the pan like a mushroom and is too big and light textured: The dough has risen too much.
- *There was too much yeast.* Reduce the yeast by ½ teaspoon next time.
- *There was too much liquid.* Next time, reduce the liquid by 1 tablespoon.
- *The proportions of the recipe were too large for the size of the baking pan.* Reduce all the quantities in the recipe by one third or one half next time.
- *The bread was baked on too warm a day.* The baking process is affected by hot surrounding temperatures; bake again on a cooler day or in the early morning or evening.

Bread is not cooked throughout: The dough was too heavy.
- *Too large a percentage of whole grain flours was used.* Next time use more bread flour.
- *Too many heavy, moist ingredients.* Next time reduce the amount of cheese, applesauce, sour cream, dried fruit, or other such ingredients.
- *The dough needed an extra knead.* Next time, reset the machine after Knead 2 and start the cycle again from the beginning to give the dough extra kneading time.
- *There was not enough yeast.* Increase the yeast by one fourth of the amount called for next time you bake the bread.

Added ingredients are clumped: When the extras were added they did not get mixed in completely.

- *The extras were added too late and did not get distributed.* Next time, add them at the beep or add them during the pause between Knead 1 and Knead 2.
- *The extras were too large or too sticky to get distributed.* Next time chop the ingredients smaller and toss them with some flour to separate them.

After baking, the loaf has a long crease down the side that slightly separates from the loaf: There was too much flour and the loaf did not rise enough.
- *There was too much flour.* Next time reduce the flour by 2 tablespoons.
- *There was not enough liquid.* Add more liquid next time in increments of 1 tablespoon.
- *The dough needed more rising time.* If your machine can be programmed for part of a cycle, next time you bake press Stop/Reset after Rise 3 and program the machine for an extra rise.

Leftover Bread Cookery

I always seem to end up with plenty of leftover bread from baking in my bread machine, most of which begins to stale in a matter of hours. So what do you do with leftover bread after you have eaten a multitude of sandwiches and tons of toast? How much room is there in the freezer? Has every neighbor been given a loaf? A few wayward crumbs thrown to visiting birds?

A loaf of bread can be the handiest staple to have in the cupboard; there is an entire world of recipes based on the leftover loaf. Many of them are quite old-fashioned, harking back to the days when no foodstuff went to waste. Besides providing for a well-stocked pantry of fresh breadcrumbs and croutons, bread provides the base for grilled sandwiches and French toast, and for a wide variety of beautiful, easy appetizers that can be topped with savory preparations of meat, fish, vegetables, or cheese. Bread can be floated in soups; used as breading, stuffing, and binding for meats, poultry, and fish; or used to create a host of filling desserts. Recipes for some of these creations are spread throughout this book, but here is an overview of some of the delicious ways you can use up leftover bread.

- Fine dry or coarse fresh breadcrumbs are the best substance for coating meats, eggplant, croquettes, and cheeses to make a crisp crust after sautéing. These are called "breading" for a reason!
- Bread slices or soaked bread or rolls are used as a filling starch like pasta, or to line casseroles, like a pastry crust, for savory *stratas* or sweet bread puddings.
- In cubes, chunks, or coarse crumbs, bread is the main ingredient for meat and vegetable stuffings; for fruit stuffings, as in baked apples; or to bulk out and bind ingredients, as in meat loaf, meatballs, and crab cakes.
- Toasted fresh breadcrumbs make a great crunchy and attractive topping for roasted vegetables,

casseroles, or spreads, such as macaroni and cheese or deviled crab. They are also used as a separate ingredient tossed with pasta, topping pizzas, or in potato salad, offering a contrast in flavor and texture.
- Fresh breadcrumbs are mixed with eggs to form a mixture like a savory breading mixture, and cooked in broth to form a variety of old-fashioned dumplings.
- Breadcrumbs are used as a thickening agent in sauces like the tomato sauce for moussaka and for *skordalia*, the wonderful Greek sauce for fish and vegetables made with garlic, nuts, bread, and olive oil.
- Without bread there would be no fondue or Welsh rabbit, made simply of melted cheeses with bread.
- Crostini, or twice-baked breads, are the base for all sorts of warm and cold canapés.
- Crunchy toasts are floated in soups, such as French onion, *pan cotto* (stale bread is added to this Tuscan broccoli and potato soup), gazpacho (bread, vinegar, tomatoes, and garlic pureed together for a cold soup), *panada* (broth, vegetables, and bread baked until the bread absorbs the broth, and eaten with a spoon), and *pistou* (the French vegetable soup with a crouton coated with pesto on the bottom).
- Pita bread can be used for lining the cooking pot used to steam rice, the way it is done in Middle Eastern kitchens.
- Dry breadcrumbs are often used in place of flour to dust baking pans to keep cakes and cheesecakes from sticking. They are important in separating layers of strudel or filo dough, as in fruit strudels.
- European and Jewish baking use dry breadcrumbs as a main ingredient in place of flour for cakes and tortes. Breadcrumbs are often used in steamed puddings and in eastern European hearty rye breads.

DAILY BREADS

White Breads and Egg Breads

WHITE BREADS

The world of baking has not always known white bread. It is the product of a sophisticated milling process that acts like a series of sieves, separating the bran and germ from the creamy white endosperm. Mills were first powered by steam in the 1700s, finally breaking the centuries-old customs of using wind, muscle, and water power for milling. This innovation proved a great success. Ingredients to make bread became easier than ever to obtain. The invention of high-speed roller mills became a hot topic among European inventors. Patents were finally granted to Swiss inventors in the mid-1800s, but it was a Hungarian, Count Szechenyi, who is credited with first putting such a system into widespread use in Budapest mills in 1870. The resulting finely bolted flour was used by the Viennese and French to create their sophisticated array of baroque coffeehouse breads and pastries. In 1879, a team of Hungarian engineers was invited to Minneapolis to set up such innovative systems of milling in America, and the General Mills Corporation was born.

White breads and egg breads are the mainstay of the home bread baker's kitchen. That is why I categorize them as daily breads; they are good made fresh every day and have basic, versatile flavors so they can be eaten at every meal and are easily consumed in a day. I consider them gourmet breads, with delicate flavor and texture, yet completely accommodating at the same time. Loving white and egg breads is like choosing vanilla ice cream—often thought of as plain. But those who love white bread, like those who love vanilla ice cream, appreciate its subtleties of flavor and the myriad foods with which it can be combined. White bread textures vary with the addition of water, milk, buttermilk, yogurt, evaporated milk, or dry milk. Non-dairy milks, too, such as coconut or soy, can be used with wonderful results. White bread can be spartan, with just a tad of oil and sugar, or rich, with lots of butter and milk. Water makes a chewy, coarse-textured loaf, while milk makes a fine-textured, softer loaf. The combination of water and milk is a favorite in bread baking; it should be your tipoff to a delicate crumb. For toast, sandwiches, dinner bread, hamburger or hot dog rolls, croutons, French toast, or for use in a *strata* or bread pudding, these are the breads to use.

HONEY WHITE BREAD

H oney is a great favorite in breadmaking—for good reason. It is a natural sweetener with up to 80 percent of its weight composed of sugar. "The land of milk and honey" was what the promised land was called in the Old Testament, and today honey, a miracle in a jar, certainly still connotes luxury. Since honey is collected mainly from leguminous plants, look for familiar clover, sage, eucalyptus, tupelo, or buckwheat honeys. I like to search out nice local honeys to use in my breads, such as star thistle honey from Sonoma County, or cherry honey from the fruit stand down the road.

1 Place all the ingredients in the pan according to the order in the manufacturer's instructions. Set crust on medium and program for the Basic cycle; press Start. (This recipe is not suitable for use with the Delay Timer.)

2 When the baking cycle ends, immediately remove the bread from the pan and place it on a rack. Let cool to room temperature before slicing.

1½-POUND LOAF

½ cup water
½ cup milk
1½ tablespoons canola oil
2 tablespoons honey

2⅞ cups bread flour
1 tablespoon gluten
1 teaspoon salt

1¾ teaspoons SAF yeast or
   2¼ teaspoons bread
   machine yeast

2-POUND LOAF

⅔ cup water
⅔ cup milk
2 tablespoons canola oil
3 tablespoons honey

3¾ cups bread flour
1 tablespoon plus
   1 teaspoon gluten
1½ teaspoons salt

2¼ teaspoons SAF yeast or
   2¾ teaspoons bread
   machine yeast

The Baker's Glossary of White Flours Ground from Wheat

Wheat comes in many varieties. Hard red winter wheat, hard red spring wheat, soft red winter wheat, hard and soft white wheat, and spelt are known as the bread wheats. The gluten-rich, genetically complicated, hard Ukrainian wheat known as Turkey Red was introduced to the American Midwest and Canada in the nineteenth century by Mennonite settlers, and provided a significant increase in wheat production. Today, hybridized high-protein winter wheat, *Triticum aestivum*, hybridized from Turkey Red and Egyptian spelt, is the world's leading cultivated grain, producing wonderfully elastic doughs.

Each kernel of wheat has three parts—the bran, endosperm, and germ. How these parts are milled or sifted out determines what type of flour is created. White flours all have the bran and the germ sifted out. Each wheat has distinctive properties that dictate what it will best be used for. The hard wheats are the most important in bread bakery language. A higher protein percentage tells you the flour is best for breads, and the dough will turn out best if worked by machines—such as the electric mixer, bread machine, or food processor—in which the flour is worked much more vigorously than it could be by hand.

The following list includes many types of white flour and my favorites for bread machine baking. Remember that all pre-bagged brands will differ slightly from each other, giving slight variations to your bread's character.

Bread Flour

For the best results in making premium white breads I use cream-colored unbleached bread flour made from hard red spring wheat that is aged without chemicals or preservatives. It has a protein content of 12 to 14 percent. High-gluten wheat flour absorbs more liquid than other flours, creating a more elastic dough and a lighter-textured bread. I like Organic Hi Protein Hi Gluten Unbleached Flour or Organic Old Mill Flour with Reduced Bran from Giusto's. Other brands of bread flour that may be found around the country are Arrowhead Mills, King Arthur, Great Valley Mills, Hudson Cream, or one of the most commonly available brands such as Pillsbury, Gold Medal, Hecker's, or Hodgson Mills.

High-Gluten Flour

High-gluten flour is ground from hard red spring wheat and has some malted barley added. It is unbleached, that is, aged without chemicals or preservatives. It functions very much like bread flour, and is fine for bread machine baking.

All-Purpose Flour

Unbleached all-purpose flour, also called refined white flour, is blended from a combination of approximately 80 percent hard wheat and 20 percent soft. Note that the content of different brands of unbleached flour varies in different locales. Unbleached flour in the southern states has a higher percentage of soft wheat, and in the northern, midwestern, and western states it contains a higher percentage of hard wheat. Unbleached flour is aged to naturally oxidize the proteins and bleach out the natural yellow pigment present in freshly milled flour (also known as green flour). Bleached flour is aged quickly with chlorine dioxide, has less gluten, and lacks the vitamin E that naturally remains in flour after milling. I consider unbleached flour superior to bleached flour for use in bread recipes.

Bolted Flour

Bolted, or sifted, is the name for whole wheat flour that has had most of its bran sifted out. Bolted flour is new to home bakers, but well known to professionals. The only brand available through retail is Giusto's Old Mill Reduced Bran Flour, stone-ground, with 80 percent of the bran sifted out. It makes fabulous sandwich or country breads on its own or in combination with other whole wheat flours (it is good with spelt, kamut, and triticale). Make your own bolted flour by combining 3 cups unbleached white flour, 1 cup fine or medium stone-ground whole wheat flour, and 3 tablespoons raw wheat germ. This is an excellent all-purpose bread flour.

Clear Flour

Clear flour is not the name of a certain type of flour, but a milling term for the high-protein bread flour that is the least refined of white flours. There can be a few grades of clear flour, depending on how much it has been sifted. Often called straight flour, it has long been available to the professional baking industry but now King Arthur sells it to home bakers. It has a darkish cast to it, reflecting the high ash content—coarse particles that are partly bran—that is left in it after minimal sifting. Clear flour can be made from a blend of wheats rather than just one, depending on what type of flour the miller wants to create. Use it in place of bread flour in white breads or in combination with whole wheat flour, and especially in rye flour doughs. Clear flour makes delicious, chewy breads with lots of flavor.

Italian-Style, French-Style, and Irish-Style Flours

These are special flour blends offered by King Arthur Flour Company. The Italian-style flour mimics the pure grade "00" flour used in Italian baking for focaccias, *grissini*, pasta, and in combination with other bread flours. The French-style flour is higher in protein, mimicking the special flour used by the Poilâne bakery in Paris for creating French breads. The Irish-style blend is a whole meal flour made especially for soda bread and brown bread. These flours are fun to use if you are a baking enthusiast.

Gluten Flour

Gluten flour is made by washing the starch from the endosperm several times, then further grinding the remaining gluten proteins before mixing them with the finest white flour, known as patent flour, in a 75/25 proportion. It is exceptionally high in protein and low in starch, particularly useful in special diet breads and in doughs made with whole grain flours that are low in, or completely lacking, gluten, especially in bread machine baking. I don't call for gluten flour, though, in this book. Do not confuse vital wheat gluten with gluten flour or high-gluten bread flour.

COUNTRY WHITE BREAD

T his is the type of loaf to make using the Delay Timer since it contains nonfat dry milk rather than fresh milk. The dry milk will not foster any harmful bacteria as it sits. Available as a powder made from whole or skim milk, I always use the skim, or nonfat, dry milk; nonfat has about 1 percent fat, while whole has about 27 percent fat. Nonfat also keeps longer. All types of dry milk have a marked increase in milk sugar, and the yeast love it. It is not necessary to dissolve the dry milk in the liquid ingredients before adding it; the powder will mix in fine when added with the dry ingredients. If you have lumps in your milk powder, be sure to break them up before adding it or they will stay intact throughout the mixing and baking and you'll have powdered milk lumps in your finished loaf.

1 Place all the ingredients in the pan according to the order in the manufacturer's instructions. Set crust on medium and program for the Basic cycle; press Start. (This recipe may be made using the Delay Timer.)

2 When the baking cycle ends, immediately remove the bread from the pan and place it on a rack. Let cool to room temperature before slicing.

1½-POUND LOAF	2-POUND LOAF
1⅓ cups water	1⅔ cups water
1 tablespoon vegetable or light olive oil	1½ tablespoons vegetable or light olive oil
1 tablespoon sugar	1½ tablespoons sugar
3 cups bread flour	4 cups bread flour
1½ tablespoons instant potato flakes	2 tablespoons instant potato flakes
3 tablespoons nonfat dry milk	¼ cup nonfat dry milk
1 tablespoon gluten	1 tablespoon plus 1 teaspoon gluten
1½ teaspoons salt	2 teaspoons salt
2 teaspoons SAF yeast or 2½ teaspoons bread machine yeast	2½ teaspoons SAF yeast or 1 tablespoon bread machine yeast

HOUSE BREAD

I like my homemade bread flecked with a bit of this and a bit of that, without any cane sugar in it so that the flavor of the fresh flours is dominant. In this case I add just a bit of rye flour, buckwheat flour, and wheat germ, which I usually seem to have on hand. Since the additions to this bread depend on what I have around, it has also been made with cornmeal or corn flour, graham flour, teff flour, kamut flour, or whole wheat flour substituted for one or another of the flours called for in the recipe. Just a little bit of something out of the ordinary is enough to subtly affect the taste of this great loaf. The main ingredient, of course, is a good, strong bread flour, as fresh as possible.

1 Place all the ingredients in the pan according to the order in the manufacturer's instructions. Set crust on medium and program for the Basic cycle; press Start. (This recipe may be made using the Delay Timer.)

2 When the baking cycle ends, immediately remove the bread from the pan and place it on a rack. Let cool to room temperature before slicing.

1½-POUND LOAF	2-POUND LOAF
1⅛ cups water	1½ cups water
2 tablespoons olive oil	2½ tablespoons olive oil
2⅞ cups bread flour	3⅞ cups bread flour
1 tablespoon buckwheat flour	1½ tablespoons buckwheat flour
1 tablespoon dark rye flour	1½ tablespoons dark rye flour
1 tablespoon toasted wheat germ	1½ tablespoons toasted wheat germ
1 tablespoon powdered fructose	1½ tablespoons powdered fructose
1 tablespoon gluten	1 tablespoon plus 1 teaspoon gluten
1½ teaspoons salt	2 teaspoons salt
2 teaspoons SAF yeast or 2½ teaspoons bread machine yeast	2¼ teaspoons SAF yeast or 2¾ teaspoons bread machine yeast

MILK BREAD

1½-POUND LOAF

1⅛ cups whole milk
1 tablespoon unsalted
  butter or margarine,
  cut into pieces

3 cups bread flour
1 tablespoon sugar
1 tablespoon gluten
1½ teaspoons salt

2 teaspoons SAF yeast or
  2½ teaspoons bread
  machine yeast

2-POUND LOAF

1⅓ cups whole milk
2 tablespoons unsalted
  butter or margarine,
  cut into pieces

4 cups bread flour
2 tablespoons sugar
1 tablespoon plus
  1 teaspoon gluten
2 teaspoons salt

2½ teaspoons SAF yeast or
  1 tablespoon bread
  machine yeast

T his is a favorite white bread that is perfect for beginning bakers and has that great homemade bread flavor. Milk is the main liquid ingredient in breads that do not fall into the category of lean breads, ones made without any fat or sweetening. Here is a little baker's lesson: When milk is used in a bread dough, it increases and strengthens the absorptive capacity of the flour, especially high-gluten bread flour. So during the rising, you will notice that the dough is a bit stiffer than it was right after mixing. Milk also decreases the acidity in a dough, allowing the yeast to work a bit more efficiently and to age, or ferment, more slowly, giving the bread a delicate flavor. Milk has plenty of sugar, in the form of lactose, so you will have a nice dark crust. Since this loaf has some fat in it, it should stay fresh for two to three days.

❶ Place all the ingredients in the pan according to the order in the manufacturer's instructions. Set crust on medium or dark, and program for the Basic cycle; press Start. (This recipe is not suitable for use with the Delay Timer.)

❷ When the baking cycle ends, immediately remove the bread from the pan and place it on a rack. Let cool to room temperature before slicing.

FRENCH SANDWICH PAIN AU LAIT

I never thought much of breads made in the style of the white French sandwich bread called pain de mie, *which translates as "the heart of the crumb" or "the middle of the bread loaf," until I took a class with Steve Sullivan, the baker at Chez Panisse at the time. This bread is similar to the one he made. While he worked we munched on the bread with slices of fresh California mozzarella and paper-thin prosciutto with a dab of olive paste, experiencing what he described as "a play of contrasting flavors." This is the bread used for grilled sandwiches, such as croque monsieurs, or to cut into shapes for tea sandwiches. While this type of bread is usually baked in a lidded loaf pan to make a perfectly square loaf, the contained environment of the bread machine provides a close second. The barley flour adds a bit of sweetness. This is a slow riser; it will rise dramatically during the baking.*

1 Place all the ingredients in the pan according to the order in the manufacturer's instructions. Set crust on medium and program for the Basic cycle; press Start. (This recipe may be made using the Delay Timer.)

2 When the baking cycle ends, immediately remove the bread from the pan and place it on a rack. Let cool to room temperature before slicing.

1½-POUND LOAF

1¼ cups water
5 tablespoons unsalted
  butter, cut into pieces

2⅞ cups bread flour
⅛ cup barley flour
⅓ cup nonfat dry milk
1 tablespoon gluten
1 teaspoon sugar
1½ teaspoons salt

2 teaspoons SAF yeast or
  2½ teaspoons bread
  machine yeast

2-POUND LOAF

1⅔ cups water
6 tablespoons unsalted
  butter, cut into pieces

3¾ cups bread flour
¼ cup barley flour
½ cup nonfat dry milk
1 tablespoon plus
  1 teaspoon gluten
1½ teaspoons sugar
2 teaspoons salt

2¼ teaspoons SAF yeast or
  2¾ teaspoons bread
  machine yeast

The Toolbox: Essential Bread Machine Baking Equipment

Brinna Sands, founder of the King Arthur Flour Baker's Catalogue and a confirmed bread machine baker, is the perfect person to ask about baking equipment. She has "a bunch" of bread machines of various models, manufacturers, and ages. I asked her to give me a definitive list of the essential equipment needed for bread machine baking, beyond the machine itself. Here is her list:

- **A set of plastic or stainless steel dry measuring cups and spoons, and a glass measuring cup for liquids.** Although this system of measure is not as reliable as measuring by weight using the metric system as professional bakers do, it is the system Americans traditionally use, and the system in which this book's recipes are measured. One way to make "dip and sweep" measuring more accurate is to bring your flour, which settles during its shelf life, back to an unpacked, aerated state. Use the handle of a wooden spoon to stir the flour and then pour it slowly into a canister, or sprinkle the flour from a large spoon into your measuring cup when measuring it for a recipe. While this may seem a bit fussy, remember that air is also a primary leavening agent.

- **A thin, half-width, heat-resistant rubber spatula.** "The blade is 1¼ by 3 inches with an 8½-inch-long handle," says Brinna. "It is perfect for rooting around the edges when you are checking the dough during the beginning of Knead 2 and making sure everything is getting mixed properly." It is simple geometry that the vertical pans have less surface area and mix more efficiently than the long horizontal pans (which are outfitted with two kneading blades instead of the standard one), in which unincorporated flour can collect in the corners that are far from the kneading blade. I use the stiff plastic spatula that came with my food processor. I also use it for loosening the sides before turning the loaf out of the pan after baking.

- **A pair of heavy-duty oven mitts.** I use a pair of deep barbecue mitts or mitts from a restaurant supply house that cover my wrists, a habit left over from my bakery days when I learned about protecting myself from heavy ovenware. Brinna likes the thick, washable cotton terrycloth oven mitts available in her catalog. Stay away from the lightweight designer mitts; they are too thin and the bread pan is HOT when removed from the machine. The reality is that oven mitts do wear out with repeated use, especially between the thumb and forefinger, and need to be replaced periodically.

- **A small cleaning brush with bristles that are safe for nonstick surfaces.** The sides and bottom of the inside of the machine need at least to be wiped clean after each baking session. "A brush is perfect for loosening up the crumbs that stick and collect in the bottom of the machine," advises Brinna. "Then you can use the hose on your vacuum cleaner to gather them all up. It's easier than turning the machine upside down and shaking them out." I use a damp cloth if there are just a few stray crumbs. Be sure the machine is unplugged before you do anything around the element.

- **A wire cooling rack.** For proper cooling, it is important that a loaf be placed on a rack that allows air to circulate all around the loaf. There are stainless steel racks, nonstick racks, and even old-fashioned wooden racks for purists. Racks may be round or rectangular, small or large. I like a nice 12-by-16-inch stainless steel cooling rack, but I keep a variety of sizes for all sorts of loaves.

- **A long-bladed serrated bread knife.** Don't ever consider using anything without a serrated edge for slicing: otherwise your bread will tear mercilessly. All brands of knives include one in their collections. If you can, wait until the bread cools before slicing. Use gentle pressure with a back-and-forth motion.

SOUR CREAM BREAD

Sour Cream Bread has a beautiful crust and a unique, moist, dense texture reminiscent of a brioche or cake. Sour cream is an ingredient much beloved by bakers of both breads and pastries. It has an inherent richness and acidity that consistently give a special texture, flavor, and keeping quality to bread. A simulated sour cream made from a vegetable oil base, such as Imo, can be substituted for fresh sour cream in this bread with good results. Since sour cream has plenty of its own butterfat, no extra butter or oil is needed in this bread recipe to make a nice loaf. You will make this good bread often; it was a favorite among my recipe testers. The delicate, cakey texture makes it great for grilled sandwiches and French toast.

1 Place all the ingredients in the pan according to the order in the manufacturer's instructions, with the water and sour cream put in first, and adding the dry ingredients in on top. Set crust on medium and program for the Basic cycle; press Start. (This recipe is not suitable for use with the Delay Timer.)

2 When the baking cycle ends, immediately remove the bread from the pan and place it on a rack. Let cool to room temperature before slicing.

1½-POUND LOAF

½ cup plus 1 tablespoon water
1 cup sour cream

3½ cups bread flour
1 tablespoon light brown sugar
2 teaspoons gluten
1¼ teaspoons salt

2 teaspoons SAF yeast or 2½ teaspoons bread machine yeast

2-POUND LOAF

¾ cup plus 1 tablespoon water
1¼ cups sour cream

4⅓ cups bread flour
1½ tablespoons light brown sugar
1 tablespoon gluten
1½ teaspoons salt

1 tablespoon SAF yeast or 1 tablespoon plus ½ teaspoon bread machine yeast

YOGURT BREAD

1½-POUND LOAF

¾ cup water
1 cup plain whole milk
   yogurt

3½ cups bread flour
1 tablespoon gluten
2 teaspoons salt

2 teaspoons SAF yeast or
   2½ teaspoons bread
   machine yeast

2-POUND LOAF

1 cup water
1⅓ cups plain whole milk
   yogurt

4¾ cups bread flour
1 tablespoon plus
   1 teaspoon gluten
2¼ teaspoons salt

2½ teaspoons SAF yeast or
   1 tablespoon bread
   machine yeast

This is a beloved recipe from the files of food writer Jacquie McMahan, adapted for the bread machine. She makes homemade yogurt in jelly glasses and sets it overnight on her Wolf range. Though this recipe was not published in any of his books, James Beard, well known for his love of good bread, taught Jacquie to make this bread during a weeklong cooking class he gave at the Stanford Court Hotel, where he baked in Fournou's Ovens. Jacquie was one of eight student in the class, the roster of which included food world notables such as Jeremiah Tower, Alice Waters, Joyce Goldstein, Flo Braker, and Chuck Williams. Everyone loved feeding Beard, so during the class, the restaurant chefs kept coming in with treats for him to taste while he was lecturing and baking bread. This bread is pure Beard—simple ingredients that bake up wholesome and flavorful. Eat it the day it is baked. It is a perfect sandwich bread.

1 Place all the ingredients in the pan according to the order in the manufacturer's instructions. I put 3¾ cups of flour in for the 1½ pound loaf (4½ cups for the 2-pound loaf) and sprinkle the rest in over the dough ball as needed, since yogurts have different consistencies. Set crust on dark and program for the Basic cycle; press Start. (This recipe is not suitable for use with the Delay Timer.) The dough ball will be slightly sticky, but it will smooth out after the kneading.

2 When the baking cycle ends, immediately remove the bread from the pan and place it on a rack. Let cool to room temperature before slicing.

GREEK BREAD

Everyday bread in Greece is call psomo, or mother's bread. *Don't substitute regular milk for the evaporated milk here, you will miss out on the especially sweet, rich flavor it provides. The most authentically Greek version of this bread is made with canned evaporated goat's milk, but the ubiquitous evaporated cow's milk is just fine.*

❶ Place all the ingredients in the pan according to the order in the manufacturer's instructions. Set crust on medium and program for the Basic cycle; press Start. (This recipe is not suitable for use with the Delay Timer.)

❷ When the baking cycle ends, immediately remove the bread from the pan and place it on a rack. Let cool to room temperature before slicing.

1½-POUND LOAF	2-POUND LOAF
⅓ cup water	½ cup water
1 cup evaporated milk or evaporated goat's milk	1⅛ cups plus 1 tablespoon evaporated milk or evaporated goat's milk
2¾ cups bread flour	3¾ cups bread flour
¼ cup whole wheat or whole grain spelt flour	¼ cup whole wheat or whole grain spelt flour
1¼ tablespoons sesame seeds	1¾ tablespoons sesame seeds
1 tablespoon gluten	1 tablespoon plus 1 teaspoon gluten
2 teaspoons sugar	1 tablespoon sugar
1½ teaspoons salt	2 teaspoons salt
2 teaspoons SAF yeast or 2½ teaspoons bread machine yeast	2½ teaspoons SAF yeast or 1 tablespoon bread machine yeast

Leftover Bread Cookery: The Art of French Toast

I think anything as rudimentary as soaking stale bread in milk and eggs, then pan-sautéing it to reconstitute texture, has universal appeal. It produces such a comforting breakfast food, but does so through such a simple technique that it can easily be taken for granted. Well, it shouldn't be.

French toast, *pain perdu*, or "lost bread," is not an exclusively French invention, as early Romans soaked dry bread in wine, eggs, and honey. Later, the Normans brought it from France to England, where it was dubbed the Poor Knights of Windsor, a name that has stuck until the present. A favorite dish of princes, old English recipes for *payn pur-dew* refer to bread soaked in an elixir of spiced sherry, eggs, spices, and cream. In Germany it is called Drunken Maidens or *Arme Ritter* (Poor Knights), with regional variations sprinkled with cinnamon and sugar or touting poppy seeds. The Swedes serve it sandwiched with ham and cheese for dinner and the Mexicans know it as a *fritada*. For the Jewish holiday of Purim it is served as "Queen Esther's Toast."

While sweet baguettes, sourdough, and challah egg bread are my favorites for French toast, cinnamon bread, any whole wheat, seed, white sandwich, croissant, or holiday sweet bread can be used. Day-old and stale are key words here; fresh bread will just end up soggy. Cream, half-and-half, whole milk, nonfat milk, commercial eggnog, or soy milk all work equally well as the soaking liquid. Use fresh eggs or a commercial liquid egg substitute equivalent. If cholesterol is a consideration, use all egg whites in the soaking mixture and light olive oil for frying. For the adult palate, add 2 to 3 tablespoons of your favorite liqueur, such as Grand Marnier, amaretto, or rum, to jazz up the batter.

Butter and maple syrup are certainly the traditional toppings, but I also like a fruit syrup such as blueberry or raspberry (try Knudsen's sugar-free pourable fruit or one from Knott's Berry Farms), sautéed or fresh fruit, powdered sugar and fresh lemon wedges, or even hot applesauce and vanilla yogurt.

Good Morning French Toast
Serves 2

This is a basic recipe for French toast. Day-old bread is best since it won't disintegrate after soaking.

3 large eggs
¾ cup milk
½ teaspoon vanilla extract
Four 1-inch-thick slices day-old bread
1 to 2 tablespoons butter, as needed

1 Using a whisk or immersion blender, beat the eggs, milk, and vanilla together in a bowl. Pour into a shallow bowl. Add the bread and soak both sides until all of the milk mixture is absorbed.

2 Melt the butter in a large skillet over medium heat, arrange the slices without crowding, and sauté until deep golden brown, 3 to 4 minutes on each side. Top with Warmed Winter Fruit (see below) or plain maple syrup.

Warmed Winter Fruit
Makes about 3 cups

6 dried apricot halves
1 tablespoon dried cherries
1 tablespoon golden raisins
2 tablespoons butter
1 small apple, peeled, cored, and sliced
1 small pear, peeled, cored, and sliced
Pinch of ground cinnamon
1 banana, sliced
½ cup canned pitted sweet cherries, drained
⅓ cup maple syrup

1 Cover the apricots, cherries, and raisins with hot water. Let soak for 10 minutes.

2 Melt the butter in a large skillet over medium-low heat. Sauté the apples and pears until soft. Drain the soaked fruit and add to the skillet with the cinnamon. Sauté for 5 minutes. Add the banana, canned cherries, and syrup, and heat for 2 minutes. Serve immediately spooned over the French toast.

Banana-Stuffed French Toast
Serves 3

Six 2-inch-thick slices day-old bread
3 small bananas, each cut into 12 diagonal slices
8 large eggs
½ cup milk
3 tablespoons maple syrup
1 teaspoon ground nutmeg

1 Preheat oven to 400°F. Line a baking sheet with parchment paper.

2 Insert a small sharp knife into the side of the crust and carefully cut a small horizontal pocket directly into the middle of each slice of bread, leaving a 1-inch border on 3 sides. Stuff each pocket with 6 slices of banana.

3 Using a whisk or immersion blender, beat the eggs, milk, syrup, and nutmeg in a bowl until foamy. Pour into a shallow bowl. Add the bread and soak both sides. Melt 1 to 2 tablespoons butter in a large skillet over medium heat, arrange the slices without crowding, and sauté until lightly browned, 3 to 4 minutes per side. Turn them once. Transfer slices to the baking sheet and bake for 15 minutes. Serve immediately.

MAPLE BUTTERMILK BREAD

1½-POUND LOAF

1 cup plus 1 tablespoon
   water
1½ tablespoons unsalted
   butter, melted
3 tablespoons maple syrup

3 cups bread flour
⅓ cup dry buttermilk powder
1 tablespoon gluten
1½ teaspoons salt

1¾ teaspoons SAF yeast or
   2¼ teaspoons bread
   machine yeast

2-POUND LOAF

1⅛ cups water
2 tablespoons unsalted
   butter, melted
¼ cup plus 1 tablespoon
   maple syrup

4 cups bread flour
½ cup dry buttermilk powder
1 tablespoon plus
   1 teaspoon gluten
2 teaspoons salt

2¼ teaspoons SAF yeast or
   2¾ teaspoons bread
   machine yeast

T his is a basic white bread that pairs tangy buttermilk with wonderful maple syrup, and is especially nice for toast and sandwiches. Who could not love maple syrup? Produced by boiling the sap of the sugar maple tree that grows in the Northeast states and eastern Canada, maple syrup has the most aromatic and enticing flavors of any natural sweetening. I always have some in my refrigerator. I always ask my literary agent to bring me a little jug for my birthday when she goes on vacation each summer in the Adirondack Mountains of upstate New York. The Fancy, or AA grade, is delicate in flavor, and the syrup becomes more robust in Grades A, B, and C, which are great for baking. Use fresh buttermilk in place of the water and dry buttermilk powder, if you wish, but you cannot use the Delay Timer with perishable ingredients.

1 Place all the ingredients in the pan according to the order in the manufacturer's instructions. Set crust on medium and program for the Basic cycle; press Start. (This recipe may be made using the Delay Timer.)

2 When the baking cycle ends, immediately remove the bread from the pan and place it on a rack. Let cool to room temperature before slicing.

BANANA SANDWICH LOAF

The subtle sweetness in this bread comes from the ripe banana. Don't worry that you add chunks of banana to the bread pan; they will get mashed during the kneading. Treat this loaf just like French bread; it is best the day it is made. There is no better bread for a peanut butter and jelly sandwich.

1 Place all the ingredients in the pan according to the order in the manufacturer's instructions. Set crust on medium and program for the Basic cycle; press Start. (This recipe is not suitable for use with the Delay Timer.)

2 When the baking cycle ends, immediately remove the bread from the pan and place it on a rack. Let cool to room temperature before slicing.

1½-POUND LOAF	2-POUND LOAF
1 cup water	1⅓ cups water
1 tablespoon vegetable or nut oil	1½ tablespoons vegetable or nut oil
1 ripe 6-ounce banana, cut into chunks	1 ripe 8-ounce banana, cut into chunks
3 cups bread flour	4 cups bread flour
¼ cup dry buttermilk powder	⅓ cup dry buttermilk powder
1 tablespoon gluten	1 tablespoon plus 1 teaspoon gluten
1½ teaspoons salt	2 teaspoons salt
2 teaspoons SAF yeast or 2½ teaspoons bread machine yeast	2¼ teaspoons SAF yeast or 2¾ teaspoons bread machine yeast

The Right Ingredient: About Gluten

Gluten (also known as vital wheat gluten) is a natural protein occurring in wheat. It adds body and volume to bread machine loaves. I have specified the proper amount of gluten needed in each recipe in this book, but if you are creating your own recipes for the bread machine, a good guideline is to add 1 teaspoon to 1 tablespoon of vital wheat gluten per cup of flour, depending on the gluten content of the flour in the recipe. Bread flour needs less gluten added; heavier whole wheat and non-gluten flours need more to make a high-rising, light-textured loaf. Advised proportions are always printed on the package. Vital wheat gluten is readily available in the flour section of supermarkets. It generally comes in a 10-ounce box that sells for less than $3.00. Hodgson Mill fortifies its gluten with vitamin C for extra punch. Vital wheat gluten is *not* the same as gluten flour; it is a more concentrated form, so do not confuse the two.

COCONUT MILK WHITE BREAD

1⅛ cups canned coconut
  milk

3 cups bread flour
1 tablespoon gluten
1½ teaspoons salt

1¾ teaspoons SAF yeast
  or 2¼ teaspoons bread
  machine yeast

2-POUND LOAF

1½ cups canned coconut
  milk

4 cups bread flour
1 tablespoon plus
  1 teaspoon gluten
2 teaspoons salt

2½ teaspoons SAF yeast or
  1 tablespoon bread
  machine yeast

D o not confuse canned coconut milk with canned cream of coconut, which is even more concentrated and sweeter than the milk. No need for extra fat or sugar in this moist, slightly dense-textured bread; the coconut milk naturally provides both. Be sure to shake the can well before opening it since the solids may have settled to the bottom. This is the perfect bread to serve with Thai food, with crawfish omelets, or with barbecued jerk chicken, cole slaw, and the "holy trinity" of Creole food—shallots, celery, and green peppers.

❶ Place all the ingredients in the pan according to the order in the manufacturer's instructions. Set crust on medium and program for the Basic cycle; press Start. (This recipe is not suitable for use with the Delay Timer.)

❷ When the baking cycle ends, immediately remove the bread from the pan and place it on a rack. Let cool to room temperature before slicing.

FRENCH BREAD

F rench bread is characterized by a crisp crust, nice volume, and a close-grained, chewy texture. It is distinctly different from a white bread made with milk, honey, and butter. The addition of egg whites makes for an extra crispy crust. If you are going to make this bread using the Delay Timer, be sure to use powdered egg whites (see page 76), which perform just like fresh egg whites when whipped with cold water. This loaf is best when eaten slightly warm, or at room temperature within eight hours of when it is baked—there is no fat in it to help keep the bread moist, and the flavor changes when it is day-old. This is an excellent loaf with all the characteristics of traditional French bread except its shape. If you would like to turn this dough out before baking and shape it into long loaves to bake in the oven, prepare it on the Dough cycle and refer to page 218.

1 Using an electric mixer, beat the egg whites until almost stiff and soft peaks are formed. Set crust on medium or dark, and program for the Basic or French Bread cycle. Place all the ingredients in the pan according to the order in the manufacturer's instructions, adding the egg whites in with the water; press Start. (This recipe is not suitable for use with the Delay Timer if using fresh eggs.)

2 When the baking cycle ends, immediately remove the bread from the pan and place it on a rack. Let cool to room temperature before slicing.

1½-POUND LOAF

2 large egg whites
1 cup water

3 cups bread flour
1 tablespoon gluten
2 teaspoons sugar
1¾ teaspoons salt

2 teaspoons SAF yeast or
2½ teaspoons bread
machine yeast

2-POUND LOAF

2 large egg whites
1¼ cups water

4 cups bread flour
1 tablespoon plus
2 teaspoons gluten
1 tablespoon sugar
2½ teaspoons salt

2¼ teaspoons SAF yeast or
2¾ teaspoons bread
machine yeast

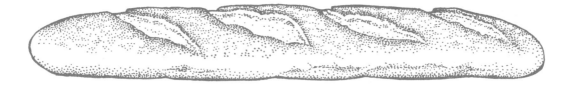

The Baker's Glossary of Grain Terms

Grains are picked clean, graded, and sifted of non-grain particles and dirt before storage. The grains are then conditioned with an application of water, heat, and air to give a uniform moisture content, which toughens the bran and softens the endosperm for easy separation. Then the grains are split open to squeeze out the germ and scrape off the bran layer from the endosperm. These parts are crushed during milling to make different processed grains and milled to make flour. The list that follows includes the terms used to distinguish the parts of the grain, names for grain products to help you decipher package labels and ingredients lists, and common milling terms.

Berry—The whole grain with a loosely attached outer hull, such as wheat or rye. (The hull gets removed by threshing.)

Bleached flour—Chlorine dioxide gas is used to age the flour and remove the yellow carotenoid pigment naturally found in wheat flour.

Bran—The protective outer coating of an individual grain seed. It is several layers thick, and is separated from the grain by polishing or from flour by bolting. It contains the fiber, a form of cellulose, and a complex sugar. Also referred to as polishings.

Celiac disease—A medical syndrome characterized by malabsorption. Symptoms are caused by eating grains containing gluten (primarily wheat, barley, rye, and oats). Also known as celiac sprue and gluten-sensitive enteropathy.

Cereal—Grain plants in the *Gramineae* family, which include wheat, rye, and barley.

Cracked, grits, steel-cut—Terms used when whole grains have been cut into small pieces. They cook faster than whole grains and come in a variety of consistencies from fine to coarse.

Endosperm—The floury storage center of the grain, under the bran layer, high in starch granules designed to nourish the seed after sprouting. It contains the gluten proteins and is the part of the grain milled to make white flour.

Flour—Whole grain ground into a fine powder. There are a variety of particle consistencies from fine to coarse for most flours. The whole grain or just the endosperm are ground to make flours of different textures and flavors.

Germ—The meal made from the inside, or embryo, of the grain kernel. The germ provides the concentrated source of oil, vitamins, and minerals. This is the seed embryo at the base of the kernel that will germinate if planted.

Gluten—The mass of complex protein cells in flour that becomes elastic when moistened and kneaded. Gluten strands encase the expanding yeast gases, forming the classic dome shape associated with yeast breads. Substantial gluten protein is found only in wheat and rye flours.

Groat—The whole grain with a tightly attached outer hull, such as buckwheat or barley, removed by cracking.

Hull—Also known as the *husk* or *testa*, the hull is the inedible shell-like outer coating of the grain. Tight hulls are removed by polishing or pearling, loose hulls by threshing, and some special varieties are hull-less.

Kernel—Small, separate, edible dry seed fruits of grain plants.

Meal—Whole grain ground into a variety of consistencies, but all of them coarser than flour. Polenta, cornmeal, and farina are meals. Depending on the processing of the whole grain, they may have the bran and germ or may not.

Pearling—The process of removing the outer bran layer from barley.

Polishing—The process of removing the outer bran layer from rice.

Rolled flakes—Grains that are steamed, cut, and then rolled flat and dried; these cook faster than cracked or whole grains.

Roasted—Whole grains that are toasted for added digestibility and flavor, such as buckwheat groats.

Seed—Dormant fruit of the grain plant.

Spikelet—An individual grass flower head that holds the seeds.

Stone-ground—Flour and meal that is made by slowly crushing grains with heavy, grooved revolving stones under pressure. Since this process is slow and the temperature is never above body heat, precious nutritive oils are preserved and the bran and germ are evenly distributed.

Testa—The hard, external shell-like coating of a seed.

Threshing—The process of separating the outer hull from the grain by beating. Other methods are pearling and polishing, which grind off the hull, retaining the bran.

Unbleached flour—Wheat flour aged by oxygen in the air for one to two months. Aging flour develops the gluten proteins and makes for stronger doughs. The flour retains a creamy color.

Whole grain—A groat or berry that still contains the bran and germ. The whole groat or berry is minimally processed, or hulled and cleaned, to rid it of the inedible outer coating.

Wheat kernel

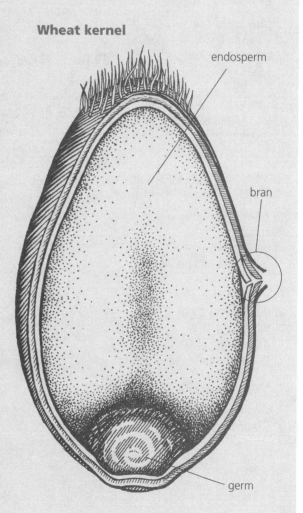

endosperm

bran

germ

VIENNA BREAD

1½-POUND LOAF

½ cup water
½ cup milk
3 tablespoons unsalted
   butter, cut into pieces

3 cups bread flour
2 tablespoons sugar
1 tablespoon gluten
1½ teaspoons salt

1¾ teaspoons SAF yeast or
   2¼ teaspoons bread
   machine yeast

2-POUND LOAF

⅔ cup water
⅔ cup milk
4 tablespoons unsalted
   butter, cut into pieces

4 cups bread flour
3 tablespoons sugar
1 tablespoon plus
   1 teaspoon gluten
2 teaspoons salt

2¼ teaspoons SAF yeast or
   2¾ teaspoons bread
   machine yeast

V*ienna bread is made like a simple French bread, but with the addition of milk and butter for flavor, softness, and an extra day's fresh keeping. However, it does not have the crisp crust of breads made without butter. It has been a favorite bread in France since the Revolution. It gets its name from once having been made with Vienna flour, a premium white flour. This bread was a favorite of my father, who was a connoisseur of white breads.*

1 Place all the ingredients in the pan according to the order in the manufacturer's instructions. Set crust on medium and program for the Basic or French Bread cycle; press Start. (This recipe is not suitable for use with the Delay Timer.)

2 When the baking cycle ends, immediately remove the bread from the pan and place it on a rack. Let cool to room temperature before slicing.

OLD-FASHIONED POTATO BREAD

R oot vegetables were among the first foods to be cultivated, and have long been an essential food source. Potatoes were a staple in the Incan cultures of Peru. They also made the journey to Europe with returning New World explorers, transforming European and eventually North American cuisines forever. It comes as no surprise, then, that this dietary staple has long been used in baking bread. Fresh mashed potatoes add a moist, fluffy texture not comparable to any other ingredient in breads. The complex carbohydrates in the potato make a perfect food for the yeast and the rest is kitchen legend; bread machine bakers love to use the floury potatoes in breads and starters. No matter how large my repertoire of baking gets, potato bread is one of my perennial favorites. I think it is the best white bread for sandwiches.

1 Combine the potato and water in a small saucepan. Simmer, covered, until the potato is tender, about 10 minutes; slip off the peels. Mash or puree the potato with its water (do not drain; you want the water). Pour the potato–water mixture into a 2-cup glass measuring cup and add additional water to make 1⅓ cups for a 1½-pound loaf or 1⅔ cups for the 2-pound loaf. Cool to room temperature.

2 Place all the ingredients in the pan according to the order in the manufacturer's instructions, adding the potato mixture with the liquid ingredients. Set crust on medium and program for the Basic cycle; press Start. (This recipe is not suitable for use with the Delay Timer.)

3 When the baking cycle ends, immediately remove the bread from the pan and place it on a rack. Let cool to room temperature before slicing.

1½-POUND LOAF

1 medium russet potato (8 to 9 ounces), cut into chunks
¾ cup water
2 tablespoons unsalted butter, cut into pieces

3 cups bread flour
1 tablespoon sugar
1½ teaspoons gluten
1½ teaspoons salt

1¾ teaspoons SAF yeast or 2¼ teaspoons bread machine yeast

2-POUND LOAF

1 medium russet potato (8 to 9 ounces), cut into chunks
1 cup water
3 tablespoons unsalted butter, cut into pieces

4 cups bread flour
1½ tablespoons sugar
2 teaspoons gluten
2 teaspoons salt

2¼ teaspoons SAF yeast or 2¾ teaspoons bread machine yeast

INSTANT-POTATO BREAD

1½-POUND LOAF

½ cup water
⅔ cup buttermilk
1½ tablespoons olive oil
1½ tablespoons dark honey

2½ cups bread flour
⅓ cup instant potato flakes
1 tablespoon gluten
1¼ teaspoons salt

1¾ teaspoons SAF yeast or
  2¼ teaspoons bread
  machine yeast

2-POUND LOAF

¾ cup water
¾ cup buttermilk
2 tablespoons olive oil
2 tablespoons dark honey

3 cups bread flour
½ cup instant potato flakes
1 tablespoon plus
  1 teaspoon gluten
1½ teaspoons salt

2 teaspoons SAF yeast or
  2½ teaspoons bread
  machine yeast

L ong ago, Peruvian Indians dried potatoes by stomping on them to press out the moisture, then left them to freeze overnight. The potatoes were later reconstituted in water over a campfire. When vegetables are dried, their vitamins, flavor, and color remain intact. Still, I used to dismiss the use of instant mashed potatoes in my breads; I always used fresh mashed potatoes. But my girlfriend and fellow bread machine baker Suzanne convinced me to add the instant flakes. The bread tasted so good, especially the loaves made in the bread machine, that now I always have a box of instant potatoes in the cupboard. The crumb on potato bread is fluffy and dense, the interior moist, and the crust crisp. This loaf can be baked on the Quick Yeast Bread cycle since the potatoes encourage the yeast. (See your manufacturer's manual for guidelines for adjusting the quantity of yeast when using this cycle.) This is a high-domed loaf. Be sure to add the flour first, to the liquid already in the pan, and then the potato flakes. Otherwise, as you are measuring the flour, the potatoes will already be soaking up the liquid, and the result will be a dry dough ball.

❶ Place all the ingredients in the pan according to the order in the manufacturer's instructions. Set crust on medium and program for the Basic cycle; press Start. (This recipe is not suitable for use with the Delay Timer.) The dough ball will be nicely formed and slightly sticky but stiff at the same time when tested. It should feel a bit sticky, so take care not to add any more than an extra tablespoon of flour. The potato flakes will soak up the extra moisture during the rises and will become smooth during the risings.

❷ When the baking cycle ends, immediately remove the bread from the pan and place it on a rack. Let cool to room temperature before slicing.

BEER BREAD

F lip the cap on your favorite beer and let it go flat at room temperature for a few hours before assembling the ingredients. Whatever the brand is, whether dark or light, domestic or imported, your choice of beer will dictate the distinctive flavor of this loaf. Serve this bread with roast pork and sauerkraut or with corned beef.

1 Pour the beer into a bowl and let stand at room temperature for a few hours to go flat.

2 Place all the ingredients in the pan according to the order in the manufacturer's instructions. Set crust on dark and program for the Basic cycle; press Start. (This recipe is not suitable for use with the Delay Timer.)

3 When the baking cycle ends, immediately remove the bread from the pan and place it on a rack. Let cool to room temperature before slicing.

1½-POUND LOAF	2-POUND LOAF
1⅛ cups (9 ounces) beer	1½ cups (12 ounces) beer
2 tablespoons olive oil	3 tablespoons olive oil
3½ cups bread flour	4½ cups bread flour
¼ cup sugar	⅓ cup sugar
¾ teaspoon salt	1 teaspoon salt
1¾ teaspoons SAF yeast or	2½ teaspoons SAF yeast or
2¼ teaspoons bread	1 tablespoon bread
machine yeast	machine yeast

How Much Does It Cost to Make a Loaf of Bread in the Bread Machine?

The total cost of a 1½-pound loaf of bread without any added ingredients like cheese, spices, nuts, dried fruit, or vegetables is very inexpensive, about 75 cents to $1.00.

Flour: A 10-pound bag of flour contains 40 cups and sells for $3.50 to $4.10. A 1½-pound loaf calls for 3 cups of flour. Cost per loaf: about 35 cents.

Yeast: The cost of 2 teaspoons of dry yeast is about 15 cents.

Milk: A recipe that calls for fresh milk or buttermilk will call for about 1¼ cups, about 30 cents worth. One to two tablespoons of dry buttermilk powder or nonfat dry milk costs about 5 cents.

Butter or oil: The standard loaf uses about 10 cents worth of butter, margarine, or vegetable oil, or 15 to 25 cents worth of premium olive oil or nut oil.

Other ingredients: Allow 5 cents more for sugar or honey and salt.

HUNGARIAN WHITE BREAD WITH FENNEL SEEDS

1½-POUND LOAF

1⅛ cups water
1½ tablespoons unsalted
   butter, melted

3 cups bread flour
1½ tablespoons sugar
1 tablespoon gluten
2½ teaspoons fennel seeds
1½ teaspoons salt

2 teaspoons SAF yeast or
   2½ teaspoons bread
   machine yeast

2-POUND LOAF

1⅓ cups water
2 tablespoons unsalted
   butter, melted

4 cups bread flour
2 tablespoons sugar
1 tablespoon plus
   1 teaspoon gluten
1 tablespoon fennel seeds
2 teaspoons salt

2½ teaspoons SAF yeast or
   1 tablespoon bread
   machine yeast

H*ungarians are known as premier bread bakers. Hungarian wheat is grown on the fertile Great Hungarian Plain that sweeps two thousand miles east from the Transylvanian Alps. Up until World War II, this wheat was treated like gold in Europe and exported to destinations all over the Continent. Hungarian flours are graded from coarse to fine and there is a saying "if you can make strudel out of it, then it is good flour for bread, crêpes, and noodles." The* kenyér, *or "daily bread," in this recipe can be made studded with aromatic caraway or fennel seeds, providing a great accompaniment to Hungary's flavorful savory dishes. The subtle addition of the seeds is a delightful surprise to the palate. This is a firm-textured bread with an incredible crumb, and is very fragrant when toasted.*

1 Place all the ingredients in the pan according to the order in the manufacturer's instructions. Set crust on medium and program for the Basic cycle; press Start. (This recipe may be made using the Delay Timer.)

2 When the baking cycle ends, immediately remove the bread from the pan and place it on a rack. Let cool to room temperature before slicing.

One-Pound Loaves

The recipes in this book are designed for 1½- and 2-pound-loaf bread machines. But all machines have the capacity to make smaller 1-pound loaves as well. The 1-pound size is also known as a sampler loaf, and is perfect for one or two people, especially if you like to make fresh bread every day. Here are a few basic recipes created to make some special 1-pound loaves. You'll find recipes for plain white and egg breads, as well as a couple whole-grain loaves and a sweet bread. Of course, to make a 1-pound loaf from any of the other recipes in this book, all you have to do is cut the measurements for the 2-pound loaf in half.

SAMPLER BRIOCHE EGG LOAF

❶ Place all the ingredients in the pan according to the order in the manufacturer's instructions. Set crust on medium and program for the Basic cycle; press Start. (This recipe is not suitable for use with the Delay Timer.) The dough ball will be soft.

❷ When the baking cycle ends, immediately remove the bread from the pan and place it on a rack. Let cool to room temperature before slicing.

1-POUND LOAF

2 large egg yolks plus water to equal ⅔ cup
4 tablespoons unsalted butter, cut into pieces and softened

1¾ cups bread flour
1 tablespoon sugar
2 teaspoons gluten
1 teaspoon salt

1⅛ teaspoons SAF yeast or 1½ teaspoons bread machine yeast

SAMPLER COUNTRY WHITE LOAF

1-POUND LOAF

¾ cup fat-free milk
1 tablespoon canola oil

1⅞ cups bread flour
2 tablespoons barley flour
2 tablespoons toasted
  wheat germ
1 tablespoon sugar
2 teaspoons gluten
1 teaspoon salt

1⅛ teaspoons SAF yeast or
  1½ teaspoons bread
  machine yeast

1 Place all the ingredients in the pan according to the order in the manufacturer's instructions. Set crust on dark and program for the Basic cycle; press Start. (This recipe is not suitable for use with the Delay Timer.)

2 When the baking cycle ends, immediately remove the bread from the pan and place it on a rack. Let cool to room temperature before slicing.

SAMPLER BUTTERMILK WHITE LOAF

1-POUND LOAF

¾ cup plus 1 tablespoon
  buttermilk
1 tablespoon dark honey
1 tablespoon butter or
  margarine, softened

2 cups bread flour
2 teaspoons gluten
1 teaspoon salt

1¼ teaspoons SAF yeast or
  1½ teaspoons bread
  machine yeast

1 Place all the ingredients in the pan according to the order in the manufacturer's instructions. Set crust on dark and program for the Basic cycle; press Start. (This recipe is not suitable for use with the Delay Timer.)

2 When the baking cycle ends, immediately remove the bread from the pan and place it on a rack. Let cool to room temperature before slicing.

SAMPLER HONEY WHOLE WHEAT LOAF

1 Place all the ingredients in the pan according to the order in the manufacturer's instructions. Set crust on dark and program for the Whole Wheat cycle; press Start. (This recipe is not suitable for use with the Delay Timer.)

2 When the baking cycle ends, immediately remove the bread from the pan and place it on a rack. Let cool to room temperature before slicing.

1-POUND LOAF

¾ cup fat-free milk
2 tablespoons honey
1 tablespoon butter, softened

1¾ cups whole wheat flour
¼ cup bread flour
1 tablespoon gluten
1 teaspoon salt

1¼ teaspoons SAF yeast or 1½ teaspoons bread machine yeast

SAMPLER OATMEAL LOAF

1 Place all the ingredients in the pan according to the order in the manufacturer's instructions. Set crust on dark and program for the Basic cycle; press Start. (This recipe is not suitable for use with the Delay Timer.)

2 When the baking cycle ends, immediately remove the bread from the pan and place it on a rack. Let cool to room temperature before slicing.

1-POUND LOAF

¾ cup buttermilk
1 tablespoon honey or maple syrup
2 teaspoons butter or margarine, softened

1¾ cups bread flour
½ cup rolled oats
2 teaspoons gluten
1 teaspoon salt

1¼ teaspoons SAF yeast or 1½ teaspoons bread machine yeast

SAMPLER HAWAIIAN SWEET LOAF

1-POUND LOAF

⅓ cup evaporated milk
One 8-ounce can crushed
  pineapple in its own juice
¼ cup pineapple juice
  reserved from draining
  the canned pineapple
1 tablespoon vegetable or
  nut oil

2 cups bread flour
⅓ cup flaked coconut
1½ tablespoons light brown
  sugar
2 teaspoons gluten
1 teaspoon salt
½ teaspoon ground ginger

1½ teaspoons SAF yeast or
  2 teaspoons bread
  machine yeast

¼ cup coarsely chopped
  macadamia nuts, rinsed
  and dried on a paper
  towel if salted

1 Place the ingredients, except the nuts, in the pan according to the order in the manufacturer's instructions. Set crust on dark and program for the Basic or Sweet Bread cycle; press Start. (This recipe is not suitable for use with the Delay Timer.) When the machine beeps, or between Knead 1 and Knead 2, add the nuts.

2 When the baking cycle ends, immediately remove the bread from the pan and place it on a rack. Let cool to room temperature before slicing.

EGG BREADS

Egg breads are simply divine. While in a practical sense, eggs add rich flavor, vibrant color, and leavening power to a dough, they have a spiritual element as well.

Eggs have long been added to bread doughs to make them special. There is a *pain du sacresant*, or sacred bread, for every culture that worships, and these breads are usually made with eggs. One of the earliest religions believed that a primeval egg split open to form heaven and earth. Modern Muslim women chant prayers while mixing dough and their baked bread is never cut with a knife, since the bread is symbolic of one of the multitude of prophets in the Koran. Challah, the traditional Jewish egg bread that is probably the most familiar egg bread, is served as prayers are said. I find the Jewish challah one of the best breads to make for any momentous event, a wedding, a birth, or during mourning. This oversized loaf seems to bless the table with its presence, just as it has for centuries.

Among early Europeans, the egg was a symbol of the four basic elements. The egg white symbolized water, the shell represented earth, the membrane air, and the yolk, with its yellow orb, fire. The Scots told fortunes with the whites. The white would be dropped in a glass of ale and turned upside down. The interpretation would be told according to the shape the white took in the liquid. It would then be used in the making of bannocks (their griddle-baked daily bread), and the baker was not allowed to speak while mixing it.

So when you are baking your egg bread, remember that these breads are not only some of the easiest to construct in the bread machine, but also the ones accompanied by daily blessings for health, sustenance, and happiness.

FRANSKBRØD

1½-POUND LOAF

1 cup water
1 large egg

3 cups bread flour
1 tablespoon sugar
1 tablespoon gluten
1¼ teaspoons salt

2 teaspoons SAF yeast or
    2½ teaspoons bread
    machine yeast

2-POUND LOAF

1⅓ cups water
1 large egg

4 cups bread flour
1½ tablespoons sugar
1 tablespoon plus
    1 teaspoon gluten
1½ teaspoons salt

2½ teaspoons SAF yeast or
    1 tablespoon bread
    machine yeast

Franskbrød is the most prevalent white bread in all of Scandinavia. It translates to "French bread," but it contains an egg, so technically it is not a true lean bread by French baking standards. The combination of the egg and water makes for a chewy loaf. This recipe is adapted from one by a great baker and food writer, Beatrice Ojakangas, who has written many bread books utilizing every baking technique, from the food processor to the bread machine. Serve this bread with dinner.

1. Place all the ingredients in the pan according to the order in the manufacturer's instructions. Set crust on medium and program for the Basic or French Bread cycle; press Start. (This recipe is not suitable for use with the Delay Timer.)

2. When the baking cycle ends, immediately remove the bread from the pan and place it on a rack. Let cool to room temperature before slicing.

BUTTER BREAD

T his egg bread is shaped into les gemeaux, or "the twins," a pair of loaves baked in the same pan. You can bake this specially shaped twin-humped loaf in your bread machine on the Basic or Variety cycles as described below. Or you can remove the dough, shape it into the twin loaf (with the seam in the middle), place it in a loaf pan (8-by-4-inch for 1½ pounds dough; 9-by-5-inch for 2 pounds), cover it with plastic wrap to rise for 45 minutes, and bake it off in your oven for 40 minutes at 350°F. If you don't want to do anything fancy with this loaf you don't have to; just run it straight through the Basic cycle. When you slather it with jam, you won't need the butter; it's already in the bread.

1 Place all the ingredients in the pan according to the order in the manufacturer's instructions. Set crust on medium and program for the Basic or Variety cycle; press Start. (This recipe is not suitable for use with the Delay Timer.)

2 If you are using the Basic cycle, after Rise 1 ends press Pause, remove the bread from the machine, and close the lid. If you are using the Variety cycle, remove the pan when Shape appears in the display. Turn the dough out onto a clean work surface and divide it into 2 equal portions. Flatten each portion into a small rectangle and roll up from a short side to form 2 fat squares of dough. Remove the kneading blade and give the pan a light greasing by spraying it with a bit of vegetable cooking spray. Place the 2 separate pieces side by side in the bottom of the bread pan (they will be touching). Return the pan to the machine.

3 Press Start to continue to rise and bake as programmed. When the baking cycle ends, immediately remove the bread from the pan and place it on a rack. Let cool to room temperature before slicing.

1½-POUND LOAF

⅞ cup water
1 large egg
5 tablespoons unsalted
    butter or margarine,
    cut into pieces

3 cups bread flour
1 tablespoon gluten
1½ teaspoons salt

2 teaspoons SAF yeast or
    2½ teaspoons bread
    machine yeast

2-POUND LOAF

1⅛ cups water
1 large egg
6 tablespoons unsalted
    butter or margarine,
    cut into pieces

4 cups bread flour
1 tablespoon plus
    1 teaspoon gluten
2 teaspoons salt

2½ teaspoons SAF yeast or
    1 tablespoon bread
    machine yeast

The Right Ingredient: About Eggs

Whole eggs add a wonderful golden color, a tender cakelike texture, and great flavor to bread that cannot be duplicated by any other ingredient. They are often used as a backup leavener for specialty and non-gluten flours in yeast breads. Since the cholesterol is concentrated in the yolk, many recipes call for just egg whites.

The liquid measurement for eggs is important in bread machine baking since eggs are considered liquid ingredients. Refer to this guide for substitutions or when developing your own recipes. Since fresh eggs cannot be used for baking with the Delay Timer, use a commercial egg substitute or dried powdered egg whites if you are not making the bread just after loading. Powdered egg whites will not make any noticeable difference in the flavor of the bread. Add the powder with the dry ingredients, or combine the powder with two parts cold water and shake, adding the resulting mixture with the liquid ingredients.

For no-fat diets, substitute two egg whites or a commercial liquid egg substitute for one large egg.

Egg substitutes work perfectly in all bread machine bread recipes. Many bakers on special diets substitute an equal measurement of mashed silken tofu for the eggs (a whole egg equals one-quarter cup).

Here is a helpful guide to using eggs and egg substitutes in baking recipes:

1 whole large egg equals ¼ cup liquid measure
1 large egg white equals 3 tablespoons liquid
1 large egg yolk equals 1 tablespoon liquid
3 small eggs equal 2 large eggs
1 whole large egg equals 2 egg yolks
2 whole large eggs equal 3 egg whites
1 whole large egg equals 1½ egg whites
1 whole large egg equals 3 tablespoons commercial liquid egg substitute
1 large egg white equals 2 tablespoons commercial liquid egg substitute
1 large fresh egg white equals 1 tablespoon egg-white powder plus 2 tablespoons cold water

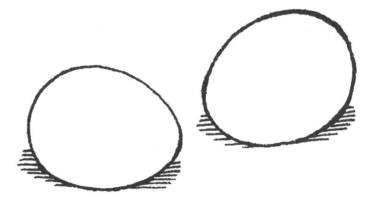

BRIOCHE BREAD

Pain brioche *is a staple of the French kitchen and every French chef masters it. While most people are familiar with the classic* petites brioches *with their topknots, butter-rich bakery brioche is often baked in a loaf pan. Pay attention to the technique for adding the room-temperature butter pieces; it is done while the machine is running during the kneading phase. Brioche bread is perfect for French toast, bread puddings, appetizer sandwiches, and for just plain old toast. Serve the warm golden slices spread with some good preserves, like pure apricot or boysenberry jam (see recipes in the Jams, Preserves, and Chutneys chapter), or with an apple butter and some cream cheese. You can also shape this dough into individual brioches or wrap it around a wheel of Brie cheese (pages 78 to 79). Prepare the recipe using the Dough cycle, scrape it into a plastic container and refrigerate it overnight, and then proceed with the instructions on page 79.*

❶ Place the ingredients, except the butter, in the pan according to the order in the manufacturer's instructions. Set crust on medium and program for the Basic cycle; press Start. (This recipe is not suitable for use with the Delay Timer.) The dough will be soft and sticky.

❷ About 10 minutes into Knead 2 (I set a kitchen timer), open the lid while the machine is running. Add a piece or two of the butter, allowing it to be incorporated before adding more pieces. It will take a full minute or two to add all the butter. Close the lid.

❸ When the baking cycle ends, open the lid and let the bread sit in the pan for 15 minutes. Gently remove the loaf from the pan and place it on a rack. Let cool to room temperature before slicing.

1½-POUND LOAF

⅓ cup milk
2 large eggs
1 egg yolk

2 cups bread flour
2 tablespoons sugar
2 teaspoons gluten
¾ teaspoon salt

1¼ teaspoons SAF yeast or
  1¾ teaspoons bread
  machine yeast

7 tablespoons unsalted
  butter, cut into pieces

2-POUND LOAF

½ cup plus 1 tablespoon
  milk
2 large eggs
2 egg yolks

2¾ cups bread flour
2½ tablespoons sugar
1 tablespoon gluten
1 teaspoon salt

1¾ teaspoons SAF yeast or
  2¼ teaspoons bread
  machine yeast

½ cup plus 2 tablespoons
  (1¼ sticks) unsalted
  butter, cut into pieces

Technique: Shaping Individual Brioches

Makes 8 to 10 individual brioches

Here the brioche dough will be shaped by hand into the charming classic rolls and baked in your home oven. Serve for brunch with jam. No butter is necessary.

1 recipe Brioche Bread dough (page 77), refrigerated overnight
1 egg, well beaten, for glaze

1 Place 8 (for the 1½-pound dough) or 10 (for the 2-pound dough) individual 3½-by-1½-inch brioche flute tins on a baking sheet. Spray each with vegetable oil cooking spray.

2 Turn the dough out onto a lightly floured work surface and divide it in half. Roll each half into a thick log, and divide each log into 4 (for the 1½-pound) or 5 (for the 2-pound) 2-inch pieces and 4 (or 5) 1-inch pieces. Round each 2-inch piece into a ball and place in a prepared tin. Form the 1-inch pieces into teardrop shapes. Press your finger into the center of each ball, straight through to the bottom. Insert the pointed end of a teardrop into the hole. Press to flatten the topknot into the piece of dough in the tin. Repeat with all the remaining pieces of dough. Cover loosely with a clean towel and let rest at cool room temperature for about 1 hour, or until doubled in bulk.

3 Preheat the oven to 400°F.

4 Brush the tops of the brioches with the beaten egg and bake for 10 to 15 minutes, or until golden brown. Remove from the tins and place on a rack. Let cool completely. Brioches are best reheated so that the texture has time to set.

Brie in Brioche

Makes one 8-inch round, serves 20 as an appetizer or 12 as part of a meal

An impressive and immensely popular appetizer for entertaining large groups, fromage en brioche *is a staple in the French cooking repertoire. I learned to make this in a brioche class twenty-five years ago, and have been making it ever since. A full round of cheese is wrapped in bread dough and baked until golden. You will find the technique easier than you'd expect. Some bakers save a bit of the dough to make decorations, like leaves, curlicues, or braids, to place on top of the loaf before baking. This bread can be served warm or at room temperature. It is very good with soup or salad. Decorate the serving plate with fresh grapes, apples, and pears. Have a brie knife on hand for cutting, and provide your guests with plates and forks.*

One 1½-pound-loaf recipe Brioche Bread dough (page 77), refrigerated overnight
One 8-inch wheel (2.2 pounds) of well-chilled, slightly firm Brie cheese (leave the rind on)
1 egg mixed with 1 teaspoon milk, for glaze

1 Line a baking sheet with parchment paper. On a lightly floured work surface, divide the dough into 2 uneven portions. Using a rolling pin, roll out the larger portion of chilled dough into a 9-inch-diameter round, about ¼ inch thick. Fold into quarters and transfer the dough to the baking sheet. Unfold and place the cheese in the center of the dough. Bring up the edges of the dough and press against the sides of the cheese.

2 Roll out the remaining portion of dough into a 10-inch-diameter round (about 1 inch larger than the first circle). Brush the entire circle with the egg glaze. Place the circle, glaze side down, on top of the cheese. Press the dough onto the sides and trim the base with a small knife to neaten. Press to seal all around the sides of the cheese so it adheres to the bottom layer of dough.

3 Brush the entire cheese with the egg glaze. Cover loosely with plastic wrap and let rise at room temperature until puffy, about 1 to 1½ hours.

4 Twenty minutes before baking, preheat the oven to 400°F.

5 Bake for 10 minutes, then lower the temperature to 350°F and bake for an additional 10 to 12 minutes, until golden brown. Remove from the oven and place the pan on a rack. Cool for at least 15 minutes before using a large metal spatula to transfer to a serving platter or marble slab for serving.

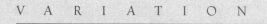

V A R I A T I O N

Apricot Brie in Brioche

This is a favorite of mine for catering. The baked Brie has a layer of apricot just under the pastry crust. There is a burst of flavor in every bite.

⅔ cup thick apricot preserves
½ cup chopped dried apricots

Mix the preserves and apricots in a small bowl. Spread evenly over the top of the Brie before placing the second layer of dough over the cheese to encase it. Bake as directed.

ZOPF (SWISS EGG BREAD)

1½-POUND LOAF

½ cup milk
⅓ cup water
1 large egg
2 tablespoons unsalted
   butter, cut into pieces

3 cups bread flour
1 tablespoon sugar
1 tablespoon gluten
1½ teaspoons salt

2 teaspoons SAF yeast or
   2½ teaspoons bread
   machine yeast

2-POUND LOAF

½ cup milk
⅔ cup water
1 large egg
3 tablespoons unsalted
   butter, cut into pieces

4 cups bread flour
1½ tablespoons sugar
1 tablespoon plus
   1 teaspoon gluten
2 teaspoons salt

2¼ teaspoons SAF yeast or
   2¾ teaspoons bread
   machine yeast

Zopf *is the traditional egg bread of Switzerland. Its name comes from Züpfe, "to braid" in Swiss German. Every home baker in Switzerland has her own version, as it is a much beloved bread. When baked in an oven, this bread is braided with one end thicker than the other, like when you braid hair. This version is from Bern and it is baked in the machine.*

1 Place all the ingredients in the pan according to the order in the manufacturer's instructions. Set crust on medium and program for the Basic cycle; press Start. (This recipe is not suitable for use with the Delay Timer.)

2 When the baking cycle ends, immediately remove the bread from the pan and place it on a rack. Let cool to room temperature before slicing.

JEWISH EGG BREAD

C hallah, meaning "offering" in Hebrew, is a traditional Jewish egg bread that, as far as I am concerned, has no peer. It is served with every Sabbath meal and on Jewish holidays. This nondairy version can be baked inside the machine, or the dough can be removed and shaped into a traditional braid or coil and then baked in the oven (see page 82).

1 Place the ingredients in the pan according to the order in the manufacturer's instructions. Set crust on medium and program for the Basic cycle; press Start. (This recipe is not suitable for use with the Delay Timer.) During Rise 3, carefully lift the lid and sprinkle just the top of the dough with the poppy or sesame seeds. Close the lid to finish the rising and baking.

2 When the baking cycle ends, immediately remove the bread from the pan and place it on a rack. Let cool to room temperature before slicing.

1½-POUND LOAF	2-POUND LOAF
¾ cup water	1 cup water
2 large eggs	2 large eggs plus 1 egg yolk
1 tablespoon honey	1½ tablespoons honey
3 tablespoons vegetable oil	¼ cup vegetable oil
3 cups bread flour	4 cups bread flour
1 tablespoon gluten	1 tablespoon plus 1 teaspoon gluten
1½ teaspoons salt	2 teaspoons salt
1¾ teaspoons SAF yeast or 2¼ teaspoons bread machine yeast	2 teaspoons SAF yeast or 2½ teaspoons bread machine yeast
1 tablespoon poppy or sesame seeds, for sprinkling	1 tablespoon poppy or sesame seeds, for sprinkling

Technique: Jewish Egg Braid or Coil

Makes 1 large braided or coiled loaf

Jewish egg bread is steeped in symbolism. The three strands of the braid represent truth, peace, and justice. The poppy seeds on top represent the manna that fell from heaven in the desert to feed the wandering tribes according to the Old Testament. You can also shape this into a coil, a circular loaf with no beginning and no end, baked for Rosh Hashanah, the Jewish New Year.

1 recipe Jewish Egg Bread dough (page 81)
1 egg white beaten with 1 tablespoon water
1 tablespoon poppy or sesame seeds, for
    sprinkling, optional

❶ Line a large baking sheet with parchment paper. Turn the dough out onto a lightly floured work surface.

❷ *To make a braided loaf:* Divide the dough into 3 equal portions. Using your palms, roll each portion into a fat cylinder, 12 inches long for the 1½-pound dough, or 14 inches long for the 2-pound dough, tapered at each end. Be sure the ropes are of equal size and shape. Place the 3 ropes parallel to each other on the baking sheet. Begin braiding from the center of the ropes rather than at the ends for a more even shape. Take one of the outside ropes and fold it over the center rope, then repeat the movement from the opposite side. Continue by alternating the outside ropes over the center rope. When completed, rotate the half braid and repeat the procedure from the middle out to the other ends. Adjust or press the braid to make it look even. Tuck the ends under, pinching the ends into tapered points.

❸ *To make a coiled loaf:* With your palms, roll the entire portion of dough into a rope about 20 inches long. Place the rope on the baking sheet, with one end in the center. Coil the rope around that end to make a loose spiral. Pinch the end under.

❹ Cover the shaped dough loosely with plastic wrap and let rise at room temperature until the dough is almost doubled in bulk, 45 minutes to 1 hour. Do not let this dough rise longer before baking or it may collapse in the oven.

❺ Twenty minutes before baking, set the oven rack in the middle of the oven and preheat it to 350°F.

❻ Beat the egg and water glaze with a fork until foamy. Using a pastry brush, brush the top of the loaf with some of the egg glaze and sprinkle with the seeds, or leave plain. Bake for 35 to 45 minutes, or until the loaf is deep golden brown and the bread sounds hollow when tapped on the bottom with your finger. Immediately remove the bread from the pan and place it on a cooling rack. Let cool to room temperature before slicing.

POPPY SEED EGG BREAD

T his loaf with all white flour rises so dramatically that one set of proportions works best in either size machine. It is very much like regular challah, but made with dairy products, and the poppy seeds are distributed throughout rather than sitting on top, so it ends up cakelike. (Store your poppy seeds in the freezer, just like nuts, to keep them fresh.) My tester, Margery Schneider, doesn't store this bread in a plastic bag, but leaves the cut loaf cut side down on her breadboard overnight to retain the crisp crust. Serve with a savory butter for dinner, or with jam for breakfast and brunch.

1½- OR 2-POUND-LOAF MACHINES
½ cup milk
3 large eggs
2 tablespoons unsalted butter, cut into pieces
3 cups bread flour
1 tablespoon sugar
1 tablespoon gluten
2 teaspoons poppy seeds
1½ teaspoons salt
1½ teaspoons SAF yeast or 2 teaspoons bread machine yeast

1 Place all the ingredients in the pan according to the order in the manufacturer's instructions. Set crust on medium and program for the Basic or Tender cycle; press Start. (This recipe is not suitable for use with the Delay Timer.)

2 When the baking cycle ends, immediately remove the bread from the pan and place it on a rack. Let cool to room temperature before slicing.

Leftover Bread Cookery: Baked Fruit Desserts

These fruit desserts are really old-fashioned. They are the kinds of desserts you would eat when you visited your grandmother when you were young.

Stuffed Baked Apples with Maple Crème Fraîche

Serves 6

Baked apples are a real pleasure. They may be old-fashioned, but they are still a wonderful dessert, especially when made with fresh fall apples. If you can get extra-large, firm stuffing apples like Rome Beauties or Granny Smiths, they are the best, since they hold their shape nicely after baking. Serve with spoonfuls of maple-infused crème fraîche on the side.

For the apples:

½ cup dried cranberries
Boiling water
6 large apples, washed and cored
Two 1-inch-thick slices homemade white, light whole wheat, or nut bread
⅓ cup (2 ounces) pecans
⅔ cup light brown sugar
1½ teaspoons ground cinnamon
½ teaspoon ground nutmeg
Pinch of ground cloves
2 tablespoons brandy or Calvados, optional
3 tablespoons unsalted butter

For the maple crème fraîche:

1½ cups crème fraîche
5 tablespoons pure maple syrup

❶ To prepare the apples, place the cranberries in a small bowl and cover with boiling water to plump for 10 minutes. Peel the apples by cutting a spiral pattern around the entire apple with a sharp paring knife, starting at the bottom and cutting up to the top. Repeat with each apple. Place in a deep baking dish with the apples touching each other and set aside.

❷ Preheat the oven to 325°F.

❸ Place the bread in a food processor and grind to coarse crumbs; you will have about 1½ cups. Add the pecans and pulse to chop. Add the brown sugar and spices; pulse to mix. Drain the cranberries, pat dry with a paper towel, and toss them with the brandy if you are using it. Combine the cranberries with the sugared crumbs.

❹ Fill each apple core with the filling mixture. Top each with ½ tablespoon butter. Pour about a cup of water (or half water and half apple juice) into the baking dish and cover the dish with aluminum foil. Bake for 25 minutes, then remove the foil and bake for an additional 45 minutes. Baste 2 or 3 times during baking.

❺ To make the maple crème fraîche, place the crème fraîche in a small bowl. Whisk in the maple syrup until smooth. Cover and refrigerate until serving.

❻ Remove the apples from the oven and let stand at room temperature in the baking dish until cool enough to serve, or cover and refrigerate overnight to serve cold or reheated.

Pear Brown Betty

Serves 6

This warm baked winter fruit dessert, similar to a crisp and popular in America since colonial times, should really be called a "brown Bethy." Be sure to use pears that are ripe but still firm or they will disintegrate when cooked. This can also be made with apples. Serve with a pitcher of heavy cream on the side.

Two 1-inch-thick slices homemade white or whole wheat egg bread
½ cup light brown sugar
¼ cup sugar
2 teaspoons ground cinnamon
½ teaspoon ground allspice
¼ teaspoon ground cloves
8 firm pears (2½ pounds), such as Bartlett or Bosc, peeled, cored, and sliced 1 inch thick
3 tablespoons fresh lemon juice
¼ cup apple or pear juice, or water
⅓ cup unsalted butter, cut into pieces

❶ Preheat the oven to 375°F. Butter an 8-by-8-inch shallow baking dish.

❷ Place the bread in a food processor and pulse to coarse crumbs; you will have about 1½ cups.

❸ Combine the crumbs, sugar, and spices in a bowl. Toss the sliced pears with the lemon juice in another bowl.

❹ Sprinkle the baking dish with 3 tablespoons of the spiced crumbs. Top with half of the pears and pour the juice or water over. Top with half of the remaining spiced crumbs; dot with 3 tablespoons of butter. Top with a final layer of fruit, crumbs, and butter pieces.

❺ Bake for 35 to 40 minutes, or until bubbly and the fruit is cooked. Cool slightly and serve warm.

VIRGINIA LIGHT ROLLS

Makes 16 dinner rolls

1½- OR 2-POUND-LOAF MACHINES

1 cup plus 1 tablespoon milk
3 tablespoons honey
2 large eggs
6 tablespoons butter or margarine, cut into pieces

4¼ cups unbleached all-purpose flour
1½ teaspoons salt

2 teaspoons SAF yeast or 2½ teaspoons bread machine yeast

4 tablespoons melted butter or margarine, for brushing

T his basic all-white dinner roll dough is slightly sweet and fluffy, producing tender rolls with that well-loved, good buttery flavor. I have given directions here for shaping the dough into finger rolls, but there are many shapes to choose from (see pages 358 to 359). Decide which whimsical shape you like and have a go. You can put seeds on these if you like. You can also prepare these ahead of time as Brown-and-Serve Dinner Rolls (page 87).

❶ Place all the ingredients in the pan according to the order in the manufacturer's instructions. Program for the Dough cycle; press Start. The dough ball will be soft, but add no more than 2 to 3 extra tablespoons of flour, as needed, if you think it necessary.

❷ Line a large baking sheet with parchment paper. When the machine beeps at the end of the cycle, press Stop and unplug the machine. Turn the dough out onto a lightly floured surface. Divide the dough in half, then roll each half into a 2- to 3-inch cylinder. With a metal dough scraper or a chef's knife, cut the cylinder into 8 equal portions. Repeat with the second cylinder, making a total of 16 equal portions. Shape each portion like a miniature loaf by patting it into an oval, then rolling up from a short side to make a small compact cylinder about 4 inches long. Place the rolls in two rows of 8 with their long sides touching. Brush some melted butter on the tops of the rolls. Cover loosely with plastic wrap and let rise at room temperature until doubled in bulk, about 45 minutes.

❸ Twenty minutes before baking, preheat the oven to 375°F.

❹ Place the baking sheet in the center of the oven and bake for 25 to 28 minutes, until golden brown. Remove the rolls from the pan and cool on a rack. Serve warm, or cool to room temperature and reheat.

Brown-and-Serve Dinner Rolls

These brown-and-serve instructions may be used for Virginia Light Rolls (page 86), as well as Soft Whole Wheat Dinner Rolls (page 109), or Squash or Pumpkin Cloverleaf Rolls (page 356).

1 Mix, rise, and shape dinner rolls as directed in the recipe. Arrange the rolls in two 9-inch round cake pans, in two 9-by-9-inch ungreased disposable aluminum baking pans, or in disposable muffin tins. Let rise until doubled in bulk at room temperature, about 30 minutes.

2 Preheat the oven to 300°F.

3 Bake in the center of the oven until the rolls are fully baked, but not browned, 15 to 20 minutes. Remove from the oven and cool completely on a rack in the pan. Place the pan of rolls in a heavy-duty plastic bag, or wrap in plastic wrap and then in a layer of aluminum foil, and refrigerate for up to 3 days or freeze for up to 3 weeks. You can bake half the rolls and eat them while fresh, and freeze the other half for later.

4 To serve: Let the pan of frozen rolls thaw in the bag at room temperature or in the refrigerator overnight. Preheat the oven to 375°F for 15 minutes. Bake the rolls until golden brown, 10 to 14 minutes. Serve immediately.

EGG BAGELS

Makes 16 bagels

1 cup water
2 large eggs
1½ tablespoons vegetable or canola oil

4 cups bread flour
1 tablespoon sugar or malt powder
1 tablespoon gluten
2 teaspoons fine kosher salt

2¼ teaspoons SAF yeast or 2¾ teaspoons bread machine yeast

3 to 4 quarts water
2 tablespoons fine kosher salt
1 egg yolk beaten with 2 tablespoons water, for glaze
Sesame, poppy, caraway, or fennel seeds, for garnishing

B*agels differ from other yeast breads because after the dough is risen and shaped the bagels are immersed in boiling water to give them their characteristic firm, chewy interior. They are really fun to make. Be easy on yourself with the forming; homemade bagels will never be as evenly shaped as commercial ones, but they taste incredible. While all bagels are not egg bagels, I find the addition of eggs makes for a slightly lighter homemade version; bagel dough tends to be very dense. Split, toast, and serve these bagels with butter and jam or with lox and cream cheese.*

1 Place the water, eggs, oil, flour, sugar, gluten, salt, and yeast in the pan according to the order in the manufacturer's instructions. Program for the Dough cycle or the Bagel cycle; press Start.

2 When the Dough cycle ends, bring the 3 to 4 quarts of water to a rolling boil in a deep stockpot. Turn the dough out onto a lightly floured work surface; the dough will be stiff. Divide the dough into fourths. Divide each quarter into 4 equal portions. Shape each portion of dough into a smooth round, tucking the excess dough underneath. Flatten with your palm. Poke a floured finger through the middle of the ball. Stretch the hole with your fingers to make it about 1 inch in diameter. Spin the dough around your finger to expand the hole; the hole will be quite large as you spin, but will shrink slightly when you stop. Set the bagel aside on the work surface while forming the others. Let the bagels rest on the work surface for 15 minutes; they will need no further rising after this.

3 Preheat the oven to 375°F and line 2 baking sheets with parchment paper.

4 Add the 2 tablespoons salt to the boiling water (this will flavor the crust). Reduce heat to medium-high to maintain a slow rolling boil. With a curved slotted spatula, lower 4 bagels into the gently boiling water. They will drop to the bottom and then rise to the surface after about 4 minutes. As they come to the surface, turn the bagels and boil them 3 minutes on the other side (a total of 7 minutes for each bagel). This goes very quickly. Remove from the boiling water with a slotted spoon and place 1 inch apart on the prepared baking sheet. Repeat with remaining bagels.

5 Place the seeds on a plate. Brush the bagels with egg glaze and press each raw bagel into the seeds to coat the top. Bake for 30 to 35 minutes, or until deep golden. Remove from the baking sheets and let cool on racks. Eat the bagels the day they are baked or freeze for up to 1 month.

ENGLISH MUFFINS

Makes 1 dozen 3-inch muffins

**1½- OR 2-POUND-
LOAF MACHINES**

1½ cups fat-free milk
2 tablespoons unsalted
   butter, melted
1 large egg

4½ cups unbleached
   all-purpose flour
2 teaspoons salt

2¼ teaspoons SAF yeast or
2¾ teaspoons bread
   machine yeast

⅓ cup yellow cornmeal
   or coarse semolina,
   for sprinkling

E nglish muffins really should be named American muffins, as they are the pure Yankee offshoot of the griddle-baked Celtic crumpet and bannock. This is my favorite recipe, adapted from the late Jane Grigson, the esteemed British food writer and journalist. These never fail to delight and amaze people who never thought of an English muffin as a homemade specialty. They are more substantial than the store-bought variety. Store these muffins, wrapped tightly in plastic, in the refrigerator or freezer after baking. To serve, pull them apart with a fork and toast them. Serve with lots of sweet butter and a fruit curd, or use them for your eggs Benedict.

1 Place all the ingredients in the pan according to the order in the manufacturer's instructions. Program for the Dough cycle; press Start. The dough ball will be soft and very slightly moist. The softer you leave the dough, the lighter the muffins. You can always add a bit more flour when you remove the dough from the machine.

2 Lightly sprinkle the work surface with cornmeal or semolina. When the machine beeps at the end of the cycle, press Stop and unplug the machine. Turn the dough out onto the work surface and, with a rolling pin, roll into a rectangle about ½ inch thick. Sprinkle the top surface with cornmeal or semolina to prevent sticking while rolling. Cut out the muffins with a 3-inch biscuit cutter or with the rim of a drinking glass. Roll out the trimmings and cut out the remaining muffins. Cover with a clean tea towel, or place them in the refrigerator if they are rising too fast while the others are baking.

3 Preheat an electric griddle to 350° to 375°F, or heat a cast-iron stovetop griddle over medium heat until a drop of water sprinkled on the griddle dances across the surface. Lightly grease the surface.

④ Immediately place several muffins on the hot griddle. Cook for about 10 minutes on each side, turning them when they are quite brown. English muffins take time to bake all the way through, and they will swell and be very puffy while baking. Remove the muffins from the griddle with a spatula and let cool on a rack.

Freezing Bread

Freezing is a simple and safe method of preserving food. Although fresh is best when it comes to yeast and quick breads, frozen baked goods do retain excellent flavor and are good to have on hand. Please remember that the freezer compartment of a refrigerator does not achieve a true deep freeze, but is intended for short-term storage. It will keep foods well for a few months, but for safe long-term storage, you should freeze at 0°F or below. Maximum storage time in a home freezer for all bread and rolls is 3 months.

To freeze bread and rolls, bake according to the recipe. For sweet rolls and sweet breads, bake completely but do not glaze or ice. Place on a rack and let cool to room temperature. Wrap whole or presliced loaves first in good-quality plastic wrap and then in aluminum foil or in a plastic freezer bag. Rolls can be stored in a double layer of freezer bags. Label and date the loaves or rolls if possible; you will be surprised at how similar everything looks when frozen.

To thaw, let the loaf or rolls stand at room temperature for about 3 hours or in the refrigerator overnight, completely wrapped to preserve moisture. Yeast breads may be refreshed, or thawed, in a 350°F oven. Place an unsliced loaf, au naturel or wrapped in aluminum foil, in a preheated oven for about 15 minutes to crisp the crust and heat it through. Sliced breads may be refreshed in a toaster without defrosting or microwaved for 15 seconds. Rolls reheat best wrapped in foil, as they dry out quickly.

After sweet bread or sweet rolls are thawed and reheated, glaze, ice, or dust with powdered sugar just before serving.

HAMBURGER BUNS AND HOT DOG ROLLS

1½-pound dough makes 8 round sandwich buns or long rolls

2-pound dough makes 12 round sandwich buns or long rolls

K*eep bags of these in the freezer for impromptu barbecues and picnics. The sandwich buns are nice and soft, perfect for sloppy joes and summer tomato and mayonnaise sandwiches. The long rolls are good for ricotta with arugula and tomatoes, turkey and cheese, and, of course, hot dogs or bratwurst. These rolls are really good—the kind you look for in the supermarket but can rarely find.*

1 Place all the ingredients in the pan according to the order in the manufacturer's instructions. Program for the Dough cycle; press Start.

1½-POUND LOAF	2-POUND LOAF
1 cup water	1¼ cups water
1 large egg	1 large egg
4 tablespoons unsalted butter, cut into pieces	6 tablespoons unsalted butter, cut into pieces
2 tablespoons sugar	3 tablespoons sugar
3 cups bread flour	4 cups bread flour
¼ cup nonfat dry milk	⅓ cup nonfat dry milk
2 tablespoons instant potato flakes	3 tablespoons instant potato flakes
1 tablespoon gluten	1 tablespoon plus 1 teaspoon gluten
1½ teaspoons salt	2 teaspoons salt
1¾ teaspoons SAF yeast or 2¼ teaspoons bread machine yeast	2 teaspoons SAF yeast or 2½ teaspoons bread machine yeast
1 egg yolk beaten with 1 tablespoon water, for glaze	1 egg yolk beaten with 1 tablespoon water, for glaze
1½ tablespoons sesame seeds, for sprinkling	1½ tablespoons sesame seeds, for sprinkling

2 Line a large baking sheet with parchment paper. When the machine beeps at the end of the cycle press Stop and unplug the machine. Immediately turn the dough out onto a lightly floured work surface. With a dough knife, divide the 1½-pound dough into 8 equal portions or the 2-pound dough into 12 equal portions. For hamburger buns form each portion into tight rounds. For long rolls, flatten each portion into an oval about 6 inches long and rolling up tightly from a long end to form a cylinder. Place the rolls on the lined baking sheet at least 1 inch apart. Press with your palm to flatten each roll. Cover loosely with plastic wrap and let rest for 30 minutes.

❸ Preheat the oven to 375°F.

❹ Brush the rolls with the egg glaze and sprinkle with sesame seeds. Bake for 15 to 22 minutes, depending on the size of the roll, until lightly browned. Remove the rolls from the sheet with a spatula and let cool completely on a rack. Slice in half horizontally to serve.

Pasta Doughs from Your Bread Machine

Until lately, unless you lived in an Italian neighborhood or were invited to an Italian family dinner, it was rare to see fresh pasta. In the past decade, the availability of a wide variety of fresh, frozen, and factory-made premium dried pastas (from old Italian families like de Cecco and Ronzoni) has exceeded all hopes—to the delight of hungry diners.

Fresh pasta dough is easily made in any bread machine that has a motor capable of mixing heavy whole grain doughs. This is one of the newly discovered uses for the bread machine. Some manufacturers, like Oster, even have a special setting just for pasta making. You make the dough in the machine, let it rest, then roll it out by hand or in a pasta machine. The no-fuss ease of making your own pasta dough in the bread machine is a satisfying culinary adventure.

Semolina di grano duro, known as semolina or durum flour, is an ingredient in most all pastas, in combination with all-purpose flour. It is an important flour because it dries out quickly, and produces pasta that cooks to a firm bite rather than becoming mushy, since it doesn't absorb a lot of water. Semolina flour is important if you are making extruded pasta. Many cooks use bread flour for their pasta, which is just as good. Egg noodles are made from unbolted all-purpose flour, which makes a tender pasta. In northern Italy, pasta is made from spelt flour, known as *farro*.

The easiest noodles to make at home are the ones that are cut from a sheet into various sizes, wide lasagna strips, ribbons of fettuccine, and thin strands of tagliarini. Each shape can be served with a number of luscious sauces, or simply with garlic, olive oil, and Parmesan cheese. I think the dough for egg pasta is the easiest for beginners; the eggs tenderize the stiff dough.

The following are the most popular shapes cut from homemade pasta. Remember that they will look different than machine-produced pastas.

- Fettuccine—Also called *tagliatelle*, this is the most common homemade noodle. The dough is rolled up and cut into slices about ¼ inch wide.

- Tagliarini—The thinnest noodle, cut into a ¹⁄₁₆-inch width. Tagliarini is great in soups. *Capellini d'angelo*, or angel's hair, is the thinnest tagliarini and can only be cut with a machine.

- Lasagna—These noodles are 2 to 3 inches wide and about 10 inches long, or the length of your baking dish. Long strips are cut from flat sheets of rolled-out dough with a plain or fluted pastry wheel. Since they cook so quickly, I often don't cut them into strips, but make the sheets close to the size of my baking dish. You don't need to precook fresh lasagna noodles before assembling the dish.

The Toolbox: Equipment for Making Pasta

In your pasta-making toolbox, you will need:

- A long hardwood rolling pin, a dough scraper, and a wooden or plastic pastry board if you will be rolling and cutting the pasta by hand.

- A pasta machine if you will be rolling and cutting by machine. (Hand-cranked models from Atlas and Imperia are the simplest and least expensive. Simac Pasta Matic and Kitchen Aid Food Preparer are also able to extrude pasta.)

- A wooden drying pole or rack, clean kitchen towels, or a baking sheet dusted with flour, for drying the pasta.

- A slotted spoon, wooden pasta fork, or Chinese mesh strainer for stirring the pasta while it cooks and a colander for draining it if you plan to cook the pasta right away.

EGG PASTA

Makes 1½ pounds pasta, 7 to 8 servings

Egg pasta is excellent with all sorts of fresh or cooked sauces—like ragù, marinara, bolognese, pesto, white clam sauce, cream sauces—and pasta frittatas, baked pastas, with sautéed mushrooms and peas, timbales, cannelloni, manicotti, and in soups.*

1½- OR 2-POUND-LOAF MACHINES
4 large eggs, lightly beaten, at room temperature
2 tablespoons warm water
1 tablespoon olive oil
2 cups unbleached all-purpose or bread flour
1 cup semolina pasta flour
1 teaspoon salt

1 Place all the ingredients in the bread pan according to the order in the manufacturer's instructions. Program for the Dough or the Pasta Dough cycle; press Start. Set a kitchen timer for 7 minutes. When the timer rings, check the dough ball that has collected on the blade. It should be firm but pliable. If it is too dry, add a couple drops of water while the machine is kneading. If it is too moist, sprinkle in some all-purpose flour, a teaspoon at a time. Reset the timer for 3 more minutes. When the timer rings, press Stop to cancel the cycle. (These recipes are not suitable for use with the Delay Timer.)

2 Remove the dough from the pan. Form into a ball, wrap in plastic wrap, and let rest at room temperature for 30 minutes. (The dough can be refrigerated at this point for up to 3 days, but bring to room temperature before rolling out.) The dough is now ready to roll out and cut as desired.

3 *To roll the dough by hand:* Dust your work surface with all-purpose flour. Divide the dough into 3 equal portions, keeping the reserved dough balls covered to prevent drying out. Place the ball of dough on the work surface and with the rolling pin, roll back and forth. Then begin to roll in one direction, away from you. Make a quarter turn and roll in the other direction until the dough stretches into a rounded rectangle about ⅛ inch thick. Roll the dough around the rolling pin and unroll to stretch the dough further (this is how the old

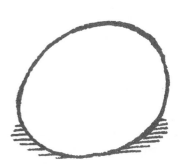

Freezing Instructions

You can freeze the pasta dough ball for up to 1 month, defrosting overnight in the refrigerator before bringing to room temperature and rolling out. Or you can freeze your noodles in single-serving bundles on a baking sheet, then transfer to a plastic freezer bag. Frozen noodles can be cooked in the boiling water, but the cooking time will be about 2 minutes longer.

Italian grandmothers do it). Keep the dough as thin and as light as possible. Work quickly, as the dough dries out.

4 *To cut the dough by hand:* Sprinkle the dough with flour and bring the 2 opposite ends of the dough together in the center. Repeat 2 more times, until you have a tight double jelly roll of pasta. Hold the roll with one hand and, with a sharp chef's knife in the other, slice into ⅛-, ¼-, or ½-inch-wide thin, medium, or wide noodles. You can slip the dull edge of the knife under the center of the dough and lift the noodles, they will unravel over the knife. Or lift the noodles with your fingers.

5 *To roll the dough with a pasta machine:* Attach the pasta machine onto your counter and set the smooth rollers to the widest opening. Dust your work surface with all-purpose flour. Divide the dough into 4 to 6 equal portions, keeping the reserved dough balls covered to prevent drying out. Place the ball of dough on the work surface and press to flatten, to a width no wider than the opening of the machine. Run the dough through the machine. Dust with flour as necessary. Fold in thirds and run through the machine again. Run the dough through the machine 2 more times, but don't fold the dough again.

6 Set the notch on the machine to the next smallest setting and run the dough through the rollers. Continue rolling and stretching the dough, using a smaller setting each time, until the smallest setting is reached. Most machines have 6 graduated settings. You can skip some settings. The dough strip will be long and delicate.

7 *To cut the dough with a pasta machine:* Adjust the cutting mechanism of the machine to the desired width and run the dough through to cut. You can run the cut pasta directly out onto a baking sheet dusted with some semolina.

8 *To dry the pasta:* Transfer the cut pasta to a drying rack, a floured towel, or a floured baking sheet. As one layer is filled, place a sheet of parchment over the pasta on the baking sheet, and continue to layer the pasta and sprinkle lightly with flour to keep from sticking. Cut into desired lengths with a sharp chef's knife. Let the pasta air dry at least 20 minutes before cooking or freezing.

9 *To cook the pasta right away:* Bring 4 quarts of water to a boil over high heat for each pound of pasta. Add 1 tablespoon of cooking oil and 1½ tablespoons salt. Then immerse the pasta. Cook for 2 to 3 minutes, stirring a few times to separate the strands, then as the water comes to a low boil again, begin to taste test. Remove a strand from the pot; it should be slightly firm to the bite, not mushy. This happens fast! Pour the cooked pasta into a colander in the sink to drain. Don't rinse with cold water. Return it to the pan in which it was cooked and toss with some butter or oil, then serve as soon as possible with your sauce.

V A R I A T I O N S

Herb Egg Pasta

Add 2 tablespoons minced flat-leaf parsley, 2 tablespoons minced fresh basil, and 2 tablespoons minced fresh marjoram to the flour in the bread pan. Use milk in place of the warm water. This pasta is excellent with cheese sauces such as *fonduta*, with ricotta and parsley, and with olive oil sauces.

Black Pepper Egg Pasta

Add 1 heaping tablespoon of finely ground black pepper to the flour in the bread pan. This pasta is very good with vegetable, tomato, and butter sauces.

WHOLE WHEAT EGG PASTA

Makes 1½ pounds pasta, 7 to 8 servings

1½- OR 2-POUND-LOAF MACHINES

4 large eggs, lightly beaten, at room temperature
3 tablespoons warm water
1 tablespoon olive oil

2 cups unbleached all-purpose flour
1 cup whole wheat or whole grain spelt flour
1 teaspoon salt

 his pasta is excellent with vegetable, sausage, tomato, and cheese sauces, like gorgonzola.

Follow the step-by-step directions for Egg Pasta beginning on page 95.

GREEN SPINACH PASTA

Makes 1½ pounds pasta, 7 to 8 servings

1½- OR 2-POUND-LOAF MACHINES

½ pound fresh spinach, washed
3 large eggs, lightly beaten, at room temperature
1 tablespoon olive oil

3 cups unbleached all-purpose flour
1 teaspoon salt

 his pasta is excellent with tomato sauces and cream sauces.

❶ Place the spinach in a food processor fitted with the metal blade. Process to a puree. Remove the spinach and place in a small mesh strainer over a small bowl. Press out 2 to 3 tablespoons spinach juice. Reserve 3 tablespoons spinach puree.

❷ Follow the step-by-step directions for Egg Pasta beginning on page 95, adding 2 tablespoons of the spinach juice and 3 tablespoons of the puree with the wet ingredients in Step 1. Adjust the texture of the dough ball using the reserved spinach juice.

SEMOLINA PASTA

Makes 1½ pounds pasta, 7 to 8 servings

T his pasta is very good with all tomato sauces, with meatballs, with vegetable sauces such as pureed broccoli, with cream sauces such as balsamella, and for baked pasta dishes.

Follow the step-by-step directions for Egg Pasta beginning on page 95.

1½- OR 2-POUND-LOAF MACHINES

⅞ cup warm water
1 tablespoon olive oil

2 cups unbleached
    all-purpose or bread flour
1 cup semolina pasta flour
1 teaspoon salt

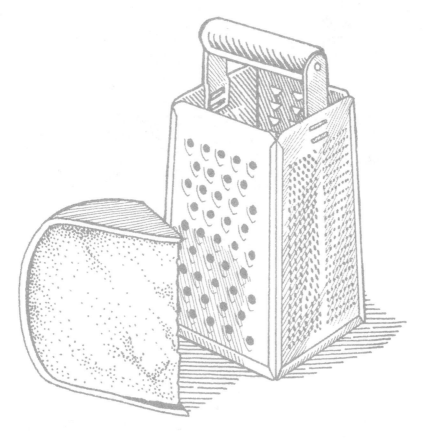

EARTH'S BOUNTY

Whole Wheat, Whole-Grain,

and Specialty Flour Breads

WHOLE WHEAT BREADS

Mention whole grain bread and one of the following images might spring to mind: heavy, dry, tooth-breaker. Any experienced baker knows there is some truth to each of those images, but in reality, whole grain breads can be hearty in flavor and still light textured. Whole wheat breads are part of a genre known as whole grain breads because whole wheat flours are ground from all the parts of the grain. A 100 percent whole wheat bread may be the quint-essential whole grain loaf, a loaf that every baker wants to master, but there is room for the hand of creativity in whole wheat breads, too. They can be made with all different pro-portions of whole wheat flour, from a few tablespoons to 50 or 75 percent. Differences in the grinds of different brands of flour also contribute slightly different textures to whole wheat breads. You will have your favorite brands of flour and will use them over and over again, but by varying the types you use, you can get a wider variety of whole wheat breads.

There are fine, medium, and coarse grinds of whole wheat flour. Which one you use can make a big difference in how your bread turns out. Unless you order from a specialty mill, like Giusto's, though, bags of whole wheat flour are not generally labeled by their grind. This means that you have to buy different flours and figure out what grinds you have by looking at them and feeling them. In fine flour, all the parts of the grain—the germ, the bran, and the endo-sperm—are equally ground. It feels smooth. The finest grind of whole wheat flour makes a moist, fine-textured, but dark-colored and rich-flavored, bread. Coarse and medium grinds disperse the bran and germ throughout the flour. You can easily see and feel them. The larger the pieces of bran, the coarser the flour. The coarser the flour, the coarser the crumb will be and the heavier the finished loaf, be-cause the sharp edges of the bran tend to cut the thin strands of stretchy gluten during rising. I note the grinds of various brands in the margin of my workbooks with comments like "Gold Medal, medium grind" or "Stone Buhr, coarse grind." Many of my recipes in this book specify what grind of whole wheat to use in order to assure the best possible loaf.

The type of machine you own will dictate, to some extent, the whole wheat and other whole grain breads you can make. For doughs that call for half whole wheat and half white flour, white whole wheat, or some whole wheat pastry flour, you can use the Basic cycle. All machines are capable of handling the dough density produced by these proportions. For breads with a higher percentage of whole wheat flour or all whole wheat flour, you must use a machine that specifically has a Whole Wheat cycle, which indicates that the machine has a motor powerful enough to handle the heavy doughs. Even on these machines, if you hear the motor straining or pausing because the dough has stalled the paddle during the kneading, open the lid and use your plastic spatula to move the dough so that the machine can do its job. I also dribble some water onto the dough ball to soften it so that it can be kneaded more easily.

The more whole wheat flour you add to a recipe, the denser the baked loaf will be, and bread machine whole wheat breads often fill only two-thirds the capacity of the bread pan when they are finished baking. To compensate for this, some recipes call for more flour than usual, so don't worry if the proportions in this chapter look different than in the other recipes in the book.

If you are using the Basic cycle and find your whole wheat dough is still a bit too dense, you can use the "extra knead" technique, developed by the Innovative Cooking Enterprises group. This technique gives whole wheat breads, as well as breads containing specialty flours and multigrain breads, a stronger structure during their rising time and a lighter texture when they are baked. Simply let your machine go through the Knead 1 and 2 segments of the cycle, then press Stop and restart the cycle from the beginning, this time allowing it to continue until the loaf is finished.

Breads containing whole wheat flour will have a stiffer dough ball than you are used to in all–white flour breads. When you check the dough ball, press it with your finger. It should be firm yet springy, with plenty of moisture and rather tacky under the surface. The moisture will be slowly soaked up by the grains during the rises. Depending on the type of flour you have used, you will feel a smooth to sandy texture when you run your fingers over the dough ball.

Adjust a dry dough ball—one that looks shaggy and leaves a lot of flour around the edge of the pan—by dribbling water in *on top* of the dough ball in ½ teaspoon increments while the machine is running, rather like working with clay, or else the water will splash

up and out of the pan (I know this from experience). This will slowly moisten the dough ball as it is kneaded.

If the dough ball is too wet, add flour in 1½-teaspoon increments or sprinkle it in from your fingers, *around the sides of the dough ball under the paddle*, while the machine is running. Be careful to avoid the rotating blade. The dough ball will automatically pick up most of the flour. If the dough looks very moist around the paddle, it is okay; this moisture will be absorbed during the remaining kneading time.

When you make your own whole grain breads, you get exactly what you put into the machine—plenty of whole grain goodness, flavor, and nutrition with minimal sweetness from sugar. The tastes of these grains and flours are natural and earthy, and the aroma during baking is like no other type of bread. You can just inhale the healthful, nutty sweetness.

LIGHT WHOLE WHEAT BREAD

A ll bakers want a good all-purpose whole wheat bread in their repertoire. Here it is. The buttermilk, called for in its powdered form, softens the grain, and there is an egg for richness and extra rising power. You can opt to use fresh buttermilk in place of the water, thereby eliminating the need for any dried buttermilk. This bread is excellent toasted.

1 Place all the ingredients in the pan according to the order in the manufacturer's instructions. Set crust on medium or dark and program for the Basic cycle; press Start. The dough ball will be moist. (This recipe is not suitable for use with the Delay Timer.)

2 When the baking cycle ends, immediately remove the bread from the pan and place it on a rack. Let cool to room temperature before slicing.

1½-POUND LOAF	2-POUND LOAF
1 cup water	1⅓ cups water
1 large egg	1 large egg
2 tablespoons vegetable or nut oil	2½ tablespoons vegetable or nut oil
2½ cups bread flour	3¼ cups bread flour
½ cup whole wheat flour	¾ cup whole wheat flour
3 tablespoons dry buttermilk powder	4 tablespoons dry buttermilk powder
2 tablespoons dark brown sugar	2½ tablespoons dark brown sugar
1 tablespoon gluten	1 tablespoon plus 1 teaspoon gluten
1½ teaspoons salt	2 teaspoons salt
2 teaspoons SAF yeast or 2½ teaspoons bread machine yeast	2½ teaspoons SAF yeast or 1 tablespoon bread machine yeast

HONEY WHOLE WHEAT BREAD

T his bread contains a bit more whole wheat flour than Light Whole Wheat Bread. There is a lot of honey for sweetness and the combination of milk and water for tenderness. This one is a slow riser, so don't despair. This bread is best eaten the day it is baked.

1 Place all the ingredients in the pan according to the order in the manufacturer's instructions. Set crust on medium and program for the Basic cycle; press Start. (This recipe is not suitable for use with the Delay Timer.)

2 When the baking cycle ends, immediately remove the bread from the pan and place it on a rack. Let cool to room temperature before slicing.

1½-POUND LOAF	2-POUND LOAF
⅓ cup water	½ cup water
½ cup milk	⅔ cup milk
¼ cup honey	⅓ cup honey
1 large egg	1 large egg
1 tablespoon butter, cut into pieces	1½ tablespoons butter, cut into pieces
2 cups bread flour	2⅔ cups bread flour
1 cup whole wheat flour	1⅓ cups whole wheat flour
1 tablespoon plus 1 teaspoon gluten	1 tablespoon plus 2 teaspoons gluten
2 teaspoons salt	2½ teaspoons salt
2¼ teaspoons SAF yeast or 2¾ teaspoons bread machine yeast	1 tablespoon SAF yeast or 1 tablespoon plus ½ teaspoon bread machine yeast

The Baker's Glossary of Whole Wheat Flours and Other Milled Wheats

There are over thirty thousand different varieties of wheat, all belonging to fourteen basic wheat species, adapted to growing conditions from the Arctic to the tropics. Wheat was unknown to the pre-Columbian peoples of the Americas until the Spanish mariners brought some to Central and South America in the 1500s.

Wheat is made into a larger variety of differently milled whole grain flours than any other grain. Sometimes the flours are stone-ground or ground from organically grown wheat; these flours are superior in flavor and breadmaking elasticity. Whole wheat flours, like all whole-grain flours, contain a high percentage of oil and should be stored in the refrigerator to protect them from rancidity.

Whole Wheat Flour

Whole wheat flours are ground from the whole wheat berry, including the oil-rich bran and germ, giving them intensely nutty flavors. They are ground into a variety of fine to coarse textures that bake up into chewy, crusty breads. Whole wheat flours tend to be slightly lower in gluten than bread flour and make dense breads, so I add plenty of extra vital wheat gluten to make a high-rising, springy loaf in the bread machine, and a good dose of fat to keep the bread moist. There must also be plenty of liquid in whole wheat bread doughs, as whole wheat flours continue to absorb it slowly during the rises. A whole wheat dough that is sticky during kneading will be surprisingly springy and only tacky to the touch by the Rise 3 part of a cycle. If you do have trouble getting these doughs to bake into nice, springy loaves, you might want to try adding a dough enhancer (see page 168).

Graham Flour

Named after whole grain proponent Sylvester Graham in the late nineteenth century, extra nutty and sweet graham flour is often confused with whole wheat flour, but it is very different. It makes a different tasting and a lighter bread because of the way it is ground; a coarse grind, it contains all of the germ but only a portion of the bran. It may be substituted one-to-one in whole wheat bread recipes. Graham flour breads are great favorites.

White Whole Wheat Flour

White whole wheat is a new strain of winter wheat that is especially sweet. Its hull is white instead of red, so the color of the whole grain flour it produces is light rather than ruddy. It has all the nutrition of whole wheat flour, but is more delicate in flavor because it lacks the phenolic compounds that are present in red-hulled varieties. It can be used as a substitute for all-purpose flour because of its light flavor, with no loss of light texture. Your bread will look like a light whole wheat bread. White whole wheat flour contains 12 to 13 percent protein. You can substitute 1 cup plus 1 tablespoon white whole wheat flour for each cup of regular whole wheat flour in a recipe.

Whole Wheat Pastry Flour

Whole wheat pastry flour is ground from soft wheat and is often used in bread doughs, such as for challah or sweet rolls, in combination with bread flour. It has just 9 to 10 percent protein, its low gluten making it best-suited for muffins and quick breads.

Wheat Bran and Wheat Germ

Unprocessed bran and wheat germ, which add color, nutrition, and fiber to breads, are by-products of milling white flours. Wheat germ and bran are separated from the endosperm, which gets ground into white flour, by the process known as bolting, likened to putting the ground grain through a fine sieve. Wheat bran is the indigestible outer coating of the wheat berry. It is pure fiber, and is used to add roughage and texture to a whole grain loaf. Wheat germ is the embryo seed section of a grain of wheat, which contains a great deal of nutrition in its natural oils, especially vitamins B and E. It must be refrigerated to prevent rancidity. Wheat germ can be used either raw or toasted; toasted it adds lots of nutty flavor to a bread. Don't add too much, though; the sharp fibers of wheat bran and wheat germ cut the gluten and will weigh down the dough considerably. Many dietitians recommend some bran or wheat germ daily in a healthy diet.

Spelt Flour

Spelt wheat (an ancient wheat known as *farro* in Italy and *dinkl* in Germany) has less protein than regular whole wheats, but it has its own unique flavor. It is the wheat that was eaten most during the Middle Ages in Europe, but was used as long as five thousand years ago in the Middle East and Anatolia, which is part of Turkey. It has a tough outer husk that keeps the inner grain protected from oxidation and pollutants, so it is a favorite of organic bakers. Spelt is a fabulous bread flour with a strong wheaty aroma that is evocative of comfort. It rises high and has a soft texture. It is sometimes considered a non-wheat flour since it is low in gluten and suitable for some gluten-restricted diets. Spelt may be substituted for regular whole wheat flour: Add 1 cup plus 1 tablespoon of spelt flour per cup of whole wheat flour or hold back on 1 to 2 tablespoons of liquid, since spelt is soft and absorbs all the liquid it needs very quickly.

Semolina or Durum Flour

Cream-colored semolina flour, also called durum flour, is the finely ground endosperm of durum wheat used extensively in pasta making. It makes a delicious, high-protein addition to Italian-style breads and can be used interchangeably with flour made from kamut, a Montana wheat with a strong oat-sweet aroma. Semolina flour is not the same as semolina meal, which is a coarse-ground cereal like farina (the ground endosperm of spring or winter wheat) or Wheatena (the ground whole grain wheat), and used in a manner similar to coarse cornmeal.

Kamut

An ancient strain of wheat that is a relative of durum wheat, kamut, now grown in Montana, is gaining in popularity. The kernels are extra-large—three times the size of regular wheat—and are very hard. They absorb liquid very slowly and often need 1 tablespoon more water per cup of flour, but bake up into a nutty and buttery tasting bread. Kamut flour can be substituted in an equal amount for whole wheat flour in any of these recipes.

Wheat Berries

A wheat berry is a whole grain of wheat. Wheat berries are often used in bread doughs, but they must be cooked or sprouted first to be edible. Add them to the machine at the beep for Extras, or between Knead 1 and Knead 2, rather than at the beginning with the rest of the ingredients. If you knead wheat berries too much, they will break down, the gluten will become stringy, and the dough will be a real mess.

Cracked Wheat

Cracked wheat is the whole wheat berry that has been coarsely ground. It may be fine, medium, or coarse, and any of these grinds can be used in these breads. You can add a little bit of uncooked cracked wheat to a bread dough, but for the best texture it must be cooked or soaked first, or you will have hard little nuggets in your bread. You can also use bulgur wheat, which is cracked wheat that has been parboiled and dried for faster cooking.

Rolled Wheat Flakes

Rolled wheat flakes are steamed whole grain wheat that has been flattened between rollers, just like rolled oats. They will show up like flecks in the bread if added raw or, if cooked or soaked, will become part of the liquid ingredients for the dough.

BUTTERMILK WHOLE WHEAT BREAD

1⅛ cups buttermilk
2 tablespoons canola oil
2 tablespoons maple syrup

1½ cups whole wheat flour
1½ cups bread flour
1 tablespoon plus
   1 teaspoon gluten
1½ teaspoons salt

2 teaspoons SAF yeast or
   2½ teaspoons bread
   machine yeast

1½ cups buttermilk
3 tablespoons canola oil
2½ tablespoons maple
   syrup

2 cups whole wheat flour
2 cups bread flour
1 tablespoon plus
   2 teaspoons gluten
2 teaspoons salt

2¼ teaspoons SAF yeast or
   2¾ teaspoons bread
   machine yeast

Buttermilk was once drained off churned butter, but today it is cultured and incubated on skim milk for consistency, which is, of course, to the consumer's benefit. It is a delicious liquid that is perfect for use in breads. The tangy, buttery flavor comes from lactose-fermenting bacteria that convert citric acid. Combined with yeast, there is a lot of fermenting going on, and the by-product is a tender, flavorful bread. This bread is a delight in all its steps, from assembling the ingredients, through the baking cycle, to finally enjoying the bread itself.

1 Place all the ingredients in the pan according to the order in the manufacturer's instructions. Set crust on medium and program for the Basic or Whole Wheat cycle; press Start. (This recipe is not suitable for use with the Delay Timer.)

2 When the baking cycle ends, immediately remove the bread from the pan and place it on a rack. Let cool to room temperature before slicing.

SOFT WHOLE WHEAT DINNER ROLLS

Makes 16 dinner rolls

F or lovers of sweet whole wheat breads, these are the best whole grain dinner rolls. You can make them in any shape you choose; see pages 358 to 359 for instructions. The sour cream makes these rolls tender and moist. Be prepared for the bread basket to be emptied!

see pages 358 to 359 for instructions.

1½- OR 2-POUND-LOAF MACHINES

⅔ cup milk
½ cup sour cream
¼ cup honey
2 large eggs
4 tablespoons butter or
  margarine, cut into pieces

3 cups unbleached
  all-purpose flour
1 cup whole wheat flour
½ cup toasted wheat germ
1½ teaspoons salt

2 teaspoons SAF yeast or
  2½ teaspoons bread
  machine yeast

❶ Place all the ingredients in the pan according to the order in the manufacturer's instructions. Program for the Dough cycle; press Start.

❷ Grease a large baking sheet or line with parchment paper. When the machine beeps at the end of the cycle, press Stop and unplug the machine. Turn the dough out onto a lightly floured surface. Divide the dough in half, then roll each half into a 2- to 3-inch cylinder. With a metal dough scraper or a chef's knife, cut the cylinder into 8 equal portions. Repeat with the second cylinder, making a total of 16 equal portions. Shape each portion like a miniature loaf by patting it into an oval, then rolling up from a short side to make a small compact cylinder about 4 inches long. Place the rolls in two rows of 8 with their long sides touching. Brush some melted butter on the tops of the rolls. Cover loosely with plastic wrap and let rise at room temperature until doubled in bulk, about 45 minutes.

❸ Twenty minutes before baking, preheat the oven to 375°F.

❹ Place the baking sheet in the center of the oven and bake for 25 minutes, until golden brown. Remove the rolls from the pans and let cool on a rack. Serve warm, or cool to room temperature and reheat before serving.

LOU'S DAILY BREAD

1½-POUND LOAF

Zest of 2 oranges, cut into very thin strips

1¼ cups fat-free milk
2 tablespoons olive or walnut oil
2 tablespoons honey

1⅝ cups whole wheat flour
1½ cups bread flour
1 tablespoon gluten
1¼ teaspoons salt

1¾ teaspoons SAF yeast or 2¼ teaspoons bread machine yeast

2-POUND LOAF

Zest of 2 oranges, cut into very thin strips

1⅔ cups fat-free milk
3 tablespoons olive or walnut oil
3 tablespoons honey

2¼ cups whole wheat flour
2 cups bread flour
1 tablespoon plus 1 teaspoon gluten
1½ teaspoons salt

2¼ teaspoons SAF yeast or 2¾ teaspoons bread machine yeast

T his is my food writer friend Lou Pappas's house bread. She is an avid baker, so it must be good since she makes it on a regular basis. She uses the whey drained off homemade yogurt cheese for the liquid; I have substituted nonfat milk, which is known as fat-free milk these days. Take care to remove only the zest—the colored part of the skin—from the orange. This is where the flavorful oil is; the white pith is quite bitter. I suggest a fine or medium grind of stone-ground whole wheat flour for this bread.

1 In a food processor, chop the orange peel fine, or chop it fine by hand.

2 Place all the ingredients in the pan according to the order in the manufacturer's instructions. Set crust on medium and program for the Whole Wheat cycle; press Start. (This recipe is not suitable for use with the Delay Timer.)

3 When the baking cycle ends, immediately remove the bread from the pan and place it on a rack. Let cool to room temperature before slicing.

HEALTHY WHOLE WHEAT CHALLAH

C hallah is usually made with all white flour. This whole wheat version is for people who like to have whole grains in all of their breads. It will have a denser texture than regular challah, but it has its own lovely character made into a twist and is richly flavored. It is moist and really great for sandwiches. This bread is a real surprise, even for bread lovers who never eat whole wheat bread.

❶ Place all the ingredients in the pan according to the order in the manufacturer's instructions. Set crust on medium or dark, and program for the Basic or Whole Wheat cycle; press Start. (This recipe is not suitable for use with the Delay Timer.) This is a moist dough ball. Do not add more flour during the kneading or the bread will be dry.

❷ When Rise 2 ends, press Pause, open the lid and lift the warm dough from the pan. Divide the dough into 2 equal portions. With the palms of your hands, roll each portion into a fat oblong sausage, about 10 inches long. Place the two pieces side by side. Holding each end, wrap one around the other, twisting each one at the same time, to create a fat twist effect. Tuck under the ends and replace in the pan in the machine. The twist shape will bake in the machine.

❸ When the baking cycle ends, immediately remove the bread from the pan and place it on a rack. Let cool to room temperature before slicing.

1½-POUND LOAF

⅔ cup water
3 large eggs
3 tablespoons vegetable oil
2 tablespoons honey

1½ cups whole wheat flour
1½ cup bread flour
1½ tablespoons gluten
1 tablespoon instant potato
flakes
1½ teaspoons salt

2 teaspoons SAF yeast or
2½ teaspoons bread
machine yeast

2-POUND LOAF

1 cup water
3 large eggs
¼ cup vegetable oil
2½ tablespoons honey

2 cups whole wheat flour
2 cups bread flour
2 tablespoons gluten
1¼ tablespoons instant
potato flakes
2 teaspoons salt

2½ teaspoons SAF yeast or
1 tablespoon bread
machine yeast

OLD-FASHIONED SESAME-WHEAT BREAD

T*his is a recipe I adapted from one I used to make in the restaurant bakery for the dinner bread basket. It has a tender crumb from the combination of milk and water, and a bit of added texture and flavor from the sesame seeds. A favorite with my recipe testers, this slightly sweet, aromatic bread with the golden brown crust is best eaten the day it is made.*

1 Place all the ingredients in the pan according to the order in the manufacturer's instructions. Set crust on medium and program for the Basic cycle; press Start. (This recipe is not suitable for use with the Delay Timer.)

2 When the baking cycle ends, immediately remove the bread from the pan and place it on a rack. Let cool to room temperature before slicing.

1½-POUND LOAF	2-POUND LOAF
¾ cup water	¾ cup water
⅜ cup milk	¾ cup milk
2 tablespoons butter, cut into pieces	3 tablespoons butter, cut into pieces
2¼ cups bread flour	3 cups bread flour
¾ cup whole wheat flour	1 cup whole wheat flour
2 tablespoons light or dark brown sugar	3 tablespoons light or dark brown sugar
1 tablespoon sesame seeds	1 tablespoon plus 2 teaspoons sesame seeds
1 tablespoon plus 1 teaspoon gluten	1 tablespoon plus 2 teaspoons gluten
1½ teaspoons salt	2 teaspoons salt
2 teaspoons SAF yeast or 2½ teaspoons bread machine yeast	2¼ teaspoons SAF yeast or 2¾ teaspoons bread machine yeast

TOASTED SESAME–WHOLE WHEAT BREAD

I n the early 1970s I used to buy a moist, dense whole wheat bread at Barbara's Bakery, a small Palo Alto bread shop owned by entrepreneur Murray Jaffe. This was their signature bread, and if you didn't get there before noon, it would be sold out. Two essential tips for the best flavor and texture: use cold-pressed sesame oil, which is paler in color and milder than the toasted sesame oil used in Asian foods, and use fine-grind whole wheat flour.

1 Place the sesame seeds in a dry skillet. Cook over medium heat, shaking constantly, until the seeds are lightly toasted, about 2 minutes. Set aside to cool.

2 Place all the ingredients in the pan according to the order in the manufacturer's instructions. Set crust on medium and program for the Whole Wheat cycle; press Start. (This recipe may be made using the Delay Timer.)

3 When the baking cycle ends, immediately remove the bread from the pan and place it on a rack. Let cool to room temperature before slicing.

1½-POUND LOAF

2 tablespoons sesame seeds

1⅛ cups water
2 tablespoons honey
3 tablespoons sesame oil

3½ cups whole wheat flour
2 tablespoons gluten
1¾ teaspoons sea salt

2½ teaspoons SAF yeast or
  1 tablespoon bread
  machine yeast

2-POUND LOAF

2½ tablespoons sesame
  seeds

1⅔ cups water
3 tablespoons honey
¼ cup sesame oil

4½ cups whole wheat flour
3 tablespoons gluten
2¼ teaspoons sea salt

1 tablespoon SAF yeast
  or 1 tablespoon plus
  ½ teaspoon bread
  machine yeast

Leftover Bread Cookery: Classic Combinations of Bread and Cheese

My Favorite Grilled Cheese Sandwich

On soup and sandwich night, my mom used to make these in a hinged electric grill, which squished the grilled sandwich perfectly. The sandwich takes on many different characters depending on the cheese you use: an Oregon Tillamook cheddar, a Vermont raw cheddar, a mild Wisconsin Colby, or perhaps the English Double Gloucester. Vary the filling with a bit of crumbled goat cheese, cooked bacon strips, fresh tomato slices, sweet hot mustard, roasted canned or fresh green chile strips, sautéed mushrooms, deli smoked turkey, or Black Forest ham. Serve with a dill pickle spear, sweet pickle chips, or gherkins. The homemade bread makes the sandwich sublime.

Slices of firm-textured homemade white, whole
   wheat, or multigrain bread, 2 slices per
   sandwich
Cheddar cheese sliced ½ inch thick
Unsalted butter or butter-flavored cooking spray

Cover a slice of bread almost to the edges with ½-inch-thick slices of cheese; place a second slice of bread on top. Melt a pat of butter in a frying pan over medium heat. Place the sandwich in the sizzling butter, moving it around to evenly soak the bread. Using a spatula, press down on the bread. Cook for 30 seconds, until golden brown and evenly toasted. Top with a pat of butter and flip the sandwich over to finish cooking on the second side; press once more with the spatula. Transfer the sandwich to a plate and cut in half. Have napkins on hand—a grilled cheese is meant to be eaten with your hands.

Welsh Rabbit
Serves 4

Welsh rabbit, or rarebit, has no bunny rabbit in it. Rabbit is an old name for Old English cheddar cheese, produced near the Welsh border, that was melted and poured over toast. This is as traditional as a homespun British dish can be. I loved this as a kid (use milk instead of beer for the young diners), and my friends who are Brits make it often for lunch or dinner. When topped with a poached egg, it is called a Golden Buck. This recipe comes from Colonial Williamsburg in Virginia, where it is served as tavern fare with mugs of cold ale.

1 tablespoon butter or margarine
1 pound medium or sharp cheddar cheese,
   shredded
¾ cup beer, divided
1 large egg, beaten
Dash of hot red pepper sauce
Dash of Worcestershire sauce
1 teaspoon Coleman's dry mustard
4 slices toast, plain or buttered, crusts removed
Hungarian ground paprika, for sprinkling

❶ In the top of a double boiler, melt the butter. Add the cheese and all but 2 tablespoons of the beer. Let the butter and cheese melt slowly over low heat.

❷ Combine the beaten egg with the hot pepper and Worcestershire sauces. Moisten the mustard with the reserved beer, and stir to make a paste. Add to the melted cheese, stirring constantly. Spoon over the toast, sprinkle with paprika, and serve at once.

Fondue Neuchâtel

Serves 6

Fondue goes in and out of fashion in this country. But in Europe it is a quintessential winter food for sharing. It was originally cooked communally over an open fire by herdsmen camped out in high Alpine meadows. The name of this fondue comes from the addition of Neuchâtel, a dry, 11-percent alcohol white wine. You can substitute Riesling or champagne. Kirsch is the traditional finishing touch, a strong clear liqueur made from mountain cherries. You can use other clear eaux-de-fruits, such as pear or raspberry brandy, if you have one on hand. It is best to start your fondue on the stovetop, and then transfer it to the bowl of a tabletop warmer. Use an earthenware or ceramic fondue pot for this fondue. Long forks are needed for dipping the bread, but provide your guests with regular forks and small plates for eating. This is bread and cheese at their best!

8 ounces Emmenthaler cheese, shredded
8 ounces Gruyère cheese, shredded
2½ tablespoons all-purpose flour
1 clove garlic, split
1½ cups dry white wine
3 tablespoons clear fruit brandy
Fresh-ground black pepper
Fresh-grated nutmeg
1 loaf fresh homemade country
  bread, cut into
  1-inch cubes

1 Combine the cheeses in a bowl. Toss with the flour. Rub the inside of a heavy saucepan with the garlic clove. Add the wine to the pan and heat to a simmer. Stirring constantly, slowly add the cheese a handful at a time, letting each addition melt before adding the next. The melted cheese will be the consistency of a light béchamel cream sauce. Stir in the brandy and the pepper and nutmeg to taste.

2 Transfer the fondue to a fondue pot, chafing dish, or *caquelon* (a Swiss earthenware casserole glazed on the inside). Keep moderately warm over a low flame. Serve the fondue immediately, accompanied by the cubes of bread.

THREE-SEED WHOLE WHEAT BREAD

S eeded light whole wheat breads are extremely popular with home bread bakers. The wonderful flavors the seeds exude in the oven heat go right into the bread. This bread is great for sandwiches and toast.

1 Place the ingredients, except the seeds, in the pan according to the order in the manufacturer's instructions. Set crust on medium and program for the Basic or Whole Wheat cycle; press Start. (This recipe is not suitable for use with the Delay Timer.) When the machine beeps, or between Knead 1 and Knead 2, add all the seeds.

2 When the baking cycle ends, immediately remove the bread from the pan and place it on a rack. Let cool to room temperature before slicing.

1½-POUND LOAF	2-POUND LOAF
1¼ cups water	1⅔ cups water
2 tablespoons sunflower seed oil	3 tablespoons sunflower seed oil
1½ cups bread flour	2 cups bread flour
1½ cups whole wheat flour	2 cups whole wheat flour
3 tablespoons nonfat dry milk	¼ cup nonfat dry milk
2 tablespoons brown sugar	3 tablespoons brown sugar
1 tablespoon gluten	1 tablespoon plus 1 teaspoon gluten
1 teaspoon salt	1½ teaspoons salt
2 teaspoons SAF yeast or 2½ teaspoons bread machine yeast	2½ teaspoons SAF yeast or 1 tablespoon bread machine yeast
⅓ cup raw sunflower seeds	½ cup raw sunflower seeds
2 tablespoons sesame seeds	2½ tablespoons sesame seeds
2 teaspoons poppy seeds	2½ teaspoons poppy seeds

IRISH POTATO BROWN BREAD

I n the late eighteenth century, potatoes became a staple in the Irish diet; they called the potato a spud. Irish immigrants brought the tuber to New England, where it is still grown today. The addition of instant potato flakes to this bread should tell you it will be a very moist bread. Instant potatoes and whole wheat are a fantastic combination.

❶ Place all the ingredients in the pan according to the order in the manufacturer's instructions. Set crust on medium and program for the Whole Wheat cycle; press Start. (This recipe is not suitable for use with the Delay Timer.)

❷ When the baking cycle ends, immediately remove the bread from the pan and place it on a rack. Let cool to room temperature before slicing.

1½-POUND LOAF

1¼ cups water
3 tablespoons butter,
 cut into pieces
2 tablespoons honey

2 cups whole wheat flour
1 cup bread flour
¼ cup instant potato flakes
1 tablespoon plus
 2 teaspoons gluten
1½ teaspoons salt

2 teaspoons SAF yeast or
 2½ teaspoons bread
 machine yeast

2-POUND LOAF

1⅔ cups water
4 tablespoons butter,
 cut into pieces
3 tablespoons honey

2½ cups whole wheat flour
1½ cups bread flour
⅓ cup instant potato flakes
2 tablespoons gluten
2 teaspoons salt

2½ teaspoons SAF yeast or
 1 tablespoon bread
 machine yeast

Bread Machine Baker's Hint: Whole-Grain Doughs

Take care to leave whole grain doughs a bit sticky to the touch. Because whole grain doughs are coarser and contain more oil, they absorb moisture more slowly than white doughs and will firm during rising. Whole wheat doughs are always more dense than all-white flour doughs, yet they should still be pliable and springy. Since they require shorter mixing and kneading times, there is a special cycle on the bread machine, the Whole Wheat cycle, just for these breads.

FLAX SEED WHOLE WHEAT BREAD

1⅛ cups water
2 tablespoons canola oil
3 tablespoons honey

2 cups bread flour
1 cup whole wheat flour
¼ cup nonfat dry milk
2 tablespoons flax seed
1 tablespoon gluten
1 teaspoon salt

2 teaspoons SAF yeast or
   2½ teaspoons bread
   machine yeast

2-POUND LOAF

1½ cups water
3 tablespoons canola oil
¼ cup honey

2⅔ cups bread flour
1⅓ cups whole wheat flour
⅓ cup nonfat dry milk
2½ tablespoons flax seed
1¼ tablespoons gluten
1½ teaspoons salt

2¼ teaspoons SAF yeast or
   2¾ teaspoons bread
   machine yeast

F lax seed, a common ingredient in European blended seed breads, is a newcomer to the American baking scene. But flax seed is growing in popularity because it contains omega-3 fatty acids, the same type as in fatty fish, said to help lower the risk of cancer. If you want to try baking with white whole wheat flour, this would be a good place to substitute it for the regular whole wheat flour. The type of honey you use will add considerable character. This bread is great for sandwiches and with soups.

1 Place all the ingredients in the pan according to the order in the manufacturer's instructions. Set crust on medium and program for the Basic or Whole Wheat cycle; press Start. (This recipe may be made using the Delay Timer.)

2 When the baking cycle ends, immediately remove the bread from the pan and place it on a rack. Let cool to room temperature before slicing.

DAKOTA BREAD

C *afé Latte in St. Paul, Minnesota, makes Dakota Bread every day from fresh milled flour. It was named for the baker's home state of South Dakota. This bread has become one of the most beloved among home bakers, appearing in numerous publications with varying amounts of seeds and grains, yet still making an incredibly light bread with an intoxicating aroma. Please note that bulgur (also known as bulgur cracked wheat), which has been partially precooked so as to cook quickly, is entirely different from plain cracked wheat. Bulgur can be used unsoaked in a recipe. Here is my version of Dakota Bread for the bread machine.*

1 Place all the ingredients in the pan according to the order in the manufacturer's instructions. Set crust on dark and program for the Basic cycle; press Start. (This recipe may be made using the Delay Timer.)

2 When the baking cycle ends, immediately remove the bread from the pan and place it on a rack. Let cool to room temperature before slicing.

1½-POUND LOAF	2-POUND LOAF
1¼ cups water	1⅝ cups water
2 tablespoons canola oil	3 tablespoons canola oil
2 tablespoons honey	3 tablespoons honey
2¼ cups bread flour	2⅞ cups bread flour
½ cup whole wheat flour	1 cup whole wheat flour
¼ cup raw bulgur cracked wheat	⅓ cup raw bulgur cracked wheat
2 teaspoons gluten	1 tablespoon gluten
1½ teaspoons salt	2 teaspoons salt
¼ cup raw sunflower seeds	⅓ cup raw sunflower seeds
¼ cup raw pumpkin seeds, chopped	⅓ cup raw pumpkin seeds, chopped
2 teaspoons sesame seeds	2 teaspoons sesame seeds
1½ teaspoons poppy seeds	2 teaspoons poppy seeds
2 teaspoons SAF yeast or 2½ teaspoons bread machine yeast	2¼ teaspoons SAF yeast or 2¾ teaspoons bread machine yeast

HARPER'S LOAF

Makes two 8½-by-4½-inch loaves

**1½- OR 2-POUND-
LOAF MACHINES**

1⅛ cups water
2 large eggs
3 tablespoons peanut oil
3 tablespoons honey
3 tablespoons unsalted
butter, cut into pieces

2 cups whole wheat flour
1½ cups bread flour
1½ teaspoons salt

2½ teaspoons SAF yeast or
1 tablespoon bread
machine yeast

2 tablespoons rolled oats,
for sprinkling
2 tablespoons sunflower
seeds, for sprinkling

The name of this bread refers to Paul Hurst, a world-renowned concert harpist and pianist who has composed and recorded a tone poem called the Sequoia Symphony with the Moscow State Radio and Television Orchestra. He is also a great bread lover. This is his favorite recipe, which came from his harp teacher and mentor, the late DeWayne Fulton. Technically an egg bread, this loaf is fluffy and tender. Use a roasted brand of peanut oil (like Livora) for the best flavor. This bread is baked into two large loaves in the oven. I like to use my Alfred clay ceramic bread pans to bake them (see Resources page 611).

1 Place all the ingredients in the pan according to the order in the manufacturer's instructions. Program for the Dough cycle; press Start.

2 Lightly brush the bottom and sides of two 8-by-4-inch loaf pans with peanut oil. Turn the dough out onto a clean work surface; it will naturally deflate. Without working the dough further, use your metal bench scraper or knife to divide the dough into into 4 equal portions. With the palms of your hands, roll into 4 fat oblong sausages, each about 10 inches long. Place 2 of the pieces side by side. Holding both pieces of dough together at one end, wrap one around the other 2 to 3 times to create a fat twist effect. Repeat to form the second loaf. Place in the pans and tuck under the ends. Brush the tops with some peanut oil. Cover loosely with plastic wrap and let rise at room temperature until the dough is almost doubled in bulk, about 1 inch over the rims of the pans, 45 minutes to 1 hour.

3 Twenty minutes before baking, set the oven rack to the middle and preheat the oven to 350°F (lower the temperature by 25° if using glass pans).

4 Brush the tops of the loaves with more peanut oil. Sprinkle the tops with the oats and sunflower seeds. Bake for 40 to 45 minutes, or until the loaves are deep golden brown, and the sides are slightly contracted from the pan. Lift one end of a loaf up out of the pan to peek underneath to check for even browning on the bottom, and tap on the top and bottom surface with your finger; it should sound hollow. An instant-read thermometer will read 200°F. Immediately remove the loaves from the pans and place on a rack. Let cool to room temperature before slicing.

Whole Wheat Nutrition

A kernel of wheat is known as the "five-in-one"; it contains protein, carbohydrates, soluble and insoluble fiber, vitamins, and minerals. The less it is processed, the more nutrition you get. For high nutrition, look for products with the germ intact, such as whole wheat flours, wheat germ, and bran. Whole grains and bran contain hemicelluloses along with the insoluble fiber. The cellulose absorbs water, preventing constipation, colon cancer, and varicose veins. The germ of wheat contains precious phytoestrogens and the B vitamins. Wheat grass and sprouted wheat are routinely used in salads or juice as part of a regenerative cleansing program. Wheat contains vitamin E, iron, magnesium, selenium, and zinc. As with all true grains, wheat and wheat products lack a substantial amount of lysine and methionine, so if you don't eat meat, wheat is best combined with beans and seeds to give you all the essential amino acids. Eat some form of vitamin C, too, when you eat whole wheat. Since wheat contains phytic acid, without the C, the minerals concentrated in the bran stay unassimilated.

No Additives

When you bake your own bread, you avoid consuming the many artificial additives and preservatives that have become commonplace in the commercial baking industry's processing, packaging, transporting, and storing of bread. A synthetic chemical can even be infused into the packaging material to make bread that has been on the shelf for weeks still smell freshly baked!

Chemical additives control molds, yeasts, rope bacteria, and other invisible organisms that make bread go stale or rancid. Chemicals help extend the shelf life of a loaf. Surprisingly, the worst enemy in the commercial baking industry is oxygen, which makes bread go stale. In 1947 antioxidants were one of the first chemical additives to be commercially produced. Dough conditioners are additives used during production to modify the physical appearance and texture of a loaf. They turn what would probably be a mediocre baked loaf into consistently high-quality bread. Anti-staling and anti-firming compounds are other important ingredients in commercial breads. When bread stales, the starch crystallizes. To inhibit this crystallization, bread emulsifiers are used. Thirty years ago, over 16 million pounds of chemical food additives were used every year in the American food industry for bread. One can only imagine how much more are used now.

Other countries that are more serious about their bread, like France and Italy, do not widely permit anti-staling agents, dough conditioners, and antioxidants. It is more common to find small batch bakeries in these countries, where it is acknowledged that bread is a food meant to be made fresh every day.

The following list contains some of the most common additives to bread and flour:

Bleached flour—artificially aged with chlorine bleach gas to cut down on expensive storage time and supposedly to increase its baking qualities by developing the protein

Potassium bromate—added to unbleached flour, labeled bromated, to speed up the aging process in a manner similar to bleached flour

Calcium peroxide—antimycotic agent used to prevent the growth of microscopic spores

BHT and BHA—preservatives, and the first anti-oxidants to hold up in the heat of baking

Potassium sorbate—preservative and antimycotic agent

Sodium benzoate—preservative and antimycotic agent; because of its natural origin, it is the least harmful additive.

Sodium propionate—antimycotic agent

ADA (azodicarbonamide)—a dough conditioner that keeps the dough from getting overworked during long machine mixing

EDTA—an antioxidant

Calcium propionate—antimycotic agent

Calcium disodium—dough conditioner

L-cysteine, Stearoyl-2-lactylate, and Sodium steryl fumarate—dough conditioners, often paired with glycerides, that allow bread to be made more easily in a machine and even out differences in batches of flour

Partially hydrogenated vegetable oil—usually combined with some palm oil to prolong shelf life and add texture and body to crumb

Mono- and diglycerides—anti-staling compounds

Chemical additives need to be regarded with suspicion. Many people have found that elusive health problems stem from being allergic to chemicals like BHT (butylated hydroxytoluene) and BHA (butylated hydroxyanisole). If you are chemical sensitive, this information is very important. If you think you do not eat much bread, and that you are not consuming many of these chemicals, consider the statistics that report that each person eats approximately 100 pounds of bread a year.

When you bake in the bread machine, it is good to allow each loaf to have its own appealing inherent taste, texture, and appearance, rather than comparing it to an aerated commercial loaf. Allow the simple pleasure of your own bread and its health value to become a priority in your diet.

WHOLE WHEAT CRESCENT DINNER ROLLS

Makes 16 dinner rolls

I n small amounts, sour cream is a wonderful addition to a dough; it helps create a moist, close-textured roll. Here the whole wheat flour is sweetened a bit with the addition of a small amount of ground almonds.

❶ Place the almonds in a dry skillet. Lightly toast over medium heat, stirring constantly, about 2 minutes. In a food processor, combine the almonds with 2 tablespoons of the whole wheat flour. Grind to a fine meal.

❷ Place all the ingredients, including the almond meal, in the pan according to the order in the manufacturer's instructions. Program for the Dough cycle; press Start.

❸ Line two baking sheets with parchment paper. When the machine beeps at the end of the cycle, immediately turn the dough out onto a lightly floured work surface; divide into 2 equal portions. With a rolling pin, roll each portion into a 10-inch round. Using a pastry wheel, cut each round into 8 pie-shaped wedges. Roll up each wedge from the wide edge at the base of the triangle and place the crescents 1 inch apart on the baking sheet, point side down. Cover lightly with plastic wrap and let rise at room temperature until almost doubled in bulk, about 30 minutes.

❹ Twenty minutes before baking, preheat the oven to 375°F.

❺ Bake the rolls, one pan at a time, for 15 to 18 minutes, or until lightly browned. Let cool partially on a rack. Eat the rolls warm.

1½- OR 2-POUND-LOAF MACHINES

¼ cup slivered blanched almonds
2 cups whole wheat flour

1 cup water
2 large eggs
4 tablespoons unsalted butter, cut into pieces
½ cup sour cream

2¼ cups bread flour
2 tablespoons light brown sugar
1 tablespoon gluten
2 teaspoons salt

2¼ teaspoons SAF yeast or 2¾ teaspoons bread machine yeast

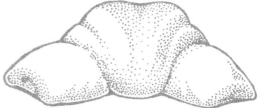

100% WHOLE WHEAT BREAD

1½-POUND LOAF

¾ cup water
¾ cup milk
2 tablespoons canola oil
¼ cup light molasses

4 cups whole wheat flour
3 tablespoons gluten
1¾ teaspoons salt

1 tablespoon SAF yeast or
   1 tablespoon plus
   ½ teaspoon bread
   machine yeast

2-POUND LOAF

1 cup water
⅞ cup milk
3 tablespoons canola oil
⅓ cup light molasses

5 cups whole wheat flour
¼ cup gluten
2¼ teaspoons salt

1 tablespoon plus
   ½ teaspoon SAF yeast
   or 1 tablespoon plus
   1 teaspoon bread
   machine yeast

*T*he first thing you may notice about this recipe is the amount of flour it calls for—it's more than the usual proportion. That is because all whole grain flour breads are naturally more compact than ones that contain some bread flour. For this bread, use the finest grind of stone-ground whole wheat flour you can find. Be sure to use a machine with a Whole Wheat cycle, otherwise your machine will labor too much during the kneading.

1 Place all the ingredients in the pan according to the order in the manufacturer's instructions. Set crust on medium and program for the Whole Wheat cycle; press Start. (This recipe is not suitable for use with the Delay Timer.)

2 When the baking cycle ends, immediately remove the bread from the pan and place it on a rack. Let cool to room temperature before slicing.

Bread Machine Baker's Hint: Flour Protein Content

It seems as though it must be simple to combine flour, water, and yeast to make bread. But to make a really great loaf, you must use the right kind, or combination, of flours. Bread machine–mixed yeast doughs work best with high-protein flours. The amount of protein, also known as gluten, varies with every type of flour. Even different brands of the same type flour will have slightly different percentages; for your information, the percentages are always listed on the side of the flour bag. The amount of protein ultimately determines the texture of your bread, whether a light, fluffy loaf (more gluten) or a dense, coarse one (less gluten).

The recipes in this book tell how much gluten to use, but if you're experimenting with your own recipes, and the flour you are using has a low percentage of protein, be sure to add some vital wheat gluten to give it a protein boost. High-protein flour and some vital wheat gluten are necessary when you are adding heavier cracked grains and other non-gluten flours and want a bread machine loaf with that moist, tender crumb that is not too airy or too dense. The general rule for using specialty flours that are low in protein, such as oat or barley, is to add no more than ½ cup of specialty flour per 3 cups of wheat flour. Rye flour is the exception; it can be used in a 1-to-1 ratio with wheat flour, half rye and half wheat. Whole wheat breads will always be a bit lighter in texture if used in combination with white flours, but whole wheat can be used in any proportion.

Here, for your reference, is a list of the approximate protein contents of various types of flour.

Stone-ground high-protein whole wheat flour	15 percent protein
Unbleached high-gluten flour	13 to 14 percent protein
Stone-ground whole wheat flour	13 to 14 percent protein
100% white whole wheat flour	13 percent protein
Bread flour	12.7 percent protein
Durum semolina flour	12.3 percent protein
French-style white flour	12 percent protein
Clear flour	11 to 12 percent protein
Unbleached all-purpose flour	10.5 to 12 percent protein
Whole wheat pastry flour	9.5 percent protein
Unbleached white pastry flour	7.3 to 9.7 percent protein
Italian-style white flour	7.9 percent protein
Cake flour	7.5 to 8.5 percent protein

TECATE RANCH WHOLE WHEAT BREAD

1½-POUND LOAF

1⅓ cups water
3 tablespoons canola oil
2 tablespoons honey
2 tablespoons molasses

3¼ cups whole wheat flour
⅓ cup wheat bran
2½ tablespoons gluten
1 tablespoon poppy seeds
1½ teaspoons salt

1 tablespoon SAF yeast
  or 1 tablespoon plus
  ½ teaspoon bread
  machine yeast

2-POUND LOAF

1¾ cups water
¼ cup canola oil
3 tablespoons honey
3 tablespoons molasses

4½ cups whole wheat flour
½ cup wheat bran
3½ tablespoons gluten
1 tablespoon plus
  1 teaspoon poppy seeds
2 teaspoons salt

1 tablespoon plus
  ½ teaspoon SAF yeast
  or 1 tablespoon plus
  1 teaspoon bread
  machine yeast

O ne of the oldest recipes still served at the Rancho La Puerta health spa in Baja, California, is this 100 percent whole wheat bread. It is also served at the Ranch's more luxurious sister spa, the Golden Door Spa, in San Diego, with chef Michel Stroot at the helm. It was originally called Zarathustra Bread because of the spa founder's research into the ancient Persian religion of Zoroastrianism, which focuses on man's good deeds. The loaf was a statement of commitment to vibrant good health and to a caring philosophy of the interdependence of mind, body, and spirit. That commitment is the basis for the cuisine served to this day at the spa. If your machine has a Whole Wheat cycle, be sure to use it here since the dough is thick and sticky, and it is best given plenty of time to rise. The result is a surprisingly light-textured whole grain bread. Be sure to wait until the bread is completely cooled before slicing, to set the beautiful crumb. No wonder they've made this for decades!

1 Place all the ingredients in the pan according to the order in the manufacturer's instructions. Set crust on dark and program for the Whole Wheat cycle; press Start. (This recipe may be made using the Delay Timer.) After 10 minutes, check the dough ball with your finger. It will be sticky. Add 1 to 2 tablespoons more flour. The dough will still be very sticky; don't worry, it will absorb the liquid during the rises. If you add too much flour, the bread will be dense, rather than springy. If you don't add the extra flour as needed, the top can collapse.

2 When the baking cycle ends, immediately remove the bread from the pan and place it on a rack. Let cool to room temperature before slicing.

WHITE WHOLE WHEAT BREAD

In this recipe from the *King Arthur Flour Company,* white whole wheat flour makes an incredibly light-textured whole grain bread that almost has you believing it is a white flour bread. If you use olive oil, be sure to use a light, flavorless one. Since this has the sweet addition of maple syrup (my favorite), it is perfect for toasting.

1 Place all the ingredients in the pan according to the order in the manufacturer's instructions. Set crust on dark and program for the Basic or Whole Wheat cycle; press Start. (This recipe may be made using the Delay Timer.)

2 When the baking cycle ends, immediately remove the bread from the pan and place it on a rack. Let cool to room temperature before slicing.

1½-POUND LOAF

1¼ cups water
2 tablespoons nut oil or olive oil
¼ cup maple syrup

3¼ cups white whole wheat flour
1 tablespoon gluten
1½ teaspoons salt

2 teaspoons SAF yeast or 2½ teaspoons bread machine yeast

2-POUND LOAF

1⅝ cups water
3 tablespoons nut oil or olive oil
⅓ cup maple syrup

4⅓ cups white whole wheat flour
1½ tablespoons gluten
2 teaspoons salt

2½ teaspoons SAF yeast or 1 tablespoon bread machine yeast

SPELT BREAD

S pelt is the natural offspring of durum wheat, and was once a common Mediterranean weed. It was the primary wheat used during the Roman empire and the Middle Ages. Roman wedding breads, called confarreatios, were made from spelt. Now grown in America as a specialty wheat, spelt is a tasty alternative to regular wheats and growing in popularity because it tastes so good and is easy to handle. Some bakers use a bit of spelt in all their whole wheat breads for the extra flavor. Spelt flour absorbs water much quicker than regular whole wheat flour since it is so soft, so be prepared to have a dough that comes together much quicker and with less liquid than regular whole wheat breads. I like a combination of spelt and bread flour best, since an all-spelt flour loaf is good, but very compact. I use a brand of organic spelt flour from Purity Foods called VitaSpelt.

1½-POUND LOAF	2-POUND LOAF
⅓ cup water	½ cup water
½ cup buttermilk	¾ cup buttermilk
1 tablespoon canola oil	2 tablespoons canola oil
1 tablespoon whipped reduced-fat margarine	1 tablespoon whipped reduced-fat margarine
2¼ cups whole grain spelt flour	3 cups whole grain spelt flour
¾ cup bread flour	1 cup bread flour
2 tablespoons dark brown sugar	3 tablespoons dark brown sugar
1 tablespoon plus 1 teaspoon gluten	1 tablespoon plus 2 teaspoons gluten
1½ teaspoons salt	2 teaspoons salt
2 teaspoons SAF yeast or 2½ teaspoons bread machine yeast	2¼ teaspoons SAF yeast or 2¾ teaspoons bread machine yeast

1 Place all the ingredients in the pan according to the order in the manufacturer's instructions. Set crust on dark and program for the Whole Wheat cycle; press Start. (This recipe is not suitable for use with the Delay Timer.) The dough ball will look sticky. Do not add too much flour, the dough will smooth out.

2 When the baking cycle ends, immediately remove the bread from the pan and place it on a rack. Let cool to room temperature before slicing.

CRACKED WHEAT BREAD

Cracked wheat bread is an often-requested recipe, a favorite yeast bread. This loaf has no dairy products aside from the butter, but you'd never know it. This is a bread that will convert you to this style of whole-grain baking.

1 Pour the boiling water over the cracked wheat in a bowl. Add the molasses, butter, and salt. Let stand 1 hour at room temperature to soften.

2 Place the ingredients in the pan according to the order in the manufacturer's instructions, adding the cracked wheat mixture and the additional water as the liquid ingredients. Set crust on medium and program for the Basic cycle; press Start. (This recipe may be made using the Delay Timer.)

3 When the baking cycle ends, immediately remove the bread from the pan and place it on a rack. Let cool to room temperature before slicing.

1½-POUND LOAF	2-POUND LOAF
¾ cup boiling water	1 cup boiling water
½ cup cracked wheat or bulgur	⅔ cup cracked wheat or bulgur
3 tablespoons molasses	¼ cup molasses
2 tablespoons unsalted butter or margarine, cut into pieces	3 tablespoons unsalted butter or margarine, cut into pieces
1½ teaspoons salt	2 teaspoons salt
¾ cup water	1 cup water
2⅔ cups bread flour	3½ cups bread flour
⅓ cup whole wheat flour	½ cup whole wheat flour
1 tablespoon gluten	1 tablespoon plus 1 teaspoon gluten
2½ teaspoons SAF yeast or 1 tablespoon bread machine yeast	1 tablespoon SAF yeast or 1 tablespoon plus ½ teaspoon bread machine yeast

Leftover Bread Cookery: The Charlotte

A baked fruit charlotte is one of the best-known desserts calling for leftover bread, second in popularity only to bread pudding. It is an old-fashioned dessert that shows up in many different cuisines. A mold is lined with buttered bread, filled with a fruit compote, and topped with a round of bread that ends up helping to contain the filling. While classic apple charlotte is the most familiar and a great favorite, the compote can be made from pears, quinces, apricots, or plums using these same directions. The summer pudding is a British variation. In it the bread dissolves into the fruit and becomes an enticing scarlet color from the berries.

When making a charlotte or summer pudding, use a firm, tight-grained day-old white or whole wheat bread. Make sure the overlapping slices are snug or else the filling will spill out. If the filling is too loose, it will soak through the bread and the charlotte will collapse when it is turned out onto a serving plate. You want to present a perfect little dome.

The following adapted recipes are the handiwork of Mary Cech, pastry instructor at the Culinary Institute of America at Greystone. She made them while working at the Cypress Club in San Francisco and at Charlie Trotter's in Chicago. She made the charlottes in individual portions using the 6-ounce coffee cups every restaurant has tons of, but in lieu of these you can use commonly available Pyrex custard cups or individual charlotte molds. If you want to make one large charlotte, use a 1-quart charlotte mold, soufflé dish, or mixing bowl. Be sure you weigh down the pudding by covering it with a plate and putting a large can on top of it while it is refrigerated. Serve the charlotte with a dollop of crème frâiche, whipped cream, or Mary's special thick old-fashioned Devonshire-style or French cream on the side.

Individual Warm Apple Charlottes
Serves 4

---

4 large Granny Smith or other tart cooking apples, peeled, cored, and cut into ¾-inch cubes

1 cup (2 sticks) butter, divided
2 ounces (⅓ cup) whole almonds
½ cup honey
½ cup apricot jam
1½-pound loaf firm-textured white or wheat bread, cut into ½-inch-thick slices, crusts removed

1 Place the apples and ¼ cup of the butter in a sauté pan. Cook over low heat for 5 minutes. Meanwhile, grind the almonds in the food processor. Remove them from the work bowl. Add the jam to the work bowl and process until smooth. Add the honey and the jam to the apples and increase the heat to high, stirring until slightly tender (not mushy) and all the liquid is reduced and the mixture is thick. Remove from the heat and stir in the almonds. Let stand at room temperature.

2 Preheat the oven to 425°F.

3 Melt the remaining ¾ cup butter in a sauté pan. Place four 6–ounce molds on a baking sheet. Reserving 4 whole slices for the tops, cut remaining slices into quarters. Using the whole slices, cut 4 rounds of bread for the tops by turning one of the molds upside down and cutting around the edge with a knife; it will fit exactly.

4 Dip each piece of bread lightly in the melted butter and press into the molds, overlapping the slices like shingles around the sides and covering the bottom (some chefs like a heart–shaped piece of bread on the very bottom, which will show up on the top when turned out). Divide the compote among the 4 molds and cover the tops with the bread rounds; press lightly.

5 Place the baking sheet in the center of the oven and bake for 20 to 25 minutes, until the tops are just crispy (the insides will be caramelized). Do not overbake. Remove from the oven and immediately invert onto individual dessert plates. Dust with some confectioners' sugar and place a large spoonful of French cream on the side.

Individual Raspberry and Strawberry Summer Puddings
Serves 4

2 pints (3 cups) raspberries
2 pints strawberries, sliced, to make 3 cups
¾ to 1 cup sugar, to taste
1½-pound loaf firm-textured white bread or day-old brioche, cut into ½-inch-thick slices, crusts removed

1 Combine the berries and ¾ cup of the sugar in a saucepan. Cook over medium heat until the berries are juicy, but still holding their shape, about 5 minutes. Taste for sweetness, and add more sugar if desired. Let cool to lukewarm.

2 Preheat the oven to 350°F. Place four 6-ounce molds on a baking sheet and grease lightly.

3 Reserving 4 whole slices of bread, cut the remaining slices into 4 long strips each. Cut 4 rounds of bread for the tops by turning one of the molds upside down on a whole slice and cutting around the edge with a knife; each round will fit exactly. Out of the same slice, cut a little round for the bottom and cut it into triangles if desired. Press the bottom round and strips of bread into the molds, covering all surfaces and reserving the round tops.

4 Divide the berry mixture among the bread-lined molds, setting aside any extra. Cover the tops with the bread rounds; press lightly. Spoon any berry liquid over the top to soak the bread, or turn each top round over to soak it through.

5 Place the baking sheet in the center of the oven and bake for exactly 15 minutes. Do not overbake. Remove from the oven and let cool. Cover with plastic wrap and chill for 4 hours or overnight. To serve, carefully invert each mold to slide the pudding out onto an individual dessert plate. Garnish with a dollop of cream and extra berries.

Mary's French Dessert Cream
Makes 1 cup

Cream is a key ingredient in many dessert recipes and a premier accompaniment when whipped until fluffy.

1 pint heavy cream
1 tablespoon light brown sugar, or to taste

Place the cream in a small saucepan. Bring to a boil over medium high heat, and reduce by half; it will take about 20 minutes. Add the sugar to taste, stir until dissolved, and pour into a covered container. Refrigerate until ready to serve.

GRAHAM BREAD

1½-POUND LOAF

1⅛ cups water
1 large egg
2 tablespoons butter,
    cut into pieces

2¼ cups bread flour
¾ cup graham flour
⅓ cup nonfat dry milk
¼ cup light brown sugar
2 teaspoons gluten
1½ teaspoons salt

2 teaspoons SAF yeast or
    2½ teaspoons bread
    machine yeast

2-POUND LOAF

1⅓ cups water
1 large egg plus 1 egg yolk
3 tablespoons butter,
    cut into pieces

3 cups bread flour
1 cup graham flour
½ cup nonfat dry milk
⅓ cup light brown sugar
1 tablespoon gluten
2 teaspoons salt

2¼ teaspoons SAF yeast or
    2¾ teaspoons bread
    machine yeast

G raham bread is a favorite Swedish bread, a bit on the sweet side. While graham flour is technically a whole wheat flour, it gives a very different flavor to bread—extra grain-sweet and nutty—because it is produced through a different milling process. There is no substitute for it, so search it out. I use Bob's Red Mill brand. You will fall in love with this bread. It is very old-fashioned, and was a staple homemade bread in the 1930s and 1940s.

1 Place all the ingredients in the pan according to the order in the manufacturer's instructions. Set crust on medium and program for the Basic or Whole Wheat cycle; press Start. (This recipe is not suitable for use with the Delay Timer.)

2 When the baking cycle ends, immediately remove the bread from the pan and place it on a rack. Let cool to room temperature before slicing.

RYE BREADS

R ye has a characteristically bitter-strong, earthy flavor. It contains only a small amount of a gluten that is more fragile than the gluten in wheat. This gives a loaf a moist, dense quality. A loaf with rye flour in it will ferment more quickly than a loaf that is all wheat and, if overkneaded, can get very sticky due to natural gums in the grain called pentosans. The presence of acid in a rye dough makes it more manageable, so you will see rye breads with ingredients like vinegar, beer, and sourdough.

There are quite a few baking products made from rye. The whole grains, known as groats or berries, are ground into light, medium, and dark rye flours, distinguished by their varying proportions of bran. Pumpernickel flour, also known as rye meal, is the coarsest grind, with the most bran and germ left in. Rolled rye flakes and cracked rye are also good additions to breads; they can be used as substitutes for rolled oats and cracked wheat. With a range of rye flours, you can make all your favorite rye breads in the bread machine, from a chewy pumpernickel or a light Swedish rye to a dark Russian rye, or even pretzel dough. Super-markets will vary in how many rye products they carry, but natural food stores and mail-order flour sources carry most of them.

Because of the saplike gum that appears naturally in rye, and because of its water-binding capacity, rye doughs will always feel moist and sticky when you test them with your finger. This makes it easy to add too much flour during kneading, so be careful not to add more

than a tablespoon or two more than the measurement given in the recipe.

When I am teaching people to make bread by hand, I always recommend rising rye doughs in tall narrow plastic buckets rather than wide bowls, as this grain has a natural tendency to rise horizontally rather than vertically. The bread machine handles this beautifully with its baking canister. The warm environment of the bread machine is also perfect for rising rye doughs, as they can easily become slack and cold, especially in winter.

Rye is an incredibly healthful grain. It has vitamin E and rutin, two premium antioxidants, is good for combating cholesterol deposits, and contains insoluble fiber. Since rye contains a type of the gluten proteins found in wheat, it is not suitable for gluten-free diets or for sufferers of celiac sprue disease.

SCANDINAVIAN LIGHT RYE

1½-POUND LOAF

1⅛ cups water
1½ tablespoons canola oil

1⅞ cups bread flour
1⅛ cups medium rye flour
2 tablespoons brown sugar
1 tablespoon plus
  1 teaspoon gluten
1½ tablespoons caraway
  seeds
1½ teaspoons salt

2½ teaspoons SAF yeast or
  1 tablespoon bread
  machine yeast

2-POUND LOAF

1½ cups water
2 tablespoons canola oil

2½ cups bread flour
1½ cups medium rye flour
3 tablespoons brown sugar
1 tablespoon plus
  2 teaspoons gluten
2 tablespoons caraway
  seeds
2 teaspoons salt

1 tablespoon SAF yeast
  or 1 tablespoon plus
  ½ teaspoon bread
  machine yeast

There is a Swedish legend that says that if a pair of lovers eat something containing caraway, they will stay faithful forever. Caraway seeds are part of every classic light rye, a bread for which I think almost every home baker in Minnesota (home to a large Scandinavian population) has a recipe. This is daily bread for much of the cold hinterlands.

❶ Place all the ingredients in the pan according to the order in the manufacturer's instructions. Set crust on medium and program for the Basic cycle; press Start. (This recipe may be made using the Delay Timer.) The dough ball will be soft and springy.

❷ When the baking cycle ends, immediately remove the bread from the pan and place it on a rack. Let cool to room temperature before slicing.

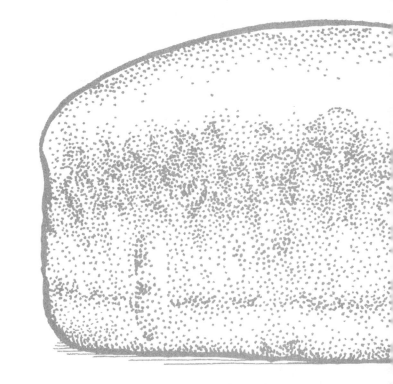

The Baker's Glossary of Rye Flours and Other Milled Ryes

You can replace up to half the wheat flour in any recipe with rye flour for a hearty whole grain loaf. Rye bread crusts are very dark brown and the crumb is fine-grained, getting more coarse and dense the higher the percentage of rye flour you use. Without the addition of wheat flour for body, rye makes a flat, crumbly, and coarse-grained loaf. Many fermented ethnic breads in Scandinavia and Russia are made in this manner, but I find they take a practiced hand and lots of rising time to get a palatable loaf by Western standards. Rye combines well with the flavors of dill, caraway, anise, and fennel, as well as cornmeal, oats, barley, wild rice, and whole wheat, so you will see lots of recipes with combinations of these ingredients in them.

Whole Rye

Whole rye is the whole grain with bran and germ intact.

Rye Flour

Rye flour is the finely ground whole grain and comes labeled as light, medium, or dark. The flour will vary in color and texture, depending on the amount of bran and germ sifted out during the milling process. What is labeled "rye flour" in a 1-pound box at the supermarket is medium rye flour.

White Rye Flour

White rye flour, or light rye flour, is not often seen outside of bakeries, but is now available from Giusto's and King Arthur. It is the ground endosperm of the rye kernel containing no germ or bran. It makes a superb light rye bread.

Rye Meal

Rye meal is medium-ground whole rye; it gives a rough texture to breads. It is also known as pumpernickel flour.

Cracked Rye

Cracked rye is the cracked groat. Like cracked wheat, it needs to be cooked or soaked before being added to a dough.

Rolled Rye Flakes

Rye flakes are whole rye grains that have been steamed and flattened by steel rollers. Use them in the same manner as rolled oats.

Triticale Flour

Developed as "the new improved grain" a few decades ago, triticale is a hybrid of rye and wheat and a favorite of whole grain bread lovers, although certainly not a mainstream flour. Low in gluten, for a bread with the best texture it should be used like rye in combination with wheat flours. Triticale is also available in whole grain form.

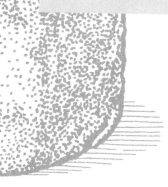

SWEDISH RYE BREAD

1½-POUND LOAF

1¼ cups water
3 tablespoons honey
2 tablespoons vegetable oil

2 cups bread flour
1¼ cups medium rye flour
1 tablespoon plus
   1 teaspoon gluten
2 teaspoons fennel seeds
1½ teaspoons grated orange
   zest or dried orange peel
1¼ teaspoons salt

2 teaspoons SAF yeast or
   2½ teaspoons bread
   machine yeast

2-POUND LOAF

1⅝ cups water
¼ cup honey
3 tablespoons vegetable oil

2¾ cups bread flour
1¾ cups medium rye flour
1 tablespoon plus
   2 teaspoons gluten
1 tablespoon fennel seeds
2 teaspoons grated orange
   zest or dried orange peel
1½ teaspoons salt

2½ teaspoons SAF yeast or
   1 tablespoon bread
   machine yeast

T*his was one of the first rye breads I ever made by hand. It is not sour. I still make this rye, but now I make it in the bread machine, with the spicy addition of a bit of orange, to make a loaf that is the best of its genre. If you are unfamiliar with the flavor of fennel seeds in bread, you are in for a treat; they make a totally different-tasting rye bread. Serve this bread with thick split pea soup.*

1 Place all the ingredients in the pan according to the order in the manufacturer's instructions. Set crust on medium and program for the Basic cycle; press Start. (This recipe may be made using the Delay Timer.)

2 When the baking cycle ends, immediately remove the bread from the pan and place it on a rack. Let cool to room temperature before slicing.

LIMPA

N ext to black bread, limpa *is the most familiar Swedish rye bread among home bakers. It was one of the breads in the first batch of recipes I received from my friend Judy Larsen. The recipes came from her mother in Minneapolis. Every household would have its own recipe, usually passed down in the family. Limpa is a sweeter rye bread than most and is always made for the holidays. Use for the ritual "dipping in the kettle"—lowering slices into hot meat or ham broth on Christmas Eve. This bread is fantastic with dinner, and great toasted.*

❶ Place all the ingredients in the pan according to the order in the manufacturer's instructions. Set crust on medium and program for the Basic cycle; press Start. (This recipe is not suitable for use with the Delay Timer.)

❷ When the baking cycle ends, immediately remove the bread from the pan and place it on a rack. Let cool to room temperature before slicing.

1½-POUND LOAF	2-POUND LOAF
¾ cup water	1 cup water
⅓ cup milk	½ cup milk
1 tablespoon molasses	2 tablespoons molasses
1½ tablespoons brown sugar	2 tablespoons brown sugar
2 tablespoons butter, cut into pieces	3 tablespoons butter, cut into pieces
1¾ cups bread flour	2½ cups bread flour
1¼ cups medium rye flour	1½ cups medium rye flour
1 tablespoon gluten	1 tablespoon plus 1 teaspoon gluten
½ teaspoon fennel seeds, crushed	¾ teaspoon fennel seeds, crushed
½ teaspoon aniseed, crushed	¾ teaspoon aniseed, crushed
1½ teaspoons grated orange zest	2 teaspoons grated orange zest
1½ teaspoons salt	1¾ teaspoons salt
2 teaspoons SAF yeast or 2½ teaspoons bread machine yeast	2¼ teaspoons SAF yeast or 2¾ teaspoons bread machine yeast

BOHEMIAN BLACK BREAD

F rom Germany to Poland to Russia, some form of this daily black bread is made. It is soft and mild, rather than dense and sour as you might expect a black bread to be. The flavor is even better on the second day. Serve this popular bread with bratwurst or roast pork, and Himmel und Erde, "heaven and earth," equal portions of potatoes, turnips, and apples mashed together with butter and milk, sprinkled with bits of cooked bacon.

❶ Place all the ingredients in the pan according to the order in the manufacturer's instructions. Set crust on medium and program for the Basic or Whole Wheat cycle; press Start. (This recipe may be made using the Delay Timer.)

❷ When the baking cycle ends, immediately remove the bread from the pan and place it on a rack. Let cool to room temperature before slicing.

1½-POUND LOAF	2-POUND LOAF
1⅛ cups water	1½ cups water
3 tablespoons butter, melted	4 tablespoons butter, melted
1½ tablespoons molasses	2 tablespoons molasses
1¾ cups bread flour	2⅓ cups bread flour
1 cup medium or dark rye flour	1⅓ cup medium or dark rye flour
¼ cup wheat bran	⅓ cup wheat bran
2 tablespoons unsweetened Dutch-process cocoa powder	3 tablespoons unsweetened Dutch-process cocoa powder
1 tablespoon gluten	1 tablespoon plus 1 teaspoon gluten
1½ teaspoons instant espresso powder	2 teaspoons instant espresso powder
1½ teaspoons caraway seeds	2 teaspoons caraway seeds
½ teaspoon fennel seeds	¾ teaspoon fennel seeds
1½ teaspoons salt	2 teaspoons salt
2 teaspoons SAF yeast or 2½ teaspoons bread machine yeast	2½ teaspoons SAF yeast or 1 tablespoon bread machine yeast

SOUR CREAM RYE

T he acid ingredients in this recipe—vinegar and sour cream—give this rye dough a moist, pliable consistency that ends up producing a beautifully moist, fine-textured loaf. Sour cream is an unusual ingredient in rye bread recipes, but here the addition makes a memorable sandwich loaf. I like to make this bread when I have a pot of borscht full of beets and potatoes on the stove. The aroma of this bread while it is baking is quite exciting. The loaf is as delicate as a cake when it comes out of the pan, so remove it carefully and cool it standing rather than on its side.

1 Place all the ingredients in the pan according to the order in the manufacturer's instructions. Set crust on medium and program for the Basic or Whole Wheat cycle; press Start. (This recipe is not suitable for use with the Delay Timer.) The dough ball will be well shaped, but tacky and spread like a puddle during the risings.

2 When the baking cycle ends, immediately remove the bread from the pan and carefully place it on a rack. Let cool to room temperature before slicing.

1½-POUND LOAF	2-POUND LOAF
⅔ cup water	¾ cup water
2 tablespoons balsamic vinegar	2½ tablespoons balsamic vinegar
⅔ cup sour cream	⅞ cup sour cream
2 tablespoons dark honey or molasses	3 tablespoons dark honey or molasses
2 tablespoons vegetable oil	3 tablespoons vegetable oil
1¾ cups bread flour	2½ cups bread flour
1¼ cups dark rye flour	1½ cups dark rye flour
1 tablespoon instant potato flakes	1½ tablespoons instant potato flakes
1 tablespoon plus 1 teaspoon gluten	1 tablespoon plus 2 teaspoons gluten
1 tablespoon caraway seeds	1 tablespoon plus 1 teaspoon caraway seeds
1 teaspoon ground coriander seeds	1½ teaspoons ground coriander seeds
1½ teaspoons salt	2 teaspoons salt
2¼ teaspoons SAF yeast or 2¾ teaspoons bread machine yeast	2½ teaspoons SAF yeast or 1 tablespoon bread machine yeast

Milling Your Own Whole-Grain Flours

While some owner's manuals recommend against using home milled flours because their density can alter crucial recipe measurements, once you have become familiar with your machine there is no reason you can't use your own milled flours and make the necessary adjustments to the liquid-flour balance. Owning and operating a home kitchen grain mill is an investment in time and money, but many bakers swear by it, opting for a bit more labor in exchange for the added flavor and nutrition. Since excellent commercial unbleached and stone-ground flours are widely available today, this really is a personal decision. But there are benefits—the milled flour can be transferred immediately to the pan, leaving virtually no time for oxidation to destroy precious vitamins and minerals. The aroma of fresh-milled flour is so enticing, once you smell it, you will be hooked.

With a home mill, you will be grinding only whole-grain flours, never white flours, which need to be sifted to remove the bran and germ. The grind settings range from very coarse to very fine. Whole grains for milling can be kept for years stored in airtight containers. One cup of the larger grains (wheat, corn, rye) will yield 1 cup flour. The smaller grains (amaranth, teff, rice, millet) yield 1 cup of flour per ¾ cup whole grain. Wheat and rye are the easiest grains to mill.

It seems that the more expensive the mill, the quieter it is and the less muscle power is required on your part. In the past, home mills have been known for being heavy, rustic, and tremendously laborious hand-cranked jobs, most certainly a link to the past. I had an incredibly heavy but fascinating hand stone mill I was given by a friend. It was a modern quern; a descendant of an ancient hand milling tool. I found out that it was a Samap from France. It made flour, as well as cracked grains, but I spent lots of time grinding.

The counter-clamped steel Corona hand mill, which caused a sensation in the 1960s during the back-to-the-land movement, is still a good method for grinding wet hominy for masa, soaked soybeans for tofu, and a variety of cracked breakfast grains. It is usually the first mill in a home grinder's life. My friends Ralph and Toni Korgold have been using theirs for decades, mixing and grinding the grains for their cooked breakfast cereal blend of the month.

The next step, the modern, lightweight plastic-bodied electric mills are incredibly efficient, living up to names like Magic Mill or Whisper Mill. They grind hard wheat berries, soybeans, and corn kernels into commercial-quality flour in one grinding, and are self-cleaning. They look perfect next to the bread machine and food processor, and take up a minimal amount of counter space.

Other electric grain mills include the Kitchen Aid, a grain mill with steel blades that is an attachment for their heavy stand mixer (I consider this best for cereal grinding), and a small electric mill by Braun. The Baker's Catalogue offers two exceptional mills. One is the Family Grain Mill by Messerschmidt of Germany, a hand mill made of heavy-duty plastic that clamps onto the side of the counter and grinds from coarse to fine. The other is the Regal Kitchen Pro (from the same company that makes bread machines), a countertop electric model that grinds everything into beautiful flour and is very reasonably priced. Two other very good mills are a large counter model by Lee, and another by Excalibur, which has been out of production for a few years. If you see one of these at a flea market or garage sale, grab it; these mills are known for their excellence and durability.

POLISH BEER RYE BREAD

R ye breads are so inherent to the cuisine of Poland that the word chleb, which translates to "bread," is what every loaf that has even a small amount of rye flour in it is called. Since my tester Mary Anne is Polish and rye breads are her favorite, we had to make a rye that combined the complex rye flavor with a very savory sourdough-like aroma during baking, just like in a professional bakery. This is a very light rye, so it is good for sandwiches. This bread garners raves!

1 Open the container of beer and let stand at room temperature for a few hours to go flat.

2 Place all the ingredients in the pan according to the order in the manufacturer's instructions. Set crust on medium and program for the Basic cycle; press Start. (This recipe is not suitable for use with the Delay Timer.)

3 When the baking cycle ends, immediately remove the bread from the pan and place it on a rack. Let cool to room temperature before slicing.

1½-POUND LOAF	2-POUND LOAF
1 cup (8 ounces) beer	1⅓ cups (11 ounces) beer
3 tablespoons apple cider vinegar	¼ cup apple cider vinegar
2 tablespoons honey	3 tablespoons honey
1 tablespoon butter, melted	2 tablespoons butter, melted
1 tablespoon minced raw shallot	1½ tablespoons minced raw shallot
2 cups bread flour	2½ cups bread flour
¾ cup light or medium rye flour	1 cup light or medium rye flour
¼ cup whole wheat flour	½ cup whole wheat flour
2 tablespoons yellow cornmeal	3 tablespoons yellow cornmeal
2 tablespoons gluten	2½ tablespoons gluten
2 teaspoons caraway seeds	2½ teaspoons caraway seeds
1½ teaspoons salt	2 teaspoons salt
1 tablespoon SAF yeast or 1 tablespoon plus ½ teaspoon bread machine yeast	1 tablespoon plus 1 teaspoon SAF yeast or 1 tablespoon plus 1½ teaspoons bread machine yeast

SUNFLOWER PUMPERNICKEL RYE

P umpernickel is a dense, rich, and textured bread. Its flavor is best at room temperature. It is the regional bread of Bavaria, a province of Germany known for hearty good food. There is a story that says the Russian dictator Lenin once carved his inkwell out of a hunk of pumpernickel rye bread. Serve this spread with cheese, use it to make tomato and red onion sandwiches, pair it with all sorts of wursts and mustard, or just toast it. This recipe makes great soft pretzels (see page 144).

1½-POUND LOAF	2-POUND LOAF
1⅓ cups water	1⅔ cups water
3½ tablespoons molasses	4½ tablespoons molasses
2 tablespoons butter, melted	3 tablespoons butter, melted
1½ cups bread flour	2 cups bread flour
1 cup medium or dark rye flour	1⅓ cups medium or dark rye flour
½ cup whole wheat flour	⅔ cup whole wheat flour
¼ cup cornmeal	⅓ cup cornmeal
3 tablespoons unsweetened Dutch-process cocoa powder	¼ cup unsweetened Dutch-process cocoa powder
2 tablespoons brown sugar	2½ tablespoons brown sugar
1½ tablespoons nonfat dry milk	2 tablespoons nonfat dry milk
1½ tablespoons gluten	2 tablespoons gluten
½ teaspoon instant espresso powder	¾ teaspoon instant espresso powder
2 teaspoons caraway seeds	1 tablespoon caraway seeds
1½ teaspoons salt	2 teaspoons salt
2½ teaspoons SAF yeast or 1 tablespoon bread machine yeast	1 tablespoon SAF yeast or 1 tablespoon plus ½ teaspoon bread machine yeast
⅓ cup raw sunflower seeds	½ cup raw sunflower seeds

1 Place the ingredients, except the sunflower seeds, in the pan according to the order in the manufacturer's instructions. Set crust on medium and program for the Basic or Whole Wheat cycle; press Start. (This recipe is not suitable for use with the Delay Timer.) When the machine beeps, or between Knead 1 and Knead 2, add the sunflower seeds.

2 When the baking cycle ends, immediately remove the bread from the pan and place it on a rack. Let cool to room temperature before slicing.

CRACKED RYE BREAD

C *racked grain breads of all kinds are bakery favorites for their nubby textures. Recipes for cracked rye breads are few and far between, though. Here is one you can make over and over again. This is a recipe I got from one of my baking mentors, Judy Larsen, and I adapted it for the bread machine. It is important to soak the cracked rye first or it won't be able to bake into the loaf. This loaf makes great cashew butter and jelly sandwiches, but it is a favorite of mine for accompanying winter soups.*

1 Pour the boiling water over the cracked rye in a bowl. Add the brown sugar, butter, and salt. Let stand 1 hour on the counter to soften.

2 Place the ingredients in the pan according to the order in the manufacturer's instructions, adding the grain and its soaking liquid as the liquid ingredients. Set crust on medium and program for the Basic or Whole Wheat cycle; press Start. (This recipe may be made using the Delay Timer.)

3 When the baking cycle ends, immediately remove the bread from the pan and place it on a rack. Let cool to room temperature before slicing.

1½-POUND LOAF	2-POUND LOAF
1¼ cups boiling water	1¾ cups boiling water
½ cup cracked rye	⅔ cup cracked rye
3 tablespoons dark brown sugar	¼ cup dark brown sugar
3 tablespoons butter	4 tablespoons butter
1¼ teaspoons salt	1½ teaspoons salt
1⅔ cups bread flour	2¼ cups bread flour
1 cup medium rye flour	1⅓ cups medium rye flour
⅓ cup nonfat dry milk	½ cup nonfat dry milk
1 tablespoon plus 1 teaspoon gluten	1 tablespoon plus 2 teaspoons gluten
1 tablespoon sesame seeds	1½ tablespoons sesame seeds
1 tablespoon wheat germ	1½ tablespoons wheat germ
2½ teaspoons SAF yeast or 1 tablespoon bread machine yeast	1 tablespoon SAF yeast or 1 tablespoon plus ½ teaspoon bread machine yeast

Technique: Making Soft Pretzels

Chewy pretzels are a great snack food. While commercial pretzels are cooked in a water-lye bath, at home, a baking soda bath does the job just fine. Here are two recipes: one for white dough pretzels that are immersed in a bath before baking, and one for rye pretzels, baked entirely in the oven. Children love these.

Soft Pretzels

Makes 12 large pretzels

1½- or 2-pound-loaf machines

For the dough:

½ cup water
1 cup milk

4 cups bread flour
1 tablespoon malt powder, preferably, or sugar
1¼ teaspoons salt

2¼ teaspoons SAF yeast or 2¾ teaspoons bread machine yeast

For the pretzel bath:

2 quarts water
2 tablespoons baking soda

For the topping:

1 egg white beaten with 1 tablespoon water
About 2 tablespoons coarse kosher or sea salt

❶ To make the dough, place all the ingredients in the bread pan according to the order in the manufacturer's instructions. Program for the Dough cycle; press Start.

❷ Line 2 large baking sheets with parchment paper. When the machine beeps at the end of the cycle, turn the dough out onto the work surface and divide into 12 equal portions (you can make smaller pretzels, dividing the dough into 18 portions). With your palms, shape each portion into a 20-inch rope. To form a pretzel shape, hold both ends of the rope and bring both ends around into the center to form a large loop. Twist the ends together once, about 3 inches from the ends. Bring the twisted end up and over the loop and attach it to the bottom center of the loop. You will have a pretzel shape that looks rather like a heart with 3 sections. Carefully transfer the pretzel to the baking sheet. Repeat with all of the dough pieces. Let rest, uncovered, at room temperature for 30 minutes.

❸ Preheat the oven to 400°F. Bring 2 quarts of water to a boil in a large, deep pan, and add the baking soda to the water. (If you want soft, breadlike pretzels, skip the boiling and go directly to Step 5 and bake in the oven.)

❹ When the 30 minutes are up, with a large spatula, carefully lift a risen pretzel, then lower it into the boiling water. You can boil 2 pretzels at once. Leaving the water at a low rolling boil, boil for 45 seconds to 1 minute, until puffy. Remove with a slotted spoon, hold over the pan to drain, then place back on the baking sheet 2 inches apart. Repeat until all the pretzels have been boiled.

❺ Brush each pretzel with the egg glaze and sprinkle with the salt. Bake one sheet at a time, in the center of the oven, for 16 to 20 minutes, until deep golden brown. Cool the pretzels on a rack. Eat them warm or store at room temperature for up to 3 days, wrapped in a single layer of foil.

Baked Rye Pretzels with Seeds
Makes 16 pretzels

1½- or 2-pound-loaf machines

For the dough:

1¼ cups water
1 tablespoon canola oil
1 large egg yolk

2¼ cups bread flour
1 cup white whole wheat flour
¼ cup medium or dark rye flour
1½ tablespoons malt powder, preferably, or sugar
1 teaspoon salt
Pinch of ground white pepper

2½ teaspoons SAF yeast or 1 tablespoon bread machine yeast

For the topping:

1 egg white beaten with 1 tablespoon water
About 2 tablespoons coarse kosher or sea salt
Sesame seeds or caraway seeds

❶ To make the dough, place all the ingredients in the pan according to the order in the manufacturer's instructions. Program for the Dough cycle; press Start.

❷ Line 2 large baking sheets with parchment paper. When the machine beeps at the end of the cycle, turn the dough out onto the work surface and divide into 16 equal portions. With your palms, shape each portion into a 16-inch rope. To form a pretzel shape, hold both ends of the rope and bring both ends around into the center to form a large loop. Twist the ends together once, about 3 inches from the ends. Bring the twisted end up and over the loop and attach it to the bottom center of the loop. You will have a pretzel shape that looks rather like a heart with 3 sections. Carefully transfer the pretzel to the baking sheet. Repeat with all of the dough, leaving 1½ inches between each pretzel. Let rest, uncovered, at room temperature for 20 minutes.

❸ Preheat the oven to 375°F.

❹ Brush each pretzel with the egg glaze and sprinkle with the salt and seeds. Bake one sheet at a time, in the center of the oven, for 15 to 20 minutes, until deep golden brown. Cool the pretzels on a rack. Eat them warm or store at room temperature for up to 3 days, wrapped in a single layer of foil.

SPECIALTY FLOUR BREADS

Specialty flours, also known as non-wheat flours, include all flours not ground from wheat. While many of these flours are not as well known as wheat, they are all exceptional for making bread in the bread machine. In your search for good whole grain breads, don't shy away from recipes that feature some of these unfamiliar grains. Their imaginative addition to wheat loaves creates breads with a fascinating variety of new flavors, aromas, and textures, for example, cornmeal millet, white barley bread, or oatmeal whole wheat. Cooked grains, such as millet, wild rice, buckwheat groats, bulgur wheat, black rice, polenta, and hominy, meld beautifully into a loaf of bread. The texture of bread made with specialty grains and flours varies from smooth and fine-textured to coarse and crumbly. There is no common definition because each flour is so different and comes not only in whole grain form, but also as fine flour, coarse meal, rolled flakes, and cracked grains. Non-wheat flours have varying amounts of protein, fiber, and nutrition. Some are easy to eat, others are an acquired taste.

If you tried to create a yeasted loaf from all, or a large percentage of, specialty flour, you would produce a dense, flat loaf because of the lack of gluten in these grains. (Gluten is present only in wheat and rye flours.) Specialty flours must be used in small proportions along with plenty of high-gluten bread flour and vital wheat gluten in order to give the loaf an internal structure. I have created recipes here that are easy to make and will be to the liking of even the fussiest bread eater. Specialty flours are added in only a small proportion, comprising from just a few tablespoons to a quarter of the total flour in the loaf. Still, each flour and grain addition will result in a different feel—a whole wheat and cornmeal loaf will have a grainy texture in comparison to a loaf with the bumpy texture of rolled oats, cracked wheat, and wild rice added to some barley flour.

The main trick to working with doughs made with specialty flours is to remember that they soak up a lot of moisture during rising, as compared to white flour breads, which soak up the moisture right away during the mixing and kneading. When you check your dough ball, leave these doughs, as you do whole wheat doughs, a bit moister than usual to avoid a finished loaf that is too dry. When you touch the grain-rich dough gently with your finger, it will pull up as you pull your finger away, yet still look like a nice ball of dough. You want the dough to retain its tacky feel, so resist the urge to sprinkle it with more than 1 or 2 teaspoons of flour during the Knead 2 segment of the cycle.

These doughs emit a wonderfully grain-sweet, yeasty aroma during the rising that I find as intoxicating as the aroma during baking. Do not be put off by slow risers. Specialty flour doughs are notorious for remaining under half their finished size during the rising times, due to their reduced gluten, and then filling the pan three-quarters to almost full during baking. If a loaf comes out too dense, add ½ teaspoon more yeast and an extra 1 to 2 teaspoons gluten the next time you make it.

Set the crust control, if your machine has it, on medium or dark for these breads. I especially like an extra-dark crust, as opposed to a medium, terra cotta-colored crust on white breads. Some flours, like barley, never darken unless there are plenty of other ingredients added.

Don't let specialty flour breads rest inside the machine on Keep Warm. It is important to remove them from the machine immediately once the beep sounds and to let them cool on a rack, or they will dry out. If your loaf is especially dense and looks like it is not quite done, don't hesitate to program the machine for more time on the Bake Only cycle, or to turn it out of the pan and bake it a bit longer in your home oven.

Where can you find these specialty flours? Almost every supermarket offers rye flour, oatmeal, and cornmeal. Whole foods supermarkets, gourmet grocery stores, and natural foods stores offer the largest selections of whole grain and non-wheat flours. Or you can always order them from mail-order resources (see pages 612 to 613).

CORNMEAL HONEY BREAD

1½-POUND LOAF

1⅛ cups water
1½ tablespoons unsalted
   butter, cut into pieces
3 tablespoons honey

2⅔ cups bread flour
⅓ cup yellow cornmeal
⅓ cup dry buttermilk powder
1 tablespoon plus
   1 teaspoon gluten
1 teaspoon salt

1¾ teaspoons SAF yeast
   or 2¼ teaspoons bread
   machine yeast

2-POUND LOAF

1½ cups water
2 tablespoons unsalted
   butter cut into pieces
¼ cup honey

3½ cups bread flour
½ cup yellow cornmeal
½ cup dry buttermilk powder
1 tablespoon plus
   2 teaspoons gluten
1½ teaspoons salt

2½ teaspoons SAF yeast
   or 1 tablespoon bread
   machine yeast

A *yeasted corn bread is something of a surprise; it is not only toothsome, but has an appealing sweet, moist, slightly gritty texture. Please use a stone-ground cornmeal for this bread if you can. I order every brand I can find, especially the ones ground at small family-owned stone mills. They are remarkable in flavor (I even give gifts of them at Christmas). This will become one of your favorite breads.*

1 Place all the ingredients in the pan according to the order in the manufacturer's instructions. Set crust on dark and program for the Basic cycle; press Start. (This recipe may be made using the Delay Timer.)

2 When the baking cycle ends, immediately remove the bread from the pan and place it on a rack. Let cool to room temperature before slicing.

CORNMEAL AND HOMINY BREAD

W hile writing a book on the breads of the American Southwest, I discovered the unique addition of canned hominy to breads, and was hooked. Hominy adds moisture and texture to an otherwise crunchy loaf, and a delicate cornlike flavor that is most complementary to the cornmeal. Be sure to refrigerate this loaf for storage; it has a lot of moisture and will begin to mold when day-old if stored at room temperature.

1 Place all the ingredients, except the hominy, in the pan according to the order in the manufacturer's instructions. Set crust on dark and program for the Basic or Fruit and Nut cycle; press Start. (This recipe is not suitable for use with the Delay Timer.) When the machine beeps, or between Knead 1 and Knead 2, add the hominy.

2 When the baking cycle ends, immediately remove the bread from the pan and place it on a rack. Let cool to room temperature before slicing.

1½-POUND LOAF

½ cup milk
½ cup water
2 tablespoons olive oil

3 cups bread flour
½ cup yellow cornmeal
2 tablespoons sugar
1½ tablespoons gluten
1½ teaspoons salt

2 teaspoons SAF yeast or
   2½ teaspoons bread
   machine yeast

1 cup canned hominy,
   rinsed

2-POUND LOAF

⅔ cup milk
⅔ cup water
3 tablespoons olive oil

4 cups bread flour
⅔ cup yellow cornmeal
3 tablespoons sugar
2 tablespoons gluten
2 teaspoons salt

2½ teaspoons SAF yeast
   or 1 tablespoon bread
   machine yeast

1½ cups canned hominy,
   rinsed

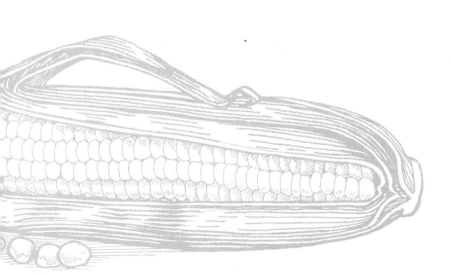

The Baker's Glossary of Specialty Flours and Grains

Barley Flour

Barley has a chewy texture and a mild, sweet flavor. Hulled pearl barley can be toasted and rolled into barley flakes, which are used like rolled oats, or ground into a low-gluten flour with a grayish color. Use a small proportion (1 cup of barley flour to 5 cups of wheat flour, or 20 percent barley flour, at the most) for a slightly bitter, moist-crumbed bread that is excellent toasted. Of course, smaller proportions of barley flour can also be used. The crusts of barley breads bake up a tan color and tend to harden as they cool. Barley combines well with the flavors of orange, rye, and whole wheat.

Buckwheat Flour

Small amounts of buckwheat flour combined with wheat flour make a surprisingly delicious light-textured bread. Usually eaten in its robust roasted form, called *kasha*, buckwheat is technically not a grain, but the seed of a red-stemmed plant related to rhubarb. Buckwheat flour is low in protein, which makes for a tender baked product with an assertive, musky, slightly bitter flavor, and the purple-gray color of its flour bakes into a dark gray-brown crust. Buckwheat grown in Europe has a rather mild taste, distinctly different from the Japanese variety of buckwheat grown in the United States, which can be quite earthy and musky. While the whole grain is an acquired taste, I have found that the addition of a small amount of buckwheat flour makes an exceptional bread that is loved upon first bite. Give it a try. At most, use 1 cup of buckwheat flour to 5 cups of wheat flour. Use buckwheat with wheat flours, rye flours, and cornmeal. It pairs very well with cinnamon and prunes.

Chestnut Flour

Chestnut flour is ground from dried chestnuts and the flavor varies depending on how the nuts have been dried. The flour's beige texture is dust-fine and silky, and the flavor distinctive. Use a small proportion (a scant 1 cup of chestnut flour to 5 cups of wheat flour at the most) in breads. Chestnut flour combines well with all nuts, assertive honeys, and whole wheats. Use chestnut flour in everything from regular loaves to pizza doughs to country breads.

Cornmeal

Yellow cornmeal comes in a variety of grinds, from fine to coarse, and makes delicious yeasted cornbreads. Degerminated cornmeal has had the germ removed for longer shelf life. *Masa harina* is finely ground golden cornmeal made from lime-treated hominy. For the best flavor, search out fresh stone-ground cornmeals. Polenta is considered a coarse grind of cornmeal.

Baked goods made with cornmeal are crumbly in texture and a bit gritty, with a characteristic pale yellow color. Because cornmeal is unique in flavor and texture, there is no substitute for it. Use a small proportion (1 to 2 cups of cornmeal to 4 to 5 cups of wheat flour) to create light-textured breads. Cornmeal's mild flavor combines well with all other grains and is great seasoned with chiles. Blue cornmeal may be substituted for yellow cornmeal in breads.

Millet

Tiny round yellow grains of millet resemble pale mustard seeds and are a common addition to whole-grain cereal mixtures. Millet has a slightly mild nutty taste, a fluffy texture, and is very easy to digest. I use the whole raw millet as a "crunchy munchy" addition to other grains and seeds in a dough that bakes up into firm, chewy textured bread. Millet combines well with the flavors of all flours, but is especially nice with wild and domestic rices, cornmeals, oats, rye, and whole wheat.

Oats

Rolled oats are the most familiar cereal grain on the market. Whole groats are hulled, steamed, and flattened into flakes. They may be ground into oat flour with a food processor or into a coarse meal suitable for breadmaking. The mild, nutty flavor and moist, nubby texture of oats is a favorite in breads, with the recipes often calling for spices, honey, nuts, and dried fruits. Use a small proportion (1 cup of rolled oats to 2 cups of wheat flour at most and a 1-to-5 ratio for oat flour). Oats combine well with the flavors of graham, whole wheat, rye, wild rice, and millet.

Potato Flour

Potato flour is ground from cooked, dried, starchy potatoes. Used mostly as a thickener, it is great for dusting loaves and makes moist doughs in lieu of adding cooked mashed potatoes to the dough. It is a premium food for the yeast, as the yeast thrives on the starch. Use a scant 1 cup of potato flour to 5 cups of wheat flour at most, since potato flour tends to be heavy. It is not the same as potato starch flour, which is used extensively in Jewish baking for sponge cakes and dinner rolls. Potato flour is also different from dehydrated instant potato flakes.

Quinoa

Quinoa (prounounced "keen-wa") is really the fruit of a plant rather than a grass, and has the highest protein content of any grain (about 17 percent). It has been grown in the Andes Mountains of South America for about three thousand years. It can be used like rice or millet. Before it is used, whole quinoa must be thoroughly rinsed because it is coated with saponin, a resin-like substance with a bitter, soapy taste that protects the grains from insects. Rinse and drain the quinoa about 5 times with cold running water. The more rinsing it undergoes, the milder the flavor of the cooked grain will be. When cooked, the disc-shaped sesame-like grains become translucent. Quinoa is used cooked in breads in the same manner as rice. There is also quinoa flour, but it is hard to find outside of health food stores. Do not confuse quinoa with amaranth, also from South America.

Rice and Rice Flour

There are thousands of varieties of rice, each with its own distinct flavor, texture, aroma, color, length of grain, and degree of translucency. Short-grain brown rice is nutty, sweet, dense, and chewy. Unpolished, it retains a layer of bran, which adds fiber and flavor. Long-grain brown (Texmati) rice is beige in color and nutty in flavor. Converted rice is parboiled before drying, and cooks up nice and fluffy. Aromatic rices, such as basmati and jasmine, are known for their distinctive fragrances. Use 1 to 2 cups of cooked rice to 6 cups of flour for the best results. Brown rices take twice as long as white rice to cook, and have more nutrients.

In addition to using cooked whole grain rice in some of my breads, occasionally I like to use rice flour in bread machine breads. Rice flour can be ground from brown or white rice, although I always use brown rice flour. There is also a sweet rice flour used in Asian cuisine, but not for breads. Rice flour is an excellent thickener and is good for dusting (use for dusting your pizza doughs when rolling out), as it absorbs moisture slowly and has a light, sweet flavor. Use a small proportion of rice flour (a scant 1 cup of rice flour to 5 cups of wheat flour) when making bread. The crust on a loaf made with rice flour will be a delicate light brown with a fine crumb. For more information on rice flours, see page 172.

Soy Flour

Soybean products were long thought unsuitable for breadmaking; on their own they make moist, compact bricks with a hearty musty, sweet flavor that many find to be an acquired taste. But soy flour in small amounts melds well with other flours, slows the rancidity in baked goods, and, with its high fat and protein content, adds considerable nutrition and moisture to loaves. Soy flour keeps well on a cupboard shelf for up to a year. Breads that contain soy flour are chewy, with a golden crust and delicate musty flavor.

The soy products that are available for baking include grits, soy flakes, a soy meal, and, my favorite,

continued on next page

a finely milled flour (ground from toasted whole soy-beans). Toasted soy products, labeled soya, have a nutty rich flavor while raw soy products are blander. The best tasting, most nutritious soy flour is stone-ground and full-fat. Defatted soy flour has the oil removed by a process using chemical solvents, so don't let the fat-free craze tempt you to buy this. The proteins in soy flour complement the ones in wheat flour, an especially nice pairing since soy has no gluten. Soy flour makes a crust that tends to brown quickly, so a good rule of thumb is to set your machine's crust setting on light. Add no more than 1 cup of soy flour per 3 to 5 cups of wheat flour, adding a tablespoon of vital wheat gluten per cup of soy flour for texture.

Teff Flour

Teff flour, available almost exclusively in health food stores and from mail-order catalogs, is a specialty flour and a staple in an ethnic cuisine not familiar to most Americans. Since the grains of teff, native to northern Africa but now grown in Idaho, are so small, they cannot be processed, so teff makes a nice whole grain flour with its bran and germ intact. Ivory-colored teff is coveted for its pure color. White breads made from it were once a sign of status in Ethiopia, as white wheat breads once were in this country. The mahogany-brown seeds have a rich, deep flavor slightly reminiscent of carob or Wheatena. Both ivory and brown teff seeds are ground into flour. Teff is known for its pleasantly sweet, almost molasses-like flavor. The mild nature of teff combines well with the sweet spices, such as cinnamon, allspice, cardamom, coriander, and ginger. It has not traditionally been used with yeast, but in combination with high-protein bread flour it can be used sparingly for a lovely bread. It is the easiest of the new grains to introduce to children, as it has a gentle palatability; try teff bread for breakfast toast.

Wild Rice

Delicious by itself or in combination with other rices, wild rice has a strong woodsy flavor and a chewy texture. It is not really a rice, but the seed of an aquatic grass native to the marshes of the Great Lakes and Canada. Some wild rice is still traditionally harvested by hand by Native Americans, but most is cultivated in man-made paddies and harvested by machine, with California being the biggest producer. Paddy rice is left to cure out in the weather, causing the characteristic shiny, dark kernels, while hand-harvested rice is parched immediately over open fires, giving it a variety of distinctly matte colors from a ruddy red-brown to a subtle gray-green. Labels usually note if the rice is hand-harvested or cultivated, but the color will tell you immediately how it was grown. Each brand of wild rice has its own particular taste, so if you have experienced a brand that was too husky for your palate, experiment with others, or use it in combination with other rices for a milder taste. All grades can be used interchangeably in bread recipes calling for wild rice, but must always be cooked first, giving breads a flecking of dark color and a deep-toned, musky flavor. A little wild rice goes a long way, but once you taste a bread that combines wild rice with oatmeal, you will know how tasty it can be.

Wild rice is generally used as a cooked whole grain in breads rather than as a flour. For the best results, use 1 to 2 cups of cooked rice to 6 cups of flour. Hard to find, but nice if you can find it, is wild rice flour. There is a pure wild rice flour, which has no gluten, and a wild rice and unbleached white flour mixture, which can be used straight from the bag for baking.

POLENTA-SUNFLOWER-MILLET BREAD

T his is one of my cache of "crunchy munchy" breads with whole millet, which looks so pretty dotting every slice. The family of common millets is just huge, and the only difference between the millet we eat and the kind the birds eat is that the bird seed is unhulled. Once you feel the great textural additions of millet and the coarse grind of cornmeal known as polenta, you'll be adding these grains often. If you find the little nubs too crunchy, just soak the millet in hot water for fifteen minutes and drain it before adding to the bread dough.

1 Place all the ingredients in the pan according to the order in the manufacturer's instructions. Set crust on medium and program for the Basic or Whole Wheat cycle; press Start. (This recipe may be made using the Delay Timer.)

2 When the baking cycle ends, immediately remove the bread from the pan and place it on a rack. Let cool to room temperature before slicing.

1½-POUND LOAF	2-POUND LOAF
1⅛ cups water	1½ cups water
3 tablespoons honey	¼ cup honey
2 tablespoons sunflower seed oil	3 tablespoons sunflower seed oil
2½ cups bread flour	3¼ cups bread flour
½ cup whole wheat flour	¾ cup whole wheat flour
¼ cup polenta	⅓ cup polenta
3 tablespoons whole raw millet	¼ cup whole raw millet
3 tablespoons raw sunflower seeds	¼ cup raw sunflower seeds
1½ tablespoons gluten	2 tablespoons gluten
1½ teaspoons salt	2 teaspoons salt
1¾ teaspoons SAF yeast or 2¼ teaspoons bread machine yeast	2½ teaspoons SAF yeast or 1 tablespoon bread machine yeast

ORANGE-BUCKWHEAT BREAD

I am fascinated with buckwheat flour. It is an acquired taste unless you are Jewish and ate kasha as a kid or eat a lot of Japanese soba-kiri noodles. But this flour is great in small amounts, and I have made converts of lots of bakers with recipes like this. Buckwheat has its botanical origin at the unique Lake Baikal area in Siberia. It is the planet's oldest and deepest fresh water lake, located in the center of the Mongolian empire and home to hundreds of plant species found nowhere else. It makes buckwheat special indeed. Cultivated since prehistoric times as a bread grain, it became a staple all around mainland Asia and, later, in Japanese and Indian diets.

❶ Place all the ingredients in the pan according to the order in the manufacturer's instructions. Set crust on dark and program for the Basic cycle; press Start. (This recipe is not suitable for use with the Delay Timer.) The dough ball will be moist and springy.

❷ When the baking cycle ends, immediately remove the bread from the pan and place it on a rack. Let cool to room temperature before slicing.

1½-POUND LOAF	2-POUND LOAF
1 cup buttermilk	1⅓ cups buttermilk
1 large egg	1 large egg
2 tablespoons unsalted butter, cut into pieces	3 tablespoons unsalted butter, cut into pieces
2 cups bread flour	3 cups bread flour
¾ cup whole wheat flour	1 cup whole wheat flour
⅓ cup light buckwheat flour	½ cup light buckwheat flour
2 tablespoons dark brown sugar	3 tablespoons dark brown sugar
Grated zest of 1 large orange	Grated zest of 1 large orange
1 tablespoon gluten	1 tablespoon plus 1 teaspoon gluten
1½ teaspoons salt	2 teaspoons salt
2¼ teaspoons SAF yeast or 2¾ teaspoons bread machine yeast	2½ teaspoons SAF yeast or 1 tablespoon bread machine yeast

Bread and Its Place on the Food Pyramid

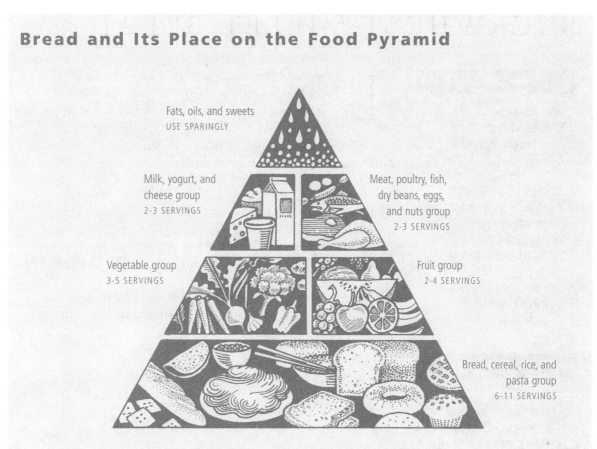

Fats, oils, and sweets
USE SPARINGLY

Milk, yogurt, and
cheese group
2-3 SERVINGS

Meat, poultry, fish,
dry beans, eggs,
and nuts group
2-3 SERVINGS

Vegetable group
3-5 SERVINGS

Fruit group
2-4 SERVINGS

Bread, cereal, rice, and
pasta group
6-11 SERVINGS

The American Food Guide Pyramid was developed by the U.S. Department of Agriculture in 1992. It was later streamlined to reflect a worldwide perspective. Food pyramids have also been developed based on other traditional diets around the world, such as Asian, Latin American, and Mediterranean. The Third International Congress on Vegetarian Nutrition added a Vegetarian Food Guide Pyramid. All these pyramids place whole grain bread and pasta, beans, nuts, and tubers at the wide base for optimum health and sensible eating patterns. The pyramids recommend eating six to eleven servings of grain products per day—as many of them as possible unrefined, unprocessed, and unhulled whole grains—in cereals, pastas, and breads.

Starchy grains make us feel satisfied and well fed. As complex carbohydrates, grains are ready fuel for the body and are chemically built of chains of glucose, a necessary energy source for the brain, nervous system, and muscle functions. The breads made from whole grains meld well with the newly labeled "super foods": olive oil, fresh herbs, lemons, garlic, and yogurt—foods that contribute to optimum health.

Once the domain of a minority of health-conscious folks, many people are now becoming more interested in using a wide variety of whole-grain flours, and supermarket selections are growing to accommodate them. Baking your own bread is the perfect way to incorporate good nutrition into your diet naturally.

BUCKWHEAT-MILLET BREAD

1½-POUND LOAF

1⅛ cups water
1 tablespoon unsalted
   butter, cut into pieces
2 tablespoons dark honey

2⅔ cups bread flour
⅓ cup light buckwheat flour
⅓ cup whole millet
1 tablespoon gluten
1½ teaspoons salt

2 teaspoons SAF yeast
   or 2½ teaspoons bread
   machine yeast

2-POUND LOAF

1½ cups water
2 tablespoons unsalted
   butter, cut into pieces
3 tablespoons dark honey

3½ cups bread flour
½ cup light buckwheat flour
½ cup whole millet
1 tablespoon plus
   1 teaspoon gluten
2 teaspoons salt

2½ teaspoons SAF yeast
   or 1 tablespoon bread
   machine yeast

I have found that breads that use a small percentage of buckwheat flour along with wheat flours have wide appeal and wonderful flavor. Here the buckwheat is paired with millet. You will find this a scrumptious toasting bread, and a wonderful bread for sandwiches filled with Swiss or white American cheese and turkey or Black Forest ham.

1 Place all the ingredients in the pan according to the order in the manufacturer's instructions. Set crust on dark and program for the Basic cycle; press Start. (This recipe is not suitable for use with the Delay Timer.)

2 When the baking cycle ends, immediately remove the bread from the pan and place it on a rack. Let cool to room temperature before slicing.

CHESTNUT FLOUR BREAD

C*hestnut flour is often in a package labeled* farina di castagne, *as it is imported from Italy. It is one of my favorite specialty flours and I look for any opportunity to use it. The fine flour is like silk—I think it could have been used for powdering royal faces for court appearances a few hundred years ago. The character of this dough will reflect the chestnut flour you use—light and nutty or dark and smoky, depending on how the chestnuts were dried before they were ground into flour. After you've eaten your fill of this bread when it's fresh, try using it for French toast or in bread pudding.*

❶ Place all the ingredients in the pan according to the order in the manufacturer's instructions. Set crust on medium or dark and program for the Basic cycle; press Start. (This recipe is not suitable for use with the Delay Timer.) The dough ball will be moist and springy.

❷ When the baking cycle ends, immediately remove the bread from the pan and place it on a rack. Let cool to room temperature before slicing.

1½-POUND LOAF	2-POUND LOAF
⅞ cup fat-free milk	1⅛ cups fat-free milk
1 large egg	1 large egg
3 tablespoons butter or margarine, cut into pieces	4 tablespoons butter or margarine, cut into pieces
2½ cups bread flour	3¼ cups bread flour
½ cup chestnut flour	¾ cup chestnut flour
2 tablespoons dark brown sugar	3 tablespoons dark brown sugar
2 tablespoons minced pecans	3 tablespoons minced pecans
1 tablespoon gluten	1 tablespoon plus 1 teaspoon gluten
1½ teaspoons salt	2 teaspoons salt
2 teaspoons SAF yeast or 2½ teaspoons bread machine yeast	2½ teaspoons SAF yeast or 1 tablespoon bread machine yeast

POLENTA-CHESTNUT BREAD

1½-POUND LOAF

1 cup plus 1 tablespoon
  buttermilk
3 tablespoons dark honey
3 tablespoons olive oil

2⅓ cups bread flour
½ cup chestnut flour
⅓ cup polenta
1½ tablespoons gluten
1½ teaspoons salt

2¼ teaspoons SAF yeast
  or 2¾ teaspoons bread
  machine yeast

2-POUND LOAF

1⅓ cups buttermilk
¼ cup dark honey
¼ cup olive oil

3 cups bread flour
¾ cup chestnut flour
½ cup polenta
2 tablespoons gluten
2 teaspoons salt

2¾ teaspoons SAF yeast
  or 1 tablespoon plus
  ¼ teaspoon bread
  machine yeast

*T*his bread combines two Italian flours, chestnut flour ground from the fruits of the chestnut trees that grow outside of Rome, and northern Italian coarsely ground cornmeal, known as polenta. Stone-ground yellow cornmeal may be substituted for polenta. It gives a nice underlying texture to this compact, moist loaf. This is a nice bread with which to make a "black-eyed Susan" for breakfast—a slice of bread that has had an "eye" cut out of its center (with the rim of a glass) and an egg cooked right in the middle of it.

1 Place all the ingredients in the pan according to the order in the manufacturer's instructions. Set crust on dark and program for the Basic cycle; press Start. (This recipe is not suitable for use with the Delay Timer.) The dough ball will be firm, yet slightly sticky.

2 When the baking cycle ends, immediately remove the bread from the pan and place it on a rack. Let cool to room temperature before slicing.

BARLEY BREAD

B*arley bread is not a bread most people commonly make. But barley flour gives considerable sweetness to a loaf, so you will find it as a minor ingredient in a number of my breads. Barley breads are rich in history; every civilization seems to have had one. The Egyptians celebrated Osiris, their god of agriculture, who grew barley watered with the sacred waters of the Nile. Early Greeks made wine-soaked breads combining barley, raisins, pomegranate seeds, and pine nuts. Thick slices of heavy barley bread were dipped in wine for breakfast in the Middle Ages. And barley bread dipped in water and salt has long been a food of religious penance for cloistered monks. I think you'll find this modern version just right for toast and jam.*

1 Place all the ingredients in the pan according to the order in the manufacturer's instructions. Set crust on medium and program for the Basic or Whole Wheat cycle; press Start. (This recipe may be made using the Delay Timer.)

2 When the baking cycle ends, immediately remove the bread from the pan and place it on a rack. Let cool to room temperature before slicing.

1½-POUND LOAF	2-POUND LOAF
1 cup plus 3 tablespoons water	1½ cups water
2 tablespoons light brown sugar	3 tablespoons light brown sugar
2 tablespoons vegetable oil	3 tablespoons vegetable oil
2¼ cups bread flour	3 cups bread flour
½ cup barley flour	⅔ cup barley flour
¼ cup whole wheat flour	⅓ cup whole wheat flour
3 tablespoons dry buttermilk powder	¼ cup dry buttermilk powder
1 tablespoon plus 2 teaspoons gluten	2 tablespoons gluten
1 teaspoon ground cinnamon	1½ teaspoons ground cinnamon
1½ teaspoons salt	2 teaspoons salt
2¼ teaspoons SAF yeast or 2¾ teaspoons bread machine yeast	2½ teaspoons SAF yeast or 1 tablespoon bread machine yeast

Bread Machine Baker's Hint: Creating Your Own Bread Machine Recipes

Once any basic recipe from the manufacturer's manual or from this book or another has been mastered, feel free to substitute and experiment with other ingredients, using the successful recipe as your measurement guide.

Here are some tips:

- Always look for the proportion of 3 ounces of liquid to 1 cup of flour. That way you will have a dough that is not too wet or too dry.

- Remember that eggs and honey count as liquid ingredients.

- You need more yeast with a recipe that has cheese or fruit and nuts added.

- You need more gluten if you use whole wheat or specialty flours.

- Whole wheat flours soak up more liquid than white flours.

- Egg breads rise higher and are more delicate than breads without eggs.

- Certain egg breads, like brioche, can have two to three times the amount of fat as a regular recipe.

- Breads with more sweetening brown faster.

Specific information about how to use and substitute various flours, sweeteners, cooked grains, dried fruits, and other ingredients appears throughout the book. (You may find the Baker's Glossaries especially helpful.) A recipe that will be baked off in the oven can have more flour, so you can make a larger loaf than you could if you were baking it in the machine (a bread pan has a higher capacity for the Dough cycle than for the baking cycles; see the manual from your manufacturer for the maximum capacities of your machine).

Allow for some trial and error. Here are recipe guidelines for creating your own bread recipes for the machine:

1½-POUND LOAF

1⅛ to 1½ cups total liquid
3 to 3½ cups flour
1 to 6 teaspoons gluten
0 to 8 tablespoons fat
0 to 4 tablespoons sweetener
½ to 1½ teaspoons salt
½ to 4 teaspoons SAF or bread machine yeast
1½ to 2 cups total fruit and nuts

2-POUND LOAF

1⅓ to 2 cups total liquid
4 to 4½ cups flour
2 to 8 teaspoons gluten
0 to 10 tablespoons fat
0 to 6 tablespoons sweetener
½ to 3 teaspoons salt
1 to 5 teaspoons SAF or bread machine yeast
2 to 3 cups total fruit and nuts

CORNELL BREAD

T he late Dr. Clive McCay worked at Cornell University in the 1930s. He developed some of the first lowfat bread recipes; his goal was to make a perfect food for correcting the protein deficiency of his patients at State Hospitals of New York. Dr. McCay's breads were so popular and in demand from the general public that he developed recipes for commercial bakeries and, later, for home bakers. The secret ingredient was soy flour—just a small amount added to a bread recipe can boost the protein content of each slice by almost 20 percent.

Super soy foods are now routinely included as part of fiber-rich diets, and soy flours are available at Whole Foods supermarkets and natural foods stores, or you can get them by mail order from Bob's Red Mill or King Arthur Flour. The lignins and antioxidant enzymes prevalent in soy products help fight cancer. The phytoestrogens are thought to reduce the incidence of breast cancer, and saponins are touted as reducing elevated blood cholesterol. This bread is a delicious way to protect your health!

1 Place the ingredients in the pan according to the order in the manufacturer's instructions. Set crust on dark and program for the Whole Wheat cycle; press Start. (This recipe is not suitable for use with the Delay Timer.)

2 When the baking cycle ends, immediately remove the bread from the pan and place it on a rack. Let cool to room temperature before slicing.

1½-POUND LOAF	2-POUND LOAF
1⅛ cups water	1½ cups water
2 tablespoons canola oil	3 tablespoons canola oil
2 tablespoons honey	3 tablespoons honey
2 tablespoons dark brown sugar	3 tablespoons dark brown sugar
1 large egg	1 large egg
1½ cups whole wheat flour	2 cups whole wheat flour
1 cup plus 2 tablespoons bread flour	1½ cups bread flour
⅓ cup full-fat soy flour	½ cup full-fat soy flour
1½ tablespoons wheat germ	2 tablespoons wheat germ
¼ cup nonfat dry milk	⅓ cup nonfat dry milk
1½ tablespoons gluten	2 tablespoons gluten
1½ teaspoons salt	2 teaspoons salt
2½ teaspoons SAF yeast or 1 tablespoon bread machine yeast	1 tablespoon SAF yeast or 1 tablespoon plus ½ teaspoon bread machine yeast

MILLET AND POTATO LONG ROLLS

Makes 10 long rolls

1½- OR 2-POUND-LOAF MACHINES

1 cup whole wheat flour
½ cup raw whole millet
¼ cup sesame seeds
½ cup instant potato flakes
1 cup boiling water

1½ cups warm water
1 large egg plus 1 egg white (reserve yolk for glaze) or equivalent of a liquid egg substitute
2 tablespoons unsalted butter or margarine, cut into pieces

3½ cups bread flour
⅓ cup light brown sugar
1½ teaspoons salt

2½ teaspoons SAF yeast or 1 tablespoon bread machine yeast

3 tablespoons sesame seeds, for sprinkling before baking

I nstead of forming a loaf, this dough is meant for soft and thick grain-rich long rolls that are perfect for sandwiches, hot dogs and sausages, and grilled meats, such as flank steak. I like my rolls kind of large, but you can make them any size you like. Millet and potatoes are a naturally complementary taste combination. Keep bags of rolls in the freezer for up to 2 months, ready to be defrosted and thrown on the grill at a moment's notice. These are great if you have to bring something to a potluck. You'll be famous.

❶ Combine ½ cup of the whole wheat flour, the millet, and sesame seeds in the workbowl of a food processor. Grind to a coarse flour and set aside. Stir the potato flakes and the boiling water together in a small bowl until thick; cool for 5 minutes.

❷ Place all the ingredients in the pan according to the order in the manufacturer's instructions. Add the mashed potatoes on top of the wet ingredients and the sesame-millet flour and the remaining ½ cup whole wheat flour with the dry ingredients. Program for the Dough cycle; press Start.

❸ Line a large baking sheet with parchment paper. When the machine beeps at the end of the cycle, press Stop and unplug the machine. Turn the dough out onto the work surface and divide into 10 equal portions. Form the rolls by patting each portion into an 8-inch oval and rolling up from a long edge, like a mini-loaf of bread. Place rolls seam side down and at least 2 inches apart on the baking sheet. Flatten each with your palm to 3 inches wide. Cover loosely with plastic wrap and let rise at room temperature until puffy, about 45 minutes.

4 Twenty minutes before baking, preheat the oven to 375°F.

5 Beat the reserved egg yolk with a teaspoon of water in a small bowl. Brush the tops of the rolls with the glaze and sprinkle with the sesame seeds. Bake in the center of the oven until lightly brown and firm to the touch, about 18 to 23 minutes. Immediately remove the rolls from the baking sheet to a rack to cool. Slice the rolls with a serrated knife.

Bread Machine Baker's Hint: Storing Grains and Whole-Grain Flours

Store naturally oil-rich whole-grain flours in airtight plastic containers or resealable plastic bags in the refrigerator or freezer, as they tend to go rancid quickly at room temperature, and can absorb excess moisture from the air. Whole-grain flours can be stored for up to three months in the refrigerator, or for up to one year in the freezer. If you can, it is best to buy these flours from stores that refrigerate them. Degerminated cornmeal, oatmeal, soy flour, and whole grains like rice can be stored indefinitely in tightly closed plastic containers or glass jars in a cool, dry, room-temperature cupboard. Wild rice has a shelf life of seven to ten years. These items are usually sold in plastic bags or boxes, so when purchasing make sure the package is tightly sealed and check for a valid freshness date. Store brown rice in the refrigerator or freeze to prevent oxidation. Store stone-ground cornmeal in the refrigerator or freezer for as long as six to nine months. Brans should all be stored in the refrigerator, and can be kept six to eight months; raw and toasted wheat germ are best refrigerated and used within three to four months.

QUINOA BREAD

1½-POUND LOAF

½ cup water
½ cup buttermilk
½ cup firm-packed cooked
  quinoa (see cooking
  information page 183)
2 tablespoons sesame oil
2 tablespoons honey

3 cups bread flour
1 tablespoon gluten
1½ teaspoons salt

2 teaspoons SAF yeast
  or 2½ teaspoons bread
  machine yeast

2-POUND LOAF

⅔ cup water
⅔ cup buttermilk
¾ cup firm-packed cooked
  quinoa (see cooking
  information page 183)
3 tablespoons sesame oil
3 tablespoons honey

4 cups bread flour
1 tablespoon plus
  1 teaspoon gluten
2 teaspoons salt

2½ teaspoons SAF yeast
  or 1 tablespoon bread
  machine yeast

Q*uinoa is a grain indigenous to the Andes Mountains of South America. Introduced to this country in the early 1980s, some domestic quinoa is being grown in the mountainous regions of Colorado and New Mexico. It is a delicate grain, easy to digest, with a mild flavor that melds well with dried fruit and dried tomatoes. Be sure to use cold-pressed sesame oil here, not the toasted variety used in Asian cooking.*

1 Place all the ingredients in the pan according to the order in the manufacturer's instructions. Set crust on dark and program for the Basic cycle; press Start. (This recipe is not suitable for use with the Delay Timer.)

2 When the baking cycle ends, immediately remove the bread from the pan and place it on a rack. Let cool to room temperature before slicing.

🍲 Bread Machine Baker's Hint: Rolled Grains

Flaked grains, such as rolled oats and barley, brans, and wheat or quinoa flakes, are added raw to doughs to give a distinct nubby feel to a finished dough. Sometimes they are first softened by soaking so they will become more a part of the dough. There will be a gentle lumpy feel to the dough depending on how much of the cooked grain is added. Cornmeals and barley grits will cause a dough to feel gritty when you run your hand over its surface. If small raw grains are added, such as millet, quinoa, and teff, expect a gritty to pebbly quality. Be sure not to add too much flour; these doughs are meant to be a bit sticky.

TEFF HONEY BREAD

T*eff is known as the tiniest grain in the world. Wayne Carlson's Teff Company of Idaho is the only commercial company growing and marketing this grain in the United States. It is sold under the moniker of Maskal Teff. Carlson supplies natural foods stores through Bob's Red Mill and Ancient Harvest companies. He also grinds and packages teff flour for the Ethiopian community in America. You will get a wonderfully unique flavor with this loaf.*

1 Place all the ingredients in the pan according to the order in the manufacturer's instructions. Set crust on dark and program for the Basic cycle; press Start. (This recipe is not suitable for use with the Delay Timer.)

2 When the baking cycle ends, immediately remove the bread from the pan and place it on a rack. Let cool to room temperature before slicing.

1½-POUND LOAF

1⅛ cups water
2 tablespoons vegetable oil
2 tablespoons honey

2¼ cups bread flour
¾ cup ivory or dark teff flour
1 tablespoon plus
   1 teaspoon gluten
1½ teaspoons salt

2½ teaspoons SAF yeast
   or 1 tablespoon bread
   machine yeast

2-POUND LOAF

1½ cups water
3 tablespoons vegetable oil
3 tablespoons honey

3¼ cups bread flour
¾ cup ivory or dark teff flour
1 tablespoon plus
   2 teaspoons gluten
2 teaspoons salt

1 tablespoon SAF yeast
   or 1 tablespoon plus
   ½ teaspoon bread
   machine yeast

CHICKPEA FLOUR BREAD

C*hickpea flour, also called garbanzo flour, is known in Indian and Pakistani baking as* gram *or* besum, *and used for naan and chapatis. It is also used extensively in Greek baking, especially on Crete, where a bread called eptazymo is made from ground toasted chickpeas. Chickpea flour is not usually used in yeast breads in America, but one taste of this bread will change that. Chickpea flour is enticingly sweet, flavorful flour ground from lightly toasted green chickpeas. This bread is made in the manner of the Greek country bread, though a tad richer (I use evaporated goat's milk and scrape the "cream" off the top of the can), and is great spread with cream cheese or goat cheese and orange marmalade. This dough can be made into Paximadia (page 324).*

1 Place all the ingredients in the pan according to the order in the manufacturer's instructions. Set crust on light and program for the Basic cycle; press Start. (This recipe is not suitable for use with the Delay Timer.)

2 When the baking cycle ends, immediately remove the bread from the pan and place it on a rack. Let cool to room temperature before slicing.

1½-POUND LOAF

1⅛ cups evaporated milk or evaporated goat's milk
1 tablespoon olive oil
1 tablespoon honey

2½ cups bread flour
½ cup chickpea flour
1 tablespoon plus
  2 teaspoons gluten
1½ teaspoons salt
¼ teaspoon ground
  cinnamon
¼ teaspoon crushed hot
  pepper flakes

2½ teaspoons SAF yeast
  or 1 tablespoon bread
  machine yeast

2-POUND LOAF

1½ cups evaporated milk or evaporated goat's milk
1½ tablespoons olive oil
1½ tablespoons honey

3⅓ cups bread flour
⅔ cup chickpea flour
2 tablespoons gluten
2 teaspoons salt
⅓ teaspoon ground
  cinnamon
⅓ teaspoon crushed hot
  pepper flakes

1 tablespoon SAF yeast
  or 1 tablespoon plus
  ½ teaspoon bread
  machine yeast

BROWN RICE FLOUR BREAD

B*rown rice flour has its germ and bran left in after grinding. A staple in gluten-free breads, brown rice flour is also a flavorful addition to wheat breads. It has a beautiful silky texture and absorbs liquid slowly, making it an excellent flour to keep on hand for dusting loaves and pizza. This is a great sandwich bread.*

1 Place all the ingredients in the pan according to the order in the manufacturer's instructions. Set crust on dark and program for the Whole Wheat cycle; press Start. (This recipe may be made using the Delay Timer.)

2 When the baking cycle ends, immediately remove the bread from the pan and place it on a rack. Let cool to room temperature before slicing.

1½-POUND LOAF	2-POUND LOAF
1¼ cups water	1⅔ cups water
2 tablespoons olive oil	3 tablespoons olive oil
2 tablespoons honey	3 tablespoons honey
1¼ cups whole wheat flour	1¾ cups whole wheat flour
1 cup bread flour	1¼ cups bread flour
¾ cup brown rice flour	1 cup brown rice flour
1½ tablespoons nonfat dry milk	2 tablespoons nonfat dry milk
1½ tablespoons gluten	2 tablespoons gluten
1½ teaspoons salt	2 teaspoons salt
1 tablespoon SAF yeast or 1 tablespoon plus ½ teaspoon bread machine yeast	1 tablespoon plus 1 teaspoon SAF yeast or 1 tablespoon plus 1½ teaspoons bread machine yeast

Bread Machine Baker's Hint: Dough Enhancers

Bread machines seem to produce the best results with the addition of dough "enhancers" or "conditioners," which are simply ingredients that help the loaf rise high and even. Professional bakers have used these ingredients, like gluten, malt powder, ascorbic acid, and lecithin, for a long time, and bread machine recipes respond well to the extra punch. Commercial bread machine mixes contain dough conditioners to assure consistent results. Although this is new terminology for home bakers, it is good information to have in case your loaves are not turning out the way you want them to. As you have already seen, I call for some gluten in all my bread machine recipes to give the extra strength needed to keep a good rise during the warm rest period. You can read about gluten in the Orientation chapter in the section on essential bread ingredients (see page 13). I always have some malt powder on hand because it is so tasty. Williams-Sonoma, the King Arthur Baker's Catalogue, and other catalogs and retail stores offer Lora Brody's Bread Dough Enhancer, which is a combination of most of these dough-enhancing ingredients.

Malt Powder

Diastatic malt powder is sprouted barley that has been roasted, ground, and dried. It is a favorite of American, French, and English professional bakers as it helps break down the starch in flour, improves texture, and acts as a sugar in relation to the yeast. Add a scant ½ teaspoon per 1½-pound loaf—this is powerful stuff. Buy Premier Malt where brewing supplies are sold or mail order it from The Baker's

Catalogue. It is excellent in bagels, white bread, whole wheat bread, French bread, and nut breads.

Lecithin

Lecithin, a soybean oil emulsifier that contributes to more efficient mixing and is often used in professional bakeries, is excellent for creating lowfat and whole grain breads; it yields a softer, more conditioned texture that contributes to higher rising without any added fat. The addition of lecithin enhances gluten activity. Widely available in health food stores, it is high in nutrients and comes in granule or liquid form: both need to be refrigerated. If using the granules, substitute the same amount of lecithin for the oil or butter measurement. If using liquid lecithin, substitute it for half the oil or butter, as the liquid is more concentrated. I use the granules; they are much less messy.

Ascorbic Acid

Ascorbic acid, or vitamin C, is a volume enhancer. It strengthens weak flours by changing the pH, and the yeast loves it. Use 1 large pinch per 3 cups of flour. Buy ascorbic acid in bulk, or you can crush some vitamin C tablets or take it out of a capsule. Hodgson's Mill offers gluten with vitamin C added to it; it is available by mail order if it is not in your local supermarket. Never add ascorbic acid if a recipe has acid ingredients; it will be too acidic. This is a real professional bakery secret weapon.

Two tablespoons of vinegar or lemon juice, or acid ingredients such as buttermilk and yogurt, are often added to heavy whole grain doughs such as pumpernickel, and have the same effect as ascorbic acid.

WILD RICE BREAD

This bread has always been very popular in my baking classes. It is a real surprise; the wild rice and the coarse, dark rye flour make a dynamite taste duo.

❶ Heat the water to a boil in a medium saucepan. Add the rice. Cover and simmer over low heat for 30 to 45 minutes, until the rice is tender. Strain the remaining cooking liquid into a 2-cup measure and add enough extra water to equal the original amount in the pan (1⅛ cups for the 1½-pound loaf or 1½ cups for the 2-pound loaf). Set the liquid and rice aside separately to cool. You will have about ⅔ cup cooked rice for the 1½-pound loaf and 1 cup for the 2-pound loaf.

❷ Place the ingredients, except the rice, in the pan according to the order in the manufacturer's instructions. Set crust on dark and program for the Basic or Fruit and Nut cycle; press Start. (This recipe is not suitable for use with the Delay Timer.) When the machine beeps, or between Knead 1 and Knead 2, add the rice.

❸ When the baking cycle ends, immediately remove the bread from the pan and place it on a rack. Let cool to room temperature before slicing.

1½-POUND LOAF	2-POUND LOAF
1⅛ cups water	1½ cups water
⅓ cup raw wild rice	½ cup raw wild rice
2½ tablespoons walnut oil	3 tablespoons walnut oil
2 teaspoons light brown sugar	1 tablespoon light brown sugar
2¾ cups bread flour	3½ cups bread flour
⅓ cup pumpernickel rye flour	½ cup pumpernickel rye flour
1 tablespoon plus 1 teaspoon gluten	1 tablespoon plus 2 teaspoons gluten
1½ teaspoons salt	2 teaspoons salt
2 teaspoons SAF yeast or 2½ teaspoons bread machine yeast	2¼ teaspoons SAF yeast or 2¾ teaspoons bread machine yeast

Gluten-Free Breads

Gluten-free baking works beautifully in the bread machine. If you don't have an allergy, this type of baking may seem superfluous to you, and the breads probably unpalatable. But if you are gluten intolerant, the idea of a slice of bread with dinner or toast for breakfast is euphoria. The challenge of gluten-free baking is to make a dough that has some of the stretchy quality of a gluten dough, so that the loaf holds together and is light textured. Gluten occurs in wheat, rye, oats, barley, and other flours, so this type of baking depends on rice, tapioca, potato starch, corn, and buckwheat flours with bits of xanthan gum and guar gum added to lend elasticity.

You need to have a strong motor in your bread machine to make these breads, one that is capable of handling whole wheat doughs, because the gluten-free doughs are like thick, sticky batters. Be sure to scrape down the sides of the pan after five minutes of mixing. These recipes have a total of 3 cups of flour,

so they will make 1½-pound loaves (which can also be baked in 2-pound-loaf machines); larger loaves will not bake correctly in the machine and will rise over the rim of the pan. The bread is dense and moist, so keep it in the freezer or refrigerator instead of at room temperature. If you want to make a 1-pound sampler loaf, reduce the recipe proportions by one-third.

The first three recipes, developed in the Red Star Yeast and Betty Crocker test kitchens, are included here courtesy of Lisa Brugellis of Welbilt of America. The recipes are included with the company's Millennium bread machine models, all of which have a special Non-Gluten Bread cycle, which turns out bread in 58 minutes. If you don't have this special cycle, use the Quick Yeast Bread cycle on your machine. For more information on gluten-free baking, look up the *Gluten-Free Gourmet* books by Bette Hagman (Henry Holt Publishers).

Bread Machine Baker's Hint: Tips for Creating Great Gluten-Free Breads

- Using a whisk, mix together the dry ingredients in a mixing bowl until evenly combined. Then add them to the bread pan.

- If you have a Welbilt bread machine be sure to add an extra 2 tablespoons of liquid to every recipe.

- Fresh eggs can be used interchangeably with commercial egg substitutes.

- Xanthan gum and guar gum can be used interchangeably.

- Cider vinegar, added with the wet ingredients, acts as a preservative in the baked loaf.

- Do not use the Delay Timer on these gluten-free

breads, as they all contain eggs for extra leavening.

- The consistency of your dough ball will be more like a very moist batter than a firm dough ball.

- Gluten-free loaves tend to be flat across the top, rather than domed as wheat breads are. This is okay.

- Cool breads completely before slicing with a serrated knife so that they hold together properly.

- Sourdough lovers, make your favorite starter using rice flour instead of wheat flour. The rice flour ferments nicely, and you can make a myriad of sourdough breads with it.

GLUTEN-FREE CINNAMON RAISIN BREAD

L isa Brugellis of Welbilt, who worked at Gourmet magazine for a few years, says this gluten-free bread is her first choice, delightful even for those who are accustomed to only wheat breads.

1 Place the ingredients, except the raisins, in the pan according to the order in the manufacturer's instructions. Set crust on medium and program for the Non-Gluten or Quick Yeast Bread cycle; press Start. (This recipe is not suitable for use with the Delay Timer.) Set a kitchen timer for 5 minutes. When the timer rings, open the lid and add the raisins. Close the lid.

2 When the baking cycle ends, immediately remove *the pan* from the machine and place it on a rack. Let cool for 10 minutes before removing the loaf from the pan. Let the loaf cool to room temperature before slicing.

1½- OR 2-POUND-LOAF MACHINES

1¼ cups water
1 teaspoon apple cider vinegar or rice vinegar
3 tablespoons vegetable or nut oil
3 large eggs, broken into a measuring cup to equal ¾ cup (add water if needed)

1¾ cups white rice flour
1⅛ cups brown rice flour
½ cup dry buttermilk powder or nonfat dry milk
3 tablespoons sugar or powdered fructose
2 teaspoons xanthan gum
1½ teaspoons ground cinnamon
1½ teaspoons salt

2¼ teaspoons SAF yeast or 2¾ teaspoons bread machine yeast

¾ cup golden raisins or dried cranberries

The Baker's Glossary of Essential Flours and Ingredients for Gluten-Free Yeast Breads

The following flours and ingredients appear in different recipes for gluten-free breads. You can also substitute small amounts of buckwheat flour, barley flour, corn flour, cornstarch, lentil flour, chickpea flour, potato flour, oat flour, and soy flour, but don't use just one of these products when making a loaf. If any of the products are difficult to find, they are available from mail-order sources. See page 613.

Arrowroot

Like cornstarch, arrowroot powder can be used in place of tapioca flour to strengthen the structure in gluten-free bread machine breads.

Bean Flours

Chickpea (garbanzo), lentil, and split pea flours are more common in Indian and Middle Eastern cuisines, but are nice flavor additions in gluten-free yeast breads.

Cornmeal Products

Yellow and white cornmeal are gluten-free grains and used in small amounts in bread machine yeast breads. Corn flour, which is finely ground, is also excellent. Cornstarch, a refined product ground from white corn, is used in combination with other flours in yeast baking, or used as a thickener.

Guar Gum

Guar gum powder, a natural gel, is added for extra fiber, which is lacking in flours other than wheat. It is ground from the seeds of the guar gum plant.

Nut Flours

Nut flours are high in natural fats and protein. They can be used exclusively in quick breads in place of wheat flour. Beautiful nut flours such as almond, filbert, pistachio, and pecan, are superb in small proportions in yeast breads, and are available by mail order from The California Press. You can also use chestnut flour, which is silky and sweet.

Potato Starch Flour

Potato starch flour is a mild, very white, fine flour that combines well with the other gluten-free flours in yeast breads. It is *not* the same as potato flour, which is heavier. Look for it in the kosher section of the supermarket, where it will be labeled potato starch.

Rice Flours

Ground from polished white rice, white rice flour is a basic flour in gluten-free bread machine baking. It has a mild flavor and combines thoroughly with other flours. Use a fine grind of white rice flour (it comes in fine, medium, and coarse). Brown rice flour is higher in fiber and nutrition than white rice flour. Because it has the bran, it should be kept in the refrigerator or freezer. Sweet rice flour is ground from glutenous rice and is used as a thickening agent in sauces, but not in bread. It is labeled Mochiko Sweet Rice Flour in Asian markets and supermarkets; do not confuse it with regular white rice flour. Rice bran is extracted from brown rice and can be used in place of wheat bran in all types of baking.

Tapioca Flour

Tapioca flour, or tapioca starch, is ground from the cassava root, known as manioc in the tropics. It was made into breads on the Caribbean Islands when Columbus landed. It has resurfaced with the growing popularity of gluten-free baking, as it adds a structure likened to gluten in breads. It is smooth and pure white. It congeals as it cools, making a chewy bread. It is used in combination with white rice flour, soy flour, and potato starch flour.

White Spelt Flour

Many bakers who have to avoid wheat or rye use organic white spelt flour, which is sifted free of bran and germ but is not bleached, bromated, or enriched. The fluffy breads have an excellent texture. Some people with gluten allergies can also tolerate kamut since it has a gluten structure different than regular wheat.

Xanthan Gum

A natural carbohydrate powder ground from the dried cell wall of a laboratory-grown microorganism, this is used to bind and substitute for the bulk and stretchy nature of gluten in wheat breads so that the yeast has a medium to contain it. Without xanthan gum, you will have a flat bread with no structure.

GLUTEN-FREE MOCK LIGHT RYE

S ince rye flour has some gluten in it, it is off limits for those with celiac disease. Here is a bread with all the flavors usually associated with rye, and it is delightful.

1 Place all the ingredients in the pan according to the order in the manufacturer's instructions. Set crust on dark and program for the Non-Gluten or Quick Yeast Bread cycle; press Start. (This recipe is not suitable for use with the Delay Timer.)

2 When the baking cycle ends, immediately remove *the pan* from the machine and place it on a rack. Let cool for 10 minutes before removing the loaf from the pan. Let the loaf cool to room temperature before slicing.

1½- OR 2-POUND-LOAF MACHINES

1¼ cups water
3 tablespoons dark molasses
1 teaspoon apple cider or rice vinegar
¼ cup vegetable or canola oil
3 large eggs, broken into a measuring cup to equal ¾ cup (add water if needed)

2¼ cups white rice flour
⅞ cup brown rice flour
½ cup nonfat dry milk
¼ cup dark brown sugar
1 tablespoon xanthan gum
1 tablespoon plus 1 teaspoon caraway seeds
Grated zest of 1 large orange or 2 teaspoons dried orange peel
1½ teaspoons salt

2¼ teaspoons SAF yeast or 2¾ teaspoons bread machine yeast

GLUTEN-FREE RICOTTA POTATO BREAD

1⅓ cups water
¾ cup ricotta cheese
1 teaspoon apple cider vinegar or rice vinegar
3 tablespoons vegetable or canola oil
3 large eggs, broken into a measuring cup to equal ¾ cup (add water if needed)

2¼ cups white rice flour
½ cup instant potato flakes
⅓ cup potato starch flour
⅓ cup tapioca flour
½ cup dry buttermilk powder or nonfat dry milk
3 tablespoons sugar or powdered fructose
2 teaspoons xanthan gum
1½ teaspoons salt
¾ teaspoon baking soda

2¼ teaspoons SAF yeast or 2¾ teaspoons bread machine yeast

P*otato starch flour makes for an exceptionally nice bread.*

❶ Place all the ingredients in the pan according to the order in the manufacturer's instructions. Set crust on medium and program for the Non-Gluten or Quick Yeast Bread cycle; press Start. (This recipe is not suitable for use with the Delay Timer.)

❷ When the baking cycle ends, immediately remove *the pan* from the machine and place it on a rack. Let cool for 10 minutes before removing the loaf from the pan. Let the loaf cool to room temperature before slicing.

GLUTEN-FREE BUTTERMILK WHITE BREAD

T*his bread will give the kitchen that wonderful smell of baking bread, craved by those for whom gluten is off limits. As soon as it cools, slice it up and toast it fresh.*

1 Place all the ingredients in the pan according to the order in the manufacturer's instructions. Set crust on medium and program for the Non-Gluten or Quick Yeast Bread cycle; press Start. (This recipe is not suitable for use with the Delay Timer.)

2 When the baking cycle ends, immediately remove *the pan* from the machine and place it on a rack. Let cool for 10 minutes before removing the loaf from the pan. Let the loaf cool to room temperature before slicing.

1½- OR 2-POUND-LOAF MACHINES

1 cup buttermilk
½ cup water
1 teaspoon apple cider vinegar or rice vinegar
4 tablespoons butter or margarine, cut into pieces
4 large egg whites, beaten until foamy

1 cup white rice flour
1 cup brown rice flour
¾ cup potato starch flour
¼ cup tapioca flour
3 tablespoons light or dark brown sugar
1 tablespoon plus ½ teaspoon xanthan gum
1½ teaspoons salt

1 tablespoon plus 1 teaspoon SAF yeast or 1 tablespoon plus ½ teaspoon machine yeast

GLUTEN-FREE CHICKPEA-, RICE-, AND TAPIOCA-FLOUR BREAD

1¼ cups water
1 teaspoon apple cider vinegar or rice vinegar
3 tablespoons maple syrup
3 tablespoons olive oil
3 large eggs, broken into a measuring cup to equal ¾ cup (add water if needed)

1 cup chickpea flour
1 cup brown rice flour
½ cup cornstarch
½ cup tapioca flour
½ cup nonfat dry milk
2 tablespoons light brown sugar
1 tablespoon plus 1 teaspoon xanthan gum
1½ teaspoons salt

2¼ teaspoons SAF yeast or 2¾ teaspoons bread machine yeast

One of my favorite sources for flour is Bob's Red Mill in Oregon. This recipe is adapted from Bob's, using the exceptional flavor of chickpea (garbanzo) flour and their excellent tapioca flour.

1 Place all the ingredients in the pan according to the order in the manufacturer's instructions. Set crust on dark and program for the Non-Gluten or Quick Yeast Bread cycle; press Start. (This recipe is not suitable for use with the Delay Timer.)

2 When the baking cycle ends, immediately remove *the pan* from the machine and place it on a rack. Let cool for 10 minutes before removing the loaf from the pan. Let the loaf cool to room temperature before slicing.

LOW-GLUTEN WHITE SPELT BREAD

W hite spelt flour, also known as gourmet wheat flour, contains significantly lower levels of gluten and is therefore more easily digestible for those who are sensitive to ordinary wheat flour. White spelt flour is often used as the base for many non-wheat breads, such as raisin bread, potato bread, and herb bread, and you can substitute white spelt flour for bread flour in other recipes. Because spelt is technically not gluten-free, it should not be consumed by anyone diagnosed with celiac disease. This is a good basic bread even if you are not on a special diet.

❶ Place all the ingredients in the pan according to the order in the manufacturer's instructions. Set crust on medium and program for the Basic cycle; press Start. (This recipe is not suitable for use with the Delay Timer.) Test the dough ball, and add 1 to 2 teaspoons spelt flour or water as needed, but leave the dough moist and slightly tacky.

❷ When the baking cycle ends, immediately remove *the pan* from the machine and place it on a rack. Let cool for 10 minutes before removing the loaf from the pan. Let the loaf cool to room temperature before slicing.

1½- OR 2-POUND-LOAF MACHINES

1 cup water
¼ cup apple juice
  concentrate, thawed
1½ tablespoons canola oil
  or soft butter

3 cups white spelt flour
¼ cup oat bran or cornmeal
1 tablespoon full-fat soy
  flour
1¼ teaspoons salt

2½ teaspoons SAF yeast
  or 1 tablespoon bread
  machine yeast

GLUTEN-FREE ALMOND AND DRIED FRUIT HOLIDAY BREAD

For the dough:

1½ cups water
2 teaspoons almond extract
1 teaspoon apple cider vinegar or rice vinegar
3 large eggs, broken into a measuring cup to equal ¾ cup (add water if needed)

2 cups white rice flour
½ cup potato starch flour
½ cup tapioca flour or arrowroot
½ cup dry buttermilk powder or nonfat dry milk
⅓ cup sugar or 3 tablespoons powdered fructose
1 tablespoon xanthan gum
1½ teaspoons ground cardamom
½ teaspoon ground mace or nutmeg
Grated zest of 1 lemon or 1 teaspoon dried lemon peel
1½ teaspoons salt

2½ teaspoons SAF yeast or 1 tablespoon bread machine yeast

½ cup mixed dried fruit bits
2 tablespoons currants
⅓ cup toasted slivered almonds

For the lemon glaze:

1 cup sifted confectioners' sugar
1 tablespoon melted butter or margarine
2 to 3 tablespoons fresh lemon juice, heated

E*ven if you can't eat wheat, there is no reason why you can't have a sweet bread. This also makes nice French toast.*

1 To make the dough, place the ingredients, except the raisins, in the pan according to the order in the manufacturer's instructions. Set crust on medium and program for the Non-Gluten or Quick Yeast Bread cycle; press Start. (This recipe is not suitable for use with the Delay Timer.) Set a kitchen timer for 5 minutes. When the timer rings, open the lid and add the dried fruit and almonds. Close the lid.

2 When the baking cycle ends, immediately remove *the pan* from the machine and place it on a rack. Let cool for 10 minutes before removing the loaf from the pan. Place it on a rack with a plate underneath.

3 To make the lemon glaze, combine the confectioners' sugar, butter, and lemon juice in a small bowl. Immediately pour over the top of the loaf, letting it dribble down the sides. Let cool to room temperature before slicing.

MULTIGRAIN BREADS

All around the world, grains of every type are used to make bread. There are the cereal grains—grains that are part of the grass family—the most common of which are wheat, rice, maize, and barley. There are also many regionally grown grains used in the staple foods of that area, such as sorghum, teff, and millets in West Africa, ragi in India, and African rice, a cousin of Asian rice. There are wild cereals that are considered a delicacy, such as wild teff, drinn, panic grass, and jungle rice.

Grains all have the same basic yet sophisticated structure. Each grain is a tiny dry fruit that contains a single seed capable of reproducing itself. An inedible, hard outer shell called the hull protects the seed. The seed is surrounded by a layer of starchy carbohydrates designed to feed a developing embryo. The embryo, or germ, contains a concentration of micronutrients, fat, and proteins. It is rich in vitamins E, A, and B-complex, calcium, and iron.

Mixed grain combinations and cereal breads are very popular in America; some bakers would never consider making any other kind of bread. In addition to all the grains you can individually add to a bread, commercial breakfast cereal blends can also be used, such as Roman Meal, Cream of Rye, Wheatena, Cream of Wheat (farina), Quaker multigrain cereal, Muesli, and six-, eight-, nine-, and ten-grain blends that are varying combinations of wheat, rye, barley, triticale, corn, oats, flax, millet, brown rice, wheat germ, wheat bran, and soy grits in varying proportions.

The following recipes call for all sorts of flours and grains. The breads they create are packed with protein and nutrition. When making whole-grain breads, you will always end up with a more substantial, dense loaf than a white flour loaf. Since these doughs are heavy, make sure they are mixing thoroughly in the bread pan. Store these breads in the refrigerator, and to serve, slice with a serrated or electric knife.

THREE-GRAIN BREAD

*T*his is my version of the rye and Indian meal bread that was a favorite in the first thirteen colonies, often paired fresh with rose geranium–apple jelly, or served day-old in slices floating in a thick soup. Every cookbook of the era has a recipe for this bread, and it is still as good today. I have substituted oil for the bacon fat.

1 Place all the ingredients in the pan according to the order in the manufacturer's instructions. Set crust on medium and program for the Whole Wheat cycle; press Start. (This recipe is not suitable for use with the Delay Timer.)

2 When the baking cycle ends, immediately remove the bread from the pan and place it on a rack. Let cool to room temperature before slicing.

1½-POUND LOAF	2-POUND LOAF
1⅛ cups fat-free milk	1½ cups fat-free milk
2 tablespoons sunflower seed oil or light olive oil	3 tablespoons sunflower seed oil or light olive oil
2 tablespoons molasses	3 tablespoons molasses
1¾ cups bread flour	2¼ cups bread flour
1 cup whole wheat flour	1¼ cups whole wheat flour
¼ cup dark rye flour	⅓ cup dark rye flour
2 tablespoons yellow cornmeal or polenta	3 tablespoons yellow cornmeal or polenta
1 tablespoon plus 1 teaspoon gluten	1 tablespoon plus 2 teaspoons gluten
1 teaspoon salt	1½ teaspoons salt
2 teaspoons SAF yeast or 2½ teaspoons bread machine yeast	2½ teaspoons SAF yeast or 1 tablespoon bread machine yeast

WHOLE-GRAIN DAILY BREAD

T his is an all-purpose recipe for use with cooked (and cooled) whole grains of any type, whether leftover rice, quinoa, or cornmeal. (See pages 182 to 183 for information on cooking whole grains.) This means the loaf can be different every time you make it. It has the most heavenly aroma while baking, and is quite light in texture.

1 Place all the ingredients in the pan according to the order in the manufacturer's instructions. Set crust on dark and program for the Basic cycle; press Start. (This recipe is not suitable for use with the Delay Timer.) Reach in and touch the dough with your fingers, being careful to avoid the rotating blade. The dough ball will be quite soft. Add another tablespoon of flour if it is too sticky around the blade.

2 When the baking cycle ends, immediately remove the bread from the pan and place it on a rack. Let cool to room temperature before slicing.

1½-POUND LOAF	2-POUND LOAF
1 cup buttermilk	1⅓ cups buttermilk
¾ cup cooked whole grain of choice, firmly packed	1 cup cooked whole grain of choice, firmly packed
2 tablespoons canola oil	3 tablespoons canola oil
2 tablespoons honey	3 tablespoons honey
2½ cups bread flour	3⅓ cups bread flour
½ cup whole wheat flour	⅔ cup whole wheat flour
¼ cup rolled oats	⅓ cup rolled oats
1 tablespoon gluten	1 tablespoon plus 1 teaspoon gluten
1½ teaspoons salt	2 teaspoons salt
2 teaspoons SAF yeast or 2½ teaspoons bread machine yeast	2½ teaspoons SAF yeast or 1 tablespoon bread machine yeast

Bread Machine Baker's Hint: Cooking Whole Grains for Use in Baking

The bread machine is the perfect mixing medium for adding whole grains to doughs for flavor and texture. Most grains are precooked or softened in water before they are added to bread dough. When considering how much cooked grain you will need, bear in mind that you will probably want to eat some of the grain just after cooking and still have enough left to use in a bread recipe, once it has chilled. You will use less water to cook a dinner grain, such as rice, than you will to cook a breakfast porridge, such as oatmeal or polenta. Coarser grains will be firmer and their shapes more distinct in a baked bread than more finely ground grains, which distribute more evenly into the texture of the bread. If you will be eating the cooked grain on its own and prefer it salted, add ¼ to ½ teaspoon sea salt (or to taste) per cup of uncooked grain *after* cooking. This is important because grains will not absorb enough water during cooking if salt is present. I do not add salt to grains to be used in baking, as the recipe will also call for salt.

Meals and grits (and small grains like millet) need only to be soaked in boiling water before being added to a bread recipe to provide taste and texture. Rolled grains can be soaked, which softens them and allows them to be incorporated into the dough, or they can be added to the dough dry so that they remain distinct in the finished loaf. Whole grains can be soaked overnight in hot water (a wide-mouth thermos works well for this) for a chewy addition. If you are cooking a grain and have extra water left over after cooking, use the grain water as part of your recipe's liquid measure. The food processor is an excellent method for grinding softer whole grains (such as rice, millet, and rolled oats) into a coarse flour, and for grinding soaked grains (such as buckwheat groats and amaranth).

When adding a steamed grain or porridge to a bread recipe that does not already call for it, reduce the total liquid in the recipe by ⅔ cup for each cup of cooked grain added.

Stove-Top Cooking Directions

Rinse the grain in a wire strainer under cool water. Bring the proper amount of water to a rolling boil. Add the raw or toasted grain to the boiling water, and bring it back to a rolling boil. Immediately reduce the heat to low, cover, and simmer until all the water is absorbed and the grain is fluffy and tender to the bite. Remove from heat and let the grain rest for 5 to 15 minutes, covered, before using.

Microwave Cooking Directions

Reduce the amount of water given in the chart by ¼ cup. Place the water in a 2-quart microwave-safe casserole. Cook on high power until boiling, 3 to 4 minutes. Stir in the grain and partially cover with plastic wrap. Cook for the same amount of time as for stove-top cooking, or until the water has been absorbed. Let stand for 5 minutes before fluffing with a fork.

No-Cook Preparation

Soaking is a good method for softening cracked grains—such as grits, couscous, and bulgur—that will be added to a dough. Place the grain in a bowl and stir in an equal amount of boiling water. Cover with plastic wrap and let stand for 15 to 30 minutes, or until softened.

Dry-Toasting Directions

Toasting grains can improve their texture and flavor. The grain begins to open during toasting, which decreases the cooking time. To toast grain, place it in a dry skillet or wok over medium heat. Cook, stirring constantly with a wooden spoon, until the grain is slightly golden and has a toasted aroma, 2 to 4 minutes, depending on the size of the grain.

Whole Grain Cooking Times

Grain	Water	Cooking Time	Yield
Quantities based on 1 cup uncooked grain.			
Amaranth*	1½ cups	20 minutes	2 cups
Pearl barley	2 cups	45 minutes	3 cups
Hull-less barley	2 cups	45 minutes	3 cups
Bulgur wheat	2 cups	15 minutes	2½ cups
Cornmeal*	3 to 4 cups	25 minutes	4 cups
Kasha*	2 cups	12 minutes	3½ cups
Unroasted buckwheat groats	2 cups	12 minutes	3½ cups
Millet (Let rest 1 hour after cooking for easiest handling.)	2 cups	30 minutes	2½ cups
Oat groats	2 cups	60 minutes	2½ cups
Rolled oats	2¼ cups	8 minutes	1½ cups
Quinoa**	2 cups	20 minutes	3½ cups
Rice (long-grain white)	2 cups	20 minutes	3 cups
Rice (short-grain white)	2 cups	20 minutes	3 cups
Rice (long-grain brown)*	2 cups	40 minutes	3 cups
Rice (short-grain brown)*	2 cups	60 minutes	3 cups
Rye berries	2½ cups	2 hours	3 cups
Spelt berries	3 cups	40 minutes	3 cups
Teff	3 cups	20 minutes	3 cups
Triticale berries	2¼ cups	1 hour	2½ cups
Wheat berries	3 cups	1 hour	3 cups
Wild rice (paddy-cultivated)	2½ cups	55 minutes	3¾ cups
Wild rice (hand-harvested) (Drain off any excess liquid.)	3 cups	30 minutes	3¾ cups

*Grains that are improved in texture and flavor by being toasted before they are steamed, which opens the grain kernel and decreases cooking time.

**Must be rinsed well before cooking to remove the bitter outer coating that keeps it from being devoured by birds in the fields. Place the whole grain in a deep bowl. Fill with cold water to cover. Swirl with your fingers; it will foam. Drain through a fine mesh strainer and place under cold running water. Rinse until the suds disappear.

HONEY WHEAT BERRY BREAD

W*heat berry bread is a standard in every whole grain baker's repertoire. Cook the wheat berries with light or dark brown sugar. This is a chewy, dark bread that is a slow riser.*

❶ Combine the wheat berries, sugar, and 1⅓ cups water in a saucepan. Bring to a boil. Reduce the heat to a simmer and partially cover. Simmer for 1 hour, until firm-chewy and slightly tender. Remove the mixture from the heat and let stand until room temperature, about 4 hours. You will have about 1⅓ cups cooked wheat berries.

1½-POUND LOAF	2-POUND LOAF
¾ cup wheat berries 3 tablespoons light or dark brown sugar 1⅓ cups water	¾ cup wheat berries 3 tablespoons light or dark brown sugar 1⅓ cups water
1 cup water ⅔ cup of the cooked and cooled wheat berries 2 tablespoons butter or margarine, cut into pieces 3 tablespoons honey	1¼ cups water 1 cup of the cooked and cooled wheat berries 3 tablespoons butter or margarine, cut into pieces ¼ cup honey
1½ cups bread flour 1½ cups whole wheat flour 1½ tablespoons gluten 1½ teaspoons salt	2 cups bread flour 2 cups whole wheat flour 2 tablespoons gluten 2 teaspoons salt
2½ teaspoons SAF yeast or 1 tablespoon bread machine yeast	1 tablespoon SAF yeast or 1 tablespoon plus ½ teaspoon bread machine yeast

❷ Place all the ingredients in the pan according to the order in the manufacturer's instructions. (Store any extra cooked wheat berries in a covered container in the refrigerator up to 3 days or freeze them.) Set crust on dark and program for the Basic cycle; press Start. (This recipe may be made using the Delay Timer.) The dough ball will be quite firm and nubby. Do not add any more liquid. This dough is a slow riser.

❸ When the baking cycle ends, immediately remove the bread from the pan and place it on a rack. Let cool to room temperature before slicing.

Bread Machine Baker's Hint: Homegrown Grain Sprouts

Makes 2 cups

Use this method for sprouting rye berries, brown rice, triticale berries, or amaranth, as well as wheat berries. For use in bread, chop or coarsely grind the sprouts in a food grinder, in a food processor using the steel blade, or with a knife. Do not overprocess; you want the sprouts to be chunky.

½ cup raw wheat berries

1 Place the whole grains in a bowl and cover with tepid water by a full inch to allow for swelling. Let stand for 6 to 8 hours, or overnight, at room temperature. The next morning, drain off the water and rinse with fresh water.

2 Divide the soaked grains between two quart jars. Cover the tops of the jars with cheesecloth or nylon net secured with a rubber band or canning lid screw-top rim band to allow for circulation. Place the jars on their sides in a warm dark place, such as a cupboard. Rinse and drain the sprouts with tepid water poured through the cheesecloth twice a day for two to three days. The berries will sprout and show little shoots. The sprout can be a tiny one just peeking out, or up to the same length as the grain; brown rice can take two days longer. Leave the jars on the counter exposed to some light if you want the sprouts to turn a bit green. Refrigerate sprouts in a plastic bag for up to 3 days.

SPROUTED WHEAT BERRY BREAD

W hole-grain bread enthusiasts always ask for this recipe. In the 1960s, when I first began baking bread, it was commonplace to find a jar of some type of sprouts on the kitchen counter when I would visit friends. You can buy sprouts in the produce section of your supermarket or health food store, or you can grow your own, which takes about three days. Note that the wheat berries are added halfway through the Knead 2 part of the cycle here, to prevent them from becoming overprocessed.

❶ Place the ingredients, except the wheat berries, in the pan according to the order in the manufacturer's instructions. Set crust on dark and program for the Basic or Whole Wheat cycle; press Start. (This recipe is not suitable for use with the Delay Timer.) Set a kitchen timer for 12 minutes. When the timer rings, open the lid and sprinkle in the wheat berries around the sides of the dough ball while the machine is running, being careful to avoid the rotating blade. Close the lid. The wheat berries will be slowly incorporated.

❷ When the baking cycle ends, immediately remove the bread from the pan and place it on a rack. Let cool to room temperature before slicing.

1½-POUND LOAF
1⅛ cups buttermilk
2 tablespoons canola oil
2 tablespoons honey
2 cups bread flour
1¼ cups graham or whole wheat flour
1½ tablespoons gluten
1½ teaspoons salt
1 tablespoon SAF yeast or 1 tablespoon plus ½ teaspoons bread machine yeast
1 cup chopped sprouted wheat berries (see page 185)

2-POUND LOAF
1½ cups buttermilk
3 tablespoons canola oil
3 tablespoons honey
2¾ cups bread flour
1½ cups graham or whole wheat flour
2 tablespoons gluten
2 teaspoons salt
1 tablespoon plus 1 teaspoon SAF yeast or 1 tablespoon plus 1½ teaspoons bread machine yeast
1¼ cups chopped sprouted wheat berries (see page 185)

GRAHAM INDIAN BREAD

T his is a variation of one of the most famous colonial American breads, which always combine coarsely ground whole wheat and cornmeal. It was made with flour fresh from the local mill. Search out the graham flour; it has a much more assertive taste than regular whole wheat flour, and it makes all the difference. This is one of my favorite cornmeal breads; it makes great toast and sandwiches.

1 Place all the ingredients in the pan according to the order in the manufacturer's instructions. Set crust on medium and program for the Whole Wheat cycle; press Start. (This recipe is not suitable for use with the Delay Timer.)

2 When the baking cycle ends, immediately remove the bread from the pan and place it on a rack. Let cool to room temperature before slicing.

1½-POUND LOAF

1 cup buttermilk
¼ cup water
2 tablespoons unsalted
   butter, cut into pieces

1½ cups bread flour
1 cup graham flour
½ cup yellow cornmeal
3 tablespoons sugar
1 tablespoon gluten
1¼ teaspoons salt

2 teaspoons SAF yeast
   or 2½ teaspoons bread
   machine yeast

2-POUND LOAF

1⅓ cups buttermilk
⅓ cup water
3 tablespoons unsalted
   butter, cut into pieces

2 cups bread flour
1¼ cups graham flour
¾ cup yellow cornmeal
¼ cup sugar
1 tablespoon plus
   1 teaspoon gluten
1¾ teaspoons salt

2½ teaspoons SAF yeast
   or 1 tablespoon bread
   machine yeast

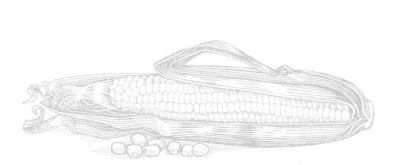

SENNEBEC HILL BREAD

T his bread, dense and nutty with six different grains that you mix yourself, is adapted from a recipe by the wonderful food writer Bernard Clayton, Jr. His treatises on breadmaking, two volumes of the Complete Book of Breads and the Breads of France *(both from Simon & Schuster, 1973 and 1978) are classics. This is also a favorite bread of my friend, the food writer Jacquie McMahan, a great gourmand. This is a wonderful bread.*

1 Place all the ingredients in the pan according to the order in the manufacturer's instructions. Set crust on dark and program for the Whole Wheat cycle; press Start. (This recipe is not suitable for use with the Delay Timer.)

2 When the baking cycle ends, immediately remove the bread from the pan and place it on a rack. Let cool to room temperature before slicing.

1½-POUND LOAF	2-POUND LOAF
1¼ cups water	1⅔ cups water
3 tablespoons canola oil	¼ cup canola oil
2 tablespoons molasses	3 tablespoons molasses
2 large egg yolks	3 large egg yolks
1½ cups bread flour	2¼ cups bread flour
¾ cup whole wheat flour	1 cup whole wheat flour
½ cup medium or dark rye flour	⅓ cup medium or dark rye flour
3 tablespoons rolled oats	3½ tablespoons rolled oats
3 tablespoons yellow cornmeal	3½ tablespoons yellow cornmeal
3 tablespoons toasted wheat germ	3½ tablespoons toasted wheat germ
½ cup nonfat dry milk	⅓ cup nonfat dry milk
1½ tablespoons gluten	2 tablespoons gluten
1½ teaspoons salt	2 teaspoons salt
2½ teaspoons SAF yeast or 1 tablespoon bread machine yeast	1 tablespoon SAF yeast or 1 tablespoon plus ½ teaspoon bread machine yeast

STONEHENGE BREAD

This combination of nubby whole grains and flours reminds me of an old-fashioned peasant loaf, such as a pain méteil, *in which some wheat flour was used to lighten up the heavy all-rye breads in the cold Northern European countries. Use the finely ground imported instant polenta that comes already mixed with buckwheat flour, if you can find it. Bake this bread for the summer solstice.*

1 Place the millet, bulgur wheat, polenta, boiling water, honey, and butter in a bowl. Let soak for 15 minutes to soften the grains, melt the butter, and cool until warm.

2 Place the ingredients in the pan according to the order in the manufacturer's instructions, adding the grains and their soaking liquid as the liquid ingredients. Set crust on dark and program for the Basic or Whole Wheat cycle; press Start. (This recipe is not suitable for use with the Delay Timer.)

3 When the baking cycle ends, immediately remove the bread from the pan and place it on a rack. Let cool to room temperature before slicing.

1½-POUND LOAF	2-POUND LOAF
3 tablespoons whole millet	¼ cup whole millet
¼ cup bulgur wheat	⅓ cup bulgur wheat
3 tablespoons polenta	¼ cup polenta
1¼ cups boiling water	1½ cups boiling water
3 tablespoons honey	¼ cup honey
3 tablespoons unsalted butter, cut into pieces	4 tablespoons unsalted butter, cut into pieces
2 cups bread flour	2⅔ cups bread flour
½ cup whole wheat flour	⅔ cup whole wheat flour
¼ cup medium rye flour	⅓ cup medium rye flour
¼ cup rolled oats	⅓ cup rolled oats
2 tablespoons bran	3 tablespoons bran
1½ tablespoons gluten	2 tablespoons gluten
1½ teaspoons salt	2 teaspoons salt
1 tablespoon SAF yeast or 1 tablespoon plus ½ teaspoon bread machine yeast	1 tablespoon plus 1 teaspoon SAF yeast or 1 tablespoon plus 1½ teaspoons bread machine yeast

NINE-GRAIN HONEY BREAD

1½-POUND LOAF

1¼ cups boiling water
½ cup 9-grain cereal
3 tablespoons honey
3 tablespoons unsalted
  butter, cut into pieces

1⅔ cups bread flour
1 cup whole wheat flour
⅓ cup dry buttermilk
  powder
1½ tablespoons gluten
1¼ teaspoons salt

2½ teaspoons SAF yeast
  or 1 tablespoon bread
  machine yeast

2-POUND LOAF

1¾ cups boiling water
⅔ cup 9-grain cereal
¼ cup honey
4 tablespoons unsalted
  butter, cut into pieces

2 cups bread flour
1⅓ cups whole wheat flour
⅔ cup dry buttermilk
  powder
2 tablespoons gluten
1½ teaspoons salt

1 tablespoon SAF yeast
  or 1 tablespoon plus
  ½ teaspoon bread
  machine yeast

T*he nine-grain cereal called for in this recipe contains cracked wheat, triticale, oats, rye, barley, corn, millet, soy, brown rice, and flax seed, giving you a lot of grain nutrients in a compact package. Dry buttermilk powder, also called for here, should be a baking staple on your pantry shelf. It gives the rich flavor of buttermilk while avoiding calories and fat. Reconstituted dry buttermilk powder has less than 1 gram of fat per cup, compared to 8 grams for fresh whole buttermilk and 2.3 grams for lowfat buttermilk.*

1 Pour the boiling water over the cracked grain cereal in a bowl. Add the honey and butter. Let stand for 1 hour to soften the grains.

2 Place the ingredients in the pan according to the order in the manufacturer's instructions, adding the cereal and its soaking liquid as the liquid ingredients. Set crust on dark and program for the Basic or Whole Wheat cycle; press Start. (This recipe may be made using the Delay Timer.)

3 When the baking cycle ends, immediately remove the bread from the pan and place it on a rack. Let cool to room temperature before slicing.

ZO'S 14-GRAIN BREAD

This bread with three different kinds of whole wheat flour was created by Heloise Leavitt, proprietor of Leavitts Kitchen Center in St. George, Utah. The kitchen equipment store caters to the Mormon community, known for its passionate love of homemade breads made from freshly ground grains. This is a recipe given out with each order for a Zojirushi Auto Bakery bread machine, the store's favorite machine and one known for making grain-rich breads in a snap. You can use any commercial brand of dough enhancer here.

1 Place all the ingredients in the pan according to the order in the manufacturer's instructions. Set crust on dark and program for the Whole Wheat cycle; press Start. (This recipe may be made using the Delay Timer.)

2 When the baking cycle ends, immediately remove the bread from the pan and place it on a rack. Let cool to room temperature before slicing.

1½-POUND LOAF	2-POUND LOAF
1⅔ cups water	2 cups water
2 tablespoons canola oil	3 tablespoons canola oil
2 tablespoons honey or sugar	3 tablespoons honey or sugar
1½ cups whole wheat flour	1¾ cups whole wheat flour
⅔ cup kamut flour	1 cup kamut flour
⅔ cup spelt flour	1 cup spelt flour
½ cup raw 9-grain cereal	⅔ cup raw 9-grain cereal
2 tablespoons raw sunflower seeds	3 tablespoons raw sunflower seeds
1 tablespoon whole millet	1½ tablespoons whole millet
1 tablespoon flax seed	1½ tablespoons flax seed
1 tablespoon sesame seeds	1½ tablespoons sesame seeds
1 tablespoon raw amaranth seeds	1½ tablespoons raw amaranth seeds
1 tablespoon lecithin granules (see page 168)	1½ tablespoons lecithin granules (see page 168)
3 tablespoons gluten	¼ cup gluten
2 tablespoons tofu powder or nonfat dry milk	3 tablespoons tofu powder or nonfat dry milk
2 teaspoons dough enhancer (see page 168)	1 tablespoon dough enhancer (see page 168)
1½ teaspoons salt	2 teaspoons salt
1 tablespoon SAF yeast or 1 tablespoon plus ½ teaspoon bread machine yeast	1 tablespoon plus ½ teaspoon SAF yeast or 1 tablespoon plus 1 teaspoon bread machine yeast

SUPER-GRAIN BREAD

S uper-grain refers to the addition of popped amaranth, cornmeal, quinoa, barley, and spelt. All these grains have a reputation for high nutrition, great flavor, and plenty of good fiber. Store this bread in the refrigerator after it has cooled.

1½-POUND LOAF	2-POUND LOAF
1 heaping tablespoon raw amaranth seeds	1½ heaping tablespoons raw amaranth seeds
½ cup water	¾ cup water
⅔ cup buttermilk	¾ cup buttermilk
1 large egg	1 large egg
2 tablespoons butter, cut into pieces	2½ tablespoons butter, cut into pieces
2 tablespoons honey	2½ tablespoons honey
1¾ cups bread flour	2⅓ cups bread flour
½ cup whole wheat or spelt flour	¾ cup whole wheat or spelt flour
2 tablespoons quinoa flour	3 tablespoons quinoa flour
2 tablespoons barley flour	3 tablespoons barley flour
2 tablespoons brown rice flour	3 tablespoons brown rice flour
2 tablespoons instant potato flakes	3 tablespoons instant potato flakes
2 tablespoons cornmeal	3 tablespoons cornmeal
2 tablespoons rolled oats	3 tablespoons rolled oats
1½ tablespoons gluten	2 tablespoons gluten
1½ teaspoons salt	2 teaspoons salt
1 tablespoon SAF yeast or 1 tablespoon plus ½ teaspoon bread machine yeast	1 tablespoon plus ½ teaspoon SAF yeast or 1 tablespoon plus 1 teaspoon bread machine yeast

1 Heat a deep, heavy saucepan over medium heat. Place the amaranth in the pan. Stir immediately with a natural-bristle pastry brush. Stir constantly. The amaranth will pop like popcorn. Immediately remove to a bowl to cool.

2 Place all the ingredients, including the popped amaranth, in the pan according to the order in the manufacturer's instructions, adding the popped amaranth with the dry ingredients. Set crust on dark and program for the Whole Wheat cycle; press Start. (This recipe is not suitable for use with the Delay Timer.) The dough ball should be moist and springy.

3 When the baking cycle ends, immediately remove the bread from the pan and place it on a rack. Let cool to room temperature before slicing.

What Are Organic Flours?

You may already be familiar with the attributes of organic flours. These are flours ground from wheats that have been grown in soils improved and maintained by natural fertilizers rather than chemical ones. The taste, smell, and texture of these flours reflect the quality of these soils, and the flours seem to react better with yeast. Organic flours are gaining in recognition and popularity; I just noticed that Gold Medal now has an organic flour on the supermarket shelf. Food writers are calling specifically for organic flours in their ingredients lists. Some bakers use only organic flours.

In exchange for high yields, modern agriculture has had to cope with other problems, such as pesticide residues entering the plants through their roots, growing crops in nutrient-depleted soil, and contaminated groundwater. Organic farming employs techniques that respect natural biological cycles. In order for foods to be labeled organic, they have to be grown in soil that has not been treated with any nonorganic substances for at least three years. The foods are grown without the aid of toxic synthetic chemicals (pesticides, insecticides, fungicides, and herbicides), and natural means are used to maintain the soil's nutrients and fertility. Specific requirements for organic certification now vary from state to state, but the USDA will soon be publishing national standards.

One of the pioneers in providing organic whole grain flours and information about how to use them was Frank Ford. Before organic was a household word, Frank grew his hard red winter wheat in Deaf Smith County, Texas, with none of the usual chemical grain fertilizers. In 1960 he set up a small stone mill and an office in an abandoned railroad car. He distributed his flours out of the back of his pickup truck.

Today, Deaf Smith wheat is a standard for excellence. As a purveyor of organic flour, Arrowhead Mills, provides fresh flours to home and commercial bakers in the United States and around the world. Arrowhead Mills flour is now on supermarket shelves across the country.

Despite much press, organic grains are still a minority in the agricultural marketplace; organic farming is labor intensive, crops give lower yields, and prices to the consumer are a bit higher because of a limited supply. But I believe the flours truly are superior. If they are available to you, I urge you to give them a try.

TRADITIONAL LOAVES

Country Breads and

Sourdough Breads

COUNTRY BREADS

Country-style breads, also called European-style artisan or peasant breads, represent the pinnacle of breads to bakers. Made in the bread machine, they are a bit of an anomaly. The entire premise of European-style country breads baked today is that they embody the artisan creed, and this tells the customer a lot about the quality of the bread and the style in which it has been made. Artisan bread baking employs old methods, so it is usually created entirely by hand and baked in a wood-fired oven to give it a very special character. *Pain cuit au feu de bois*, or bread baked in a wood-fired oven, has a passionate following. It is the primary baking technique that says natural, authentic, and traditional.

Many old world–style bakers stubbornly hold on to old methods, regarding the bread machine as a savage, interrupting the natural flow of the universal laws of baking by removing the process from the warmth of their hands. But others have modified their opinions to a more positive stance. Obviously the closed electric oven chamber of a bread machine will never produce a loaf with the crust or familiar long or round shape of a traditionally baked loaf, but baking country bread in the machine does have its attributes. Even when baking with a machine, you can still use a baker's care and feel, choosing fresh ingredients and using classic recipes. And there is the entire spectrum of aromas and sensations associated with bread-making that remain constant no matter what means you use. Any machine can make good country breads; the newer ones with their state-of-the-art technology—developed, in

part, with just these breads in mind—produce especially good results.

Country breads, no matter the origin of any given recipe, are all known for the same simplicity of raw ingredients that allows the flavor of the flour to really dominate. When first-rate ingredients—organic flours, natural leaven and yeasted starters, pure spring water, and unrefined sea salt—are used in making them, the quality of these loaves really becomes apparent. These are, on the whole, simple breads, whose characters can be changed by a slight variation in the proportion of flour or how long a starter sits. Sugar and fat are virtually nonexistent in these breads, making them favorites with people who are concerned about cholesterol and calories.

Many country breads use starters, or pre-ferments, for leavening. The recipes that follow begin with breads that do not use starters. Later in this section, when you come to the recipes that use starters, you will be using your machine to make the starters as well as the doughs. The starters are made on the Dough cycle, then left to sit in the machine for a specified number of hours. The new Welbilt machines have a special setting just for starters, keeping the pre-ferments gently warm at an even 85°F for up to twenty-four hours; I think more manufacturers will be adding this feature in the future. The closed environment of any bread machine offers a nice place for a starter to develop. The amount of time a starter sits will vary from recipe to recipe. The consistencies of the starters will vary, too, ranging from very soupy, to thick and creamy, to springy, almost like a small amount of bread dough. When the starter is ready, the dough ingredients are added right into the bread pan with it, a new cycle is chosen, and the machine does its work.

Baking off a loaf is the culmination of the baker's art. Many of the breads I've included are baked right in the machine, and for these the baking temperature is, of course, already decided. This automation is perfect for beginning bakers. No fancy equipment, no jostling in the oven, no need to pay attention to timing. Set the crust control on medium or dark for country breads (remember that the real difference here is the amount of time that it bakes; a darker crust will usually bake about seven minutes longer than a medium one). The closed bread machine environment naturally has a lot of steam in it, another very desirable element. The evaporation of the water from the dough creates almost a miniature steam-injected oven, an environment that has always been a challenge for the home baker to recreate. This moisture around the loaf contributes to the texture and appearance of the final loaf. It is important for the caramelizing of the sugars in the flour, which gives the crust its brown color. While the thick crusts produced in oven baking are great, a thinner crust produced by the machine allows the dough to come up to its full shape and helps prevent a dense, heavy loaf.

All of these breads can be baked in the oven after the initial mixing in the machine. Many bakers like to combine the ease of preparing the starter and dough in the machine with the use of traditional techniques—such as rising the dough in a banettone or baking the bread on a baking stone—in preparing a loaf.

Some of the recipes in this collection are based on classic recipes whose character can't be approximated without the denser crust the oven provides. These doughs need to be taken out of the machine, shaped, and baked in the oven. This allows you to take advantage of the beautiful hands-on shaping techniques that make loaves unique. Loaves prepared this way end up close cousins to, and sometimes even better than, ones made by more common home mechanical mixing techniques, such as the heavy-duty electric stand mixer or the food processor. It was a great surprise and delight to me that these loaves were some of the best I have ever made in the entire thirty years I have been baking.

For doughs prepared in the machine and baked off in the oven, the machine's Dough cycle has some great advantages built into it. The chart in your manufacturer's manual that details the different parts of the cycles will show you that the Dough cycle has two kneading periods with a short rest in between. I view this little rest as the *autolyse* in artisan baking. A tremendously important rest period, it allows the enzymes in the dough that create the acids that contribute to the final flavor to be released. Some recipes deliberately manipulate the dough to include these all-important rest periods. Also, as in artisan baking there is not one, but two or three rising times; this contributes to the bread's texture. If you are using the Basic or the French Bread cycle, you can reset it for another rise, or reset the cycle to begin the whole thing over again, allowing the dough to get the advantages of being kneaded and risen a second time.

As when preparing other breads, it is important to lift the lid of the machine and check the consistency of the dough at various points, adding flour or water as needed. While the technique of adding a bit of water or flour in increments to adjust a dough may seem novel to the budding bread machine baker, it has been done for centuries by artisan bakers. French bakers use the terms *bassinage* to describe adding some water during the kneading cycle and *contre-frasage* to describe adding flour. But pay close attention to each recipe; often the properties of these doughs will vary from one recipe to the next. Sometimes the doughs are meant to be moist to the point of slackness, yet still elastic, a very desirable consistency that makes a loaf with lots of uneven holes in it. Every type of flour will produce a different dough, even different white flours, whether bread flour, all-purpose, or clear flour.

Fermentation of the dough begins at the completion of the kneading and ends when the dough is deflated for shaping. The closed environment of the bread machine is a mock-up of the proofing boxes that are so important to professional bakers. The controlled temperature and humidity inside your bread machine are very

important to your resting dough, and the bread machine provides this environment naturally, without any effort on your part. You won't have any sudden changes in temperature to stress your dough and damage its quality. I do not recommend the use of One Hour, Quick Yeast Bread, or Rapid cycles for country breads; you want to use all the rising time needed to develop your dough.

Always remove the bread from the baking pan as soon as it has completed baking. You don't want your loaf to sit in the machine and become soggy and lose its crisp crust. Bread machine–baked country loaves have a higher percentage of inner crumb to outer crust, but the firm texture and feel of the bread will be comparable to regular oven-baked country loaves.

Breadmaking is a fulfilling and highly creative task. No matter what method you use, you must still use your senses to feel, smell, touch, and taste, measures that artisan bakers internalize as part of their craft. What you might not achieve in a classically shaped appearance will be compensated for in the satisfaction of making a country bread of an excellent texture, with good nutrition, noticeably different from those that are mass-produced, that brings pleasure to people around you. Don't forget— during baking you'll still have that ethereal aroma that is present in the kitchen of all good bakers. And after all, it is the baker who transforms the grain into bread.

PEASANT BREAD

T his is one of the first lean breads, or breads made without butter, to master. It is a simple country bread made in what is called the direct method, and used from Portugal and the Pyrenees to Poland and Greece. There is no starter, and the bread undergoes an extra kneading cycle to develop the gluten. This produces a delightfully crusty outside and a tender, chewy inside. The character of this bread will change slightly depending on the type of olive oil used—French oil is more acidic and fruity; Spanish oil is known for being smooth with an olivey aftertaste; Greek oil is thick and robust; and Italian oil is fruity and clean, but even within these categories, each brand will have its own flavor.

1 Place all the ingredients in the pan according to the order in the manufacturer's instructions. Set crust on dark and program for the Basic or French Bread cycle; press Start. (This recipe may be made on the French Bread cycle using the Delay Timer.) If using the Basic cycle, after Knead 2, press Stop, reset the machine, and start the cycle again, allowing the dough to be kneaded an extra time. The dough ball will be smooth, slightly moist, and springy.

2 When the baking cycle ends, immediately remove the bread from the pan and place it on a rack. Let cool to room temperature before slicing.

1½-POUND LOAF

1⅛ cups water
2 tablespoons olive oil

3¼ cups bread flour
2 teaspoons gluten
2 teaspoons sugar
1½ teaspoons salt

2 teaspoons SAF yeast
or 2½ teaspoons bread
machine yeast

2-POUND LOAF

1½ cups water
3 tablespoons olive oil

4¼ cups bread flour
1 tablespoon gluten
1 tablespoon sugar
2 teaspoons salt

2½ teaspoons SAF yeast
or 1 tablespoon bread
machine yeast

CHUCK WILLIAMS'S COUNTRY FRENCH

1½-POUND LOAF

1¼ cups water

2¼ cups bread flour
¾ cup whole wheat flour
2 teaspoons gluten
1½ teaspoons salt

1¾ teaspoons SAF yeast
    or 2¼ teaspoons bread
    machine yeast

2-POUND LOAF

1⅔ cups water

3 cups bread flour
1 cup whole wheat flour
1 tablespoon gluten
2 teaspoons salt

2¼ teaspoons SAF yeast
    or 2¾ teaspoons bread
    machine yeast

This is a loaf created by Williams-Sonoma mail-order catalog and shop founder Chuck Williams. The recipe was originally developed for baking in a La Cloche baker, a covered ceramic baking pan that they offer. On the next page I give instructions for baking it in a La Cloche in a home oven, but it makes a wonderfully satisfying bread baked fully in the machine. Time it so the bread is ready for dinner.

1 Place all the ingredients in the pan according to the order in the manufacturer's instructions. Set crust on dark and program for the Basic or French Bread cycle; press Start. (This recipe may be made using the Delay Timer.)

2 When the baking cycle ends, immediately remove the bread from the pan and place it on a rack. Let cool to room temperature before slicing.

Technique: Baking with a La Cloche Ceramic Baking Dish

A La Cloche baking dish is an unglazed clay baking dish with 2-inch sloping sides and a domed cover that is used for baking oversized country loaves. La Cloches are popular among home bakers, who use them to achieve very nicely shaped loaves with extra-crisp crusts. There is a 12¼-inch round La Cloche for round loaves, and a 15¼-by-5¼-inch rectangular La Cloche baker that makes an elongated French bread shape (the loaf ends up looking like a fat baguette). Any recipe in this chapter can be baked in the oven in a La Cloche. A La Cloche works best with doughs that do not contain sugar, as high-sugar doughs tend to adhere to the porous surface of the baker and when the sugar burns it is virtually impossible to clean off. Always use heavy oven mitts, like barbecue mitts, when handling a La Cloche; it is very hot just out of the oven. Here is how to use a La Cloche baking dish:

1 Prepare the bread recipe using the Dough cycle. Sprinkle the dish with flour, cornmeal, or coarse semolina (farina), and place the dough, shaped into either a round or a rectangle, in the center of the dish. Move the dough around to cover the bottom and up the sides a bit. Cover with the domed cover and let rise at room temperature for 30 minutes.

2 Remove the cover. Using a sharp knife, slash the top surface of a round loaf decoratively in an X, or slash diagonal lines down the top of a rectangular loaf, no more than ¼ inch deep. Before placing the baker in the oven, rinse the inside of the cover with tap water; drain off excess drips but do not dry (this moisture creates steam during baking). Place the cover back over the slightly risen dough ball and place the baker in the center of a cold oven. Turn the oven temperature to 450°F.

3 After 30 minutes, remove the cover with heavy oven mitts to allow the loaf to brown thoroughly. Bake for another 10 to 15 minutes, until the finished loaf is golden brown, crisp, and sounds hollow when tapped with your finger. Carefully remove the dish from the oven and transfer the loaf to a rack. Let cool for 15 minutes before serving warm.

4 To clean La Cloche or other ceramic baking pans, tap out the excess flour and crumbs, and scrub off any stuck-on bits with a brush and water only; soap residue can impart a taste into the next loaf you bake. Towel dry and let stand at room temperature for at least 30 minutes before replacing the cover and storing in the cupboard.

SEMOLINA COUNTRY BREAD

1½-POUND LOAF

1⅓ cups water
2 tablespoons olive oil

1¾ cups bread flour
1¼ cups semolina flour
1 tablespoon plus 1 tea-
    spoon sesame seeds
1 tablespoon gluten
1½ teaspoons salt

2 teaspoons SAF yeast
    or 2½ teaspoons bread
    machine yeast

2-POUND LOAF

1¾ cups water
3 tablespoons olive oil

2¼ cups bread flour
1¾ cups semolina flour
2 tablespoons sesame seeds
1 tablespoon plus
    1 teaspoon gluten
2 teaspoons salt

2¼ teaspoons SAF yeast
    or 2¾ teaspoons bread
    machine yeast

P ane di Semola *is made using a simple straight dough. Be sure to use the finely ground semolina flour that is used for making pasta rather than the coarser grind that is similar to farina, a protein-rich flour also ground from durum wheat. This bread is a good one to choose if you will be using the Delay Timer. It is fantastic warm with garlic butter melting in, and also makes great bruschetta.*

1 Place all the ingredients in the pan according to the order in the manufacturer's instructions. Set crust on dark and program for the French Bread or Basic cycle; press Start. (This recipe may be made using the Delay Timer.)

2 When the baking cycle ends, immediately remove the bread from the pan and place it on a rack. Let cool to room temperature before slicing.

PAIN ORDINAIRE AU BEURRE

S imple daily bread—French-style—is a home baker's delight. This bread must be eaten the day it is baked, preferably within a few hours, to enjoy the crisp, chewy crust. Try making this bread using French-style flour from The Baker's Catalogue (see Resources page 610), a domestic flour blended to match a sample of the flour used in Poilâne's bakery in Paris.

1 Place all the ingredients in the pan according to the order in the manufacturer's instructions. Set crust on medium or dark and program for the Basic or French Bread cycle; press Start. (This recipe may be made using the Delay Timer.)

2 When the baking cycle ends, immediately remove the bread from the pan and place it on a rack. Let cool to room temperature before slicing.

1½-POUND LOAF

1¼ cups water
1 tablespoon unsalted
   butter, cut into pieces

3 cups unbleached
   all-purpose flour
2 teaspoons gluten
1½ teaspoons fine sea salt

2 teaspoons SAF yeast
   or 2½ teaspoons bread
   machine yeast

2-POUND LOAF

1⅔ cups water
1½ tablespoons unsalted
   butter, cut into pieces

4 cups unbleached
   all-purpose flour
1 tablespoon gluten
2 teaspoons fine sea salt

2¼ teaspoons SAF yeast
   or 2¾ teaspoons bread
   machine yeast

CLASSIC BAGUETTES

Makes 2 baguettes

1½- OR 2-POUND-LOAF MACHINES

1½ cups water

3¼ cups unbleached all-purpose flour
2 teaspoons gluten with vitamin C
1¾ teaspoons salt

2½ teaspoons SAF yeast or 1 tablespoon bread machine yeast

The baguette is technically a new shape in the bread world; the long ones appeared in Paris during the 1930s in response to the public wanting more crust than crumb. The bread machine makes a French bread that is light and airy due to the mechanical action of the kneading blade, a type of mixing that just cannot be reproduced by hand. It also enables the dough to stay more moist, resulting in a thin, crisp crust. This recipe is for a classic French baguette adapted from a Joe Ortiz recipe designed for the food processor. It works incredibly well mixed in the bread machine and baked in the oven. You must use baguette trays (two 18-by-2-inch trays) to make the loaves; they are too soft to stand on their own on a baking sheet. I love how long and thin the baguettes are after they are baked in a very hot oven. And I was delighted to be able to tear into a hot loaf and have crumbs shatter on the counter. "Perfect!" exclaimed my neighbors when I brought them a still-hot wand.

1 Place all the ingredients in the pan according to the order in the manufacturer's instructions. Program for the Dough cycle; press Start. The dough ball will be sticky. Do not add any more flour at this point.

2 Grease two baguette trays. When the machine beeps at the end of the cycle, press Stop and unplug the machine. Immediately remove the bread pan from the machine and turn the wet dough out onto a floured work surface using a dough card. Knead a few times with your dough card (the dough will be too sticky to knead with your hands) to incorporate just enough flour (no more than ¼ cup) so that the dough is not in a puddle and you can shape the loaves. You want this dough to stay as wet as possible. Divide the dough into 2 equal portions.

3 Flatten each portion into a thin 10-by-6-inch rectangle with the palm of your hand. Starting with a long side, roll one up, using your thumbs to help roll tightly. With the side of your hand, define a depression lengthwise down the center of the dough. Repeatedly fold the dough over in thirds the long way to make a tight log and pinch the seams to seal. Stretch the log by rolling it back and forth on the table with your palms a few times until about 15 inches long. Gently transfer to the prepared pan seam side down. Stretch the log to fit the 18-inch pan. No dough will hang over the ends of the pan. Repeat with the other piece of dough. Cover loosely with a clean tea towel and let dough rise at room temperature until two and a half times its size in bulk, about 1 hour.

4 With a small, sharp knife, slash the surface of the baguettes 3 or 4 times on the diagonal, no more than ¼ inch deep. This must be done gently, as the delicate dough will deflate slightly. Cover again.

5 Place a baking stone or tiles on the center rack and preheat the oven to 450°F.

6 Lightly brush the tops of the loaves with cold water. Place the pans directly on the stone and bake for 20 to 25 minutes, or until the surfaces of the loaves are a deep golden brown and sound hollow when tapped with your finger. Immediately remove the bread from the pans and place them on a rack. Eat hot or within 2 hours.

Bread Machine Baker's Hint: Gluten with Vitamin C

Vitamin C, or ascorbic acid, is sometimes added to dough as a volume enhancer. You will see that some of my country bread recipes call for gluten that has had some vitamin C added. This product is available in grocery stores and by mail order from Hodgson's Mill (see Resources, page 611). You can also make your own: Crush a vitamin C tablet and add just a pinch to the amount of gluten called for in the recipe.

FRENCH WHOLE
WHEAT BREAD

Makes 1 long loaf

**1½- OR 2-POUND-
LOAF MACHINES**

1¼ cups plus 1 tablespoon
  buttermilk
½ cup water

2½ cups whole wheat flour
½ cup whole grain spelt
  flour or additional ½ cup
  whole wheat flour
1 tablespoon gluten with
  vitamin C
1½ teaspoons salt

1 tablespoon plus
  1 teaspoon SAF yeast
  or 1 tablespoon plus
  2 teaspoons bread
  machine yeast

T*he French like 100 percent whole wheat breads, too, but their version looks a lot different than American loaves. I like to call this loaf, known as* pain complet, *a torpedo, since it is elongated and pointed at the ends, dense and crusty. It is made just like a classic baguette, but with a richer dough, and ends up with a moist, tight crumb. This loaf is a favorite with French bakers, who sometimes add nuts, raisins, currants, or chopped dried apricots (my favorite) to make a good fruit bread for breakfast. The dried fruit adds a tart sweet flavor to the unsweetened dough. Made with nuts, it is especially nice with cheese and salads. As with all French breads, eat this within a few hours of baking to savor its inherent appeal.*

1 Place all the ingredients in the pan according to the order in the manufacturer's instructions. Program for the Dough cycle; press Start. The dough ball will be sticky, but very springy when you press your finger into the dough. Do not add any more flour at this point. The dough will smooth out during the kneading.

2 When the machine beeps at the end of the cycle, press Stop and unplug the machine. Open the lid and use your fingers to deflate the dough. Close the lid, set a kitchen timer for 30 minutes, and let the dough rise in the machine. Line a baking sheet with parchment paper.

3 When the timer rings, remove the bread pan from the machine and scrape the dough out onto a lightly floured work surface with a dough card. Knead a few times and pat into a 12-by-6-inch rectangle. Roll up from a long edge into a fat loaf and roll back and forth with your palms to make pointed ends. Fold the log of dough in half lengthwise and pinch the seams to seal. Roll the dough back and forth again, and pull out the pointed ends to make a loaf about 14 inches long. Place on the baking sheet and cover with a clean tea towel. Let rise at room temperature until doubled in bulk, about 1 hour.

4 Twenty minutes before baking, place a baking stone or tiles on the center rack and preheat the oven to 400°F.

5 Holding kitchen shears at a 45° angle, snip the surface 4 or 5 times down the length of the loaf, no more than 1 inch deep. Place the pan directly on the stone and bake for 32 to 38 minutes, or until the surface of the loaf is a deep, dark brown and sounds hollow when tapped with your finger. The loaf will be very firm. Immediately remove the bread from the pan and place it on a cooling rack. Eat warm or within 2 hours.

VARIATIONS

French Whole Wheat Bread with Dried Fruit

1½ cups dark or golden raisins, currants, or chopped dried apricots

In Step 3, pat the dough into a 12-inch-long rectangle about 1½ inches thick as directed. Sprinkle the dried fruit all over the dough and press it in. Tightly roll up the dough, encasing the dried fruit. Shape, rise, and bake as directed.

French Whole Wheat Bread with Nuts

1½ cups coarsely chopped walnuts, pecans, almonds, or hazelnuts (you want big pieces, which will be scattered throughout the dough)

In Step 3, pat the dough into a 12-inch-long rectangle about 1½ inches thick as directed. Sprinkle the nuts all over the dough and press them in. Tightly roll up the dough, encasing the nuts. Shape, rise, and bake as directed.

PANE ITALIANO

1½-POUND LOAF

1⅓ cups water

2½ cups bread flour
⅔ cup semolina flour
1 tablespoon instant potato
   flakes
1 tablespoon sugar
2 teaspoons gluten
1½ teaspoons salt

2 teaspoons SAF yeast
   or 2½ teaspoons bread
   machine yeast

2-POUND LOAF

1⅔ cups water

3¼ cups bread flour
⅞ cup semolina flour
1½ tablespoons instant
   potato flakes
1½ tablespoons sugar
1 tablespoon gluten
2 teaspoons salt

2¼ teaspoons SAF yeast
   or 2¾ teaspoons bread
   machine yeast

T*he simple homemade breads of Italy have become real favorites of American bakers. For good reason: they taste of the earth and of good fresh ingredients. Use organic bread flour here, if you can, or replace the bread flour with clear flour or a portion of Italian-style flour available from The Baker's Catalogue. The creamy, high-protein semolina flour called for is also known as semolina pasta flour or durum flour.*

1 Place all the ingredients in the pan according to the order in the manufacturer's instructions. Set crust on medium or dark and program for the Basic or French Bread cycle; press Start. (This recipe may be made on the French Bread cycle using the Delay Timer.) If using the Basic cycle, after Knead 2, press Stop, reset the machine, and start the cycle again, allowing the dough to be kneaded an extra time. The dough ball will be moist.

2 When the baking cycle ends, immediately remove the bread from the pan, and place it on a rack. Let cool to room temperature before slicing.

Leftover Bread Cookery: Vegetable Garden Pancakes

Makes 4 servings or 12 appetizer bites

I love vegetable pancakes with dinner instead of potatoes or rice. They are simple, but they look very special. These vegetable pancakes are great for brunch, as a simple but flavorful side dish to roast meats, or as an appetizer.

For the pancakes:

3 tablespoons unsalted butter or margarine
1 to 2 tablespoons olive oil
1 large yellow onion, finely chopped
½ red bell pepper, finely chopped
2 stalks celery, finely chopped
1 medium zucchini, grated
1½ cups grated carrots or parsnips, or a
   combination of the two
One 10½-ounce package chopped spinach, thawed
   and squeezed dry
3 large eggs
¾ cup fine breadcrumbs, toasted
Salt and fresh-ground black pepper or salt-free
   herb blend
Olive oil, for sautéeing

For the garnish:

1 cup sour cream
1 cup chopped fresh tomato
¼ cup minced fresh chives

1 Melt the butter and oil together over medium heat in a large sauté pan. Add the onions and cook for 5 minutes. Add the red pepper, celery, zucchini, and carrots. Cook for 5 minutes more over medium heat, until softened. Add the spinach and cook for 1 minute. Remove from the heat and cool 15 minutes to room temperature.

2 Beat the eggs in a medium bowl. Add the breadcrumbs and stir to moisten evenly. Add the vegetable mixture and season with the salt and pepper or herb blend to taste. Form into patties, 12 small ones for appetizers or 8 larger ones for a side dish. Place on a plate and refrigerate, covered with plastic wrap, for at least 30 minutes, or until close to serving, up to 4 hours.

3 Heat a large sauté pan over medium heat until a drop of water skates over the surface. Add olive oil to cover the bottom of the pan, and allow it to heat. Add the pancakes and cook until the edges are dry and the bottoms are golden brown, about 2 minutes. Turn and cook the opposite sides until golden, about 2 minutes more. Serve immediately or keep warm in a 200°F oven, covered with foil, until ready to serve. Garnish with sour cream and chopped tomato and chives. Serve immediately.

PANINO BRUSCHETTA

Makes 9 round rolls

1½- OR 2-POUND-LOAF MACHINES

For the dough:

½ cup water
½ cup milk
1 large egg
1 tablespoon olive oil

3¼ cups bread flour
1 tablespoon yellow cornmeal or polenta
1 tablespoon whole wheat flour
1½ teaspoons salt
1 teaspoon sugar

2¼ teaspoons SAF yeast or 2¾ teaspoons bread machine yeast

For the garlic oil:

¼ cup olive oil
2 cloves garlic, pressed

Coarse sea salt or kosher salt, for sprinkling

I talian sandwich eaters head to paninotecas, *the equivalent of our delis.* Panino *means sandwich, but it is also the word for the little breads used to make them. There are many types of bread doughs used in making* panini (*the plural of* panino), *and each region has a specialty.* Panini *can be round, square, or elongated. In Venice there are* rosettas, *which remind me of Kaiser rolls with a top knob; in Milan there are* michetta, *which have a hole in the middle; and in Piedmont there are butterfly-like* biovettes; *in Genoa* focaccia *flatbread is cut into portions.* Panino Bruschetta *are good fresh from the oven or split and grilled to make fresh-sliced tomato and arugula sandwiches. They are reminiscent of bruschetta with their topping of garlic and olive oil.*

1 Place all the dough ingredients in the pan according to the order in the manufacturer's instructions. Program for the Dough cycle; press Start.

2 When the machine beeps at the end of the cycle, open the lid and poke the dough with your fingers to deflate. Close the lid, unplug the machine, and let the dough stand in the machine for 45 minutes longer.

3 Line a large baking sheet with parchment paper and dust with flour. Turn the dough out onto a lightly floured work surface. With a rolling pin, roll the dough out into a 10-by-6-inch rectangle that is 1 inch thick. Cut out circles of dough with a 3-inch biscuit cutter or drinking glass. Reroll scraps and cut out more circles. Place the circles on the baking sheet about 2 inches apart; 3 across and 4 down. Cover loosely with a clean tea towel and let rest for 25 minutes.

4 Twenty minutes before baking, place a baking stone on the lower third rack and preheat the oven to 400°F.

5 To make the garlic oil, combine the olive oil and garlic in a small saucepan or microwave-proof bowl. Heat until just warm.

6 Brush the tops of the rolls with the garlic oil and sprinkle with salt. Bake for 12 to 15 minutes, until golden brown. Remove the rolls from the baking sheet and cool on racks.

The Toolbox: Equipment for Oven-Baked Country Breads

Country bread doughs can be fully baked in the bread machine, but they are fantastic doughs for bakers who want to shape their loaves by hand and bake their breads in a conventional oven. For this reason, some of the recipes in this chapter are executed totally in the machine and some require your hands to shape the loaves into the proper traditional shapes they are known for in the baking world. Hand-shaping techniques give each type of loaf its own character, texture, and crumb-to-crust proportion, despite the fact that most of the breads are made from exactly the same simple ingredients: flour, water, salt, and yeast. The following *batterie de cuisine* is an important list for a baker who wishes to master the array of country breads.

- Wooden board or marble slab (about 18-by-18-inch) for finishing, kneading, and shaping

- Plastic dough card, or dough scraper (consider this an extension of your hand), great for scraping wet doughs out of the bread pan and for cleaning the work surface of accumulated dough

- Metal bench knife for portioning

- Parchment paper for lining baking sheets

- Baking pans: heavy gauge aluminum or steel 18-by-13-inch half-sheet baking pans, ceramic baking sheet, perforated baking sheets

- Black steel baguette trays, 18 by 2 inches with two attached cradles

- French bâtard cradle pan, 15½-by-8-by-4-inch

- Breadstick pans

- Banetton or a medium colander and clean tea towels

- Timer

- Kitchen shears and small sharp knife or *lamé* for slashing before baking

- Ceramic baking stone (12- or 16-inch round or 16-by-14-inch rectangle) or 12 to 16 unglazed quarry tiles

- Heavy-duty oven mitts that are big enough to protect your wrists and lower arm, or barbecue mitts

- Large metal cooling rack

GRISSINI

Makes 24 grissini

**1½- OR 2-POUND-
LOAF MACHINES**

1½ cups water
¼ cup olive oil

1 teaspoon salt
1½ cups semolina flour
2½ cups unbleached
all-purpose flour

1 tablespoon SAF yeast
or 1 tablespoon plus
½ teaspoon bread
machine yeast

About ½ cup additional
olive oil, for dipping
About 1¼ cups semolina
flour, for sprinkling and
rolling

Grissini *is the Italian word for breadsticks. They are shaped by hand and then baked at a high temperature in the oven. They look very different than mass-market, machine-extruded breadsticks, which all look exactly alike; these are charmingly knobby and irregular. Bake until they are crisp. Otherwise, if they are soft like bread, they will bend and break when you stand them in a crock to serve. If you are unsure about making them freeform, you can use a breadstick tray, which is made up of a series of very thin cradles. Serve these breadsticks in an appetizer buffet, plain or with butter, or wrapped with smoked turkey or prosciutto. They are also wonderful with soup.*

❶ Place all the dough ingredients in the pan according to the order in the manufacturer's instructions. Program for the Dough cycle; press Start.

❷ Dust a work surface with semolina flour. When the machine beeps at the end of the cycle, turn the dough out onto the work surface and pat it into a thick 12-by-6-inch rectangle without kneading or overworking the dough. Leave this to rise on the work surface, especially if it is a marble slab, or transfer it to an 17-by-11-inch baking sheet that has been dusted with semolina flour. Brush the top of the dough with olive oil. Cover with plastic wrap and let rise at room temperature until doubled in bulk, about 1 hour.

❸ Place a baking stone on the center rack and preheat the oven to 425°F. Brush 2 heavy 17-by-11-inch baking sheets with olive oil. Place the additional olive oil and semolina flour in two shallow bowls.

4 Press the dough all over to gently deflate it and place it on a floured work surface. Using a pastry or pizza wheel, cut the dough into four equal pieces lengthwise; the dough will deflate a bit more. Cut each piece into 6 thick strips lengthwise. Pick up each end of each strip and stretch to the desired length or quickly roll out each strip with your palms, stretching from the center out to the ends, to a size that will fit your baking sheet. Dip each strip in the olive oil and then roll it in semolina flour. Place the strips spaced evenly apart on the baking sheets. Each sheet will hold 12 *grissini*. Bake each sheet separately in the center of the oven for 15 to 20 minutes, or until the *grissini* are lightly browned and crisp. Remove the *grissini* from the baking sheets to cool completely on racks.

A Baker's Glossary of Bread Starters

Country breads have a language all their own, which includes terms that can be quite confusing at times, especially those describing the different starters. The following list of definitions, including the meanings of some foreign words, is an invaluable reference while you are deciphering and working on European-style country bread recipes.

Biga—A thick, rather firm-textured, Italian bread dough sponge starter made of flour, water, and yeast.

Build—Term used to describe the adding of more liquid and flour to a starter to increase its volume before using it in a dough.

Chef—This is the foundation step to creating a natural starter; after building and feeding it will develop into a *levain*. Also known as a *chef levain*.

Levain—Also a starter, *levain* is the French word for leavening. A *levain naturel* consists only of flour and water and is fermented by wild airborne yeasts. A *levain levure* is fortified with some commercial yeast and ready to use a few hours after the building of a *chef*.

Mother or madre—An American term used to describe a sourdough starter

Pâte fermentée—This is the "old dough" method of pre-fermentation, in which a piece of dough is taken from a previous batch of dough to be added to a new batch. *Pâte fermentée* can also be made fresh each time you bake. This starter is as thick as a regular bread dough, made with a ratio of 3 parts flour to 1 part water.

Poolish—A liquidy French bread dough starter made of flour, water, and yeast. It is named for its Polish origin and composed of half water and half flour.

Pre-ferment—A term referring to any type of starter or sponge that is initially fermented before being made into a bread dough.

Sourdough—A thin starter created from flour, water, and naturally occurring airborne wild yeasts. Commercial yeasts may also be used.

Sponge—A bread starter that is made from an initial mixing of some liquid with some commercial or natural yeasts and flour to form a batterlike mixture that pre-ferments before being added to a dough.

Starter—Any natural or commercial yeast-reinforced sourdough, sponge, or piece of old dough that is added to a dough for leavening power, shortening the baking process and enhancing the flavor of the bread.

PAIN DE MAISON SUR POOLISH

T*he* poolish *was a turn-of-the-century breadmaking technique, but of late it has revitalized the artisan bread movement. A starter dough is prepared and left to sit for at least six hours before the dough is mixed. The final mixing and kneading phase is known as the* petrissage. *In the bread machine, you get to skip the long hours of hard work needed to make a nice loaf of bread from this classic sponge starter recipe. The instructions given here are for baking the bread in the machine, but I also like to hand shape this bread into* boules *(see page 223) and bake them in the oven. This loaf is dense and slightly sour.*

1 To make the *poolish* starter, place the water, flour, and yeast in the bread pan. Program for the Dough cycle, and set a kitchen timer for 10 minutes. When the timer rings, press Stop and unplug the machine. Let the starter sit in the machine for about 6 hours.

2 To make the dough, combine the water and the yeast, stirring to dissolve. Pour into the bread pan with the *poolish* and add the flour, sugar, gluten, and salt. Set crust on dark and program for the French Bread cycle; press Start. (This recipe is not suitable for use with the Delay Timer.) The dough ball will be slightly wet and slack, but smooth and elastic.

3 When the baking cycle ends, check the bread. If the crust is still pale and loaf is not done, reset for Bake Only for 12 minutes longer. When the bread is done, immediately remove it from the pan and place it on a rack. Let cool to room temperature before slicing.

1½-POUND LOAF

For the poolish:

1 cup water
1¼ cups organic bread flour
¼ teaspoon SAF or bread
    machine yeast

For the dough:

⅓ cup water
1½ teaspoons SAF yeast
    or 2 teaspoons bread
    machine yeast
2 cups organic bread flour
1 tablespoon sugar
1 tablespoon gluten
1½ teaspoons salt

2-POUND LOAF

For the poolish:

1⅓ cups water
1⅔ cups organic bread flour
⅓ teaspoon SAF or bread
    machine yeast

For the dough:

½ cup water
1½ teaspoons SAF yeast
    or 2 teaspoons bread
    machine yeast
2⅔ cups organic bread flour
1½ tablespoons sugar
1 tablespoon plus
    1 teaspoon gluten
2 teaspoons salt

PAIN DE PARIS

B*aguette dough used to be called* pain de Paris, *or Parisian bread. The French Bread cycle will give this dough three full rises with rests in between called* autolyses, *which are terribly important for developing the gluten structure, and therefore a good, chewy texture and strong flavor. While this dough is best when formed into the familiar long rod (program for the Dough cycle in Step 3 and see page 218), it can also be fully baked in the machine as instructed here. It has a traditional French starter known as a* pâte fermentée, *or "old dough," a pre-ferment that is as thick and silky as a bread dough. This is a delicious bread, which I am very proud to share with you.*

1 To make the *pâte fermentée* starter, place the starter ingredients in the bread pan. Program for the Dough cycle; press Start. Set a kitchen timer for 10 minutes. When the timer rings, press Pause and set the timer again for 10 minutes. Let the starter rest for 10 minutes (the *autolyse*). When the timer rings, press Start to continue and finish the Dough cycle. When the machine beeps at the end of the cycle, press Stop and unplug the machine. Gently deflate the spongy starter, and let it sit in the bread machine for 3 to 12 hours, deflating it about every 4 hours. (If you are making the starter ahead of time, remove it from the machine at this point and refrigerate it for up to 48

1½-POUND LOAF	2-POUND LOAF
For the pâte fermentée:	*For the pâte fermentée:*
½ cup water	½ cup water
1¼ cups bread flour	1¼ cups bread flour
Pinch of sea salt	¼ teaspoon sea salt
½ teaspoon SAF or 1 teaspoon bread machine yeast	½ teaspoon SAF or 1 teaspoon bread machine yeast
For the dough:	*For the dough:*
1 cup minus 1 tablespoon water	1⅓ cups water
2 cups bread flour	3 cups bread flour
1½ teaspoons gluten with vitamin C	2½ teaspoons gluten with vitamin C
¾ teaspoon SAF yeast or 1¼ teaspoons bread machine yeast	1¼ teaspoons SAF yeast or 1¾ teaspoons bread machine yeast
½ cup *pâte fermentée*	¾ cup *pâte fermentée*
1 teaspoon sea salt	1½ teaspoons sea salt

hours. Bring to room temperature before making the dough.) You will have about 1½ cups starter.

2 Rinse out a plastic dry measure with cold water. With the measuring cup still wet, measure out ½ cup (for the 1½-pound loaf) or ¾ cup (for the 2-pound loaf) of starter and set it aside for the dough (it will slide right out of the measuring cup). If you have not already stored the *pâte fermentée* earlier, you can store the rest of the starter (enough for 2 to 3 batches of Pain de Paris) in the refrigerator for up to 48 hours (see page 227 for more information). Or discard it and make a new batch the next time you make this bread.

3 To make the dough, place the water, flour, gluten and yeast in the pan according to the order in the manufacturer's instructions. (You don't have to wash out the bread pan from the starter.) Set crust on dark and program for the French Bread cycle; press Start. After Knead 1, press Pause. Add the reserved *pâte fermentée* and the salt. Press Start to continue. The dough will be moist and smooth.

4 When the baking cycle ends, immediately remove the bread from the pan and place it on a rack. Let cool to room temperature before slicing.

Technique: Shaping Long Loaves of Pain de Paris for Oven Baking

Makes 2 baguettes

1 recipe Pain de Paris dough (page 216)
1 egg white beaten with 1 tablespoon of water, for glaze

1 Line a baking sheet with parchment paper or grease two thin 2-inch-wide baguette pans. Turn out the dough onto a lightly floured work surface. Divide the dough into 2 equal portions.

2 Flatten each portion into a thin 10-by-6-inch rectangle with the palm of your hand. Starting on a long side, roll up, using your thumbs to help roll tightly. With the side of your hand, define a depression lengthwise down the center of the dough. Fold over and pinch seams to seal. Gently transfer, seam side down, to the prepared pan. No dough will hang over the ends of

the pan. Repeat with the second piece of dough. Cover loosely with plastic wrap and let rise at room temperature until fully doubled in bulk, about 30 minutes.

3 Twenty minutes before baking, place a baking stone or tiles on the center rack of the oven and preheat to 425°F.

4 Beat the egg white and water with a fork until foamy. Brush the surface of the loaves with the glaze. With a small, sharp knife, slash the surface 3 or 4 times on the diagonal, no more than ¼ inch deep. Place the pans directly on the stone and bake for 20 to 25 minutes, or until the loaves are golden brown and sound hollow when tapped with your finger. Remove the loaves from the pans immediately to cool on a rack.

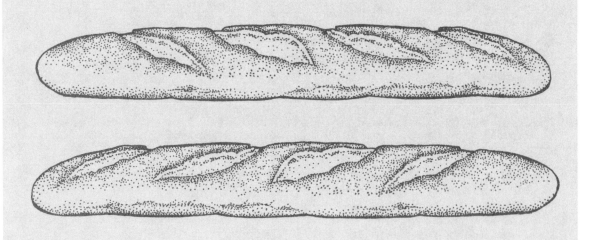

PAIN À L'ANCIENNE

Makes 1 round loaf

P ain à l'ancienne *is daily bread for much of rural France. A country relative of the* pain de Paris *and the baguette,* pain à l'ancienne *is a more rustic bread because it is made with a bit of whole wheat flour. You will get the best results from a stone-ground, coarse grind of whole wheat flour; you want lots of flecks throughout the loaf. When I stayed outside of Cahors, near Villefranche de Rouergue, I visited a baker who worked alone in what looked like an abandoned stone cottage. He baked loaves like this one, and we leaned over a crooked stone fence and called out to him to buy his bread. He left his oven inside the cottage, walked into the yard, and handed us the large round bread over the fence. The crust was incredibly dark, almost brown-black, a darker crust than I was used to. This loaf needs to be baked in the oven—if you have a La Cloche (see page 201), use it, but the bread bakes nicely on baking sheets, too.*

1 To make the *pâte fermentée* starter, place the starter ingredients in the bread pan. Program for the Dough cycle; press Start. Set a kitchen timer for 10 minutes. When the timer rings, press Pause and set the timer again for 10 minutes. Let the starter rest for 10 minutes (the *autolyse*). When the timer rings, press Start to continue and finish

1½-POUND LOAF	2-POUND LOAF
For the pâte fermentée:	*For the pâte fermentée:*
½ cup water	½ cup water
Pinch of sea salt	Pinch of sea salt
1¼ cups bread flour	1¼ cups bread flour
½ teaspoon SAF or 1 teaspoon bread machine yeast	½ teaspoon SAF or 1 teaspoon bread machine yeast
For the dough:	*For the dough:*
1¼ cup plus 1 tablespoon water	1⅔ cups water
2½ cups bread flour	3⅓ cups bread flour
⅓ cup whole wheat flour	½ cup whole wheat flour
2 teaspoons gluten with vitamin C	1 tablespoon gluten with vitamin C
2 teaspoons light brown sugar or malt powder	1 tablespoon plus 1 teaspoon light brown sugar or malt powder
1½ teaspoons SAF yeast or 2 teaspoons bread machine yeast	2 teaspoons SAF yeast or 2½ teaspoons bread machine yeast
¾ cup *pâte fermentée*	1 cup *pâte fermentée*
1½ teaspoons sea salt	2 teaspoons sea salt
Yellow cornmeal, for sprinkling	Yellow cornmeal, for sprinkling

the Dough cycle. When the machine beeps at the end of the cycle, press Stop and unplug the machine. Gently deflate the spongy starter, and let it sit in the bread machine for 3 to 12 hours, deflating it about every 4 hours. (If you are making the starter ahead of time, remove it from the machine at this point and refrigerate it for up to 48 hours. Bring to room temperature before making the dough.) You will have about 1½ cups starter.

2 Rinse out a plastic dry measure with cold water. With the measuring cup still wet, measure out ¾ cup (for the 1½-pound loaf) or 1 cup (for the 2-pound loaf) of starter and set is aside for the dough (it will slide right out of the measuring cup). If you have not already stored the *pâte fermentée* earlier, you can store the rest of the starter in the refrigerator for up to 48 hours (see page 227 for more information). Or discard it and make a new batch the next time you make this bread.

3 To make the dough, place the water, flours, gluten, brown sugar, and yeast in the pan according to the order in the manufacturer's instructions. (You don't have to wash out the bread pan from the starter.) Set crust on medium and program for the Dough cycle; press Start. After Knead 1, press Pause. Cut the reserved *pâte fermen-tée* into pieces, and add it to the machine with the salt. Press Start to continue. The dough will start out lumpy, but will become a moist and smooth firm dough ball as the kneading continues and the starter is incorporated.

4 When the machine beeps at the end of the Dough cycle press Stop and unplug the machine. Set a kitchen timer for another hour and leave the dough in the machine to continue to rise in the warm atmosphere.

5 Line a baking sheet with parchment paper and sprinkle with the cornmeal. When the timer rings, using a plastic dough card, turn the dough out onto the work surface, it will naturally deflate. Using as little flour as possible, knead lightly into a round shape with both hands; pull the sides of the dough underneath to make it tighter. Pinch the bottom seam to close the dough. The surface will be smooth and even, with no tears. Dust lightly all over with flour and place, smooth side up, on the baking sheet to leave room for expansion. If you want to use an 8-inch woven reed rising basket or a colander lined with a clean tea towel, dust it with flour and place the dough ball in it, smooth side down. Cover loosely with plastic wrap and let rise at room temperature until doubled in bulk, about 1 hour.

6 Twenty minutes before baking, place a ceramic baking stone or tiles on the lower third oven rack and preheat to 450°F.

7 If using the rising basket, run your hand around the sides to loosen the dough and gently turn out onto the baking sheet. If you have risen the loaf already on the baking sheet, you will skip this step.

8 Dust the top with flour. Using a sharp knife, slash the top with a triangle, no more than ¼ inch deep. Place the baking sheet directly on the baking stone. Bake for 10 minutes. Reduce the oven temperature to 375°F and continue to bake until golden brown and crusty, 25 to 30 minutes longer. The loaf will be dark brown, crusty, and sound hollow when tapped on the top and bottom with your finger. Remove from the pan and let cool on a rack for at least 1 hour. This bread is best served completely cooled the day it is baked.

Technique: Shaping Country Breads

Shaping bread dough, called rounding by professional bakers, requires your full attention so that the finished loaf will be the right texture and consistency. This is an area of baking that expands along with your knowledge and technique. You can shape any of the recipes in this chapter into the following classic rustic shapes. Remember, since they are not baked in pans, they will have an asymmetrical beauty of their own forged in the heat of the oven.

Unless directed, use as little flour as possible on your work surface while shaping. Have some extra flour on hand for dusting the tops of the loaves. Professionals use "gray" or clear flour for dusting country breads. Take a section of dough and press it with your palms onto the work surface to remove the accumulated carbon dioxide. It will remain in a rounded form. Take one side of the dough and fold it toward the center and press. Fold in the other side and press in the center. By folding you will have a side with a seam and a smooth side that has some surface tension, which will eventually be the top of the loaf. Shape as directed and note that the loaves should always be evenly shaped and not torn anywhere on the surface. Bake in a preheated hot oven, 425°F, with a ceramic baking stone or tiles, if you have them.

Any of the shapes can be made from 1½ or 2 pounds dough.

The glaze referred to in these shaping instructions is the classic lean bread glaze, 1 egg white with 1 tablespoon water beaten until foamy and brushed onto the dough with a pastry brush.

Bâtard
Makes 1 large loaf

In the same family as the baguette and *ficelle*, *bâtard* translates to "bastard," as it is a cross between a round loaf and a baguette. It is a large oblong torpedo-shaped loaf that looks like a shorter, fat baguette. You will need a whole recipe of dough to form one loaf. Pat the dough into a rectangle, tightly roll up and fold into thirds the long way, as for a baguette, then shape into a 12-inch elongated oval (the ends can be blunt or tapered) with a thick middle section. Gently transfer, seam side down, to a greased and dusted 15½-by-8-by-4-inch French bâtard cradle pan or a greased and dusted 17-by-12-inch baking sheet. Slash the top 3 times on the diagonal with a sharp knife no deeper than ¼ inch, or make one long slash down the middle of each loaf.

Let rise until doubled in bulk, about 1 hour. Glaze, and bake in a hot oven for 35 to 40 minutes, or until the surface of the loaf is golden brown in color and sounds hollow when tapped on the top and bottom with your finger. Immediately remove the loaf from the pan to a cooling rack.

Ficelle
Makes 3 or 4 thin loaves

This loaf is long, like a baguette, but only about 2 inches in diameter after baking. Divide the dough into 4 even portions. Flatten each into a thin 14-by-6-inch rectangle with your palm. Tightly roll up and fold into thirds the long way, as for a baguette. Gently transfer, seam side down, to baguette pans or baking sheets that have been greased and sprinkled with cornmeal. Rise, glaze, and slash as for the bâtard. Bake in a hot oven for 18 to 22 minutes, or until the surfaces of the loaves are golden brown in color and the loaves sound hollow when tapped on the top and bottom with your finger. Immediately remove the loaves from the pan and transfer to a cooling rack.

Pain de Campagne

Makes 1 large loaf

This is an oversized round country loaf shaped from one large mass of dough. In France the diameter could be as great as 12 to 14 inches. The doughs from these recipes will make a slightly smaller loaf. One and a half pounds of dough will produce about an 8- to 10-inch round. Roughly pat all of the dough into a thick, uneven circle. Pull up the sides and knead into the center of the loaf to create a tight round ball. Place seam side down on a baking sheet that is lined with parchment paper or greased and sprinkled with oatmeal. Let rise until doubled in bulk, about 1 hour. Glaze or dust with flour, and, using a sharp knife, slash the top in a netlike tic-tac-toe or triangle pattern, no deeper than ¼ inch. Bake in a hot oven for 45 to 50 minutes, or until the surface of the loaf is golden brown in color and sounds hollow when tapped on the top and bottom with your finger. Immediately remove the loaf from the pan and transfer to a cooling rack.

Boule

Makes 2 medium loaves

This is a small round country loaf, about 6 inches in diameter, a favorite shape. Divide the dough into 2 equal portions. Form each into a tight round as for *pain de campagne*. Place seam side down on a baking sheet lined with parchment paper or greased and sprinkled with cornmeal. Let rise until doubled in bulk, about 45 minutes. Glaze or dust with flour, and, using a sharp knife or kitchen shears, slash an X or a square on top, no deeper than ¼ inch. Bake in a hot oven for 25 to 30 minutes, or until the surfaces of the loaves are golden brown in color and sound hollow when tapped on the top and bottom with your finger. Immediately remove the loaves from the pan and transfer to a cooling rack. *Boules* can also be shaped with a three-stand braid (known as *la boule tressée*) or two twisted or spiraled strands that form a rope (known as a *pain cordon* or *pain spiral*), fashioned from extra dough, laid across the tops and gently attached with an egg glaze after the final rise. These decorated loaves need no slashing.

La Couronne

Makes 1 large loaf

The crown, which is a circle with a hole in the center, is one of the oldest shapes for bread. It could be carried on the arm into the fields or stored on a wooden pole. There are special molds for making crowns, or they can be shaped by hand. They are pretty on a buffet table with the center filled with grapes or a cheese ball. Roughly pat all of the dough into a thick, uneven circle. Pull up the sides and knead into the center of the loaf to create a loose round. Using the tips of all five of your fingers, held tightly together, use both hands to pierce the center of the round of dough. Pull the inside open and gradually work around the inside of the hole, expanding it to about 3 inches in diameter. Place the ring on a baking sheet lined with parchment paper or greased and sprinkled with flour. Place a small greased custard cup in the center to define the hole. Let rise until doubled in bulk. Glaze or dust with flour. Bake in a hot oven for 40 to 45 minutes, or until the surface of the loaf is golden brown in color and it sounds

continued on next page

hollow when tapped on the top and bottom with your finger. Immediately remove the loaf from the pan and transfer to a cooling rack.

Champignon
Makes 6 small loaves

These hearth loaves are shaped like rustic little mushrooms. This shape has been made for centuries and was a favorite for harvest celebrations. The shape is traditional for *petit brioche*, but here they are freestanding. Divide dough into 6 even portions (you can also shape it into one large loaf). Further divide each piece into 2 uneven portions. Form the larger piece into a tight round. Form the smaller piece into a round, roll it out into a disc the same diameter as the larger dough ball, and place atop the larger ball. With a floured finger, poke a hole in center of the stacked rounds to adhere them to each other. Place, top up, on a baking sheet lined with parchment paper or greased and sprinkled with flour. Rise only 15 to 20 minutes, as the mushroom shape becomes less defined the longer it rises. Gently redefine the hole to keep the top intact, although it may tip to one side or the other after baking. Dust with flour and bake in a hot oven for 20 to 25 minutes, or until the surfaces of the loaves are golden brown in color and sound hollow when tapped on the top and bottom with your finger. Immediately remove the loaves from the pan and transfer to a cooling rack.

Pain Épis
Makes 2 long loaves

This loaf is cut with a kitchen shears to resemble a shaft of wheat. Line a large baking sheet with parchment paper. Cut the dough into 2 equal portions and form each into a 18-inch-long rectangle, then tightly roll up and fold into thirds the long way, forming a tight log, as for a baguette. Gently transfer, seam side down, to the prepared baking sheets. Holding kitchen shears at a 45 degree angle to the loaf, and using quick motions (to prevent sticking and give a more earthy appearance), make cuts in the dough, halfway across. Cut at 3-inch intervals down the length of the dough, and with your other hand, turn each piece over, stretching every other one over the top of the dough to the other side so that the pieces alternate sides, resembling a head of wheat. You will have 6 to 8 cuts, depending on the size of the loaf. Let rise at room temperature for only 25 minutes. Bake for 30 to 35 minutes, or until the surfaces of the loaves are golden brown in color and sound hollow when tapped on the top and bottom with your finger. Immediately remove the loaves from the pan and transfer to a cooling rack. Take care with the *l'épis* after baking; its sections can break apart easily.

PAIN AU SEIGLE

Makes 2 round loaves

Frenchrye bread, like all other French breads, has a specific definition. By law it must contain at least 65 percent rye flour. Some of the loaves are over a foot in diameter. This loaf, pain au seigle, literally country bread with rye, contains only a portion of rye flour. Note that this rye has no caraway seeds, which are so often paired with rye that some people mistake the flavor of caraway for the flavor of rye. This is a bread that was first popular in the mountainous regions of France, the Pyrenees and Brittany. It has a starter, since rye breads rise better with some type of acid ingredient (that is why beer and vinegar are regularly added to Scandinavian ryes). Serve this bread with butter and marmalade; with cheese, cold cuts, charcuterie, pâté; toasted topped with melted cheese and floating in onion soup; or as the French do, with oysters. I prefer a simple treatment—toasted with honey and butter.

❶ To make the *pâte fermentée* starter, place the starter ingredients in the bread pan. Program for the Dough cycle; press Start. Set a kitchen timer for 10 minutes. When the timer rings, press Pause and set the timer again for 10 minutes. Let the starter rest for 10 minutes (the *autolyse*). When the timer rings, press Start to continue and finish the Dough cycle. When the machine beeps at the end of the cycle, press Stop and unplug the machine. Gently

1½-POUND LOAF	2-POUND LOAF
For the pâte fermentée rye starter:	*For the pâte fermentée rye starter:*
½ cup water	½ cup water
1 cup bread flour	1 cup bread flour
¼ cup medium rye flour	¼ cup medium rye flour
Pinch of sea salt	Pinch of sea salt
½ teaspoon SAF or 1 teaspoon bread machine yeast	½ teaspoon SAF or 1 teaspoon bread machine yeast
For the dough:	*For the dough:*
1¼ cups water	1½ cups plus 1 tablespoon water
2 cups bread flour	2¾ cups bread flour
1 cup medium rye flour	1¼ cups medium rye flour
2 teaspoons dark brown sugar or malt powder	3 teaspoons dark brown sugar or malt powder
1½ teaspoons SAF yeast or 2 teaspoons bread machine yeast	2 teaspoons SAF yeast or 2½ teaspoons bread machine yeast
½ cup rye *pâte fermentée*	¾ cup rye *pâte fermentée*
1½ teaspoons sea salt	2 teaspoons sea salt

deflate the spongy starter, and let it sit in the bread machine for 3 to 12 hours, deflating it about every 4 hours. (If you are making the starter ahead of time, remove it from the machine at this point and refrigerate it for up to 48 hours. Bring to room temperature before making the dough.) You will have about 1½ cups starter.

❷ Rinse out a plastic dry measure with cold water. With the measuring cup still wet, measure out ½ cup (for the 1½-pound loaf) or ¾ cup (for the 2-pound loaf) of starter and set it aside for the dough (it will slide right out of the measuring cup). If you have not already stored the *pâte fermentée* earlier, you can store the rest of the starter in the refrigerator for up to 48 hours (see page 227 for more information). Or discard it and make a new batch the next time you make this bread.

❸ To make the dough, place the water, flours, brown sugar, and yeast in the pan according to the order in the manufacturer's instructions. (You don't have to wash out the bread pan from the starter.) Program for the Dough cycle; press Start. After Knead 1, press Pause. Cut the reserved starter into pieces, then add the starter pieces and the salt to the bread pan. Press Start to continue. The dough ball will be moist and have a sticky feel. Do not add any more flour.

❹ Line a baking sheet with parchment paper. When the machine beeps at the end of the cycle, press Stop and unplug the machine. Turn the dough out onto a lightly floured work surface. Knead the dough a few times by hand, adding another tablespoon or two of flour just to have the dough hold its shape; it will still be soft. Divide the dough into 2 portions. Shape each portion into a tight round. Place on the baking sheet, seam side down. (Or shape to fit round cloth-lined small baskets or colanders

Bread Machine Baker's Hint: Storing *Pâte Fermentée*

Pâte fermentée literally means "old dough" in French. It was traditionally a small piece of dough the baker saved each time he made a batch of bread to serve as the leavening for his next batch.

In recipes that call for *pâte fermentée*, I include instructions for making the starter new each time. You need to prepare it a day before mixing the dough, though, so plan accordingly. You can also use leftover *pâte fermentée* from a previous batch, or you can make a batch of the starter ahead of time and store it in the refrigerator or freezer until you are ready to bake your bread.

Make the *pâte fermentée* according to the directions in the recipe. You will have about 1½ cups starter. Remove what you are going to use immediately, or store the whole batch. Transfer the starter to a covered container and refrigerate for up to 48 hours. Be sure there is some extra room in the container you choose; the *pâte fermentée* will grow in size as it sits in the refrigerator. The cover for the container should not be quite airtight, allowing the

starter to breathe a little. You can also freeze the starter, but if you do, it will be easier if you portion it out first. Measure out portions for the 1½-pound or 2-pound loaves and freeze them in individual freezer-strength self-sealing plastic bags for up to 1 month. (A helpful hint for measuring—if you rinse a plastic measuring cup with water, then dip it, still wet, into the dough, the dough will easily slide out of the cup and into the bag.)

To use starter that has been stored in the refrigerator, allow it to come to room temperature before adding it to the machine along with the rest of the dough ingredients. If frozen, let the starter defrost in the refrigerator overnight and then come to room temperature before using.

The *pâte fermentées* used in Pain de Paris (page 216) and Pain á l'Ancienne (page 219) are interchangeable. The rye *pâte fermentée* is not interchangeable with other recipes, but may be stored this same way.

lightly dusted with flour.) Cover the dough loosely with a clean tea towel and let rise for about 1 hour.

5 Twenty minutes before baking, place a baking stone on the lowest rack of the oven, if desired, and preheat to 425°F.

6 Dust the tops of the loaves with flour and rub in; this will give the bread a rustic look after baking. Slash each loaf decoratively with an X using a sharp knife.

7 Place the baking sheet on another baking sheet of the same size (called double panning), to prevent burning the bottoms. Bake for 30 to 35 minutes, or until the loaves are brown, crisp, and sound hollow when tapped with your finger. Remove from the oven and remove the loaves from the baking sheet to cool on a rack. Let cool completely before slicing.

PAIN AU LEVAIN

Makes 2 round loaves

For the chef starter:

1 cup buttermilk
2 tablespoons water
1¼ cups bread flour
3 tablespoons dark rye flour
½ teaspoon SAF or bread machine yeast

For the levain:

All of the chef starter
½ cup water
1 cup bread flour
¼ cup dark rye flour
¼ teaspoon SAF or bread machine yeast

For the dough:

⅓ cup water
1⅓ cups bread flour
2 tablespoons light brown sugar
2 teaspoons salt
¼ teaspoon SAF yeast or ¾ teaspoon bread machine yeast

T *his is good plain bread, country style. You will run the Dough cycle several times; to make the chef, or French-style starter, which sits overnight to ferment, and then to make the* levain *sponge, which sits for a few hours before mixing the final dough. My chef starter is nontraditional, but the buttermilk makes for a quick, aromatic starter, flecked with golden specks of butter, that would normally take a week to develop. This loaf utilizes a levain-levure, a starter that is made with some commercial yeast (different than a levain naturel, a true sourdough without any manufactured yeasts and all fermentation by wild airborne yeasts). You can remove a walnut-sized piece of the dough, called a levain or old dough, and place it in a jar in the refrigerator. This little ball of dough can be used in place of the chef starter when you make your next batch of bread; it needs to be used within a week. If you keep cutting off a little ball of dough whenever you make the bread, the flavor of your loaves will evolve just like in the old Parisan cellar bakeries. This bread is baked in the oven to get that good crust and round shape and has a fine, chewy texture.*

❶ To make the chef starter, place all the starter ingredients in the bread pan. Program for the Dough cycle, and set a kitchen timer for 10 minutes. When the timer rings, press Stop and unplug the machine. Let the starter sit in the bread machine for 8 to 12 hours. The thick batter will smell pleasantly sour.

❷ To make the *levain*, place the water, flours, and yeast in the bread pan with the bubbly chef starter. Program for the Dough cycle, and set a timer for 7 minutes. When the timer rings, press Stop and unplug the machine. You will have a beautiful, shiny dough ball that is very sticky and flecked with bits of rye. Let the sponge sit in the bread machine for 3 hours. Check halfway through in case it fills the entire pan and you need to stir it down. It will lighten as it rises, filling the pan.

3 To make the dough, place all the dough ingredients in the bread pan with the *levain*. Program for the Dough cycle; press Start. The dough will be shiny and very moist. Don't be tempted to add more flour. There will be a definite fresh fermented smell.

4 Line a baking sheet with parchment paper. When the machine beeps at the end of the cycle, press Stop and unplug the machine. Turn the dough out onto a lightly floured work surface. Knead the very soft dough for 2 to 3 minutes by hand, adding another 1 or 2 tablespoons of flour just to have the dough hold its shape; it will still be soft. Divide in half to make 2 equal portions and shape into 2 tight rounds. Place the loaves on the baking sheet. (Or shape to fit a long or round cloth-lined basket lightly dusted with flour for rising before turning out onto a prepared baking sheet or onto the hot baking stone.) Cover the dough loosely with a clean tea towel and let rise for about 1 hour in the refrigerator.

5 Twenty minutes before baking, place a baking stone on the lowest rack of the oven, if desired, and preheat to 425°F. (Optional: To form a crisp crust, 15 minutes before baking, pour hot water into a broiler pan and place the pan on the bottom rack to steam the oven for the initial baking period.)

6 Slash the loaf decoratively with an X using a sharp knife. Dust the tops with flour and rub in.

7 Place the baking sheet on another baking sheet of the same size (called double panning), to prevent burning the bottoms of the loaves. Bake for 30 to 35 minutes, or until the loaves are brown, crisp, and sound hollow when tapped with your finger. Remove from the oven and place on a rack to cool completely before slicing.

PANE TOSCANA

1½-POUND LOAF

1⅓ cups water

2⅔ cups bread flour
⅓ cup whole wheat flour
1 tablespoon gluten

1¾ teaspoons SAF yeast
  or 2¼ teaspoons bread
  machine yeast

Pinch of sugar
Pinch of salt (see Note)

2-POUND LOAF

1¾ cups water

3½ cups bread flour
½ cup whole wheat flour
1 tablespoon plus
  1 teaspoon gluten

2¼ teaspoons SAF yeast
  or 2¾ teaspoons bread
  machine yeast

Pinch of sugar
Pinch of salt (see Note)

P*ane Toscana, or Tuscan bread, is a staple in Northern Italy and usually homemade. It has been made for centuries, always without salt, meant to provide contrast to the saltier foods it is eaten with. Fifteen years ago, my Aunt Marge sent me a clipping, now yellowed with age, from the New Brunswick, New Jersey,* Daily News. *It was a recipe for Tuscan peasant bread. It was the first time I had seen this recipe with a bit of whole wheat flour added, and it fast became a standard loaf in my repertoire. It also called for a pinch of salt, more to the American palate. Years later I realized this recipe came from Egi Maccioni, the wife of Sirio Maccioni, the owner of Le Cirque 2000 restaurant in New York City. This is the bread called for in Italian-style bread salads, canapes with sliced smoked salmon, and in ribolita, the Tuscan minestrone made with bread instead of pasta. "But it is not good for toast," said Egi. "I don't know why, it just isn't." Use the coarsest grind of whole wheat flour you can find for this bread.*

1 To make the sponge, place the water, 1 cup of the bread flour, the whole wheat flour, the gluten, and the yeast in the pan according to the order in the manufacturer's instructions. Program for the Dough cycle, and set a kitchen timer for 10 minutes. When the timer rings, press Stop and unplug the machine. Let the sponge rest in the machine for 1 hour.

2 To make the dough, add the remaining 1⅔ cups bread flour (for the 1½-pound loaf) or 2½ cups (for the 2-pound loaf), the sugar, and salt to the sponge in the bread pan. Set the crust on dark and program for the French Bread cycle; press Start. The dough ball will be moist and a bit slack.

❸ When the baking cycle ends, immediately remove the bread from the pan and place it on a rack. Let cool to room temperature before slicing. This bread keeps for 3 days at room temperature.

NOTE:
With a medium-sized hand, a two-finger pinch is about 1⁄16 teaspoon and a three-finger pinch will be about double that amount. Use the amount that suits your palate.

V A R I A T I O N

Pane Toscana with Green and Black Olives

For the 1½-pound loaf:

⅔ cup pitted green and black olives, any combination

For the 2-pound loaf:

¾ cup pitted green and black olives, any combination

Follow the recipe as directed, programming the machine as specified in Step 2. When the machine beeps, or between Knead 1 and Knead 2, add the olives. Continue as directed.

OLIVE OIL BREAD

T*his olive oil bread, pane all'olio, uses a biga, an Italian starter. It is one of the easiest breads to make of those that require starters. White flour, water, and yeast are mixed together, then left to sit in the machine for many hours before the dough is mixed. The bread is baked fully in the machine, and ends up with a delicate crumb and very, very good flavor. Use a fruity extra-virgin olive oil in this dough and serve some more for dipping when you eat the fresh loaf. This bread is good made into bruschetta.*

1 To make the *biga* starter, place starter ingredients in the bread pan. Program for the Dough cycle and set a timer for 10 minutes. When the timer rings, press Stop and unplug the machine. Let the starter sit in the machine for 12 to 18 hours.

2 To make the dough, with a rubber spatula, break up the starter into 6 or 8 pieces and leave in the machine. Place all the dough ingredients in the bread pan. Set crust on dark and program for the French Bread cycle; press Start. The dough will be moist and smooth, but flaccid.

3 When the baking cycle ends, immediately remove the bread from the pan and place it on a rack. Let cool to room temperature before slicing.

1½-POUND LOAF

For the biga starter:

¾ cup water
1½ cups bread flour
½ teaspoon SAF yeast or bread machine yeast

For the dough:

¼ cup water
3 tablespoons olive oil
1½ cups bread flour
2 teaspoons sugar
1 teaspoon gluten
1½ teaspoons salt
1¼ teaspoons SAF yeast or 1¾ teaspoons bread machine yeast

2-POUND LOAF

For the biga starter:

1 cup water
2 cups bread flour
½ teaspoon SAF yeast or bread machine yeast

For the dough:

½ cup water
¼ cup olive oil
2 cups bread flour
1 tablespoon sugar
2 teaspoons gluten
2 teaspoons salt
1½ teaspoons SAF yeast or 2 teaspoons bread machine yeast

The Right Ingredient: Olive Oil

You will notice that a good many of my breads use olive oil as the fat in the recipe. This is especially true of the country breads, which traditionally use olive oil instead of butter or other oils. I use a variety of olive oils when baking, to match the right kind of olive oil to the character of the bread; an extra-virgin will provide a more assertive flavor than a pure oil like Sasso. I usually have a sweet, mild or light olive oil for all-purpose baking, such as Napa Valley Naturals or a lite Bertolli. Some bakers go so far as to seek out an olive oil from the region in which the bread was traditionally made, for example, using olive oil from the Liguria region of Italy in certain Italian country breads.

Olive oil has long been the companion of the baker in the kitchen. It has a wonderful taste and is good for all types of baking, everything from quick breads to flat breads and yeast breads, and for frying. Olive oil has the added bonus of being low in cholesterol and saturated fat. Along with canola, walnut, macadamia and almond oils, it is among the healthiest oils to consume. It complements the taste of flour and other ingredients, both sweet and savory, in bread.

There are many grades and price ranges to choose from when buying olive oil. Perhaps you favor a domestic olive oil, an imported brand, or an organic olive oil. Each oil has its own unique flavor. This is why many bakers don't have just one olive oil of choice—they keep a few varieties on the shelf to impart different flavors to different breads. I remember the first Spanish olive oil I bought, Lérida, which was a striking gold color and came in a pretty square bottle. I always have a bottle of Stutz extra-virgin on hand. In most recipes, I do not specify anything about the type of olive oil, but simply call for "olive oil." You can use any type at all, but I encourage you to explore the many choices available. Domestic brands I use include Sciabica's, Stutz, Consorzio,

B.R. Cohn Sonoma Estate, and McEvoy Ranch. There are imported brands, such as Olio Extra Vergine Buonsapore (used at Chez Panisse restaurant). Bulk oils, readily available in supermarkets, include Sasso, Colavita, and Bertolli.

Store olive oil in a cool, dark place. Do not refrigerate, as it makes the oil cloudy, and do not store the oil next to the stove, where it can be damaged in the presence of heat.

Grades of Olive Oil

The grade of olive oil, usually placed under the brand name, is easily identified on the label. Some artisan oils have the extraction date stamped on the back. Olive oils that are bright to olive green in color are pressed from green, unripe, olives. Yellow and golden oils are pressed from ripe black olives picked at the end of the season.

- **Extra-virgin olive oil** is cold-pressed (that is, no heat or chemicals are used to extract the oil), and has a distinctive fruity taste and an acidity of less than 1 percent. Circular stone presses and hydralic presses are used to extract the oil. It is considered a premium quality oil. Within this category are virgin and fine virgin.

- **Pure olive oil** is the most available type of olive oil. It has a more subdued flavor than extra-virgin. It also costs less than extra-virgin, and is often a blend of oils from different types of olives. It comes from pressings that occur after the extra-virgin oil has been extracted; some heat and chemical solvents are used.

- **Lite olive oil** is not lower in calories or fat, but is so named because it is very light in color and has a milder flavor than other olive oils. It has a tad of extra-virgin oil blended in.

ITALIAN WHOLE WHEAT BREAD

Makes 1 round loaf

T*he texture of this light whole wheat bread, known as pane integrale, made with a starter that sits for a few hours, is quite moist and soft, just like the dough. It has a delicate, evocative texture and aroma. This is a nice dinner and sandwich bread. You can bake the entire loaf in the machine, but be sure to use the dark crust setting, as this loaf is quite pale even when the center is baked. I like to bake this loaf in the oven to get more of the great crust and a bit less inner crumb. This is a superb homemade-style country bread; I like to serve it spread with cheese.*

1 To make the sponge starter, place the starter ingredients in the bread pan. Program for the Dough cycle, and set a timer for 10 minutes. When the timer rings, press Stop and unplug the machine. Let the sponge sit in the machine for 4 hours, or as long as overnight. The environment will be nice and warm.

2 To make the dough, place all the dough ingredients in the bread pan with the sponge. Program for the Dough cycle; press Start. The dough ball will be very moist, tacky, and smooth.

3 Line a baking sheet with parchment paper and sprinkle with cornmeal. When the machine beeps at the end of the cycle, press Stop and unplug the machine. Turn the dough

1½-POUND LOAF

For the sponge starter:

1⅓ cups water
1⅛ cups bread flour
¾ cup whole wheat flour
¼ teaspoon SAF yeast or bread machine yeast

For the dough:

1 cup bread flour
1 tablespoon sugar
1 tablespoon gluten
1½ teaspoons salt
1¾ teaspoons SAF yeast or 2¼ teaspoons bread machine yeast

Yellow cornmeal, for sprinkling

2-POUND LOAF

For the sponge starter:

1⅔ cups water
1½ cups bread flour
1 cup whole wheat flour
¼ teaspoon SAF yeast or bread machine yeast

For the dough:

1¼ cups bread flour
1¼ tablespoons sugar
1 tablespoon plus 1 teaspoon gluten
2 teaspoons salt
2 teaspoons SAF yeast or 2½ teaspoons bread machine yeast

Yellow cornmeal, for sprinkling

out onto a clean work surface; shape into a tight round. Place on the baking sheet, cover loosely with plastic wrap, and let rise at room temperature until almost tripled in bulk, 1 to 1½ hours.

4 Twenty minutes before baking, place a baking stone on a rack in the lower third of the oven and preheat to 450°F.

5 Slash the surface of the loaf once down the center, no deeper than ½ inch, using a sharp knife. Place the baking sheet directly on the hot stone in the oven. Reduce the oven temperature to 425°F. Bake for 35 to 40 minutes, until golden brown and the top sounds hollow when tapped. The loaf will not be very dark brown due to the wheat flour and small amount of sugar. Cool the loaf directly on a rack for at least 20 minutes before slicing and serving.

PANE FRANCESE

Makes 1 oblong loaf

1½- OR 2-POUND-LOAF MACHINES

For the biga sponge:

1⅛ cups water
1 teaspoon SAF yeast or bread machine yeast
2 cups bread flour (organic, if possible)

For the dough:

¼ cup water
1¼ cups bread flour (organic, if possible)
2 teaspoons gluten with vitamin C
1½ teaspoons salt

I adapted this recipe from one in The Village Baker by Joe Ortiz (Ten Speed Press, 1996). This was originally developed for the food processor, but I make it in the bread machine instead. What a great recipe—the smell! The texture! It uses a lievito naturale for leavening power, a yeasted biga sponge that is very soft and looks like a perfect soft vanilla ice cream swirl after mixing. Pane francese means French bread in Italian, but this loaf is a bit flatter than true French bread, and is reminiscent of the earthy breads made by early Roman bakers. This bread develops a sturdy, crackly-crisp crust and moist interior filled with uneven holes that will make you feel like one of the most accomplished bakers in the world. It is baked in the oven—if baked in the machine you would miss out on that fabulous crust.

1 To make the starter, place the *biga* ingredients in the bread pan. Program for the Dough cycle and set a kitchen timer for 5 minutes. When the timer rings, press Stop and unplug the machine. Let the starter sit in the machine for 8 to 10 hours.

2 To make the dough, place all the dough ingredients in the bread pan with the *biga*. Program for the Dough cycle; press Start. The dough will be moist and smooth, but flaccid. Take a deep breath while it is mixing; this is what bread dough is supposed to smell like—fresh and yeasty.

3 When the machine beeps at the end of the cycle, press Stop and unplug the machine. Set a timer for 1 hour and leave the dough in the machine to continue to rise in the warm atmosphere.

4 When the timer rings, using a dough card, scrape the dough out of the bread pan onto a floured work surface. Knead a few times and pat into a 12-inch oval. Roll up

from a long edge into an oblong-rectangular loaf. Dust
the work surface lightly with a bit of flour to prevent
sticking and set the loaf on the floured surface. Cover the
loaf with a clean tea towel and let rest for 30 minutes.

5 Line a baking sheet with parchment paper. Carefully
pick up the loaf and place it on the baking sheet. As you
pick it up from both ends and carry it, it will naturally
stretch and extend slightly, which will create a flattish
loaf about 14 inches long and 5 inches wide. Dust the
top with flour. Cover again and let rest for 20 minutes.

6 Place a baking stone or tiles on the center rack of the
oven if desired, and preheat to 450°F.

7 Do not slash or glaze the loaf. Place the pan directly on
the oven rack, or on the stone if using, and immediately
reduce the oven temperature to 425°F. Bake for 30 to
35 minutes, or until the surface of the loaf is a deep
golden brown and sounds hollow when tapped with
your finger. Immediately remove the loaf from the pan
and place it on a cooling rack. Serve warm or at room
temperature.

LITTLE ITALIAN BREAD ROLLS

Makes 3 small breads

This recipe for pane all'olio Bolognese *is based on one found in the March 1980 issue of one of my all-time favorite food magazines, the now defunct* Cuisine. *It is a good, simple recipe with a nice three-hour* biga *starter and a three-hour rise for flavor, but it is the shaping that makes these rolls special. I give instructions for three special shapes. Two decades ago, very few people aside from native Italians knew about the intricate shapes into which these oversized rolls could be made. With the vast increase of interest in foods from all areas of Italy, authentically shaped bread and rolls are now more commonplace in the United States. These white rolls are crusty and beautiful. Please search out leaf lard; it is most flavorful in the rolls and gives them an authentic taste.*

1 To make the *biga* starter, place the starter ingredients in the pan according to the order in the manufacturer's instructions. Program for the Dough cycle and set a kitchen timer for 10 minutes. When the timer rings, press Stop and unplug the machine. Let the starter rest in the machine for 3 hours.

2 To make the dough, add all the dough ingredients to the starter in the pan. Program for the Dough cycle; press Start. After Knead 2, press Reset, and program for the Dough cycle again, allowing the dough to be kneaded a second time. When the machine beeps at the end of the cycle, press Stop and unplug the machine. Let the finished dough sit in the machine for 2 hours.

3 Turn the dough out onto a clean work surface; divide it into 3 equal portions. Flatten each portion into a 7-inch round with your palms. Roll up each round into a tight log. Cover with oiled plastic wrap, and let rest for 10 minutes. With a rolling pin, roll each log into a 10-by-3-inch rectangle. Cover again with the plastic wrap and let them rest for 5 minutes.

4 Preheat the oven to 450°F. Line a large baking sheet with parchment paper and sprinkle with cornmeal.

5 To make *carciofo*, rolls that resemble artichokes, cut 2-inch slits that go about three-quarters of the way across, spaced ½ inch apart, down one long side of the dough. Starting at a short end, roll up the dough. Place, with the fringed edge standing up, on the baking sheet. With your fingers, pull down the strips of dough to make a petal effect. Repeat with the other 2 rectangles.

6 To make *montasu*, or scrolls, roll up the 2 short ends of the rectangle toward the center with your thumbs pressing and pushing, until the two rolls almost meet in the middle, with a 1-inch space between the two. Twist one roll 90° and lay it on top of the other roll. Press firmly in the center to adhere the two rolls together and hold the shape. Place on the baking sheet. Repeat with the other 2 rectangles.

7 To make the *crocetta*, little cross rolls, roll up the 2 short ends of the rectangle towards the center, until they almost meet, but leave a 1-inch space in between. Twist one roll 2 complete turns to form a double twist in the center section. Pull one roll up and over the second roll, centering the double twist on the second roll. Twist and turn the top roll under the bottom, forming a cross. Place on the baking sheet. Repeat with the other 2 rectangles.

8 Let stand, uncovered, for 10 minutes. Brush gently with water and bake for 10 minutes. Reduce the oven temperature to 400°F and bake for an additional 10 to 15 minutes, until crusty and golden brown. Place the baking sheet on a rack to cool. Serve the rolls within a few hours.

CIABATTA

Makes 2 large loaves

For the biga starter:

½ cup water
1½ cups plus 3 to 4 tablespoons unbleached all-purpose flour
¼ teaspoon SAF or bread machine yeast

For the dough:

⅞ cup warm water
2 tablespoons milk
2 teaspoons olive oil or canola oil
1½ teaspoons SAF yeast or 2 teaspoons bread machine yeast
2 cups bread flour
1½ teaspoons salt

Ciabatta *is one of the hottest Italian-style country breads made in artisan bakeries in this country today. Carol Field paved the way by including the recipe in her landmark book* The Italian Baker *(Harper & Row, 1985), and every serious baker I know aspires to master it. This is one of the best country breads you can make. It has a superb crust and flavor. The word* ciabatta *describes the look of the loaf, like a flat slipper or old shoe, hence the regional nickname "slipper bread" around Lake Como. This dough is a perfect candidate for the bread machine because it is so wet that it couldn't be mixed by hand, except by a very experienced baker. (So don't be tempted to add more flour when you see how wet the dough is!) In addition, the mechanical kneading time of about twenty-three minutes is just right for this dough. This bread uses a lievito naturale, or biga, a starter that is firm like a bread dough and rests overnight, so be sure to plan for a two- to three-day process leading up to the shaping of the bread and the baking of it in the oven. You will need a six-quart plastic bucket for refrigerating the dough. The combination of techniques produces a chewy bread with big, uneven holes, known as occhi or "eyes," throughout the crumb. Half of this recipe could also make a dozen long grissini (see page 212), or divide the recipe into 8 portions and make ciabattini, or sandwich rolls. This formula is my adaptation of one given to me by P. J. Hamel of the King Arthur Flour test kitchen. When this loaf comes out of the oven, I always think it is magic!*

1 To make the *biga* starter, place the water, 1¼ cups of the flour, and the yeast in the bread pan. Program for the Dough cycle. After about 5 minutes, scrape down the sides and slowly add another ¼ cup of flour. When Knead 2 ends, remove the small dough ball from the machine and place it on a work surface. Hand knead in about 3 tablespoons more flour. You will have a smooth dough ball firmer and a bit drier than one for bread, stiff yet resilient. Return the dough to the bread pan and close the lid (you could press Pause, but I just leave the lid open. This takes all of about 30 seconds). The machine will continue with the rise phases of the Dough cycle.

When the cycle ends, press Stop and unplug the machine. Let the starter sit in the bread machine for 9 to 12 hours, or overnight. The dough will rise and fall back upon itself, become moist, and smell yeasty. (If you can't make the dough right away, store the *biga* in a self-sealing plastic bag in the refrigerator for up to 3 days. Bring to room temperature before making the dough, or warm it in the microwave for 10 seconds, before breaking up the *biga* into pieces and making the dough.)

2 To make the dough, with your fingers, tear the slightly sticky starter into walnut-size pieces and put them back in the machine. Place the water, milk, oil, and yeast in the bread pan with the biga pieces. Add 1½ cups of the bread flour and the salt. Program for the Dough cycle; press Start. At the start of Knead 2, add the remaining ½ cup of flour. The dough will be very wet and sticky like a yeasted savarin batter. Don't add any more flour, just leave the dough alone except for scraping the sides into the center. The dough will end up elastic and shiny, but relaxed and slack, sticking to the sides of the pan. If you tried to mix it by hand, you couldn't knead it on a work surface.

3 When the machine beeps at the end of the cycle, the dough will have almost filled the pan. The top will be smooth, but if you stick your finger in, it will be sticky. Spray a deep 6-quart plastic bucket with olive oil cooking spray or brush with oil. Scrape the risen dough into the container, give the top a light spray or brush with oil, cover, and refrigerate for 6 hours to overnight, but no longer than 24 hours. This long, cool rise is important for the slow fermentation and the flavor of the finished *ciabatta*, so don't skimp on it.

4 Line a large, heavy baking sheet with parchment paper (some bakers use aluminum foil) and sprinkle heavily with flour. Turn the chilled dough out onto a lightly floured work surface, sprinkle lots of flour on top, and pat into a long rectangle about 5 inches wide. Divide into 2 equal rectangles across the middle and place each portion on the baking sheet. Cover with a clean tea towel and let rest at room temperature for 20 minutes to relax the dough.

5 Dust the tops of the loaves with some flour. Using the flat section of your fingers below the fingertips and holding them in an open splayed position, press, push, and stretch the dough, making a rectangle about 10 by 5 inches (the width of your hand). Your fingers will not press in some areas, so you will have a dimpling, flattening effect, which will end up producing the characteristic uneven texture in the baked loaf. Cover again and let rest at room temperature until tripled in bulk, about 1½ hours. The loaves will stay flattish looking. Don't worry, they will rise dramatically in the oven.

6 Twenty minutes before baking, place a baking stone on the lower third oven rack and preheat to 425°F.

7 Spray or sprinkle the loaves with some water and place the baking sheet on the hot stone. You can slip the parchment off the baking sheet and bake directly on the stone, if you like. Bake for 20 to 25 minutes, until golden brown. Prop open the oven door about 5 inches and let the *ciabatta* cool in the oven at least 15 minutes. Remove from the oven and serve. Wrap in plastic to store.

TWO-WEEK BIGA
(Classic Italian Starter)

Makes about 4 cups biga

While it is convenient enough to make a new biga each time you bake, if you bake a lot, you can make a large batch of biga using this recipe and use it in increments for up to two weeks in any of the six recipes that follow. If you like to bake country breads, like I do, this is a real boon in saving time, especially since bigas require none of the feeding or waiting that traditional sourdough starters do. Obviously a two-day-old biga will be a bit different than a fourteen-day-old biga. The older biga will be more fermented and therefore impart a slightly different flavor, but this biga is delicious every step of the way and will have the same rising power whether it was made two days ago or ten. The aroma of this biga is fresh and clean, and the breads made with it are delightful through all stages of mixing and baking.

Bigas can be quite loose or they can be firm, like this one. This one is used like an "old dough," or a piece of dough saved from the last batch and added to a new batch for flavor and leavening. The full flavor produced by this method shows the grain at its best; you get a natural chewiness and delightful flavor. The lump of starter is added to the machine along with the wet ingredients, and it gets incorporated throughout the dough during the mixing and kneading. Please note that for the breads made with Two-Week Biga, I add the yeast along with the water and biga.

Note that you can use either unbleached all-purpose flour or bread flour in this biga recipe with good results. Also, you can make half of this biga recipe, if you like, but surprisingly, once you've got a batch in the refrigerator and begin to taste how good the breads are that are made with it, you'll be using it all up. My guess is that once you get used to this type of starter, you won't ever be without it.

1½- OR 2-POUND-LOAF MACHINES
1⅔ cups warm water ⅓ teaspoon SAF yeast 　or ½ teaspoon bread 　machine yeast 3¾ cups unbleached 　all-purpose or bread flour

1 Place the water and yeast in the bread pan. Add the flour. Program your machine for the Dough cycle and press Start. Immediately set a timer for 10 minutes. When the timer rings, press Stop and unplug the machine. You will have a stiff dough ball that will loosen and become moist as it sits. Let the starter sit in the machine for about 6 hours. The dough will rise and fill the pan, becoming moist, and smelling yeasty.

2 Prepare a lidded plastic container (I use a short 1-quart container) to store the *biga* by spraying the inside bottom and sides of it with vegetable oil cooking spray. The plastic container should be large enough to hold at least three times the amount of *biga* you have. (This will accommodate the *biga* as it rises inside the refrigerator.) Scrape the *biga* out of the bread pan and into the container using a spatula or dough card; the dough will be very sticky. I find it helpful to label the *biga* with the date and time it was made before refrigerating it. Store the *biga* in the refrigerator, where it will continue fermenting. It will be ready to use in 18 to 24 hours. You will need to deflate the *biga* by stirring it with your finger or the tip of a knife after about 12 hours, 24 hours, and 48 hours (since it is a live culture, it slowly rises while chilled). Store in the refrigerator for up to 2 weeks.

You can also freeze the *biga*. Since it would be difficult to measure portions from a frozen batch of starter, portion the starter before freezing. For details on measuring, see step 3. Store each half cup of *biga* in a separate freezer-quality self-sealing plastic bag. The *biga* may be frozen for up to 1 month. Then defrost it in the fridge overnight before using.

3 To use the *biga*, rinse out a measuring cup with cold water. Leave the measuring cup wet. Use a small knife or large spoon to cut away a section of the refrigerated *biga* and pack it into the measuring cup until it is full. Bring the *biga* to room temperature before making the bread dough, or warm it in the microwave for 10 seconds. I measure it out, then just leave it on the counter covered with some plastic wrap for an hour or so until I am ready to load the machine. It is okay that the *biga* rises as it warms; just dump it into the pan, whatever its volume, along with the water.

Mastering the *Biga*

I had traveled many times to the first Il Fornaio store on Union Street in San Francisco—a California-based franchise bakery chain modeled on one of the same name in Italy. The first bread I made styled after one of theirs was a chocolate bread. In 1982, I was offered a position at the fledgling Il Fornaio company for which I would have trained at their baking academy, but I took another job, opting to work in Alaska sourdough country instead. I started working with *bigas* in the late 1980s. Although I had been baking for years, the manipulation and use of the *biga* were new to me, and my first attempts were less than enthusiastic. On the advice of Carol Field, the food writer who first brought the *biga* to American shores, I kept at it and let the unfamiliar technique evolve into my repertoire.

I met chef and baker Franco Galli, formerly of Il Fornaio America, at a book party celebrating the publication of *The Il Fornaio Baking Book* (Chronicle Books, 1993), which he authored. Up to that time, the crusty, rustic Italian breads made by the Il Fornaio Bakery were a bit out of reach of the home baker. Of course the secret to their wonderful breads was the starter and they detailed it and much more in this informative book.

The recipes in this section are styled after and inspired by ones created by master baker Franco Galli. I guarantee that you, too, will be a great baker when you master them.

PAGNOTTA

Makes 1 large loaf

1½- OR 2-POUND-LOAF MACHINES

1⅔ cups warm water
½ cup Two-Week Biga
    (page 243)
¾ teaspoon SAF yeast
    or 1¼ teasoons bread
    machine yeast

3¾ cups bread flour
1½ teaspoons salt

Pagnotta *translates simply to "round loaf." It is a floury country bread I adore. It has a very crisp knobby crust and moist, dense interior that reminds me (even though this is not a sourdough bread) of my favorite bread made by Boudin—at this writing the last big commercial sourdough bakery in San Francisco's North Beach—which bakes in the Italian tradition. The rustic shape turns out a bit different with every baking. The aroma of this bread is very grain-rich, so the flour you use is of utmost importance. You can also use this dough to make a dozen* pagnottine, *square rolls, for guests. See page 248.*

❶ Place all the ingredients in the pan, according to the order in the manufacturer's instructions, adding the starter and yeast with the water. Program for the Dough cycle; press Start. The dough will be shiny, very moist to the point of being slightly sticky, and soft. Don't be tempted to add more flour. When the machine beeps at the end of the cycle, press Stop and unplug the machine. Gently deflate the dough with your finger. Set a kitchen timer and let the dough rest for another hour in the warm environment of the machine.

❷ Turn the dough out onto a lightly floured work surface. Using your dough card, fold the edges over into the center. You can add another tablespoon or two of flour as you work, just to have the dough hold its shape, but it will still be soft. Working around the loaf in a circular motion, each fold will lay on top of each other, making a tight round with an uneven surface that would normally be on the bottom of the loaf. The smooth side will be touching the work surface. Spread a thick layer of flour on the work surface and turn the loaf over so that the smooth side will face up. Cover with a clean tea towel and let rise at room temperature for about 45 minutes.

3 Twenty minutes before baking, place a baking stone on the lowest rack of the oven, if desired. Place a clean baking sheet in the oven to heat it up, and preheat the oven to 425°F.

4 Carefully remove the hot baking sheet from the oven and place on a rack or on top of the stove. Sprinkle with flour. Using a flat surface such as the underside of a sauté pan lid and your dough card, gently slide the loaf off the work surface and turn it over onto the lid so that the bottom is now on top. This is easier than it sounds. Slide the loaf onto the hot baking sheet; it will appear to deflate slightly. This is okay. The rough side of the loaf will be facing up. Immediately place in the oven.

5 Bake for 10 minutes. Reduce the oven temperature to 400°F and bake for an additional 30 to 35 minutes, or until the crust is deep brown, very crisp, and the loaf sounds hollow when tapped with your finger. I insert an instant-read thermometer into a soft crease on the side; it should read about 200°F. Remove the bread from the oven and place on a rack. Let cool completely before slicing.

Technique: How to Shape and Bake Italian Dinner Rolls

Makes 1 dozen little rolls

I love the way these rolls are shaped, into little squares.

1 recipe Pagnotta dough (page 246)

1 Brush a small 5- to 7-inch square or rectangular dish with olive oil. Turn the dough out into the dish. Press the dough into an even layer with your fingertips. Cover with a clean tea towel and let rest at room temperature for 1½ hours.

2 Invert the dish to turn the dough out onto a heavily floured work surface. With a knife, pastry wheel, or metal bench knife, divide the dough into 2 equal pieces. With your fingers, deflate until flat, and begin rolling up a rectangle of dough by folding it over in ½-inch increments, which will create surface tension. The dough roll will be about 1¾ inches in diameter. Press down to flatten slightly into a square log and be sure the seam side is down. The roll will

be completely covered with flour. Repeat with the second piece. Cover with the clean tea towel and let rest on the work surface until doubled in bulk, about 45 minutes to 1 hour.

3 Twenty minutes before baking, place a baking stone on the lowest rack, if desired, and preheat the oven to 425°F. Line a large baking sheet with parchment paper.

4 With your metal bench knife or a sharp knife, cut each log into 6 equal pieces. Dust with more flour, if necessary. These look nice when made really floury. You will have a little square with an expanding open area, called "the wound," at the cut edge. This is desirable. Transfer the rolls to the baking sheet placing them about 1 inch apart.

5 Bake until golden brown and crusty, 22 to 28 minutes. The rolls will expand and puff up considerably. Cool on the sheet for 10 minutes and serve immediately, or cool completely and reheat before serving.

PANE BIGIO

Makes 2 round loaves

Bigio *translates to "gray," and this loaf with a small percentage of whole wheat flour and bran does have a grayish-brown cast when baked.* Pane bigio, *the Italian counterpart to the French* pain de campagne, *is a nice, simple country bread, best eaten fresh, within a few hours of baking.*

❶ Place all the dough ingredients in the pan according to the order in the manufacturer's instructions, adding the starter and yeast with the water. Program for the Dough cycle; press Start. The dough will be smooth, slightly moist and sticky, and a bit soft. Don't add more flour. When the machine beeps at the end of the cycle, press Stop and unplug the machine. Gently deflate the dough with your finger. Set a timer for an hour and let the dough rest another hour in the machine.

❷ Line a baking sheet with parchment paper and sprinkle with cornmeal. When the timer rings, turn the dough out onto a lightly floured work surface. Divide the dough into 2 equal pieces, and using your dough card, gently knead each into a ball. Place the balls on the baking sheet a few inches apart. Cover with a tea towel and let rise until doubled in bulk, about 45 minutes.

❸ Twenty minutes before baking, place a baking stone on the lowest rack of the oven, if desired, and preheat to 425°F.

❹ Sprinkle the top of each loaf with flour and rub in. Slash a crosshatch or triangle into the tops, no more than ¼ inch deep. Bake for 30 to 35 minutes, or until the crusts are deep brown, very crisp, and sound hollow when tapped with your finger. I insert an instant-read thermometer into a soft crease on the side; it should read about 200°F. Remove from the oven and place the loaves on a rack. Let cool completely before slicing.

1½- OR 2-POUND-LOAF MACHINES

1¼ cups warm water
½ cup Two-Week Biga (page 243)
1 teaspoon SAF yeast or 1½ teaspoons bread machine yeast

2⅛ cups bread flour
¾ cup whole wheat or graham flour
2 tablespoons bran or wheat germ
1 teaspoon gluten with vitamin C added
1½ teaspoons salt

¼ cup yellow cornmeal, for sprinkling

Pain de Campagne from a Vermont Kitchen

Brinna Sands of King Arthur Flour is an avid bread machine baker and student of traditional baking techniques, so I asked her to contribute a recipe for this book. She sent me a three-page recipe for a European-style country bread in prose form. It was so evocative of the stream of consciousness of a philosophical baker, that I decided to include it for you just as she sent it. Brinna measures her ingredients in a very different manner than the rest of the recipes in this book, so I have included regular measurements should you find hers daunting.

Brinna Sands's Pain de Campagne

I'm hoping that if I commit this recipe to print, as it stands now, that I will stop obsessing about it and be able to move on. What I'm really afraid of is that, even then, I may not want to move on because this bread has become, for better or worse, our current daily bread. The struggle I'm having is that it flies in the face of all the whole grains, *levains*, and starters I've been committed to over the years. It is, after all, a primarily white, yeast-leavened, bread-machine kneaded loaf that is the antithesis of all things I used to hold important. But I love it. Everyone loves it. It's terrific right out of the oven, a half an hour out of the oven, the next day, the day after that, and finally as toast, bread pudding, *strata*, croutons, crumbs. . . . What makes it so compelling? Try it and see. I'm not sure I have the answer.

The Day Before Baking

The *Biga*

Perhaps the fact that this is made with a *biga* somewhat mitigates my guilt about making it. A *biga* is an Italian name for a kind of pre-fermented dough. I'm calling it a *biga* because a *biga* can be almost any form of pre-ferment, from a sponge (two parts water to one part flour by weight) to a dough (1 part water

to 1¼ to 1½ parts flour by weight). The French have more precise names for these things, names that are harder to remember and say than *biga*. And "biga" seems to be a good name for a creature that has taken up habitation in your kitchen or refrigerator and keeps reappearing. Besides, this loaf is more Italian than French in heritage.

A pre-ferment is what a baker uses to speed up the time between mixing a dough and pulling finished loaves out of the oven, without sacrificing texture and flavor. By making up a sponge or dough with a touch of yeast, and letting it work for anywhere from 2 to 48 hours, you can add it to a newly made dough that will inherit the flavors it has had time to develop.

So in making a bread with a *biga*, you add one more step. But it's only remembering to make the *biga* that can be called "work" because it's a cinch to make. Place your bread machine bucket on a scale and measure into it:

6 ounces (¾ cup) water
1 ounce (3 tablespoons) pumpernickel or whole rye meal
7 to 8 ounces (approximately 1½ cups) unbleached all-purpose or bread flour
¼ teaspoon instant yeast (SAF yeast or ½ teaspoon bread machine yeast, not rapid-rise)

Put the bread pan in the machine, start the Dough cycle, and allow to mix just long enough to thoroughly blend all the ingredients, 5 to 6 minutes. Then hit Reset and go away. You can leave this *biga* right in the machine until you're ready for the next step, or you can take the bucket out of the machine, cover it with plastic wrap, and let it sit. If you aren't going to get to it after 12 hours or so, put it, covered, into the fridge. It will keep very nicely there for a couple more days.

The Day of Baking

The Dough

The dough for this bread is quite wet, one that a bread machine does really well developing. The final bread will be light, with good-sized holes in it, and chewy with an assertive crust.

Take your bread machine pan, uncover it if it's covered, and put it back on your scale. Add:

12 ounces (1½ cups) water
1⅕ ounces (¼ cup) pumpernickel or whole rye meal
15 to 16 ounces (approximately 3¼ to 3½ cups)
   unbleached all-purpose or bread flour
Scant tablespoon salt
1½ teaspoons instant yeast (SAF yeast or
   2 teaspoons bread machine yeast, not rapid-rise)

Put the pan back into the machine and set it on the Dough cycle. After it's had a chance to mix, get in there with a rubber spatula and scrape any residue off the sides of the machine and incorporate it into the dough. After the machine has finished its cycle, let the dough continue to rise until it has just crowned over the top of the pan.

Turn the dough out onto a lightly floured board, and, with the help of a bench knife or bowl scraper, fold the edges of the dough into the center, gently pressing out the accumulated gases. Turn it over and shape it into a round loaf, tucking the edges into the middle of the bottom until it's neat and tidy and well shaped.

Rising and Baking

If you have a baking stone in your oven, you can bake your loaf right on the stone. To do this, place the shaped loaf on a piece of flour-dusted parchment, cover and let rise until it's well developed, an hour or more. Twenty minutes to a half hour before you want to bake your bread, preheat your oven to 450°F. Just before the bread goes into the oven, slash the top in whatever artful way you wish. This allows the loaf to continue to expand in the oven without shredding and gives it your signature appearance. If you don't have a stone, place your shaped loaf on a baking sheet or a dark pizza pan that's at least 12 inches in diameter.

You'll develop a much better crust if you can add steam to the oven for the first few minutes the bread is baking. This can be done either by spraying the loaf fairly copiously with water before it goes in, or by placing a metal pan under the baking stone or rack you want to bake the bread on, allowing it to preheat with the oven. Pour a half to 1 cup of very hot water in the pan just before you slide in your loaf. Be very careful. Steam can burn. Good oven mitts are very useful here.

Bake the bread for about 45 minutes. Keep an eye on your loaf. If it seems to be browning too much, turn the heat down and continue baking at 400°F. Remove from the oven and place on a cooling rack. In a minute or so the loaf will begin to speak. Cool pretty thoroughly before you cut into it so the interior structure has a chance to set.

Eating

The easiest way to get at this loaf is to cut it in half, stand a half on edge and cut slices starting at one end. Store the other half on edge to prevent it from drying out. Eat it with whatever excuse you need (because it's there; to eat with butter, jam, soup, or tea; or best of all, the presence of a friend with whom the bread just needs to be broken).

Afterthoughts

Perhaps it's because the gestation of this loaf is so long, or because the loaf is so fulsome and round, or because it speaks when it is done. Maybe it's because the bread machine makes it so easy to create. Or maybe it's just because it's the perfect vehicle for so many of the things that make life a good place to be. Whatever the reason, it's at this point that I go back to the beginning and start another *biga*.

ITALIAN
SEMOLINA BREAD

Makes 1 round loaf

**1½- OR 2-POUND-
LOAF MACHINES**

1 cup warm water
¼ cup Two-Week Biga
(page 243)
1 teaspoon SAF yeast
or 1½ teaspoons bread
machine yeast
2 tablespoons olive oil

1½ cups bread flour
1 cup semolina flour
1 teaspoon gluten with
vitamin C added
1¼ teaspoons salt

¼ cup farina, for sprinkling

T*his is such a wonderful bread, but the only way you will know that is to bake it immediately. The crust is crisp and crackly; the interior is moist and close textured. It is perfect. The aroma drives me wild; it smells like a field of fresh grain. This is what country bread was meant to be—a plain bread with gigantic character. So eat it with dinner, with meat and cheese, or just dip it in olive oil and enjoy.*

❶ Place all the dough ingredients in the pan according to the order in the manufacturer's instructions, adding the starter and yeast with the water. Program for the Dough cycle; press Start. The dough will be smooth, slightly moist and sticky, and a bit soft. Don't be tempted to add more flour. When the machine beeps at the end of the cycle, press Stop and unplug the machine. Gently deflate the dough with your finger. Set a kitchen timer and let the dough rest another hour in the warm environment of the machine.

❷ Turn the dough out onto a floured work surface. Using your dough card, gently knead into a ball. Cover with a clean tea towel and let rise at room temperature until doubled in bulk, about 45 minutes.

❸ Knead the risen dough ball once more into a tight round, pressing the air out of it. Sprinkle the work surface with flour and place the loaf on it, seam side down. Cover with the towel and let rise again, for 40 minutes.

❹ Twenty minutes before baking, place a baking stone on the lowest rack of the oven, if desired, and preheat to 425°F. Line a baking sheet with parchment paper and sprinkle with the farina.

5 Slide the loaf off the work surface with your dough card and transfer to the baking sheet. With a small sharp knife, make 5 slashes in a radiating pattern, like the rising sun or the fingers of your outstretched hand, into the top, no more than ¼ inch deep. The pattern will cover the entire top surface.

6 Bake for 35 to 40 minutes, or until the crust is dark brown, very crisp, and sounds hollow when tapped with your finger. The loaf will look done earlier, as the crust browns quickly, but needs the full time to bake the interior. Remove from the oven and place the loaf on a rack. Let cool completely before slicing.

PANE DI CEREALE

Makes 1 round loaf

1½- OR 2-POUND-LOAF MACHINES

½ cup raw cracked grain cereal
1½ cups water

¼ cup Two-Week Biga (page 243)
¾ teaspoon SAF yeast or 1¼ teaspoons bread machine yeast
2 tablespoons olive oil
1 tablespoon honey

1½ cups whole wheat or graham flour
1½ cups bread flour
1 teaspoon gluten with vitamin C
1½ teaspoons salt

2 tablespoons yellow cornmeal, for sprinkling

T he health craze has hit all developed countries, as this bread containing lots of healthy cracked grains shows. Use any hearty cracked grain cereal. They come in six-grain, seven-grain, nine-grain, and twelve-grain varieties. There's also hot apple granola that contains cracked wheat, rye, barley, and oats. You can use whatever type you wish, but take note that these raw cracked-grain cereals are different than regular boxed cereals or instant hot breakfast cereals, so you may have to seek them out. This makes a soft whole-grain bread, very different from its crusty cousins in the rest of this chapter, but very tasty.

1 Place the cereal and 1 cup of the water in a bowl. Let stand at room temperature for 1 hour.

2 Place all the dough ingredients in the pan, adding the starter and yeast with the remaining ½ cup water and the soaked grains. Program for the Dough cycle; press Start. The dough will initially look very wet. The grains will absorb the extra moisture during the kneading. When the machine beeps at the end of the cycle, press Stop and unplug the machine. Gently deflate the dough with your finger. Set a timer and let the dough rest for another hour in the warm environment of the machine.

3 Turn the dough out onto a lightly floured work surface. Using your dough card, fold the edges over into the center. Knead into a tight round. Spread a thick layer of flour on the work surface and turn the loaf over so that the bottom side will face down and the bottom face up. Cover with a clean tea towel and let rise at room temperature, about 45 minutes.

4 Twenty minutes before baking, place a baking stone on the lowest rack of the oven, if desired, and preheat to 400°F. Line a baking sheet with parchment paper and sprinkle with cornmeal.

5 Using your dough card, gently slide the loaf off the work surface and turn it over onto the baking sheet; it will appear to deflate slightly. Immediately place in the oven.

6 Bake for 35 to 40 minutes, or until the crust is deep brown and the bread sounds hollow when tapped with your finger. Remove from the oven and place on a rack. Let cool completely before slicing.

PANE ALL'UVA

Makes 2 loaves

2 cups (10 ounces) dark or golden raisins

1½ cups warm water
¼ cup Two-Week Biga (page 243)
2 teaspoons SAF yeast or 2½ teaspoons bread machine yeast
2 tablespoons olive oil

4 cups bread flour
1¼ teaspoons salt

Cornmeal, for sprinkling

My dear friend Qui Grenier loves Italian raisin bread. A visit with her usually includes tea and toast, usually raisin toast with butter. Let me just say that when you are hungry, and the bread and conversation are this good, it's easy enough for two people to toast their way through an entire loaf. Be prepared: Italian raisin bread has no sugar, and you may be surprised at how different this bread tastes from American raisin bread. The loaves are low and sort of flat, but they slice nicely. Slice and freeze any bread leftover after one day, as the loaf begins to dry out when day-old.

❶ Place the raisins in a bowl and cover with hot water. Let them stand for 1½ hours, or while your bread machine completes the Dough cycle as instructed in Step 2.

❷ Place all the dough ingredients, except the raisins, in the bread pan, according to the order in the manufacturer's instructions, adding the starter and yeast with the water. Program for the Dough cycle; press Start. The dough will be smooth and firm. When the machine beeps at the end of the cycle, press Stop/Reset and program again for the Dough cycle. Press Start. Drain the raisins and pat as dry as possible, as any moisture will be incorporated into the dough. Gradually sprinkle in the raisins while the machine is kneading. If the dough looks too sticky after the raisins are incorporated, sprinkle another 1 to 2 tablespoons flour around the paddle while the machine is running.

❸ Line a baking sheet with parchment paper and sprinkle with cornmeal. When the machine beeps at the end of the cycle, press Stop and unplug the machine. Turn the dough out onto a lightly floured work surface. Using your dough card, gently knead into a ball and divide into 2 equal pieces. Pat each piece into an 8-inch-long rectangle and fold the long edges into the center. Form into a round, then work out into a 4-by-8-inch rectangle. Taper the ends by rolling and pressing onto the work surface. You will have a flattish, fat torpedo shape. Place the loaves on the baking sheet crosswise with a few inches between them. Cover with a clean tea towel and let rise at room temperature until doubled in bulk, about 45 minutes.

4 Twenty minutes before baking, place a baking stone on the lowest rack of the oven, if desired, and preheat the oven to 425°F.

5 Brush the tops of the loaves with some olive oil. I just dribble some over the center and some onto the brush and quickly brush. Bake for 35 to 40 minutes, or until deep brown and firm to the touch. The crust will be soft. Transfer from the pan to a rack and immediately brush the tops once more with olive oil; it will soak right in. Let cool completely before slicing.

SAFFRON AND OLIVE OIL CHALLAH

Makes 1 braided loaf

1½- OR 2-POUND-LOAF MACHINES

⅔ cup water
Small pinch saffron threads

⅓ cup Two-Week Biga
  (page 243)
½ teaspoon SAF yeast
  or 1 teaspoon bread
  machine yeast
2 large eggs
¼ cup olive oil

2½ cups bread flour
2 tablespoons sugar
1¼ teaspoons salt

1 egg beaten with
  1 tablespoon of water,
  for glaze
1 tablespoon poppy or
  sesame seeds, for
  sprinkling, optional

T he addition of olive oil to the more traditional challah ingredients makes for a beautiful egg bread, suitable for Friday evening Sabbath meals. I was surprised at how little yeast this dough requires. It does rise slowly, but don't despair. It seems to pick up speed during its last rise and in the oven, making an exceptional loaf. One slice of this ultra-tender bread will remind you that there is a good reason why challah is called the "cake of bread." The low yeast and sugar contents let the sweetness of the grain shine, accented by the biga. The crust is thin, dark, and rich; it shatters delectably when sliced. You can omit the saffron if you want, which was added in days of old by Jewish bakers, especially in winter, to make the pale yellow color more pronounced. Challah keeps fresh for days. It is good for dinner on day one, sandwiches and toast thereafter.

1 Bring the water to a boil in a saucepan or microwave. Add the saffron and let it steep at room temperature for 20 to 30 minutes, until just warm.

2 Place the saffron water and other dough ingredients in the pan according to the order in the manufacturer's instructions, adding the starter and yeast with the liquids. Program for the Dough cycle. The dough ball will be firm, yet smooth and soft. When the machine beeps at the end of the cycle, press Stop and unplug the machine. Set a kitchen timer and let the dough rest for another 30 minutes in the warm environment of the machine (no need to deflate).

3 Line a baking sheet with parchment paper or grease a 9-by-5-inch loaf pan. When the timer rings, immediately remove the dough and place on a lightly floured work surface; divide into 3 equal portions. Using your palms, roll each portion into a fat cylinder, 12 inches in length and tapered at each end. Be sure the ropes are of equal size and shape. Place the 3 ropes parallel to each other. Begin braiding like you are braiding hair. Adjust or press the braid to make it look even. If the loaf is to be free-form, taper the ends for a long loaf, or press together to make the braid a compact square. If you are baking it in the loaf pan, tuck the ends under to make a rectangle that will fit into the pan. Cover loosely with plastic wrap and let rise at room temperature until the dough is doubled in bulk, about 1 hour.

4 Twenty minutes before baking, preheat the oven to 350°F.

5 Beat the egg and water glaze with a fork until foamy. Using a pastry brush, brush the top of the loaf with some of the glaze and sprinkle with the seeds, or leave plain. Bake for 40 to 45 minutes, or until the loaf is deep golden brown and the bread sounds hollow when tapped on the top and bottom with your finger. Immediately remove the loaf from the pan or sheet and transfer to a cooling rack. Let cool to room temperature before slicing.

Leftover Bread Cookery: Baked Egg Dishes for Any Meal

Vegetable Frittata

Makes one 10-inch frittata, serves 8

This egg casserole is baked in a deep springform pan, unusual for a fritatta, and served in wedges like a cake. Although it takes a bit of time to assemble, it can be baked a day ahead and reheated. Serve hot, room temperature, or cold, for brunch or supper. This is great party food.

¼ cup olive oil
1 large yellow onion, chopped
½ pound fresh mushrooms, sliced
3 medium zucchini, sliced ¼ inch thick
3 summer squash, sliced ¼ inch thick
1 red bell pepper, seeded and cut into ¼-inch-thick strips
1 yellow bell pepper, seeded and cut into ¼-inch-thick strips
6 large eggs
¼ cup cream or evaporated milk
3 tablespoons chopped fresh basil leaves
Salt and black pepper to taste
1 to 2 slices day-old country bread, cut into ½-inch cubes
½ pound cream cheese, cut into chunks
2 cups shredded Jarlsberg or Swiss cheese

❶ Preheat the oven to 350°F. Grease the bottom and sides of a 10-inch springform pan. If it might leak, cover the outside bottom and up the sides with a sheet of aluminum foil or plan to place it on a baking sheet to catch the leaks.

❷ Heat the olive oil in a large skillet. Sauté the onion, mushrooms, squash, and peppers stirring occasionally, until crisp-tender, about 15 minutes. While the vegetables are cooking, whisk together the eggs, cream, basil, and seasonings in a large bowl. Add the bread cubes and cheeses.

❸ Add the sautéed vegetables to the bread mixture and stir with a large rubber spatula to incorporate. Scrape into the prepared pan and pack the mixture tightly. Place on the baking sheet if you are using one.

❹ Bake for about 1 hour, until firm to the touch, puffed, and golden brown. Serve or cool to room temperature and refrigerate. Reheat in a 350°F oven until warmed through, about 15 minutes.

Wine, Bread, and Cheese Soufflé

Serves 4

This rustic casserole is a cross between a traditional soufflé and a quiche. It has a crust of garlic-scented bread slices and a filling that is made with a dry white wine, like a sauvignon blanc. The type of wine you use will affect the character of the dish. This is a wonderful meal if you're in a hurry.

½ cup (1 stick) unsalted butter or margarine, at room temperature
2 to 3 cloves garlic, pressed

8 slices day-old homemade country bread,
   (no more than ¾ inch thick) cut in half on
   the diagonal
½ cup dry white wine
½ cup milk
3 large eggs
¼ teaspoon salt
¼ teaspoon ground black pepper
¼ teaspoon paprika
1 teaspoon Dijon mustard
Splash of white Worcestershire sauce
2 cups shredded Swiss cheese, such as Jarlsberg
   or Emmenthaler

1 Preheat the oven to 325°F.

2 Cream together the butter and garlic in a small bowl. Spread the bread slices on one side with the garlic butter. Arrange, butter side down, to line the sides and bottom of a 1½-quart casserole or 7½-inch soufflé dish. It does not matter if there are some uneven spaces between the slices, but place slices as close together as possible.

3 Whisk together the wine, milk, eggs, salt, pepper, paprika, mustard, and Worcestershire sauce in a medium bowl until smooth, about 1 minute. Add the cheese and stir to combine. Pour into the lined casserole.

4 Bake for 30 to 35 minutes, or until golden brown and the filling is puffed and set. Serve immediately. This dish can be made up to 8 hours ahead, covered with plastic wrap, and refrigerated. Reheat before serving in a 325°F oven for 10 minutes or until heated through.

SOURDOUGH BREADS

Another branch of country bread-making is sourdough baking, the oldest method commonly used to create hearty, rustic breads. If you have been making the starter breads in the earlier section of this chapter, you are already working with the principles that apply to sourdough baking. A piece of "soured" dough saved from a previous batch of baking or batter is added to the new batch to add flavor and leavening to the baked loaf. In the world of natural starters, it is interesting to note that many people will eat only breads made from natural leavenings, as they consider breads made with commercial yeasts lacking in the proper taste, texture, and nutrition. The sourdough method of raising bread, known as *préfermentation* in France, is almost as old as bread itself. It is quite a fragile process, as natural leaveners are constantly re-sponding to ever-changing conditions in their environment.

Although sourdough breads are made all over the world, the recipes I include here are in the American sourdough tradition. They hark back to the days when gold prospectors traveled across America with their starters in hand, since there was no refrigeration to store fresh compressed yeast. Sourdough starters were the reliable answer to leavening daily bread in the early West. American sourdoughs differ from their European siblings in that they are usually pan loaves with some fat and sugar added. Breads like San Francisco sourdough are made in the European tradition.

Sourdough starter baking existed long before the commercial cultivation of yeast, which is a relatively new development. Despite the multi-tude of technological advances in the last few thousand years, the leavening process of harness-ing "wild" (noncommercial strains of) airborne yeasts has remained essentially the same as when the Egyptians discovered thousands of years before Christ that the barm scooped off the top of their beer vats had the ability to raise their wheat flour doughs. To make a starter, equal parts of flour and water are mixed and then left to stand at room temperature. The mixture provides a pleasant medium for invisible spores to propagate and begin to ferment or sour. Some of the starter is mixed in when making a bread dough, providing leavening and a varying degree of acidic flavor to the finished bread. A starter that has become heavily acidic needs to be "fed" to dilute the acidity, as strong acidity can inhibit rising power.

Before cultivated yeast was available, bakers used various starter methods, such as salt rising (a milk, cornmeal, sugar, and salt mixture was heated and then left to stand at room tempera-ture), raw or mashed potato starters, starters activated with dry hops, or yeast-rich frothy barm skimmed off of beer and ale and then propagated in carbohydrate-rich potato water.

Wild yeast sourdough is a fermentation notorious for its temperamental results. Some geographic locations are better than others for getting a stronger starter. Pollution is one thing that seems to decrease wild yeast potency, so if your starter batter does not activate with bubbles within a few days, a pinch of cultivated yeast will need to be added to attract the wild yeasts. Depending on your "catch," your starter

can be delicious or terrible. Many baking afi-
cionados simply get some starter from a friend
who is cultivating some, as it is so much easier
and more predictable than catching your own
from scratch. Sourdough culture requires a lot
of observation and flexibility from its devotees.

The secret to sourdough baking and to
controlling a starter is time, and plenty of it.
A starter, also known as a "mother" or a "chef,"
is left to ripen at room temperature for many
days to develop the desired degree of sourness,
which differs for every baker and for every type
of bread. In between feedings—the periodic
additions of flour and liquid to a starter—the
sugars in the flour break down, producing pungent acids that give the bread its distinct flavor.
The starter bubbles and expands with enzyme
action and smells like an earthy perfume,
slightly sour and apple-like, from the malolactic
fermentation. (A batch that smells bad must be
thrown out because it has been contaminated
by another strain of bacteria, and the process
must be started over.) This is, incidentally, the
same bacterial-acid conversion process that
occurs in winemaking, a fact I discovered when
a wine merchant was sniffing at the various
starters I had bubbling away in the bakery one
day, and noted the similarity in scents. Once
you use some of this liquidy starter in baking,
you can continue to keep and feed the remaining starter, or you can remove a piece from the
dough and use a portion of that the next time.
You can end up with a great loaf of bread and
keep a wonderful starter going from a very
small initial amount of starter. Starters are
slowly built by adding fresh flour and water,
usually over the course of a few days to a week,
reactivating the starter and making it fresh and
strong again. Ingredients such as ground ginger,

cumin, caraway seeds, onion, apple, honey,
sugar, or yogurt can be added as a boost,
encouraging the activity of the bacteria. You
may also choose to discard any remaining
starter each time you bake, and make your
starter fresh each time.

A thicker, doughlike piece of starter will
always ferment more slowly than one that has
more liquid. Remember that the same rules
apply to sourdough starters as apply to commercial yeasts when it comes to heat and
cold—excessive heat, over 100°F, will kill the
delicate yeasts. Starters of any type can be
frozen, though, and fed and used when they
are thawed, an important technique to keep
seldom-used starters going. (I wish I had
known it years ago when I was given some
special starters and couldn't keep them going
for lack of use.)

So many bakers never work with sourdoughs
because they just can't develop an acceptable
starter. As I did not want this to be the case
with you, my starters are fortified with some
commercial yeast or use some of the freeze-
dried starters that are commercially available.

Among the starter recipes included here
is a selection of "fast" starters. These include
Next-Day White Sourdough Starter, Next-Day
Rye Sourdough Starter, Suzanne's Sourdough
Starter, German Beer Starter, and French
Buttermilk Starter. Each can be made from
scratch in 1½ to 3 days with ease and pre-
dictability. These quick starters are also important for bakers who make sourdough breads
only sporadically, as they can easily be made
fresh each time you want to bake. The Grapeyeast Starter is more traditional, and does
require more time to make.

Each starter has its own characteristic flavor

and rising power. Most of the starters given here can be used interchangeably in any of the sourdough bread recipes in this book, and you can also vary the flours you use to make the starters. For certain recipes I have suggested certain starters, but feel free to experiment. A German Beer Starter may not be the best choice to use in Sourdough Banana Nut Bread. All you have to do is consider the ingredients you have put into the starter and how they will mesh with the ingredients of the bread, and you will have a delicious outcome. If, by chance, you already have a good starter sitting in your refrigerator, by all means take it out, feed it, and get to baking! If you make gluten-free breads, you can use white or brown rice flour in place of the wheat flour in your sourdough starter; it ferments nicely.

You can make anything from pizza dough to French bread to pancakes with a sourdough starter. Please note that this type of baking is different than any other in this book. It has a much more developed flavor with a bit of a punch. You will know when you are baking sourdough bread because even its aroma while baking will be tangy.

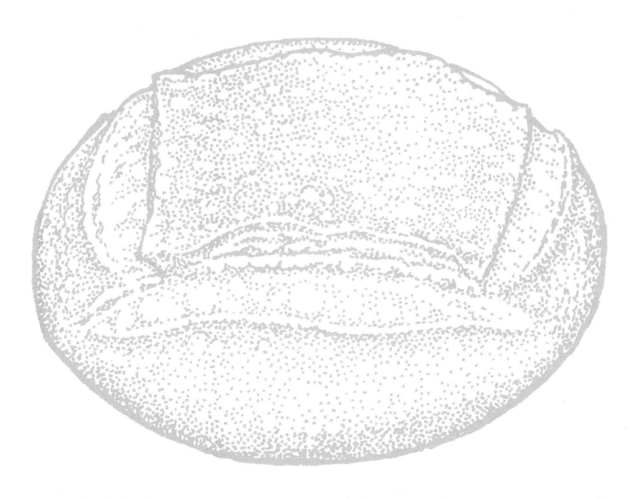

NEXT-DAY WHITE SOURDOUGH STARTER

Makes 2 ½ cups starter

T his is my version of a sourdough starter that is ready to use after thirty-two hours. If you start it early in the morning, it will be ready to use the afternoon of the following day. It is a sure thing for first-time sourdough bakers, eliminating an often variable product. I use a dry culture starter from Goldrush Sourdough, which is readily available on supermarket shelves and from The Baker's Catalogue. It makes a clean, tangy starter.

INGREDIENTS

One ½-ounce package commercial dry sourdough starter
2 cups bread flour
Pinch of active dry, bread machine, or SAF yeast
2 cups warm water (85°F)
½ medium apple, peeled, cored, and cut into chunks

For the first feeding:

¼ cup bread flour
¼ cup warm water

1 Combine the packaged starter with the flour and yeast in a medium bowl. Whisk in the warm water until the mixture is smooth. Stir in the apple chunks. Transfer to a plastic container or crock. Cover with a few layers of cheesecloth and secure with a rubber band; then cover loosely with plastic wrap. Let stand at warm room temperature for 24 hours (80°F is optimum), stirring the mixture 2 to 3 times. It will be bubbly and begin to ferment, giving off a tangy, sour aroma. It will be the consistency of a pancake batter.

2 Remove the apple chunks. Add the first feeding flour and water and whisk to combine. Let stand for 8 hours longer. The starter will be ready to use. If you desire a more sour starter, or do not wish to use it right away, cover the starter loosely and store it in the refrigerator for 24 hours. For information about maintaining your starter, see page 267.

NEXT-DAY RYE SOURDOUGH STARTER

Makes 2 ½ cups starter

One ½-ounce package
   commercial dry
   sourdough starter
1½ cups dark rye flour
½ cup bread flour
Pinch of active dry, bread
   machine, or SAF yeast
2 cups warm water (85°F)
1 thin slice onion
¼ large clove garlic
4 caraway seeds

For the first feeding:

¼ cup rye flour
¼ cup warm water

Some sours utilize rye flour and add a bit of onion, a classic old touch that contributes greatly to the flavor and encourages fermentation. This is a fast version of rye bread starter that uses a packaged dry culture to add flavor. It has a wonderful aroma evocative of all that sourdough baking epitomizes. This starter is ready to use after thirty-two hours. Begin it early in the morning, and you'll have Sourdough Rye Bread for dinner the following night.

1 Combine the starter package with the flours and yeast in a medium bowl. Whisk in the warm water until smooth. Stir in the onion, garlic, and caraway. Transfer to a plastic container or crock. Cover with a few layers of cheese-cloth and secure with a rubber band; then cover loosely with plastic wrap. Let stand at warm room temperature for 24 hours (80°F is optimum), stirring the mixture 2 to 3 times. It will be bubbly and begin to ferment, giving off a tangy, sour aroma. It will be the consistency of a pancake batter.

2 Remove the onion and garlic pieces. Add the first feeding flour and water, and whisk to combine. Let stand for 8 hours longer. The starter will be ready to use. If you desire a more sour starter, or do not wish to use it right away, cover the starter loosely and store it in the refrigerator for 24 hours. For information about maintaining your starter, see page 267.

Technique: Building and Maintaining a Sourdough Starter

Time and nourishment are two of the key elements in developing a starter with a good, strong flavor. This process is also called "building" a starter or mother. Usually a sourdough starter does not get used up when a dough is made from it. Although many of the starter recipes I include here are easy enough to make fresh each time you want sourdough bread, you may also wish to keep and replenish leftover starter for your next baking. In order to maintain a starter in good condition, replenish it each time you use some. Also feed a starter whenever you haven't used it for 2 weeks. The directions that follow may be applied to any of the starters in this book.

The quantities I give here are for replenishing a starter by a lot; if you are feeding a starter you have not used, you can feed it with less, as long as you add equal amounts of flour and water.

Sourdough starter
1 to 1⅓ cups any flour
1 to 1⅓ cups water
1 heaping tablespoon plain yogurt or a pinch of sugar, optional

1 Let the refrigerated starter come to room temperature. Stir the separated grayish-yellowish liquid back into the mixture. If you are only feeding the starter and have not just used some of it, you may wish to discard half of it if you don't want to accumulate too much. Pour the remaining starter into a medium bowl. Add 1 to 1⅓ cups of flour (unbleached all-purpose, medium to course-grind whole wheat,

medium rye flour, or other, depending on the type of starter), and an equal amount of water. If I really want to increase the activity of the starter I also add a heaping tablespoon of plain yogurt or a pinch of sugar, as extra food for the yeast. If you have about 1 cup of starter to replenish, the proportions given here will mix into a thick, creamy mass.

2 Wash out the container in which the starter had been stored using soap and hot water, or run it through the dishwasher, to get rid of any remaining bacteria. Then return the starter to its original container and cover it with several thicknesses of cheesecloth held in place with a rubber band. Let the starter stand at room temperature, stirring several times a day, until bubbly, overnight to 2 days, depending on how sour you want it. It will continue to bubble and expand. If the starter turns color, has an unpleasant aroma, or grows any type of mold, the starter is out of balance and must be completely discarded. Do not leave the starter at room temperature longer than 5 days without feeding it.

3 After the starter has been allowed to stand at room temperature to ferment, cover it with a layer of plastic wrap held in place with a rubber band, or transfer it to a freezer-quality self-sealing bag, and refrigerate it. The best starters are those used and replenished daily to weekly.

SUZANNE'S SOURDOUGH STARTER

Makes 2 cups starter

INGREDIENTS

One 8-ounce container
  sour cream (not imitation,
  lowfat, or nonfat)
½ cup warm water
3 tablespoons apple cider
  vinegar
⅛ teaspoon active dry, bread
  machine, or SAF yeast
¾ to 1 cup unbleached
  all-purpose or bread flour

My friend Suzanne Rosenblum believes that it is best to make a new starter for each batch of bread. For this starter, use an unpasteurized apple cider vinegar that has the "mother" floating in it, if you can. This starter does not need to be fed (Suzanne believes that feeding changes the initial sour flavor); when it gets to the desired point of sourness, it is ready to use. The whole process takes as little as three days. I also like this starter made with all or part whole wheat or spelt flour. Divine!

1 Whisk the sour cream until smooth in a medium bowl. Add the water and vinegar, and sprinkle with the yeast. Add the flour. I prefer to use the full cup, but Suzanne likes her starter liquidy, so she adds only ¾ cup. Add a bit more flour to adjust the consistency to that of a pancake batter.

2 Transfer to a plastic container or crock. Cover with a few layers of cheesecloth and secure with a rubber band; then cover loosely with plastic wrap. Let stand at warm room temperature for 24 hours (80°F is optimum). It will start to bubble immediately and have a fresh, creamy smell that will gently sour. You can begin using the starter after 2 to 5 more days. The longer it sits, the more sour it will become. If you have not used the starter 6 days after you made it, store it in the refrigerator, covered loosely, until you are ready to use it. For information about maintaining your starter, see page 267.

GERMAN BEER STARTER

Makes 1¼ cups starter

T his is a luscious starter, strong, and perfect for whole grain breads (I also use it for Sourdough French Bread, page 278). It will bubble quickly because of the added punch from the beer, which the yeast loves. There are all sorts of interesting beers available now from microbreweries; try using one such as a pumpkin ale, to make this starter.

INGREDIENTS

¾ cup unbleached
   all-purpose or bread flour
2 tablespoons rye flour
Large pinch of active dry,
   bread machine, or SAF
   yeast
1 cup flat beer

1 Whisk together the flours, yeast, and beer in a medium bowl. The mixture will be smooth and thick. Transfer to a plastic container or crock. Cover with a few layers of cheesecloth and secure with a rubber band; then cover loosely with plastic wrap.

2 Let stand at warm room temperature for 24 hours to 48 hours (80°F is optimum), stirring a few times. It will be bubbly and smell strongly fermented. Use immediately or store in the refrigerator, covered loosely, until you are ready to use it. For information about maintaining your starter, see page 267.

Overnight Sourdough Pancakes

Makes about twenty 4-inch pancakes

Since a sourdough starter is best if used at least once a week, here is a good way to keep it active. Anyone with a sourdough starter enjoys being able to make these tangy pancakes, as well as a variety of breads. This is an excellent "all-purpose" pancake recipe with a delightful flavor—you can substitute part of the unbleached flour with whole wheat flour or buckwheat flour for variety. I call for blueberries here, but you can use different varieties of fresh berries in the summer, and frozen unthawed, unsweetened berries in the winter. To make this into waffle batter, add 2 tablespoons of melted butter.

1½- or 2-pound loaf machines

For the pancake sponge:

1 cup warm water
1 cup evaporated milk
½ cup sourdough starter
2 cups unbleached all-purpose flour

For the pancake batter:

2 large eggs, beaten
2 tablespoons maple syrup or honey
1 tablespoon light olive oil
1 teaspoon baking soda dissolved in 1 tablespoon water
½ teaspoon baking powder
½ teaspoon salt
1½ to 2 cups fresh blueberries or one 12-ounce package frozen unthawed blueberries, optional

❶ To make the pancake sponge, the night before you want to make the pancakes, place the water, milk, and starter in the bread pan. Add the flour. Program for the Dough cycle, and set a kitchen timer for 10 minutes. When the timer rings, press Stop and unplug the machine. You will have a batter. If you leave it thin, it will make crisp pancakes; a thicker batter, which I like, will make more hearty pancakes. Let the sponge sit in the machine overnight. The batter will rise and fill the pan, become moist, and smell yeasty.

❷ To make the pancakes, the next morning, add the eggs, maple syrup or honey, oil, baking soda, baking powder, and salt to the sponge. Plug in the machine, program for the Dough cycle, and press Start. Watch the mixing for a few minutes. Press Stop as soon as the batter is ready. Do not overmix; the batter should be smooth yet have small lumps. Press Stop, unplug the machine, and you are ready to make the pancakes.

❸ Heat a griddle or heavy skillet over medium heat until a drop of water skates over the surface, then lightly grease it. Pour the batter onto the griddle using a ¼-cup measure. Sprinkle with some berries, if you like. Cook until bubbles form on the surface, the edges are dry, and the bottoms are golden brown, about 2 minutes. Turn once, cooking the opposite sides until golden, about 1 minute more. The second side will take half the amount of time to cook as the first side. Serve immediately with maple syrup, or keep warm in a 200°F oven until ready to serve.

FRENCH BUTTERMILK STARTER

Makes 1½ cups starter

I always seem to have cultured buttermilk around. With a cup left in the carton, I decided to add yeast and some flour, and let it stand for twenty-four hours. Voila! C'est magnifique! I got a smooth, thick fermented starter that has become my favorite. Buttermilk is thinnest at the time of purchase and thickens as it sits. You may want to adjust how much flour you add according to the thickness of your buttermilk. If your buttermilk has exceeded its pull date, the starter may be ready to use after 1 day, but I suggest you let it ferment for at least three days to use it at its best.

INGREDIENTS

¾ cup unbleached all-purpose or bread flour
Large pinch of active dry, bread machine, or SAF yeast
1 to 1¼ cups lowfat buttermilk

For the first feeding:

2 tablespoons unbleached all-purpose or bread flour
3 tablespoon water

1 Whisk together the ¾ cup flour, yeast, and buttermilk in a medium bowl; the mixture should be thick like a pancake batter. Add a bit more flour to adjust the consistency, if necessary. Transfer to a plastic container or crock. Cover with a few layers of cheesecloth and secure with a rubber band; then cover loosely with plastic wrap. Let stand at warm room temperature 24 hours (80°F is optimum). It will be bubbly, begin to ferment, and smell delightful. There will be tiny yellow dots of butter from the buttermilk on the top.

2 After 36 hours when the starter begins to smell sour, feed it with the 2 tablespoons of flour and the water; whisk to combine. Let stand for 1 to 2 more days, until the desired degree of sourness is achieved. This starter can be used 3 or 4 days after it is initially mixed. The longer you let it sit, the more sour it will be; you can judge how sour the starter has become by the way it smells. If you are not ready to use it after 3 or 4 days, let it stand a few more days to continue to sour, or store it in the refrigerator, covered loosely, until you are ready to use it. For information about maintaining your starter, see page 267.

GRAPEYEAST NATURAL STARTER

Starters cultivated from fresh grapes are a very popular type of natural starter. Get your grapes from the arbor in your yard, an old wild vine, an organic farmer's stand at a weekend farmers' market, or a local organic winery in late August or early September. The source of the grapes is important, as sulphured grapes have had the wild yeasts killed that collect naturally on their skins, and that is the culture you want to cultivate. This home recipe is adapted from one given to me by Karen Mitchell of the Model Bakery in St. Helena, California, and is the basis for her pain du vin sourdough round. The starter takes anywhere from nine days to two weeks to prepare.

1 Place the grape bunches in a 4-quart deep plastic bucket (the yeast is on the outside of the skins). Use the back of a large spoon to crush the grapes, pressing out the must (unfermented grape juice) and leaving the skins hanging on the stem. Remove the stem and skins, and leave the crushed grapes, whole seeds, and the must in the bucket. Cover with a double layer of cheesecloth fastened with a rubber band and let stand at warm room temperature (80° to 90°F) to naturally ferment for 5 to 7 days. Do not add anything else to the bucket during this time.

2 Strain the contents of the bucket through a wire mesh over a bowl, reserving the juice. Discard the solids. You will end up with about half as much juice as solids. Pour the juice into a measuring cup and note the measure, then pour the juice into a clean plastic bucket. Add flour equal to the amount of grape juice and whisk to create a thick slurry. Cover with a double layer of cheesecloth and let stand at room temperature to naturally ferment for 3 days. The starter, known as a *chef* at this point, will bubble and foam.

3 On the third day, add the mineral water and 1½ cups of flour to the starter, adding a bit more flour if you desire a thicker starter. Whisk until smooth. Re-cover the starter, now a classic *levain*, and let rest at room temperature for 24 hours to 3 days, depending on how sour you want it. (Some bakers pre-ferment sour starter for up to one month at room temperature with occasional feedings.)

4 At this point, this starter can be stirred down and used immediately. Or cover the starter loosely and store it in the refrigerator for up to 1 week. For information about maintaining your starter, see page 267.

Bread Machine Baker's Hint: Tips for Sourdough Starters

- The grayish liquid that forms on the top is the "hootch"; stir it back in.

- A glass springtop jar without its rubber seal is a good container for a starter.

- Do not keep a starter in a container with a tight lid because the gases in the container expand as the starter ferments.

- Do not store a starter in a stainless steel or aluminum container; these would retard the enzymatic activity.

- Sourdough starters will ferment quickly at a warm room temperature, about 80°F. If your room is cooler, it will take longer to achieve the desired sourness.

- Once a sourdough starter is bubbly and there is a liquid forming on the top, it needs to be fed or refrigerated until use.

- If a starter has been refrigerated, bring it to room temperature before adding it to a dough. You can remove it from the refrigerator the day before you will be baking and let it sit out overnight.

- If a starter turns pink, orange, or black, has an unpleasant aroma, gets wrinkled looking, or grows any type of mold, it should be discarded immediately. Do not take a chance by using a questionable starter.

- Never add salt to a starter; it retards the natural enzymatic activity.

- If you don't have time to use or maintain a starter, you can freeze it. For optimum potency, freeze for no longer than 2 months.

WHITE SOURDOUGH BREAD

1½-POUND LOAF

¾ cup sourdough starter
(pages 265 to 272)
½ cup fat-free milk
2 tablespoons unsalted
    butter, melted
1½ tablespoons honey

3 cups bread flour
1½ teaspoons salt

1½ teaspoons SAF yeast
    or 2 teaspoons bread
    machine yeast

2-POUND LOAF

1 cup sourdough starter
    (pages 265 to 272)
¾ cup fat-free milk
3 tablespoons unsalted
    butter, melted
2 tablespoons honey

4 cups bread flour
2 teaspoons salt

1¾ teaspoons SAF yeast
    or 2¼ teaspoons bread
    machine yeast

*T*his is a light-textured, yet chewy sandwich loaf. Your bacteria-laden starter will give a unique flavor to this old-fashioned American pan bread that will depend on where you live and what wild yeasts your starter has picked up. I make this loaf with the Next-Day White (see page 265) or French Buttermilk (page 271) starter. The dough also makes very nice rolls; see the Variation.

❶ Place all the ingredients in the pan according to the order in the manufacturer's instructions. Set crust on dark and program for the Basic cycle; press Start. (This recipe is not suitable for use with the Delay Timer.)

❷ When the baking cycle ends, immediately remove the bread from the pan and place it on a rack. Let cool to room temperature before slicing.

V A R I A T I O N

Sourdough Poppy Seed Rolls
Makes 10 rolls from the 1½-pound dough, 15 rolls from the 2-pound dough

1 egg beaten with 1 tablespoon milk, for glaze
2 tablespoons poppy seeds

Make the dough on the Dough cycle. Turn the dough out onto a floured work surface and divide the 1½-pound dough into 10 or the 2-pound dough into 15 equal pieces. Flatten and form each piece into an oval. Place on a baking sheet lined with parchment paper and brush each roll with the egg glaze. Sprinkle with poppy seeds. Let rise until doubled in bulk, about 40 minutes. About midway through this rise, preheat the oven to 400°F. Bake the rolls for 20 to 25 minutes, until they are golden brown. Transfer the rolls from the pan to cool on a rack.

CLASSIC SOURDOUGH RYE

T*his is a nice, easy-to-make sandwich loaf that features the classic combination of sourdough, caraway, and rye flour baked all the way through in the machine. For the best flavor and texture use light rye flour, which is ground from just the endosperm like white wheat flour. This bread is best made with Next-Day Rye Sourdough Starter.*

1 To make the sponge, place the sponge ingredients in the bread pan. Program for the Dough cycle; press Start. When the machine beeps at the end of the cycle, press Stop and unplug the machine. Let the sponge starter sit in the machine for 8 hours, or as long as overnight.

2 To make the dough, place all the dough ingredients in the bread pan with the sponge according to the order in the manufacturer's instructions. Set crust on medium and program for the Basic or French Bread cycle; press Start. (This recipe is not suitable for use with the Delay Timer.) The dough ball will be moist, tacky, and smooth.

3 When the baking cycle ends, immediately remove the bread from the pan and place it on a rack. Let cool to room temperature before slicing.

1½-POUND LOAF	2-POUND LOAF
For the sponge:	*For the sponge:*
¾ cup Next-Day Rye Sourdough Starter (page 266)	1 cup Next-Day Rye Sourdough Starter (page 266)
1⅛ cups water	1½ cups water
1⅛ cups light or medium rye flour	1½ cups light or medium rye flour
½ teaspoon SAF or bread machine yeast	½ teaspoon SAF or bread machine yeast
For the dough:	*For the dough:*
1 tablespoon unsalted butter, melted	1½ tablespoons unsalted butter, melted
2¼ cups bread flour	3 cups bread flour
1 tablespoon sugar	1½ tablespoons sugar
1 tablespoon caraway seeds	1 tablespoon plus 1 teaspoon caraway seeds
1½ teaspoons salt	2 teaspoons salt
1 teaspoon SAF yeast or 1½ teaspoons bread machine yeast	1¼ teaspoons SAF yeast or 1¾ teaspoons bread machine yeast

Bread Machine Baker's Hint: Sourdough Baking Tips

- Use sourdough starters at room temperature. If a starter has been refrigerated, let it stand out on the counter overnight before you bake with it.

- Starters should be fed every 10 to 14 days when not in use to keep them fresh and active. There is nothing worse than a bright pink or black starter that has broken down and become unusable from lack of food and the presence of unfriendly bacteria! See page 273 for more details about feeding. You can freeze any of your sourdough starters if you are baking only sporadically. For optimum potency, freeze for no longer than 2 months.

- Sourdough starters should always smell fresh and yeasty. If a starter smells bad, discard it immediately and make a new starter. Never chance working with a starter that may have taken in harmful bacteria.

- Use a glass liquid measuring cup to measure your starter. Just pour it from the cup into the bread pan; then measure the recipe's milk or water using the same cup, without rinsing it out. The liquid will bring any remaining starter along with it as you add it to the pan.

- If the flavor of your sourdough starter is too strong, add ½ teaspoon of baking soda, which neutralizes acid, into the flour portion of the feeding or primary batter ingredients. You can also add the bit of bak- ing soda to the ingredient list when making the bread dough.

- While most bread machine breads benefit from the addition of gluten, I found that gluten in combination with sourdough starter made too light textured a bread, so I have not included it in these recipes. If your bread is too dense, add 2 to 3 teaspoons gluten to your recipe next time you bake it.

- You don't need as much yeast to raise a loaf when adding sourdough starter. The starter has substantial rising power on its own.

- The dough ball for a sourdough bread will be firm and shiny. After the kneading, the ball will relax and look slack. This is okay.

- It is very important that sourdough breads cool completely before you slice them. This is more true for sourdoughs than for other types of bread. Even when a bread is just warm, the moist crumb has not set yet and you will clump and tear the slices, even if using a serrated knife.

- You can use sourdough starter in a regular bread recipe. Add 1 cup of sourdough starter and decrease the liquid in the recipe by ⅔ cup and the flour by ⅓ cup. Use the same amount of yeast as called for in the recipe.

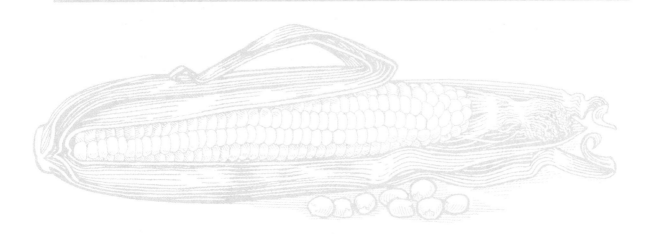

SOURDOUGH CORNMEAL BREAD

M y friend, California rancho cooking expert Jacquie McMahan, always asks for breads that incorporate cornmeal. Here's a sourdough cornmeal combination. I've also included a variation with corn kernels, cheese, olives, and green chiles added, in case you are having a Mexican or Southwestern-inspired meal. Use any white flour sourdough starter. Toast some of this bread to eat with your poached eggs. Cornmeal bread is also great with strawberry jam.

1 Place all the ingredients in the pan according to the order in the manufacturer's instructions. Set crust on medium and program for the Basic cycle; press Start. (This recipe is not suitable for use with the Delay Timer.)

2 When the baking cycle ends, immediately remove the bread from the pan and place it on a rack. Let cool to room temperature before slicing.

V A R I A T I O N

Sourdough Chile-Cheese Cornmeal Bread

¾ cup fresh or defrosted baby corn kernels
½ to ¾ cup grated sharp Cheddar cheese
⅓ to ½ cup canned diced green chiles
2 to 3 tablespoons chopped black olives

Program the machine as specified for Sourdough Cornmeal Bread, but add the corn, cheese, chiles, and olives at the pause between Knead 1 and Knead 2. The exact amount of these ingredients is not important; use less for a 1½-pound loaf, and add more for the 2-pound.

1½-POUND LOAF

1¼ cups white flour sourdough starter (pages 265 to 272)
½ cup plus 2 tablespoons fat-free milk
2 tablespoons olive oil or lard
3 tablespoons honey or molasses

2½ cups bread flour
⅔ cup yellow cornmeal
1½ teaspoons salt

1½ teaspoons SAF yeast or 2 teaspoons bread machine yeast

2-POUND LOAF

1½ cups white flour sourdough starter (pages 265 to 272)
⅞ cup plus 1 tablespoon fat-free milk
3 tablespoons olive oil or lard
4 tablespoons honey or molasses

3½ cups bread flour
¾ cup yellow cornmeal
2 teaspoons salt

2 teaspoons SAF yeast or 2½ teaspoons bread machine yeast

SOURDOUGH FRENCH BREAD

Makes 1 round loaf

1½- OR 2-POUND-LOAF MACHINE

2 cups white flour sourdough starter (pages 265 to 272)
½ cup water

3¼ to 3½ cups bread flour
2 teaspoons salt

2¼ teaspoons bread machine yeast

Yellow cornmeal, for sprinkling

T his loaf is baked in the oven so it can develop that chewy crust dappled with little bubbles and that moist interior just like the loaves from the old San Francisco bakers. You can use any white flour sourdough starter, but be sure that it is at least five days old and real sour. You want the punch. This dough is made on the first day, but baked on the second, so plan accordingly. If your bread rises more slowly than the time frame given here, don't despair, just let it continue to rise. This bread has a dense, moist crumb and delightful sour aroma.

1 Place all the dough ingredients in the bread pan according to the order in the manufacturer's instructions. Use 3 cups of the flour at first, adding more as needed, depending on the consistency of your starter. Program for the Dough cycle; press Start. The dough ball will be firm, then get shiny and soften. When the machine beeps at the end of the cycle, press Stop and unplug the machine. Gently deflate the dough with your finger. Let the dough rest for another 3 hours in the environment of the machine. If it is rising slowly, I have left it in there for up to 8 hours. Check by poking with your finger; it will be springy.

2 Turn the dough out onto a lightly floured work surface. Using a dough card, fold the edges over into the center to make a round loaf, adding flour as needed to prevent sticking. Spread a thick layer of flour on the work surface and turn the loaf over so that the smooth side will be face down in the flour. Cover with a clean tea towel and let rest at room temperature for about 1 hour.

3 Knead the loaf into a tight round again to deflate it. Line an 8-inch round bowl or colander with a clean tea towel. Sprinkle heavily with flour. Place the round of dough in it, smooth side down. Wrap tightly with plastic wrap and refrigerate for 12 to 24 hours. It will rise slowly.

4 Twenty minutes before baking, place a baking stone on the lowest rack of the oven, if desired, and preheat to 450°F. Line a baking sheet with parchment paper and sprinkle with some cornmeal.

5 Remove the dough from the refrigerator and gently turn it out and over onto the baking sheet (the smooth side will be on top now). It will appear to deflate slightly and probably look very moist. This is okay. Gently slash a cross-hatch or square into the top of the loaf, no more than ¼ inch deep with a small sharp knife. Immediately place in the hot oven.

6 Bake for 12 minutes. Reduce the oven temperature to 375°F and bake for an additional 25 to 30 minutes, or until the crust is deep brown, very crisp, and the loaf sounds hollow when tapped with your finger. I insert an instant-read thermometer into a soft crease on the side; it should read about 200°F. Remove the bread from the oven and place it on a rack. Let cool completely before slicing.

Bread Machine Baker's Hint: Reheating Bread

Reheat bread in a 350°F oven. Place the unsliced loaf, au naturel or wrapped in aluminum foil, in a preheated oven for 10 to 15 minutes to crisp the crust. It should just heat through. Sliced breads and rolls reheat best when wrapped. You can also reheat bread in a microwave oven. Place an unwrapped loaf or slice on a paper towel. Microwave on medium-high only until slightly warm, about 15 seconds. If bread or rolls are overheated in the oven or in a microwave, they will become hard and tough as they cool.

SOURDOUGH WHOLE WHEAT BREAD

1½-POUND LOAF

1 cup any sourdough starter
(pages 265 to 272)
⅓ cup fat-free milk
3 tablespoons canola oil
¼ cup molasses

1¾ cups bread flour
1¼ cups whole wheat flour
1½ teaspoons salt

1¼ teaspoons SAF yeast
or 1¾ teaspoons bread
machine yeast

2-POUND LOAF

1⅓ cups any sourdough
starter (pages 265 to 272)
½ cup fat-free milk
3½ tablespoons canola oil
⅓ cup molasses

2½ cups bread flour
1½ cups whole wheat flour
2 teaspoons salt

1¾ teaspoons SAF yeast
or 2¼ teaspoons bread
machine yeast

H*ere is your basic sourdough whole wheat bread for all sorts of uses—dinner, sandwiches, toast. Be sure to check the dough consistency, as the liquid will vary according to how thick your starter is. So don't worry if it looks a bit dry; you can adjust it. I like this made with any of the starters, but especially the Next-Day White Sourdough Starter (page 265) made with whole wheat flour. This dough can also be made into a wonderful cinnamon bread. See page 281 for the changes that must be made to the dough-making process, and for complete filling and shaping instructions.*

❶ Place all the ingredients in the pan according to the order in the manufacturer's instructions. Set crust on dark and program for the Whole Wheat cycle; press Start. (This recipe is not suitable for use with the Delay Timer.) Check the consistency of the dough during Knead 2; add a little more milk or flour as needed.

❷ When the baking cycle ends, immediately remove the bread from the pan and place it on a rack. Let cool to room temperature before slicing.

Sourdough Whole Wheat Cinnamon Bread

Makes 1 loaf

Penuche is a melted filling of sugar, butter, vanilla, and nuts. The word means "brown sugar" or "raw sugar" in Spanish. Sourdough Whole Wheat Bread (page 280) makes a sensational wrapper for this filling. To prepare the recipe to make cinnamon bread, substitute an equal amount of brown sugar or honey for the molasses. If you will be baking the cinnamon bread in your machine, program it for the Basic or Variety cycle. If you will be baking the cinnamon bread in the oven, use the Dough cycle. This bread is divine and makes wonderful toast.

1½- or 2-pound-loaf machines

For the dough:

1 recipe Sourdough Whole Wheat Bread dough (page 280); substitute brown sugar or honey for the molasses

For the penuche filling:

2 tablespoons butter, at room temperature
1 teaspoon vanilla extract or vanilla powder
¼ cup light brown sugar
¼ cup dark brown sugar
1 tablespoon ground cinnamon
¼ cup finely chopped walnuts, optional

1 Add the ingredients and program the machine as specified for Sourdough Whole Wheat Bread. At the end of Rise 2 on the Basic cycle, press Pause, or when the display shows Shape in the Variety cycle, remove the pan and close the lid. Immediately turn the dough out onto a lightly floured work surface; pat into an 8-by-12-inch fat rec-tangle. With a fork, cream the butter and the vanilla extract in a small bowl. If you are using vanilla powder, toss it with the brown sugar. Spread the surface of the dough with a thin layer of butter. Sprinkle with the brown sugars, cinnamon, and nuts, if using, leaving a 1-inch space all the way around. Starting at a short edge, roll up jelly-roll fashion into a fat loaf. Tuck the ends under and pinch the bottom seam. Coat the bottom of the dough with cooking spray.

2 *To bake in the bread machine:* Remove the kneading blade and place the dough back in the pan; press Start to continue to rise and bake as programmed. When the baking cycle ends, immediately remove the bread from the pan and place it on a rack. Let cool to room temperature before slicing.

3 *To bake in the oven:* Place the loaf in a greased 9-by-5-inch loaf pan (for the 1½-pound loaf) or two 7-by-4-inch loaf pans (for the 2-pound loaf). I use disposable aluminum pans from the supermarket for these loaves since the filling often leaks. Spray the top of the loaf with cooking spray and cover lightly with plastic wrap. Let rise at room temperature until doubled in bulk, about 45 minutes.

4 Twenty minutes before baking, place a baking stone on the lower rack of the oven and preheat to 350°F.

5 Bake for 45 to 50 minutes, or until golden brown and the sides have slightly contracted from the pan. If the crust browns too quickly, place a piece of aluminum foil loosely over the top. Cool on a rack.

LEVAIN LOAF

Makes 2 small loaves

For the sponge:

1 cup lukewarm bottled
    mineral water
½ cup Grapeyeast Natural
    Starter (page 272) or
    other sourdough starter
½ teaspoon bread machine
    yeast
¾ cup bread flour
¾ cup whole wheat flour

For the dough:

Sponge, above
1 teaspoon SAF or
    1½ teaspoons bread
    machine yeast
1¾ cups bread flour
1½ teaspoons fine sea salt

Yellow cornmeal, for
    sprinkling

T *his is my version of Karen Mitchell's* pain du vin. *The amount of flour this loaf will take depends on the consistency of your starter. If your starter is soupy, it will take a bit more; if it is very sticky, it will take less. You can opt not to use the yeast, but plan on doubling your rising times.*

❶ To make the sponge, place the water, starter, and yeast in the bread pan. Add the flours on top. Program for the Dough cycle; press Start. Set a kitchen timer for 10 minutes. The sponge will be very wet and sticky. Don't be tempted to add more flour. When the timer rings, press Stop and unplug the machine. Let rest at room temperature in the machine for 24 hours.

❷ The next day, stir down the sponge by running the Dough cycle for 3 minutes.

❸ To make the dough, sprinkle the yeast over the sponge. Add the flour and the salt. Program for the Dough cycle and press Start. The dough will be shiny, very moist to the point of being slightly sticky, and soft. Don't be tempted to add more flour. When the machine beeps at the end of the cycle, press Stop and unplug the machine. Gently deflate the dough with your finger. Set a timer and let the dough rest for another 1½ hours in the warm environment of the machine.

❹ Line a baking sheet with parchment paper and sprinkle with cornmeal. Turn the dough out onto a lightly floured work surface. Divide the dough into 2 equal pieces. Using a dough card, gently knead each piece into a ball. Place the balls on the baking sheet a few inches apart. Cover with a clean tea towel and let rise at room temperature until doubled in bulk, about 1 hour.

5 Twenty minutes before baking, place a baking stone on the middle rack of the oven, if desired, and preheat to 425°F.

6 Sprinkle the top of each loaf with flour and rub in to coat. Slash an X into the tops, no more than ¼ inch deep, with a small sharp knife. Bake for 35 to 40 minutes, or until the crusts are deep brown, very crisp, and sound hollow when tapped with your finger. The loaves will be full and high. I insert an instant-read thermometer into a soft crease on the side; it should read about 200°F. Remove the loaves from the oven and place on a rack. Let cool completely before slicing.

Technique: How to Position a Loaf and Bake It in the Oven

Baking is the process that turns your dough into an edible food. The heat quickly penetrates the mass, encouraging the last gasp of fermentation and raising the temperature inside the loaf, which kills the yeast. You will see a rapid increase in the size of the loaf once it begins baking, this is called oven spring. This is why some loaves that look kind of scraggly going into the oven look very nice when they are finished baking. The starch sets and the natural sugars in the flour caramelize, giving you the brown color of the crust.

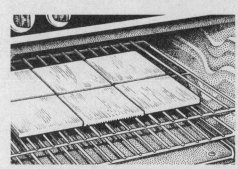

The first thing to do when preparing to bake a loaf in the oven is to make sure the oven rack is in the center or lower third of the oven. Professional bakeries bake country breads on the floors of brick ovens; you can simulate their setup by placing a ceramic baking stone or tiles on the oven rack for the baking sheet to rest on. Alternatively, the loaves will turn out well using just a baking sheet and no stones. Shaped loaves are often shoveled into the oven with a wooden paddle called a peel, but none of my baking instructions in this book require the use of a peel. When you place the bread on a baking sheet, you are assured that it will be in the correct position, usually centered, on the baking sheet. There is many a tale about the home baker who used a peel and had the bread land somewhere in the oven other than on the stone or had their bread stick to the peel and become shaped like a horseshoe.

The next preparation step is to set the oven temperature specified in the recipe.

The type of flour and size of the loaf determine how long a loaf will bake. The larger the loaf, the longer the bake off. Smaller loaves can be baked at a higher temperature for a short time because of the small proportion of inner crumb. That is why baguettes and rolls can bake at 450°F, but a large round bakes at 375°F.

When is the bread done? First, consider the length of time it has been in the oven. I usually set a timer for 10 minutes less than the baking time called for in the recipe. When the timer rings, I begin to check for doneness. I look at the color of the crust first. If it is too pale, the loaf is definitely under-done. You can raise the temperature of the oven, or just let it bake longer. The crust on country breads should be firm to hard when you tap it with your finger. I take it as a good sign if it is hard, since it will soften slightly as it cools (as the water vapor in the middle of the hot loaf evaporates out to the crust), but that crisp crust is often hard to get in a home oven. A crispy crust means the bread will be nice and chewy for the eater. The slash marks you made will be torn open by the rising into an uneven, rustic pattern. Tap the loaf, and listen for a hollow sound. A thud means it is not baked on the inside. To be absolutely sure the loaf is baked, you can measure the temperature with an instant-read thermometer. When it registers 190° to 200°F, the loaf is done.

Use thick oven mitts to transfer the finished loaves from the oven to the top of the stove or a rack. I often let a large loaf cool right on the baking sheet. When the loaf first begins to cool, you will hear some crackling noises as the crust contracts.

While sourdough loaves must cool completely before slicing, other country breads come with the bonus of being able to be devoured warm. Enjoy the satisfying shattering of the crust, the moist inner crumb, and the slight yeasty aroma. I always check out the first slice to inspect the pattern of the air pockets. Then, finally, comes the satisfaction of a job well done.

SOURDOUGH BUCKWHEAT BREAD

B uckwheat flour and sourdough have a natural affinity, as you will see when you make this excellent bread. Use any white flour starter. I also like to use this bread for stuffings.

❶ Place all the ingredients in the pan according to the order in the manufacturer's instructions. Set crust on dark and program for the Basic cycle; press Start. (This recipe is not suitable for use with the Delay Timer.)

❷ When the baking cycle ends, immediately remove the bread from the pan and place it on a rack. Let cool to room temperature before slicing.

1½-POUND LOAF	2-POUND LOAF
1 cup white flour sourdough starter (pages 265 to 272)	1¼ cups white flour sourdough starter (pages 265 to 272)
¼ cup buttermilk	½ cup buttermilk
1 large egg	1 large egg
Grated zest of 1 orange	Grated zest of 1 orange
2 tablespoons unsalted butter, melted	3 tablespoons unsalted butter, melted
2 cups bread flour	2⅔ cups bread flour
½ cup whole wheat flour	⅔ cup whole wheat flour
½ cup buckwheat flour	⅔ cup buckwheat flour
3 tablespoons light brown sugar	3½ tablespoons light brown sugar
1½ teaspoons salt	2 teaspoons salt
1½ teaspoons SAF yeast or 2 teaspoons bread machine yeast	1¾ teaspoons SAF yeast or 2¼ teaspoons bread machine yeast

SOURDOUGH SUNFLOWER SEED HONEY BREAD

S weet and nutty—this is how I like whole wheat breads. This one has just enough walnuts to give a hint of them. They are especially nice toasted very slightly to take the starchiness out of their flavor.

❶ Place the ingredients in the pan according to the order in the manufacturer's instructions. Set crust on dark and program for the Whole Wheat cycle; press Start. (This recipe is not suitable for use with the Delay Timer.)

❷ When the baking cycle ends, immediately remove the bread from the pan and place it on a rack. Let cool to room temperature before slicing.

1½-POUND LOAF	2-POUND LOAF
1 cup sourdough starter (pages 265 to 272)	1⅓ cups sourdough starter (pages 265 to 272)
½ cup fat-free milk	⅔ cup fat-free milk
¼ cup margarine, cut into pieces	⅓ cup margarine, cut into pieces
1 cup bread flour	1½ cups bread flour
2 cups whole wheat flour	2½ cups whole wheat flour
¼ cup dark brown sugar	⅓ cup dark brown sugar
⅓ cup raw sunflower seeds	½ cup raw sunflower seeds
2 tablespoons chopped walnuts	3 tablespoons chopped walnuts
1½ teaspoons salt	2 teaspoons salt
1½ teaspoons SAF yeast or 2 teaspoons bread machine yeast	1¾ teaspoons SAF yeast or 2¼ teaspoons bread machine yeast

SOURDOUGH RAISIN BREAD

F or the hard-core sourdough lovers I couldn't leave out a raisin bread. Use dark, golden, extra-large Monukka, or currants, and soak them well before adding so they will be soft. You can also use this dough to make a beautiful olive bread; see the Variation.

① Place the raisins in a bowl and cover with hot water. Let stand for 1½ hours at room temperature to soften. Drain the raisins and pat as dry as possible, as any moisture will be incorporated into the dough.

② Place the ingredients in the pan according to the order in the manufacturer's instructions. Set crust on dark and program for the Basic cycle; press Start. (This recipe is not suitable for use with the Delay Timer.) Add the raisins during the first 10 minutes of Knead 2. Gradually sprinkle in the raisins while the machine is kneading. If the dough looks too sticky after the raisins are incorporated, sprinkle another 1 to 2 tablespoons of flour around the paddle while the machine is running.

③ When the baking cycle ends, immediately remove the bread from the pan and place it on a rack. Let cool to room temperature before slicing.

V A R I A T I O N

Sourdough Olive Bread

For either size loaf, delete the raisins from the recipe and reduce the salt to ¾ teaspoon. In Step 2, add 1¼ cups pitted and halved black olives and ½ cup pitted and halved green olives (drain on paper towels before adding) in place of the raisins. Continue as directed.

1½-POUND LOAF

1½ cups raisins

½ cup sourdough starter (pages 265 to 272)
½ cup fat-free milk
2 large eggs
2 tablespoons margarine, cut into pieces

3 cups bread flour
2 tablespoons sugar
1½ teaspoons salt

1 teaspoon SAF yeast or 1½ teaspoons bread machine yeast

2-POUND LOAF

1¾ cup raisins

¾ cups sourdough starter (pages 265 to 272)
⅔ cup fat-free milk
2 large eggs
3 tablespoons margarine, cut into pieces

4 cups bread flour
2½ tablespoons sugar
2 teaspoons salt

1¼ teaspoons SAF yeast or 1¾ teaspoons bread machine yeast

SOURDOUGH BANANA NUT BREAD

T his is a really nice sweet and sour bread with lots of goodies in it. It is good for peanut butter and jelly or smoked turkey or Black Forest ham sandwiches, or for toast.

1 Place all the ingredients in the pan according to the order in the manufacturer's instructions. Set crust on medium and program for the Basic cycle; press Start. (This recipe is not suitable for use with the Delay Timer.)

2 When the baking cycle ends, immediately remove the bread from the pan and place it on a rack. Let cool to room temperature before slicing.

1½-POUND LOAF	2-POUND LOAF
½ cup sourdough starter (pages 265 to 272)	¾ cups sourdough starter (pages 265 to 272)
¼ cup buttermilk	½ cup buttermilk
½ cup sliced bananas	⅔ cup sliced bananas
1 large egg	1 large egg
2 tablespoons nut oil	3 tablespoons nut oil
2½ cups bread flour	3⅓ cups bread flour
½ cup whole wheat flour	⅔ cup whole wheat flour
½ cup chopped macadamia nuts or pecans	⅔ cup chopped macadamia nuts or pecans
3 tablespoons chopped dried pineapple or dates	4 tablespoons chopped dried pineapple or dates
2 tablespoons light brown sugar	3 tablespoons light brown sugar
1¼ teaspoons salt	1½ teaspoons salt
1¾ teaspoons SAF yeast or 2¼ teaspoons bread machine yeast	2¼ teaspoons SAF yeast or 2¾ teaspoons bread machine yeast

SOURDOUGH BREAD WITH FRESH PEARS AND WALNUTS

I adore pears in any type of baking. Greeks, Chinese, French, and Italians all sing the praises of the pear in their cooking. For this recipe, be sure to get firm, underripe pears that will hold up during baking, such as a Bartlett, D'Anjou, or the russet Bosc, which is described as a buttery pear that does not melt.

1 Place the ingredients, except the pears, in the pan according to the order in the manufacturer's instructions. Set crust on medium and program for the Basic or Sweet Bread cycle; press Start. (This recipe is not suitable for use with the Delay Timer.) About 5 minutes into the kneading, sprinkle the pears into the dough, a few at a time, until all the pears are added.

2 When the baking cycle ends, immediately remove the bread from the pan and place it on a rack. Let cool to room temperature before slicing.

1½-POUND LOAF	2-POUND LOAF
¾ cup sourdough starter (pages 265 to 272)	1 cup sourdough starter (pages 265 to 272)
⅓ cup buttermilk	½ cup buttermilk
1½ teaspoons vanilla extract	2 teaspoons vanilla extract
2 tablespoons butter, cut into pieces	3 tablespoons butter, cut into pieces
3 cups bread flour	4 cups bread flour
⅓ cup rolled oats	½ cup rolled oats
3 tablespoons light brown sugar	4 tablespoons light brown sugar
⅓ cup walnuts	½ cup walnuts
2 teaspoons apple pie spice	1 tablespoon apple pie spice
1½ teaspoons salt	2 teaspoons salt
1¼ teaspoons SAF yeast or 1¾ teaspoons bread machine yeast	1¾ teaspoons SAF yeast or 2¼ teaspoons bread machine yeast
1½ cups peeled, cored, and chopped fresh pear (1 to 2 large pears)	2 cups peeled, cored, and chopped fresh pear (about 2 large pears)

The Right Ingredient: About Salt

While salt isn't truly required as a flavor enhancer, it is considered an essential ingredient for its ability to accent other flavors in the bread. A lack of salt is very noticeable as a flat taste in a finished loaf. Salt also plays another important role; the little bit that most bread recipes call for acts as a stabilizer so that the yeast does not overferment. It helps to condition and toughen the protein strands so that they do not break easily during the rising process and the dough expands smoothly. Too much salt can inhibit yeast activity, though, so be sure you use the exact amount called for in a recipe.

If you are on a salt-restricted diet and wish to reduce the salt in a recipe, be sure to reduce the yeast measurement proportionally or use the full amount of a lite salt. Without the right amount of salt, the dough will rise too fast. This is especially true in the environment of the bread machine, which is warm and very hospitable to the yeast.

Plain iodized table salt (mechanically removed from rock salt deposits with potassium iodine and magnesium silicate added to prevent caking) and fine sea salt (from saline deposits at the edge of the sea, containing no preservatives or anti-caking agents) can be used interchangeably in recipes. I prefer the flavor of a fine-grind sun-evaporated sea salt, and even call for fine sea salt in some country breads in which the flavor of each ingredient is so integral to the finished loaf. Sun-evaporated, unrefined sea salts retain their complementary minerals, calcium, potassium, and magnesium, which gives them a distinct flavor reminiscent of the sea. I like fine La Baleine, an iodized sun-evaporated sea salt from the Mediterranean, or Balboa fine-crystal salt from San Francisco Bay. An entire line of different salts for the gourmet bread-maker are available by mail order, including pretzel salt, extra fine salt for focaccia and breadsticks, Maldon Crystal Sea Salt from England (it has pyramid-shaped flakes), good for use in bread as well as for sprinkling, and Fleur de Sel De Guerande from Brittany. *Fleur de sel*, literally "flower of salt," is gathered off the top layer of salt that collects in sun-evaporation pans over the water. It is known as "the caviar of salts," and used as a condiment rather than an ingredient. The pretty white crystals can be sprinkled directly onto sweet butter that has been spread on *pain de campagne*, for example. Another exceptional salt is Light Grey Celtic Sea Salt, which is a bit moist and gets ground in a salt mill; it is a favorite with specialty artisan bakers. Kosher salt (which is mined, but contains no additives) is less salty than regular salts and a favorite of ethnic bakers. Along with coarse sea salt kosher salt must be ground before being used in dough (it won't dissolve), otherwise it may be sprinkled in its larger pieces on top of focaccia, bagels, pretzels, and breadsticks before baking, for a pretty finishing touch.

When you are using the Delay Timer to make bread, add the salt to the bread pan just after you've added the liquid, at the beginning of the dry ingredients. The flour then acts as a buffer between the salt and the yeast, so that the salt does not inhibit the yeast as the ingredients are sitting in the pan. Some recipes and owner's manuals say that salt and yeast should never come in contact, but I find this precaution necessary only when using the Delay Timer. If you are mixing and baking the bread right away, it really doesn't matter what comes in contact with what. As you can see from my recipes, in fact, I usually add the salt and yeast next to one another at the end; I believe the salt gets distributed more evenly this way.

ORANGE SOURDOUGH BREAD WITH CRANBERRIES, PECANS, AND GOLDEN RAISINS

T*he sweet-sour taste combination of the raisins and cran-berries in this bread is one of my favorites. Use a white flour sourdough starter, like the French Buttermilk.*

1 Place the ingredients, except the fruit and nuts, in the pan according to the order in the manufacturer's instructions. Set crust on medium and program for the Basic cycle or Fruit and Nut cycle; press Start. (This recipe is not suitable for use with the Delay Timer.) When the machine beeps, or between Knead 1 and Knead 2, add the fruits and nuts. If you are using the Basic cycle, you may also mix all the ingredients together at the beginning, if you wish.

2 When the baking cycle ends, immediately remove the bread from the pan and place it on a rack. Let cool to room temperature before slicing.

1½-POUND LOAF	2-POUND LOAF
½ cup French Buttermilk Starter (page 271), or any white flour sourdough starter	¾ cup French Buttermilk Starter (page 271), or any white flour sourdough starter
¾ cup orange juice	1 cup orange juice
2 tablespoons butter, cut into pieces	3 tablespoons butter, cut into pieces
3¼ cups bread flour	4¼ cups bread flour
3 tablespoons sugar	¼ cup sugar
1 teaspoon salt	1½ teaspoons salt
1¾ teaspoons SAF yeast or 2¼ teaspoons bread machine yeast	2 teaspoons SAF yeast or 2½ teaspoons bread machine yeast
½ cup dried cranberries	⅔ cup dried cranberries
⅓ cup golden raisins	½ cup golden raisins
⅓ cup chopped pecans	½ cup chopped pecans

SOURDOUGH PUMPKIN SPICE BREAD

M y girlfriend Suzanne and I like to order some of our spices in bulk from McCormick. This last batch included a pound of apple pie spice mixture—a combination of cinnamon, nutmeg, and allspice—which is now in everything sweet that I bake. I ended up developing and making this recipe for Halloween. Serve this bread with cream cheese and Spiced Vanilla Honey (page 599) or Cinnamon Date Cheese (page 602).

1 Place all the ingredients in the pan according to the order in the manufacturer's instructions. Set crust on dark and program for the Basic cycle; press Start. (This recipe is not suitable for use with the Delay Timer.)

2 When the baking cycle ends, immediately remove the bread from the pan and place it on a rack. Let cool to room temperature before slicing.

1½-POUND LOAF	2-POUND LOAF
¾ cup sourdough starter (pages 265 to 272)	1 cup sourdough starter (pages 265 to 272)
1 cup canned pumpkin puree	1⅓ cups canned pumpkin puree
¼ cup water	⅓ cup water
2 tablespoons vegetable or nut oil	3 tablespoons vegetable or nut oil
3½ cups bread flour	4½ cups bread flour
3 tablespoons dark brown sugar	¼ cup dark brown sugar
2 teaspoons apple pie spice	1 tablespoon apple pie spice
1½ teaspoons salt	1¾ teaspoons salt
1¼ teaspoons SAF yeast or 2¼ teaspoons bread machine yeast	1½ teaspoons SAF yeast or 1¾ teaspoons bread machine yeast

SOURDOUGH CARROT POPPY SEED BREAD

C*arrots, poppy seeds, and dried apricots make one of my favorite breads, good for breakfast as well as dinner.*

1 Place all the ingredients in the pan according to the order in the manufacturer's instructions. Set crust on dark and program for the Basic cycle; press Start. (This recipe is not suitable for use with the Delay Timer.)

2 When the baking cycle ends, immediately remove the bread from the pan and place it on a rack. Let cool to room temperature before slicing.

1½-POUND LOAF	2-POUND LOAF
¾ cup sourdough starter (pages 265 to 272)	1 cup sourdough starter (pages 265 to 272)
½ cup buttermilk	⅔ cup buttermilk
1½ tablespoons olive or walnut oil	2 tablespoons olive or walnut oil
2½ cups bread flour	3⅓ cups bread flour
½ cup whole wheat flour	⅔ cup whole wheat flour
1¼ cups shredded raw carrots	1½ cups shredded raw carrots
2 tablespoons minced dried apricots	3 tablespoons minced dried apricots
1 tablespoon poppy seeds	1¼ tablespoons poppy seeds
1 tablespoon sugar	1¼ tablespoons sugar
1½ teaspoons salt	2 teaspoons salt
1¼ teaspoons SAF yeast or 1¾ teaspoons bread machine yeast	1¾ teaspoons SAF yeast or 2¼ teaspoons bread machine yeast

SOURDOUGH COTTAGE CHEESE BREAD WITH FRESH HERBS

T his is a loaf to showcase fresh herbs, so don't use dried here. For a spicier bread you can substitute chives for the watercress. Be sure to slice this bread with a serrated bread knife, since the crumb is delicate when the bread is fresh. Serve warm with fresh goat cheese for spreading, or with simple pasta dishes or roast chicken. Day-old, it is good toasted in thick slices or cubed for croutons.

1½-POUND LOAF

¾ cup sourdough starter (pages 265 to 272)
¾ cup cottage cheese
2 tablespoons olive oil

3 cups bread flour
¼ cup chopped fresh watercress leaves, loosely packed
1 tablespoon chopped fresh chives
1 tablespoon chopped fresh basil
1 tablespoon chopped fresh dill
2 teaspoons chopped fresh marjoram
¼ teaspoon dried lemon rind or ½ teaspoon fresh lemon zest
1½ teaspoons salt

1½ teaspoons SAF yeast or 2 teaspoons bread machine yeast

2-POUND LOAF

1 cup sourdough starter (pages 265 to 272)
1 cup cottage cheese
3 tablespoons olive oil

4 cups bread flour
¼ cup chopped fresh watercress leaves, loosely packed
1 tablespoon chopped fresh chives
1 tablespoon chopped fresh basil
1 tablespoon chopped fresh dill
2 teaspoons chopped fresh marjoram
¼ teaspoon dried lemon rind or ½ teaspoon fresh lemon zest
2 teaspoons salt

1¾ teaspoons SAF yeast or 2¼ teaspoons bread machine yeast

1 Place all the ingredients in the pan according to the order in the manufacturer's instructions. Set crust on dark and program for the Basic cycle; press Start. (This recipe is not suitable for use with the Delay Timer.)

2 When the baking cycle ends, immediately remove the bread from the pan and place it on a rack. Let cool to room temperature before slicing.

SOURDOUGH TOMATO BREAD WITH FETA

T*his bread has a complex flavor and aroma. Feta cheese is both strong and salty, and goes well with the sweetness of the tomato. You can substitute crumbled fresh goat cheese for the feta, if you like.*

1 Place all the ingredients in the pan according to the order in the manufacturer's instructions. Set crust on dark and program for the Basic cycle; press Start. (This recipe is not suitable for use with the Delay Timer.) The dough will look dry at first, but will moisten as the tomatoes break up.

2 When the baking cycle ends, immediately remove the bread from the pan and place it on a rack. Let cool to room temperature before slicing.

1½-POUND LOAF

¾ cup sourdough starter (pages 265 to 272)
¾ cup chopped canned tomatoes with some liquid
2 tablespoons olive oil

3 cups bread flour
⅔ cup crumbled feta cheese
½ teaspoon salt

1¼ teaspoons SAF yeast or 1¾ teaspoons bread machine yeast

2-POUND LOAF

1 cup sourdough starter (pages 265 to 272)
¾ cup chopped canned tomatoes with some liquid
3 tablespoons olive oil

4 cups bread flour
¾ cup crumbled feta cheese
¾ teaspoon salt

1¾ teaspoons SAF yeast or 2¼ teaspoons bread machine yeast

SOURDOUGH PESTO BREAD

P esto is a thick paste made of fresh basil, pine nuts, garlic, and Parmesan cheese that originated in Italy. You can make your own and use it in this bread, or use a commercial brand, found in the produce section or with the fresh pasta selection at the supermarket. Pesto has a pungent nature and is excellent with farinaceous foods like bread and pasta. Here it is added into the dough. Serve this herb bread before dinner with wine, or as a complement to Italian meals.

❶ Place all the ingredients in the pan according to the order in the manufacturer's instructions. Set crust on dark and program for the Basic or French Bread cycle; press Start. (This recipe is not suitable for use with the Delay Timer.)

❷ When the baking cycle ends, immediately remove the bread from the pan and place it on a rack. Let cool to room temperature before slicing.

1½-POUND LOAF	2-POUND LOAF
1 cup sourdough starter (pages 265 to 272)	1⅓ cups sourdough starter (pages 265 to 272)
⅓ cup fat-free milk	½ cup fat-free milk
2 tablespoons olive oil	3 tablespoons olive oil
3 tablespoons pesto	¼ cup pesto
3 cups bread flour	4 cups bread flour
1 tablespoon sugar	1½ tablespoons sugar
1½ teaspoons garlic powder	1¾ teaspoons garlic powder
1 teaspoon dried marjoram	1¼ teaspoons dried marjoram
1 teaspoon dried basil	1¼ teaspoons dried basil
1 teaspoon salt	1½ teaspoons salt
1½ teaspoons SAF yeast or 2 teaspoons bread machine yeast	1¾ teaspoons SAF yeast or 2¼ teaspoons bread machine yeast

SOURDOUGH ENGLISH MUFFINS

Makes 1 dozen 3-inch muffins

T hese English muffins are tangy, just as they should be. Keep a stash in the freezer so that you won't have to buy them at the grocery store. Homemade English muffins are worth the work. I found an old-fashioned smooth-rimmed biscuit cutter with a tiny red handle at a tag sale at my local church that I use just for these muffins. They are fantastic with Lemon Curd with Mint (page 600). Split with a fork or with your fingers.

1½- OR 2-POUND-LOAF MACHINES
1 cup sourdough starter (pages 265 to 272)
½ cup fat-free milk
2 tablespoons unsalted butter, melted
1 large egg
3¾ cups bread flour
1½ teaspoons salt
2 teaspoons SAF yeast or 2½ teaspoons bread machine yeast
⅓ cup yellow cornmeal or coarse semolina, for sprinkling

1 Place all the ingredients in the pan according to the order in the manufacturer's instructions. Program for the Dough cycle; press Start. The dough ball will be soft and very slightly moist. The softer you leave the dough, the lighter the muffin will be. You can add a bit more flour when you remove the dough from the machine.

2 Lightly sprinkle the work surface with cornmeal. When the machine beeps at the end of the cycle, using a dough card scrape the dough out onto the work surface and, with a rolling pin, roll it into a rectangle about ½-inch thick. Sprinkle the top with cornmeal to prevent sticking. Cut out the muffins with a 3-inch biscuit cutter or the rim of a drinking glass. Roll out the scraps and cut out the remaining muffins. Cover the muffins with a clean tea towel or place them in the refrigerator if they are rising too fast while the others are baking.

3 Preheat an electric griddle to 350° or 375°F, or heat a cast-iron griddle over medium heat until a drop of water sprinkled on the griddle dances across the surface. Lightly grease the surface. Place several muffins on the hot griddle. Cook for about 10 minutes on each side, turning when they are quite brown. English muffins take time to bake all the way through, and will swell and be very puffy while baking. Remove the muffins from the griddle with a spatula and cool on a rack.

Leftover Bread Cookery: *Stratas* (Savory Bread Puddings)

Strata is a culinary term coined in the 1950s for an old-fashioned casserole composed of layers of ingredients, the same technique used for constructing a lasagne or quiche, except that bread is used as the main starch. If you have never made a savory bread pudding *strata*, it can sound unusual, but the results are spectacular. *Stratas* are real convenience foods. Some can be assembled up to 12 hours ahead of time and refrigerated. They make a wonderful brunch served with fresh fruit, or a hearty lunch or Sunday supper served with a green salad. If I have time to make it, I like to eat a few tablespoons of chunky homemade salsa on the side.

The firm texture and low-fat quality of French or Italian country breads make them well-suited for *stratas*. But any white, whole wheat sandwich, or egg bread, (even English muffins) can be used; cut the bread into ½-inch-thick slices to fit your casserole dish. Strata ingredients vary from bacon and spinach with jack cheese or asparagus, mushroom, and Brie to roasted red peppers, chorizo sausage, and chèvre. Whatever meat you use, be sure it is already cooked and cooled before going in the *strata*. The pudding is held together with a mixture of milk and eggs. I find that commercial liquid egg substitues work well, too. Take care not to overbake a *strata*, or the custard will be rubbery.

Cheese, Ham, and Chile Strata

Serves 8 generously

This is my favorite strata. I've made it for many power breakfasts when catering.

1 medium loaf firm day-old bread, sliced thin and crusts removed (about 15 slices, cut into halves)
3 cups (10 to 12 ounces) coarsely chopped cooked ham, such as honey-baked

2 large cans (7 ounces each) diced, roasted green chiles
1 pound mild cheddar cheese, shredded (about 4 cups)
5 cups milk
10 large eggs
1½ teaspoons dried basil or oregano
Fresh-ground black pepper to taste

1 Arrange a quarter of the bread slices, slightly overlapping, in the bottom of a shallow 4-quart casserole. Top with a third of the ham; then a layer of the green chiles and then 1 cup of the cheese. Arrange another layer of bread over this, barely covering the filling. Continue to layer the ham, chiles, cheese, and bread to make a total of 4 layers of bread and 3 layers of filling, finishing with the bread slices on top. (You will have 1 cup of cheese left for topping.)

2 Whisk together the milk, eggs, and seasonings in a large bowl. Slowly pour over the bread. Sprinkle the top with the last cup of the cheese, cover tightly, and refrigerate at least 2 hours to overnight.

3 When ready to bake, preheat the oven to 325°F.

4 Bake uncovered for 50 minutes to 1 hour, or until the center is puffed and golden; a knife inserted into the center will come out clean. Let stand for 10 minutes before serving hot.

Fast Winter Salsa

Makes 1½ cups

1 clove garlic
4 scallions, cut into chunks
1 to 2 jalapeño chiles, seeded, or chipotle chiles
  en adobo
1 handful of rinsed and dried fresh cilantro
One 16-ounce can fancy stewed or plum tomatoes,
  drained
Juice of 1 lime

Place the garlic, onions, chiles, and cilantro
in the bowl of a food processor fitted with
the metal blade. Chop coarsely using short
pulses. Add the tomatoes and pulse until
chunky; season with lime juice. Keeps for
3 days in the refrigerator.

Jesse's Bread and Cabbage Strata (Pannecoi)

Serves 6

*This is an earthy family recipe from restaurateur
and food writer Jesse Cool, who is a passionate
vegetable eater. Make sure you buy a fresh cabbage with bright, crisp outer leaves; it will taste
less "cabbagey." I make a simple marinara sauce
with a bit of basil to use here, but a commercial
brand is also good in a pinch; just remember that
it will be more salty than homemade. Pannecoi
is a great side dish for roasted meats, or makes a
great vegetarian entree when served with a salad.*

3 tablespoons olive oil
1 day-old loaf homemade Pane Italiano (page 208)
  or Semolina Country Bread (page 202), sliced
  ½ inch thick and cut in half
½ head white or savoy cabbage, sliced thin
1 medium yellow onion, sliced very thin
2 cups chicken broth
2 cups marinara sauce, canned or homemade
8 ounces mozzarella cheese, sliced
¾ cup grated Parmesan or Asiago cheese

❶ Preheat the oven to 350°F.

❷ Drizzle the olive oil in the bottom of a
deep 13-by-9-inch baking dish or casserole,
and place a layer of the bread slices over the
olive oil. Cover the bread with an inch of
cabbage, and then with a layer of onions.
Season with salt and pepper. Drizzle with
⅔ cup of the chicken broth. Spoon a layer
of ⅔ cup marinara sauce and a layer of
mozzarella. Sprinkle with Parmesan. Repeat
the process, making 2 more layers of bread,
cabbage, onions, broth, sauce, and cheese.
Top with the last layer of cheese.

❸ Bake for 1 hour 15 minutes to 1 hour
30 minutes, until set and all the liquid is
absorbed. Remove from the oven and let
stand for 10 minutes before serving.

ALL KINDS OF FLAVORS

Breads Made with
the Produce of the Garden,
Orchard, and Creamery

HERB, NUT, SEED, AND SPICE BREADS

Hail to the first unknown baker who added earthy culinary herbs to a bread dough. It must have been long ago, because there are pictorial records from Egyptian tombs that give directions for herbed loaves. The harmonious blending of grains, ingredients with distinctive fragrances, exotic spices, and nuts ushers one into a sphere of innovative taste experiences and invisible clouds of aroma. These flavors may be incorporated into every type of bread, from the simplest French loaf to a rich egg bread. Bakers are invited to embellish at their whim, adding delicate, balmy dill; warm, bold oregano; assertive, licorice-like tarragon; or resiny thyme. Any herb, nut, or spice added to a bread immediately makes it more distinctive. And breads with these additions have a wide appeal, complementing all sorts of foods and culinary traditions.

The way herbs are used in a cuisine can become a "trademark," so much so that the geographic region of many an ethnic bread can be identified by its flavors. The modern regional cuisine of Provence, for example, is based on the flavors of wild herbs that grow in France's sunbaked southeast corner, a pungent blend of rosemary, thyme, lavender, savory, and oregano. The blend of these spices has become well known as *herbes de Provence*, a blend with a scent sometimes more akin to perfume than to culinary flavoring. The Greeks love both pungent oregano and basil, a holy herb in the Eastern Orthodox Church. The Italians also take their herbs seriously, using lots of borage, mint, sage, basil, and flat-leaf parsley. Certainly the most famous Italian bread, pizza, is a show-case for herbs. Scandinavian cuisine and fresh dill are forever partners, and traditional Mexican cooking relies on *heirbas de olor*, "the aromatic herbs": Mexican laurel, rosemary, cilantro, Mexican tarragon, Spanish oregano, and sage. Hungarians, Poles, and Russians bake with marjoram, garlic, paprika, parsley, dill, and caraway. In baking, these herbs can be integrated into breads in one of three ways: by adding the fresh or dried herbs to the dough; by brushing the dough with an herb-infused oil before baking as for focaccia; or by baking the bread atop a bed of aromatic branches, such as rosemary or fennel on a grill.

Nuts and seeds are other natural ingredients that go well in breads. They exude their precious, health-giving oils into a dough in the presence of heat, and so lend their character to the dough. For some bread lovers, the lack of nuts in a loaf actually makes it incomplete. Many nuts that were once considered only of local interest are now available worldwide. Commonly available nuts, including walnuts, pecans, hazelnuts (filberts), pistachios, pine nuts (pignolia), chestnuts, cashews, peanuts, and almonds, can be used toasted or raw. They come whole, slivered, blanched, sliced, ground into meal-like flours, and made into oil-rich, spreadable butters.

The array of seeds that can be used in breads ranges markedly in size, shape, and flavor. Sunflower seeds, pumpkin seeds, and flax seeds, the new darlings of the health set, are smaller in size than nuts, but contribute similar qualities. They are great favorites in bread as much for their crunch as for their flavor. Then there are the ancient seeds—poppy seeds, sesame seeds, fennel seeds, and coriander seeds, flavors that have been used by bakers for thousands of years. These tiny seeds are packed with flavor; some of them are known as spices.

In addition to earthy shriveled seeds, spices include curled barks and buds, berries, and gnarled roots from precious trees and plants. They come with a wealth of lore steeped in myth. Spices' ability to heighten the effect of food, their antiseptic properties that masked unsavory flavors resulting from a lack of refrigeration, and their use in traditional rituals, provided the impetus for some of the greatest explorations. Cities like Venice and Alexandria; people like Marco Polo, Vasco da Gama, and Christopher Columbus; the Crusades and the East India Trading Company, all figure into the historical evolution that brought spices to the Western world and made them an integral part of our kitchens.

The world of flavored breads from the machine is one that asks the baker's senses to see, taste, smell, and feel the variety of warm colors, flavors, and textures. These breads are artful and fragrant. No esoteric knowledge is needed, just a light touch and a whimsical, creative spirit. But keep in mind that flavors in bread are most dramatic as a tantalizing whisper rather than a dominating flavor.

One note about how to store some of the flavorings used in this section: Store your herbs and spices in a cool area of the kitchen, away from the heat of the stove or direct sunlight. Keep the containers tightly closed. Use them regularly and check for potency once a year, replacing as needed. Freeze seeds, such as caraway, sesame, and poppy, in the jars in which they were purchased. Refrigerate nuts in airtight containers or packaging for up to two to three months; they will keep for a year or longer in the freezer.

HERB BREAD

A n old-fashioned aromatic bread with a nice, light texture, this loaf is good for dinner, made into croutons or a stuffing, or toasted with melted cheese the next day. It uses a combination of dried herbs that are basic in any cook's cupboard, and is a snap to make. I usually use walnut or almond oil, but olive oil is nice, too. Enjoy the scent while this is rising and baking!

1 Place all the ingredients in the pan according to the order in the manufacturer's instructions. Set crust on medium or dark and program for the Basic cycle; press Start. (This recipe may be made using the Delay Timer.)

2 When the baking cycle ends, immediately remove the bread from the pan and place it on a rack. Let cool to room temperature before slicing.

1½-POUND LOAF	2-POUND LOAF
1⅛ cups water	1½ cups water
1½ tablespoons nut oil or olive oil	2 tablespoons nut oil or olive oil
3 cups bread flour	4 cups bread flour
1 tablespoon sugar	1½ tablespoons sugar
1 tablespoon gluten	1 tablespoon plus 1 teaspoon gluten
1½ teaspoons salt	2 teaspoons salt
1 teaspoon dried marjoram	1¼ teaspoons dried marjoram
1 teaspoon dried basil	1¼ teaspoons dried basil
1 teaspoon dried tarragon	1¼ teaspoons dried tarragon
2 teaspoons SAF yeast or 2½ teaspoons bread machine yeast	2¼ teaspoons SAF yeast or 2¾ teaspoons bread machine yeast

FRESH DILL BREAD

T his is a very aromatic bread; you will surely enjoy the smell while it is baking. The onion is added at the beginning of the cycle so that the action of the mixing and kneading makes the pieces smaller and distributes them throughout the dough. Eventually the onions more or less disintegrate into the dough, rather than appear as noticeable chunks in the finished loaf. This is a slow riser, but the baked result is a fluffy, tasty bread.

1 Place all the ingredients in the bread pan according to the order in the manufacturer's instructions. Set crust on medium and program for the Basic cycle; press Start. (This recipe is not suitable for use with the Delay Timer.)

2 When the baking cycle ends, immediately remove the bread from the pan and place it on a rack. Let cool to room temperature before slicing.

1½-POUND LOAF	2-POUND LOAF
½ cup water	¾ cup water
1 large egg	1 large egg
4 ounces cream cheese, at room temperature and cut into pieces	5 ounces cream cheese, at room temperature and cut into pieces
2 tablespoons unsalted butter, cut into pieces	3 tablespoons unsalted butter, cut into pieces
3¼ cups bread flour	4⅓ cups bread flour
1 tablespoon gluten	1 tablespoon plus 1 teaspoon gluten
⅓ cup finely chopped yellow onion	½ cup finely chopped yellow onion
¼ cup chopped fresh dill	6 tablespoons chopped fresh dill
1½ teaspoons salt	2 teaspoons salt
2 teaspoons SAF yeast or 2½ teaspoons bread machine yeast	2½ teaspoons SAF yeast or 1 tablespoon bread machine yeast

BROOKLYN BOTANIC GARDEN HERB BREAD

T*he restaurant at the venerable botanic landmark in New York City serves this bread. It has an unconventional combination of seeds and herbs, caraway, sage, and nutmeg. This bread is great for stuffings.*

1 Place all the ingredients in the bread pan according to the order in the manufacturer's instructions. Set crust on dark and program for the Basic cycle; press Start. (This recipe is not suitable for use with the Delay Timer.)

2 When the baking cycle ends, immediately remove the bread from the pan and place it on a rack. Let cool to room temperature before slicing.

1½-POUND LOAF	2-POUND LOAF
¾ cup milk	1 cup milk
1 large egg	1 large egg
2 tablespoons unsalted butter, cut into pieces	3 tablespoons unsalted butter, cut into pieces
3 cups bread flour	4 cups bread flour
1 tablespoon gluten	1 tablespoon plus 1 teaspoon gluten
1 tablespoon caraway seed, crushed	1 tablespoon plus 1 teaspoon caraway seed, crushed
1 teaspoon dried sage	1¼ teaspoons dried sage
1 teaspoon fresh grated nutmeg	1¼ teaspoons fresh grated nutmeg
1¼ teaspoons salt	2 teaspoons salt
2 teaspoons SAF yeast or 2½ teaspoons bread machine yeast	2½ teaspoons SAF yeast or 1 tablespoon bread machine yeast

Bread Machine Baker's Hint: Preserving Fresh Herbs

Culinary herbs are defined as "the fragrant leaves of soft-stemmed plants." Growing your own means having fresh herbs available at all times, although hothouse varieties are now available year-round in the supermarket. Whether you buy bunches of herbs at the produce section or grow your own, it is common that a bunch of herbs is just too much to use at one time. Rather than letting the herbs die, it is easy to preserve the surplus by drying or freezing. My mom always has a few batches of basil in the freezer. She chops and portions the extra as soon as she gets home from the supermarket so that the herbs are as fresh as possible at the time of freezing. My friend Mary Cantori has a huge herb garden and regularly dries herbs. By continually harvesting from the plants, she also keeps plots pruned. I am the lucky recipient of a few baggies full of marjoram, summer savory, and basil—my favorites—from her every Christmas. Growing your own herbs is also the way to enjoy varieties of herbs you never see sold commercially. My friend, food writer and expert on California rancho cooking Jacquie Higuera McMahan, has a large clump of Spanish oregano that she cultivates, which was transplanted from her family's California rancho decades ago. It is a more subtle and sweet aromatic than the Greek variety we commonly see here.

How to Dry Fresh Herbs
Fresh herbs are more potent and aromatic than dried, but the mild, distinct flavors of dried herbs are favorites, too. This method of preserving is especially good for bay, oregano, summer savory, marjoram, tarragon, thyme, safflower pistils, and rosemary. Take heed of the quality of the herbs you dry; herbs from healthy plants will give the best results. Be sure that no pesticides or sprays have been used on the herbs.

Gently wash the leaves with cool to tepid water, as hot water can dissolve precious aromatic oils. Remove the leaves from the stem, unless the herbs will be hung to dry or used as a *bouquet garni*. Spread the leaves on a double layer of paper towels placed on a plate or flat basket. Let them air dry at room temperature for 3 days to one week in a clean area away from direct sunlight. If you harvest your own herbs and have enough for a bunch, tie a string around the stems and hang the bunch in a dry, warm, dark area, such as in the garage or in a closet. Strip off the whole leaves when the plants have dried enough to become brittle. Home-dried herb leaves are coarser and larger than commercial dried herbs, which is preferable, since the smaller pieces lose their precious fragrance faster. Store the whole dried leaves—in paper bags or airtight containers in a dark place to prevent discoloration—no longer than 6 months. About 1 teaspoon of dried herbs is equal to 1 tablespoon of fresh.

How to Freeze Fresh Herbs
My mother buys her fresh herbs at the farmer's market, then chops and divides them into small packets for easy additions to breads and sauces later on. This method of preserving is especially good for mint, cilantro, basil, sage, marjoram, epazote, and chives.

For a flavor close to fresh, wash the leaves and strip them from the stem as for drying. Chop the leaves or leave them whole, as desired. Place herbs in small plastic freezer bags and freeze. Break off portions of the frozen herbs to use as needed. The herbs can be used frozen or defrosted, but should be used as soon as possible after they are taken from the freezer. Do not refreeze. Use them as you would fresh herbs in recipes.

ROSEMARY-LEMON BREAD

 his recipe is adapted from one by food writer and former chef of Greens Restaurant Deborah Madison. Although Deborah always professes that bread is not her forte, she is an avid bread lover and does make great bread. This one is wonderful for the spring and is nice, as my friend Lynn Alley likes it, dressed up with an icing-like lemon glaze and sprinkled with rosemary flowers.

1 Preheat the oven to 350°F.

2 To skin the nuts, bring the 2 cups water to a boil in a saucepan. Add the baking soda and the nuts. Boil for 3 to 5 minutes; the water will turn black. Drain the nuts in a colander and run them under a stream of cold water. Discard the cooking water. Using your fingers, slip off each skin, and place on a clean dish towel. Pat dry and place on a clean baking sheet. Toast the nuts in the oven for 10 to 15 minutes, stirring twice. Cool on the baking sheet. Chop the nuts and set aside.

1½-POUND LOAF	2-POUND LOAF
For the dough:	*For the dough:*
2 cups water	2 cups water
3 tablespoons baking soda	3 tablespoons baking soda
½ cup (2 ounces) whole hazelnuts	¾ cup (3 ounces) whole hazelnuts
⅔ cup milk	1 cup milk
1 large egg	1 large egg plus 1 egg yolk
2 tablespoons unsalted butter, cut into pieces	3 tablespoons unsalted butter, cut into pieces
3 tablespoons honey	¼ cup honey
2¾ cups bread flour	3¾ cups bread flour
1½ teaspoons chopped fresh rosemary	2 teaspoons chopped fresh rosemary
Grated zest of 1 large lemon	Grated zest of 1 large lemon
1 tablespoon gluten	1 tablespoon plus 1 teaspoon gluten
1½ teaspoons salt	1¾ teaspoons salt
2 teaspoons SAF yeast or 2½ teaspoons bread machine yeast	2¼ teaspoons SAF yeast or 2¾ teaspoons bread machine yeast
¾ cup golden raisins	1 cup golden raisins
For the lemon icing:	*For the lemon icing:*
¾ cup sifted confectioners' sugar	¾ cup sifted confectioners' sugar
2 tablespoons warm fresh lemon juice	2 tablespoons warm fresh lemon juice

❸ To make the dough, place the remaining dough ingredients, except the hazelnuts and raisins, in the pan according to the order in the manufacturer's instructions. Set crust on medium and program for the Basic or Fruit and Nut cycle; press Start. (This recipe is not suitable for use with the Delay Timer.) When the machine beeps, or between Knead 1 and Knead 2, add the raisins and hazelnuts. Add an extra tablespoon or two of water if the dough ball seems dry.

❹ When the baking cycle ends, immediately remove the bread from the pan and place it on a rack. Let cool to room temperature before slicing, or drizzle with the lemon icing.

❺ To make the lemon icing, if you are using it, whisk the sugar and the lemon juice in a small bowl. Place the rack with the hot bread over a piece of waxed or parchment paper to catch the drips. Drizzle the glaze over the entire loaf, letting some drip down the sides. Let the loaf stand at room temperature until it is completely cool and the glaze is set.

MOUNTAIN HERB BREAD

My favorite herb bread recipe that I adapted for the bread machine was a gift from my friend Connie Rothermel, who got it on one of her skiing jaunts to the then little-known resort of Crested Butte, Colorado, almost twenty years ago. It is a delicious, simple dinner or sandwich loaf deeply speckled with a complex combination of dried herbs and wildflower honey, giving the effect of having been an inspiration of the moment.

1 Place all the ingredients in the pan according to the order in the manufacturer's instructions. Set crust on dark and program for the Basic cycle; press Start. (This recipe is not suitable for use with the Delay Timer.)

2 When the baking cycle ends, immediately remove the bread from the pan and place it on a rack. Let cool to room temperature before slicing.

1½-POUND LOAF	2-POUND LOAF
1¼ cups water	1⅔ cups water
2 tablespoons olive oil	2½ tablespoons olive oil
¼ cup wildflower honey	¼ cup wildflower honey
2 cups bread flour	2¾ cups bread flour
1 cup whole wheat flour	1¼ cups whole wheat flour
3 tablespoons light brown sugar	¼ cup light brown sugar
3 tablespoons nonfat dry milk	¼ cup nonfat dry milk
1 tablespoon gluten	1 tablespoon plus 1 teaspoon gluten
1½ tablespoons minced fresh parsley	2 tablespoons minced fresh parsley
1½ teaspoons dried basil	2 teaspoons dried basil
1 teaspoon dried dill weed	1¼ teaspoons dried dill weed
1 teaspoons dried summer savory	1¼ teaspoons dried summer savory
¾ teaspoon dried marjoram	1 teaspoon dried marjoram
½ teaspoon dried tarragon	¾ teaspoon dried tarragon
¼ teaspoon dried thyme	⅓ teaspoon dried thyme
1½ teaspoons salt	2 teaspoons salt
2 teaspoons SAF yeast or 2½ teaspoons bread machine yeast	2¼ teaspoons SAF yeast or 2¾ teaspoons bread machine yeast

BUTTERMILK BREAD WITH LAVENDER

T*his recipe was inspired by a stunning book called* The Lavender Garden *(Chronicle Books, 1998) by Robert Kourik, which gives lore and growing information for all types of lavender suitable for home gardens like my own. Lavender, which grows as a shrub, has long been used for culinary purposes. If you think this odd, remember that lavender is a member of the mint family and is the dominant flavor in the combination herbes de Provence, from the area in France known for its lavender fields. For the sweetest effect in baking use just the corollas, or inner petals, rather than the entire flower head, which is quite tough and woody. This bread is made using the petals and some fresh leaves, which makes it more pungent than it would be with the flowers alone. It is a perfect bread for summer entertaining.*

❶ Place all the ingredients in the pan according to the order in the manufacturer's instructions. Set crust on dark and program for the Basic cycle; press Start. (This recipe is not suitable for use with the Delay Timer.)

❷ When the baking cycle ends, immediately remove the bread from the pan and place it on a rack. Let cool to room temperature before slicing.

1½-POUND LOAF	2-POUND LOAF
⅓ cup water	½ cups water
¾ cup buttermilk	⅞ cup buttermilk
3 tablespoons olive oil	¼ cup olive oil
3 cups bread flour	4 cups bread flour
2 tablespoons finely chopped fresh lavender leaves	3 tablespoons finely chopped fresh lavender leaves
1 teaspoon finely chopped fresh lavender flowers	1¼ teaspoons finely chopped fresh lavender flowers
Grated zest of 1 small lemon	Grated zest of 1 small lemon
1 tablespoon gluten	1 tablespoon plus 1 teaspoon gluten
1½ teaspoons salt	2 teaspoons salt
2 teaspoons SAF yeast or 2½ teaspoons bread machine yeast	2¼ teaspoons SAF yeast or 2¾ teaspoons bread machine yeast

WHOLE WHEAT BASIL BREAD

B asil is an herb that is used in religious ceremonies in the Eastern Orthodox Church but is also part of the daily cuisine in Mediterranean countries. It is an extremely aromatic and well-liked herb; I don't know anyone who does not love it. Be sure to pack the chopped basil into the measuring cup when you make this bread; you want lots of it in this bread. This bread is excellent with pasta and your homemade tomato sauce, and with egg dishes.

❶ Place all the ingredients in the pan according to the order in the manufacturer's instructions. Set crust on dark and program for the Basic cycle; press Start. (This recipe is not suitable for use with the Delay Timer.)

❷ When the baking cycle ends, immediately remove the bread from the pan and place it on a rack. Let cool to room temperature before slicing.

1½-POUND LOAF	2-POUND LOAF
¾ cup buttermilk	1 cup buttermilk
⅓ cup water	½ cup water
2 tablespoons butter, cut into pieces	3 tablespoons butter, cut into pieces
2 tablespoons honey	3 tablespoons honey
3 cups white whole wheat flour	4 cups white whole wheat flour
¼ cup chopped fresh basil	⅓ cup chopped fresh basil
¼ cup pine nuts, chopped	⅓ cup pine nuts, chopped
1 tablespoon gluten	1 tablespoon plus 1 teaspoon gluten
1½ teaspoons salt	2 teaspoons salt
2 teaspoons SAF yeast or 2½ teaspoons bread machine yeast	2½ teaspoons SAF yeast or 1 tablespoon bread machine yeast

HERB LIGHT RYE BREAD

T*he flavor in this loaf comes from the combination of heavy-scented cultivated seeds—dill, poppy, caraway, and celery. Except for the poppy, which is a flower, these seeds are all from umbelliferous plants. All the aromatic seeds have been used in Mediterranean baking since the Egyptian and Greek Empires. The seeds' essential oils are released during baking. This is a great dinner bread.*

1 Using a mortar and pestle, combine the dill seeds, poppy seeds, and celery seeds and crush them together coarsely. Or place the seeds between 2 sheets of waxed paper and crush them with a rolling pin.

2 Place all the ingredients in the pan according to the order in the manufacturer's instructions, adding the crushed seeds with the dry ingredients. Set crust on dark and program for the Basic cycle; press Start. (This recipe is not suitable for use with the Delay Timer.)

3 When the baking cycle ends, immediately remove the bread from the pan and place it on a rack. Let cool to room temperature before slicing.

1½-POUND LOAF	2-POUND LOAF
½ teaspoon dill seed	¾ teaspoon dill seed
½ teaspoon poppy seeds	¾ teaspoon poppy seeds
¼ teaspoon celery seeds	⅓ teaspoon celery seeds
⅞ cup water	1⅛ cups plus 1 tablespoon water
1 large egg	1 large egg
1½ tablespoons minced shallot	2 tablespoons minced shallot
1 tablespoon molasses	1½ tablespoons molasses
2¼ cups bread flour	3 cups bread flour
¾ cup medium or dark rye flour	1 cup medium or dark rye flour
1 tablespoon gluten	1 tablespoon plus 1 teaspoon gluten
1½ teaspoons caraway seed	1⅓ teaspoons caraway seed
1¾ teaspoons salt	2¼ teaspoons salt
2 teaspoons SAF yeast or 2½ teaspoons bread machine yeast	2½ teaspoons SAF yeast or 1 tablespoon bread machine yeast

SOUR CREAM SEMOLINA BREAD WITH HERB SWIRL

T his bread is incredibly good. It is pretty, too, with its green swirl pattern in every soft slice. It has an intoxicating aroma during baking, not only from the herbs, but also from the semolina flour, which blends so well with bread flour. Semolina flour is also known as durum flour; it is the flour used in pasta making. Serve this bread to your favorite guests.

1½-POUND LOAF	2-POUND LOAF
For the dough:	*For the dough:*
¾ cup water	1 cup water
1 tablespoon olive oil	1½ tablespoons olive oil
½ cup sour cream	⅔ cup sour cream
1½ cups bread flour	2¼ cups bread flour
1 cup semolina flour	1¼ cups semolina flour
2 teaspoons sugar	1 tablespoon sugar
1 tablespoon gluten	1 tablespoon plus 1 teaspoon gluten
1½ teaspoons salt	1¾ teaspoons salt
2 teaspoons SAF yeast or 2½ teaspoons bread machine yeast	2½ teaspoons SAF yeast or 1 tablespoon bread machine yeast
For the herb swirl:	*For the herb swirl:*
⅓ cup chopped fresh flat-leaf parsley	⅓ cup chopped fresh flat-leaf parsley
3 to 4 tablespoons chopped fresh herbs, such as dill, basil, chervil, marjoram or tarragon	3 to 4 tablespoons chopped fresh herbs, such as dill, basil, chervil, marjoram or tarragon
1¼ teaspoons dried herb mixture, such as Italian herbs	1¼ teaspoons dried herb mixture, such as Italian herbs

1 Place all the dough ingredients in the pan according to the order in the manufacturer's instructions.

2 *To mix and bake the dough in the machine:* Set crust on medium and program for the Basic or Variety cycle; press Start. (This recipe is not suitable for use with the Delay Timer.) After Rise 2 of the Basic cycle has ended, press Pause, or when the display shows Shape in the Variety cycle, remove the pan and close the lid. Immediately remove the dough and place it on a lightly floured work surface; pat into a 12-by-8-inch fat rectangle. Brush with 2 tablespoons olive oil. Sprinkle with the parsley and the rest of the herbs, leaving a 1-inch space all the way around. Starting at a short edge, roll up jelly-roll fashion. Tuck the ends under and pinch the bottom seam. Coat the bottom of the dough with cooking spray. Remove the kneading blade and place the dough back in the pan; press Start to continue to rise and bake as programmed.

3 When the baking cycle ends, immediately remove the bread from the pan and place it on a rack. Let cool to room temperature before slicing.

4 *To mix the dough in the machine and bake it in the oven:* Program the machine for the Dough cycle; press Start. The dough ball will be soft and springy. Follow the shaping instructions in Step 2, then place the loaf in a greased 8-by-4-inch loaf pan (for the 1½-pound loaf) or 9-by-5-inch loaf pan (for the 2-pound loaf) instead of putting the loaf back into the bread machine. Spray the top with cooking spray and cover lightly with plastic wrap. Let rise at room temperature until doubled in bulk, about 45 minutes. Bake in a preheated 375°F oven for 35 to 40 minutes, or until golden brown and the sides have slightly contracted from the pan. Remove the bread from the pan and cool it on a rack.

Leftover Bread Cookery: Stuffed Vegetables

Mushrooms Stuffed with Pancetta and Herbs

Makes 40 stuffed mushrooms, serves 15

Pancetta is an uncured Italian bacon that does not impart as assertive or salty a taste as regular bacon. These are my favorite stuffed mushrooms.

2½ cups fresh coarse ground breadcrumbs from homemade white, whole wheat, or herb bread
¼ cup Parmesan cheese
¼ cup chopped flat-leaf parsley
2 teaspoons mixed Italian herbs, other herb blend, or salt-free herb blend
6 ounces raw pancetta, chopped
2 tablespoons olive oil
3 large shallots, chopped
½ cup plain yogurt

40 medium-large fresh mushrooms
¼ cup olive oil

❶ In a food processor pulse the breadcrumbs, cheese, parsley, and herbs and process until evenly combined. Sauté the pancetta until crisp in a medium sauté pan. Add to the crumbs in the processor workbowl.

❷ Without washing the pan, add the olive oil and sauté the shallots until translucent in the rendered pancetta fat and oil. Add to

the food processor workbowl along with the yogurt. Process until the mixture is evenly moistened and just comes together. Remove to a covered container and refrigerate until needed. The stuffing can be made 1 day ahead of serving.

❸ Wash and stem the mushrooms. Place on a baking sheet. Stuff each cap with a rounded tablespoon of filling. Broil for 3 to 4 minutes, until lightly browned. Serve immediately.

Stuffed Eggplant

Serves 2

I consider stuffed eggplant to be real home cooking. This version contains meat, making it a main dish rather than a vegetable side. Serve it next to pasta with butter and parsley and a simple salad.

2 slices homemade white, whole wheat, or herb bread, crusts removed
⅓ cup flat-leaf parsley
1 large eggplant (at least 1 pound)
1 tablespoon olive oil
½ pound ground sirloin
1 yellow onion, finely chopped
¼ of a large red pepper, finely chopped
3 plum tomatoes, chopped
½ cup coarse grated mozzarella cheese
1½ teaspoons dried marjoram or oregano

¼ teaspoon crushed hot red pepper flakes
Salt and black pepper, to taste
¼ cup plus 1 tablespoon olive oil
2 tablespoons grated Asiago cheese

❶ Place the bread in a food processor and grind to coarse crumbs; you will have 1 cup. Add the parsley and chop to make parsleyed crumbs. Remove to a bowl and set aside.

❷ Preheat the oven to 350°F.

❸ Halve the eggplant lengthwise. Scoop out the insides, leaving ½-inch sides. Sprinkle the inside of the shells with salt. Set in a shallow 8-by-8-inch baking dish. Chop the eggplant that was scooped out.

❹ Heat 1 tablespoon olive oil in a large sauté pan over medium-high heat. Add the ground meat and brown for about 10 minutes. Add the onion, pepper, and eggplant; sauté until soft, 5 to 8 minutes. Remove from the heat and add the tomatoes and cheese. Add the seasonings. Divide the filling in half and pile into the eggplant shells.

❺ Toss the crumbs with the ¼ cup olive oil. Sprinkle on top of the stuffed shells; sprinkle with Asiago. Bake for 45 minutes. Serve hot, with some hot marinara sauce on the side, if desired.

OLIVE OIL–PINE NUT BREAD

I n the early days of Greens Restaurant in San Francisco this bread was served as an appetizer, with wine. There is some wine right in the recipe, which gives the bread considerable character. This bread is a good choice to serve for dinner, but day-old it is also great for croutons or as a savory base for melted cheese.

❶ Place the ingredients, except the pine nuts, in the pan according to the order in the manufacturer's instructions. Set crust on medium and program for the Basic or French Bread cycle; press Start. (This recipe is not suitable for use with the Delay Timer.) Five minutes into Knead 2, sprinkle in the pine nuts.

❷ When the baking cycle ends, immediately remove the bread from the pan and place it on a rack. Let cool to room temperature before slicing.

1½-POUND LOAF	2-POUND LOAF
½ cup water	⅔ cup water
½ cup dry white wine	⅔ cup dry white wine
¼ cup olive oil	⅓ cup olive oil
2 cups bread flour	2⅔ cups bread flour
¾ cup whole wheat flour	1 cup whole wheat flour
¼ cup rye flour	⅓ cup rye flour
1 tablespoon gluten	1 tablespoon plus
1 tablespoon sugar	1 teaspoon gluten
1½ teaspoons salt	1 tablespoon plus
	2 teaspoons sugar
2 teaspoons SAF yeast	2 teaspoons salt
or 2½ teaspoons bread	
machine yeast	2½ teaspoons SAF yeast
	or 1 tablespoon bread
⅓ cup pine nuts, coarsely	machine yeast
chopped	
	½ cup pine nuts, coarsely
	chopped

CALIFORNIA NUT BREAD

Shelled nuts are tremendously popular, so popular that they have been described as having halos because they give so much gustatory pleasure. When you add the nuts to this bread coarsely chopped, you end up with chunks of the nut in the bread, as well as some ground up from the action of the blade. Choose from some of the most popular varieties—hazelnut, walnut, pecan, macadamia, pistachio, peanut, or almond. Each nut has a corresponding nut oil, which is important to use in this bread, for flavor and to make the dough pliable. You can use a lightly toasted nut oil or a cold-pressed one. Be sure to use only one flavor nut with its oil per batch of bread, but as you bake this bread again and again using different nuts, you will be surprised at the variety you can achieve from just this one recipe.

❶ Preheat the oven to 350°F.

❷ Spread the nuts evenly on a baking sheet. Bake until lightly toasted, about 5 to 7 minutes. Remove from the oven and let cool.

❸ Place the ingredients, except the nuts, in the pan according to the order in the manufacturer's instructions. Set crust on medium or dark and program for the Basic cycle; press Start. (This recipe is not suitable for use with the Delay Timer.) When the machine beeps or between Knead 1 and Knead 2, add the nuts. Test the dough with your fingers. If it is very firm and dry, maybe even lumpy, add another tablespoon of buttermilk to soften it up a bit.

❹ When the baking cycle ends, immediately remove the bread from the pan and place it on a rack. Let cool to room temperature before slicing.

1½-POUND LOAF

¾ cup (3 to 4 ounces) nutmeat pieces

1¼ cups buttermilk
⅓ cup nut oil

3 cups bread flour
1 tablespoon dark brown sugar
1 tablespoon gluten
1½ teaspoons salt

2½ teaspoons SAF yeast or 1 tablespoon bread machine yeast

2-POUND LOAF

1 cup (4 to 5 ounces) nutmeat pieces

1⅔ cups buttermilk
½ cup nut oil

4 cups bread flour
1½ tablespoons dark brown sugar
1 tablespoon plus 1 teaspoon gluten
2 teaspoons salt

1 tablespoon SAF yeast or 1 tablespoon plus ½ teaspoon bread machine yeast

PECAN RAISIN BREAD

P ecans, a member of the hickory family, are an American nut. While related to the walnut, pecans have a rich, buttery nature of their own. Pecan halves look very much like the rugged walnut half, but have more oil. There are at least five hundred varieties of pecans, all of whose original habitats are in the southern United States, from Georgia to Texas. Many bakers who do not favor walnuts love pecans. Although raisins and pecans are often combined in sweet breads, this one is savory. Serve this bread for dinner or eat it toasted.

❶ Preheat the oven to 350°F.

❷ Spread the nuts on a baking sheet. Bake for 10 minutes, stirring twice. Cool on the baking sheet. Chop the nuts into large pieces and set aside.

❸ Place the ingredients, except the nuts and the raisins, in the pan according to the order in the manufacturer's instructions. Set crust on medium and program for the Basic or Fruit and Nut cycle; press Start. (This recipe is not suitable for use with the Delay Timer.) When the machine beeps, or between Knead 1 and Knead 2, add the nuts and the raisins.

1½-POUND LOAF	2-POUND LOAF
1 cup (about 4 ounces) pecan halves	1¼ cups (about 6 ounces) pecan halves
1 cup plus 2 tablespoons water	1½ cups water
1 tablespoon butter, cut into pieces	1½ tablespoons butter, cut into pieces
2½ cups bread flour	3⅓ cups bread flour
½ cup dark rye flour	⅔ cup dark rye flour
1 tablespoon dark brown sugar	1½ tablespoons dark brown sugar
1 tablespoon plus 1 teaspoon gluten	1 tablespoon plus 2 teaspoons gluten
1½ teaspoons salt	2 teaspoons salt
2¼ teaspoons SAF yeast or 2¾ teaspoons bread machine yeast	2½ teaspoons SAF yeast or 1 tablespoon bread machine yeast
⅓ cup dark raisins	½ cup dark raisins

4 When the baking cycle ends, immediately remove the bread from the pan and place it on a rack. Let cool to room temperature before slicing.

Bread Machine Baker's Hint: The Right Amount of Dough for Your Machine

To get the best results from your bread machine, it is important not to underfill or overfill your machine. The recipes in this book are all designed to fit properly into 1½- and 2-pound-loaf machines. When developing your own recipes, though, or using the Dough cycle to mix a favorite bread recipe, you need to keep the capacity in mind. A general guideline is that 1½- and 2-pound-loaf machines need a minimum of 1½ cups dry ingredients to work properly. The maximum for a 1½-pound-loaf machine is 3 to 3½ cups dry ingredients, and in machines with a 2-pound-loaf capacity, the maximum is 4 to 5 cups dry ingredients. Consult your owner's manual for the exact recommendations for your model. When figuring the amount of dry ingredients you are adding, include ingredients other than flour, such as wheat germ or oatmeal. Eggs are counted as liquid ingredients. Be careful to measure ingredients accurately, and never try making a loaf larger (or a larger amount of dough) than your machine is designed to handle.

TOASTED WALNUT BREAD

T his is the all-time favorite bread machine recipe of one of my recipe testers, Margery Schneider. She clipped it from a Fleischmann's Yeast ad in a magazine years ago. It has a particularly nice nut-induced color. Be sure to chop the nuts only coarsely; they will break up during the kneading. She serves this bread with potato soup for dinner or with Marmalade Butter (pages 598 to 599) for breakfast.

1 Preheat the oven to 350°F.

2 Spread the walnuts on a baking sheet and place in the center of the oven for 4 minutes to toast lightly. Set aside to cool.

3 Place the ingredients, except the walnuts, in the pan according to the order in the manufacturer's instructions. Set crust on medium and program for the Basic or Fruit and Nut cycle; press Start. (This recipe is not suitable for use with the Delay Timer.) When the machine beeps, or between Knead 1 and Knead 2, add the walnuts.

4 When the baking cycle ends, immediately remove the bread from the pan and place it on a rack. Let cool to room temperature before slicing.

1½-POUND LOAF	2-POUND LOAF
¾ cup (3 to 4 ounces) walnut pieces	1 cup (4 to 5 ounces) walnut pieces
1 cup water	1⅓ cups water
2 large egg whites, lightly beaten	2 large egg whites, lightly beaten
1½ tablespoons butter, cut into pieces	2 tablespoons butter, cut into pieces
3 cups bread flour	4 cups bread flour
2 tablespoons sugar	3 tablespoons sugar
2 tablespoons nonfat dry milk	3 tablespoons nonfat dry milk
1 tablespoon gluten	1 tablespoon plus 1 teaspoon gluten
¾ teaspoon salt	1 teaspoon salt
1½ teaspoons SAF yeast or 2 teaspoons bread machine yeast	2 teaspoons SAF yeast or 2½ teaspoons bread machine yeast

SUNFLOWER OATMEAL BREAD

W*hen I worked in a restaurant bakery so long ago, I had an assistant for many years whose name was Celeste. She made this bread one day, and luckily I wrote down the recipe because she doesn't even remember it. It has remained one of my favorite breads for twenty years. For years I taught it in my baking classes and now I have adapted it, most successfully, for the bread machine. It is moist, nubby, and richly flavored. This bread, for me, is a breakfast toast bread, spread with butter and one of my homemade jams.*

1 Place all the ingredients in the bread pan according to the order in the manufacturer's instructions. Set crust on medium and program for the Basic cycle; press Start. (This recipe is not suitable for use with the Delay Timer.)

2 When the baking cycle ends, immediately remove the bread from the pan and place it on a rack. Let cool to room temperature before slicing.

1½-POUND LOAF	2-POUND LOAF
½ cup water	⅔ cup water
⅝ cup buttermilk	⅞ cup buttermilk
1 large egg	1 large egg
1½ tablespoons butter, cut into pieces	2 tablespoons butter, cut into pieces
2 tablespoons honey	3 tablespoons honey
1 tablespoon molasses	1½ tablespoons molasses
2½ cups bread flour	3⅓ cups bread flour
½ cup rolled oats	⅔ cup rolled oats
½ cup whole wheat flour	⅔ cup whole wheat flour
½ cup raw sunflower seeds	⅔ cup raw sunflower seeds
1 tablespoon gluten	1 tablespoon plus 1 teaspoon gluten
1½ teaspoons salt	2 teaspoons salt
2 teaspoons SAF yeast or 2½ teaspoons bread machine yeast	2¼ teaspoons SAF yeast or 2¾ teaspoons bread machine yeast

PAXIMADIA

Makes 10 pieces paximadia

1½- OR 2-POUND-LOAF MACHINES

1¼ cups water
2 tablespoons olive oil
2 tablespoons honey

2½ cups whole wheat flour
1 cup bread flour
1 teaspoon pumpkin pie spice blend, or ½ teaspoon each ground cinnamon and cloves
1 teaspoon salt

2 teaspoons SAF yeast or 2½ teaspoons bread machine yeast

F ood writer Lynn Alley has a love affair with Greek cooking. One day she was invited to visit her friend Aimilia Manassakis, who is a native of Crete and now runs the Greek Village Restaurant in Carlsbad, California, to watch her bake homemade paximadia. Paximadia *is a crunchy twice-baked bread rusk, affectionately known as Greek toast, created in Greek villages by rebaking bread in the residual dying heat of wood-fired ovens. While most Americans have never heard of* paximadia, *it is still the bread of choice throughout modern Greece, at home for breakfast or in restaurants. It is served with strong coffee and soft cheese and honey. The rusks are also crumbled into salads, served with olives and feta cheese for lunch, or drizzled with olive oil to eat as an appetizer with wine. This is Lynn's bread machine adaptation of Aimilia's wonderful recipe. Lynn makes it with freshly milled whole wheat flour from her GrainMaster Whisper Mill. Since it contains no butter or eggs, it is suitable for serving during Lent.*

1 Place all the ingredients in the bread pan according to the order in the manufacturer's instructions. Program for the Dough cycle; press Start. The dough ball will be firm, yet springy and moist.

2 Line a baking sheet with parchment paper. Turn the dough out onto a clean work surface. Knead to form a freefrom oblong oval loaf 11 by 4 inches. Place, seam side down, on the baking sheet. Using a serrated knife, carefully cut the loaf all the way through with a gentle back and forth sawing motion, into 1- to 1¼-inch slices to make 10 slices. After cutting all the pieces, place one hand on each end of the loaf and gently press together to make a whole loaf with separations that you can see clearly. Cover loosely with plastic wrap. Let rest at room temperature for 20 minutes.

3 Meanwhile, preheat the oven to 350°F.

4 Bake for 35 to 40 minutes, or until deep brown and the bottom sounds hollow when tapped with your finger. Remove the bread from the oven and transfer the loaf to a rack to cool. Leave the parchment on the baking sheet; you will use it again.

5 When the loaf is completely cooled, at least 2 hours, separate the slices by tearing them apart with your hands, the way it is done in Greece. Set the oven at its lowest setting, about 200°F. Place the slices on their flat sides on the parchment-lined baking sheet. Place in the oven and let the toasts dry out slowly, about 5 hours. Remove from the oven and cool completely. Store in an airtight tin.

ZUNI INDIAN BREAD

Native Americans do not call themselves such; they call themselves The People. They have a long history of baking nourishing and thoughtful breads, often with minimal ingredients. This is a recipe similar to ones made by the Pueblos, baked in an outdoor adobe beehive oven called a horno. The recipe given here is a perfect example of traditional bread ingredients being blended with modern ways—it is made from start to finish in the bread machine. Use any fine or medium stone-ground yellow, blue, white, or red cornmeal, all used for baking in the pueblo villages of the American Southwest. It is important that this bread cool completely before you slice it.

1 Place all the ingredients in the pan according to the order in the manufacturer's instructions. Set crust on dark and program for the Whole Wheat cycle; press Start. (This recipe is not suitable for use with the Delay Timer.)

2 When the baking cycle ends, immediately remove the bread from the pan and place it on a rack. Let cool to room temperature before slicing.

1½-POUND LOAF
1 cup buttermilk
1 large egg
2 tablespoons sunflower seed oil
2 cups bread flour
⅔ cup whole wheat flour
⅓ cup cornmeal
½ cup raw sunflower seeds
2 tablespoons dark brown sugar
1½ tablespoons gluten
1½ teaspoons salt
2¼ teaspoons SAF yeast or 2¾ teaspoons bread machine yeast

2-POUND LOAF
1⅓ cups buttermilk
1 large egg
3 tablespoons sunflower seed oil
2½ cups bread flour
1 cup whole wheat flour
½ cup cornmeal
⅔ cup raw sunflower seeds
3 tablespoons dark brown sugar
2 tablespoons gluten
2 teaspoons salt
2½ teaspoons SAF yeast or 1 tablespoon bread machine yeast

ORANGE-CUMIN BREAD

C umin is a familiar spice in Mediterranean baking. The strongly aromatic seeds are harvested from an umbellifer similar to caraway, which has been cultivated since ancient times. Cumin seeds act as an unexpected and harmonious foil to the fruity tang of oranges in this bread. Prepare a grilled longhorn cheddar and tomato sandwich using slices of this bread, and wash it down with a tall glass of iced tea made from hibiscus blossoms— such as Red Zinger tea—garnished with wedges of lime. This loaf makes beautiful, out-of-the-ordinary toast, as the warmth of the toaster brings out the flavor of the cumin.

1 Place all the ingredients in the pan according to the order in the manufacturer's instructions. Set crust on dark and program for the Basic cycle; press Start. (This recipe is not suitable for use with the Delay Timer.) The dough ball will be firm and smooth, yet springy.

2 When the baking cycle ends, immediately remove the bread from the pan and place it on a rack. Let cool to room temperature before slicing.

1½-POUND LOAF	2-POUND LOAF
½ cup orange juice	⅔ cup orange juice
⅔ cup fat-free milk	⅞ cup fat-free milk
3 tablespoons butter, cut into pieces	4 tablespoons butter, cut into pieces
2⅔ cups bread flour	3½ cups bread flour
⅓ cup whole wheat flour	½ cup whole wheat flour
¼ cup light brown sugar	⅓ cup light brown sugar
1 tablespoon gluten	1 tablespoon plus 1 teaspoon gluten
1½ teaspoons cumin seed, crushed in a mortar and pestle	2 teaspoons cumin seed, crushed in a mortar and pestle
1½ teaspoons salt	2 teaspoons salt
2 teaspoons SAF yeast or 2½ teaspoons bread machine yeast	2¼ teaspoons SAF yeast or 2¾ teaspoons bread machine yeast

MOROCCAN BREAD WITH SESAME AND ANISEED (KISRA)

Makes 2 round loaves

1¼ cups water

2¾ cups bread flour
½ cup whole wheat flour
2 teaspoons sesame seeds
2 teaspoons aniseeds
2 teaspoons salt

2 teaspoons SAF yeast
or 2½ teaspoons bread
machine yeast

2 tablespoons yellow
cornmeal, for sprinkling

1½ cups water

3⅓ cups bread flour
⅔ cup whole wheat flour
1 tablespoon sesame seeds
1 tablespoon aniseeds
2½ teaspoons salt

2½ teaspoons SAF yeast
or 1 tablespoon bread
machine yeast

2 tablespoons yellow
cornmeal, for sprinkling

For your Moroccan-inspired meals, make a loaf of kisra with the flavors of sesame and anise. This recipe is adapted from one by Paula Wolfert, an expert on the foods of Morocco. It is traditionally shaped and baked in thick, flattened discs like pita, but without the pocket, and the directions for baking it this way are given here. If it is baked on an earthenware griddle over an open fire, it is called khboz instead. Be sure to use a coarse grind of whole wheat flour, preferably stone-ground, to obtain the proper texture of this bread. Serve it with a salad of grated carrots with dates; a tagine, such as the classic stew of chicken with prunes and apricots; and couscous with olives. The bread is meant to be dense in texture to use for scooping up the tagine. Or try using it to scoop up an appetizer of Hummus (page 605).

1 Place all the dough ingredients in the pan according to the order in the manufacturer's instructions. Program for the Dough cycle; press Start.

2 Turn the dough out onto a work surface and divide it into 2 equal portions. Knead each portion into a ball and let rest for 10 minutes covered with a clean tea towel. With your fingers, moisten the surface of each dough ball with some olive oil; press with your palm to flatten each into a disc 1 inch thick and 6 inches in diameter. Dust the work surface with a bit of flour to keep the dough from sticking to it and cover the discs with the towel. Let rest for 1½ to 2 hours, until puffy. Prick the surface of each loaf with the tines of a fork to gently release the gas.

3 Preheat the oven to 400°F. Sprinkle a baking sheet with cornmeal and place the loaves on the baking sheet.

4 Immediately place the loaves in the oven (it won't be up to temperature or hot yet) and bake for exactly 12 minutes. Reduce the oven temperature to 300°F and bake for an additional 35 to 40 minutes, or until the breads are brown and sound hollow when tapped on the bottom with your finger. Remove to a rack to cool before cutting into wedges to serve.

The Right Ingredient: Fats Used in Breads

Fat brings out the flavor, provides the desirable mouth-feel, and makes the texture of bread softer, especially the sandwich-type loaves made in the bread machine. Remember that in most cases it is not the type of fat you use, but the proportions. I found that recipes made by hand that usually needed no fat did need a dab when adapted to the bread machine to keep the texture soft and balance out the other ingredients. Fat lubricates the developing gluten and makes a loaf that slices without tearing or falling apart.

Use butter or margarine for delicate, rich breads with beautiful crusts (sticks of butter have the increments measured on the side for exact portioning), croissants, and sweet breads. Use vegetable oil such as sunflower, canola, corn, or safflower for hearty, whole-grain breads; good olive oil for Italian or low-cholesterol breads; peanut and sesame oils for Oriental breads; lard (which is surprisingly less saturated than butter) for ethnic breads; and nut oils, such as hazelnut, walnut, pecan, and pistachio for artisan and sweet breads.

Cut the butter into pieces before placing it in the bread pan; the mixing action will incorporate it evenly. Avoid low-fat margarine unless called for; it ends up more a liquid than a fat addition and throws off a recipe. To substitute oil for butter in a recipe, reduce the amount of liquid by 1 tablespoon to balance the recipe.

The best omega-3 oils for optimum health include olive oil, walnut oil, canola oil, and flax seed oil. Saturated fats include cheese along with butter (the animal fats). Monosaturated fats that are still good for you include olives, peanuts, and avocados.

POTATO BREAD WITH CARAWAY SEEDS

T he Roman legions brought caraway with them on their treks north when they occupied lands up to the Danube River in their settlement at Aquincum. Perhaps that is when the tradition of baking with caraway seeds began in what is now Hungary. Caraway is one of the four prominent seasonings of Hungarian baking, along with marjoram, dill, and thyme. One of the most famous Hungarian breads is this one, made with potatoes and aromatic caraway seeds. It is served with meals—alongside a good gulyás (beef and green pepper stew), with stuffed cabbage with tomato sauce, or accompanying pork chops baked on a bed of sauerkraut. This is a fast recipe, since you don't have to cook potatoes to make it. I use a potato water made with instant mashed potatoes, in combination with potato starch flour. If you have potato water left over from making mashed potatoes, please go ahead and use it, leaving out the instant flakes. This is a soft bread with a crisp crust.

1½-POUND LOAF	2-POUND LOAF
1⅓ cups warm water	1⅔ cups warm water
2 tablespoons instant potato flakes	3 tablespoons instant potato flakes
1½ tablespoons butter or lard	2 tablespoons butter or lard
2⅔ cups bread flour	3½ cups bread flour
⅓ cup potato starch flour	½ cup potato starch flour
1½ tablespoons sugar	2 tablespoons sugar
2 teaspoons gluten	1 tablespoon gluten
2 teaspoons caraway seeds	1 tablespoon caraway seeds
1½ teaspoons salt	2 teaspoons salt
1¾ teaspoons SAF yeast or 2¼ teaspoons bread machine yeast	2 teaspoons SAF yeast or 2½ teaspoons bread machine yeast

1 Place the instant potato flakes in the water in a bowl. Let stand for 5 minutes. The flakes will expand and soften, and the water become cloudy.

2 Place the ingredients in the pan according to the order in the manufacturer's instructions, adding the potato water with the butter or lard as the liquid ingredients. Set crust on dark and program for the Quick Yeast Bread or Rapid cycle; press Start. (This recipe is not suitable for use with the Delay Timer.)

The dough ball will be smooth and soft. If the dough rises more than two-thirds of the way up the pan, gently deflate the dough a bit. This will keep the dough from hitting the window during baking.

3 When the baking cycle ends, immediately remove the bread from the pan and place it on a rack. Let cool to room temperature before slicing.

DAVID SOOHOO'S BAO

Makes 6 buns

1½- OR 2-POUND-LOAF MACHINES

For the bao dough:

⅔ cup water
4 tablespoons unsalted butter, melted
1 large egg

3½ cups bread flour
5 tablespoons sugar
1 tablespoon nonfat dry milk

1 tablespoon bread machine yeast

For the filling:

¼ cup water
1 tablespoon rice wine or dry sherry
2 tablespoons oyster sauce
1 tablespoon hoisin sauce
2 tablespoons soy sauce
1 teaspoon sesame oil
1 tablespoon sugar
3 tablespoons all-purpose flour
¼ pound prepared *char siu* (Chinese barbecued pork)
3 tablespoons diced yellow onion or scallions, green part only

For the egg glaze:

1 large egg beaten with 1 tablespoon sugar

1½ tablespoons white sesame seeds

Bao *buns, encasing a filling of* char siu *pork, are a popular dim sum item in Cantonese restaurants. Traditionally, they are steamed until fluffy white. Immigrant chefs who came to America discovered that when baked, the buns turned golden, resulting in a sort of Asian hamburger, which pleased the locals.*

Chef David SooHoo and his wife, food writer Elaine Corn, own Bamboo restaurant in Sacramento, California, and the baked pork bao is the most popular appetizer on their restaurant menu. It took David five years to develop this particular recipe, a repeated draw at his cooking classes, but he has been making bao *since he was a teenager cooking in his father's restaurant. Today he easily prepares the dough in his BreadMaker bread machine, comparing the results to other rich egg breads like challah and brioche. SooHoo doubles this dough recipe (you need a 2-pound-loaf capacity machine to do this), knowing the dough is ready when it pushes up the lid a bit. He also likes to stuff the bao with 1-inch cubes of cheese, such as cheddar or Brie. David says it takes three times to master any recipe, and especially the handwork involved in the shaping of these buns, which utilizes techniques that are repeated throughout Chinese cuisine. For that real Chinatown flavor, buy the meat ready-made from an Asian grocery's deli department, where it is cooked the traditional way—in a hanging oven.*

❶ To make the dough, place all the dough ingredients in the pan according to the order in the manufacturer's instructions, but adding only 2 cups of the bread flour. Program for the Dough cycle; press Start. About 5 minutes into Knead 2, slowly add the remaining 1½ cups flour. The dough will be stiff at first, but by the end of the kneading phase it will be pliable and smooth. It is important not to add more water; if the batter is too moist, the *bao* will flatten as they bake.

❷ While the dough is rising, prepare the filling: Make the gravy by combining the water, rice wine or sherry, oyster sauce, hoisin, soy sauce, sesame oil, and sugar in the top of a double boiler. Whisk in the flour. Place over simmering water and, stirring constantly, cook until thick and smooth. The gravy should be the consistency of mayonnaise. Remove from the water bath and cool in the refrigerator.

3 Chop the pork into a large dice and place it in a large bowl with the onions. Add the gravy and mix. Cover and refrigerate until needed.

4 Line a large baking sheet with parchment paper. When the machine beeps at the end of the cycle, press Stop and unplug the machine. Turn the dough out onto a clean wooden work surface. Roll into a fat 3-inch-wide log. Cut the log into 6 equal portions. Place a disc of dough on a wooden work surface (don't shape on cool marble or ceramic because it will stiffen the dough). With the palm of your hand, press down on the center and rotate your palm, spiraling out from the center. The dough will shape into a 3-inch-diameter circle (not lopsided, please) with a pretty spiral pattern radiating from the center like a flower. Don't use any flour. Repeat with the remaining portions of dough.

5 Using a 1½-ounce ice cream scoop (size 40) or another utensil, place a scoop of about 2 tablespoons of the filling in the center of the round of dough. Bring the dough up over the filling and, holding the two sides between your thumb and third finger and pinching with your pointer finger, pleat the edges to encase the filling. Place the *bao* on their sides, and at least 4 inches apart, on the prepared baking sheet. Cover loosely with plastic wrap and let rise at room temperature until doubled in bulk, 45 minutes to 1 hour. If the filling is cold, the *bao* will take 1½ hours to rise.

6 Twenty minutes before baking, preheat the oven to 350°F.

7 Brush each *bao* with the egg glaze and sprinkle with sesame seeds. Bake in the center of the oven for 30 to 40 minutes, until big, puffy, and golden brown. If you have a convection oven, this will take about 20 minutes. Eat the *bao* the day they are baked, or freeze in plastic freezer bags for up to 2 months. Reheat in a microwave (no need to defrost) for 2 to 3 minutes for a quick dinner.

Mixes and Some Special Breads Created from Them

When experimenting with the types of breads you can make in your bread machine, you may well want to taste the different commercial boxed mixes that are available. Although bread machine recipes, even from scratch, are only moments away from being mixed in the machine, some bakers like to use mixes. There are many brands and types of bread machine mixes available, some on supermarket shelves and some by mail order. Most small mills package some sort of bread machine mix made of their own flours, which is a real treat. All brands seem to offer homestyle or country white breads and hearty or honey whole wheat breads. Some, like Hodgson Mill and Eagle Mills, use stone-ground wheat. Most mixes include bread boosters like gluten, lecithin, vitamin C, and malted barley flour. Beyond these basics, the offerings vary from brand to brand. Some offer mixes for cracked wheat, honey wheat berry, nine-grain, herb and cheese, and some sort of cinnamon bread. There seems to be a wider variety of bread mixes available by mail order than on supermarket shelves. The King Arthur Baker's Catalogue offers multigrain sunflower and maple whole wheat mixes. Williams-Sonoma has a good cinnamon-raisin mix in bulk and some sweet bread mixes to which you add your own spices with the eggs and milk. White mixes usually have a variation to make egg bread. Krusteaz and Fleischmann's mixes use bleached flour, while others list unbleached flour. The mixes I tried did not list any preservatives.

Every brand of bread mix bakes up into a loaf with a slightly different profile when it comes to texture (most are quite light- to medium-textured by my standards), aroma (only the Hodgson Mill and King Arthur mixes really smelled as fresh as when you make your own), moistness (all I sampled were very moist and lasted for two to three days at room temperature), sweetness (I like to have more control over the sweetness content, and like to use alternate sweeteners like fructose and maple syrup), crust (most crusts were thin, yet slightly crispy), and salt content (the mixes ranged from about 150 mg to almost 300 mg per mix). None I tested had any cholesterol reading. If you have any special dietary needs at all, you must check the side panel on the box.

Mixes contain their own yeast packets. If you are tempted to add a pinch more yeast, don't. When I did so, the breads rose too fast and were too delicate after baking. Sometimes I did add a few tablespoons more liquid without any disastrous results, and some gluten if none was listed in the ingredients on the side panel.

If you want to make a 2-pound loaf, use one and a half 1-pound mixes. I did find, though, that the 1½-pound loaf is a good-sized loaf. Bread mixes can be mixed on the Dough cycle and hand-shaped into loaves to place in bread pans and bake in the oven.

Although every so often I want a plain bread from a mix, I found that the mixes dress up well. Don't hesitate to add your favorite ingredients to make a personalized loaf. To a plain country white dough I added a tablespoon of hazelnut oil and then pressed the dough out on a baking sheet as for a focaccia, dimpled it after it was risen, and poured a lot of hazelnut oil all over the top. Then I sprinkled it with crumbled dried marjoram and coarse salt and baked it. It turned out chewy and the crust was incredible soaked with the nut oil. Have a little bit of marinara sauce left over from dinner? Let a French or Italian dough rise on the pan, dimple it, and spread with some of the marinara. I had some Parmesan cheese, which I sprinkled on top, and baked a wonderful pizza bread. I used the same dough and pressed fresh blueberries into the top, then sprinkled the whole thing with raw sugar before baking. It was fabulous for breakfast. You could use hazelnut oil or another nut oil. I was really impressed with the bread I got

continued on next page

using a mix as the base, and often shaped it and baked it in my oven after mixing it in the bread machine. I was especially thrilled with the focaccia I created; they were moist and chewy. I recommend cutting focaccia made this way with kitchen shears rather than a knife.

When you make the recipes that follow, or experiment with your own additions to mixes, always open the lid and test the dough with a spatula 10 minutes into the kneading cycle, just as for other bread machine recipes. Often one to three teaspoons of water need to be added. It seems to be different each time. Use the following recipes as a guide (with any type of mix you like as the base) to creating unique breads in a flash. No one will ever guess they came from a mix.

FRESH HERB BREAD

1½-POUND LOAF

1 cup plus 2 tablespoons water (for 14-ounce mix) or 1¼ cups water (for 1-pound mix)
One 14-ounce or 1-pound box white or whole wheat bread machine mix
½ cup chopped fresh herbs, any combination of parsley, chervil, basil, marjoram, sage, chives, mint, thyme, or lovage
¼ cup chopped hazelnuts
Grated zest of 1 lemon
2 teaspoons gluten
1 yeast packet (included in mix)

1 Place all the ingredients in the pan according to the order in the manufacturer's instructions. Set the crust for dark and program for the Basic cycle; press Start.

2 When the baking cycle ends, immediately remove the bread from the pan and place it on a rack. Let cool to room temperature before slicing.

TOMATO FLATBREAD WITH MARJORAM

Makes 1 focaccia

❶ Place all the dough ingredients in the pan according to the order in the manufacturer's instructions. Program for the Dough cycle; press Start. The dough will be pink.

❷ Brush a rectangular baking sheet with some olive oil and sprinkle with cornmeal. When the machine beeps at the end of the cycle, immediately remove the bread pan and turn the dough out onto the baking sheet. With oiled fingers or a rolling pin, press and flatten the dough into a 1–inch-thick oval. Cover with plastic wrap and let rise at room temperature until doubled in height and puffy, 40 minutes.

❸ Twenty minutes before baking, place a baking stone on the lowest rack of a cold oven and preheat it to 400°F.

❹ With your fingers held open, press into the dough all the way to the baking sheet to dimple. Drizzle with the ¼ cup olive oil and sprinkle with the herbs and the coarse salt. Bake for 18 to 23 minutes, until browned. Serve cut into squares with kitchen shears the day it is made, warm or at room temperature.

1½-POUND LOAF

For the dough:

1 cup plus 2 tablespoons water (for 14-ounce mix) 1¼ cups (for 1-pound mix) crushed tomatoes with their liquid or tomato sauce
2 tablespoons olive oil
One 14-ounce or 1-pound box white or whole wheat bread machine mix
1 yeast packet (included in mix)

Olive oil, for brushing
Yellow cornmeal, for sprinkling

For the topping:

¼ cup extra-virgin olive oil
1 tablespoon dried marjoram, crushed
2 teaspoons dried basil, crushed
Coarse sea salt, for sprinkling

RED WINE–WALNUT WHOLE WHEAT BAGUETTES

Makes 2 baguettes

1½-POUND LOAF

½ cup water (for 14-ounce mix) or ¾ cup water (for 1-pound mix)
¼ cup plus 1 tablespoon (for 14-ounce mix) or ½ cup plus 1 tablespoon (for 1-pound mix) dry red wine, such as Merlot
One 14-ounce or 1-pound box Whole Wheat Bread Machine Mix
½ cup chopped walnuts
1 yeast packet (included in mix)

1 Place all the ingredients in the pan according to the order in the manufacturer's instructions. Program for the Dough cycle; press Start.

2 Grease an 18-by-2-inch-wide baguette tray. When the machine beeps at the end of the Dough cycle, scrape the wet dough out with a dough card onto a floured work surface. Knead a few times with your dough card. Divide the dough into 2 equal portions. Flatten each portion into a thin 10-by-6-inch rectangle with the palm of your hand. Starting at a long end, roll up each, using your thumbs to help roll tightly. With the side of your hand, define a depression lengthwise down the center of the dough. Repeatedly fold the dough over in thirds the long way to make a tight log and pinch seams to seal. Stretch each log by rolling it on the table back and forth with your palms a few times to elongate. Gently transfer, seam side down, to the prepared pan. No dough will hang over the ends of the pans. Cover loosely with a clean tea towel and let rise at room temperature until doubled in bulk, about 40 minutes.

3 Twenty minutes before baking, line the center rack of the oven with a baking stone or tiles and preheat the oven to 450°F.

4 With a small, sharp knife, slash the surface 3 or 4 times on the diagonal, no more than ¼ inch deep. Place the pan directly on the stone and bake for 20 to 25 minutes, or until the surfaces of the loaves are a deep golden brown and sound hollow when tapped with your finger. Remove the loaves from the pans immediately to a cooling rack. Eat hot or within 2 hours.

GREEN CHILE BREAD

Makes 1 loaf

1 Place all the dough ingredients in the pan according to the order in the manufacturer's instructions. Program for the Dough cycle; press Start.

2 Line a baking sheet with parchment paper and sprinkle it with cornmeal. When the machine beeps at the end of the cycle, turn the dough out onto a lightly floured work surface. Pat into a 10-by-16-inch rectangle. Spread with the mayonnaise and sprinkle with the scallions. Sprinkle with the cheese and green chiles. Fold the two short ends of the dough into the center and bring up the two long ends to encase the filling. Pinch the seams to seal. Place on the baking sheet, seam side down. Cover loosely with plastic wrap and let rise at room temperature 20 minutes.

3 Preheat the oven to 375°F.

4 With a small sharp knife, slash the tops with 3 diagonal slashes down the top to expose the filling. Bake until golden brown, 30 to 35 minutes. Cool on the pan and serve at room temperature (let the cheese firm up), sliced with a serrated knife.

1½-POUND LOAF

For the dough:

1 cup plus 2 tablespoons water (for 14-ounce mix) or 1¼ cups water (for 1-pound mix)

1 tablespoon olive oil or walnut oil

One 14-ounce or 1-pound box white or whole wheat bread machine mix

1 yeast packet (included in mix)

For the filling:

¼ cup mayonnaise

½ cup chopped scallions

8 ounces Monterey Jack cheese, grated (2 cups)

½ cup canned roasted green chiles, drained and chopped

Yellow cornmeal, for sprinkling

FIG AND WALNUT BREAD

1½-POUND LOAF

1 cup water (for 14-ounce mix) or 1 cup plus 2 tablespoons water (for 1-pound mix)

One 14-ounce or 1-pound box white bread machine mix

2 teaspoons gluten

1 yeast packet (included in mix)

¾ cup chopped dried figs

¼ cup chopped walnuts

1 Place the ingredients, except the figs and walnuts, in the pan according to the order in the manufacturer's instructions. Set the crust for dark and program for the Basic or Fruit and Nut cycle; press Start. When the machine beeps, or between Knead 1 and Knead 2, add the figs and walnuts.

2 When the baking cycle ends, immediately remove the bread from the pan and place it on a rack. Let cool to room temperature before slicing.

POLISH POPPY SEED BREAD

1½-POUND LOAF

1 cup (for 14-ounce mix) or 1 cup plus 2 table-spoons (for 1-pound mix) fat-free milk

1 egg yolk

1 teaspoon almond extract

One 14-ounce or 1-pound box white bread machine mix

½ cup chopped slivered blanched almonds

⅓ cup currants

1 tablespoon poppy seeds

1 tablespoon light brown sugar

2 teaspoons gluten

1 yeast packet (included in mix)

1 Place all the ingredients in the pan according to the order in the manufacturer's instructions. Set the crust for medium and program for the Basic cycle; press Start.

2 When the baking cycle ends, immediately remove the bread from the pan and place it on a rack. Let cool to room temperature before slicing.

SAVORY VEGETABLE AND FRUIT BREADS

W e are certainly used to vegetables in soup or as a side dish for dinner, but in baked bread? I remember the first time I had a vegetable in bread— it was zucchini bread, a quick bread. I couldn't believe a vegetable could take on such a different character. The vegetable lent not only a wonderful flavor to the bread, but also added a very special kind of moisture to it. From then on, I began to make all sorts of quick breads with carrots, sweet potato, pumpkin, and corn. The first yeast bread I ever made with vegetables was one that called for potatoes. Then I made a recipe from my favorite British food writer, Jane Grigson, that paired raw onions with walnuts. It was fantastic. A trip to Berkeley to Narsai David's bakery found me staring at a loaf made with grated raw potatoes and beets. Pink bread!

From then on, I began to see the edible stems, roots, fruits, and leaves that we call vegetables—things like tomatoes, pumpkin, winter squash, parsnips, spinach, and garlic—as dominant ingredients in yeast breads rather than strictly as toppings or fillings, as for pizza or ravioli. The vegetables lend their characteristic flavors, along with a full palate of muted colors. Yeast breads that contain vegetables and sweet fruits carry the aura of being extra healthy by including optimum nourishment in a loaf. Fruit, often thought

of as a sweet bread ingredient, complements savory breads, too.

While this may seem to us like nouvelle cuisine, bakers have been fortifying breads with their garden produce, especially tubers and bulbs, since man was a hunter-gatherer. The Egyptians were creative bakers and loved to put onion, the lily of the Nile, in their breads. Small cakes of pounded cereal, onion, and poppy seeds have been found in archaeological digs at the Swiss lakeside dwellings. The combination of such a variety of products we get from the earth blend together to make good breads. If you try some of these recipes, your baking repertoire will expand considerably.

BLACK OLIVE BREAD

1½-POUND LOAF

1⅛ cups fat-free milk
¼ cup olive oil
1 tablespoon honey

2½ cups bread flour
½ cup rye flour
1 tablespoon plus
  1 teaspoon gluten
½ teaspoon salt

2¼ teaspoons SAF yeast
  or 2¾ teaspoons bread
  machine yeast

1 full cup pitted black olive
pieces

2-POUND LOAF

1⅓ cups fat-free milk
⅓ cup olive oil
1½ tablespoons honey

3¼ cups bread flour
¾ cup rye flour
1 tablespoon plus
  2 teaspoons gluten
¾ teaspoon salt

2½ teaspoons SAF yeast
  or 1 tablespoon bread
  machine yeast

1¼ full cups pitted black
olive pieces

This is a rustic bread that is studded with chunks of black olives. It will have a different character depending on what type of olive you use: canned California black olives are the mildest; Greek Kalamata, soft-fleshed and strong-flavored; intense jet-black Moroccan blacks; or purple-black Alfonsos from Chile. (One of my recipe testers tried using different varieties in the loaf. She thought she favored a combination of green and black olives, until she moved on to green olives stuffed with garlic.) Just remember to pit the olives first, or the bread will be full of surprises! Drain the olives well on paper toweling before adding them, or you will have to add a bit more flour to soak up the brine. This bread is made on the French Bread cycle to give it three full rises.

1 Place the ingredients, except the olives, in the pan according to the order in the manufacturer's instructions. Set crust on medium and program for the French Bread cycle; press Start. (This recipe is not suitable for use with the Delay Timer.) The dough ball will be slightly sticky. Halfway through Knead 2, open the machine and add the olives. If you like big chunks of olives, press Pause at the beginning of Rise 1 instead, remove the dough, pat it into a rectangle, and sprinkle with the olives. Roll up the dough and gently knead a few times to distribute the olives. Return the dough ball to the machine and press Start to resume the rising.

2 When the baking cycle ends, immediately remove the bread from the pan and place it on a rack. Let cool to room temperature before slicing.

PAIN D'AIL

I n Provençe, garlic is said to be the poor man's, or every-man's, spice. Simply a garlic French bread, this is a good dinner bread. Store fresh garlic bulbs in a cool, dry place; they do not need to be refrigerated. Use a garlic press to pulverize the cloves for this recipe, or crush the cloves with the flat side of a knife blade to release their wonderful flavor. If you get the odor of garlic on your fingers, you can remove it by rubbing them on a stainless steel spoon under running water. The metal neutralizes the garlic like magic. You can also use roasted garlic in this bread, if you wish; the flavor will be more subdued. This bread is good served with roasted meats and rice casseroles.

1 Peel the garlic cloves and press into the butter. Mash together.

2 Place all the ingredients in the pan according to the order in the manufacturer's instructions. Add the garlic butter with the liquid ingredients. Set crust on medium and program for French Bread cycle; press Start. (This recipe may be made using the Delay Timer.)

3 When the baking cycle ends, immediately remove the bread from the pan and place it on a rack. Let cool to room temperature before slicing.

1½-POUND LOAF

3 cloves garlic
2 tablespoons unsalted
  butter, softened

1¼ cups water

3⅛ cups bread flour
1 tablespoon gluten
1 tablespoon sugar
1½ teaspoons salt

2 teaspoons SAF yeast
  or 2½ teaspoons bread
  machine yeast

2-POUND LOAF

4 cloves garlic
3 tablespoons unsalted
  butter, softened

1½ cups water

4 cups bread flour
1 tablespoon plus
  1 teaspoon gluten
1½ tablespoons sugar
1¾ teaspoons salt

2½ teaspoons SAF yeast
  or 1 tablespoon bread
  machine yeast

BALSAMIC-CARAMELIZED ONION BREAD

T*his bread is the brainchild of my tester, Mary Anne McCready. This was her favorite method of preparing onions, and they ended up in and on everything, from vegetables to roasts. It was only a matter of time before they ended up in her bread. The slow cooking of the onions with the balsamic vinegar makes for a very sweet vegetable addition to a savory bread. While the bread is baking, be prepared to suffer as its tantalizing smell fills the kitchen. This bread is very aromatic with vinegary undertones. There is a little-known religious sect called the Worshippers of the Onion in Paris; they would love this loaf as a sacrament. The top ends up a nice, crunchy dark brown.*

1½-POUND LOAF

For the onions:

3 tablespoons olive oil
2 tablespoons balsamic
    vinegar
1 large onion (about
    ¾ pound) thinly sliced

For the dough:

¾ cup water

1 tablespoon sugar
2½ cups bread flour
½ cup light or medium rye
    flour
1 tablespoon gluten
1½ teaspoons salt

2 teaspoons SAF yeast
    or 2½ teaspoons bread
    machine yeast

2-POUND LOAF

For the onions:

3 tablespoons olive oil
2 tablespoons balsamic
    vinegar
1 large onion (about
    ¾ pound) thinly sliced

For the dough:

1 cup water

5 teaspoons sugar
3⅓ cups bread flour
⅔ cup light or medium rye
    flour
1 tablespoon plus
    1 teaspoon gluten
2 teaspoons salt

2½ teaspoons SAF yeast
    or 1 tablespoon bread
    machine yeast

1 To prepare the onions, place the olive oil and the vinegar in a medium sauté pan. Add the onions. Slowly cook over low heat for about 20 minutes, stirring occasionally, until the onions are limp and soggy; do not brown. Pour off any excess liquid into a measuring cup and add water to make the liquid measurement for the dough; you might have 1 to 2 tablespoons, or nothing. Set the onions aside to cool to room temperature. You will have about a full cup of onions.

2 To make the dough, place the dough ingredients in the pan according to the order in the manufacturer's instructions. Set crust on medium or dark and program for the Basic or Fruit and Nut cycle; press Start. (This recipe is not suitable for use with the Delay Timer.) When the machine beeps, or between Knead 1 and Knead 2, add the caramelized onions. The dough will initially look dry, so don't be tempted to add liquid; there will be plenty in the onions. If the dough seems too wet 3 minutes after the addition of the onions, add a tablespoon more flour in increments.

3 When the baking cycle ends, immediately remove the bread from the pan and place it on a rack. Let cool to room temperature before slicing.

TOMATO BREAD

1¼ cups water
3 tablespoons tomato paste
⅓ cup chopped oil-packed
   sun-dried tomatoes, with
   their oil

2¾ cups bread flour
½ cup whole wheat flour
1½ tablespoons gluten
1½ teaspoons salt

2 teaspoons SAF yeast
   or 2½ teaspoons bread
   machine yeast

1½ cups water
¼ cup tomato paste
½ cup chopped oil-packed
   sun-dried tomatoes, with
   their oil

3⅔ cups bread flour
⅔ cup whole wheat flour
2 tablespoons gluten
2 teaspoons salt

2¼ teaspoons SAF yeast
   or 2¾ teaspoons bread
   machine yeast

T his tomato bread calls for dried tomatoes. During the drying process, the acid that is present in fresh tomatoes is removed, making this vegetable/fruit easier to digest. Use the imported Italian tomato paste in a tube if you can find it (sometimes stashed at the deli counter), although canned tomato paste is fine. This bread is good with all sorts of cheeses, and is nice shaped into baguettes and baked in the oven.

❶ Place all the ingredients in the pan according to the order in the manufacturer's instructions. Set crust on medium or dark and program for the Basic cycle; press Start. (This recipe may be made using the Delay Timer.)

❷ When the baking cycle ends, immediately remove the bread from the pan and place it on a rack. Let cool to room temperature before slicing.

SWEET POTATO BREAD

T his is a surprise bread, bright orange with bits of tart cranberries throughout. Some people like to add ⅛ cup finely chopped pecans along with the cranberries. It is not a sweet bread, so you can serve it with dinner and for sandwiches. You can make the sweet potato puree yourself by putting fresh-baked or leftover baked sweet potatoes through a food mill or a food processor. Or you can use canned, vacuum-packed sweet potatoes. One 9-ounce can drained and mashed will yield ¾ cup.

1 Place the ingredients, except the cranberries, in the pan according to the order in the manufacturer's instructions. Set crust on medium and program for the Basic or Fruit and Nut cycle; press Start. (This recipe is not suitable for use with the Delay Timer.) When the machine beeps, or between Knead 1 and Knead 2, add the cranberries; they will break up some with the action of the blade.

2 When the baking cycle ends, immediately remove the bread from the pan and place it on a rack. Let cool to room temperature before slicing.

1½-POUND LOAF	2-POUND LOAF
½ cup fat-free milk	⅔ cup fat-free milk
¾ cup pureed sweet potatoes	1 cup pureed sweet potatoes
3 tablespoons sour cream	¼ cup sour cream
3 cups bread flour	4 cups bread flour
1 tablespoon gluten	1 tablespoon plus 1 teaspoon gluten
1½ teaspoons salt	2 teaspoons salt
Grated zest of 1 orange	Grated zest of 1 orange
2 teaspoons SAF yeast or 2½ teaspoons bread machine yeast	2½ teaspoons SAF yeast or 1 tablespoon bread machine yeast
⅔ cup fresh whole cranberries	⅞ cup fresh whole cranberries

ZUCCHINI BREAD

T he cylindrical zucchini squash has been grown as a staple vegetable in the Americas since the Aztecs, long before it was known as Italian summer squash. A more delicate cousin of winter squashes like pumpkins, zucchini are really a soft-shelled, immature version. They are available all year round and are a favorite home garden crop, where they can grow to astounding proportions. The shredded raw vegetable makes for a colorful, flavorful dinner bread, adding considerable moisture to the dough. Try this bread for grilled cheese sandwiches.

❶ Place all the ingredients in the pan according to the order in the manufacturer's instructions. Set crust on medium and program for the Basic cycle; press Start. (This recipe is not suitable for use with the Delay Timer.)

❷ When the baking cycle ends, immediately remove the bread from the pan and place it on a rack. Let cool to room temperature before slicing.

1½-POUND LOAF	2-POUND LOAF
¾ cup fat-free milk	1 cup fat-free milk
1 cup shredded zucchini (4 ounces)	1½ cups shredded zucchini (6 ounces)
2 tablespoons olive oil	3 tablespoons olive oil
2 cups bread flour	2⅔ cups bread flour
1 cup whole wheat flour	1⅓ cups whole wheat flour
1 tablespoon dark brown sugar	2 tablespoons dark brown sugar
Grated zest of 1 lemon	Grated zest of 1 lemon
1 tablespoon gluten	1 tablespoon plus 1 teaspoon gluten
1½ teaspoons salt	2 teaspoons salt
2 teaspoons SAF yeast or 2½ teaspoons bread machine yeast	2¼ teaspoons SAF yeast or 2¾ teaspoons bread machine yeast

CHERRY-WHEAT BERRY BREAD

T his wonderful bread is adapted from a recipe developed by my friend, food consultant Judith Dunbar Hines. When she worked for L'Esprit Dried Foods she created this recipe to use the company's wonderful dried cherries, which were new on the retail market at the time. This is a slightly sweet loaf that makes good turkey sandwiches the day after Thanksgiving.

❶ Combine the wheat berries and the 1 cup of water in a saucepan. Bring to a boil. Reduce the heat, partially cover, and simmer for about 45 minutes, until chewy and tender. Drain off the excess water and let cool to warm.

❷ Place the ingredients, except the wheat berries and the cherries, in the pan according to the order in the manufacturer's instructions. Set crust on dark and program for the Basic cycle; press Start. (This recipe is not suitable for use with the Delay Timer.) When the machine beeps, or at the pause between Knead 1 and 2, add the wheat berries and the cherries. The dough ball will be quite soft and nubby.

❸ When the baking cycle ends, immediately remove the bread from the pan and place it on a rack. Let cool to room temperature before slicing.

1½-POUND LOAF	2-POUND LOAF
⅓ cup wheat berries	½ cup wheat berries
1 cup water	1 cup water
1 cup water	1¼ cups water
1 large egg white	1 large egg white
2 tablespoons canola oil	3 tablespoons canola oil
¼ cup honey	⅓ cup honey
3 cups bread flour	4 cups bread flour
2 teaspoons gluten	1 tablespoon gluten
1½ teaspoons salt	2 teaspoons salt
2½ teaspoons SAF yeast or 1 tablespoon bread machine yeast	1 tablespoon SAF yeast or 1 tablespoon plus ½ teaspoon bread machine yeast
½ cup tart dried cherries tossed with 1 tablespoon flour	⅔ cup tart dried cherries tossed with 1 tablespoon flour

PRUNE BREAD

P runes are the fruit of gourmets. They are dried specifically from prune plums, as other types of plums without a firm flesh and a high sugar content just ferment when they dry. The thriving prune industry in California was started in the nineteenth century by an immigrant Frenchman, with the variety of plums known as Prune d'Agen, named after a town in Aquitaine in southwest France. It takes three pounds of these fresh plums to make a pound of succulent prunes. In this recipe, prunes will integrate right into the dough. I like to buy the vacuum-packed cans of pitted prunes (they are very moist); if the ones you buy are drier, soak the prunes in hot water for an hour and drain them before chopping. Some people don't consider this bread complete without nuts, so go ahead and add ¼ cup chopped walnuts or pecans, if you must. This excellent bread is good spread with cream cheese or toasted.

1½-POUND LOAF	2-POUND LOAF
1⅛ cups water	1½ cups water
3 tablespoons unsalted butter, cut into pieces	4 tablespoons unsalted butter, cut into pieces
2¼ cups bread flour	2¾ cups bread flour
¾ cup whole wheat flour	1¼ cups whole wheat flour
2 tablespoons light brown sugar	3 tablespoons light brown sugar
1 tablespoon gluten	1 tablespoon plus 1 teaspoon gluten
1¼ teaspoons salt	1¾ teaspoons salt
1 teaspoon ground cinnamon	1¼ teaspoons ground cinnamon
¼ teaspoon fresh-ground nutmeg	⅓ teaspoon fresh-ground nutmeg
2 teaspoons SAF yeast or 2½ teaspoons bread machine yeast	2½ teaspoons SAF yeast or 1 tablespoon bread machine yeast
9 pitted prunes (about 3 ounces), chopped	12 pitted prunes (about 4 ounces), chopped

❶ Place the ingredients, except the prunes, in the pan according to the order in the manufacturer's instructions. Set crust on dark and program for the Basic or Fruit and Nut cycle; press Start. (This recipe is not suitable for use with the Delay Timer.) When the machine beeps, or between Knead 1 and Knead 2, add the prunes. If you like big chunks of prunes, press Pause at the beginning of Rise 1, remove the dough, pat it into a rectangle, and sprinkle with the prunes. Roll up the dough and gently knead it a few times to distribute the prunes. Return the dough ball to the machine and press Start to resume the rising.

2 When the baking cycle ends, immediately remove the bread from the pan and place it on a rack. Let cool to room temperature before slicing.

Leftover Bread Cookery: Pork Chops with Cranberry Prune Stuffing

Serves 4

Pork, cranberries, and prunes—a toothsome combination. Buy the wonderfully thick-cut pork chops for this entree. It is a convenient dinner, baked in the oven. Serve the pork chops with roasted potatoes and homemade applesauce.

¼ loaf homemade white, whole wheat, Prune Bread (page 350), or other flavored bread
2 tablespoons olive oil
1 large or 2 medium shallots, chopped
Grated zest of 1 orange
1 teaspoon chopped fresh sage
½ cup canned whole cranberry sauce
⅓ cup chopped pitted prunes
½ cup canned chicken broth
4 loin pork chops, 1 to 2 inches thick, bone-in

1 Preheat the oven to 350°F.

2 Cut the bread into chunks and whirl in the food processor to make about 1⅓ cups fresh breadcrumbs. In a medium sauté pan, heat the olive oil and cook the shallots until limp, but not browned, 5 minutes. Turn off the heat. Add the orange zest, sage, cranberry sauce, prunes, and 3 to 4 tablespoons of chicken broth to moisten; stir to combine.

3 Oil the bottom of a shallow roasting pan or baking dish. With a small sharp knife, make a pocket in each chop by cutting from the outer side of the meat through the center to the bone. Season inside and out with salt and pepper. Stuff each pocket with a quarter of the stuffing. Lay side by side in the baking dish and pour the remaining chicken broth over.

4 Cover with foil and bake for 30 minutes. Uncover and bake for 25 to 30 minutes longer, or until the pork chops are tender. Serve immediately.

ROSEMARY-GOLDEN RAISIN BREAD

Makes 1 round loaf

1½- OR 2-POUND-LOAF MACHINES

3 cups bread flour
1 teaspoon dried rosemary

⅔ cup water
¼ cup extra-virgin olive oil
2 large eggs

⅓ cup nonfat dry milk
¼ cup sugar
1½ teaspoons salt

2 teaspoons SAF yeast
  or 2½ teaspoons bread
  machine yeast

½ cup golden raisins

I go wild for this bread, even though at one time I didn't like rosemary in bread. A small amount of rosemary, never more, adds just a hint of herbal flavor to this unusual Italian egg bread, often served for Easter. Pane rosmarino is baked in the oven so that its crust can turn a luscious dark brown.

1 In the workbowl of a food processor, combine 1 cup of the flour with the rosemary. Pulse to pulverize the rosemary.

2 Place the ingredients, including the rosemary flour but not the raisins, in the pan according to the order in the manufacturer's instructions. Program for the Dough cycle; press Start.

3 Line a baking sheet with parchment paper. When the machine beeps at the end of the cycle, using a dough scraper, turn the dough out onto a clean work surface. Pat into an uneven oval loaf shape. Sprinkle with the raisins and fold in half. Knead gently to distribute evenly. Even out and smooth the dough. Shape into a tight round. Place on the baking sheet and brush the top with olive oil. Cover loosely with plastic wrap and let rise at room temperature until doubled in bulk, about 1 hour.

4 Twenty minutes before baking, preheat the oven to 350°F.

5 Brush the surface of the loaf again with olive oil, and, using a sharp knife, slash an X on the top, no deeper than ½ inch. Bake in the center of the oven for 30 to 35 minutes, until dark brown and the bottom sounds hollow when tapped. Place the loaf on a rack. Let cool to room temperature before slicing.

CARROT BREAD WITH CRYSTALLIZED GINGER

C*arrots are so sweet that no sugar is needed to make this bread. It is studded with bits of crystallized ginger that melt into the bread and burst with flavor in your mouth. You can use leftover steamed carrots and puree them, or, more conveniently, use a jar of junior baby food carrots. This bread is sure to become a favorite.*

❶ Place all the ingredients in the pan according to the order in the manufacturer's instructions. Set crust on dark and program for the Basic cycle; press Start. (This recipe is not suitable for use with the Delay Timer.)

❷ When the baking cycle ends, immediately remove the bread from the pan and place it on a rack. Let cool to room temperature before slicing.

1½-POUND LOAF	2-POUND LOAF
3 tablespoons fat-free milk	¼ cup fat-free milk
One 6-ounce jar junior baby food strained carrots or ¾ cup pureed carrots	One 6-ounce jar junior baby food strained carrots or ¾ cup pureed carrots
2 large eggs	2 large eggs
2 tablespoons unsalted butter, cut into pieces	3 tablespoons unsalted butter, cut into pieces
3 cups bread flour	4 cups bread flour
¼ cup chopped crystallized ginger	⅓ cup chopped crystallized ginger
1 tablespoon gluten	1 tablespoon plus 1 teaspoon gluten
1½ teaspoons salt	2 teaspoons salt
1¾ teaspoons SAF yeast or 2¼ teaspoons bread machine yeast	2 teaspoons SAF yeast or 2½ teaspoons bread machine yeast

Bread Pan Shapes

There are now three different shapes of pans on the bread machine market: a tall cylindrical oval or cube, a vertical rectangle, and a long horizontal loaf, which looks the most like a traditional loaf. Some bakers prefer the cylindrical shape—it tends to mix better since there is less surface area on the bottom of the pan, often eliminating the need to go in and scrape around the edges of the pan for consistent mixing. The most common shape is the vertical rectangle. This is a rectangular shape, but it has tall sides and is not so far removed from a cube. Vertical rectangle pans are known for having the dough collect in one end of the pan and bake into a slope, but this is easy to avoid. Just check the dough as it is rising, and if you need to push it to the center, do so using a rubber spatula. The long horizontal pans have the widest mixing areas, and usually have two kneading blades to mix effectively.

I always cool any loaf right side up. For regular servings, turn a tall loaf on its side to cut it into wedges or into slices (the slices fit nicely into plastic sandwich bags). Slice the vertical rectangular and horizontal loaves as you would a standard oven pan loaf. A 1½-pound loaf from any pan yields about 10 to 16 slices and a 2-pound loaf yields anywhere from 14 to 20 slices.

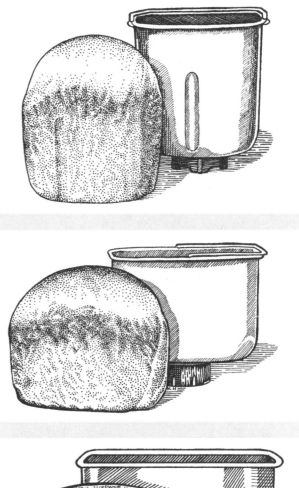

APPLESAUCE BREAD

F*ruit purees have become very popular in bread as they contain zero fat, are low in calories, and provide fiber as well as a nice flavor. Use canned or homemade. Be sure to adjust the liquid here, depending on how thick your applesauce is. If the sauce is very watery, add a bit less apple juice. If you add the optional brown sugar and ½ cup of chopped walnuts, this bread will be especially good for toast. If you don't add the sugar, the loaf will not be sweet and can be served with a bratwurst, potato pancake, and sauerkraut dinner.*

❶ Place all the ingredients in the pan according to the order in the manufacturer's instructions. Set crust on medium and program for the Basic or Sweet Bread cycle; press Start. (This recipe is not suitable for use with the Delay Timer.)

❷ When the baking cycle ends, immediately remove the bread from the pan and place it on a rack. Let cool to room temperature before slicing.

1½-POUND LOAF	2-POUND LOAF
¼ cup apple juice	½ cup apple juice
½ cup unsweetened applesauce	¾ cup unsweetened applesauce
1 large egg	1 large egg
2 tablespoons unsalted butter, cut into pieces	3 tablespoons unsalted butter, cut into pieces
3 cups bread flour	4 cups bread flour
3 tablespoons light brown sugar, optional	¼ cup light brown sugar, optional
1 tablespoon gluten	1 tablespoon plus 1 teaspoon gluten
1½ teaspoons salt	2 teaspoons salt
1 teaspoon ground cinnamon or apple pie spice	1¼ teaspoons ground cinnamon or apple pie spice
⅓ teaspoon baking soda	½ teaspoon baking soda
2 teaspoons SAF yeast or 2½ teaspoons bread machine yeast	2¼ teaspoons SAF yeast or 2¾ teaspoons bread machine yeast

SQUASH OR PUMPKIN CLOVERLEAF ROLLS

Makes 16 cloverleaf dinner rolls

1½- OR 2-POUND- LOAF MACHINES

1 winter squash (about
   1⅓ pounds), or 1 cup
   canned pumpkin puree

½ cup water
½ cup milk
⅓ cup butter, melted

4½ cups unbleached
   all-purpose flour
3 tablespoons light or dark
   brown sugar
Grated zest of 1 orange
2 teaspoons salt

2¼ teaspoons SAF yeast
   or 2¾ teaspoons bread
   machine yeast

I have a passion for the big, hard winter squash that comes
in myriad sizes, shapes, and colors: the globular green
buttercup, the pear-shaped tan butternut, the sugar pumpkin, bright orange turban, striped turban, bumpy acorn, or the dense
oval Hubbard (which is sometimes substituted for pumpkin since it
has a lower moisture content). Any variety of squash yields equally
good results. If you are really in a hurry, you can certainly use
canned pumpkin here with no loss of flavor. I give instructions for
shaping each roll into a cloverleaf here, but you can use this dough
to make any of the shapes described on pages 358 to 359.

1 Preheat the oven to 350°F.

2 If you are using winter squash, wash the squash and cut
off the top with a sharp chef's knife. Take care when
cutting, because some varieties are very hard. Cut in half
and scrape out the seeds and spongy fibers. Leave butternut squash or pumpkin in halves, or cut larger squash
into large cubes leaving the skin intact. Place in a baking
dish, flesh down, and add a half inch of water. Cover and
bake for 1 to 1½ hours, depending on the size of the
pieces, or until the flesh is tender when pierced with a
knife. Drain, cool, then scoop out the squash flesh and
discard the skin. Puree the pulp until smooth in a food
mill or food processor. You should have about 1 cup.
Cool, cover, then refrigerate or freeze until needed.
Warm slightly in the microwave before placing in the
bread machine.

3 Place all the ingredients in the pan according to the
order in the manufacturer's instructions. Program for
the Dough cycle; press Start. (This recipe is not suitable
for use with the Delay Timer.)

4 Grease 16 standard muffin cups (one full pan plus 4 cups in a second pan). When the machine beeps at the end of the cycle, immediately remove the dough and place on a lightly floured work surface; divide into 4 equal portions. Divide each of those pieces into 4 equal portions. Divide each of the 16 portions into 3 portions and form these into small balls about the size of a walnut. You want them all about the same size; this is important or else the rolls will look funny after baking. Arrange 3 balls of dough touching each other in each of the muffin cups. Cover loosely with plastic wrap and let rise until doubled in bulk, about 30 minutes.

5 Meanwhile, preheat the oven to 375°F.

6 Bake for 15 to 18 minutes, or until golden brown. Immediately remove the rolls from the pan. Let cool on racks or serve warm.

NOTE:

To prepare the rolls in advance and bake them later, brush the tops of the shaped dough with melted butter. Cover loosely with 2 layers of plastic wrap, leaving some room for expansion and taking care to tightly wrap all the edges. Immediately refrigerate for 2 to 24 hours. When ready to bake, uncover and let stand at room temperature no more than 20 minutes. Bake as directed.

Technique: How to Shape and Bake Soft Dinner Rolls

Sure we love focaccia and fresh loaves of rustic bread for dinner. But American-style soft dinner rolls, shaped into a host of pretty, traditional shapes, never go out of style or favor. The bread machine makes the dough a snap. (You can even use a commercial bread machine mix if you like, but the rolls won't be quite as good.) Piping hot with melted butter, dinner rolls need no embellishment. They are meant to melt in your mouth and to be a bit chewy at the same time. I was a lucky child—growing up, my mother kept all sorts of fancy dinner rolls in the freezer and brought some out every night for dinner. We had finger rolls with poppy seeds, crescent-shaped butterhorns, cloverleafs, or just plain round puffy rolls. I especially liked the fantans, which, like a deck of cards, could be pulled apart in tender stages.

Dinner roll dough is not the same as bread dough; it is a bit more delicate and soft. The doughs have butter or margarine, milk, and sometimes egg for richness. They don't need to be worked hard like dough for a loaf, so dinner roll recipes call for all-purpose flour. Not as much gluten is needed. They have a fine crumb. While the hand shaping is not hard, there is a bit of precision involved or else they will look lopsided, even though little irregularities will disappear as the rolls puff in the oven. Look for the other dinner roll recipes in this book, Virginia Light Rolls (page 86), an all–white flour version, and Soft Whole Wheat Dinner Rolls (page 109), for similar doughs that can also be baked in the beautiful shapes below. A basket of homemade dinner rolls with your lunch or supper of roast turkey, ham, pork loin, or chicken spells, well, you know, old-fashioned comfort and a grand day of baking.

Parker House Rolls

Makes 16 rolls

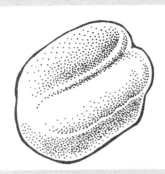

Grease a 13-by-9-inch baking dish (if you use glass, reduce the oven heat by 25°). Roll out the dough into a flat 12-by-12-inch square about ½-inch thick. Using a 2½-inch round biscuit cutter with a smooth edge, cut out rounds. Using the handle of a wooden spoon to mark the fold, press (not all the way through) to make the mark lengthwise a little off center, dividing the roll into two sections—one ⅓ of the area and the other ⅔. Brush with melted butter. Fold the small half over the larger half. Press the folded edge gently with your finger to adhere. Repeat with the remaining rounds. Place in the baking pan, sides just touching. Let rise 45 minutes and bake for 25 to 28 minutes.

Snails

Makes 8 rolls

Cut the dough in half and divide it into 8 equal portions. Roll each portion into a 8-inch-long rope, ½ inch in diameter. Starting at one end and holding the other edge stable, wind the strip of dough around itself to form a loose spiral. Tuck the edge firmly under. Repeat with the remaining portions. Place the snails about 2 inches apart on the baking sheet. Let rise 45 minutes and bake for 15 to 18 minutes.

Fantan Rolls
Makes 12 rolls

Grease the cups of a standard muffin tin. With a rolling pin, roll the dough into a rectangle 18-by-14 inches, ⅛ to ¼-inch thick. Brush the surface with melted butter. Cut the rectangle in half lengthwise, then cut each half into 3 long strips of equal width. Stack the strips on top of each other to form a layered pile. With a sharp knife, cut in half. Cut each half into 6 equal portions. Place each portion in a muffin cup with the cut edge facing up (they will fan open as they bake). Brush each with melted butter. Let rise 45 minutes and bake for 15 to 18 minutes.

Butterhorns
Makes 16 rolls

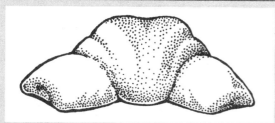

Cut the dough in half to make 2 equal portions. On a lightly floured work surface, roll each half into a 10-inch circle. Brush with melted butter. With a sharp knife or pastry wheel, cut each circle into 8 equal wedges. Beginning at the wide end, firmly roll each wedge up toward the point. Place, point side down on the prepared baking sheets and curve the ends inward. Place the rolls about 2 inches apart on the baking sheet. Let rise 45 minutes and bake for 15 to 18 minutes.

Stuffing Breads

Stuffings for meat and poultry are a satisfying part of a meal and have universal appeal. They are comfort food. Over time, the humble stuffing has evolved into a really wonderful-tasting part of the meal. Having started out as a practical and thrifty stretcher for often lean game meats, stuffing is now a cornerstone of the Thanksgiving meal, and makes a Sunday chicken a special occasion. Stuffing enhances the flavor of a bird and absorbs its juice as it roasts. In fact, bread has come to be considered such a vital accompaniment to cooked birds that game birds that aren't stuffed, like partridges or doves, are often placed, bacon-wrapped, on a bed of sliced, toasted bread for serving. Stuffings can also be used in preparing fish, pork, and vegetables.

Almost all day-old breads, whether white, whole wheat, multigrain, or flavored, are excellent stuffing bases. Many of the flavored breads in this chapter make especially nice stuffings. If you begin with a bread that is already very savory, all you need to do is moisten the cubed bread with an egg or broth and you have a stuffing. The recipes in this section have been developed with just that in mind. This is not to say these stuffing breads can't be enjoyed out of hand—they are wonderful on their own. But I also see them as flavorful, convenient cooking shortcuts and I have included, in this section as well as in the rest of the chapter and the book, some very special entree recipes that call for stuffings. For real convenience, keep a loaf of stuffing bread in the freezer, at the ready.

Here are some hints for successful stuffings:

- A 1½-pound loaf of bread will yield about 10 cups of cubes, and a 2-pound loaf will yield about 12 cups of bread cubes.

- Figure on 1 cup of stuffing per person, baking the extra in a pan on the side. A 12-pound turkey will hold 4 to 5 cups stuffing; a Cornish hen will take about 1 cup; a large roasting chicken or capon will hold 3 to 4 cups; pork chops or trout hold about a ½ cup.

- Day-old bread is best for stuffings, unless your recipe calls for fresh. If you do not have any day-old bread, you can dry your fresh bread for stuffing.

Cut it into ¾-inch cubes (with or without crusts) and scatter the cubes on an ungreased baking sheet. Bake in a preheated 300°F oven until they are crisp but not browned, about 10 to 20 minutes. Or, place the cubes on an ungreased baking sheet and leave them on the kitchen counter, uncovered, to air-dry for 8 hours or overnight.

- If you are using really stale bread, soak it in chicken broth or milk to soften it first. Slightly stale bread doesn't need soaking.

- Cut or chop the onions, nuts, fruits, and any other added ingredients to be approximately the same size as the bread cubes.

- Sauté onions before adding them to a stuffing.

- Never use raw meat, especially pork products, in stuffings. Pork sausage, giblets, oysters, or any type of raw meat must be cooked through before being added to a stuffing. The internal temperature of the meat or poultry will not be high enough to cook meat in a stuffing properly.

- Adding leafy vegetables or herbs, such as Swiss chard or parsley, lightens the texture of a stuffing.

- Stuff poultry right before roasting it. Never stuff it the night before, or it can spoil. If you make the stuffing ahead of time, refrigerate it until it is time to stuff the bird or meat. Other meats that are rolled and stuffed, like lamb and veal, are the exception, and can be prepared the night before.

- Spoon the stuffing in loosely, rather than packing it, to retain a nice texture after roasting and allow room for the stuffing to expand as it cooks.

- Any stuffing that will not fit into the bird or meat can go into a covered casserole (and can be refrigerated until there is room in the oven). Before baking the dressing, moisten it with ½ cup broth, white wine, or water, to substitute for the roasting juices. Bake, covered with foil, at 350°F, until the stuffing registers 165°F on an instant-read thermometer.

- After the meal, remove all the stuffing from the bird and refrigerate it separately. Rolled meats and stuffed pork chops don't require this precaution.

CHICKEN STUFFING BREAD

H ere is a basic stuffing bread for chicken. I use my favorite combination of dried herbs from the garden to make it, and then use it to stuff the cavity of a whole bird or to push under the skin of boneless chicken breasts. But do try this bread on its own, too. It is as good eaten out of hand as it is for stuffing.

1 Place all the ingredients in the pan according to the order in the manufacturer's instructions. Set crust on dark and program for the Basic cycle; press Start. (This recipe is not suitable for use with the Delay Timer.)

2 When the baking cycle ends, immediately remove the bread from the pan and place it on a rack. Let cool to room temperature before slicing.

1½-POUND LOAF	2-POUND LOAF
1⅛ cups fat-free milk	1½ cups fat-free milk
2 tablespoons butter, cut into pieces	3 tablespoons butter, cut into pieces
3 cups bread flour	4 cups bread flour
1 tablespoon sugar	1½ tablespoons sugar
1 tablespoon gluten	1 tablespoon plus 1 teaspoon gluten
2 tablespoons chopped fresh chives	3 tablespoons chopped fresh chives
1 tablespoon dried marjoram	1½ tablespoons dried marjoram
1 teaspoon dried basil	1½ teaspoons dried basil
1 teaspoon dried thyme	1½ teaspoons dried thyme
1½ teaspoons salt	2 teaspoons salt
2 teaspoons SAF yeast or 2½ teaspoons bread machine yeast	2½ teaspoons SAF yeast or 1 tablespoon bread machine yeast

Leftover Bread Cookery: Stuffed-Under-the-Skin Roast Chicken

Serves 4

My mom makes a fabulous roast chicken, and when it is stuffed it is even better. While this recipe has the stuffing strategically placed under the skin, if you triple the stuffing recipe, you can stuff the cavity instead. Fresh breadcrumbs are a must. Serve this chicken with garlic mashed potatoes.

For the herb stuffing:

1 large shallot, minced
1 clove garlic, pressed
3 tablespoons butter or margarine
¼ cup chopped fresh flat-leaf parsley
1 tablespoon minced fresh herbs, such as tarragon, thyme, or sage
⅔ cup fresh coarse breadcrumbs from white, whole wheat, or flavored bread

For the chicken:

One 5½-pound roasting chicken
Juice of 1 lemon
Salt and fresh-ground black pepper

❶ Preheat the oven to 400°F.

❷ To make the stuffing, combine the shallot, garlic, and butter in a microwave-proof bowl. Partially cover with plastic wrap and heat on high until soft, about 3 minutes. Combine the rest of the stuffing ingredients in a medium bowl with the shallot mixture.

❸ To prepare the chicken, rub the inside and skin of the chicken with the lemon juice and sprinkle with salt and pepper. Place in a roasting pan. With your fingers, break the membrane at the vent opening at one side of the breast bone and work your forefinger under the skin to make a pocket on the breast and thigh, taking care not to tear the skin while you are doing this. Repeat on the other side. This is easier than it sounds.

❹ Spread half the stuffing in an even layer under the skin with your fingers. Repeat with the other side. Tie the legs together with kitchen twine. Rub the outside of the chicken with some olive oil.

❺ Reduce the oven temperature to 375°F and place the chicken in the center of the hot oven. Roast for 1½ hours, until golden brown and the juices run clear when the meat is pierced with a knife. Cover with foil and let rest 10 minutes before carving.

FRESH HERB AND NUT STUFFING BREAD

I recommend that you keep bags of cubed stuffing bread in the freezer, then it will be ready any time you want to make a stuffed food for dinner. Fresh herbs, which are delicate and pungent, make a very different stuffing bread than dried herbs do. Use your own combination of dill, chives, oregano, marjoram, lovage, thyme, or chervil, combined with plenty of parsley.

❶ Place all the ingredients in the pan according to the order in the manufacturer's instructions. Set crust on dark and program for the Basic cycle; press Start. (This recipe is not suitable for use with the Delay Timer.)

❷ When the baking cycle ends, immediately remove the bread from the pan and place it on a rack. Let cool to room temperature before slicing.

1½-POUND LOAF

1 cup plus 3 tablespoons water
1½ tablespoons walnut oil

3 cups bread flour
1 tablespoon light brown sugar
½ cup mixed fresh herbs, minced
¼ cup walnuts
1 tablespoon gluten
1½ teaspoons salt

2 teaspoons SAF yeast or 2½ teaspoons bread machine yeast

2-POUND LOAF

1½ cups plus 1 tablespoon water
2 tablespoons walnut oil

4 cups bread flour
1½ tablespoons light brown sugar
¾ cup mixed fresh herbs, minced
⅓ cup walnuts
1 tablespoon plus 1 teaspoon gluten
2 teaspoons salt

2½ teaspoons SAF yeast or 1 tablespoon bread machine yeast

FRESH HERB STUFFING BREAD WITH FENNEL SEED AND PEPPER

Y ou can choose your own herb mix for this bread. Use one or any combination of parsley, basil, chervil, Spanish oregano, thyme, or marjoram. Grind the black, white, or red peppercorns in a hand grinder; you want coarse pieces. This bread can be used either the day it is made or day-old for poultry stuffings.

1 Place all the ingredients in the pan according to the order in the manufacturer's instructions. Set crust on medium and program for the Basic cycle; press Start. (This recipe may be made using the Delay Timer.)

2 When the baking cycle ends, immediately remove the bread from the pan and place it on a rack. Let cool to room temperature before slicing.

1½-POUND LOAF

1⅛ cups water
2 tablespoons olive oil

2½ cups bread flour
½ cup whole wheat flour
⅓ cup chopped fresh herbs
3 tablespoons chopped
   walnuts or pine nuts
1½ tablespoons sugar
1½ tablespoons dry
   buttermilk powder
2 teaspoons gluten
1¼ teaspoons salt
1 teaspoon fennel seed
½ teaspoon grated lemon
   zest
½ teaspoon ground black,
   white, or red peppercorns

2 teaspoons SAF yeast
   or 2½ teaspoons bread
   machine yeast

2-POUND LOAF

1½ cups water
3 tablespoons olive oil

3 cups bread flour
1 cup whole wheat flour
½ cup chopped fresh herbs
4 tablespoons chopped
   walnuts or pine nuts
2 tablespoons sugar
2 tablespoons dry
   buttermilk powder
1 tablespoon gluten
1½ teaspoons salt
1¼ teaspoons fennel seed
¾ teaspoon grated lemon
   zest
¾ teaspoon ground black,
   white, or red peppercorns

2¼ teaspoons SAF yeast
   or 2¾ teaspoons bread
   machine yeast

CORNMEAL STUFFING BREAD

C ornmeal stuffings are usually made with a baking powder cornbread, but a yeasted one like this that incorporates corn kernels also works beautifully. You can make this bread, have a few slices with dinner, and then cube and freeze the rest to have on hand for stuffing. Use it to stuff a turkey, or to fill large, fresh Anaheim chiles before baking.

1 Place all the ingredients in the pan according to the order in the manufacturer's instructions. Set crust on dark and program for the Basic cycle; press Start. (This recipe is not suitable for use with the Delay Timer.)

2 When the baking cycle ends, immediately remove the bread from the pan and place it on a rack. Let cool to room temperature before slicing.

1½-POUND LOAF	2-POUND LOAF
One 11-ounce can of corn with liquid	One 11-ounce can of corn with liquid
¼ cup buttermilk	⅓ cup buttermilk
2 tablespoons canola or olive oil	3 tablespoons canola or olive oil
2 tablespoons honey	3 tablespoons honey
2 cups bread flour	2¾ cups bread flour
1 cup yellow cornmeal	1¼ cups yellow cornmeal
¼ cup minced fresh parsley	⅓ cup minced fresh parsley
1½ tablespoons poultry seasoning	1¾ tablespoons poultry seasoning
½ teaspoon garlic powder	¾ teaspoon garlic powder
1 tablespoon plus 1 teaspoon gluten	1 tablespoon plus 2 teaspoons gluten
1¼ teaspoons salt	1½ teaspoons salt
2 teaspoons SAF yeast or 2½ teaspoons bread machine yeast	2½ teaspoons SAF yeast or 1 tablespoon bread machine yeast

PROSCIUTTO STUFFING BREAD

T his bread makes a more assertive stuffing than the ones made just with herbs, since the prosciutto adds a strong salty flavor. Use coarsely ground black pepper from your pepper grinder. Have the deli slice the prosciutto paper-thin, then chop it before you add it to the bread pan. Be sure to store this bread in the refrigerator, as the prosciutto makes it very perishable. This is good with fish or chicken as a stuffing bread, or to eat with soup and salad.

❶ Place all the ingredients in the pan according to the order in the manufacturer's instructions. Set crust on medium and program for the Basic cycle; press Start. (This recipe is not suitable for use with the Delay Timer.)

❷ When the baking cycle ends, immediately remove the bread from the pan and place it on a rack. Let cool to room temperature before slicing.

1½-POUND LOAF	2-POUND LOAF
⅞ cup water	1¼ cups water
¼ cup olive oil	⅓ cup olive oil
3 cups bread flour	4 cups bread flour
3 ounces prosciutto, coarsely chopped	4 ounces prosciutto, coarsely chopped
1 tablespoon gluten	1 tablespoon plus 1 teaspoon gluten
1 tablespoon sugar	1 tablespoon plus 1 teaspoon sugar
1 teaspoon ground black pepper	1¼ teaspoons ground black pepper
½ teaspoon salt	¾ teaspoon salt
1½ teaspoons SAF yeast or 2 teaspoons bread machine yeast	2 teaspoons SAF yeast or 2½ teaspoons bread machine yeast

Leftover Bread Cookery: Whole Trout with Prosciutto Stuffing

Serves 6

This is a really fast entree; once the bread is made, you have about 40 minutes from prep to table. Of course, the fresher the better with trout; look for clear eyes, shiny skin, and firm flesh. Plan to cook it the same day it is purchased or caught. Serve this entree with lemon rice and steamed baby green beans.

½ loaf Prosciutto Stuffing Bread (opposite)
3 medium shallots, chopped
3 tablespoons olive oil
⅓ cup chopped fresh flat-leaf parsley
6 whole trout (about 1 pound each), cleaned with bone in and head and tail left on
Pinch of salt
Lemon wedges, for serving

❶ Preheat the oven to 475°F.

❷ Cut the bread into chunks and whirl in the food processor to make about 3 cups fresh breadcrumbs. Heat the olive oil in a medium sauté pan, and cook the shallots until limp, but not browned, about 5 minutes. Turn off the heat. Add the breadcrumbs and the parsley; toss to combine.

❸ Oil a large 14-by-12-inch shallow roasting pan or baking dish. Sprinkle each trout inside and out with a bit of salt. Lightly fill each cavity with the stuffing and rub each fish with some olive oil. Lay side by side in the baking dish.

❹ Bake for 15 to 18 minutes, or until fish is opaque near the bone when pierced with a knife. Serve immediately, with lemon wedges on the side.

CHEESE BREADS

C heese and bread—there's a natural pairing. For the palate that desires variety but appreciates simplicity, a bit of cheese makes a simple dough into something really special. Knowledgeable cheese lovers may dote on the rustic European cheeses like Locatelli (in the Romano family), rich creamy St. André with its powdery rind and woven straw mat (used instead of Brie), Emmenthaler from the Jura Mountains (in place of a less flavorful domestic Swiss), young fresh whole milk ricotta (heaven on a spoon), and fresh mozzarella that needs to be sliced in an old-fashioned egg slicer because it is so slippery (the softer the cheese, the fresher it needs to be). Regular old bakers like myself love the cheeses from their childhood, such as Colby, cheddar, Parmesan, feta, and Monterey Jack. They are easy to find and their predictable flavors delight over and over again. You will find a whole range of cheeses incorporated into these recipes.

Cheese is ephemerally flavored; treat it with care and respect, whether it is an accompaniment to your fresh baked breads, melted between grilled slices, or an integral part of the ingredient list or filling. In your breads, expect the cheese to influence the character of the loaf; the texture will be more moist and the flavor more distinct. In bread machine baking, cheese is counted proportionally as part of the liquid ingredients and, unless it is called for in little cubes or chunks, can be added with the main ingredients at the beginning of the cycle. Don't be tempted to use the dark crust setting for any cheese breads since they have a tendency to overbrown easily; a light or medium crust is best. These breads should be stored in the refrigerator once they have cooled.

RICOTTA AND FRESH CHIVE BREAD

R icotta was originally a fresh, soft cheese made with the whey left over from producing mozzarella. It is a smooth, small curd, Italian white cheese that is made in America, too. Ricotta may be made from either whole milk or part-skim (the closest in flavor to traditional Italian ricotta), each very different in taste. This is a recipe I got from one of my recipe testers who lives in California's Napa Valley. She raved about it and said it was her first real success at breadmaking. It is chock full of fresh chives, which have a more subtle flavor than scallions or regular onions, and add a nice flecked appearance to every slice. Since it is such a delicately flavored bread, eat this fresh. It loses its subtle nature after being frozen. Serve this with pasta dishes.

1 Place all the ingredients in the pan according to the order in the manufacturer's instructions. Set crust on medium and program for the Basic cycle; press Start. (This recipe is not suitable for use with the Delay Timer.)

2 When the baking cycle ends, immediately remove the bread from the pan and place it on a rack. Let cool to room temperature before slicing.

1½-POUND LOAF	2-POUND LOAF
1 cup water ⅓ cup whole or part-skim ricotta cheese	1⅓ cups water ½ cup whole or part-skim ricotta cheese
3 cups bread flour 1 tablespoon light brown sugar 1 tablespoon gluten 1½ teaspoons salt ½ cup chopped fresh chives Dash of ground black pepper	4 cups bread flour 1½ tablespoons light brown sugar 1 tablespoon plus 1 teaspoon gluten 2 teaspoons salt ¾ cup chopped fresh chives Dash of ground black pepper
2½ teaspoons SAF yeast or 1 tablespoon bread machine yeast	1 tablespoon SAF yeast or 1 tablespoon plus ½ teaspoon bread machine yeast

COTTAGE CHEESE DILL BREAD

I would be remiss not to include this recipe, as it is wildly popular with home bakers. And for good reason. An herbaceous bread that has its roots in Mennonite country, it has successfully made the transition from a traditional yeast bread and casserole loaf to the bread machine. Many people add the shallot raw, but I like to cook it a bit first. I recommend using small curd cottage cheese, and dried dill weed that is not faded—a signal that it would be lacking in flavor. The texture of this bread is quite moist and delicate, making great toast and savory bread puddings.

❶ Heat the oil in a small skillet, and sauté the shallot until translucent. Set aside to cool to warm.

❷ Place the ingredients in the pan according to the order in the manufacturer's instructions, adding the shallot with the liquid ingredients. Set crust on dark and program for Basic cycle; press Start. (This recipe is not suitable for use with the Delay Timer.) The dough ball will look very dry at first and take a few minutes to come together. Resist the urge to add more liquid.

❸ When the baking cycle ends, immediately remove the bread from the pan and place it on a rack. Let cool to room temperature before slicing.

1½-POUND LOAF	2-POUND LOAF
2 tablespoons olive oil	3 tablespoons olive oil
1 medium shallot, chopped	1 large shallot, chopped
1 cup cottage cheese	1⅓ cups cottage cheese
¼ cup fat-free milk	⅓ cup fat-free milk
1 large egg plus 1 egg yolk	1 large egg plus 1 egg yolk
2½ cups bread flour	3⅓ cups bread flour
1 tablespoon sugar	2 tablespoons sugar
1 tablespoon gluten	1 tablespoon plus 1 teaspoon gluten
2 tablespoons dried dill weed	2½ tablespoons dried dill weed
1¼ teaspoons salt	1¾ teaspoons salt
2 teaspoons SAF yeast or 2½ teaspoons bread machine yeast	2¼ teaspoons SAF yeast or 2¾ teaspoons bread machine yeast

FARMSTYLE COTTAGE CHEESE BREAD

C ottage cheese breads were once very familiar to home bakers in rural areas, due to the excess of fresh dairy products. Milk and starter were heated together until large curds formed, then the mixture was drained and salted. The delicate sour taste and acid of cottage cheese make for a tender bread. While all cottage cheese is made from skim milk, when it is as low as 1 percent, the tub will be labeled "lowfat"; that is what I call for here. Cottage cheese is excellent piled on fresh bread with applesauce, jam, or olives. This is a wonderful sandwich bread and it is a great keeper, staying fresh for three days. This dough is also suitable for making soft pretzels (follow instructions for baked pretzels, page 145).

1 Place all the ingredients in the pan according to the order in the manufacturer's instructions. Set crust on medium and program for the Basic cycle; press Start. (This recipe is not suitable for use with the Delay Timer.) The dough ball will be slightly moist.

2 When the baking cycle ends, immediately remove the bread from the pan and place it on a rack. Let cool to room temperature before slicing.

1½-POUND LOAF

¾ cup water
¾ cup small-curd lowfat
  cottage cheese
2 tablespoons olive oil

2½ cups bread flour
½ cup whole wheat flour
2 tablespoons sugar
1 tablespoon gluten
1½ teaspoons salt

2 teaspoons SAF yeast
  or 2½ teaspoons bread
  machine yeast

2-POUND LOAF

1⅛ cups water
1 cup small-curd lowfat
  cottage cheese
3 tablespoons olive oil

3¼ cups bread flour
¾ cup whole wheat flour
3 tablespoons sugar
1 tablespoon plus
  1 teaspoon gluten
2 teaspoons salt

2½ teaspoons SAF yeast
  or 1 tablespoon bread
  machine yeast

BUTTERMILK CHEESE BREAD

1½-POUND LOAF

1 cup buttermilk
½ cup water

3½ cups bread flour
1 cup shredded Swiss
  cheese (4 ounces)
1½ tablespoons sugar
1¼ teaspoons baking
  powder
1½ teaspoons salt

2 teaspoons SAF yeast
  or 2½ teaspoons bread
  machine yeast

2-POUND LOAF

1¼ cups buttermilk
⅔ cup water

4½ cups bread flour
1¼ cups shredded Swiss
  cheese (5 ounces)
2 tablespoons sugar
1½ teaspoons baking
  powder
2 teaspoons salt

2½ teaspoons SAF yeast
  or 1 tablespoon bread
  machine yeast

*S*wiss cheese conjures up a picture of a firm cheese riddled with holes, some the size of a dime and some the size of a quarter. The domestic Swiss that is available in prepackaged hunks has a mild taste in comparison to some of the hundred varieties that fall under the moniker of this cheese. In some parts of the world, Swiss is a cheese esteemed on a par with Brie. Whatever type of Swiss you use, it is a wonderful cheese in, or with, bread. Serve this bread with a thick beef and barley soup, fresh ham, or simply use it to make an outstanding sandwich.

1 Place all the ingredients in the pan according to the order in the manufacturer's instructions. Set crust on medium and program for the Basic cycle; press Start. (This recipe is not suitable for use with the Delay Timer.)

2 When the baking cycle ends, immediately remove the bread from the pan and place it on a rack. Let cool to room temperature before slicing.

CRESCIA AL FORMAGGIO

Y*ou can vary the flavor of this traditional Italian bread by using Asiago cheese, the poor man's Parmesan, or the genuino Romano sheep's milk cheese, Locatelli, a favorite of native Italians. Both are hard grating cheeses. Be prepared for this bread to rise very high in the pan during the last rise before baking. It is a great picnic bread eaten out of hand with cold meats and fruit.*

❶ Place all the ingredients in the pan according to the order in the manufacturer's instructions. Set crust on medium and program for the Basic or Tender cycle; press Start. (This recipe is not suitable for use with the Delay Timer.) The dough ball will be sticky.

❷ When the baking cycle ends, immediately remove the bread from the pan and place it on a rack. Let cool to room temperature before slicing.

1½- OR 2-POUND-LOAF MACHINES

½ cup plus 1 tablespoon water
3 large eggs
3 tablespoons olive oil

3¼ cups bread flour
¾ cup grated Asiago or Locatelli cheese
1½ tablespoons nonfat dry milk
1 tablespoon sugar
2 teaspoons gluten
½ teaspoon salt

2 teaspoons SAF yeast or 2½ teaspoons bread machine yeast

Bread Machine Baker's Hint: Baking with Cheese

- 1 cup of shredded firm cheese, such as Gruyère or cheddar, is equal to 4 ounces whole.

- 3 ounces of shredded firm cheese will effectively increase the liquid in a recipe by 1 ounce, or 2 tablespoons.

- 2 cups of cottage cheese equal 1 pound.

- ⅓ cup of soft fresh goat cheese is equal to about 2 ounces.

ROQUEFORT CHEESE BREAD WITH WALNUTS

E ven on a French map, it is virtually impossible to find the village of Roquefort-sur-Soulzon in the Rouergue countryside of southern France. If you have ever driven in France, you know that the country is filled with tiny provincial hamlets that never appear on any map, often home to only a few dozen families. In the rocky area around the gorge-lined Tarn River are four limestone plateaus called the Grand Causses dotted with craggy old caves. The caves have been used for centuries to make the famous sheep's milk cheese that takes the name of the town that first made it. Roquefort is a strong, salty cheese with blue-green veins. The complementary combination of Roquefort cheese, rye flour, and walnuts is a classic one in French country cooking (the strain of penicillin mold used in each batch of Roquefort is first cultured on rye bread). They are all together in this bread. You can vary this recipe by using English Stilton, another world-famous blue cheese, in combination with pistachio nuts. Serve the bread before dinner with pears and a red wine like Zinfandel, or with a big steak and entree salad meal.

1½-POUND LOAF	2-POUND LOAF
1 cup water	1⅓ cups water
2 tablespoons cream sherry	3 tablespoons cream sherry
4 ounces Roquefort cheese, crumbled	5 ounces Roquefort cheese, crumbled
1 tablespoon walnut oil	1½ tablespoons walnut oil
1 tablespoon unsalted butter, cut into pieces	1½ tablespoons unsalted butter, cut into pieces
2¾ cups bread flour	3⅔ cups bread flour
¼ cup medium or dark rye flour	⅓ cup medium or dark rye flour
1 tablespoon light brown sugar	1½ tablespoons light brown sugar
1 tablespoon gluten	1 tablespoon plus 1 teaspoon gluten
½ teaspoon salt	¾ teaspoon salt
½ cup chopped walnuts or pecans	⅔ cup chopped walnuts or pecans
2 teaspoons SAF yeast or 2½ teaspoons bread machine yeast	2¼ teaspoons SAF yeast or 2¾ teaspoons bread machine yeast

❶ Place all the ingredients in the pan according to the order in the manufacturer's instructions. Set crust on medium and program for the Basic cycle; press Start. (This recipe is not suitable for use with the Delay Timer.)

2 When the baking cycle ends, immediately remove the bread from the pan and place it on a rack. Let cool to room temperature before slicing.

Bread Machine Baking in Cyberspace

If you have access to the Internet and you love baking bread in the bread machine, chances are you have heard that there are a number of sites devoted to sharing recipes and information, such as the Bread Board at Prodigy. This is the place to let your high-tech inner self run wild. The free online sites I have listed below include bread chats and literally hundreds of recipes, information on various machines, book reviews, Web sites, and cyberspace mailing lists for as much information as you can handle. Once you log on to one of these sites, there are usually cross-references so you can search out other related sites. These are good places to have questions answered and to communicate with other bakers with the same interests. You can also order mail-order product catalogs, flour, and other ingredients online. Here are a few of the sites I frequent:

- Recipe File
  www.busycooks.about.com
  This site offers bread machine recipes.

- Bread Machine Review
  www.sonic.net/webpub/bread-machine/breadmachine.html
  Includes reviews of bread machines, cookbooks, and commercial bread mixes.

- The Gluten-Free Pantry
  www.glutenfree.com
  This site is especially for bakers who have gluten-free dietary needs.

- Bread Machine Magic
  www.breadmachinemagic.com
  The authors of the three splendid *Bread Machine Magic* (St. Martin's/Griffin) cookbooks have their own website and weekly discussion group Tuesdays on AOL at 10 P.M. EST (keyword: Cooking Club).

- Bread Machine Industry Association Information Website
  www.breadmachine.org.
  This site offers information about bread machines and bread machine cookbooks.

PARMESAN NUT BREAD

P armesan is one of the great cheeses of the world, the essence of Italian food. It is made only from April to November, when the cows can eat fresh grass, and this contributes to the flavor. Parmesan is a hard grating cheese that has been aged at least two years. This bread bakes up tall, so serve it in long wedges. It is great to serve with minestrone, buttered pasta, or simple salads.

❶ Place the ingredients, except the nuts, in the pan according to the order in the manufacturer's instructions. Set crust on medium and program for the Basic cycle; press Start. (This recipe is not suitable for use with the Delay Timer.) When the machine beeps, or between Knead 1 and Knead 2, add the nuts.

❷ When the baking cycle ends, immediately remove the bread from the pan and place it on a rack. Let cool to room temperature before slicing.

1½-POUND LOAF	2-POUND LOAF
1 cup water	1⅓ cups water
1½ tablespoons olive oil	2 tablespoons olive oil
3 cups bread flour	4 cups bread flour
⅔ cup grated Parmesan cheese	¾ cup grated Parmesan cheese
1 tablespoon gluten	1 tablespoon plus 1 teaspoon gluten
Pinch of sugar	Pinch of sugar
½ teaspoon salt	¾ teaspoon salt
2 teaspoons SAF yeast or 2½ teaspoon bread machine yeast	2½ teaspoons SAF yeast or 1 tablespoon bread machine yeast
⅓ cup pine nuts, coarsely chopped	½ cup pine nuts, coarsely chopped
½ cup walnuts, coarsely chopped	⅔ cup walnuts, coarsely chopped

ROASTED GARLIC AND DRY JACK BREAD

T his bread is the specialty of handcrafted bread baker Craig Ponsford at his bakery, Artisan Bakers, in Sonoma, California. Craig's loaf is a beautiful round starter bread baked in the wood-fire tradition, but the combination of flavors stand on their own even in the bread machine. Craig uses Bear Flag Dry Jack cheese, a specialty of northern California's Vella Company, which has the factory of its seventy-year old family business across the town square from Craig's bakery. Dry jack, a California original, was developed during World War I as a substitute for Parmesan cheese, which could not be imported.

1 Preheat the oven to 350°F.

2 Place the garlic in a small baking dish and bake until soft when touched with your finger, 40 to 45 minutes. Remove from the oven and let cool to room temperature.

3 Cut the head of roasted garlic in half horizontally. Place all the ingredients in the pan according to the order in the manufacturer's instructions, squeezing out the cloves of garlic and dropping them into the bread pan along with the water. Set crust on medium and program for the Basic or French Bread cycle; press Start. (This recipe is not suitable for use with the Delay Timer.)

4 When the baking cycle ends, immediately remove the bread from the pan and place it on a rack. Let cool to room temperature before slicing.

1½-POUND LOAF

3 to 4 ounces (1 to 2 heads) garlic

1¼ cups water

3 cups bread flour
½ cup grated dry jack cheese
2 teaspoons gluten
1¾ teaspoons salt

2½ teaspoons SAF yeast or 1 tablespoon bread machine yeast

2-POUND LOAF

3 to 4 ounces (1 to 2 heads) garlic

1½ cups water

4 cups bread flour
⅔ cup grated dry jack cheese
1 tablespoon gluten
2¼ teaspoons salt

1 tablespoon SAF yeast or 1 tablespoon plus ½ teaspoon bread machine yeast

COUNTRY PANCETTA-CHEESE BREAD

Makes 1 round loaf

T*his round loaf is styled after ones made in Rome, and is practically a lunch in itself, especially if served with a green salad and a bottle of Chianti wine. Pancetta comes in a sausage-like roll and is available sliced in the deli of your super-market. This loaf also makes lovely savory toast to accompany sim-ple soups, such as cream of spinach or artichoke. Be sure to let it cool completely, so that the cheese can solidify into creamy little pockets.*

1½-POUND LOAF	2-POUND LOAF
1⅛ cups water	1½ cups water
1 tablespoon olive oil	1½ tablespoons olive oil
2 cups bread flour	2⅔ cups bread flour
½ cup semolina durum flour	⅔ cup semolina durum flour
¼ cup whole wheat flour	⅓ cup whole wheat flour
¼ cup yellow cornmeal or polenta	⅓ cup yellow cornmeal or polenta
1 tablespoon gluten	1 tablespoon plus 1 teaspoon gluten
Pinch of sugar	Pinch of sugar
1 teaspoon salt	1¼ teaspoons salt
2 teaspoons SAF yeast or 2½ teaspoons bread machine yeast	2½ teaspoons SAF yeast or 1 tablespoon bread machine yeast
2 ounces pancetta, sliced thin	3 ounces pancetta, sliced thin
4 ounces whole-milk mozzarella, cut into ⅓-inch cubes	6 ounces whole-milk mozzarella, cut into ⅓-inch cubes
Yellow cornmeal or polenta, for sprinkling	Yellow cornmeal or polenta, for sprinkling

❶ Place the ingredients, ex-cept the pancetta, mozza-rella, and cornmeal, in the pan according to the order in the manufacturer's in-structions. Program for the Dough cycle; press Start.

❷ While the dough is rising, cook the pancetta in a skillet over moderate heat until crisp. Drain on paper towels, cool, and coarsely crumble.

❸ Line a baking sheet with parchment paper and sprinkle it with cornmeal. When the machine beeps at the end of the cycle, press Stop and unplug the ma-chine. Turn the dough out onto a lightly floured work surface. Pat the dough into a large, thick oval. Sprinkle the pancetta and the moz-zarella over the dough. Fold the dough into thirds and gently knead to evenly distribute the pancetta and cheese. Form into one round loaf and place on the baking sheet. Cover with a clean tea towel and let rest at room temperature until doubled in bulk, about 40 minutes.

4 Twenty minutes before baking, place a baking stone on the lower third rack of the oven, if desired, and preheat the oven to 425°F.

5 With a small sharp knife, slash the top of the loaf with an X, no more than ¼ inch deep. Place in the oven, placing the pan on the stone if using one. Bake for 15 minutes. Reduce the oven temperature to 350°F and bake for an additional 30 to 35 minutes, or until the crust is golden brown and the loaf sounds hollow when tapped with your finger. Remove the loaf from the pan and place it on a rack. Let cool to room temperature before slicing.

 Bread Machine Baker's Hint: How to Tell if a Loaf Is Done

A nicely baked loaf of bread has a golden color to its crust and sounds hollow when it is tapped with the fingers. When your loaf comes out of the pan, you can test to see if it is thoroughly baked inside with the help of an instant-read thermometer. This method is especially useful for rich doughs, which do not sound hollow when tapped. To test a loaf for doneness, insert an instant-read thermometer into the bottom or side of the bread. Breads are thoroughly baked at 190° to 200°F. But remember that a loaf has not technically finished baking until it is has cooled completely outside of the oven.

HOT JALAPEÑO BREAD WITH LONGHORN CHEESE

1½-POUND LOAF

1 cup water

3 cups bread flour
1 cup shredded longhorn
cheddar cheese
(4 ounces)
3 tablespoons nonfat dry
milk
3 canned jalapeño chiles,
seeded and diced
1 tablespoon sugar
1 teaspoon salt

2 teaspoons SAF yeast
or 2½ teaspoons bread
machine yeast

2-POUND LOAF

1⅓ cups water

4 cups bread flour
1¼ cups shredded longhorn
cheddar cheese
(5 ounces)
4 tablespoons nonfat dry
milk
4 canned jalapeño chiles,
seeded and diced
1½ tablespoons sugar
1½ teaspoons salt

2½ teaspoons SAF yeast
or 1 tablespoon bread
machine yeast

T*he jalapeños here are added at the beginning of the bread cycle so that they get incorporated into the entire dough. Even so, be prepared for the little burst of heat on your tongue after each bite. The canned jalapeños called for are convenient to use and easily found in the supermarket. Pat them with a paper towel to soak up the excess moisture before chopping them. Longhorn is an orange Wisconsin cheddar known for its excellent melting quality and nice melding with Tex-Mex flavors. This loaf bakes up into a beautiful, earthy color. It is great with bean salads.*

1 Place all the ingredients in the pan according to the order in the manufacturer's instructions. Set crust on medium and program for the Basic cycle; press Start. (This recipe is not suitable for use with the Delay Timer.)

2 When the baking cycle ends, immediately remove the bread from the pan and place it on a rack. Let cool to room temperature before slicing.

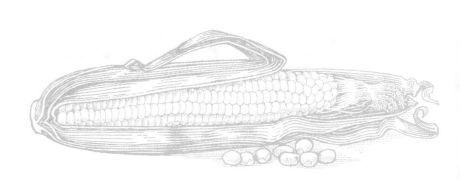

BEER BREAD WITH CHEDDAR

W henever I spoke of the beer bread in this recipe collection, the immediate response of any listener was always, "Does it have cheese in it?" So for all those lovers of beer and cheese, here it is, and it is rich—like a pound cake. Cheddar cheese, a cheese with lots of tang and often densely colored with annatto, used to be a product of the Midwest dairy states, but quickly became the most popular cheese from the Southwest to New England. Use a young, mild Colby (they are sometimes sold just three days old, and usually not older than three months), a cheese known for its firm texture, to complement the strong flavor of the beer.

❶ Open the container of beer and let stand at room temperature for a few hours to go flat.

❷ Place all the ingredients in the pan according to the order in the manufacturer's instructions. Set crust on medium and program for the Basic cycle; press Start. (This recipe is not suitable for use with the Delay Timer.)

❸ When the baking cycle ends, immediately remove the bread from the pan and place it on a rack. Let cool to room temperature before slicing.

1½-POUND LOAF

1 cup (8 ounces) beer

3½ cups bread flour
¾ cup shredded Colby or
  mild cheddar cheese
  (3 ounces)
¼ cup sugar
¾ teaspoon salt

1¾ teaspoons SAF yeast
  or 2¼ teapoons bread
  machine yeast

2-POUND LOAF

1⅓ cups (11 ounces) beer

4½ cups bread flour
1¼ cups shredded Colby
  or mild cheddar cheese
  (5 ounces)
⅓ cup sugar
1¼ teaspoons salt

2¼ teaspoons SAF yeast
  or 2¾ teaspoons bread
  machine yeast

KHACHAPURI
(Stuffed Cheese Breads)

Makes 8 individual stuffed cheese breads

1½- OR 2-POUND-LOAF MACHINES

For the dough:

1¼ cups plain yogurt
1 tablespoon olive oil

3 cups bread flour
½ teaspoon salt

1¼ teaspoons SAF yeast
   or 1¾ teaspoons bread
   machine yeast

For the filling:

1½ cups shredded
   Monterey Jack
   (6 ounces)
4 ounces feta cheese,
   crumbled
¼ cup minced Italian
   flat-leaf parsley
1 large egg
1 tablespoon finely
   chopped fresh cilantro
1 teaspoon finely chopped
   fresh mint

1 egg white, beaten with
   1 teaspoon water,
   for glaze

Khachapuri, *a word meaning "filled bread," is a popular street and restaurant food in Georgian Russia, but also a homemade specialty. There are many versions and types of cheese fillings, but the filling usually includes* suluguni, *a stringy cheese that is not available in this country. Here the* khachapuri *are stuffed with a filling of mild melting cheese and fresh herbs popular in the area around Georgia, Turkey, and Armenia—mint and coriander. Originally these breads were baked on clay griddles over open fires. In this version from food writer and cooking instructor Lynn Alley, the breads are made in individual portions, great as appetizers with red or white wine, or as an accompaniment to soup.*

1 To make the dough, place all the dough ingredients in the pan according to the order in the manufacturer's instructions. Program for the Dough cycle; press Start. If the yogurt is very thick, be prepared to add 1 to 2 tablespoons of water to the dough. The dough ball should be smooth, slightly soft, and elastic.

2 Meanwhile, make the cheese filling. Combine all of the filling ingredients in a small bowl and toss to combine. Cover and refrigerate until needed.

3 Spray 8 cups of a nonstick standard muffin tin with vegetable cooking spray. At the beep, remove the dough from the pan and turn out onto a clean work surface. Divide the dough in half, then further divide each half into quarters to make 8 pieces. Using a rolling pin, and on a work surface lightly dusted with flour to prevent sticking, roll out each portion into a 7- to 8-inch round, about ¼ inch thick. Alternately, you can press each section of dough with your palm and stretch the dough if you don't have a small rolling pin. Fold the dough lightly into quarters and transfer to a muffin cup. Unfold the dough and press to fit into the cup, leaving a skirt of dough draped over the sides. Place 2 heaping tablespoons of the cheese filling into the dough, mounding it higher in the center. Pick up the skirt of the dough and pleat in loose folds laying over each other over the filling. You can leave it folded flat or gather up the top ends and twist into a small knob. Repeat with all the portions of dough. Cover loosely with plastic wrap and let rest at room temperature for 10 minutes.

4 Preheat the oven to 400°F.

5 Brush the tops of the breads with the egg white glaze. Bake for 25 to 30 minutes, or until golden brown. Remove the pan to a rack and cool in the pan 15 minutes. Remove from the pan and cool for at least 15 minutes before serving. These can be frozen for up to a month in plastic freezer bags. To serve, defrost in the refrigerator in the bag, then warm in a 300°F oven for 8 minutes to soften the cheese. Serve immediately.

 Bread Machine Baker's Hint: Optimum Temperatures

To ensure proper rising, it's preferable to use room temperature ingredients (that includes eggs) and ever-so-slightly warm liquids when loading a bread machine. There is some leeway here; many bakers report using cold eggs and liquids straight from the refrigerator with room temperature flours and yeast with great results. The dough will just rise slower.

To counteract warm climates, or during the summer, place the baking canister in the refrigerator to chill it before adding the ingredients which can be cold. Machines with preheat cycles can have ingredients layered into the bread pan straight out of the refrigerator.

FETA AND SPINACH BREAD

1½-POUND LOAF

⅞ cup water
¾ cup frozen chopped
  spinach (defrosted and
  squeezed dry)
2 tablespoons olive oil

3 cups bread flour
4 ounces crumbled feta
  cheese
1 tablespoon sugar
½ teaspoon salt

1¾ teaspoons SAF yeast
  or 2¼ teaspoons bread
  machine yeast

2-POUND LOAF

1⅛ cups water
1 cup frozen chopped
  spinach (defrosted and
  squeezed dry)
3 tablespoons olive oil

4 cups bread flour
5 ounces crumbled feta
  cheese
1½ tablespoons sugar
1 teaspoon salt

2¼ teaspoons SAF yeast
  or 2¾ teaspoons bread
  machine yeast

F eta cheese is always associated with Greek cooking. It is a firm white sheep's milk cheese that crumbles easily and holds its shape during baking. It is stored in brine, so feta should be rinsed in cold water before using. If storing it again, cover it with fresh water. Feta has a strong salty nature, so you don't need to add as much salt to this dough as to others. Because of its strong flavor, a little feta goes a long way. With only a quarter the fat of a cheese like cheddar, feta and bread made with it are suitable for lowfat diets. You do not need to cook the frozen spinach to prepare it for this recipe. After it is thawed in a colander, just squeeze out the excess water with your fingers. This loaf, known as spanakópsomo and traditionally made with wild greens, is not a sandwich bread—it is too delicate. Instead, serve this bread with red wine and olives before dinner. I like it with omelettes or with a roast lamb meal, served with roasted garlic–infused olive oil for dipping. This bread has a beautiful aroma while baking.

1 Place all the ingredients in the pan according to the order in the manufacturer's instructions. Set crust on medium and program for the Basic cycle; press Start. (This recipe is not suitable for use with the Delay Timer.)

2 When the baking cycle ends, immediately remove the bread from the pan and place it on a rack. Let cool to room temperature before slicing.

Bread Machine Baker's Hint: What Size Loaf for Oven Baking?

If you decide to bake any of the kneaded and risen doughs from these recipes in your oven rather than in the machine, the following information about pan sizes will be helpful. If you have programmed the machine for the Basic or Whole Wheat cycles, just press Stop/Reset to clear after Rise 2, and unplug the machine. Or make the recipe on the Dough cycle. Turn the dough out onto a lightly floured work surface, form the loaf, and place it in or on the pan. Let rise, covered lightly with plastic wrap, at room temperature until doubled in bulk, about 45 minutes to 1 hour, before baking.

1-pound recipe fills one 8½-by-4½-by-2½-inch loaf pan

1½-pound recipe fills one 9-by-5-by-3-inch loaf pan

1½-pound recipe yields 1 medium or 2 small round or oval loaves

1½-pound recipe yields 2 baguettes

2-pound recipe fills two 8½-by-4½-by-2½-inch loaf pans

2-pound recipe yields 1 large, 2 medium, or 3 small round or oval loaves

CIRCLES, SQUARES, AND CRESCENTS

Pizzas and Other Flatbreads

I remember the first time I heard a friend say she made the best pizza at home. I just didn't think such a thing existed. I mean, you need the special oven, and the technique of throwing the dough into the air to stretch it seemed very difficult. It just seemed beyond the home baker's realm. Through my own experience, however, I found this wasn't true, and what has been happening in the past ten years is nothing short of a phenomenon—everyone who loves to bake seems to be making pizza. When I was teaching cooking classes, making pizza was one of the most requested topics. What was more remarkable was that my students were able to turn out pizzas that were every bit as good as parlor-made, but with the added benefit that the pizzas could be made to please a host of finicky eaters. This flatbread is so popular that it warrants a chapter named largely for it. After all, I have had a number of bread machine owners tell me that pizza dough is the only thing they make with their machine.

Other flatbreads, too, have hit a nerve with amateur and professional bakers alike. The most prominent of these is focaccia, a very old, traditional homemade flatbread of Italy. Irregularly handshaped or pressed into a pan to form a large flat loaf, focaccia gets a simple coating of olive oil, herbs, or garlic. Made from dough with essentially the same proportions as pizza dough, focaccia differs from pizza in that it can be sweet or savory, and uses fewer—but a wider variety of—toppings. Its surface is dimpled, and indentations collect the olive oil that is drizzled over it. Focaccias have a thick breadlike texture because they are allowed to rise before baking, rather than the characteristic thin crispness of pizza, which is baked immediately after shaping and topping.

Other regions have their versions of focaccia, too. In a Paris pizzeria, I watched rounds of pliable, untopped pizza dough get tossed into a very hot wood-burning oven and emerge puffed up, to be sprinkled simply with olive oil and salt. A classic country bread, this is known by different names in different regions of Italy and France—*schiacciata* in Tuscany, *fugassa* in Venice, *fougasse* in Provence, and *pogne* in Savoie—so don't be confused; the names can be used interchangeably. Because of their innate simplicity and ease of preparation, *focacce* lend themselves to endless delightful flavor variations and embellishments.

Focaccia is shaped in a wide variety of earthy, rustic sizes from round or oval to freeform or rectangular. The freeform version is often slashed in various places, giving the look of intricate cutwork, allowing the dough to open up into a decorative pattern referred to as a ladder. This is particularly popular in the *fougasse* of Provence. Restaurants and trattorias offer focaccia cut into finger-sized lengths for snacking or small five- to six-inch rounds cut horizontally for sandwiches. Uncut, the flatbread is studded with nuts or cheeses, olives or vegetables. Topped with fresh grapes or raisins, it is a traditional, and to many Americans unusual, favorite.

While pizza and focaccia are the most familiar flatbreads to their dedicated bakers and eaters, there is an entire family of flatbreads that comes from every culture in the world. They are ever-present daily bread in lands where fuel once was, or still is, a precious commodity, so these breads cook quickly. Flatbreads are eaten hot and fresh. While unleavened flatbreads, such as tortillas, are very thin indeed, the yeasted flatbreads to which this chapter is devoted can be anywhere from paper-thin, like lavash, to a few inches thick, as focaccia. In between are *naan*, the word for bread in much of Asia and India, with dozens of interpretations, and the ballooning pita, also basic daily fare eaten in much of the Middle East. These are kneaded doughs, which the bread machine prepares very nicely. These breads are meant to be eaten with meals, but are great for appetizers, too.

Since the doughs of pizza and flatbreads are so basic—water, flour, yeast, oil, and salt—take note of the quality and flavor of each ingredient you use, because you will definitely taste it. Some bakers use bottled spring water for their flatbreads. In some recipes, olive oil plays a very important role: use pure virgin and extra-virgin oils with different rich characters. For focaccia the olive oil is used not only in the dough, but for

brushing the pan, drizzling on top before and after baking, and often for dipping later at the table. Organic stone-ground flours offer a unique, fresh wheat flavor.

Flatbreads need your touch to be finished to perfection. Since the shaping is the key to their taste and texture, they must always be baked outside of the machine.

BASIC PIZZA DOUGH

*Makes 2 thin 12- to 14-inch, one 14-inch deep-dish, four 8-inch,
6 individual crusts, or one 17-by-11-inch rectangular crust*

1½- OR 2-POUND-LOAF MACHINES

1⅓ cups water
¼ cup extra-virgin olive oil

3½ cups unbleached
　all-purpose flour
1 tablespoon sugar
1½ teaspoons salt

2 teaspoons SAF yeast
　or 2½ teaspoons bread
　machine yeast

Sometimes I wonder whether the bread machine was invented just to mix and rise pizza dough, since so many bakers seem to do only that with their machines. After the dough cycle is complete, the dough is removed, shaped by hand, topped as desired, and baked off in your kitchen oven. Be sure to use unbleached all-purpose flour; it will be easier to roll out. You can use all or just a portion of the dough—it can conveniently be refrigerated overnight, or frozen.

❶ Place all the ingredients in the pan according to the order in the manufacturer's instructions. Program for the Dough or Pizza Dough cycle and press Start. The dough ball will be soft.

❷ When the machine beeps at the end of the cycle, press Stop and unplug the machine. Immediately remove the bread pan from the machine and turn the dough out onto a lightly floured work surface. Divide into the desired number of portions. Flatten each portion into a disc by kneading a few times then folding the edges into the center. Cover with a damp towel on the work surface to rest for 30 minutes until the dough has increased about 20 percent in size.

❸ Roll out and shape the dough as directed in your pizza recipe. Or place the dough in plastic food storage bags and refrigerate for up to 24 hours. To use, let rest for 20 minutes at room temperature before rolling out. The dough balls may also be stored in the freezer for up to 3 months; let the dough defrost in the refrigerator overnight before using.

SEMOLINA PIZZA DOUGH

*Makes 2 thin 12- to 14-inch, one 14-inch deep-dish, four 8-inch,
6 individual crusts, or one 17-by-11-inch rectangular crust*

B e sure to use fine semolina durum flour, the kind used for
making pasta, not a coarse grind like farina. A favorite
Italian ingredient, semolina is a very high protein flour
that adds a lot of chewiness to the dough.

1½- OR 2-POUND-LOAF MACHINES
1½ cups water
3 tablespoons olive oil
3⅓ cups unbleached all-purpose flour
⅔ cup semolina pasta flour (durum flour)
1 tablespoon sugar
2 teaspoons salt
2 teaspoons SAF yeast or 2½ teaspoons bread machine yeast

1 Place all the ingredients in the pan according to the
order in the manufacturer's instructions. Program for
the Dough or Pizza Dough cycle and press Start.

2 When the machine beeps at the end of the cycle, press
Stop and unplug the machine. Immediately remove the
bread pan from the machine, and turn the dough out
onto a lightly floured work surface. Divide into the
desired number of portions. Flatten each portion into
a disc by kneading a few times and then folding the
edges into the center. Cover with a damp towel on the
work surface to rest for 30 minutes until the dough has
increased about 20 percent in size.

3 Roll out and shape the dough as directed in your pizza
recipe. Or place the dough in plastic food storage bags
and refrigerate for up to 24 hours. To use, let rest for
20 minutes at room temperature before rolling out. The
dough balls may also be stored in the freezer for up to
3 months; let the dough defrost in the refrigerator overnight before using.

How to Top Your Pizzas

While pizza cries out for improvisation *alla momento*, here are a few classic tried-and-true recipes with lots of flavor and character. Some have light toppings; others have lots of sauce and cheese. Use whatever crust you want. I have a stash of home-dried herbs (see page 307) such as marjoram and basil just for using on pizza; they have more flavor than commercial dried herbs. I like to use rice flour for sprinkling on the work surface when rolling out the dough, and corn-meal for sprinkling on the pan, but you can use what-ever method works for you.

Essential Tomato-Herb Pizza Sauce

Makes 2 cups

This is an excellent tomato sauce for pizza. The recipe comes from my friend Laura Quemada, whose family has been making it for decades. It takes only 15 minutes of cooking before it is ready to use.

1 to 2 tablespoons olive oil
¼ large yellow onion, finely chopped
Two 8-ounce cans tomato sauce
1 clove garlic, pressed, or ½ teaspoon garlic powder
1 teaspoon dried oregano or marjoram leaves
Salt and fresh-ground black pepper

Heat the oil in a large skillet over medium heat and sauté the onion until soft and the edges begin to brown. Add the tomato sauce, garlic, oregano, and salt and pepper to taste. Bring to a low boil and adjust heat to low. Simmer, uncovered, for 15 minutes. Remove from the heat and cool. Leave the onion chunky or use an immersion blender to puree. The sauce will keep in the refrigerator for 3 days, and in the freezer for up to 1 month.

Pizza Margherita

Makes one 14-inch pizza

1 recipe pizza dough of choice
1 cup Essential Tomato-Herb Pizza Sauce
8 ounces mozzarella cheese, thinly sliced
10 large fresh basil leaves, cut into thin slices
Olive oil, for drizzling

❶ Twenty to thirty minutes before baking, place baking tiles or a pizza stone on the lowest rack of a cold oven and preheat it to 450° to 500°F. Brush a 14-inch pizza pan with olive oil and sprinkle with cornmeal or semolina.

❷ Place the dough on a lightly floured work surface. Using the heel of your hand, press to flatten it. Roll out the dough in a circle, then lift it onto the pan and gently pull and press it into a circle to fit the pan. Shape a ½-inch rim around the edge of the crust.

❸ Spread the dough with the tomato sauce, leaving a ½-inch border. Lay the mozzarella over the top. Sprinkle with basil and drizzle with olive oil.

❹ Place the pizza pan on the hot stone and bake for 12 to 15 minutes, or until the dough is crisp and brown. Remove from the oven and slide the pizza off the pan onto a cutting board. Cut into wedges immedi-ately with a chef's knife or pizza wheel and serve.

Pizza Vegitariana

Makes one 14-inch pizza

1 recipe Whole Wheat Pizza Dough (page 396) or
    other dough of choice
About 1 cup Essential Tomato-Herb Pizza Sauce
    (page 392)
4 ounces mozzarella cheese, thinly sliced
2 medium zucchini, thinly sliced
1 or 2 roasted red peppers, cut into strips, or
    4 roasted eggplant slices
1 package frozen artichoke hearts, defrosted
2 to 3 cloves garlic, minced
½ cup grated Parmesan or Asiago cheese
Olive oil, for drizzling

❶ Twenty to thirty minutes before baking, place baking tiles or a pizza stone on the lowest rack of a cold oven and preheat it to 450° to 500°F. Brush a 14-inch pizza pan with olive oil and sprinkle with cornmeal.

❷ Place the dough on a lightly floured work surface. Using the heel of your hand, press to flatten it. Roll out the dough in a circle, then lift it onto the pan and gently pull and press it into a circle to fit the pan. Shape a ½-inch rim around the edge.

❸ Spread the dough with the tomato sauce, leaving a ½-inch border. Lay the mozzarella over the top. Top with layers of the vegetables. Sprinkle with the garlic and Parmesan cheese. Drizzle with olive oil.

❹ Place the pizza pan on the hot stone and bake for 14 to 18 minutes, or until the dough is crisp and brown. Remove from the oven and slide the pizza onto a cutting board. Cut into wedges immediately with a chef's knife or pizza wheel and serve.

Classic Pepperoni Pizza

Makes one 14-inch pizza

1 recipe pizza dough of choice
About 1 cup Essential Tomato-Herb Pizza Sauce
    (page 392)
4 ounces pepperoni, peeled and thinly sliced
1 cup shredded provolone cheese (4 ounces)
6 ounces mozzarella cheese, thinly sliced
¼ pound fresh mushrooms, sliced
1 green bell pepper, seeded and cut into rings
Olive oil, for drizzling

❶ Twenty to thirty minutes before baking, place baking tiles or a pizza stone on the lowest rack of a cold oven and preheat it to 450° to 500°F. Brush a 14-inch pizza pan with olive oil and sprinkle with cornmeal or semolina.

❷ Place the dough on a lightly floured work surface. Using the heel of your hand, press to flatten it. Roll out the dough in a circle, then lift it onto the pan and gently pull and press it into a circle to fit the pan. Shape a ½-inch rim around the edge of the crust.

❸ Spread the dough with the tomato sauce, leaving a ½-inch border. Dot with pepperoni slices. Lay the cheeses over the top. Top with the mushrooms and peppers. Drizzle with olive oil.

❹ Place the pizza pan on the hot stone and bake for 14 to 18 minutes, or until the dough is crisp and brown. Remove from the oven and slide the pizza off the pan onto a cutting board. Cut into wedges immediately with a chef's knife or pizza wheel and serve.

continued on next page

Cheese Pizza

Makes one 14-inch pizza

1 recipe pizza dough of choice
4 ounces crumbled goat cheese
1 cup shredded fontina cheese (4 ounces)
1 cup shredded provolone cheese (4 ounces)
4 ounces mozzarella cheese, thinly sliced
4 fresh plum tomatoes, diced
Dried basil
Olive oil, for drizzling

1 Twenty to thirty minutes before baking, place baking tiles or a pizza stone on the lowest rack of a cold oven and preheat it to 450° to 500°F. Brush a 14-inch pizza pan with olive oil and sprinkle with cornmeal or semolina.

2 Place the dough on a lightly floured work surface. Using the heel of your hand, press to flatten it. Roll out the dough in a circle, then lift it onto the pan and gently pull and press it into a circle to fit the pan. Shape a ½-inch rim around the edge of the crust.

3 Sprinkle the dough with the goat cheese, then the fontina and provolone. Lay the mozzarella and tomato over the top. Sprinkle with basil and drizzle with olive oil.

4 Place the pizza pan on the hot stone and bake for 14 to 18 minutes, or until the dough is crisp and brown. Remove from the oven and slide the pizza off the pan onto a cutting board. Cut into wedges immediately with a chef's knife or pizza wheel and serve.

Caramelized Onion and Gorgonzola Pizza

Makes one 14-inch pizza

3 tablespoons butter
3 tablespoons olive oil
3 large yellow onions, thinly sliced
1 recipe pizza dough of choice
4 ounces crumbled gorgonzola cheese
½ cup chopped walnuts

1 Melt the butter and oil together in a large sauté pan. Add the onions and cook over very low heat, stirring occasionally, until soft and golden (not browned), about 1 hour.

2 Twenty to thirty minutes before baking, place baking tiles or a pizza stone on the lowest rack of a cold oven and preheat it to 450° to 500°F. Brush a 14-inch pizza pan with olive oil and sprinkle with cornmeal or semolina.

3 Place the dough on a lightly floured work surface. Using the heel of your hand, press to flatten it. Roll out the dough in a circle, then lift it onto the pan and gently pull and press it into a circle to fit the pan. Shape a ½-inch rim around the edge of the crust.

4 Spread the onions over the crust. Sprinkle with the gorgonzola and walnuts.

5 Place the pizza pan on the hot stone and bake for 12 to 15 minutes, or until the dough is crisp and brown. Remove from the oven and slide the pizza off the pan onto a cutting board. Cut into wedges immediately with a chef's knife or pizza wheel and serve.

Mediterranean Pizza
Makes one 14-inch pizza

1 recipe pizza dough of choice
6 ounces mozzarella cheese, thinly sliced
3 cups chopped fresh spinach (about 1 bunch)
8 ounces crumbled feta cheese
½ cup black olives, chopped
3 slices red onion
2 plum tomatoes, seeded and chopped
Olive oil, for drizzling

❶ Twenty to thirty minutes before baking, place baking tiles or a pizza stone on the lowest rack of a cold oven and preheat it to 450° to 500°F. Brush a 14-inch pizza pan with olive oil and sprinkle with cornmeal or semolina.

❷ Place the dough on a lightly floured work surface. Using the heel of your hand, press to flatten it. Roll out the dough in a circle, then lift it onto the pan and gently pull and press it into a circle to fit the pan. Shape a ½-inch rim around the edge of the crust.

❸ Lay the mozzarella over the top of the dough. Sprinkle with the spinach and feta. Scatter the olives over the top and lay some red onion rings all over. Sprinkle with the tomatoes. Drizzle with olive oil.

❹ Place the pizza pan on the hot stone and bake for 14 to 18 minutes, or until the dough is crisp and brown. Remove from the oven and slide the pizza off the pan onto a cutting board. Cut into wedges immediately with a chef's knife or pizza wheel and serve.

White Clam Pizza
Makes one 14-inch pizza

3 tablespoons minced fresh garlic
¼ cup olive oil
1 recipe pizza dough of choice
Two 6½-ounce cans minced clams, drained
¼ teaspoon hot pepper flakes
⅓ cup minced fresh flat-leaf parsley
½ cup grated Parmesan cheese

❶ Twenty to thirty minutes before baking, place baking tiles or a pizza stone on the lowest rack of a cold oven and preheat it to 450° to 500°F. Brush a 14-inch pizza pan with olive oil and sprinkle with cornmeal or semolina.

❷ Combine the garlic and olive oil in a small bowl.

❸ Place the dough on a lightly floured work surface. Using the heel of your hand, press to flatten it. Roll out the dough in a circle, then lift it onto the pan and gently pull and press it into a circle to fit the pan. Shape a ½-inch rim around the edge of the crust.

❹ Brush the dough with the garlic oil. Sprinkle with the clams, hot pepper flakes, parsley, and Parmesan. Drizzle with the remaining garlic oil.

❺ Place the pizza pan on the hot stone and bake for 14 to 18 minutes, or until the dough is crisp and brown. Remove from the oven and slide the pizza off the pan onto a cutting board. Cut into wedges immediately with a chef's knife or pizza wheel and serve.

WHOLE WHEAT PIZZA DOUGH

*Makes 2 thin 12- to 14-inch, one 14-inch deep-dish, four 8-inch,
6 individual crusts, or one 17-by-11-inch rectangular crust*

1½- OR 2-POUND-LOAF MACHINES

1⅓ cups water
¼ cup olive oil

2½ cups unbleached
all-purpose flour
1 cup whole wheat flour
1½ teaspoons salt

2 teaspoons SAF yeast
or 2½ teaspoons bread
machine yeast

W hole wheat adds a grainy texture and extra-nutty flavor to this crust. The more whole wheat flour you use, the harder the dough will be to roll out because of the bran and germ, so be prepared to patch up holes if your dough tears while shaping. Don't be tempted to use a higher proportion of whole wheat flour until you have mastered this recipe as it is. This is the crust to choose for vegetable pizzas or those with lots of cheese.

1 Place all the ingredients in the pan according to the order in the manufacturer's instructions. Program for the Dough or Pizza Dough cycle and press Start.

2 When the machine beeps at the end of the cycle, press Stop and unplug the machine. Immediately remove the bread pan from the machine, and turn the dough out onto a lightly floured work surface. Divide into the desired number of portions. Flatten each portion into a disc by kneading a few times then folding the edges into the center. Cover with a damp towel on the work surface to rest for 30 minutes until the dough has increased about 20 percent in size.

3 Roll out and shape the dough as directed in your pizza recipe. Or place the dough in plastic food storage bags and refrigerate for up to 24 hours. To use, let rest for 20 minutes at room temperature before rolling out. The dough balls may also be stored in the freezer for up to 3 months; let the dough defrost in the refrigerator overnight before using.

CORNMEAL PIZZA DOUGH

Makes 2 thin 12- to 14-inch, one 14-inch deep-dish, four 8-inch,
6 individual crusts, or one 17-by-11-inch rectangular crust

T his is my friend Suzanne Rosenblum's crust, especially
nice for her Chicago-Style Deep-Dish Pizza (see page
402) because of its nutty, crunchy texture. I especially like
to make smaller thick 8-inch crusts pressed into springform pans
from this dough in the manner of one of my favorite pizzerias,
Viccolo, which was inspired by Pizzeria Uno in Chicago.

1½- OR 2-POUND-LOAF MACHINES
1½ cups water
¼ cup olive oil
3⅔ cups unbleached all-purpose flour
⅓ cup medium-grind yellow cornmeal
1 teaspoon salt
2 teaspoons SAF yeast or 2½ teaspoons bread machine yeast

❶ Place all the ingredients in the pan according to the
order in the manufacturer's instructions. Program for
the Dough or Pizza Dough cycle and press Start.

❷ When the machine beeps at the end of the cycle, press
Stop and unplug the machine. Immediately remove the
bread pan from the machine, and turn the dough out
onto a lightly floured work surface. Divide into the
desired number of portions. Flatten the dough into a
disc by kneading a few times then folding the edges
into the center. Cover with a damp towel on the work
surface to rest for 30 minutes until the dough has increased about 20 percent in size.

❸ Roll out and shape the dough as directed in your pizza
recipe. Or place the dough in plastic food storage bags
and refrigerate for up to 24 hours. To use, let rest for
20 minutes at room temperature before rolling out.
The dough balls may also be stored in the freezer for
up to 3 months; let the dough defrost in the refrigerator
overnight before using.

PISSALADIÈRE

Makes one 15-by-10-inch pizza

INGREDIENTS

¼ cup olive oil
4 large yellow onions,
    peeled and thinly sliced
Salt and fresh-ground black
    pepper
2 teaspoons fresh thyme or
    1 teaspoon dried thyme
1 recipe Basic Pizza Dough
    (page 390)
20 oil-cured black olives,
    pitted and cut into coarse
    pieces
5 plum or beefsteak
    tomatoes, seeded and
    thinly sliced
Olive oil, for drizzling

P issaladière *is the famous rustic pizza of southern France. A snack bread usually served at room temperature, it has no cheese, just vegetables. Lots of sweet onions are piled on a crisp crust, and the whole thing is garnished with black olives and fresh tomatoes, ingredients that show up in almost all Provençal food.* Pissaladière *can have anchovies on it, too, but I prefer it with just olives and tomatoes. I make it on a baking sheet, but if you have a black steel rectangular pan, all the better.*

❶ Heat the oil in a large sauté pan over medium-high heat. Add the onions and cook, stirring occasionally, until soft and golden, about 20 minutes. Do not allow the onions to brown. Season with salt and pepper to taste and add the thyme.

❷ Twenty minutes before baking, place baking tiles or a pizza stone on the lowest rack of a cold oven and preheat it to 450°F. Brush a 15-by-10-by-1 inch pan with oil.

❸ On a lightly floured work surface, using the heel of your hand, press the pizza dough to flatten it. Roll out the dough into a large rectangle, then lift it onto the pan and gently pull and press it into the pan. Shape a ½-inch rim around the edge. Let the dough rest for 15 minutes, until it is puffy.

❹ Spread the dough with the onions, leaving a 1-inch border. Scatter the olives over the top and lay some tomato slices on top in rows. Drizzle with olive oil.

5 Place the pan on the hot stone and bake for 18 to 24 minutes, or until the dough is crisp and brown. Remove from the oven and slide the pizza off the pan onto a cutting board. Cut into wedges immediately with a chef's knife or pizza wheel and serve. Or let the pizza cool to room temperature before serving, as it is done in Nice.

The Toolbox: Equipment for Pizza, Focaccia, and Other Flatbreads

Since flatbreads are shaped and baked outside the machine, the following equipment is helpful for making them.

- Wooden board or marble slab (about 18-by-18-inch) for rolling out and shaping

- Metal dough scraper for cleaning the work surface of excess dough

- Heavy ball-bearing or thin wooden rolling pin

- 2- to 3-inch-wide pastry brushes for oiling and saucing

- Large plastic or metal salt shaker filled with all-purpose flour or rice flour for sprinkling and dusting the dough

- Ceramic baking stone (12- or 16-inch round or 16-by-14-inch rectangle) or 12 to 16 unglazed quarry tiles

- Baking pans such as heavy gauge aluminum or steel 17-by-12-inch baking sheets, ceramic baking sheets, ceramic pizza pans, power pans (12-inch round pans that have the Swiss cheese–like holes to crisp the crust directly on the hot stone), 14-inch pizza pans, deep-dish pizza pans with both ½-inch and 3-inch rims, screens, metal cake pan, springform pan, or tart pan with removable bottom (see page 401 for more information about baking pans)

- Heavy-duty oven mitts or barbecue mitts from a restaurant supply company that are big enough to protect your wrists and lower arms

- Large, wide heavy-duty metal spatula for handling baked pizzas

- Pizza wheel (the cutter with a round metal blade), kitchen shears, 10- to 12-inch chef's knife, or Chinese cleaver for cutting pizzas

TORTA RUSTICA WITH RIGATONI AND SAUSAGE

Makes one 10-inch torta

INGREDIENTS

½ pound hot Italian sausage
½ pound sweet Italian sausage
4 tablespoons unsalted butter
1 large yellow onion, finely chopped
2 large cloves garlic, minced
2 teaspoons dried basil
1 teaspoon dried oregano or marjoram
½ teaspoon dried thyme
¼ cup all-purpose flour
1 cup hot milk
1 large egg, lightly beaten
Salt and fresh-ground black pepper
1 heaping cup dry rigatoni, cooked and drained
One 16-ounce can peeled Italian tomatoes, drained and chopped
1½ cups grated Parmesan cheese
¼ cup chopped fresh flat-leaf parsley
1 recipe Semolina Pizza Dough (page 391)

T orta rustica *is an Italian savory deep-dish pie. This hearty, satisfying torta is as old as the hills of Tuscany, containing pasta as well as meat and cheese. It is ideal for a small winter buffet party or for a summer picnic with salad, fruit, and cheese.*

❶ Place the sausages in a medium saucepan and cover with water. Cook, uncovered, over medium heat until cooked through and firm, about 15 minutes. Cool, then skin the sausages and slice ½ inch thick. Set aside.

❷ Melt the butter in a large skillet over low heat. Add the onion, garlic, and herbs. Cook over low heat until the onion is soft, about 10 minutes. Sprinkle with the flour and cook for 30 seconds, stirring constantly. Using a whisk, slowly add the hot milk and cook, stirring to remove any lumps, until mixture thickens and begins to boil, about 5 minutes. Whisk the egg into the bubbling mixture. Remove from the heat and season with salt and pepper to taste. With a large spatula, fold in the cooked rigatoni, sausage, tomatoes, Parmesan, and parsley.

❸ Ten minutes before baking, place a baking stone on the center rack of the oven, if desired, and preheat it to 375°F. Spray a 10-inch springform pan with olive oil cooking spray.

❹ Place the pizza dough on a lightly floured work surface. Using a rolling pin, roll out the dough to a circle 20 inches in diameter. Quickly and gently fold the dough into quarters and transfer to the pan. Unfold immediately, letting the excess hang over the sides of the pan. Spread the filling evenly over the dough. Gather up the overhanging dough by folding it into the center, and twist the center to make a knob. Spray the top with olive oil cooking spray and prick the top all over with the tines of a fork.

5 Bake the *torta* for 50 to 60 minutes, or until golden brown. Remove from the oven to a wire rack. Cool for 10 minutes before removing the springform sides. Let stand for at least 30 minutes before serving hot, or cool to room temperature, but let stand for no more than 4 hours. Cut into thick wedges to serve. Wrap any leftovers tightly and store in the refrigerator.

Bread Machine Baker's Hint: Which Pans for Pizzas and Flatbreads?

While every expert has a favorite, almost any type of pan can give good results. I tend to use tin-lined steel or heavy-gauge aluminum round power pans (the pans with the Swiss cheese holes in the bottom) and large round deep-dish pans from Chicago Metallic, or large 18-by-12-inch baking sheets, with very good results. The steel pans do need to be seasoned according to the manufacturer's instructions before their first use, and are just rinsed and dried thereafter. If you use black-finish pans, they also will need to be seasoned. You can place a screen under the pizza on the baking sheet to catch the inevitable drips. Never put these pans in the dishwasher; they will rust mercilessly. I also really like the ceramic baking sheets from Sassafras, and red clay pizza pans from Tufty Ceramics. Made of the same materials as baking stones but shaped as standard pans, they eliminate any need for a baking stone. For some pizzas I use an 8-inch aluminum springform pan, such as for small cornmeal-crust pizzas, so that I can build up a 2-inch side of dough to encase the filling.

SUZANNE'S CHICAGO-STYLE DEEP-DISH PIZZA

Makes one 14-inch deep-dish pizza

INGREDIENTS

1 large onion, coarsely chopped
½ pound ground sirloin
½ pound ground pork
1 teaspoon whole fennel seed
3 fresh plum tomatoes
1 recipe Cornmeal Pizza Dough (page 397)
1 pound mozzarella cheese, shredded
¾ cup grated Romano cheese
1½ teaspoons dried oregano
1½ teaspoons dried basil
One 16-ounce can Hunt's Spaghetti Sauce or 2 cups Essential Tomato-Herb Pizza Sauce (page 392)
⅓ cup olive oil

D eep-dish pizza is a purely American invention. The first definitive regional adaptation of Italian pizza, it was developed by Pizzeria Uno in Chicago after World War II, with great success. In this deep-dish version, the cornmeal-laced dough is pressed into the pan with your fingers, without any fuss, then the cheese forms the first layer, which keeps the crust from getting soggy. You can certainly use your own homemade sauce, but Suzanne says Hunt's works the best.

1 Place the onion and meats in a medium sauté pan. Cook over medium heat until the meat is no longer pink and onion is cooked; blot up excess fat with a paper towel. Add the fennel seed. Set aside to cool.

2 Skin and chop the tomatoes. Place in a sieve and drain for 10 minutes.

3 Twenty to thirty minutes before baking, place a pizza stone on the lower third rack of the oven and preheat it to 400°F.

4 Brush a 14-inch deep-dish pizza pan with oil and press in the pizza dough, making sure it is even on the bottom and up the sides to the rim; do not stretch. Let rest for 15 minutes.

5 Toss the mozzarella, Romano, and herbs together in a bowl. Sprinkle the dough with two-thirds of the cheese mixture. Then spread with the entire can of sauce and drizzle with some olive oil. Distribute the meat mixture over the top for the next layer. Top with the tomatoes and the remaining cheese mixture. Drizzle with the remaining olive oil.

6 Bake for 15 minutes, then lower the oven temperature to 350°F, and bake for an additional 40 to 45 minutes. Cover with foil for the last 10 minutes if the cheese is too brown. When done, the crust will be golden brown; lift with a metal spatula to check the bottom. Remove the pizza from the oven and let it rest on a rack for 10 minutes before cutting. Serve while still hot.

Making Your Own Frozen Pizza

Frozen pizzas are convenient for entertaining or for a fast meal. The pizza can be partially baked, cooled to room temperature, then frozen for up to a week. Here is how to do it: Bake the pizza for half the required time, let it cool on a wire rack, then slide it onto a baking sheet. Place in the freezer, uncovered, for 30 minutes. Remove from the freezer, wrap in plastic wrap and then in aluminum foil if it is a large pizza, or slip a smaller pizza into a self-sealing plastic freezer bag. Label and date the pizza before returning it to the freezer. To bake and serve, 15 minutes before baking, place a baking stone in the oven, and preheat it to 425°F. Remove the pizza from the freezer. Unwrap the pizza and slide it directly onto the hot stone or place it on a baking sheet and then on the stone. Bake until the pizza is hot and the cheese is bubbling.

SAUSAGE AND PEPPER CALZONE

Makes three 4½-inch calzones

1½- OR 2-POUND-LOAF MACHINES

For the dough:

1⅛ cups water
3 tablespoons olive oil

2½ cups unbleached
   all-purpose flour
½ cup semolina pasta flour
   (durum flour) or whole
   wheat flour
1½ teaspoons salt

2¼ teaspoons SAF yeast
   or 2¾ teaspoons bread
   machine yeast

For the filling:

¾ pound sweet or hot
   Italian sausage
3 to 4 tablespoons olive oil
2 to 3 red bell peppers
   (1 pound), cut in half
   and sliced
1 medium yellow onion,
   thinly sliced
Salt and fresh-ground black
   pepper
⅓ cup grated Parmesan or
   Asiago cheese

Calzone means "trouser leg" in Italian, probably a reference to the calzone's earliest shape, which was elongated like a tube. Calzones, which are now recognizable in their half-moon shapes, can be filled with any combination of items that might constitute pizza topping. Calzones stand in the company of a number of other little stuffed breads, all of which play roles similar to our American sandwich: Cornish pasties, Russian pirogi, and the South American empanada. You can shape this dough into calzones of any size.

❶ To make the dough, place all the dough ingredients in the pan according to the order in the manufacturer's instructions. Program for the Dough cycle and press Start.

❷ While the Dough cycle is running, prepare the filling. Prick the sausages with a fork and place in a medium skillet. Add ½ inch of water, cover, and simmer until the water evaporates, about 15 minutes. Uncover and continue to cook and brown the sausages on all sides. Remove from the heat and cool. Cut into ¼-inch slices. Refrigerate until needed.

❸ Combine the oil, peppers, and onions in another skillet. Cook over medium-high heat until soft and gently browned. Remove from the heat, season with salt and pepper to taste, and let cool at room temperature.

❹ Twenty to thirty minutes before baking, preheat the oven to 425°F. Oil or line a large baking sheet with parchment paper.

❺ When the machine beeps at the end of the cycle, press Stop and unplug the machine. Immediately remove the bread pan from the machine, and turn the dough out onto a lightly floured work surface. Divide the dough into 3 equal portions. Flatten each portion with your hand and, using a rolling pin, roll out each one into a 9-inch round. Dust the work surface lightly with flour as needed to prevent sticking

6 Place a third of the filling and sausage slices over half of one round of dough, leaving a 1-inch border. Sprinkle with 2 tablespoons of the cheese. Brush the edge of the dough with water and fold over to form a half-moon-shaped turnover. Press the edges together to seal, then fold over the entire border in 1-inch sections to make a braided edge. Transfer the calzone to the baking sheet. Cut a few slits in the top to allow for steam to escape. Repeat with the remaining two pieces of dough.

7 Bake for 25 to 30 minutes, until golden brown and crisp. Slide the calzones from the baking pan onto a rack. Let cool for 10 minutes before slicing or eating out of hand.

V A R I A T I O N

Mini Calzones
Makes 12 calzones

In Step 5, divide each portion of dough into quarters. Roll out each into a 4- to 5-inch round and fill as directed. Seal, slit, and bake for 12 to 15 minutes. These can be frozen on a baking sheet, then stored in a plastic freezer bag, and re-heated. These are good for two-bite snacks.

CHEESE PIZZA TORTA

Makes one 8-inch torta

3 tablespoons yellow cornmeal or coarse semolina, for dusting
½ cup mozzarella cheese, shredded (2 ounces)
½ cup Italian fontina cheese, shredded (2 ounces)
½ cup smoked provolone, shredded (2 ounces)
3 ounces soft goat cheese (such as Montrachet or domestic chabis) or feta, crumbled (½ cup)
½ cup grated Parmesan
1 recipe Basic Pizza Dough (page 390)
⅓ cup Essential Tomato-Herb Pizza Sauce (page 392) or commercial marinara sauce
Fresh-ground black pepper
1 egg beaten with 1 tablespoon milk, for glaze

T *his is a layered cheese pizza pie that is served in wedges hot from the oven. Try it accompanied by a glass of mellow red Zinfandel.*

❶ Place a baking stone on the lower third oven rack and preheat the oven to 375°F. Grease an 8-inch springform pan and dust with cornmeal or semolina.

❷ Combine all the cheeses, except ¼ cup of the Parmesan, in a small bowl and toss together.

❸ Place the dough on a lightly floured work surface. Divide the dough into 3 equal portions. With a rolling pin, roll the dough out to very thin 9-inch rounds. Carefully place 1 round in the prepared pan and press the excess dough up the sides of the pan. Spread with half of the tomato sauce. Sprinkle with half of the cheese mixture and a few grinds of pepper, leaving a 1-inch border all around. Brush the edge of the dough with the egg glaze. Position the second dough round on top, again pressing the excess dough up the sides of the pan, spread with the tomato sauce, and sprinkle evenly with the remaining cheese mixture and a little more pepper. Brush the edge of the dough with the egg glaze. Place the last dough round on top. Bring the edges of the two bottom layers of dough up to the top, and roll the edges together in sections to seal in the cheeses; the edges will naturally form a rope pattern. Brush the top all over with the egg glaze and sprinkle with the reserved ¼ cup Parmesan.

❹ Immediately place the pan in the oven and bake until thoroughly browned, about 30 to 35 minutes. Remove from the oven to a wire rack and remove the springform sides. Let rest for 10 minutes. Slide the *torta* onto a cutting board, cut it while hot with a serrated knife, and serve.

GARLIC FOCACCIA

Makes 2 flatbreads

T his recipe for focaccia is adapted from one by the test kitchen of the SAF yeast company. It is almost like a pizza bianco, *a pizza without the sauce. I love that it has garlic powder in the crust, in addition to the fresh garlic brushed over the top. It is so tender that you can cut wedges out of it directly from the freezer with no work at all. Be sure to use garlic powder in the dough, not garlic salt, which would inhibit the action of the yeast. This one is for garlic lovers!*

❶ Place the dough ingredients in the pan according to the order in the manufacturer's instructions. Program for the Dough cycle; press Start.

❷ Brush a 17-by-11-inch baking sheet with olive oil and sprinkle heavily with cornmeal or semolina. When the machine beeps at the end of the cycle, press Stop and unplug the machine. Immediately remove the bread pan and turn the dough out onto a lightly floured work surface. Divide the dough into 2 portions. Use the heel of your hand to press and flatten a piece of the dough until it is ¼ inch thick. Lift it onto the pan. Repeat with the other portion of dough. The two portions will fit on the baking sheet with a few inches in between. Brush the tops with olive oil. Cover gently with plastic wrap and let rise at room temperature until puffy, about 25 minutes.

❸ Twenty minutes before baking, place a baking stone on the lowest rack of a cold oven and preheat it to 450°F.

❹ Brush the dough again with olive oil and sprinkle with the garlic. If there is any olive oil left over, pour it over the top. Reduce the oven temperature to 400°F. Place the pan on the hot stone and bake for 15 minutes, or until the focaccias are nicely browned. Slide onto a rack to cool or serve warm from the oven.

1½- OR 2-POUND-LOAF MACHINES

1⅛ cups water
2 tablespoons extra-virgin olive oil

3¼ cups bread flour
1½ teaspoons salt
1 teaspoon garlic powder
¼ teaspoon dried oregano

2 teaspoons SAF yeast or 2½ teaspoons bread machine yeast

Cornmeal or coarse semolina, for sprinkling
¼ cup extra-virgin olive oil, for brushing
6 large cloves garlic, minced

ROMAN BREAD

Makes 1 flatbread

R oman bread is the house bread at the Casa Vieja restaurant near Arizona State University. My recipe tester, Mary Anne, has made this bread dozens of times to accompany dinner. The onion is added at the beginning with all the other ingredients, so it gets incorporated right into the dough. Sometimes Mary Anne sprinkles it with grated Asiago cheese in place of the salt or with another dried herb, such as basil, before baking. There is never any left over, but if there were, it would be great bread for making stuffing.

1 To make the dough, place the ingredients in the pan according to the order in the manufacturer's instructions. Program for the Dough cycle; press Start.

2 Brush a large rectangular baking sheet with olive oil. When the machine beeps at the end of the cycle, press Stop and unplug the machine. Immediately remove the bread pan and turn the dough out onto the baking sheet. With oiled fingers or a rolling pin, press and flatten the dough into a 1-inch-thick oval. Cover with plastic wrap and let rise at room temperature until doubled in bulk, about 40 minutes.

3 Twenty minutes before baking, place a baking

1½-POUND LOAF

For the dough:
1 cup water

3 cups bread flour
1 tablespoon sugar
⅓ cup chopped yellow
  onion
1½ teaspoons salt

2 teaspoons SAF yeast
  or 2½ teaspoons bread
  machine yeast

For the topping:
3 tablespoons olive oil
1½ tablespoons dried
  rosemary, crushed
Coarse sea salt, for
  sprinkling

2-POUND LOAF

For the dough:
1½ cups water

4 cups bread flour
1 tablespoon plus
  1 teaspoon sugar
½ cup chopped yellow
  onion
2 teaspoons salt

1 tablespoon SAF yeast
  or 1 tablespoon plus
  ½ teaspoon bread
  machine yeast

For the topping:
¼ cup olive oil
2 tablespoons dried
  rosemary, crushed
Coarse sea salt, for
  sprinkling

stone on the lowest rack of a cold oven and preheat it to 425°F. If you are not using a baking stone, preheat the oven to 400°F.

4 Using a small, sharp knife, slash the top of the dough with a big tic-tac-toe grid, no more than ½-inch deep. Drizzle with the olive oil and sprinkle with the rosemary. Bake for 20 to 25 minutes, until browned. When the bread comes out of the oven sprinkle it with the coarse salt. Serve cut into squares the day it is made, warm or at room temperature.

ITALIAN WHOLE WHEAT FLATBREAD

Makes one 15-by-10-inch flatbread

1½- OR 2-POUND-LOAF MACHINES

⅔ cup water
1 cup milk
3 tablespoons extra-virgin olive oil

3 cups unbleached all-purpose flour
1 cup whole wheat flour

2¼ teaspoons SAF yeast or 2¾ teaspoons bread machine yeast

3 to 4 tablespoons extra-virgin olive oil, for drizzling
2 teaspoons coarse sea salt, for sprinkling

T he Italians eat a wide variety of flatbread appetizers. This one is made with whole wheat flour. In true Tuscan style, there is no salt in the dough but there is plenty on top to balance out the flavor. The combination of milk and water makes a tender bread. Serve this flatbread at the end of the day, warm if possible, cut into pieces, accompanied by some fontina cheese, grapes and figs, and a Chianti wine.

1 Place the dough ingredients in the pan according to the order in the manufacturer's instructions. Program for the Dough cycle; press Start. The dough will be soft, but still form a dough ball.

2 Brush a 15-by-10-by-1-inch metal jelly roll pan with olive oil. When the machine beeps at the end of the cycle, press Stop and unplug the machine. Immediately remove the bread pan and turn the dough out onto the prepared pan. Using the heel of your hand, press and flatten the dough to fit the pan. Cover gently with oiled plastic wrap and let rise at room temperature until doubled in bulk, about 1 hour.

3 Twenty minutes before baking, place a baking stone on the center rack of a cold oven and preheat it to 450°F.

4 Using your fingertips or knuckles, gently dimple the dough all over the surface. Drizzle the olive oil over the dough, letting it pool in the indentations. Reduce the oven temperature to 425°F. Bake for 25 to 30 minutes, or until nicely browned. Sprinkle the bread with the sea salt. Let cool for 10 minutes in the pan, then cut into squares, or slide onto a rack to cool.

WINE FOCACCIA

*Makes one 14-inch
or one 13-by-9-inch flatbread*

T he difference between a pizza crust and focaccia is simply
that focaccia is thicker. Instead of being baked immediately
after shaping to make a thin crisp, the dough is left to rise
a second time before baking. Serve this focaccia the same day it is
baked, cut into squares, accompanied by olives and white wine.

**1½- OR 2-POUND-
LOAF MACHINES**

For the dough:

1⅛ cups water
½ cup dry white wine
3 tablespoons extra-virgin
  olive oil

4 cups bread flour
2 teaspoons salt

2 teaspoons SAF yeast
  or 2½ teaspoons bread
  machine yeast

Cornmeal or coarse
  semolina, for sprinkling

For the topping:

¼ cup extra-virgin olive oil
3 tablespoons dried basil
  or ⅓ cup finely chopped
  fresh basil

❶ To make the dough, place the dough ingredients in the
pan according to the order in the manufacturer's instructions. Program for the Dough cycle; press Start.

❷ Brush a 14-inch round pizza pan or 13-by-9-inch metal
baking pan with olive oil and sprinkle heavily with cornmeal or semolina. When the machine beeps at the end of
the cycle, press Stop and unplug the machine. Immediately remove the bread pan and turn the dough out onto
a lightly floured work surface. Using the heel of your
hand, press and flatten it. Lift the dough onto the pan
and gently pull and press it, stretching it to fit the pan.
Cover gently with oiled plastic wrap and let rise at room
temperature until doubled in bulk, about 45 minutes.

❸ To prepare the topping, combine the oil and basil in a
small bowl. Let sit for 20 minutes at room temperature.

❹ Meanwhile, place a baking stone on the lowest rack
of a cold oven and preheat it to 450°F. If you are not
using a baking stone, preheat the oven to 400°F.

❺ Using your fingertips, gently poke indentations about
¼ inch deep all over the dough surface. Drizzle the herb
oil over the dough, letting it pool in the indentations.
Reduce the oven temperature to 400°F if using a stone.
Place the pan on the stone or oven rack and bake for
25 to 30 minutes, or until nicely browned. Let cool
for 15 minutes in the pan. Serve warm from the oven.

SCHIACCIATA

Makes one 14-inch flatbread

1½- OR 2-POUND-LOAF MACHINES

For the biga:

½ cup water
1 cup bread flour
½ teaspoon SAF yeast or bread machine yeast

For the dough:

1 cup water
1 tablespoon extra-virgin olive oil

2½ cups bread flour
1 teaspoon sea salt

1¼ teaspoons SAF yeast or 1¾ teaspoons bread machine yeast

3 tablespoons extra-virgin olive oil, for drizzling
Coarse sea salt, for sprinkling

The Italian schiacciata (*pronounced ski-ah-CHAH-tah*) *is a Tuscan flatbread known in other areas of Italy as a focaccia. It is known as the bakers' hors d'oeuvre and is a superb appetizer just as it is here, plain, served with wine. Toppings you might wish to try are a thin layer of tomato sauce sprinkled with chopped scallions and some Parmesan cheese, or a drizzle of thin basil pesto with pine nuts. This flatbread is made with a* biga, *or starter; for more information on* bigas, *see the Country Breads section of the Traditional Loaves chapter.*

❶ To make the starter, place the *biga* ingredients in the bread pan. Program for the Dough cycle, press Start, and set a kitchen timer for 10 minutes. When the timer rings, press Stop and unplug the machine. Let the *biga* rest in the machine for 2 hours.

❷ To make the dough, place all the dough ingredients in the pan with the *biga*. Program for the Dough cycle; press Start. The dough ball will be moist and smooth.

❸ Brush a 14-inch round pizza pan with oil. When the machine beeps at the end of the cycle, press Stop and unplug the machine. Immediately remove the bread pan and turn the dough out onto the prepared pan. Do not knead or work the dough. Dip your fingertips in cold water to keep them from sticking, and spread the dough in the pan. Leave the indentations from your fingers. Cover gently with oiled plastic wrap and let rise at room temperature until puffy, about 1 hour.

❹ Twenty minutes before baking, place a baking stone on the lowest rack of a cold oven and preheat it to 375°F.

5 Using your fingertips, press the dough gently all over the top to dimple. Drizzle the olive oil into the indentations. Bake for 30 to 35 minutes, or until nicely browned. Slide the bread onto a rack to cool. Sprinkle with the coarse salt. Eat warm or at room temperature.

The Right Ingredient: Yeast

All breads and doughs made in the machine require the use of a dry granular yeast that does not need preliminary fermentation by dissolving it in water. Fast-acting yeast and bread machine yeast both meet this requirement; quick-rise yeast can also be used.

The most commonly available fast-acting yeast is labeled as "SAF Perfect Rise" yeast, produced by the S. I. LaSaffre Company. It is sold in two-pack strips and in 3-ounce resealable bags. The other yeast that performs well in the bread machine, as its name might suggest, is bread machine yeast. It, too, is able to be mixed into a dough along with the dry ingredients, requiring no previous activation in a warm liquid. Bread machine yeast, available from Red Star and Fleischmann's, is sold in 4-ounce jars. Both fast-acting and bread machine yeasts can tolerate a wider range of temperatures than other active dry yeasts, so they will grow and multiply at lower temperatures in the bread machine's pan. As these yeasts perform differently from one another, you will see that in most recipes in this book, a different quantity of yeast is given for each type. Active dry yeast and fresh cake yeast should *not* be used in the bread machine.

Whatever yeast you are using, be sure to check the expiration date stamped on the back of the package. Fresh yeast works best, and outdated yeast may not work at all.

If your dough is over-risen, cut back the yeast by ¼ teaspoon in your next bakings until you get the density you like.

PROVENÇAL OLIVE AND ANCHOVY FLATBREAD

Makes 2 flatbreads

For the pâte fermentée:

½ cup water

1¼ cups unbleached all-purpose flour
Pinch of sea salt

½ teaspoon SAF yeast or 1 teaspoon bread machine yeast

For the dough:

1⅛ cups water

3 cups unbleached all-purpose flour
1 teaspoon sea salt

1½ teaspoons SAF yeast or 2 teaspoons bread machine yeast

30 pitted black olives (don't need to be perfect whole olives)
One 2-ounce tin flat anchovy fillets in oil, chopped, 1 tablespoon of the oil reserved

I n the south of France—known affectionately as the Midi, and home for decades to Pablo Picasso—this recipe is a classic. The region has lots of ancient olive trees, and a number of their well-loved breads incorporate plenty of olives from many different types of trees. So when you make this flatbread, feel free to do the same, although this bread traditionally uses black olives. Use large, small, oil-cured, brine-cured, white, green, purple, or black olives. The flatbread is usually made with double the amount of anchovies I call for here, but I've adapted this recipe for American palates; add more anchovies if you like. This recipe uses a pâte fermentée *starter. See the Country Breads section of the Traditional Loaves chapter for more information about these starters. The flatbread is shaped into large rectangles that end up looking like long baseball gloves with open slits in the middle when the bread expands. Eat this bread the day it is baked.*

❶ To make the *pâte fermentée* starter, place the starter ingredients in the bread pan. Program for the Dough cycle; press Start. Set a kitchen timer for 10 minutes. When the timer rings, press Pause and set the timer again for 10 minutes. Let the starter rest for 10 minutes (the *autolyse*). When the timer rings, press Start to continue and finish the Dough cycle. When the machine beeps at the end of the cycle, press Stop and unplug the machine. Gently deflate the spongy starter, and let it sit in the bread machine for 3 to 12 hours, deflating it about every 4 hours. (If you are making the starter ahead of time, remove it from the machine at this point and refrigerate it for up to 48 hours. Bring to room temperature before making the dough.)

❷ To make the dough, place all the dough ingredients in the pan with the starter. (You don't have to wash out the pan from the starter.) Program for the Dough cycle;

press Start. Between Knead 1 and Knead 2, press Pause and add the olives and anchovies with the 1 tablespoon of oil. Press Start to continue the cycle. The dough will be moist and smooth, but flaccid.

3 Line an 18-by-12-inch baking sheet with parchment paper. When the machine beeps at the end of the cycle, press Stop and unplug the machine. Immediately remove the bread pan and turn the dough out onto a lightly floured work surface. Divide the dough in half. With a rolling pin, roll a piece of the dough into a freeform 8-by-10-inch rectangle and place it on the baking sheet. Lay your hand gently on the dough with your fingers spread apart. With the tip of a sharp knife, make four cuts into the dough between your fingers through to the baking pan, but not extending all the way to the edge of the pan. Roll out the second *fougasse*, place it on the baking sheet leaving 2 inches between the two *fougasses*, and slash as for the first. Cover gently with a clean tea towel and let rise at room temperature until puffy, about 30 minutes.

4 Twenty minutes before baking, place a baking stone on the lowest rack of a cold oven and preheat it to 425°F.

5 With the rolling pin, gently roll over the surface of the *fougasses* once to deflate them slightly; pull open the slits if needed. Bake for 25 to 30 minutes, or until nicely browned. Slide the breads onto a rack to cool. Eat warm or at room temperature.

GRAPE SCHIACCIATA COFFEE CAKE

Makes one 14-inch coffee cake

1½- OR 2-POUND-LOAF MACHINES

For the dough:

⅓ cup milk
⅓ cup water
1 large egg
3 tablespoons extra-virgin olive oil
5 tablespoons butter, room temperature, cut into pieces
1 teaspoon vanilla extract

3 cups unbleached all-purpose flour
2 tablespoons raw sugar, preferably, or granulated sugar
1¼ teaspoons salt

2 teaspoons SAF yeast or 2½ teaspoons bread machine yeast

For the grape topping:

⅔ cup raw sugar, preferably, or granulated sugar
1½ teaspoons aniseed, crushed
1½ pounds (about 3 cups) small red or black seedless grapes, stemmed
¼ cup crystallized ginger, finely chopped

Extra-virgin olive oil, for brushing

T his most famous Italian sweet flatbread is made at vendemmia, *the autumn wine grape harvest, using fresh-picked wine grapes and liberally sprinkled sugar and crushed aniseed. Many wine country households cultivate a few backyard vines next to their fig trees, just for baking purposes. Schiacciata con l'Uva can be eaten for breakfast or tea as a coffee cake instead of toast, bagels, or a croissant. This is my California version.*

❶ To make the dough, place the ingredients in the pan according to the order in the manufacturer's instructions. Program for the Dough cycle; press Start. The dough ball will be sticky and just hold its shape.

❷ While the dough is rising, combine the sugar and aniseed for the topping in a small bowl and set aside.

❸ Brush a 14-inch pizza pan with olive oil. When the machine beeps at the end of the cycle, press Stop and unplug the machine. Immediately remove the bread pan and turn the dough out onto a lightly floured work surface. Using the heel of your hand, press the dough to flatten it. Roll the dough out in a circle, then lift it onto the pan and gently pull and press it into a circle to fit the pan. Shape a ½-inch rim around the edge of the crust. Brush with olive oil.

❹ Arrange the grapes on the dough and press them in. Sprinkle lightly with the crystallized ginger, then with the anise sugar. Let rise until puffy, uncovered about 25 minutes.

❺ Fifteen minutes before baking, place a baking stone on the middle rack of the oven and preheat it to 425°F.

6 Reduce the heat to 375°F and bake the coffee cake directly on the stone for 25 to 30 minutes, until golden brown. Slide the bread off the pan onto a rack to cool. Serve warm or at room temperature, cut into thick wedges.

The Toolbox: About Baking Stones

The baking stone, also called a pizza stone, is a heavy unglazed stone slab that goes on one of the racks inside the oven. The goal of using a pizza stone is to make your home oven simulate a wood-burning oven lined with bricks. When the pizza or flatbread is placed in the oven, the heat from the tiles is immediately transferred into the dough. The dough springs up under the intense heat, making the crust chewy and light, rather than soft like regular bread. My Sicilian baking friend gave me a good tip: use two stones, one on the lowest and one on the uppermost rack, to create a great mini–stone oven.

There are different types of baking stones. Some companies offer round or rectangular fired clay slabs. Others market terra-cotta baking tiles that fit conveniently into a baking sheet, which is then placed on the rack. Die-hard home pizza bakers swear by lining the rack with unglazed tiles, easily available from a tile outlet, since you can make the area covered by the tiles as large as you want. I use a large rectangular stone as I can fit more pans on it. The round ones are about the size of a pizza or focaccia.

Stones and tiles need to be seasoned before they are used for the first time. This usually requires that you rinse the stone or tiles with cool water, then place them in the oven and heat it to 250°F. Bake them without anything else in the oven for 1 hour, and then let them cool in the oven. But follow the instructions you receive from the manufacturer.

Always preheat a baking stone prior to baking, according to recipe directions, for anywhere from 10 to 20 minutes on an oven rack in any position. The stone needs to be good and hot. A baking stone requires no oiling, but should be sprinkled with cornmeal just before baking if you will be placing your pizza directly on it. This prevents sticking. You need a peel, a flat wooden or metal shovel, to slide a pizza directly onto a stone, which I find fun to use. But for the occasional baker, baking a pizza in a pan set on top of a baking stone works efficiently, and yields great results. Besides, peels are a bit tricky to use.

A pizza stone can be left in the oven all the time, but I have one that I use specifically for pizza, as the stones tend to blacken a lot with use. This is okay. The black color does not mean it is dirty, nor will it affect the taste of the pizza, but it is my preference, for this reason, not to leave the stone in the oven all the time. After baking, allow the stone to cool completely in the oven before removing it for storage. To avoid being burned, I don't ever handle it while it is hot; the stone holds and retains a lot of heat. Never place even a slightly warm stone on a cold surface or it will crack immediately and you will have to piece it together or buy a new one.

Clean a baking stone by rinsing it with plain water and scrubbing off any accumulated bits with a brush. No soap, please, as it will affect the taste of the next pizza you bake.

WALNUT FOUGASSE

Makes one 12-inch flatbread

1½- OR 2-POUND-LOAF MACHINES

1¼ cups fat-free milk
⅓ cup walnut oil

3 cups unbleached
  all-purpose flour
¾ cup coarsely chopped
  walnuts
1½ teaspoons salt

2½ teaspoons SAF yeast
  or 1 tablespoon bread
  machine yeast

3 tablespoons walnut oil,
  for brushing

I*n the south of France a focaccia-style flatbread is called a* fougasse. *This version is adapted from a recipe by baker Rose Levy Beranbaum, who was introduced to this bread by Alice Waters of Chez Panisse restaurant fame. It is a picnic bread or appetizer par excellence.*

❶ Place all the ingredients in the pan according to the order in the manufacturer's instructions. Program for the Dough cycle; press Start.

❷ Brush a 12-inch round pizza pan with 1 tablespoon of the walnut oil. When the machine beeps at the end of the cycle, press Stop and unplug the machine. Immediately remove the bread pan and turn the dough out directly onto the pan and press and flatten the dough with your fingers. Lift and gently pull the dough, stretching it to fit the round pan. Cover gently with plastic wrap and let rise at room temperature until puffy, about 20 minutes.

❸ Twenty minutes before baking, place a baking stone on the lowest rack of a cold oven and preheat it to 425°F; if you are not using a baking stone, preheat the oven to 400°F.

❹ Brush the top of the dough with 2 tablespoons of walnut oil. With a small, sharp knife, cut 7 short diagonal slashes, right through to the bottom of the pan, 3 inches long and a few inches apart, like the spokes of a wheel. With your fingers, push the slashes open. Bake until the *fougasse* is crisp and brown, 20 to 25 minutes. Slide the hot bread off the pan to cool on a rack. Eat warm or at room temperature.

LA POMPE DE NOËL

Makes one 12-inch flatbread

T*his rustic dessert* fougasse *is one of the thirteen traditional desserts that are served on Christmas Eve in Provence. It is by far one of the oldest, yet most unusual, of holiday breads, and traditionally contains* huile vierge, *the choice top grade of French olive. I learned this recipe from master baker Diane Dexter when substitute-teaching for one of her classes at Tante Marie's Cooking School in San Francisco. I ate a similar sweet* fougasse *when I visited Najac, the medieval French castle town in the Rouergue, where there is an annual* fougasse *festival. Orange-flower water, a traditional ingredient, is available at liquor stores and in the spice section of some grocery stores.*

1 Place all the dough ingredients in the pan according to the order in the manufacturer's instructions. Program for the Dough cycle; press Start.

2 Brush a 12-inch round pizza pan with olive oil. When the machine beeps at the end of the cycle, press Stop and unplug the machine. Immediately remove the bread pan and turn the dough out onto the pan. With floured fingers, press and flatten the dough, lifting and gently pulling it to stretch it into the pan; it will be about ⅜ inch thick. Cover gently with oiled plastic wrap and let rise at room temperature until puffy, about 30 minutes.

3 Twenty minutes before baking, place a baking stone on the lowest rack of a cold oven and preheat it to 375°F.

4 Brush the top of the dough with the olive oil. With a small, sharp knife, cut 7 short diagonal slashes, right through to the bottom of the pan, 3 inches long and a few inches apart, like the spokes of a wheel. With your fingers, push the slashes open. Bake until crisp and brown, 20 to 24 minutes. Slide the hot bread from the pan onto a rack to cool. Eat at room temperature or wrap tightly in plastic to serve the next day.

1½- OR 2-POUND-LOAF MACHINES

½ cup water
1 teaspoon orange-flower water
½ cup extra-virgin olive oil
1 large egg

3 cups unbleached all-purpose flour
⅞ cup sugar
Grated zest of 1 medium orange
1½ tablespoons candied orange peel, finely chopped (page 516)
½ teaspoon salt

2 teaspoons SAF yeast or 2½ teaspoons bread machine yeast

3 tablespoons extra-virgin olive oil, for brushing

NAAN

Makes 6 naan

1½- OR 2-POUND-LOAF MACHINES

1 tablespoon peanut oil
½ cup plain yogurt
½ cup milk

2 cups bread flour
¾ teaspoon salt
⅛ teaspoon baking soda

2 teaspoons SAF yeast
or 2½ teaspoons bread
machine yeast

¼ cup whole wheat pastry
flour, for dusting
3 tablespoons unsalted
butter, melted, for
brushing
1 tablespoon nigella seeds

W hen asked about a bread that typifies Muslim Northern India and Afghanistan, naan—*which is the name for this bread and also the generic word for bread in those areas—is the first one that comes to mind. It has become very popular outside this region, too; every Pacific Rim restaurant seems to offer* naan *because of its buttery flavor and moist texture. These long oval flatbreads are baked in a* tandir *oven, which is a deep clay floor oven. The shaped dough is placed on a* gaddi *(cushioned pad) and the* naan *are baked by slapping the dough onto the walls of the hot oven. One end of the dough hangs out over the fire, producing a pretty teardrop oval of bread about twenty inches long. Homemade* naan *are easy to bake in a conventional oven, and are usually made smaller out of convenience. Yogurt is a nice tangy addition to this dough, accenting the flour and replacing the fermented yogurt starter called for in many recipes. In India* naan *is made from white flour, but Afghan bakers use chapati flour, a very fine whole wheat flour that you can find in an ethnic grocery. Substitute an equal amount for the bread flour called for here. If you like, in place of the butter, use ghee, the clarified butter that is the preferred fat in India. Nigella seeds are sometimes called black sesame seeds or black onion seeds. They are traditionally sprinkled over the* naan. Naan *are meant to be eaten just out of the oven. Serve them with goat's milk yogurt or soft goat cheese, as they are eaten in Asia every day, or to accompany roasted meats and stews.*

❶ Place the oil, yogurt, milk, flour, salt, baking soda, and yeast in the pan according to the order in the manufacturer's instructions. Program for the Dough cycle; press Start.

❷ Line 2 large baking sheets with parchment paper and brush with melted butter. When the machine beeps at the end of the cycle, press Stop and unplug the machine. Immediately remove the dough and place on a work surface dusted with whole wheat pastry flour; divide into 2 equal portions. Divide each portion into thirds, and form the 6 portions into walnut-size balls. Let the dough balls rest on the side of the work surface while you work. With a floured rolling pin, roll each into a 4- to 5-inch flat uneven round or oval shape, about ½ inch thick. As they are shaped, place them on a baking sheet. Cover with a clean tea towel while you are rolling out the rest of the *naan*. Each should rest for about 20 minutes.

❸ Preheat the oven to 450°F.

❹ Flatten each round with your palm, then stretch on one side to make an 8-by-4½-inch elongated oval shape. Brush the top of each *naan* with the melted butter and sprinkle lightly with nigella seeds. Bake, one pan at a time, without turning, until golden brown and crisp in places, for 5 to 8 minutes. Serve immediately while warm and fresh, or wrap in a clean tea towel until serving.

MIDDLE EASTERN LAVASH

Makes 8 cracker breads

1½- OR 2-POUND-LOAF MACHINES

1½ cups warm water
4 tablespoons butter, melted

4 cups unbleached all-purpose flour
1 tablespoon sugar
2 teaspoons salt

2 teaspoons SAF yeast or 2½ teaspoons bread machine yeast

¼ cup sesame seeds, for sprinkling

The paper thin daily flatbread of the Arab, Armenian, and Middle Eastern countries around the Mediterranean basin, lavash is basically a naan- or tortilla-type dough rolled very thin. It is baked on a saaj, which looks like a large upside down wok over an open fire. You can bake it in your oven on baking sheets and get a good rendition. When soft, lavash is good for wrapping around hunks of cheese and grilled meats. It keeps well in an airtight container, or in the freezer; just heat in the oven for a few minutes before serving to soften it up.

1 Pour the water, butter, flour, sugar, salt, and yeast into the pan according to the order in the manufacturer's instructions. Program for the Dough cycle; press Start. After 3 minutes of kneading, check the dough to adjust the consistency; you want a soft dough. Drizzle in a bit more water if needed.

2 Preheat the oven to 425°F. Cut 2 or 4 large pieces of parchment paper to fit 2 to 4 large, heavy-duty baking sheets.

3 When the machine beeps at the end of the cycle, press Stop and unplug the machine. Immediately remove the dough and place it on a lightly floured work surface; divide it into 8 equal portions and form them into balls. Flatten the balls with the palm of your hand. Let the balls rest for 10 minutes on the side of the work surface covered with a clean towel. Place one of the baking sheets in the lower third of the oven to preheat it for 5 to 10 minutes. With a floured rolling pin, and lightly dusting the work surface as needed, roll a dough ball into a flat 12-by-9-inch rectangular shape, as thin as possible (almost translucent). Carefully remove the hot baking sheet from the oven. Drape the dough over the rolling pin and gently unroll it onto the baking sheet.

Brush quickly with cold water and sprinkle with sesame seeds.

4 Bake the single bread on the pan, without turning, until lightly browned and slightly bubbly, for 10 to 14 minutes. Slip the bread off the baking sheet and transfer to a wire rack to cool. Roll out and bake the 4 remaining breads, rolling out each one just before baking. Leave the breads on the rack to cool uncovered, if you like the bread crispy. If you like the breads soft, sprinkle with a bit of cold water and cover with a clean tea towel; when all the breads are baked, wrap in aluminum foil and let stand for 30 minutes to soften before serving.

WHOLE WHEAT PITA

Makes 10 pitas

1½- OR 2-POUND-LOAF MACHINES

1¼ cups warm water
Pinch of sugar
2 tablespoons olive oil

1½ cups whole wheat
 pastry flour
1½ cups bread flour
1½ teaspoons salt

1½ teaspoons SAF yeast
 or 2 teaspoons bread
 machine yeast

P erhaps the simplest and most basic of all yeast breads to make is pita. Also known as Middle Eastern pocket bread, this small round of dough about the size of a tortilla puffs dramatically when baked in a hot oven. It can also be made in a size large enough for a whole family, and torn into pieces when it is served. Pitas are another ancient Mediterranean daily bread. Although pitas puff up in the oven, they collapse as they cool, leaving a pocket inside that is perfect for filling. Pitas should be eaten the day they are baked, as soon as they are cool. You can also wrap them in a clean kitchen towel just after they are made to keep them warm for a short time until serving.

❶ Place all the ingredients in the pan according to the order in the manufacturer's instructions. Program for the Dough cycle; press Start. The dough ball will be soft, but not sticky.

❷ Line 2 baking sheets with parchment paper or heavily flour a peel. When the machine beeps at the end of the cycle, press Stop and unplug the machine. Turn the dough out onto a work surface lightly dusted with whole wheat pastry flour; divide it in half. Cover one half with plastic wrap to prevent it from forming a skin. Divide the first half into 5 equal portions and form each into a rough ball. Let rest for 10 minutes, covered, while dividing the second section of dough in the same way. This rest makes the dough easier to roll out.

❸ Using a rolling pin, on the work surface dusted with whole wheat pastry flour, roll each ball into a 5- to 6-inch circle about ¼ inch thick. Move the dough circles by draping them one at a time over a flour-dusted rolling pin and place them on a floured kitchen towel to rest for about 25 minutes and puff slightly before transferring to the baking sheets.

4 During the last 15 minutes the pitas are resting, place a baking stone on the bottom rack of the oven and preheat it to 450°F.

5 Transfer the circles to the baking sheet; 5 will fit on one pan. Bake, one pan at a time, directly on the hot stone. Do not open the oven door for a full 4 minutes, as the puffing begins almost immediately as the steam pushes the two halves of the bread apart. Watch carefully that the pitas do not overbake or burn. Bake for 12 to 14 minutes, until fully puffed, like a pillow, and just light brown, not dark. Remove the puffed hot breads with a wide metal spatula and stack between clean kitchen towels to keep soft.

LÁNGOS

Makes 12 individual flatbreads

1 medium russet potato
  (about ½ pound)
2 cups water

3 cups unbleached
  all-purpose flour
3 tablespoons cornstarch
2 tablespoons nonfat dry
  milk
Large pinch of sugar
Large pinch of salt

2 teaspoons SAF yeast
  or 2½ teaspoons bread
  machine yeast

Canola oil for frying
Garlic powder or salt-free
  garlic seasoning blend,
  for sprinkling

On baking days in Hungary, leftover bread dough gets divided into fist-sized pieces and flattened into thin rounds, as the Hungarians saw the Turks do during the Turkish occupation. A staple bread served with bean soups or goulash meat stews, lángos (pronounced langosh) took on its own Hungarian touch with slash marks here and there, fried and rubbed with garlic before eating. This version, made with a potato dough, is a recipe given to me by a relative, Erin Kovacs, which she translated from her mother-in-law's Hungarian cookbook. Sprinkle the flatbread with garlic powder while it is hot, and serve with bowls of cold sour cream and grated Parmesan on the side for piling onto the bread.

1 Slice the potato and place in a saucepan with the water (do not peel). Cover and bring to a boil. Simmer until tender, about 20 minutes. Drain, reserving the liquid, then peel the potato. Mash or rice the potato and set aside to cool. Measure out ¾ cup of the potato water (discard any extra) and cool to about 90°F or room temperature.

2 Place all the ingredients in the pan according to the order in the manufacturer's instructions, adding the potato and the ¾ cup potato water as the liquid ingredients. Program for the Dough cycle; press Start.

3 Line a baking sheet with parchment paper. When the machine beeps at the end of the cycle, press Stop and unplug the machine. Turn the dough out onto a lightly floured work surface. Divide the dough in half. Divide each half into 6 equal portions and form each into a ball. Place the balls of dough on the baking sheet at least 2 inches apart. Cover loosely with plastic wrap and let rest at room temperature until doubled in bulk, about 45 minutes to 1 hour.

4 On a lightly floured work surface, flatten each ball, then pull to a 6-inch rough circle. Hungarian bakers never roll the dough. It will be a bit larger than the size of the palm of your hand. With a small sharp knife, cut 3 or 4 small slits, 1 to 1½ inches long, like the spokes of a wheel, around the round. Pull to open the slits. Place on the baking sheet. Shape the remaining dough balls. Dust with flour and loosely cover again. Let rise until puffy, about 30 minutes.

5 Line another baking sheet with a few layers of paper towels. Fill a deep skillet or Dutch oven with 1½ inches of canola oil. Heat the oil until it measures 375°F on a deep-fat thermometer. The oil must be very hot to fry the breads properly. Transfer a *lángos* into the fat with a metal spatula, top side down first; you will probably be able to cook 2 at once. Fry, turning once, for a total of 2 to 3 minutes. Carefully lift from the oil with the spatula, let drain a moment, and then place on the paper towels. Repeat with the remaining breads. Sprinkle with the garlic powder while hot. Serve warm or at room temperature.

Lángos can be stored in plastic bags for a day at room temperature, and reheated before serving. To reheat, place on a baking sheet and warm in a preheated 350°F oven, 8 to 10 minutes.

SWEET LOAVES

Chocolate, Fruit, and

Other Sweet Breads

BREAKFAST BREADS

I love the sights and smells associated with sweet morning bread baking. Fruit, nut, spice, sugar, all come together in the dough. Whether you are making a barely sweet slice of toast you can dunk in your coffee or a beautifully crafted bread to serve for a brunch, these yeasted sweet breads are a welcome and enticing part of baking. They have a richness in taste and texture that is not found in other types of bread. Favorite mouthwatering fillings are encased by the dough to create a pretty, delicate pattern when sliced (Cinnamon Swirl Bread anyone?).

With the parade of edible treats comes the inevitable decision: What to bake? Stick to the old tried and true? Or, perhaps, experiment with a new recipe? Whatever your choice, these sweet breads are unique in flavor and shape, right down to their whimsical final touches. A slice off a loaf chock full of dried fruit and baked in the machine is a perfect gift or accompaniment to brunch or breakfast.

Many of these special recipes are just a push of a button away with the Dough cycle; you shape them yourself into beautiful rings and braids. Others are just as happily made in the shape of the bread pan. These are old-fashioned recipes, culled from American and European baking traditions, and may evoke some of your own memories: cinnamon swirl, raisin bread, maple oatmeal bread, granola bread. Remember that baking is not just making a recipe, but an activity that interweaves food with family life and customs.

The flavors of these breads are varied with sweet spices, nuts, extracts, vanilla bean, citrus, and glistening dried fruit. These ingredients are the baker's jewels. I love lavishly studded sweet breads. Some of these breads may have longer lists of ingredients than other recipes in the book, but there is the same ease of preparation when they are made in the bread machine. Machines often have a Fruit and Nut cycle or an Extras choice within the all-purpose cycles that will give an audible signal when to add extra ingredients. After you have baked for a while, you won't even need the signal. Firm additions, like dried fruit, can be added during kneading or with all the other ingredients at the beginning. Nuts don't need to be chopped; just let the paddle break them up during the kneading. When should you add them? A good time to add pieces of nuts and fruits is at the beginning of Knead 2 (after the pause before the dough ball begins to form), or you can just open the lid and sprinkle them in gradually while the machine is kneading. Just be sure to add them early in the cycle, since the dough ball is well formed ten minutes after starting the program.

These loaves are often especially delicate due to the addition of eggs to the dough, and rise a bit more slowly than other breads due to the addition of sugar. But you can use either the Basic or Sweet Bread cycles interchangeably here. The Sweet Bread cycle bakes at a slightly lower temperature than the Basic cycle. Usually it is best to set the crust control on light or medium to prevent overbrowning in either cycle. Be sure to let these loaves cool completely before slicing; no matter how enticing the urge to have a bite, their cakelike crumb will not have set until they are cool.

Although optional, glazing is an important finishing touch for a very fancy loaf, a lively accent of concentrated sweetness and glossy visual appeal. The essences such as mint, vanilla, and almond, and alcoholic spirits such as rum, amaretto, and brandy, have a place to blend in their bold flavors here. With fruit jewels and nuts set into the crust, you will have a bread with a picture-book look that highlights a table like no other food.

Bread Machine Baker's Hint: Tips for Sweet Breads

• Because of all the perishable ingredients called for, like milk, buttermilk, and eggs, and the extra embellishments that need to be added mid-cycle, I do not use the Delay Timer for any of the recipes in this chapter.

• I avoid most commercial candied fruits because they lack distinctive flavor and contain artificial colors and preservatives. Homemade candied peels have an intense bittersweet flavor and firm texture. If you have access to an unsprayed orange or lemon tree, or to organically grown citrus fruits, you can make your own (see pages 505 and 516). I buy glacéed dried fruit from Australia or France or I glaze my own dried fruit (see page 505). Plain dried fruits are also excellent. To add variety substitute dried cranberries, blueberries, tart or sweet cherries, or currants for raisins. Mail-order resources for dried fruits and imported glacéed fruits may be found on page 614.

• For convenience, bake the loaves well ahead of when you will need them, and then freeze them. Defrost the loaves in their wrapping at room temperature. Then add the final glaze and decorations before serving. The loaves will slice and taste as perfect as the day they were baked.

CINNAMON SWIRL BREAD

T here has to be a recipe for a classic cinnamon bread in every collection; it is just too popular and delectable not to be included. In this bread machine version, the dough is removed from the machine, stuffed and rolled up, and either put back in the machine or placed in your home oven for baking off. (I keep a stash of disposable aluminum loaf pans from the supermarket for this type of sweet loaf that can leak during baking—they work beautifully.) This bread is heavenly!

1½-POUND LOAF	2-POUND LOAF
For the dough:	*For the dough:*
1 cup water	1⅓ cups water
2 tablespoons unsalted butter, cut into pieces	3 tablespoons unsalted butter, cut into pieces
¼ cup sugar	⅓ cup sugar
3 cups bread flour	4 cups bread flour
⅓ cup dry buttermilk powder	¼ cup dry buttermilk powder
1 tablespoon gluten	1 tablespoon plus 1 teaspoon gluten
1¼ teaspoons salt	1½ teaspoons salt
2 teaspoons SAF yeast or 2½ teaspoons bread machine yeast	2½ teaspoons SAF yeast or 1 tablespoon bread machine yeast
For the cinnamon swirl:	*For the cinnamon swirl:*
2 tablespoons unsalted butter, melted, for brushing	2 tablespoons unsalted butter, melted, for brushing
⅓ cup light brown sugar	⅓ cup light brown sugar
1 tablespoon ground cinnamon	1 tablespoon ground cinnamon

1 Place all the ingredients in the pan according to the order in the manufacturer's instructions. If you wish to mix and bake the dough completely in the machine, set crust on medium and program for the Basic or Variety cycle. If you wish to bake the loaf in your kitchen oven, program for the Dough cycle. Press Start. (This recipe is not suitable for use with the Delay Timer.)

2 *To bake in the machine:* After Rise 2 ends on the Basic cycle, or when the display shows Shape in the Variety cycle, press Pause, remove the pan, and close the lid. Immediately turn the dough out onto a lightly floured work surface; pat into an 8-by-12-inch fat rectangle. Brush with the melted butter. Sprinkle with the sugar and cinnamon, leaving a 1-inch space all the way around the edge. Starting at a short edge, roll the dough up jelly-roll fashion. Tuck the ends under and pinch the bottom seam. Coat the bottom of the dough with cooking spray, remove the kneading blade, and place the dough back in the pan; press Start to continue to rise and bake as programmed. When the baking cycle ends, immediately remove the bread from the pan.

3 *To bake in the oven:* Preheat the oven to 350°F. Grease a 9-by-5-inch loaf pan (for 1½ pounds dough) or two 7-by-4-inch loaf pans (for 2 pounds dough).

When the machine beeps at the end of the cycle, remove the pan and turn the dough out onto a lightly floured work surface. Pat the 1½ pounds dough into one, or the 2 pounds dough into two 8-by-12-inch rectangles. Brush the rectangle(s) with melted butter. Sprinkle with the brown sugar and cinnamon, leaving a 1-inch edge all the way around. Starting at a short end, roll up jelly-roll fashion. Tuck the ends under and pinch the bottom seam.

Place the single large loaf in the prepared 9-by-5-inch pan or the two smaller loaves in the 7-by-4-inch pans. Spray the top(s) with cooking spray and cover lightly with plastic wrap. Let rise at room temperature until doubled in bulk, about 45 minutes. Bake for 35 to 40 minutes, or until golden brown and the sides have slightly contracted from the pan. If the crust browns too quickly, place a piece of aluminum foil loosely over the top.

4 Place the bread on a rack and let cool to room temperature before slicing. Dust with plain or vanilla confectioners' sugar, if desired.

DUTCH SUGAR LOAF

O nce in the early 1980s I took a baking class in San Francisco from Bernard Clayton, a prodigious food writer when it comes to bread and pastry. He made this bread in the class. I couldn't have been more uninterested in a bread with crushed sugar cubes baked into it, but one bite and I had an epiphany. It was fantastic! There were these moist pockets of sweet goo. Use white or brown sugar cubes. I use Ala Perruche brand with the parrot on the box, imported from France and made from African sugar cane. The cubes are a bit less refined than regular C & H sugar cubes. This is a great breakfast bread.

1. Place the sugar cubes in a heavy clear plastic freezer bag and, using the smooth side of a meat hammer, crack the cubes. Don't crush them; you want the chunks to be no smaller than quarter cubes, if possible. Add the spices to the bag and toss to coat. Set aside.

2. Place the ingredients, except the spice-coated sugar cubes, in the pan according to the order in the manufacturer's instructions. Set crust on medium, and program for the Sweet Bread cycle; press Start. (This recipe is not suitable for use with the Delay Timer.) Five minutes into the kneading segment, press Pause and sprinkle in half of the sugar cube mixture. Press Start to resume the

1½-POUND LOAF	2-POUND LOAF
⅔ cup sugar cubes	¾ cup sugar cubes
1½ teaspoons ground cinnamon	2 teaspoons ground cinnamon
Small pinch of ground cloves	Small pinch of ground cloves
1⅛ cups fat-free milk	1⅓ cups fat-free milk
1 tablespoon unsalted butter or margarine, cut into pieces	2 tablespoons unsalted butter or margarine, cut into pieces
3 cups bread flour	4 cups bread flour
1 tablespoon gluten	1 tablespoon plus 1 teaspoon gluten
1¼ teaspoons salt	1¾ teaspoons salt
2 teaspoons SAF yeast or 2½ teaspoons bread machine yeast	2½ teaspoons SAF yeast or 1 tablespoon bread machine yeast

cycle. Three minutes later, press Pause and add the rest of the sugar cube mixture. Press Start to resume the cycle.

3 When the baking cycle ends, immediately remove the bread from the pan and place it on a rack. Let cool to room temperature before slicing, or sugar syrup will ooze out.

N O T E :

Although I have made this bread with success in my bread machine, readers have commented that the sharp edges of the sugar cubes can scratch the softer Teflon and nonstick coatings in the bread pan during the vigorous kneading cycle. If you want to make this bread and yet want to be cautious with your bread pan, stop the machine after 5 minutes of the kneading cycle and remove the dough. Place it onto a work surface and pat into a thick rectangle. Sprinkle the surface with half the crushed sugar cubes. Fold the dough over in thirds and lightly knead for 2 minutes, until the dough is smooth and springy. Pat again into a rectangle and sprinkle with the rest of the sugar cubes; fold the dough in half and lightly knead 1 to 2 minutes more to distribute the sugar. Clear the program on your bread machine and set the machine to the Bake Only cycle; place the dough into the bread pan, seam side down, close the cover, and press Start. Continue with the recipe for baking and cooling.

MAPLE OATMEAL BREAD

1⅓ cups buttermilk
⅓ cup pure maple syrup
2 tablespoons unsalted
  butter, cut into pieces

3 cups bread flour
¾ cup rolled oats
1 tablespoon gluten
1½ teaspoons salt

2 teaspoons SAF yeast
  or 2½ teaspoons bread
  machine yeast

1⅔ cups buttermilk
½ cup pure maple syrup
3 tablespoons unsalted
  butter, cut into pieces

4 cups bread flour
1 cup rolled oats
1 tablespoon plus
  1 teaspoon gluten
2 teaspoons salt

2½ teaspoons SAF yeast
  or 1 tablespoon bread
  machine yeast

I use quick-cooking imported Irish oatmeal for this recipe. The flavor of Irish-grown oats is the richest of any I have eaten, and the loaf retains a characteristic nubby texture. There is a good dose of maple syrup in this bread, the luscious sweetener made of the boiled-down sap of a maple tree—I like to taste its flavor distinctly in the finished loaf. I look for B Grade maple syrup, which is sometimes labeled "for baking." It is a bit more concentrated, better for baking than for pouring over pancakes. Oatmeal and maple syrup is a combination made in baker's heaven.

1 Place all the ingredients in the pan according to the order in the manufacturer's instructions. Set crust on dark and program for the Basic cycle; press Start. (This recipe is not suitable for use with the Delay Timer.) The dough ball will be firm but springy. If it seems too stiff, dribble with some water during kneading.

2 When the baking cycle ends, immediately remove the bread from the pan and place it on a rack. Let cool to room temperature before slicing.

OLD-FASHIONED RAISIN BREAD

I t is hard to believe that at one time—in a world where raisins had to be seeded with your fingers before eating— raisins were so rare that they were not used in baking at all, but served as a dessert delicacy by themselves. They were plumped in brandy and wrapped in lemon leaves like a little gift. Today, California raisin production allows us to use raisins liberally and, along with cinnamon bread, raisin bread is one of the most common sweet breads made by home bakers. It is as good for peanut butter and jelly sandwiches as it is toasted for breakfast.

1 Place the raisins in a small bowl to heat in the microwave or in a small pan to heat on the stove. Cover with water and heat to boiling. Let stand for 10 minutes to plump, then drain on paper towels.

2 Place the ingredients, except the raisins, in the pan according to the order in the manufacturer's instructions. Set crust on medium and program for the Sweet Bread or Fruit and Nut cycle; press Start. (This recipe is not suitable for use with the Delay Timer.) When the machine beeps, or between Knead 1 and Knead 2, add the raisins.

3 When the baking cycle ends, immediately remove the bread from the pan and place it on a rack. Let cool to room temperature before slicing.

1½-POUND LOAF

1 cup dark raisins

1⅛ cups buttermilk
1 large egg
2 tablespoons canola oil
2 tablespoons dark brown
  sugar

3 cups bread flour
1 tablespoon gluten
1½ teaspoons salt

2 teaspoons SAF yeast
  or 2½ teaspoons bread
  machine yeast

2-POUND LOAF

1⅓ cups dark raisins

1½ cups buttermilk
1 large egg
2½ tablespoons canola oil
3 tablespoons dark brown
  sugar

4 cups bread flour
1 tablespoon plus
  2 teaspoons gluten
2 teaspoons salt

2¼ teaspoons SAF yeast
  or 2¾ teaspoons bread
  machine yeast

C.R.O.W.W.

T*his is a denser, more toothsome raisin bread, especially for whole wheat lovers, with cinnamon in every bite. C.R.O.W.W. stands for Cinnamon Raisin Oatmeal Walnut Whole wheat bread. The oats give moisture, the buttermilk tenderness, and molassesey dark brown sugar and dried fruit provide the sweetness. I also like to substitute extra-large Monuka raisins, small dried currants, or chopped dark dried figs for the raisins. Since the dough is so dense and a slow riser, I often check the top of the loaf at the end of baking and, if it is too pale, reset and program Bake Only for an additional 7 to 10 minutes of baking. This is a favorite daily bread of mine.*

1½-POUND LOAF

1 cup buttermilk
2 large egg whites, lightly beaten
3 tablespoons canola oil

1½ cups bread flour
1½ cups whole wheat flour
¼ cup rolled oats
¼ cup dark brown sugar
2 tablespoons gluten
1½ teaspoons salt
1¼ teaspoons ground cinnamon
1¼ teaspoons vanilla powder

2½ teaspoons SAF yeast or 1 tablespoon bread machine yeast

½ cup raisins or currants
¼ cup chopped walnuts

2-POUND LOAF

1⅓ cups buttermilk
2 large egg whites, lightly beaten
¼ cup canola oil

2 cups bread flour
2 cups whole wheat flour
⅓ cup rolled oats
⅓ cup dark brown sugar
2½ tablespoons gluten
2 teaspoons salt
1½ teaspoons ground cinnamon
1½ teaspoons vanilla powder

1 tablespoon SAF yeast or 1 tablespoon plus ½ teaspoon bread machine yeast

⅔ cup raisins or currants
⅓ cup chopped walnuts

❶ Place the ingredients, except the fruit and nuts, in the pan according to the order in the manufacturer's instructions. Set crust on dark and program for the Basic or Fruit and Nut cycle; press Start. (This recipe is not suitable for use with the Delay Timer.) When the machine beeps, or between Knead 1 and Knead 2, add the fruit and nuts. Do not be tempted to add more than a tablespoon of extra flour. This is a moist dough ball that will initially look very sticky, especially around the blade. It will transform to tacky by the end of the kneading and be smooth and shiny with the rises.

❷ When the baking cycle ends, immediately remove the bread from the pan and place it on a rack. (See headnote for possible extra baking time.) Let cool to room temperature before slicing.

Bread Machine Baker's Hint: Working with Dried Fruit

Chopping Dried Fruit
Use a knife or kitchen shears to chop or cut fruit into pieces. Spray the knife or shears first with a light coating of vegetable oil cooking spray or rub on some plain vegetable oil using an oil-soaked paper towel. This will prevent the fruit from sticking to the blade.

Measuring Dried Fruit
Lightly pack chopped dried fruit into a dry measuring cup. The fruit should be firm to the touch in the cup. If a weight measure is given, you don't have to use a measuring cup. Just weigh out the amount of fruit you need on your scale, chop it if the recipe instructs, and add it to the dough.

Adding Dried Fruit to a Dough
Toss the dried fruit with a few teaspoons of flour so that when you add it to the dough, it will not clump. When baking in the bread machine, I add the dried fruit in one of two manners. The first is to add the dried fruit at the pause between Knead 1 and Knead 2, just before the dough ball is formed. If there is really a lot of dried fruit to be added, press Pause on the machine after Rise 1. Remove the dough from the pan and place it on a work surface. Pat the dough into a flat rectangle, and sprinkle it with the dried fruit. Knead the dough lightly to distribute the fruit. Return the dough to the pan and press Start to continue the cycle. The dough will continue to rise and bake in the machine with all the dried fruit mixed into it. There is a Fruit and Nut dispenser on some machines. If using the dispenser, you would program the machine at the start for additions. I don't use the dispenser because it has only a ½-cup capacity, and I rarely add that small an amount.

Plumping Dried Fruit
When dried fruit is added to sweet bread doughs or batters, it will not soften further during rising and baking; therefore it is best to soak the fruit in a warm liquid before adding it.

Soak dried fruit for at least one hour before adding it to a dough. This process is referred to as "macerating." You can use water, wine, a liqueur that has a flavor complementary to the bread you are making, or a fruit juice to restore moisture, soften, and add flavor to the dried fruit.

If the fruit is very hard, combine 1 cup of the dried fruit (such as apricots, peaches, figs) with 1 cup of water (or other liquid) in a small saucepan. Bring to a boil. Simmer gently in the liquid for about 10 minutes, or until the fruit is soft. Do not cover the saucepan while plumping the fruit; excess sulfur dioxide, used to preserve color and freshness in dried fruit, needs to evaporate. Let the fruit cool in the liquid. You can also soften fruit in a microwave: Combine the fruit and liquid in a microwave-proof bowl. Cover and microwave on high for 3 minutes. Stir. If still hard, microwave another minute. Let stand for 2 minutes before uncovering. Let cool and chop.

GREEK CURRANT BREAD

G reeks use currants, dried from Zante grapes from Corinth, in their raisin breads. This bread is called stafidopsomo in Greece, and has undertones of spices—cinnamon and cloves—and honey, which always show up in Greek sweet breads. The orange-flower water is a nice touch, but optional. Mastika is derived from a tree gum and is a characteristic flavor in Greek breads. It is often difficult to acquire in the United States; the best way may be to have someone bring some back for you from a trip to Greece. Allspice is a fine substitute here.

❶ Place the currants in a small bowl. Add the orange juice, cinnamon stick, cloves, and mastika or allspice. Toss to combine. Cover and let stand at room temperature for 1 hour. The currants will be soft and plump. Remove and discard the cinnamon stick and cloves.

❷ Drain and reserve any extra orange juice from the currants. Add to the juice enough water to equal 2 tablespoons if you are making the 1½-pound loaf or 3 tablespoons if you are making the 2-pound loaf.

❸ Place the ingredients, except the currants, in the pan according to the order in the manufacturer's instructions, adding the juice and water mixture

1½-POUND LOAF	2-POUND LOAF
1¼ cups currants	1⅓ cups currants
3 tablespoons orange juice	¼ cup orange juice
One 2-inch piece cinnamon stick	One 2-inch piece cinnamon stick
2 whole cloves	2 whole cloves
Pinch of ground mastika or allspice	Pinch of ground mastika or allspice
1 cup evaporated milk	1⅛ cups plus 1 tablespoon evaporated milk
1½ teaspoons orange-flower water	2 teaspoons orange-flower water
3 tablespoons honey	¼ cup honey
3 cups bread flour	4 cups bread flour
1 tablespoon gluten	1 tablespoon plus 1 teaspoon gluten
1½ teaspoons salt	2 teaspoons salt
2 teaspoons SAF yeast or 2½ teaspoons bread machine yeast	2½ teaspoons SAF yeast or 1 tablespoon bread machine yeast

with the liquid ingredients. Set crust on medium and program for the Sweet Bread or Fruit and Nut cycle; press Start. (This recipe is not suitable for use with the Delay Timer.) When the machine beeps, or between Knead 1 and Knead 2, add the currants.

4 When the baking cycle ends, immediately remove the bread from the pan and place it on a rack. Let cool to room temperature before slicing.

Bread Machine Baker's Hint: Yeast and the Dark Sweet Spices

Spices are considered condiments, cherished for their flavor rather than their nourishing qualities. Spices have been used since ancient times, but were once quite rare. Without spices, the world of sweet breads would be dull indeed.

The delicious dark sweet spices that find a comfortable home in bread baking include cinnamon, cloves, nutmeg, mace, cardamom, and pepper—all aromatic products of tropical plants. The plants that produce these essences and oils have been treasured since the time of the Egyptians, not only for their ability to elevate baking from the simple to the sublime, but for their medicinal remedies and perfumes as well.

Every so often I will bake a loaf of sweet bread laden with some of these spices and lo and behold, I end up with a flat loaf. It turns out that these spices have marked antiseptic and antimycotic properties from the active ingredients in their volatile oils that can inhibit, or even completely destroy, the action of the yeast. The oils are what give spices their particular flavor and aroma. In these recipes, there should be plenty of yeast and eggs for leavening, the dough should be pliable and rise easily, there should not be too many added heavy ingredients—such as nuts or dried fruit—to weigh down the delicate doughs, and the spices should be used in small enough quantities that the breads turn out perfect. But if you are troubleshooting a less-than-perfect loaf, you may want to look at how much of these spices are in your bread and cut back a bit, or add them after the second rise in a sugary swirl.

Though it is not a dark, sweet spice, I should mention ginger here, which is at the other end of the spectrum. Powdered ginger has the opposite effect in yeast breads. The yeast loves the ginger. It turns up often in recipes, with a pinch added to encourage the yeast's activity.

PRUNE AND POPPY SEED BREAD

T he combination of sweet prunes and aromatic poppy seeds is a surprise at first. But one bite and you will be hooked; it is a compatible taste pairing. Poppy seeds are grown extensively in the alpine areas of Central Europe and grace breads and coffee cakes from Vienna to Russia. They add a nutty, crunchy quality to this great breakfast bread.

1 Place the ingredients, except the prunes, in the pan according to the order in the manufacturer's instructions. Set crust on medium and program for the Basic or Fruit and Nut cycle; press Start. (This recipe is not suitable for use with the Delay Timer.) When the machine beeps, or between Knead 1 and Knead 2, add the prunes.

2 When the baking cycle ends, immediately remove the bread from the pan and place it on a rack. Let cool to room temperature before slicing.

1½-POUND LOAF	2-POUND LOAF
½ cup milk	⅔ cup milk
⅓ cup water	½ cup water
2 tablespoons unsalted butter, cut into pieces	3 tablespoons unsalted butter, cut into pieces
1 large egg	1 large egg
2 cups bread flour	3 cups bread flour
1 cup whole wheat pastry flour	1 cup whole wheat pastry flour
¼ cup poppy seeds	¼ cup plus 1 tablespoon poppy seeds
2 tablespoons sugar	3 tablespoons sugar
Grated zest of 1 lemon	Grated zest of 1 lemon
1 tablespoon gluten	1 tablespoon plus 1 teaspoon gluten
1½ teaspoons salt	2 teaspoons salt
2 teaspoons SAF yeast or 2½ teaspoons bread machine yeast	2½ teaspoons SAF yeast or 1 tablespoon bread machine yeast
½ cup chopped pitted prunes	¾ cup chopped pitted prunes

CRANBERRY-GOLDEN RAISIN BREAD WITH CARDAMOM

Scandinavian raisin breads always have a favorite spice added—cardamom. It is surprising that a spice that is native to the Malabar coast of India is so ingrained in a baking tradition so far away from where it is grown. Cardamom was popular in the time of the early Greeks and Romans, perfuming many of their honey breads. It is the third most costly spice, after saffron and vanilla. You can crush your own cardamom seeds between sheets of waxed paper with a rolling pin. For this recipe, you can also add the fruit at the beginning of the cycle, if you wish.

1 Place the ingredients, except the fruit, in the pan according to the order in the manufacturer's instructions. Set crust on light and program for the Sweet Bread or Fruit and Nut cycle; press Start. (This recipe is not suitable for use with the Delay Timer.) When the machine beeps, or between Knead 1 and Knead 2, add the fruit.

2 When the baking cycle ends, immediately remove the bread from the pan and place it on a rack. Let cool to room temperature before slicing.

1½-POUND LOAF	2-POUND LOAF
1¼ cups water	1⅔ cups water
2 tablespoons unsalted butter, melted	2½ tablespoons unsalted butter, melted
2 tablespoons light brown sugar	3 tablespoons light brown sugar
3 cups bread flour	4 cups bread flour
¼ cup nonfat dry milk	⅓ cup nonfat dry milk
1 tablespoon gluten	1 tablespoon plus 2 teaspoons gluten
1½ teaspoons salt	2 teaspoons salt
1 teaspoon ground cardamom	1¼ teaspoons ground cardamom
2 teaspoons SAF yeast or 2½ teaspoons bread machine yeast	2½ teaspoons SAF yeast or 1 tablespoon bread machine yeast
⅔ cup golden raisins	¾ cup golden raisins
⅔ cup dried cranberries	¾ cup dried cranberries

BANANA OATMEAL BREAD WITH MACADAMIA NUTS

T his bread was created for my sister Meg, who once had such a loaf from a bakery in Seattle. "Not too sweet," she demanded as she described it. "The bananas, macadamias, oats, and whole wheat flour are perfect together." I call for salted macadamias since they are so readily available vacuum-packed. If you use unsalted macadamia nuts, be sure to add an extra ½ teaspoon of salt or the bread will taste flat. Chop the nuts with a knife, as they are quite oily and will clump if chopped in a food processor. This is definitely a bread for toasting.

1½-POUND LOAF	2-POUND LOAF
1 cup milk	1⅓ cups milk
2 tablespoons unsalted butter, cut into pieces	3 tablespoons unsalted butter, cut into pieces
One 6-ounce banana, sliced (¾ to ⅞ cup)	One 8-ounce banana, sliced (1 to 1⅛ cups)
2 cups bread flour	2½ cups bread flour
1 cup whole wheat pastry flour	1½ cups whole wheat pastry flour
⅔ cups rolled oats	¾ cup rolled oats
2 tablespoons sugar	3 tablespoons sugar
1 tablespoon gluten	1 tablespoon plus 1 teaspoon gluten
1 teaspoon salt	1¼ teaspoons salt
2¼ teaspoons SAF yeast or 2¾ teaspoons bread machine yeast	1 tablespoon SAF yeast or 1 tablespoon plus ½ teaspoon bread machine yeast
⅓ cup chopped salted macadamia nuts	½ cup chopped salted macadamia nuts

❶ Place the ingredients, except the nuts, in the pan according to the order in the manufacturer's instructions. Set crust on medium and program for the Sweet Bread or Fruit and Nut cycle; press Start. (This recipe is not suitable for use with the Delay Timer.) When the machine beeps, or between Knead 1 and Knead 2, add the macadamia nuts.

❷ When the baking cycle ends, immediately remove the bread from the pan and place it on a rack. Let cool to room temperature before slicing.

ORANGE BREAD WITH WHITE CHOCOLATE, APRICOTS, AND WALNUTS

T*he combination of white chocolate, apricots, and walnuts is one of my favorites. It is paired here with a distinctly orange dough to make a superb breakfast bread. The mandarin oranges break up during kneading and give the dough the liquid it needs. This bread is very cakelike, so remove it gently from the pan after baking and let it cool completely before slicing.*

❶ Place the ingredients, except the white chocolate chips, apricots, and walnuts, in the pan according to the order in the manufacturer's instructions. Set crust on medium and program for the Basic or Sweet Bread cycle; press Start. (This recipe is not suitable for use with the Delay Timer.) The dough ball will initially look dry; do not be tempted to add more liquid. When the machine beeps, or between Knead 1 and Knead 2, add the chips, apricots, and walnuts.

❷ When the baking cycle ends, immediately remove the bread from the pan and place it on a rack. Let cool to room temperature before slicing.

1½-POUND LOAF	2-POUND LOAF
1½ cups mandarin orange segments (one and three-fourths 11-ounce cans), liquid reserved	1¾ cups mandarin orange segments (two 11-ounce cans), liquid reserved
2 tablespoons reserved orange liquid or orange liqueur	3 tablespoons reserved orange liquid or orange liqueur
3 tablespoons unsalted butter, cut into pieces	4 tablespoons unsalted butter, cut into pieces
3 cups bread flour	4 cups bread flour
¼ cup sugar	⅓ cup sugar
2 teaspoons gluten	1 tablespoon gluten
1½ teaspoons salt	2 teaspoons salt
2 teaspoons SAF yeast or 2½ teaspoons bread machine yeast	2¼ teaspoons SAF yeast or 2¾ teaspoons bread machine yeast
½ cup white chocolate chips	⅔ cup white chocolate chips
⅓ cup minced dried apricots	½ cup minced dried apricots
⅓ cup chopped walnuts	½ cup chopped walnuts

CINNAMON-APPLE-PECAN BREAD

G et ready to put your nose right up to this warm loaf and breathe in deep; it is so fantastically ambrosial. In place of dried apples, you can use pre-chopped apple nuggets. My recipe testers and I ended up liking this bread with lots of cinnamon. This is the ultimate breakfast bread.

❶ Place the ingredients, except the apples and pecans, in the pan according to the order in the manufacturer's instructions. Set crust on medium and program for the Basic or Fruit and Nut cycle; press Start. (This recipe is not suitable for use with the Delay Timer.) When the machine beeps, or between Knead 1 and Knead 2, add the apples and pecans.

❷ When the baking cycle ends, immediately remove the bread from the pan and place it on a rack. Let cool to room temperature before slicing.

1½-POUND LOAF	2-POUND LOAF
1⅛ cups buttermilk	1½ cups buttermilk
2 tablespoons walnut oil	2½ tablespoons walnut oil
3 cups bread flour	4 cups bread flour
3 tablespoons light brown sugar	¼ cup light brown sugar
1 tablespoon gluten	1 tablespoon plus 1 teaspoon gluten
1¼ teaspoons salt	1½ teaspoons salt
1 tablespoon ground cinnamon	1⅓ tablespoons ground cinnamon
2 teaspoons SAF yeast or 2½ teaspoons bread machine yeast	2½ teaspoons SAF yeast or 1 tablespoon bread machine yeast
½ cup chopped dried apples	⅔ cup chopped dried apples
⅓ cup chopped pecans	½ cup chopped pecans

Technique: How to Store, Toast, Grind, or Blanch Nuts

Nuts come in their own protective wrapping with naturally built-in nutrition and nourishment. They add unique character and flavor to sweet bread doughs and batters as their high percentage of natural fat is absorbed into the bread dough during baking. Use raw or toasted nut pieces or ground nuts in both sweet and savory loaves. Almonds and hazelnuts have thin skins that can be removed. Store all shelled nuts in the refrigerator (for up to 9 months) or in the freezer (for no longer than 2 years), as they turn rancid quickly.

Toasting

Toasting nuts gives them a more pronounced fragrance and flavor and a crisper texture. These are the methods for toasting raw pine nuts, almonds (whole, blanched, slivered, or sliced), walnuts, edible whole acorns, or pecans (whole or pieces). Slivered or sliced nuts and pine nuts will toast much quicker than nut pieces or halves.

- **In a conventional oven**—Preheat the oven to 325°F. Place the nuts on an ungreased baking sheet, and bake on the center rack of the oven for 8 to 12 minutes, depending on the size, stirring once. When the nuts are toasted they will be hot and very pale golden. Do not let the nuts turn dark, or they will taste burnt. Remove the nuts from the oven and cool to room temperature before using in a bread dough.

- **In the microwave oven**—Place the nuts in a single layer on a shallow paper plate or double layer of paper towels. Toast the nuts on high power for about 4 minutes per ½ cup, stirring every 1 to 2 minutes to prevent burning and to facilitate even browning. This method toasts nuts very quickly, so watch carefully.

- **In a skillet**—When a recipe calls for ¼ cup or less of toasted nuts, they can be toasted in a heavy skillet on the stovetop. Place whole or chopped nuts in a dry skillet over low heat. Stir constantly or shake the pan until the nuts are slightly colored and aromatic, 2 to 4 minutes. Remove from the pan to cool.

Grinding

Ground nuts are used in breads as a replacement for part of the flour. Grind nuts in a European-style hand nut grater, an electric blender, or a food processor. Be sure the nuts are dry before grinding. Add 1 to 2 tablespoons of sugar or flour during grinding, to absorb the nut oil and prevent the formation of a paste. Grind, blend, or process the nuts until very fine. Properly ground nuts have a powdery, fluffy quality. Lightly spoon the nut flour into a measuring cup.

Blanching

Almonds may be blanched to remove their skins. Fill a medium saucepan three-quarters full of water and bring to a boil. Add the whole shelled almonds and remove the pan from the heat. Let stand 3 minutes. Immediately rinse the nuts under cold running water. Squeeze the nut kernel out of its loosened brown layer of skin by holding the nut between your thumb and index finger and pressing. Let the nuts dry on a layer of paper towels for at least 2 hours. (I usually buy almonds already blanched and slivered; it is a lot easier than blanching them myself.)

CRANBERRY-PUMPKIN BREAD

T*his is a nice sweet bread for fall. Although canned pumpkin is just fine, you can make your own pumpkin puree from a Sugar Pie or Blue Hubbard winter squash. Jack-o'-lantern pumpkins are not for baking, as their flesh is watery and tasteless. If you wish to gild the loaf, drizzle it with Confectioners' Sugar Icing (page 449).*

1 Sprinkle the dried cranberries with the brandy in a small bowl. Cover with plastic wrap and let stand at room temperature for 1 hour to macerate.

2 Place the ingredients, except the cranberries, in the pan according to the order in the manufacturer's instructions. Set crust on medium and program for the Sweet Bread cycle; press Start. (This recipe is not suitable for use with the Delay Timer.) When the machine beeps, or between Knead 1 and Knead 2, add the cranberries and any extra brandy in the bowl.

3 When the baking cycle ends, immediately remove the bread from the pan and place it on a rack. Let cool to room temperature before slicing.

1½-POUND LOAF	2-POUND LOAF
⅔ cup dried cranberries	1 cup dried cranberries
2 tablespoons brandy	3 tablespoons brandy
⅔ cup water	1 cup water
⅓ cup pumpkin puree	½ cup pumpkin puree
2 tablespoons nut oil	3 tablespoons nut oil
3 cups bread flour	4 cups bread flour
3 tablespoons light brown sugar	¼ cup light brown sugar
2 tablespoons dry buttermilk powder	3 tablespoons dry buttermilk powder
1 tablespoon gluten	1 tablespoon plus 1 teaspoon gluten
1½ teaspoons salt	2 teaspoons salt
1½ teaspoons pumpkin or apple pie spice	1¾ teaspoons pumpkin or apple pie spice
2 teaspoons SAF yeast or 2½ teaspoons bread machine yeast	2½ teaspoons SAF yeast or 1 tablespoon bread machine yeast

Confectioners' Sugar Icing

Makes enough for 1 braid, one 1½- or 2-pound loaf,
1 dozen cinnamon rolls, or a coffee cake

This is the elementary white sugar glaze that tops any sweet or holiday bread, or turns an otherwise savory bread into a sweet treat. The glaze can be embellished in many ways—this is where to use all those wonderful flavor extracts and citrus oils. Choose a flavor for your icing that complements the ingredients in the bread, for example, add cream sherry to icing for Toasted Walnut Bread (page 322) or Frangelico to icing for Old-Fashioned Raisin Bread (page 437) or Sour Cream Bread (page 53). You can even glaze a homemade white bread and stud the top of the loaf with nuts for a special presentation. You will use this recipe over and over, and for good reason. You'll want to lick the spoon, it is so delicious.

¾ cup sifted confectioners' sugar
1 to 1½ tablespoons warm milk
1 teaspoon butter, softened
1 teaspoon vanilla extract or other flavoring

❶ Whisk the ingredients together in a small bowl until smooth. Adjust the consistency of the glaze by adding more milk, a few drops at a time.

❷ Remove the bread from the machine and place it on a rack with a sheet of parchment paper or a large plate underneath. Using an oversized spoon, drizzle or pour the glaze over the top of the loaf in a back and forth motion. As the glaze cools, it will set.

V A R I A T I O N S

Intense Vanilla: Add 1 teaspoon vanilla powder to the confectioners' sugar and add ½ teaspoon ground vanilla beans along with the vanilla extract.

Almond: Substitute 1 teaspoon almond extract for the vanilla.

Anise: Substitute 1 teaspoon anise extract for the vanilla.

Lemon: Substitute 1 teaspoon lemon oil or extract or 1 teaspoon fresh lemon juice for the vanilla.

Orange: Substitute fresh orange juice or thawed frozen concentrate for the milk.

Mocha: Substitute 1 teaspoon liquid coffee extract for the vanilla.

Coconut: Substitute 1 teaspoon coconut extract for the vanilla.

Sweet Spice: Add ½ teaspoon ground cinnamon, cardamom, mace, or nutmeg.

Frangelico or Amaretto: Substitute the liqueur for the milk.

Cream Sherry: Substitute the sherry for the milk.

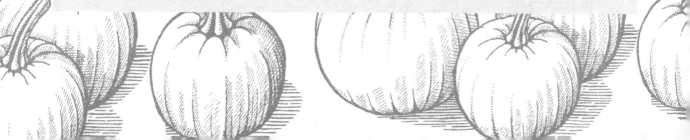

ORANGE-CINNAMON BREAD

T he cinnamon tree is native to Sri Lanka and to China, where it is called cassia. Long ago the bark was gathered in the wild by natives and sold to Arab seatraders. The strips of bark are dried in the sun, then rolled and further dried to the characteristic color. The first cinnamon plantation was planted in 1765 by the Dutch, producing enough cinnamon for kitchens around the world to have some cinnamon in them. This special sweet loaf is always exceptionally popular. Serve it plain, sprinkled with confectioners' sugar, or drizzled with the vanilla-orange glaze, reminiscent of an old-fashioned frozen Creamsicle.

1½-POUND LOAF

For the dough:

½ cup orange juice
⅓ cup milk
1 large egg
3 tablespoons unsalted
    butter, cut into pieces

3 cups bread flour
¼ cup sugar
Grated zest of 1 orange
1 tablespoon gluten
2 teaspoons ground
    cinnamon
1¼ teaspoons salt

2 teaspoons SAF yeast
    or 2½ teaspoons bread
    machine yeast

For the vanilla-orange glaze:

¾ cup sifted confectioners'
    sugar
1½ to 2 tablespoons
    orange juice
1 teaspoon vanilla extract

2-POUND LOAF

For the dough:

⅔ cup orange juice
½ cup milk
1 large egg
4 tablespoons unsalted
    butter, cut into pieces

4 cups bread flour
⅓ cup sugar
Grated zest of 1 orange
1 tablespoon plus
    1 teaspoon gluten
2½ teaspoons ground
    cinnamon
1½ teaspoons salt

2¼ teaspoons SAF yeast
    or 2¾ teaspoons bread
    machine yeast

For the vanilla-orange glaze:

¾ cup sifted confectioners'
    sugar
1½ to 2 tablespoons
    orange juice
1 teaspoon vanilla extract

1 To make the dough, place all the dough ingredients in the pan according to the order in the manufacturer's instructions. Set crust on medium and program for the Basic cycle; press Start. (This recipe is not suitable for use with the Delay Timer.)

2 When the baking cycle ends, immediately remove the bread from the pan and place it on a rack. Place a plate or piece of waxed paper under the rack.

❸ To prepare the glaze, combine the confectioners' sugar, orange juice, and vanilla in a small bowl; beat with a small whisk until smooth. With a large spoon, drizzle the bread with the glaze, letting it drip down the sides. Cool to room temperature to set the glaze before slicing.

 Bread Machine Baker's Hint: Crust Control

Most of the recipes in this book call for a medium or normal setting on the crust control, but you must always judge how your machine is functioning; light or dark might be better in some cases. Also, consider the type of loaf you are making: country loaves are good with a dark crust, regular loaf breads are good with a medium or dark crust; sweet breads brown quickly because of the sugar, so use light or medium. Substituting honey, molasses, sugar cane syrup, barley malt syrup, or maple syrup for sugar can make a crust exceptionally dark. Turn down the crust control to light for breads made with these sweeteners. If you think your machine is not functioning the way it should, call the customer service number for your machine (page 5). One of my recipe testers kept getting a crust that was too light, even on the darkest setting, and after inquiring with the manufacturer, was instructed to exchange the machine because it was not performing properly.

PERSIMMON BREAD

T he ancient persimmon tree comes from the mountains of China, and has migrated to countries like Italy, France, and America. Persimmons, also known as kaki fruit, are an exciting bright orange fall fruit, hanging on their leafless trees long after the fruits of summer have disappeared. The two varieties for eating are the tomato-shaped Fuyu and the globular Hachiya. The Fuyu, when ripe, is crisp like an apple and eaten raw, but the Hachiya becomes jelly-like in consistency, perfect for baking. While used mostly in quick breads, the persimmon makes a beautiful, delicious addition to yeast breads. It is moist and spicy. You can add the raisins, or leave them out for a perfectly smooth bread.

1½-POUND LOAF	2-POUND LOAF
2 large Hachiya persimmons	2 large Hachiya persimmons
⅔ cup milk	1 cup milk
1 large egg	1 large egg
1 tablespoon amber rum	1½ tablespoons amber rum
2 tablespoons butter, cut into pieces	3 tablespoons butter, cut into pieces
3 cups bread flour	4 cups bread flour
2 tablespoons dark brown sugar	3 tablespoons dark brown sugar
2 teaspoons gluten	1 tablespoon gluten
1½ teaspoons apple pie spice	2 teaspoons apple pie spice
1½ teaspoons salt	2 teaspoons salt
2 teaspoons SAF yeast or 2½ teaspoons bread machine yeast	2½ teaspoons SAF yeast or 1 tablespoon bread machine yeast
⅔ cup golden raisins	⅞ cup golden raisins

❶ Cut the soft persimmons in half and scoop out the inner flesh with a large spoon. Measure out and reserve ⅔ cup for the 1½-pound loaf or ¾ cup for the 2-pound loaf. (See Note.)

❷ Place the ingredients, except the raisins, in the pan according to the order in the manufacturer's instructions, adding the reserved persimmon pulp with the liquid ingredients. Set crust on dark and program for the Basic or Fruit and Nut cycle; press Start. (This recipe is not suitable for use with the Delay Timer.) When the machine beeps, or between Knead 1 and

Knead 2, add the raisins. The dough ball will be soft and springy.

❸ When the baking cycle ends, immediately remove the bread from the pan and place it on a rack. Let cool to room temperature before slicing. The bread is very tender, so be sure not to cut it before it cools.

NOTE:
Use the persimmon pulp at once, or add some fresh lemon juice and store it in the refrigerator for up to 2 days. Persimmons can be frozen whole, then defrosted before being scooped out. One large ripe Hachiya persimmon yields about ½ to ¾ cup pulp.

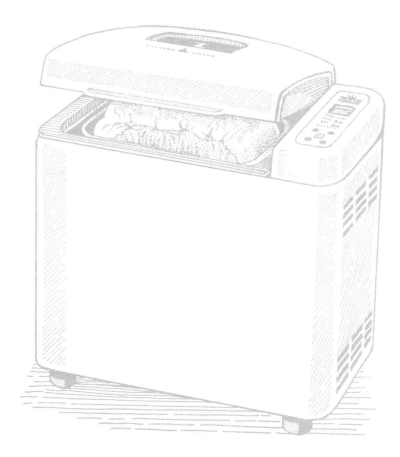

ITALIAN LEMON-RICOTTA BREAD

T he beautiful, evocative flavors of Italy are in this delicate sweet bread—lemon, anise, walnuts, and raisins. Anise is a favorite kitchen garden flavor that has been used in breads since antiquity. If you are not familiar with it, take a deep breath of Pernod liqueur and you will experience its fragrance. Serve this bread toasted for dessert or as an incredible French toast for breakfast.

1 Place all the ingredients in the pan according to the order in the manufacturer's instructions. Set crust on medium and program for the Basic cycle; press Start. (This recipe is not suitable for use with the Delay Timer.)

2 When the baking cycle ends, immediately remove the bread from the pan and place it on a rack. Let cool to room temperature before slicing.

1½-POUND LOAF
⅓ cup milk
⅔ cup ricotta cheese
2 large egg yolks
1½ teaspoons anise extract
7 tablespoons unsalted butter, cut into pieces
3 cups bread flour
⅓ cup walnuts
⅓ cup golden raisins
3 tablespoons sugar
Grated zest of 1 lemon
1 tablespoon gluten
1½ teaspoons salt
2¼ teaspoons SAF yeast or 2¾ teaspoons bread machine yeast

2-POUND LOAF
½ cup milk
¾ cup ricotta cheese
3 large egg yolks
2 teaspoons anise extract
½ cup (1 stick) plus 1 tablespoon unsalted butter, cut into pieces
4 cups bread flour
½ cup walnuts
½ cup golden raisins
3½ tablespoons sugar
Grated zest of 2 lemons
1 tablespoon plus 1 teaspoon gluten
2 teaspoons salt
2½ teaspoons SAF yeast or 1 tablespoon bread machine yeast

PAN D'ANGIOL (BREAD OF THE ANGELS)

I happen to have a passion for anything almond, especially almond paste. Almond paste is a confection made from equal parts almonds and powdered sugar, with glucose, corn syrup, and egg white added as stabilizers. It is a pliable, paste-like super-sweet food, and is readily available in supermarket baking sections. This bread is made with three almond ingredients—crumbled almond paste, almond extract, and the nuts themselves. It is a wonderful sweet bread that doesn't even need butter. It is food from the angels!

1 Place the ingredients, except the cherries and almonds, in the pan according to the order in the manufacturer's instructions. Set crust on medium and program for the Basic or Fruit and Nut cycle; press Start. (This recipe is not suitable for use with the Delay Timer.) When the machine beeps, or between Knead 1 and Knead 2, add the cherries and almonds.

2 When the baking cycle ends, immediately remove the bread from the pan and place it on a rack. Let cool to room temperature before slicing.

1½-POUND LOAF	2-POUND LOAF
1¼ cups milk	1⅓ cups milk
½ teaspoon almond extract	¾ teaspoon almond extract
1 tablespoon butter, cut into pieces	1½ tablespoons butter, cut into pieces
3 tablespoons almond paste, cut into pieces	4 tablespoons almond paste, cut into pieces
3 cups bread flour	4 cups bread flour
3 tablespoons sugar	¼ cup sugar
1 tablespoon gluten	1 tablespoon plus 1 teaspoon gluten
1½ teaspoons salt	2 teaspoons salt
2 teaspoons SAF yeast or 2½ teaspoons bread machine yeast	2½ teaspoons SAF yeast or 1 tablespoon bread machine yeast
½ cup chopped dried sour cherries	⅔ cup chopped dried sour cherries
½ cup slivered blanched almonds	⅓ cup slivered blanched almonds

SPICY PEAR BREAD

Makes 1 loaf

I am surprised so few bakers know about birnenwecken, also sometimes called birnbrot, a delightful Swiss bread made with a dried pear filling. It is a specialty of old Swiss home bakers. Most regions of Switzerland have their own variety with slightly different spices. The filling is encased in a firm dough, which keeps the bread fresh for at least a month. The bread likes to age for a week, but I enjoy it fresh with a glass of wine or mug of hot chocolate.

1 To make the dough, place all the dough ingredients in the pan according to the order in the manufacturer's instructions. Program for the Dough cycle; press Start. The dough ball will be firm, yet pliable.

2 While the dough is rising, make the filling. Combine the wine, kirsch, sugar, zest, and spices in a small saucepan and bring to a boil. Lower heat and add the dried fruit. Simmer, uncovered, for 10 minutes. Remove from the heat, cover, and let stand until room temperature and all of the liquid is absorbed, about 1 hour. Place in a food processor and pulse to make a thick jam that is not totally smooth.

3 Line a baking sheet with parchment paper. To assemble the loaf, when the machine beeps at the end

1½- OR 2-POUND-LOAF MACHINES

For the dough:

¼ cup plus 1 tablespoon milk
¼ cup water
1 large egg
3 tablespoons unsalted butter, partially melted

2½ cups unbleached all-purpose flour
¼ cup sugar
1 teaspoon salt

2 teaspoons SAF yeast or 2½ teaspoons bread machine yeast

For the fruit filling:

¾ cup dry red wine
¼ cup kirsch
¼ cup sugar
Grated zest of 1 lemon
½ teaspoon ground cinnamon
¼ teaspoon fresh-ground nutmeg
8 ounces dried pears, chopped (2 cups)
6 ounces dried figs, stemmed and chopped (1½ cups)
4 ounces pitted prunes (1 heaping cup)
¼ cup raisins

1 egg yolk beaten with 1 tablespoon milk, for glaze

of the cycle, press Stop and unplug the machine. Turn the dough out onto a lightly floured work surface. With a rolling pin, roll out into a 12-by-16-inch rectangle. With a metal spatula, spread the filling evenly over the dough, leaving ½-inch borders on three sides and a 1-inch border on one long side. Beginning at the long edge with the ½-inch border, roll up jelly-roll fashion to make a log. Moisten the 1-inch border with some water and seal. Pinch the bottom seam, leaving the ends open. Press to even the ends. Using the tines of a fork, prick the dough all over. Brush with the egg glaze. Let rest at room temperature, covered loosely with a clean tea towel, until doubled in bulk, about 45 minutes.

4 Twenty minutes before baking, preheat the oven to 350°F.

5 Brush the roll once more with the egg glaze. Bake for 30 to 40 minutes, until golden brown and firm to the touch. Let cool on the baking sheet.

DRIED APRICOT
WHOLE WHEAT BREAD

T his recipe uses fruit juice for the liquid, which ends up being part of the sweetening as well. The bread contains oatmeal and whole wheat flour, so there is also plenty of fiber in every slice. You can vary the juice and dried fruit combination—try orange juice and dried cranberries, pineapple juice and dried pineapple, prune juice and dried prunes, or cherry juice and dried cherries. You can use whatever you have on hand, but not thick nectars in place of the juice.

❶ Place the ingredients, except the apricots, in the pan according to the order in the manufacturer's instructions. Set crust on medium and program for the Whole Wheat or Fruit and Nut cycle; press Start. (This recipe is not suitable for use with the Delay Timer.) When the machine beeps, or between Knead 1 and Knead 2, add the apricots. The dough ball will be soft and moist.

❷ When the baking cycle ends, immediately remove the bread from the pan and place it on a rack. Let cool to room temperature before slicing.

1½-POUND LOAF	2-POUND LOAF
¾ cup apple or pear juice	1 cup apple or pear juice
6 tablespoons water	7 tablespoons water
2 tablespoons honey	2½ tablespoons honey
2 tablespoons nut or vegetable oil	2½ tablespoons nut or vegetable oil
1½ cups bread flour	2⅓ cups bread flour
1 cup whole wheat flour	1 cup whole wheat flour
½ cup rolled oats	⅔ cup rolled oats
1 tablespoon gluten	1 tablespoon plus 1 teaspoon gluten
1¼ teaspoons salt	1½ teaspoons salt
2 teaspoons SAF yeast or 2½ teaspoons bread machine yeast	2½ teaspoons SAF yeast or 1 tablespoon bread machine yeast
½ cup finely chopped dried apricots	⅔ cup finely chopped dried apricots

GRANOLA BREAD

I had my first slice of granola bread twenty-five years ago. My boyfriend's grandmother brought me a loaf from her local market. I toasted every slice, loving the elusive nutty sweetness and the few raisins dotting each slice. After that first loaf, I searched every grocery store for the bread, but never found it again. When I created this bread, I wanted to re-create that loaf from long ago, and I did. Use your favorite granola from the supermarket, or make your own. Granola bread remains one of my favorites.

1 Place all the ingredients in the pan according to the order in the manufacturer's instructions. Set crust on medium and program for the Basic cycle; press Start. (This recipe is not suitable for use with the Delay Timer.)

2 When the baking cycle ends, immediately remove the bread from the pan and place it on a rack. Let cool to room temperature before slicing.

1½-POUND LOAF

1⅛ cups buttermilk
2 tablespoons vegetable oil
2 tablespoons honey

2⅛ cups bread flour
¾ cup whole wheat flour
1¼ cups granola
1 tablespoon gluten
1½ teaspoons salt
1 teaspoon ground cinnamon

2 teaspoons SAF yeast or 2½ teaspoons bread machine yeast

2-POUND LOAF

1½ cups buttermilk
3 tablespoons vegetable oil
3 tablespoons honey

2¾ cups bread flour
1 cup whole wheat flour
1⅓ cups granola
1 tablespoon plus 1 teaspoon gluten
2 teaspoons salt
1½ teaspoons ground cinnamon

2½ teaspoons SAF yeast or 1 tablespoon bread machine yeast

COFFEE CAKES AND SWEET ROLLS

While even the simplest homemade bread is a treat, rich, sweet, beautifully shaped coffee cakes and sweet rolls are yeast baking's contribution to making breakfast special. They are perfect when the occasion calls for something festive and showy. Some of these recipes are also homey baking at its best; all the bakers I know want to make caramel-coated morning buns and streusel-crumb-topped coffee cakes soon after making their first loaf of bread. Coffee cakes and rolls have appeal for both novice and experienced bakers, who will enjoy making these simple but delicious recipes over and over. There is as great a pleasure in making these breads as there is in eating them. They are impressive, delectable, and eye-catching.

Coffee cakes and sweet rolls are constructed from doughs much like any bread dough, but usually contain more sugar, eggs, and butter to produce a softer dough that bakes up more cakelike in texture. What makes sweet rolls and coffee cakes special is their shape, which is usually determined by the special pans they are baked in. Old-fashioned names like *kugelhopf*, coffee rings and wreaths, brioche, and *babka* all find their places here. There is often the addition of sweet and sour cream, fruit, and nuts to these doughs. These are the imaginative elements that contribute to their reputation for being fancy. These breads may be made on the Basic or Sweet Bread cycle, if baked in the machine, or mixed on the Dough cycle and removed to be filled and formed before being baked in the oven. There may be a special frosting or soft crumb top adorning the dough.

These sweet breads are good on their own without butter or jam. Turned out after baking, they are ready to be served without any further fuss, accompanied by just a bit of warmth left over from the baking.

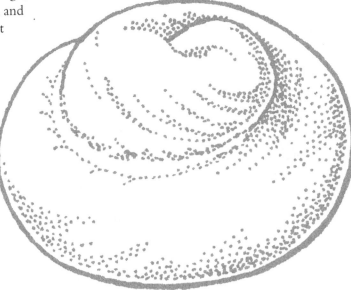

CINNABUN COFFEE CAKE

Makes one 13-by-9-inch coffee cake, serves 6

T*his is a coffee cake with all the flavors of a cinnamon bun, but conveniently made in a cake shape for ease. It is topped with light oat and nut crumbs, and tastes best warm from the oven or reheated.*

1 To make the dough, place all the dough ingredients in the pan according to the order in the manufacturer's instructions. Program for the Dough cycle; press Start. The dough will be soft and sticky, like a thick batter. Don't add any extra flour.

2 While the Dough cycle is running, prepare the topping. Combine the flour, sugar, oats, pecans, and cinnamon in a small bowl. Rub the butter in with your fingers to make clumped crumbs. You can also do this quickly in a food processor.

3 Grease a 13-by-9-inch metal or Pyrex baking dish. When the machine beeps at the end of the cycle, press Stop and unplug the machine. With a large rubber spatula, scrape the batter into the pan. Using floured fingers, spread the batter evenly to fill the pan to the edges. Sprinkle with the topping. Cover loosely with plastic wrap and let rest at room temperature for 30 minutes.

4 Meanwhile, preheat the oven to 375°F (350°F if using a glass pan).

5 Bake for 20 to 25 minutes, or until the edges are golden brown and a cake tester inserted into the center comes out clean. Place the pan on a wire rack and prepare the icing. With a large spoon, drizzle the top in a back-and-forth pattern. Serve warm, out of the pan.

1½- OR 2-POUND-LOAF MACHINES

For the dough:

⅞ cup milk
1½ teaspoons vanilla extract
1 large egg yolk
2 tablespoons unsalted butter, cut into pieces

2¼ cups unbleached all-purpose flour
¼ cup sugar
1 teaspoon salt

2 teaspoons SAF yeast or 2½ teaspoons bread machine yeast

For the oat crumb topping:

¾ cup unbleached all-purpose flour
¾ cup light brown sugar
½ cup rolled oats
½ cup chopped pecans
1½ teaspoons ground cinnamon or apple pie spice
½ cup (1 stick) unsalted butter, at room temperature

Confectioners' Sugar Icing (page 449)

SWEET BABKA WITH CHOCOLATE SWIRL

Makes 2 loaves

1½-POUND LOAF

For the dough:

1¼ cups water
2 tablespoons unsalted
    butter, cut into pieces

3 cups bread flour
⅓ cup nonfat dry milk
2 tablespoons sugar
1½ teaspoons salt

2 teaspoons SAF yeast
    or 2½ teaspoons bread
    machine yeast

For the chocolate prune swirl:

¾ cup semisweet chocolate
    chips
¾ cup snipped dried prunes
¼ cup chopped walnuts

OR

For the chocolate spice swirl:

⅔ cup sugar
2½ tablespoons
    unsweetened Dutch-
    process cocoa powder
2 teaspoons ground
    cinnamon

Plain or vanilla (see page
    513) confectioners' sugar,
    for dusting, optional

T*he word* babka *is the Polish word for grandmother, as well as the name of this sweet bread. Usually baked in a fluted round mold with a center tube, the loaves were said to resemble a woman's full skirt of centuries past. This recipe is baked in a loaf pan. One basic dough is used to create two different and delightful swirled breakfast creations—choose the filling you like. The dough is removed from the machine, stuffed and rolled up, and baked in the oven. I keep a stash of disposable aluminum loaf pans, available in any supermarket, on hand for baking sweet breads. The breads bake beautifully in them, and if any of the sweet filling leaks out, it doesn't stick.* Babka *is a traditional Easter coffee bread.*

1 Place all the dough ingredients in the pan according to the order in the manufacturer's instructions. Program for the Dough cycle; press Start. The dough ball will be soft.

2 Grease two 7-by-3-inch loaf pans (for the 1½-pound loaf) or two 8-by-4-inch loaf pans (for the 2-pound loaf). Combine the dry ingredients for the swirl filling you have chosen in a small bowl.

3 When the machine beeps at the end of the cycle, press Stop and unplug the machine. Turn the dough out onto a lightly floured work surface. Divide the dough in half. Pat each piece into a 10-by-14-inch rectangle. Brush each lightly with some melted butter. Sprinkle each with half of the filling, leaving a 1-inch space all the way around. Starting at a short edge, roll up jelly-roll fashion. Tuck the ends under and pinch the bottom seams.

4 Place the loaves seam side down in the pans. Spray the tops lightly with cooking spray and cover lightly with plastic wrap. Let rise at room temperature until doubled in bulk, about 45 minutes.

5 Twenty minutes before baking, preheat the oven to 350°F.

6 Bake the loaves for 30 to 40 minutes, or until golden brown and the sides have contracted slightly from the pan. Cool on a rack and dust with plain or vanilla powdered sugar, if desired.

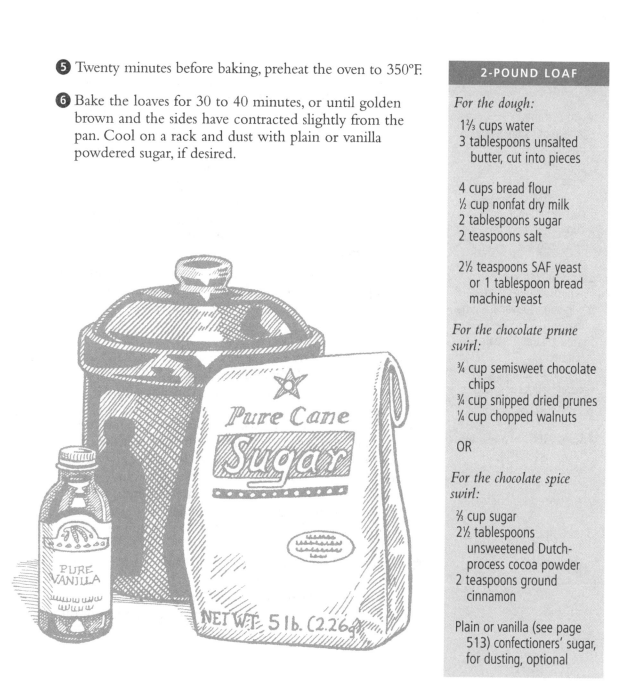

2-POUND LOAF

For the dough:

1⅔ cups water
3 tablespoons unsalted
butter, cut into pieces

4 cups bread flour
½ cup nonfat dry milk
2 tablespoons sugar
2 teaspoons salt

2½ teaspoons SAF yeast
or 1 tablespoon bread
machine yeast

For the chocolate prune swirl:

¾ cup semisweet chocolate
chips
¾ cup snipped dried prunes
¼ cup chopped walnuts

OR

For the chocolate spice swirl:

⅔ cup sugar
2½ tablespoons
unsweetened Dutch-
process cocoa powder
2 teaspoons ground
cinnamon

Plain or vanilla (see page
513) confectioners' sugar,
for dusting, optional

ALSATIAN KUGELHOPF

Makes 1 large or 2 small tube cakes

1½- OR 2-POUND-LOAF MACHINES

½ cup currants
2 tablespoons golden raisins
¼ cup Gewürztraminer wine

⅔ cup whole milk
¼ cup water
2 large eggs

3 cups unbleached all-purpose flour
¼ cup sugar or vanilla sugar (page 513)
Grated zest of 1 small lemon
1 teaspoon salt
½ cup (1 stick) unsalted butter, cut into pieces

2 teaspoons SAF yeast or 2½ teaspoons bread machine yeast

⅓ cup sliced almonds

3 tablespoons confectioners' sugar, for dusting

*M*y grandfather was born in Strasbourg, Alsace, when it was still part of Germany. Kugelhopf is the bread most associated with the area, similar to brioche because the same technique is used to make it, but a bit coarser and drier in texture. It is said to have been invented in Vienna, where it is a coffeehouse favorite known as gugelhugf. Marie Antoinette favored it, making it fashionable in eighteenth-century Paris. The famed Carême, her pâtissier royal, learned his recipe from the chef to the Austrian ambassador. Kugelhopf is baked outside of the machine in a fluted tube pan; this one is baked in a pan with a nine-cup capacity, which is smaller than the traditional swirled Turk's Head tube pan. Soak the raisins and currants in the wine of Alsace, Gewürztraminer, the wine that smells sweet yet tastes dry. Kugelhopf is never served the day it is baked, but sits overnight to age to the right texture. Serve it with sweet butter.

❶ Place the currants and raisins in a small bowl and cover with the wine. Macerate for at least an hour at room temperature. Drain the fruit, reserving any liquid.

❷ Place the ingredients, except the currants, raisins, and almonds, in the pan according to the order in the manufacturer's instructions. Program for the Dough cycle; press Start. (I set the machine for the 1-pound loaf since it has the shortest Knead phase.) Five minutes into the kneading segment, press Pause and add the currants and raisins and the almonds. Press Start to resume the cycle.

❸ Generously grease a 9-cup fluted tube pan or two 4½-cup kugelhopf molds. When the machine beeps at the end of the cycle, press Stop and unplug the machine. Set a kitchen timer for 1 hour and let the dough rest in the machine. When the timer rings, remove the dough and scrape into the tube pan with a rubber spatula, filling it no more than two-thirds full. Cover with plastic wrap and place a tea towel on top. Let rise at room temperature until the dough is almost to the top of the mold, about 1 hour.

4 Twenty minutes before baking, preheat the oven to 350°F (lower the temperature by 25° if using a pan with a dark finish).

5 Remove the towel and wrap from the mold and bake for about 35 to 40 minutes (the small pans bake for 28 to 32 minutes), until browned and the sides have pulled away from the pan. A cake tester inserted into the center will come out clean. Invert onto a rack. While still warm, drizzle the reserved soaking liquid into the center of the cake. Let cool completely. Wrap in foil to store at room temperature for 1 to 2 days. Dust with confectioners' sugar before serving.

APPLE CHALLAH

Makes 1 braided loaf

For the dough:

¾ cup water
2 large eggs
3 tablespoons vegetable oil

3 cups bread flour
3 tablespoons sugar
½ teaspoons salt

2 teaspoons SAF yeast
or 2½ teaspoons bread
machine yeast

For the apple filling:

3 medium tart baking
apples, peeled, cored,
and diced
Juice of 1 lemon
2 tablespoons honey
½ teaspoon ground
cinnamon

2 tablespoons granulated
or pearl sugar, for
sprinkling

C hallah is a traditional Jewish egg bread that has no peer as far as I am concerned, because of its delicate cakelike texture. This nondairy version makes a traditional stuffed braided apple and honey bread suitable for Rosh Hashanah. Some bakers like to use two or three different types of apples in their fillings, rather than just one, for different flavors and textures. This loaf is baked in the oven.

❶ To make the dough, place all the dough ingredients in the pan according to the order in the manufacturer's instructions. Program for the Dough cycle; press Start.

❷ To prepare the filling, combine the apples with the lemon juice, honey, and cinnamon in a medium bowl. Toss to coat evenly. Cover with plastic wrap and chill until filling the dough. Drain before using.

❸ When the machine beeps at the end of the cycle, press Stop and unplug the machine. Turn the dough out onto a lightly floured work surface. Divide it into 3 equal portions. Roll each portion into a 12-by-3-inch rectangle. Brush with some melted butter and place ⅓ of the filling down the center of each strip. Starting from a long edge, roll up each rectangle jelly-roll fashion, and pinch the seam to seal.

❹ Line a baking sheet with parchment paper. Place the 3 ropes parallel to each other and begin braiding, alternating the outside ropes over the center. Place the challah on the baking sheet. Sprinkle the top with sugar and cover lightly with plastic wrap. Let rise at room temperature until doubled in bulk, 45 minutes to 1 hour.

5 Fifteen minutes before baking, preheat the oven to 350°F.

6 Bake for 35 to 40 minutes, or until golden brown. Cool on a rack.

The Baker's Glossary of Sugars and Other Sweeteners

Sugar has been a coveted ingredient for centuries. Sugarcane is native to the South Pacific island of New Guinea, from there it spread to India, and then to the Middle East with the mariner spice trade. The ever ingenious Arabian apothecaries were the first to refine sugar in 700 A.D. It was then shipped to Venice, and the wealthy and the royal had an alternative sweetener to honey. It became an important ingredient in chocolate and coffee drinks in the coffeehouse explosion of the 1600s and has been popular ever since.

Ordinary sugar is pure sucrose and is the most common sweetener in baking. It is soluble in water (but insoluble in alcohol, so it makes a nice crystallized layer of glaze when mixed with some tasty liqueur), enhances other flavors, and gives a rich dark golden brown color from caramelization. Sugar competes with starch and gluten for moisture in flour and relaxes gluten, so the crumb is finer. This is why you get a moist, tender, delicately flavored loaf. Sugar also helps keep a loaf fresh. The type of sugar you use will add to the flavor of your bread. Here is a list to help you distinguish among the types available.

Granulated sugar refers to ordinary white sugar and the standard-size sugar crystal. When I call for sugar in an ingredient list, this is the sugar I mean. Use it in syrups and breads with lots of liquid. It can be made from sugarcane or beets. Bacteria cannot grow in sugar, so it is commonly used in preserving.

Superfine sugar is sold in 1-pound boxes and has the smallest crystal of any sugar. It is known as castor sugar in England. Some bakers use this as their all-purpose sugar because it dissolves so quickly (you can use it in breads), especially in whipped cream and cold sauces.

Confectioners' or powdered sugar is milled granulated sugar with some cornstarch added. It dissolves really fast (you can see that when you make an icing and add only a few teaspoons of liquid; it seems to dissolve instantly). It is a favorite for dusting breads.

Crystal or decorating sugar (also called pearl sugar) has the largest crystals and gives a sparkling, jewel-like finish to breads. It comes in its natural color and different colors as well; the crystals look like little bits of glass, they are so pretty. Decorative sugar is a great touch for finishing holiday breads.

Sanding sugar is sized between regular granulated and crystal sugar. It is also good for decorating breads.

Sugar cubes, or lump sugar, is a combination of different-size granulated sugars compressed into little blocks. It can be made from brown or white sugar. I love to crush these and add them to bread. (See Dutch Sugar Loaf, page 434.) I especially like Ala Perruche brand cubes made from African sugarcane and imported from France; they are less refined.

Brown sugar is either light or dark, depending on how much molasses has been added back into the granulated sugar. Obviously, dark brown sugar will have a more pronounced molasses flavor. I favor the Dark Muscovado sugar from African sugarcane distributed under the India Tree brand. Brown sugar can be used cup for cup in place of granulated sugar.

Turbinado and Demerara sugars, from Mauritius and Guyana, are partially refined with 15 percent of the molasses left in. They are coarsely crystallized (Demerara is slightly larger and is found in the raw sugar packets in restaurants) and essentially the same as the C & H raw sugar in the supermarket. Many bakers use this instead of regular granulated sugar. You can use it like light brown sugar.

Maple sugar is crystallized maple syrup. It is a regional favorite in New England, a great flavor enhancer in both white and whole wheat breads.

It can be substituted cup for cup for other granulated sugars.

Fructose is found in ripe fruits and honey, but made from cornstarch. It has double the sweetness and is more soluble in water than sucrose, regular granulated sugar. It has the same sweetening power as granulated sugar in baking.

Molasses is the brown syrup that is left after refining granulated sugar. Light molasses, Barbados, is from the first extraction and has a lovely sweet flavor; dark is from later ones and is much stronger. Blackstrap is from the final extraction; I don't use it in breads because it is bitter and heavy with ash. If your bottle just says molasses, it is probably between light and dark. Sorghum molasses is a regional sweetener, which comes from a grass, found mainly in the South.

To substitute molasses in a recipe that calls for sugar, use ½ cup molasses for each cup of granulated sugar called for and reduce the liquid ingredients by ⅓ cup for each cup of sugar called for. (If you were using molasses in a recipe that called for 2 cups of sugar, you would use 1 cup of molasses and decrease the liquid by ⅔ cup.)

Honey is a thick, sweet, semiviscous liquid produced by nectar-gathering bees. Its flavor is determined by the flowers that the bees gather pollen from. Generally, light-colored honeys are mild in flavor and darker honeys stronger. The flavor and aroma of honey are accentuated by the slow heat of the bread machine, and delightfully permeate the bread.

Pure maple syrup is made from sap that is gathered from the maple trees that grow in the northeastern United States and Canada. The sap is boiled down to make a luxuriously thick, pourable liquid. It is a premium sweetener in breads. Imitation maple-flavored syrups are different, and do not perform the same way in baking. Fancy (also known as Light Amber) is the first of the season, pale and delicate. Grade A and Grade B syrups (Medium and Dark Amber) are progressively darker and more potent in flavor. Grade A is perfect for all-purpose table use and in baking. Grade B is quite robust in flavor, like molasses. Less expensive than Grade A, it is good in whole wheat breads. Refrigerate maple syrup after opening.

To substitute honey or maple syrup for granulated sugar in a recipe, use ¾ cup of the liquid sweetener for each cup of granulated sugar called for and reduce the liquid ingredients by ¼ cup per cup of granulated sugar listed in the recipe.

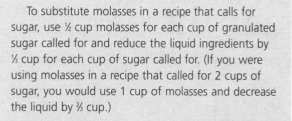

BLUEBERRY CRUMB CAKE

Makes one 18-by-12-inch coffee cake; serves 16

I first became acquainted with food writer Richard Sax when he critiqued one of my cookbooks for Chocolatier magazine, and during the last decade of his life, we corresponded regularly. His book Classic Home Desserts (Chapters, 1994) is a must-have for any serious dessert lover. This exceptionally rich crumb cake is a recipe of Richard's that originated at the Rock Hill Bakehouse. Author Michael McLaughlin borrowed it and added a layer of blueberries under the crumb top. Now I've added even more blueberries and adapted it for the bread machine, which is perfect for this firm dough that gets refrigerated overnight and is topped and baked the next morning. There are never enough good recipes designed to serve a group of 16 to 20, so here you go. Whether for a potluck brunch or your own Sunday family gathering, this fantastic crumb cake is worth the time spent making it. Cut it into squares and serve it out of the pan while it is still warm.

1½- OR 2-POUND-LOAF MACHINES

For the dough:

¾ cup sour cream
1 large egg plus 2 egg yolks
¼ cup water

4 cups unbleached all-purpose flour
Grated zest of 1 large orange
¼ cup sugar
1½ teaspoons salt

1 tablespoon plus ½ teaspoon SAF yeast or 1 tablespoon plus 1 teaspoon bread machine yeast

¾ cup (1½ sticks) unsalted butter, cut into pieces

For the streusel topping:

1⅓ cups unbleached all-purpose flour
⅔ cup sugar
1 tablespoon ground cinnamon or apple pie spice
1½ teaspoons vanilla extract or 2½ teaspoons vanilla powder
½ cup (1 stick) plus 3 tablespoons unsalted butter, chilled and cut into pieces

3 cups fresh blueberries, rinsed and picked over, or frozen unsweetened blueberries, unthawed
½ cup confectioners' sugar, for dusting

❶ The night before baking, make the dough. Place the dough ingredients, except the butter, in the pan according to the order in the manufacturer's instructions. Program for the Dough cycle; press Start. Set a kitchen timer for 10 minutes. The dough will be firm, but springy.

❷ When the timer rings, open the lid. While the machine is running, add a piece or two of the butter at a time, allowing the butter to be incorporated before adding

more pieces. It will take a minute or two to add all the
pieces. Close the lid.

3 When the Knead 2 phase ends, set a timer for 30 minutes and let the dough rise in the machine. Then press
Stop and unplug the machine. Remove the dough to
a greased 4-quart plastic bucket (I spray it with butter-
flavored cooking spray), cover with plastic wrap, and
refrigerate overnight.

4 To make the topping, in the workbowl of a food processor, combine the flour, sugar, and cinnamon. With the
motor running, dribble in the vanilla, then stop and add
the butter pieces. Pulse to make a crumbly mass that
forms large clumps. Do not overmix. Place in a covered
plastic container. Refrigerate overnight, if making the
day before, or make it in the morning.

5 In the morning, line an 18-by-12-by-1-inch jelly roll
pan with parchment paper. Spray the sides and bottom
with butter-flavored cooking spray. Turn the dough out
onto a lightly floured work surface; it will be cold and
stiff. With a rolling pin, roll out into a rectangle that
will fit the pan. Transfer to the pan, pressing to fit the
bottom. Cover with plastic wrap and set aside to rise at
room temperature until doubled in bulk, about 3 hours.

6 Preheat the oven to 350°F.

7 Uncover the pan and sprinkle the top with the blueberries, pressing them gently into the dough. Loosen the
topping with a fork and sprinkle in a thick layer over
the entire pan, covering all the dough and berries. Bake
for 30 to 35 minutes, or until golden brown on top
and around the edges and a cake tester inserted into the
cake comes out clean. Place the pan on a wire rack and
lightly dust with sifted confectioners' sugar. Serve warm.

MORNING STICKY BUNS

Makes 12 buns

1½- OR 2-POUND-LOAF MACHINES

For the dough:

1¼ cups fat-free milk
1 teaspoon vanilla extract
3 tablespoons unsalted
  butter, cut into pieces

3 cups unbleached
  all-purpose flour
3 tablespoons sugar
1¼ teaspoons salt

2 teaspoons SAF yeast
  or 2½ teaspoons bread
  machine yeast

For the cinnamon filling:

¾ cup light or dark brown
  sugar
1 tablespoon ground
  cinnamon
6 tablespoons unsalted
  butter, softened

For the caramel:

⅓ cup unsalted butter
1 cup light or dark brown
  sugar
¼ cup light corn syrup
1 cup chopped pecans

A *fter mastering cinnamon bread, sticky buns are the next big step for a sweet bread baker. Everyone loves them and everyone wants to make them. I teach this recipe to almost all my classes and surprisingly enough, it is requested as often as pizza and croissants. Here I have included directions for rising the rolls in the pan overnight. In the morning, all you have to do is bake them.*

1 To make the dough, place all the dough ingredients in the pan according to the order in the manufacturer's instructions. Program for the Dough cycle; press Start. The dough ball will be soft, yet at the same time smooth and springy. Combine the sugar and cinnamon for the filling in a small bowl. Set aside.

2 To make the caramel, 10 minutes before the end of the Dough cycle, grease the sides and bottom of a 13-by-9-inch glass or metal baking pan (I prefer to use a metal or disposable aluminum pan if I will be rising the buns overnight in the refrigerator—a glass pan cold from the refrigerator could break when placed in a hot oven.) Combine the butter, brown sugar, and corn syrup in a small skillet or heavy saucepan over low heat, stirring constantly. When the butter is melted and the sugar is dissolved, remove from the heat. Immediately pour into the baking pan. Spread evenly over the bottom with a rubber spatula. Sprinkle with the nuts. Set aside.

3 When the machine beeps at the end of the cycle, press Stop and unplug the machine. Turn the dough out onto a lightly floured work surface. Roll it into a 12-by-15-inch rectangle. Add the filling: Leaving a 1-inch border around all the edges, spread the surface evenly with the 6 tablespoons soft butter, then sprinkle evenly with the sugar and cinnamon, which will be quite a light filling. Roll up jelly-roll fashion starting from a long edge, and pinch the seam to seal. With a serrated knife using a gentle sawing motion, cut the roll into 12 equal portions, each slice about 1½ inches thick. Place the slices close together on top of the caramel, spiral cut side down. Cover loosely with plastic wrap and let the rolls rise at room temperature for 45 minutes, or until puffy and even with the rim of the pan. (The rolls can be refrigerated before this last rise, covered tightly with a double layer of plastic wrap, leaving the rolls to rise slowly and be baked in the morning. Remove the pan from the refrigerator and let rest for 20 minutes before baking.)

4 Meanwhile, preheat the oven to 350°F.

5 Bake the buns until the tops are brown, 30 to 35 minutes. Remove from the oven and let stand no more than 5 minutes on a wire rack. Place the cooling rack on top of the pan and, securely holding the hot pan with oven mitts, invert the pan on top of the rack, taking care not to touch the hot caramel. Let cool for at least 20 minutes, then transfer to a serving plate. Pull the buns apart and serve warm.

ROSE ROLLS WITH
ROSE BUTTERCREAM

Makes 16 rolls

For the dough:

¾ cup milk
½ cup water
1 large egg
½ cup (1 stick) unsalted
  butter, cut into pieces

4 cups unbleached
  all-purpose flour
½ cup sugar
2 teaspoons salt

2½ teaspoons SAF yeast
  or 1 tablespoon bread
  machine yeast

For the filling:

One 22-ounce can cherry
  pie filling

For the rose buttercream:

1 cup sifted confectioners'
  sugar
Pinch of salt
2 tablespoons warm milk
½ teaspoon vanilla extract
  or 1¼ teaspoons vanilla
  powder added to the
  sugar
½ teaspoon rose water,
  optional
1½ tablespoons unsalted
  butter, room temperature

F irst of all, I love the name of these beautiful breakfast
rolls. Second, they are a fast version of my favorite fruit-
filled Danish pastry. While I normally make all my fruit
fillings from scratch, I can't help but love the convenience of using
the ready-made here. You can also use blueberry pie filling, if you
wish, but the cherry is hard to beat.

❶ To make the dough, place all the dough ingredients
in the pan according to the order in the manufacturer's
instructions. Program for the Dough cycle; press Start.
The dough ball will be soft. When the machine beeps at
the end of the cycle, press Stop and unplug the machine.
Turn the dough out and shape it into a thick square that
will fit into a greased 4-quart plastic bucket (I spray it
with butter-flavored cooking spray). Cover with plastic
wrap, and refrigerate for 2 hours or overnight.

❷ Line 2 baking sheets with parchment paper. Gently press
the dough to deflate it and place on a lightly floured
work surface. Roll out the dough into a 12-by-16-by-¼-
inch rectangle. With a sharp knife or pastry wheel, cut
the dough lengthwise into 16 one-inch-wide strips.
Holding your palms on each end of a strip, twist one in
the opposite direction from the other at the same time.
Wrap the entire strip around one end to form a coiled
pinwheel. Tuck the tail underneath. Repeat with the
other strips of dough. Place the pinwheels on the baking
sheets at least 2 inches apart (8 per pan). Do not crowd.
Cover with plastic wrap and set aside to rise at room
temperature until doubled in bulk, 1 to 1½ hours. (You
can cover these with a double layer of plastic wrap and
let rise in the refrigerator overnight, then fill and bake in
the morning.)

❸ Preheat the oven to 400°F.

4 Using your fingertips, gently press to the bottom on the center of each coil to form an indentation for the filling. Place about 2 tablespoons of the pie filling into the center. Be careful not to use too much filling or it will bubble over during baking. You want filling surrounded by dough.

5 Place a second baking sheet of the same dimensions under one of the pans holding pastries to double pan and prevent the bottoms from burning. Bake for 13 to 16 minutes. Remove the pan from the oven and place on a wire rack. Double pan and place the second batch of rolls in the oven.

6 As the second batch bakes, frost the first batch. Make the buttercream frosting by whisking all the frosting ingredients together in a small bowl; beat until smooth and thick, yet pourable. Glaze the pastries while still warm and on the baking sheet, drizzling the glaze back and forth with the end of a spoon, a pastry bag fitted with a small plain tip, or the tips of your fingers. Move the pastries from the baking pan to a wire rack to cool. The frosting will set as it cools. When the second batch of rolls is finished, frost the same way. Let the pastries cool on the racks for 15 minutes before eating.

PETITS PAINS AU CHOCOLAT

Makes 15 little sweet breads

1½- OR 2-POUND- LOAF MACHINES

⅔ cup milk
2 large eggs
4 tablespoons unsalted butter, cut into pieces and softened

2½ cups unbleached all-purpose flour
2 tablespoons light brown sugar
1 teaspoon salt

2 teaspoons SAF yeast or 2½ teaspoons bread machine yeast

8 ounces semisweet chocolate, chopped or broken into ½-ounce pieces

1 egg beaten with 1 teaspoon milk, for glaze

C hocolate-filled pastries, often made from labor-intensive brioche dough, line up side-by-side with other morning pastries such as Danishes, brioche à tête, and croissants. *But here is a recipe for chocolate pastries that uses a much easier sweet egg dough (that chills overnight, so plan accordingly) to make the perfect pouch for a good melted chocolate filling. If you can, use a high-quality brand of semisweet chocolate, like Callebaut, Scharffen Berger, or Guittard. Cut off chunks from a thick block, or, if you are using thin blocks, here is a tip for breaking them easily into pieces: Dip a 10-inch chef's knife into hot water for a minute, dry it off, and then, exerting as little pressure as possible, cut the chocolate into strips; reheat the knife as needed. These pastries are great for brunch, still slightly warm, with coffee. Go ahead and dunk them.*

❶ Place the ingredients, except the chocolate, in the pan according to the order in the manufacturer's instructions. Program for the Dough cycle; press Start. The dough will be sticky. Grease a deep bowl. When the machine beeps at the end of the cycle, press Stop and unplug the machine. Using a dough card, turn the dough out into the bowl, scraping the sides of the pan and supporting the dough as it comes out. Cover with 2 layers of plastic wrap and refrigerate for 4 hours to overnight.

❷ Line 2 large baking sheets with parchment paper and brush with melted butter. Turn the cold dough out onto a work surface dusted with flour. With a metal bench knife, divide into 15 equal portions. With a floured rolling pin, roll out each portion to a 4-inch square about ¼ inch thick. Place ½ ounce of chocolate in the center of each square. Fold each corner up into the center to encase the chocolate. Pinch to seal. Place seam side down on the baking sheet, about 1 inch apart. Cover loosely with plastic wrap and let rise at room temperature until puffy, about 1 hour.

3 Twenty minutes before baking, preheat the oven to 350°F.

4 Brush each pastry with some egg glaze. Bake, one pan at a time, for 15 to 18 minutes, until light golden brown and dry to the touch. Transfer to a rack to cool, although these are good eaten warm.

HOT CROSS BUNS

Makes 12 buns

1½- OR 2-POUND-LOAF MACHINES

For the dough:

¾ cup fat-free milk
½ teaspoon vanilla extract
2 large eggs
4 tablespoons unsalted
   butter, cut into pieces

2¾ cups unbleached
   all-purpose flour
⅓ cup white whole wheat
   flour or additional ⅓ cup
   unbleached all-purpose
   flour
¼ cup light brown sugar
1½ teaspoons salt
1 teaspoon ground mace

2½ teaspoons SAF yeast
   or 1 tablespoon bread
   machine yeast

⅔ cup dried currants
⅓ cup finely chopped dried
   apricots or dried plums

For the icing:

¾ cup sifted confectioners'
   sugar
¼ teaspoon vanilla extract,
   almond extract, lemon
   oil, or *Fiori di Sicilia*
1¼ tablespoons fat-free
   milk

L ittle Celtic breads decorated with a Greek cross are a very old tradition; this mystic earth-centered symbol was once used to ward off evil spirits that might visit the baker. The cross symbol embodied quadrant concepts, like the four corners of the earth (forerunners of latitude and longitude lines) and the four seasons, before becoming a Christian symbol. Hot cross buns were common street food in the Elizabethan era. So don't wait until Easter to make these; they are a good brunch offering all year long.

❶ To make the dough, place the dough ingredients, except the dried fruit, in the pan according to the order in the manufacturer's instructions. Program for the Dough cycle; press Start. The dough ball will be soft.

❷ Line a baking sheet with parchment paper. When the machine beeps at the end of the cycle, press Stop and unplug the machine. Immediately turn the dough out onto a lightly floured work surface. Pat the dough into a large freeform rectangle and sprinkle with the dried fruit. Press in. Fold the dough into thirds and knead a few times to distribute the fruit evenly. Divide the dough in half. Roll each portion into a 10-inch-long log and, with a bench knife, cut into 6 equal portions. Form each portion into a round bun and place the buns 2 inches apart on the baking sheet. Let rise, uncovered, at room temperature until doubled in bulk, about 40 minutes.

❸ Twenty minutes before baking, preheat the oven to 375°F.

❹ With a sharp knife, gently cut a cross, no deeper than ½ inch, over the surface of each bun. Bake for 15 to 20 minutes, or until browned.

5 While the buns are baking, prepare the icing: Whisk the icing ingredients together in a small bowl. Beat hard until the icing is smooth and a bit firm for piping. Remove the rolls from the oven and place the baking sheet on a rack. Place the icing in a pastry bag fitted with a small plain tip, and pipe a cross over the top of each hot bun into the indentation where you cut the cross before baking. Let stand for at least 20 minutes to set before devouring.

MARITOZZI ROMANI

Makes 8 large rolls

**1½- OR 2-POUND-
LOAF MACHINES**

½ cup golden raisins
¼ cup sweet white wine,
 like Asti Spumante

⅞ cup fat-free milk
1 large egg
4 tablespoons unsalted
 butter, cut into pieces

3 cups unbleached
 all-purpose flour
¼ cup sugar
1¼ teaspoons salt

2 teaspoons SAF yeast
 or 2½ teaspoons bread
 machine yeast

¼ cup coarsely chopped
 pine nuts
¼ cup finely chopped
 orange confit (page 481)

1 egg beaten with 1 tablespoon of the drained
 wine from the raisins,
 for glaze

Maritozzi *translates to "big husband" (from* marito, *the Italian word for husband), and are* panini dolci, *sweet and tender rolls that have been made in Rome during Lent since medieval times. They have pine nuts, raisins, and candied orange peel. A great breakfast roll, these are good with coffee and tea.*

1 In a small bowl, cover the raisins with the wine. Macerate for at least an hour at room temperature.

2 Place the ingredients, except the raisins, pine nuts, and orange confit, in the pan according to the order in the manufacturer's instructions. Program for the Dough cycle; press Start. (This recipe is not suitable for use with the Delay Timer.) The dough ball will be soft.

3 Line a baking sheet with parchment paper. Drain the raisins, reserving 1 tablespoon of the liquid for the glaze. When the machine beeps at the end of the cycle, press Stop and unplug the machine. Turn the dough out onto a lightly floured work surface. Pat the dough into a large freeform rectangle and sprinkle with the raisins, pine nuts, and orange confit. Press in. Fold the dough into thirds and knead a few times to evenly distribute the fruit and nuts. Divide the dough in half, then divide each half into 4 equal portions. Shape each portion into a tight round and place on the baking sheet, at least 3 inches apart. Cover with a clean tea towel and let rise until doubled in bulk, about 45 minutes.

4 Twenty minutes before baking, preheat the oven to 400°F.

5 Brush the tops of the rolls with the glaze. Bake for 20 to 25 minutes, or until golden brown. Cool on a rack.

Orange Confit

Makes about 1 cup candied fruit plus ¾ cup syrup

"Confit" is a French culinary term for fruit preserved in a sugar syrup, as well as for savory cooked meat preserved in its own fat. I love this recipe for orange confit. It is as easy to make as it is delicious. You simmer the chopped zest in a simple syrup, then store it in its syrup in the refrigerator. When you have a recipe that calls for candied orange peel, you just remove a tablespoon or two as needed. (Try some in your raisin bread.) You can use the syrup in place of some of the liquid in the recipe, too, or use it on its own in another recipe. I like to heat the syrup and brush it over a hot sweet bread. This recipe can also be made with lemons.

3 large organic or unsprayed oranges
1¼ cups sugar
2 tablespoons light corn syrup
2 tablespoons mild honey
1 cup water

1 With a vegetable peeler or sharp paring knife, cut the orange skin, or zest, off of the fruit. Try not to get any of the white pith, which is bitter. Finely chop or julienne the zest. (Use the fruit for another purpose.)

2 Combine the sugar, corn syrup, honey, and water in a medium-sized heavy saucepan. Bring to a boil, then turn the heat to low. Cook, stirring constantly with a wooden spoon, until the sugar dissolves, about 30 seconds. Add the zest and return to a boil. Cook at a low rolling boil over medium heat about 10 to 20 minutes, until the zest is firm-cooked and the syrup thickens. The syrup should be translucent with a pale orange cast. Pierce the zest with the tip of a small knife to test for doneness. Remove from the heat and let the mixture cool. Pour into a spring-top jar for storage and refrigerate for up to 1 month. The syrup will thicken further as the confit chills.

BREAD MACHINE FRENCH BUTTER CROISSANTS

Makes 16 large croissants

1½- OR 2-POUND-LOAF MACHINES

1½ cups (3 sticks) cold
  unsalted butter
1 cup unbleached
  all-purpose flour or
  white whole wheat flour

1 cup cool milk
2 large eggs
2 tablespoons vegetable oil

3 tablespoons sugar
1½ teaspoons salt
3 cups unbleached
  all-purpose flour or
  white whole wheat flour

1 tablespoon plus
  ½ teaspoon SAF yeast
  or 1 tablespoon plus
  1½ teaspoons bread
  machine yeast

⅓ cup unbleached
  all-purpose or white
  whole wheat flour,
  for sprinkling
1 large egg beaten with
  1 teaspoon water, for
  glaze, optional

L ong the domain of the professional baker, croissants are
  famous for their multitude of layers, achieved by the same
  folding technique used in creating Danish pastries. This is
a classic recipe for les pains croissant au beurre. It is a must for
every serious sweet bread baker to master. When I review my past
baking class schedules, I find that making croissants has been a top
request from students (as popular as making pizza), so here is a
modified version for bread machine bakers. Instead of rolling in a
butter package (dough wrapped around a mass of butter), frozen bits
of butter are incorporated right into the dough. Use unsalted butter,
as it has a superior flavor and stays cold longer than salted butter,
which contains a higher percentage of moisture. The dough is mixed
only a short time, so be prepared to remove the dough after about
ten minutes in the machine. The oil in the dough works as a tender-
izer and the egg adds leavening, flavor, and texture. Beautiful croissants have never been so easy. Don't use a Preheat cycle with this
dough; if your machine has it, you will need to skip or bypass it
here. Serve these croissants with coffee or tea le matin.

❶ Cut each stick of butter into 16 slices. Place 1 cup of the
flour in a large plastic freezer bag. Add the butter pieces,
press out the air, and close the bag; toss to coat evenly.
Place the bag in the freezer for 4 hours or overnight to
freeze the butter. The bag can stay in the freezer for up
to 4 days before assembling the recipe.

❷ Place the milk, eggs, vegetable oil, sugar, salt, 3 cups flour,
and yeast in the pan according to the order in the manufacturer's instructions. Program for the Dough cycle; press
Start. Set a kitchen timer for 5 minutes and let the dough
mix and knead, scraping down the sides of the pan once
or twice. Check the dough ball; it will be sticky. Remove
the bag of butter pieces from the freezer. When the timer
rings, press Pause. Add the frozen butter and any of its

excess flour to the pan and place a paper towel over the pan to prevent the flour from flying; press Start. Set the timer for 4 minutes. Check the dough ball again. There will be a very soft, cold dough with butter pieces sticking out; it will be tacky. When the timer rings, press Stop and unplug the machine.

3 Dust an ungreased baking sheet with 1 tablespoon of flour. Scrape the dough out of the pan and onto the sheet and sprinkle another tablespoon of flour on top of the dough. With floured fingers, spread the dough to lie flat in a large freeform 9-by-6-inch rectangle about 1 inch thick, taking care to square the edges. Cover tightly with plastic wrap, making certain all the dough is covered to avoid forming dry patches. Refrigerate in the coldest part of the refrigerator until thoroughly chilled, about 30 minutes. If you're in a hurry, place it in the freezer for 10 minutes.

4 Place the chilled dough on a lightly floured work surface. With a heavy rolling pin, roll into an elongated 9-by-18-inch rectangle; the exact size is not important but be sure to keep the edges square. Pull one third over from one side to cover the center and fold the remaining third of the dough from the other side over the center. As you fold, the surface that was on the bottom ends up on top. The three layers will be stacked on top of each other with no dough hanging over. Place the folded edge of the dough at 12 o'clock and neaten the rectangle.

5 Roll out the dough again into the elongated rectangle using firm strokes. Fold it again into thirds. Use a soft brush to dust off any excess flour on the surface. Place the dough in a large plastic freezer bag (you can use the one the butter was in) and refrigerate it for 15 minutes

Equipment for Making Croissants

Since croissants are shaped and baked outside the bread machine, you will need a few well-chosen tools to make them efficiently. Perhaps the most important is the right work surface. I find a floured slab of marble the easiest to use; the dough stays cold. Some people use a wooden board or cotton pastry frame. Your work space should be about 15-by-22 inches. In addition, you will need:

- Large, heavy, ball-bearing rolling pin for rolling out the dough

- Metal pastry scraper (also called a bench knife) for handling the dough

- 1½-inch soft pastry brush for cleaning off the dough

- Ruler or tape measure for sizing the croissants

- 8- or 10-inch chef's knife or a pastry wheel for cutting the croissants

- Wide-width plastic wrap for wrapping the dough

- Two heavy-gauge, large baking sheets with a 1-inch rim for baking

- Parchment paper for lining the baking sheets

- Cooling rack

to chill. The chilling period rests the gluten and firms the butter to allow continued rolling. (You will do this rolling and folding action a total of 4 times; this technique creates the layering. Many bakers mark on a piece of paper what turn they have just finished or make indentations into the dough with their finger before putting it back in the refrigerator to keep track—it is very easy to forget.)

6 Repeat the process of rolling out and folding into thirds 2 more times. Take care not to tear the dough or allow the butter to get too soft while rolling. Remember to adjust the corners as you are working to keep the edges square, and to move the dough constantly to avoid sticking. Dust with flour as needed; you will use up the entire extra ⅓ cup. Chill the dough in the refrigerator at any point that it becomes sticky (it may need chilling between the third and fourth rollings), and remember to always place the dough with the folded edge at 12 o'clock. If you can work very quickly and the temperature of the dough has not warmed up and started to melt the butter, you can do two turns at once. The dough will become smooth and supple during the rolling. When you have done this 4 times, refrigerate the dough in the plastic bag overnight, or up to 24 hours. The dough will expand and fill the bag as it rests in the refrigerator.

7 Line 2 large baking sheets with parchment paper or aluminum foil. Gently press the dough in the bag to deflate it, remove it from the bag, and then cut it in half down the middle to make 2 square pieces of dough. Place one half back in the bag and refrigerate. Place the other half on a lightly floured work surface and roll it out into a 10-by-21-inch rectangle about ¼ inch thick.

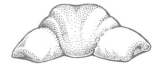

Keep lifting and moving the dough to prevent sticking or tearing. Roll the dough on a diagonal to achieve an even width. With a knife or pastry wheel and measuring tape, mark at 7 and 14 inches along one long edge, which will divide the dough into 3 equal sections. On the opposite long edge, mark at 3½ inches, 10½ inches, and 17½ inches.

8 With a large knife or pastry wheel, connect the points, cutting 5 perfect triangles and 2 half-triangles on the ends. Take care to cut cleanly and not pull on the dough. Press the two half-triangles together to make one. You will have 6 large triangles. If any edges are uneven, just trim them. Save any extra strips of dough; they can be placed on top of the croissants before you roll them and be incorporated into the roll. Slash a cut about 1 inch long into the center of the base of each triangle.

9 To shape: With the base of a triangle facing you, spread the slit and roll over the bottom edge to start the roll. With your fingers stretched out on the base and the other hand holding the point, tightly roll the base up towards the point, moving only one hand. You will stretch the point slightly and press down on the dough as you roll to keep the croissant from sliding around. Place each croissant on a baking sheet with the tip on the bottom, and bend it into a crescent shape by curving the tapered ends towards the center leaving only an inch or two between the points (they spread during baking). Do not crowd the croissants on the baking sheet; leave about 4 inches between them. Shape the remaining croissants. Repeat with the second half of the dough. Formed croissants may be frozen at this point, for up to 2 months. Let rise, uncovered, at room temperature until

How to Freeze and Thaw Croissants

To Freeze Baked Croissants
As soon as they have completely cooled, freeze croissants in plastic freezer bags. To serve, place the frozen croissants on a baking sheet and heat in a preheated 350°F oven, uncovered, for about 10 minutes to thaw, warm, and restore flakiness.

To Bake Frozen Raw Formed Croissants
As mentioned in Step 9 of the croissant recipe, you can freeze raw, formed croissants for up to 2 months. Put the raw croissants on a baking sheet lined with parchment paper or on stiff plastic lids if your freezer is small. Cover them with plastic wrap or slide them into freezer bags, and place in the freezer for 4 hours or until frozen. Once the croissants are frozen, transfer them into freezer bags. When you are ready to bake the croissants, remove them from the freezer and place them on a baking sheet lined with parchment paper. Cover lightly with plastic wrap and let them defrost in the refrigerator for 12 to 18 hours, or overnight at room temperature. Let stand, uncovered, at room temperature for about 1 hour, until puffy and no longer chilled, and bake in a preheated oven as directed in the recipe.

doubled in bulk, about 1½ hours. You can do this rise in the refrigerator overnight, covered, and bake the croissants in the morning.

10 Twenty minutes before baking, preheat the oven to 425°F.

11 When the croissants are light and springy to the touch, and have just lost their chill, they are ready to bake. Brush with the egg glaze if you like a shiny glaze. If you are using parchment paper, place another baking sheet of the same dimension under the pan with the croissants to "double pan" and protect the bottoms from burning. Bake, one pan at a time, for 10 minutes. Reduce the oven temperature to 375°F and bake for an additional 10 to 12 minutes. Remove from the baking sheet to cool on racks for at least 15 minutes before eating.

V A R I A T I O N

Almond-Filled Croissants

Makes 6 croissants

For the almond filling:

1 cup (one 8-ounce can) almond paste, at room temperature
1 large egg white, beaten
¼ teaspoon vanilla extract
¼ teaspoon almond extract
1 tablespoon flour

½ recipe croissant dough, chilled overnight and cut into triangles
Sifted confectioners' sugar, for dusting

Beat the filling ingredients together in a medium bowl until light and fluffy. Place 2 heaping tablespoons of filling in the center of the base of each triangle before rolling in Step 9. Roll up, let rise, and bake as for croissants. Dust with confectioners' sugar before serving. If you have any left-over filling, it can be stored in the refrigerator for up to 1 month.

SWEET CHEESE PUFF CROISSANTS

Makes about 24 puffs

N atural cream cheese, unlike most packaged cream cheeses, contains no stabilizers, like vegetable gum, so it is very soft. It sort of melts in your mouth. This is the type of cream cheese called for here, but the packaged variety will also work fine. You will also need miniature muffin tins 2¼ inches in diameter for this two-bite pastry. Good for breakfast or on the tea table.

INGREDIENTS

1 pound natural, preferably, or packaged cream cheese
⅔ cup sugar
1 large egg
1½ teaspoons vanilla extract or grated zest of 1 large orange
½ recipe Bread Machine French Butter Croissant dough (page 482), chilled overnight
Sifted confectioners' sugar or vanilla confectioners' sugar (see page 513), for dusting

1 Using an electric mixer or food processor, cream the cheese and sugar until smooth; add the egg and vanilla or zest. Chill for 1 hour.

2 Roll out the chilled croissant dough on a lightly floured work surface to a 16-by-16-inch square that is ¼ inch thick. Sprinkle some flour on top so that the rolling pin will not stick. Using a ruler, cut the dough with a pastry wheel into 3-inch squares. You will have about 24 squares.

3 Place a tablespoon of the cream cheese filling in the center of each square. Bring the 4 corners together into the center and pinch in a knot to close and form a square puff. Set the puffs in ungreased 2¼-inch diameter muffin cups. Let rise, uncovered, at room temperature until puffy, about 30 minutes.

4 Twenty minutes before baking, preheat the oven to 375°F.

5 Bake the puffs for 15 to 18 minutes, or until golden brown and the filling is set. Cool for 10 minutes in the pan and then remove to a cooling rack. Dust with confectioners' sugar before serving.

CHOCOLATE BREADS

Chocolate comes from the seeds of the cacao tree indigenous to Central and South America. Cacao beans were accepted as taxes and used for currency and were a royal food among the Aztecs and Mayans for centuries before the Spanish conquest. Chocolate was shipped back to Europe with the plunder of the Aztec civilization, and quickly became a rich drink for continental royalty and high society. In the sixteenth century, it was the top luxury export from the New World.

Bread recipes may call for unsweetened (or baking), semisweet, bittersweet, milk, or white chocolate, or unsweetened cocoa powder. Some bakers chop their own chocolate off a block, others like to use chocolate chips. Chocolate chips are specially formulated to hold their shape under high heat, so don't use them unless you want the chocolate to retain its shape in the loaf. Unsweetened chocolate contains no sugar, so it must be used in combination with sugar in a recipe. Use a semisweet or bittersweet chocolate for incorporating into a dough. Semisweet and bittersweet chocolate are technically the same, but in general bittersweet chocolate will have a stronger flavor. Milk chocolate is the sweetest, and white chocolate is not really chocolate at all; it contains cocoa butter, butterfat, sugar, milk, and lecithin, but no chocolate liquor.

If a bar of chocolate is labeled "couverture," it is a type of chocolate that contains a high percentage of cocoa butter to make it easy to work with when melted. You can use couver-ture in any recipes that call for bittersweet or semisweet chocolate. You may come across a super-dark chocolate, which is a new category of chocolate. To my palate it tastes too close to unsweetened chocolate to substitute for semisweet. Mexican chocolate contains almonds, sugar, cinnamon, cloves, and nutmeg, which are ground together and pressed into discs.

I call for cocoa powder in many of my chocolate bread recipes. Not only does it blend well with the dry ingredients, but it is much easier to use than block chocolate, which must be melted first. Like unsweetened chocolate, cocoa contains no sugar and must be used in combination with sugar in a recipe. It also has far less fat and fewer calories than block chocolate because it contains no cocoa butter. However, this also means the flavor is less rich, so you have to add some other flavor elements to balance it out. There are two types of cocoa powder: regular and Dutch process. I always use Dutch process, which has a stronger flavor and a richer color than regular cocoa. It is treated with a mild alkali, such as baking soda, to neutralize its natural acidity.

Store block chocolate in airtight wrapping in a cool, dark place. If a white coating or white streaks, called bloom, appear on your chocolate, they are a reaction to a change in temperature or moisture, but the chocolate is fine to use. Well stored dark chocolate is good for years; milk and white chocolates should be used within a year. Stored in a cool, dark place, cocoa keeps indefinitely.

CHOCOLATE CHALLAH

C hallah is a traditional Jewish egg bread, often described as more of a cake than a bread, that adapts well to the addition of chocolate, both in the dough and with chips added to create pockets of melted chocolate. This version is completely unconventional, but delightful nonetheless. Serve it with whipped cream cheese for brunch.

❶ Place the ingredients, except the chocolate chips, in the pan according to the order in the manufacturer's instructions. Set crust on medium and program for the Basic or Sweet Bread cycle; press Start. (This recipe is not suitable for use with the Delay Timer.) At the beep, add the chocolate chips.

❷ When the baking cycle ends, immediately remove the bread from the pan and place it on a rack. Let cool to room temperature before slicing.

1½-POUND LOAF	2-POUND LOAF
1 cup water	1¼ cups water
1 large egg plus 1 egg yolk	2 large eggs
2 tablespoons vegetable oil	3 tablespoons vegetable oil
2 teaspoons vanilla extract	1 tablespoon vanilla extract
3 cups bread flour	4 cups bread flour
½ cup sugar	⅔ cup sugar
¼ cup unsweetened Dutch-process cocoa powder	⅓ cup unsweetened Dutch-process cocoa powder
1 tablespoon gluten	1 tablespoon plus 1 teaspoon gluten
1½ teaspoons salt	2 teaspoons salt
1¾ teaspoons SAF yeast or 2¼ teaspoons bread machine yeast	2 teaspoons SAF yeast or 2½ teaspoons bread machine yeast
½ cup semisweet chocolate chips	⅔ cup semisweet chocolate chips

The Perfect Chocolate Glaze

If you would like to coat one of your breads with a chocolate glaze, here is the one to use. Begin preparing the glaze as soon as you remove the loaf from the bread pan to cool, so you can glaze the bread while it is still warm.

4 ounces bittersweet chocolate
6 tablespoons unsalted butter
1 tablespoon light corn syrup

❶ Place a plate or piece of waxed paper under the cooling rack holding the bread to catch the drips from the glaze.

❷ Melt the ingredients together in a double boiler over simmering water, stirring gently with a small whisk until smooth. Remove from the heat and immediately drizzle the bread slowly with the glaze, letting some drip down the sides. Cool to room temperature to set the glaze before slicing.

MEXICAN CHOCOLATE BREAD

S outhwestern and Mexican bakers have a special love of spices. Even their chocolate contains hints of cinnamon, coffee, and orange. Sometimes I grate Mexican brown sugar, piloncillo, *a cross between our light and dark brown sugars, to use in place of the brown sugar called for here. For the chocolate chips, I often use coarsely grated Ibarra brand chocolate from Mexico. Whether you use these special ingredients or not, you will be surprised at how succulent this sweet bread is, right down to the last bite.*

1 Place all the ingredients in the pan according to the order in the manufacturer's instructions. Set crust on medium and program for the Sweet Bread cycle; press Start. (This recipe is not suitable for use with the Delay Timer.)

2 When the baking cycle ends, immediately remove the bread from the pan and place it on a rack. Let cool to room temperature before slicing.

1½-POUND LOAF	2-POUND LOAF
½ cup milk	1 cup milk
½ cup orange juice	½ cup orange juice
1 large egg plus 1 egg yolk	2 large eggs
3 tablespoons unsalted butter, cut into pieces	4 tablespoons unsalted butter, cut into pieces
2½ cups bread flour	3½ cups bread flour
¼ cup light brown sugar	⅓ cup light brown sugar
3 tablespoons unsweetened Dutch-process cocoa powder	¼ cup unsweetened Dutch-process cocoa powder
1 tablespoon gluten	1 tablespoon plus 1 teaspoon gluten
1¼ teaspoons salt	1½ teaspoons salt
1 teaspoon instant espresso powder	1½ teaspoons instant espresso powder
¾ teaspoon ground cinnamon	1 teaspoon ground cinnamon
½ cup bittersweet chocolate chips	⅔ cup bittersweet chocolate chips
2 teaspoons SAF yeast or 2½ teaspoons bread machine yeast	2½ teaspoons SAF yeast or 1 tablespoon bread machine yeast

Technique: Melting Chocolate

Chocolate is widely used as an ingredient in sweet yeast and quick breads, and in fillings and sauces. Melt chocolate slowly in a double boiler over low heat, on the stovetop or in the microwave. Chocolate responds quickly to changes in temperature. Whatever method you use, first coarsely chop the chocolate for even melting. Chocolate burns very easily, so don't let its temperature go above 125°F. If overheated, chocolate will become grainy and taste scorched. Water causes chocolate to seize, so be sure the container you melt it in is dry. Different types and brands of good-quality chocolate melt at different rates and have different consistencies. Semisweet, bittersweet, and milk chocolates tend to hold their shape when melted and must be stirred with a whisk or rubber spatula to create a smooth consistency.

- **In a double boiler:** Place coarsely chopped chocolate over hot, just below simmering, water. Let the chocolate stand in the double boiler over the heat until melted, stirring occasionally. Because milk and white chocolates are so heat sensitive, as soon as the water is just below simmering, set the chocolate above it and remove the double boiler from the heat. Let stand until the chocolate is melted. Always melt chocolate uncovered. When you are using a double boiler, make sure the water in the lower pan doesn't touch the upper pan.

- **In a conventional oven:** Place coarsely chopped chocolate in an ovenproof glass or other ovenproof dish in a preheated 300° to 350°F oven. Check the chocolate every 5 minutes and remove it when it is melted.

- **In a microwave oven:** Place coarsely chopped chocolate in a microwave-safe container and partially cover with plastic wrap. Microwave at 50 percent power for 2 to 4 minutes, depending on the amount of chocolate you are melting. It should be shiny and slightly melted. Stir the chocolate and then microwave it for 1 minute more. Continue checking the chocolate, stirring it, and microwaving it for a minute at a time, until it is completely melted. Milk and white chocolates take less time to melt than dark or unsweetened.

- **To substitute cocoa powder for melted baking chocolate:** Use 3 tablespoons unsweetened cocoa powder and 1 tablespoon vegetable oil or butter for every ounce of unsweetened baking chocolate called for.

Recommended Brands

Once difficult for the home baker to procure, fine imported and domestic block chocolates are now much more readily available in supermarkets. Look for small baking bars of Valrhona Le Noir Gastronomie bittersweet chocolate from France, El Rey from Venezuela, Lindt Excellence from Switzerland, and Callebaut from Belgium. Van Leer's bittersweet from Jersey City, Scharffen Berger extra-bittersweet from San Francisco, and Merckens white chocolate from Massachusetts are especially fine domestic chocolates. Baker's, Tobler, and Guittard semisweet are easily found and are also very good. For chocolate chips, Nestlé, Merckens, and Guittard are all good in these breads and are easily found.

CHOCOLATE BREAD WITH DATES AND PISTACHIOS

I love dates in bread—they are very sweet just on their own, and lend their sweetness to the bread. The date palm is a versatile, important plant. It is a tree that continues to grow and give fruit for over 100 years, letting old leaves fall off as new ones are formed, the stack growing higher and higher. There is a myth that after the world was created, Allah made the date palm out of the material left over from fashioning Adam. This is a delightful bread, replete with the exotic flavors of the desert—dates and pistachios. Serve slices of it spread with cream cheese.

1 Place the ingredients, except the dates and pistachios, in the pan according to the order in the manufacturer's instructions. Set crust on medium and program for the Basic or Sweet Bread cycle; press Start. (This recipe is not suitable for use with the Delay Timer.) When the machine beeps, or between Knead 1 and Knead 2, add the dates and pistachios.

2 When the baking cycle ends, immediately remove the bread from the pan and place it on a rack. Let cool to room temperature before slicing.

1½-POUND LOAF	2-POUND LOAF
⅞ cup water	1⅛ cups water
1 large egg	1 large egg plus 1 egg yolk
3 tablespoons vegetable oil	¼ cup vegetable oil
3 cups bread flour	4 cups bread flour
½ cup sugar	⅔ cup sugar
¼ cup unsweetened Dutch-process cocoa powder	⅓ cup unsweetened Dutch-process cocoa powder
1 tablespoon gluten	1 tablespoon plus 1 teaspoon gluten
1¼ teaspoons salt	1½ teaspoons salt
2 teaspoons SAF yeast or 2½ teaspoons bread machine yeast	2½ teaspoons SAF yeast or 1 tablespoon bread machine yeast
⅔ cup snipped pitted dates	⅞ cup snipped pitted dates
¼ cup chopped pistachios	⅓ cup chopped pistachios

CHOCOLATE CHERRY BREAD

T he southwestern corner of Germany just across the river from Alsace and bordering Switzerland—the region of Baden in the Black Forest—is known for having the best food in the country. The combination of chocolate and cherries is a traditional culinary favorite there, a reflection of the fertile orchards of the area. Serve slices of this dessert bread with cups of hot tea or a sparkling white wine after a traditional meal that would make your Grossmutter proud: smoked pork chops and sauerkraut, skillet potato pancakes, steamed asparagus, and crusty rye bread. This loaf is simply wonderful with cream cheese.

1½-POUND LOAF	2-POUND LOAF
1 cup milk	1⅓ cups milk
1 large egg	1 large egg
½ teaspoon vanilla extract	¾ teaspoon vanilla extract
½ teaspoon almond extract	¾ teaspoon almond extract
3 tablespoons unsalted butter, cut into pieces	4 tablespoons unsalted butter, cut into pieces
2⅞ cups bread flour	3¾ cups bread flour
⅓ cup unsweetened Dutch-process cocoa powder	½ cup unsweetened Dutch-process cocoa powder
¼ cup light brown sugar	⅓ cup light brown sugar
1 tablespoon gluten	1 tablespoon plus 1 teaspoon gluten
1¼ teaspoons salt	1½ teaspoons salt
2 teaspoons SAF yeast or 2½ teaspoons bread machine yeast	2½ teaspoons SAF yeast or 1 tablespoon bread machine yeast
¾ cup snipped glacéed tart dried cherries (page 505)	⅞ cup snipped glacéed tart dried cherries (page 505)

❶ Place the ingredients, except the cherries, in the pan according to the order in the manufacturer's instructions. Set crust on medium and program for the Basic or Sweet Bread cycle; press Start. (This recipe is not suitable for use with the Delay Timer.) When the machine beeps, or between Knead 1 and Knead 2, add the cherries.

❷ When the baking cycle ends, immediately remove the bread from the pan and place it on a rack. Let cool to room temperature before slicing.

Leftover Bread Cookery: Bread Puddings

A fabulous way to use up the leftovers of a good soft white, challah, sweet bread, chocolate bread, or brioche is to make a bread pudding. One of my old cookbooks describes bread pudding as "a dish of many virtues," referring to its incredible versatility. Bread puddings can be laced with spirits like brandy and rum, flavored with fresh and canned fruits, from blueberries and figs to peaches and plums, topped with meringues and luscious sauces; you can even make a chocolate bread pudding or one that is served flambéed. All the puddings contain the basics: bread cubes, sugar, milk, and eggs. I am surprised at how many distinctively different desserts can be made with these ingredients as a base. Not only can the flavors vary, but the textures can be different, too, by using different ratios of bread to milk to eggs—puddings of different densities will result.

Since I adore custard in any form, I prefer a bread pudding that merges the dense texture of the moist bread with a flan-like silky custard. As quick and easy as bread puddings are to assemble and bake, somehow I think they have gotten a bad reputation by consistently being too bready. You can increase or decrease the amount of bread in any recipe given here; experiment until you achieve the texture you like. Fresh bread needs to be toasted first, but if your bread is a day or two old, you can skip toasting if you cut the cubes and let them sit out at room temperature overnight, just as for stuffing.

Please do note: After a bread pudding comes to room temperature, be sure to store the uneaten portion, covered, in the refrigerator.

Every-Night Bread Pudding
Serves 4 to 6

This is an old-fashioned bread pudding that is easy to whip up for dessert any night of the week. I make it with all milk, but you can use heavy cream or half-and-half for up to half the amount of milk if you want to make it richer. There is also a lovely white chocolate sauce to pour over. I've included some of my favorite variations, too, each better than the next.

3½ cups (about ½ loaf) day-old white, wheat, panettone, chocolate, or egg bread, crusts removed and cut into ¾-inch cubes
2 cups whole milk
⅔ cup sugar
3 large eggs
2 teaspoons vanilla extract
½ teaspoon almond extract
2 tablespoons cold unsalted butter, diced
3 tablespoons sliced almonds, for sprinkling, optional

❶ Preheat the oven to 350°F.

❷ Place the bread cubes on a baking sheet. Toast until golden brown, 10 to 15 minutes.

❸ Lower the oven temperature to 325°F and butter an 8-by-8-inch Pyrex baking dish.

❹ Transfer the bread to a large mixing bowl. Scald the milk in a small saucepan over medium heat (or heat it in the microwave). Pour over the bread and let stand for 15 minutes.

❺ With an electric mixer, beat the sugar and eggs until thick and light. Add the extracts. Pour into the milk-bread mixture and stir briefly. Scrape into the baking dish. Dot the top with butter and sprinkle with the almonds, if you are using them.

continued on next page

6 Cover the pudding with foil that has been sprayed with butter-flavored cooking spray. Bake for 35 to 40 minutes, or until the custard is set, but still moist, and the sides are firm. It will look underbaked. Serve warm or at room temperature, plain or with fresh sliced strawberries, a scoop of rum raisin ice cream, whipped cream, or this white chocolate sauce on the side.

White Chocolate Sauce

⅓ cup heavy cream
1 tablespoon Kahlua coffee liqueur
7 ounces white chocolate, roughly chopped

In a small saucepan, scald the cream. Remove from the heat. Add the Kahlua and chocolate and stir until melted. Keep warm in a hot water bath until serving.

V A R I A T I O N S

Prune Bread Pudding
Toss 1 cup halved, pitted prunes with 3 tablespoons ruby port in a small bowl and macerate for 1 hour at room temperature. Gently stir the prunes into the pudding mixture before placing in the baking dish.

Eggnog Bread Pudding
Substitute 1 cup heavy cream for 1 cup of the milk. Add ½ teaspoon brandy extract *and* ½ teaspoon rum extract in place of the almond extract. Sprinkle the top of the pudding with freshly grated nutmeg before baking.

Butterscotch Bread Pudding
Substitute light brown sugar for the white sugar. Eliminate the almond extract. Stir 1 cup butterscotch chips into the pudding mixture before placing in the baking dish.

Fresh Fruit Bread Pudding
Place ½ to 1 cup of fresh blueberries, chopped fresh pears, chopped fresh apricots, or chopped fresh peaches in the bottom of the greased baking dish. Pour the pudding mixture over the fruit.

Chocolate Bread Pudding
Serves 20

The recipe for this ultra-rich bread pudding is from Greg Topham, executive chef of East Meets West, an upscale catering company in Boston. This is a recipe Greg first learned when he was ten years old, from a Polish woman who came to live in his home. East Meets West makes this chocolate bread pudding, which is gooey rather than eggy, for clients during the winter holidays. Using high-quality chocolate is very important to the integrity of this pudding; Greg uses Valhrona bittersweet and Bensdorp cocoa. This recipe makes a large quantity; it is nice to have a special knock-out dessert large enough to serve company or take to a potluck. Serve this pudding warm with vanilla ice cream on the side, although it needs no garnish. You will be able to eat the large, cold squares out of hand when this is day-old.

Three 1½- to 2-pound loaves day-old brioche, crusts removed and cut into 1-inch cubes (if the loaves are medium-sized, I use 3 loaves, if they are large, 2)
3 pounds bittersweet chocolate, roughly chopped
2 cups whole milk
2 cups sugar
10 large eggs
½ cup unsweetened Dutch-process cocoa powder
1 tablespoon vanilla extract
4 cups cold heavy cream
½ cup (1 stick) cold unsalted butter, diced
½ cup granulated or raw sugar, for sprinkling

1 Preheat the oven to 350°F.

2 Place the bread cubes on a large baking sheet. Toast until golden brown, about 15 minutes. Combine half of the chocolate and the milk in the top of a double boiler and melt the chocolate over simmering water that does not touch the bottom of the pan. Stir with a whisk. Set the remaining 1½ pounds of chopped chocolate aside.

3 Butter a 2-gallon ceramic baking dish (Greg uses large ceramic roasting pans available from Crate and Barrel) or two deep 4-quart casseroles. Place the toasted bread cubes in a single layer in the casserole(s).

4 In the bowl of a heavy duty electric mixer fitted with the whisk attachment, whip together the sugar, eggs, cocoa, and vanilla on medium speed until smooth, creamy, and thick. The mixture will coat your finger in a thick layer and form very slowly dissolving ribbons that fall back into the bowl when the whisk is lifted out of the mixture. With a large balloon whisk, stir together the egg mixture, the cream, and the warm chocolate mixture. Pour over the bread cubes, cover with plastic wrap, and refrigerate for 30 minutes to soak. (At this point the pudding can be refrigerated for up to 8 hours before continuing.)

5 Preheat the oven to 325°F. Stir the remaining chopped chocolate into the pudding and press down to make sure all the ingredients are soaked with the liquid. Sprinkle the top with the butter. Sprinkle lightly with the sugar.

6 Cover the pudding with foil that has been sprayed with butter-flavored cooking spray. Bake for 40 to 50 minutes, or until the custard is set like a quiche and it wiggles slighly (a knife inserted into the center may not come out clean because of the pools of melted chocolate). Serve warm or at room temperature, or refrigerate and reheat the next day in a 200°F oven for 20 minutes.

PAIN AUX TROIS PARFUMS

T*he combination of pistachios, chocolate, and mint, the three perfumes, is sublime. Serve each slice with a candied mint leaf for a superb party dessert.*

❶ Place the ingredients, except the chocolate chips and pistachios, in the pan according to the order in the manufacturer's instructions. Set crust on light and program for the Sweet Bread cycle; press Start. (This recipe is not suitable for use with the Delay Timer.) When the machine beeps, or between Knead 1 and Knead 2, add the chocolate chips and pistachios.

❷ When the baking cycle ends, immediately remove the bread from the pan and place it on a rack. Let cool to room temperature before slicing.

1½-POUND LOAF	2-POUND LOAF
½ cup milk	¾ cup milk
½ cup water	½ cup water
1 large egg plus 1 egg yolk	1 large egg plus 1 egg yolk
3 tablespoons pistachio oil or melted unsalted butter	4 tablespoons pistachio oil or melted unsalted butter
1 teaspoon mint extract	1¼ teaspoons mint extract
2⅔ cups bread flour	3½ cups bread flour
¼ cup sugar	⅓ cup sugar
3 tablespoons unsweetened Dutch-process cocoa powder	4 tablespoons unsweetened Dutch-process cocoa powder
1 tablespoon plus 1 teaspoon gluten	1 tablespoon plus 2 teaspoons gluten
1 teaspoon salt	1½ teaspoons salt
2 teaspoons SAF yeast or 2½ teaspoons bread machine yeast	2½ teaspoons SAF yeast or 1 tablespoon bread machine yeast
½ cup bittersweet chocolate chips	⅔ cup bittersweet chocolate chips
⅓ cup chopped pistachios	½ cup chopped pistachios

Technique: The Final Touch

Candied Mint Leaves

Select nice-looking medium-sized mint leaves from peppermint, spearmint, bergamot, or orange mint plants, all from the mentha *family, for decorating your holiday sweet breads.*

1 egg white, or powdered egg whites reconstituted with water to equal 1 egg white
Juice of 1 lemon
½ cup superfine sugar
1 bunch mint leaves

1 Line a baking sheet with parchment. Combine the egg white with the juice of the lemon in a small bowl. Stir gently until just mixed, do not beat. Place the sugar in another bowl. Dip each leaf into the egg white mixture. Hold over the bowl of sugar and sprinkle each side with sugar. Place on the lined baking sheet. Let dry at room temperature, uncovered, for 24 hours.

2 Transfer the leaves to a shallow airtight plastic container, separating the layers with parchment paper. Store in the refrigerator for up to 4 weeks.

ITALIAN CHOCOLATE BREAD WITH AMARETTO ICING

For the nuts:

2 cups water
3 tablespoons baking soda
2 ounces whole hazelnuts
  (½ cup)

For the dough:

⅞ cup milk
1 large egg
2 tablespoons amaretto
  liqueur
3 tablespoons unsalted
  butter, cut into pieces

2⅞ cups bread flour
⅓ cup sugar
2 tablespoons unsweetened
  Dutch-process cocoa
  powder
1 tablespoon gluten
1¼ teaspoons salt
1 teaspoon ground
  cinnamon

2 teaspoons SAF yeast
  or 2½ teaspoons bread
  machine yeast

For the amaretto icing:

½ cup sifted confectioners'
  sugar
1¼ tablespoons amaretto
  liqueur
1 to 2 teaspoons hot milk

When I first discovered amaretto liqueur, I loved to have it on hand when I had parties. I would have a bottle on the table, and my guests and I would have some in our coffee, over ice cream, and even drink little sips of the viscous liquid on its own. Amaretto is made from bitter almonds and apricot kernels, which add more almondy flavor. This is a rich, fruity liqueur that stands up well in the heat of baking and accents the flavors in chocolate and nuts nicely. I buy Amaretto di Saronno, a family-made brand from northwest Italy.

1 Preheat the oven to 350°F.

2 To skin the nuts, bring the water to a boil in a saucepan. Add the baking soda and the nuts. Boil for 3 to 5 minutes; the water will turn black. Pour the nuts into a colander and run under a stream of cold water. Using your fingers, slip off each skin, and place the nuts on a clean dish towel. Pat dry and place on a clean baking sheet. Toast the nuts for 10 to 15 minutes, stirring twice. Cool on the baking sheet. Coarsely chop the nuts.

3 To make the dough, place all the ingredients in the pan according to the order in the manufacturer's instructions, adding the nuts with the dry ingredients. Set crust on medium and program for the Sweet Bread cycle; press Start. (This recipe is not suitable for use with the Delay Timer.)

4 When the baking cycle ends, remove the bread from the pan and place it on a rack with a sheet of parchment paper or a large plate underneath.

5 To make the icing, combine the icing ingredients in a small bowl and whisk until smooth. Adjust the consistency by adding more milk, a few drops at a time. Using an oversized spoon, drizzle or pour in a back and forth motion over the top of the loaf. As the glaze cools, it will set up.

2-POUND LOAF

For the nuts:

2 cups water
3 tablespoons baking soda
3 ounces whole hazelnuts (¾ cup)

For the dough:

1¼ cups milk
1 large egg
3 tablespoons amaretto liqueur
4 tablespoons unsalted butter, cut into pieces

3¾ cups bread flour
½ cup sugar
3 tablespoons unsweetened Dutch-process cocoa powder
1 tablespoon plus 1 teaspoon gluten
1½ teaspoons salt
1¼ teaspoons ground cinnamon

2½ teaspoons SAF yeast or 1 tablespoon bread machine yeast

For the amaretto icing:

½ cup sifted confectioners' sugar
1¼ tablespoons amaretto liqueur
1 to 2 teaspoons hot milk

HOLIDAY BREADS

I love baking for Christmas and Easter, having lots of good homemade bread around is just part of all the festivities. Brisk weather is balanced by the warm aromas emanating from the kitchen. Early spring warmth and color are enhanced by a golden loaf of fresh bread resting on a piece of lace. This is an unspoken language that translates into comfort and nurturing. Distinctly flavored holiday sweet breads are dramatic looking and well loved, preferred by many over the heavier desserts and cakes of the season.

In many cases, particular breads commemorate specific holidays. In the recipes that follow, I have tried to retain them in their most traditional forms, keeping the techniques as authentic as possible, but adapting them for the bread machine with great success. Many of these rich doughs have a reputation for being notoriously time-consuming, but the bread machine makes them a lighter task by far.

I remember every gathering or event where I first viewed or tasted one of these breads: an Orthodox Russian Easter brunch where the outdoor buffet table was dominated by the towering *kulich*, the window of an Italian bakery filled with mushroom-shaped domes of *gran panettone* bread with raisins poking out of the crusts, a baking class I took decades ago from master baker Diane Dexter where I made my first orange-flavored *pompe de noël*, Viennese *streisel*, and Swiss *birnenwecken*.

There are no secret techniques—available only to sophisticated bakers—required to produce these loaves. Careful attention to measuring and to the details, as well as adding the fruits and nuts at the time outlined in the recipe, will ensure that a baking masterpiece is well within reach for any baker.

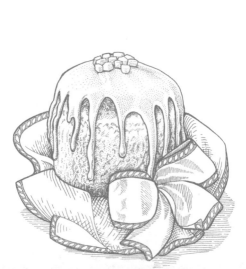

HUNGARIAN SPRING BREAD

I *love waking up on Easter morning and having a beautiful loaf of sweet bread waiting to be eaten. Hungarian bakers are known for their sweet breads and strudels and, of course, for the sour cream in their doughs. This coffee bread would normally be made in a kugelhopf or bundt pan, but I just make it in the bread machine and give it a nice lemon icing. Serve it within twenty-four hours of baking.*

❶ To make the dough, place the dough ingredients, except the raisins, lemon peel, and pecans, in the pan according to the order in the manufacturer's instructions. Set crust on medium and program for the Sweet Bread cycle; press Start. (This recipe is not suitable for use with the Delay Timer.) Sprinkle the fruit and nuts with the tablespoon of flour. When the machine beeps, or between Knead 1 and Knead 2, add the raisins, lemon peel, and nuts. The dough ball will look dry at first and take about 7 minutes to smooth out. It will still be moist.

❷ To make the icing, combine the icing ingredients in a small bowl and whisk until smooth. Adjust the consistency by adding more milk, a few drops at a time. I like this quite thick, but still pourable.

❸ When the baking cycle ends, remove the bread from the pan and place it on a wire rack with a sheet of parchment paper or a large plate underneath. Using an oversized spoon, drizzle the icing over the top of the loaf in a back and forth motion. As the glaze cools, it will set.

1½- OR 2-POUND-LOAF MACHINES

For the dough:

¾ cup sour cream, at room temperature
⅓ cup buttermilk
1 large egg plus 1 egg yolk
1½ teaspoons vanilla extract
½ teaspoon almond extract
3 tablespoons unsalted butter or margarine, cut into pieces and softened

3 cups bread flour
¼ cup sugar
1½ teaspoons salt

2½ teaspoons SAF yeast or 1 tablespoon bread machine yeast

⅓ cup golden raisins
⅓ cup diced lemon confit (page 481) or candied lemon peel (page 516)
¼ cup pecan pieces
1 tablespoon unbleached all-purpose flour

For the lemon icing:

¾ cup sifted confectioners' sugar
1 teaspoon grated lemon zest
1 teaspoon fresh lemon juice or syrup from the lemon confit
1 to 1½ tablespoons warm milk
1 teaspoon soft butter

CARDAMOM EASTER BRAID

Makes 1 large loaf

I love the look, the enticing aroma, and the flavor of this large sweet bread braid. Fresh-ground cardamom has been a favorite of mine ever since my baker-friend Judy Larsen introduced me to it thirty years ago when she gave me her mother's Scandinavian white bread recipe delicately flavored with the spice. This is a variation of that bread. Judy would also top this braid with a confectioners' sugar icing.

1 Place the dough ingredients, except the raisins or fruit, in the pan according to the order in the manufacturer's instructions. Program for the Dough cycle; press Start.

2 Line a large baking sheet with parchment paper. When the machine beeps at the end of the cycle, press Stop and unplug the machine. Immediately turn the dough out onto a lightly floured work surface. Pat into a fat rectangle and sprinkle with the raisins or fruit. Fold the dough over in thirds and knead gently to distribute evenly. Cover with a clean tea towel and let rest on the work surface for 15 minutes to relax the dough.

3 Divide the dough into 3 equal portions. Using your palms, roll each section into a fat rope about 15 inches long and tapered at each end. Be sure the ropes are of equal size and shape. Place the 3 ropes parallel to each other and braid like you are braiding hair. Adjust or press the braid to make it look even. Transfer to the baking sheet. Tuck the ends under, pinching the ends into tapered points. Cover loosely with plastic wrap and let rise at room temperature until the dough is almost doubled in bulk, about 1 hour.

4 Twenty minutes before baking, set the oven rack in the middle of the oven and preheat it to 375°F.

5 Beat the egg white and water for the glaze with a fork until foamy. Using a pastry brush, brush the tops of the loaves with the egg glaze and sprinkle liberally with the sugar. Bake for 40 to 45 minutes, or until the loaves are golden brown and the bread sounds hollow when tapped on the bottom with your finger. Cool on the baking sheet on a rack. Let cool to room temperature before slicing.

Holiday Glacéed Dried Fruit
Makes about ½ pound glazed fruit

This is one of my favorite recipes—I use it as an alternative to buying candied fruit in the supermarket. Glacéed fruits are a standard pantry item for holiday baking.

1¼ cups sugar
¼ cup honey
3 tablespoons light corn syrup
⅓ cup water
8 ounces dried fruit, such as apricots, cherries, pineapple, figs, peaches, or pear halves

1 Combine the sugar, honey, corn syrup, and water in a deep, heavy saucepan. Cook over low heat, stirring constantly with a wooden spoon, until the sugar dissolves, about 3 minutes. Using a pair of metal tongs, immerse the fruits in the syrup, taking care not to splash the syrup or crowd the fruit. Bring the mixture to a low boil without stirring. Immediately reduce the heat to medium-low and simmer. Cook the fruit slowly, for exactly 15 minutes, stirring gently to avoid burning, and occasionally basting any exposed tops. The fruit will plump up.

2 Place a large wire cooling rack over a layer of parchment or waxed paper on the counter. Fill a pan or metal bowl large enough to hold the saucepan with the fruit, with warm water.

3 Remove the pan from the heat and immediately place it in the pan of warm water to cool the syrup slightly. Carefully remove the individual pieces of fruit with the tongs, letting the extra syrup drip back into the pan. Place the fruit on the wire rack to cool completely at room temperature, for at least 8 hours. Store in an airtight container in layers separated by parchment or waxed paper that has been lightly sprayed with a thin film of vegetable oil cooking spray, for up to 3 weeks in the refrigerator.

SUZANNE'S EASTER BREAD WITH VANILLA CREAM CHEESE FROSTING

My friend Suzanne Rosenblum bakes this rich egg bread (using liquid egg substitutes) in a rectangular glass pan, which makes it a perfect fit for the medium Federal Express box, and ships it all over the United States to members of her family for Easter. She encloses directions for icing the bread (½ can each of Duncan Hines Vanilla Frosting and Duncan Hines Cream Cheese Frosting mixed together with 2 teaspoons of hot water). I have included a cream cheese icing from scratch, but you can choose whatever frosting is convenient for you. Cut this bread into squares to serve for Easter brunch or for a breakfast treat with coffee.

1½- OR 2-POUND-LOAF MACHINES

For the dough:

1 cup half-and-half
4 large eggs, or commercial liquid egg substitute equivalent
6 tablespoons unsalted butter or margarine, cut into pieces

4½ cups unbleached all-purpose flour
½ cup sugar
2 teaspoons salt

2¼ teaspoons SAF yeast or 2¾ teaspoons bread machine yeast

½ cup dried figs, stemmed and chopped
½ cup pitted dried prunes or dates, chopped
⅓ cup dried pineapple, chopped
1 tablespoon unbleached all-purpose flour, for sprinkling

For the cream cheese frosting:

One 3-ounce package cream cheese, room temperature
4 tablespoons butter, at room temperature
1 teaspoon vanilla extract
2¼ cups sifted confectioners' sugar

1 To make the dough, place the dough ingredients, except the dried fruit, in the pan according to the order in the manufacturer's instructions. Program for the Dough cycle; press Start. At the end of Knead 2, press Reset and program the cycle over again, giving the dough another full kneading. The dough will be sticky and have the consistency of a soft, smooth batter.

2 Grease the bottom and sides of a 13-by-9-inch baking pan. When the machine beeps at the end of the cycle, press Stop and unplug the machine. Turn the dough out into a deep greased bowl. Sprinkle the fruit with the tablespoon of flour. Sprinkle the dough with the chopped dried fruit and fold over the edges in the bowl to encase the fruit. Gently knead to distribute the fruit. The dough will remain very soft, almost sticky.

3 Scrape the dough into the prepared pan, pressing into the corners. Cover loosely with plastic wrap sprayed with vegetable oil cooking spray and let rise at room temperature until 1 inch above the rim of the pan, about 1 hour.

4 Twenty minutes before baking, preheat the oven to 350°F (lower the temperature by 25° if using a glass pan).

5 Bake for 35 to 40 minutes, until the bread is golden brown, the top is firm to the touch, and a cake tester inserted into the center comes out clean. Remove from the oven and invert onto a wire rack. Immediately invert again onto another rack to cool upright. When cool, wrap in plastic and store at room temperature for up to a day before icing. Store in the refrigerator after icing.

6 To make the frosting, beat the cream cheese, butter, and vanilla with an electric mixer until light and fluffy. Gradually add the confectioners' sugar, beating well. Add enough sugar to make a soft frosting that is between spreading and pouring consistency. Add a teaspoon of hot water if it is too stiff. Use immediately. Place the bread on a serving platter or board. Spread the frosting all over the top. It is okay if the frosting drips down the sides of the bread.

The Perfect Gift—Homemade Bread

Whether sent in the mail or delivered by hand, homemade bread made in the bread machine is a welcome gift at any time of the year. As a hostess gift, for a birthday, christening, or for any holiday, it is a wonderful way to treat the special people in your life. For Christmas, giving the gift of bread allows you to eliminate much of the fuss, the shopping rush, and the expenses often associated with the holiday. Plus, you'll surround yourself with evocative aromas as you bake at home.

My dear friend Judy Larsen is a great home bread baker and the one who gave me some of my first bread recipes, handed down from her mother. She always came to dinner or celebrated a holiday by giving loaves of bread. Graham bread was a surefire hit, and her white bread was embellished in all different ways for all sorts of occasions. One Christmas, she braided the loaf, glazed it with a vanilla–confectioners' sugar icing, and decorated it with candied red cherry halves on every bump down the braid (the cherries stayed in place because she placed them while the icing was wet; they adhered naturally when it dried). The loaf looked wonderful and tasted even better. Judy's beautiful loaves are largely what spurred me to take up holiday breadmaking. I began using regular and glazed nut halves for decorations, and whole silver almonds or dragées, which look really unique and festive.

If you have many people on your gift list, make a list of those you want to bake for (remember to be realistic about the amount of time you have) and collect the proper canisters, containers, boxes, labels, mailing tape, and packing material you will need for gift-giving or shipping. You will also need paper doilies, ribbon, plastic storage bags, foil, or plastic wrap, colored cellophane or tissue paper, and cardboard cake rounds, in addition to any decorative touches you decide on. The Baker's Catalogue and Miles Kimball have fabulous bread bags designed especially for bread machine loaves, (see Resources pages 610 and 614).

Begin baking early, and keep the breads in the freezer, waiting to glaze and decorate them until close to delivery or shipping dates. Choose recipes you have made before, or new ones that are appropriate to your baking ability. Be aware beforehand of what the recipes entail. If you are making panettone, for example, there may be special shopping for needed ingredients, and you would have to prepare the orange confit ahead of time. If the recipient is a baker, I usually include the recipe, written on some beautiful paper; this is something else you could do ahead of time, if you wish.

Breads for Christmas should be sent by the end of the second week in December for Christmas delivery. At other times of the year, one week ahead of when you want the bread to arrive is soon enough to mail it. If the loaf was baked outside the machine, you can send it right in the pan in which it was baked. Wrap the bread first in plastic wrap and then in aluminum foil (some bakers eliminate plastic wrap because they feel it changes the flavor of the bread), or in plastic bags.

I also like to wrap the bread by placing it on a cardboard round the same size as the bottom of the loaf, covering it with real or paper grape leaves or a paper, silver, or gold doily, and setting it on semi-transparent cellophane paper. Then I pull the ends of the cellophane up above the top of the loaf and tie them with ribbon (any width, color, or texture), raffia, or silver twine. Silk or dried flowers, cinnamon sticks, or little papier-mâché decorations can be tied into the bow.

Once the loaf is well wrapped, put some insulating material, such as bubble wrap or styrofoam peanuts, in the bottom of a box. Set the loaf inside and fill the box with more insulating material. You may also wish to insert the whole box into a larger, heavier cardboard box, filling the gaps between the boxes with added insulation. Use tape to secure the lid.

Hand-delivered bread can be decorated and wrapped as needed. I sometimes just line a basket with lemon leaves or a new cloth napkin, adorn the handle with a bow, and place the bread in it to carry in on my arm.

After all that baking, be sure to have a few extra loaves in the freezer to serve at your own table on Christmas morning or when guests stop by for tea!

EASTER RYE BREAD WITH FRUIT

T he first time I had this bread was the first time I tasted a sweet rye bread. But it is traditional in Scandinavia, where they bake a wide repertoire of breads with rye flour, especially for holidays and celebrations. Cardamom seeds, in their papery pods, look like miniature Christmas tree ornaments. To use whole cardamom in baking, crumble the pod, set the seeds on a piece of waxed paper, and fold over the waxed paper to encase the seeds. Then crush them with a rolling pin. Or use a mortar and pestle. Fresh-ground seeds are really nice, although already ground cardamom will also work fine. You can add the raisins at the beginning for this recipe, if you prefer.

1½-POUND LOAF	2-POUND LOAF
¾ cup water	1 cup water
3 tablespoons brandy	3 tablespoons brandy
1 large egg	1 large egg
3 tablespoons vegetable oil	¼ cup vegetable oil
2¼ cups bread flour	3 cups bread flour
¾ cup light or medium rye flour	1 cup light or medium rye flour
½ cup chopped almonds	⅔ cup chopped almonds
3 tablespoons dark brown sugar	¼ cup dark brown sugar
1 tablespoon gluten	1 tablespoon plus 1 teaspoon gluten
1½ teaspoons crushed cardamom seeds	2 teaspoons crushed cardamom seeds
Grated zest of 1 lemon	Grated zest of 1 lemon
Grated zest of 1 orange	Grated zest of 1 orange
1¼ teaspoons salt	1½ teaspoons salt
2½ teaspoons SAF yeast or 1 tablespoon bread machine yeast	1 tablespoon SAF yeast or 1 tablespoon plus ½ teaspoon bread machine yeast
1 cup golden raisins	1¼ cups golden raisins

1 Place the ingredients, except the raisins, in the pan according to the order in the manufacturer's instructions. Set crust on medium and program for the Sweet Bread or Fruit and Nut cycle; press Start. (This recipe is not suitable for use with the Delay Timer.) When the machine beeps, or between Knead 1 and Knead 2, add the raisins.

2 When the baking cycle ends, immediately remove the bread from the pan and place it on a rack. Let cool to room temperature before slicing.

KULICH

Makes 1 cylindrical loaf

For the fruit:

¼ cup rum raisins (page
511), with 3 tablespoons
of their rum
¼ cup currants
½ cup finely chopped dried
apricots

For the dough:

1 cup whole milk or light
cream
4 large egg yolks
2 teaspoons vanilla extract
6 tablespoons unsalted
butter, cut into pieces

4 cups unbleached
all-purpose flour
½ cup sugar
Grated zest of 1 lemon
2 teaspoons salt

2½ teaspoons SAF yeast
or 1 tablespoon bread
machine yeast

½ cup slivered blanched
almonds, lightly toasted

Confectioners', raw, or
pearl sugar, for dusting

R ussian Orthodox Christians celebrate Easter with this
sweet bread. Kulich, a bread in the tradition of brioche, is
a tall loaf, shaped rather like a puffy mushroom and traditionally decorated with strips of dough that form the Cyrillic alphabet
initials for the words "Christ is Risen." If this seems like a lot of
significance placed on what is just a loaf of bread, consider that a
homebaked loaf used as part of an Easter celebration would have been
taken to church to be blessed by the priest before serving. I give instructions for baking this loaf in a smooth-sided round mold in the
oven, since the mushroom shape is so important to the spirit of the
bread. Serve this for brunch spread with Pasqua Cheese (page 601).

❶ Combine the raisins and rum, currants, and dried
apricots in a small bowl. Cover and macerate at room
temperature for 1 hour.

❷ Place the dough ingredients, except the fruit and
almonds, in the pan according to the order in the
manufacturer's instructions. Program for the Dough
cycle; press Start.

❸ Grease a 7-inch (#18) charlotte mold, 5-pound honey
tin, or 2-pound coffee can. Fold a length of aluminum
foil in half lengthwise to make a collar 6 inches high.
Wrap around the mold and secure with kitchen twine.
This will extend the sides of the pan for a tall loaf.
When the machine beeps at the end of the cycle, press
Stop and unplug the machine. Turn the dough out
onto a lightly floured work surface and pat into a fat
rectangle. Sprinkle with the almonds and fruit. Fold
the dough over and knead gently to distribute evenly.
Knead into a ball. Place the dough in the prepared
mold. Cover loosely with greased plastic wrap and let
rise until about ½ inch above the rim of the pan (not
the foil), about 45 minutes.

4 Twenty minutes before baking, preheat the oven to 350°F, with a rack set on the lower third position.

5 Bake the *kulich* until golden brown and a cake tester inserted into the center comes out clean, about 35 to 40 minutes. If the top browns too quickly, cover loosely with a piece of aluminum foil. Immediately remove the baked loaf from the mold by sliding it out onto a rack. Brush the warm top with some melted butter and dust with confectioners' sugar or sprinkle with raw or pearl sugar. Cool completely and serve at room temperature. Top with a fresh rose if you like. If made ahead, wrap the plain bread airtight and freeze for up to 3 months. Thaw in the wrappings and rewarm in a 350°F oven for 20 minutes, then decorate.

Two Flavorful Ways to Plump Dried Fruit

Rum Raisins

Rum raisins are so simple to prepare and add so much dimension to holiday sweet breads. Drained, they can be an ingredient in breads, bread puddings, muffins, and ice creams (just fold into slightly softened vanilla ice cream and refreeze). In place of the raisins, you can use dried cherries or dried cranberries.

  2 cups dark or muscat raisins
  2 cups dark rum

Place the raisins in a spring-top jar. Cover with the rum. Replace the jar cover tightly and let the raisins stand at room temperature overnight if using the next day. For longer storage, keep in the refrigerator. Raisins will be soft and plump. Each time you remove some raisins to use, make sure the remaining raisins are still covered with rum. Refrigerated, these keep indefinitely.

Vanilla Raisins

You can use these raisins in any recipe that calls for regular raisins. They are ethereal!

  1 cup dark raisins
  1 cup golden raisins
  ¼ cup vanilla extract, heated to warm in the microwave

Place the raisins in a small bowl and toss them with the warm vanilla extract. Cover and let stand at room temperature for 3 hours to overnight. The raisins will be ready to use. For longer storage, place raisins in the refrigerator.

The Right Ingredient: Vanilla

Vanilla extract is as familiar to the home baker as chocolate. It is the most widely used spice, with a comforting perfume and delicate floral flavor. It is an extract from a flowering tropical orchid vine with edible fruit pods indigenous to Mexico, also grown in Indonesia, Tahiti, the Seychelles, and Madagascar in the Bourbon Islands.

The long, green vanilla bean pod is fermented, or cured, in the sun in a baking and sweating process for several weeks until it shrivels up. This develops the vanillin, the primary flavor of vanilla, that is encased within the skinlike walls of the pod. The word vanilla comes from the Spanish word *vainilla*, meaning "small scabbard," and *vaina*, or "string bean," which is what the pod looks like, especially when the pods are in a bunch. It has been used by apothecaries in a syrupy tincture as a stomach calmative, and shows up in perfumes (remember Shalimar by Guerlain?), candles, tobacco, and tea (my favorite is a small tin from France with black tea infused with vanilla), in addition to being used as a culinary spice.

In bread machine baking, you can use a vanilla extract, powdered vanilla, or whole beans. I use all types of vanilla. It gives great character to breads, and works well with many other accent flavors, like coffee, cocoa, sweet spices, raisins, other extracts such as almond, lemon, or orange, and spirits such as rum or brandy. It is wonderful with corn.

Vanilla Extract

Vanilla extract, in varying qualities, is the most readily available form of vanilla for the home baker. Pure amber-colored liquid extracts, made from beans, alcohol, and water in a cold-percolated method, are available in small bottles from supermarkets, specialty food stores, and by mail order. I asked food writer and vanilla expert Patricia Rain which was the best extract to use in baking. She said that the level of quality has to do with the alcohol content of the extract. You want to use a vanilla with 35 to 44 percent alcohol, which will preserve the 250 fragrance and flavor components inherent in every bean. Brands like Cook's, Nielsen-Massey (available through Williams-Sonoma), Spice Islands, and Penzeys Spice House are good choices.

Extract is also the strongest pure flavoring of vanilla available to the home baker, although there are now some extracts labeled double strength or "two fold," which need to be used sparingly (use half as much as regular vanilla). While extract smells alcoholic if you sniff it in the bottle, the alcohol's flavor evaporates in the heat of the oven, leaving only the vanilla flavor behind. Extract has a watery consistency; it is never thick. One teaspoon of extract is sufficient to flavor a pound of bread dough. Too much vanilla will make a loaf taste harsh.

Vanilla extract lasts three years in a tightly capped bottle stored in a cool, dry place away from light or in the refrigerator. I store pieces of vanilla bean in my extract. The flavor of imitation extracts, which are made from a wood pulp by-product of the paper industry and flavored with a coal tar derivative, just cannot compare to true extract.

Bottles labeled only "vanilla extract" are a blend of different types and grades of vanilla. Extracts from single growing regions will be labeled Bourbon, Mexican, or Tahitian. Madagascar Bourbon vanilla is the most affordable and most common; it has a strong, almost musky, yet classic vanilla aroma that I like with nuts, in cinnamon rolls, and in icings. The best Mexican extract is rare and expensive, but it is available in the United States. What you buy in those cheap liter bottles in the *mercado* are usually synthetic (they will contain 2 percent or less alcohol), possibly with toxic coumarin as a booster, so pass on the Mexican vanilla unless you know what you're looking for. High-end Tahitian extract is showing up more often on the market. It is expensive, has a floral, licorice-like aroma, and is considered a gourmet delicacy, even by professional bakers. It is especially nice in doughs with fresh and dried fruits.

Some bakers make their own blend of extracts.

There are many instructions, too, for making your own vanilla extract by placing the beans in brandy or vodka. I have never had great luck with this, as it takes *lots* of beans (one to three are just not enough) to get anywhere near the intense flavor of a premium vanilla extract.

Vanilla Powder

Powdered vanilla, which is very popular in Europe, is made by spraying ribbons of vanilla onto sheets of dextrose in radiant ovens. It is creamy white instead of the brown color associated with the extract and bean. It is available from Nielsen-Massey (this brand has no sugar), McCormick, and Cook's in 2-ounce jars (in many supermarkets). The powder may end up in one big, dry lump in the jar; if it does, just crumble off what you need. Long used in cake mixes, vanilla powder is also nice in streusel crumb toppings, in doughs along with vanilla extract, in all-white flour sweet doughs, and with chocolate. Use measure for measure when substituting powder for extract.

Whole Vanilla Beans

Whole beans are definitely more time-consuming to use than vanilla extract, but they give the purest vanilla flavor without the alcohol. Different beans will give different flavors to your breads. Choose from Mexican (the most brittle and shriveled), Madagascar or Bourbon (long and slender; if these have reflective crystals on them, use them—they have a high concentration of vanillin), Indonesian, and Tahitian (the most expensive, the plumpest, and most moist). If a vanilla bean is very moist, I keep it in a plastic freezer bag in the freezer to prevent mildew. Otherwise, store sleek, flexible beans in plastic or in a glass jar in a cool, dark place. If your bean is brittle, soak it in warm water or milk until pliable before splitting. You can use a bean a few times, wiping it dry after use. Beans should smell like vanilla; never use a bean that smells off or bad.

To use a vanilla bean to flavor a bread machine bread, cut the bean in half, then split it in half again lengthwise using a small knife. Scrape the seeds into the milk or other liquid you are using in the recipe, then throw in the oil-rich skin (that is where all the flavor is). Let the liquid steep for 10 minutes before removing the bean, and the liquid is ready to be added to the bread machine. I like the flecks that appear in a bread from the seeds; they remind me of eating real vanilla ice cream when I was a kid.

You can also use vanilla beans to add their flavors to sugars or coffee. I place pieces of vanilla bean (a single bean chopped into 4 or 5 pieces) in a spring-top jar and cover them with 3 to 4 cups of granulated or confectioners' sugar. The sugar takes on a vanilla flavor as it sits in the jar. The beans remain potent for about six months, and you can just keep adding more sugar to cover. Use vanilla sugar, in addition to the extract called for, in place of the regular sugar in a sweet bread or icing. Vanilla confectioners' sugar is great for dusting a fresh loaf of sweet or holiday bread. Pieces of vanilla bean can be added to the drip basket with the ground coffee to brew up a vanilla-infused pot. Or you can use the same method as with the sugar—bury pieces of a vanilla bean in your stored coffee beans, and they will take on the vanilla flavor.

Ground Vanilla Beans

Whole vanilla beans can be finely ground and dried into powder, giving a distinct and strong vanilla flavor. Ground beans are now available from Nielsen-Massey and Cook's. Use a pinch in bread doughs. You will be able to see the vanilla flecks in the finished loaf. I now use this type of vanilla.

Patricia Rain gave me a technique for how to grind whole beans, so you can make your own. This is a good way to use up beans that have been used three or four times already. Place the beans on a clean baking sheet and dry them in a 200°F oven for 10 minutes just to toast. You can do this in a skillet, but I like the oven method better. Remove from the oven and cool before breaking into pieces and grinding in a coffee grinder. The entire bean is edible. Store in a plastic container or in a glass jar in a cool, dark place.

PORTUGUESE SWEET BREAD

T*his is a buttery Portuguese holiday bread known as* Pão Doce, *a descendant of the traditional festival bread native to mainland Portugal and the Azores known as* Folar da Páscoa. *The large Portuguese population in New England has brought so much fame to this ethnic bread, though, that Portuguese sweet bread is now almost synonymous with New England. Often the loaf has a whole colored egg, a symbol of the Resurrection, set into its top, covered with a cross of dough. The bread has subtle hints of lemon and vanilla and is quite sweet. It is so good toasted and served with jam or lemon curd for breakfast. But it is just as good with a sweet wine for dessert.*

1½-POUND LOAF

⅔ cup evaporated milk
¼ cup plus 1 tablespoon
    water
2 large eggs
3 tablespoons butter,
    melted
½ teaspoon lemon extract
1 tablespoon vanilla
    extract or vanilla powder

3 cups bread flour
⅓ cup light brown sugar
1 tablespoon instant potato
    flakes
2 teaspoons gluten
1½ teaspoons salt

2½ teaspoons SAF yeast
    or 1 tablespoon bread
    machine yeast

2-POUND LOAF

¾ cup evaporated milk
⅓ cup plus 1 tablespoon
    water
2 large eggs
4 tablespoons butter,
    melted
½ teaspoon lemon extract
1 tablespoon plus
    1 teaspoon vanilla
    extract or vanilla powder

3¾ cups bread flour
½ cup light brown sugar
1½ tablespoons instant
    potato flakes
1 tablespoon gluten
2 teaspoons salt

3 teaspoons SAF yeast
    or 1 tablespoon plus
    ½ teaspoon bread
    machine yeast

1 Place all the ingredients in the pan according to the order in the manufacturer's instructions. Set crust on dark and program for the Basic or Sweet Bread cycle; press Start. (This recipe is not suitable for use with the Delay Timer.)

2 When the baking cycle ends, immediately remove the bread from the pan and place it on a rack. Let cool to room temperature before slicing.

PUMPKIN CHALLAH

Makes 2 braided loaves

Y ou can make this egg bread with any type of winter squash puree, but canned pumpkin is best since it is very thick and rich-flavored. This is a totally untraditional challah, but it is great for holiday dinners. Serve it with a savory butter for dinner, use it to make sandwiches with leftover turkey.

1 Place all the ingredients in the pan according to the order in the manufacturer's instructions. Program for the Dough cycle; press Start. The dough ball will be firm, pliable, and smooth.

2 Line a large baking sheet with parchment paper. When the machine beeps at the end of the cycle, press Stop and unplug the machine. Turn the dough out onto a lightly floured work surface; divide into 6 equal portions. Using your palms, roll each section into a fat cylinder about 12 inches long and tapered at each end. Be sure the ropes are of equal size and shape. Place 3 of the ropes parallel to each other and braid like you are braiding hair. Transfer the loaf to the baking sheet. Pinch the ends into tapered points and tuck them under. Repeat with the remaining portions. Both loaves will fit on the baking sheet cross-wise with 4 inches in between. Cover loosely with plastic wrap and let rise at room temperature until the dough is almost doubled in bulk, 45 minutes to 1 hour. Do not let it rise longer or it may collapse in the oven.

3 Twenty minutes before baking, set a rack in the middle of the oven and preheat it to 350°F.

4 Brush the tops of the loaves with the egg glaze. Bake 40 to 45 minutes, or until the loaves are golden brown and sound hollow when tapped on the bottom with your finger. Let cool on the baking sheet to room temperature before slicing.

1½- OR 2-POUND-LOAF MACHINES

½ cup water
¾ cup canned pumpkin
 puree
3 large eggs
3 tablespoons light brown
 sugar
3 tablespoons walnut or
 canola oil

4⅔ cups unbleached
 all-purpose flour
2 teaspoons salt
1 teaspoon gluten
¼ teaspoon ground ginger
¼ teaspoon nutmeg
¼ teaspoon ground
 cinnamon

2½ teaspoons SAF yeast
 or 1 tablespoon bread
 machine yeast

1 egg white beaten with
 1 tablespoon water,
 for glaze

Candied Grapefruit Peel

Makes about 2½ cups

Use this wonderful confection on its own or in combination with orange and lemon confit in your baking. It is also good for munching on after dinner. If you prefer not to use whole grapefruits when you really only need the peel, store the peel from your breakfast grapefruits in a bag in the freezer until you have enough to make this ingredient. You can also make candied lemon or orange peels with this recipe.

4 medium organic or unsprayed grapefruit
1½ cups sugar
½ cup water
2 tablespoons light corn syrup
About ¼ cup additional sugar, for sprinkling

1 Cut the peel on each grapefruit into quarters and remove each section whole from the fruit. Reserve the fruit for another use. Freeze the peel pieces for 2 to 3 hours to tenderize. When the peels are frozen, they are ready to slice. Slice the peel thin by hand or in a food processor with a ¼-inch slicing disc.

2 Place the peel in a large nonreactive saucepan and cover with cold water. Simmer over medium heat, uncovered, for about 10 to 15 minutes, until tender. Remove from the heat and let stand for 1 hour. Drain and set aside. Repeat this process two more times to leech out the bitterness. Drain and press out any extra water.

3 To make the syrup, place the sugar, water, and corn syrup in the same saucepan you used for the peel. Bring to a boil, then immediately turn the heat to low, and stir until the sugar is dissolved. Add the grapefruit peel. Simmer for about 20 to 25 minutes. The peel should be boiling gently, and will become semi-transparent. Turn the heat to high and reduce any remaining liquid to a thick syrup, stirring constantly, about 3 minutes.

4 Immediately drain the peel in a metal colander, and discard any syrup. Place the pieces in a single layer on a baking sheet lined with parchment or waxed paper.

5 Let the peel stand at room temperature to dry, for 12 hours to overnight. As it dries, sprinkle the peel with sugar to keep the pieces from sticking. To store, place the peel between layers of waxed paper in self-sealing freezer bags and freeze for up to a year. Let the candied peel stand for a few minutes at room temperature before chopping to add to a recipe.

HOLIDAY RAISIN BREAD WITH CANDIED PEELS

F*or centuries and centuries in places as diverse as the Middle East, India, China, Egypt, and ancient Greece, people coated fruits with honey to preserve them. Candied peels, known as* frutti confetti, *were considered a condiment and dessert; they served as the final course of many a meal, as well as official presents for royalty and the pope in the Middle Ages. Confectioners were considered artists just like sculptors, painters, and goldsmiths. Candied citrus peels were an integral part of the food preservation that was done in every household. Try making your own candied peels to use in this bread (see page 516). I especially like it spread with an orange Confectioners' Sugar Icing (page 449).*

❶ Place the ingredients, except the raisins and candied peels, in the pan according to the order in the manufacturer's instructions. Set crust on light and program for the Sweet Bread or Fruit and Nut cycle; press Start. (This recipe is not suitable for use with the Delay Timer.) When the machine beeps, or between Knead 1 and Knead 2, add the raisins and candied peels.

❷ When the baking cycle ends, immediately remove the bread from the pan and place it on a rack. Let cool completely before slicing.

1½-POUND LOAF	2-POUND LOAF
1⅛ cups milk 2 tablespoons honey	1⅓ cups milk 3 tablespoons honey
3 cups bread flour 1 tablespoon gluten 1½ teaspoons salt	4 cups bread flour 1 tablespoon plus 1 teaspoon gluten 2 teaspoons salt

2 teaspoons SAF yeast
  or 2½ teaspoons bread
  machine yeast
	2½ teaspoons SAF yeast
	  or 1 tablespoon bread
	  machine yeast

⅓ cup rum raisins
  (page 511)
¼ cup chopped candied
  grapefruit peel or
  candied lemon peel
  (opposite)
⅓ cup chopped candied
  orange peel (opposite)
	½ cup rum raisins
	  (page 511)
	⅓ cup chopped candied
	  grapefruit peel or
	  candied lemon peel
	  (opposite)
	½ cup chopped candied
	  orange peel (opposite)

AMARETTO BREAD

I know its richness makes it a naughty pleasure, but I adore commercial eggnog with its flavors of nutmeg and spirit extracts. Oh, the consistency!—creamy and smooth. Here is a bread in which eggnog contributes the essence of the holiday season to every bite. Since different brands of eggnog have different viscosities, be prepared to add another tablespoon or so here if yours is especially thick. This loaf is wonderful for toast and great for bread pudding. You can also glaze it with an Amaretto Icing (see page 500).

1½-POUND LOAF
¾ cup (3 ounces) whole almonds
1 cup plus 1 tablespoon commercial eggnog
¼ cup amaretto liqueur
2 large egg yolks
2 tablespoons unsalted butter, cut into pieces, or almond oil
3 cups bread flour
1 tablespoon sugar
1 tablespoon gluten
1¼ teaspoons salt
2½ teaspoons SAF yeast or 1 tablespoon bread machine yeast
¼ cup Almond Confectioners' Sugar, for dusting (opposite)

2-POUND LOAF
1 cup (4 ounces) whole almonds
1⅓ cups commercial eggnog
⅓ cup amaretto liqueur
2 large egg yolks
3 tablespoons unsalted butter, cut into pieces, or almond oil
4 cups bread flour
2 tablespoons sugar
1 tablespoon plus 1 teaspoon gluten
1½ teaspoons salt
1 tablespoon SAF yeast or 1 tablespoon plus ½ teaspoon bread machine yeast
¼ cup Almond Confectioners' Sugar, for dusting (opposite)

1 Preheat the oven to 350°F.

2 Coarsely chop the almonds and spread them evenly on a clean baking sheet. Bake until lightly toasted, about 5 to 7 minutes. Remove from the oven and let cool.

3 Place the ingredients, except the almonds, in the pan according to the order in the manufacturer's instructions. Set crust on medium and program for the Basic cycle; press Start. (This recipe is not suitable for use with the Delay Timer.) When the machine beeps, or between Knead 1 and Knead 2, add the almonds. Touch and press the dough with your fingers. It should be soft and pliable.

4 When the baking cycle ends, immediately remove the bread from the pan and place it on a rack. Let cool to room temperature; then dust with Almond Confectioners' Sugar before slicing.

Almond Confectioners' Sugar

Either as an ingredient in a bread or for dusting over the top, a flavored nut-sugar powder is an old professional trick. Almonds are the perfect nut to use, since they are lowest in oil. This makes a fluffy sugar that keeps at room temperature for up to 1 month in an airtight container.

1 cup blanched almonds
1¼ cups confectioners' sugar

Place the nuts in the workbowl of a food processor with half of the confectioners' sugar. Process until finely ground and fluffy. Add the rest of the sugar and process until a fine powder is created. Use for dusting holiday breads and sweet rolls.

ANISE CHRISTMAS BREAD

T*his is a simple, beautiful, Mexican-style holiday bread flavored with candied cherries and anise extract. It is a perfect bread for end-of-the-year festivities since anise is traditionally served at the end of a meal to signify a wish for good fortune. The dough turns a lovely pink hue as the cherries are incorporated into it by the kneading blade. If you like a fancier loaf, glaze it with Confectioners' Sugar Icing (page 449) after baking.*

1 Place the ingredients, except the cherries or apricots, in the pan according to the order in the manufacturer's instructions. Set crust on medium and program for the Sweet Bread or Fruit and Nut cycle; press Start. (This recipe is not suitable for use with the Delay Timer.) When the machine beeps, or between Knead 1 and Knead 2, add the fruit. The dough ball will be moist; resist the impulse to add more flour.

2 When the baking cycle ends, immediately remove the bread from the pan and place it on a rack. Let cool completely before slicing.

1½-POUND LOAF	2-POUND LOAF
⅞ cup water	1⅛ cups water
1 large egg	1 large egg plus 1 egg yolk
2 tablespoons unsalted butter, cut into pieces	3 tablespoons unsalted butter, cut into pieces
¾ teaspoon anise extract	1 teaspoon anise extract
2½ cups bread flour	3½ cups bread flour
3 tablespoons sugar	¼ cup sugar
2 tablespoons dry buttermilk powder	3 tablespoons dry buttermilk powder
1 tablespoon gluten	1 tablespoon plus 1 teaspoon gluten
1¼ teaspoons salt	1½ teaspoons salt
2¼ teaspoons SAF yeast or 2¾ teaspoons bread machine yeast	2½ teaspoons SAF yeast or 1 tablespoon bread machine yeast
¾ cup whole glacéed cherries or chopped glacéed apricots (page 505)	1 cup whole glacéed cherries or chopped glacéed apricots (page 505)

CHAMPAGNE-SOAKED BABA

Baba is a traditional bistro dessert. Its round cylindrical shape crosses over perfectly to tall bread machine pans. This is a grand baba, as opposed to individual petite babas. Baba is plump like a plush toy—soaked in a spirited champagne syrup, glazed, and then cut into wedges or slices to serve with sweetened whipped cream. Serve it the day it is made or no more than one day later for the best texture. For special occasions, I top the baba with a fresh, unsprayed rose by cutting a two-inch stem, then covering it with plastic wrap and pressing it into the top to secure.

1 To make the dough, place all the dough ingredients in the pan according to the order in the manufacturer's instructions. Set crust on medium and program for the Sweet Bread cycle; press Start. (This recipe is not suitable for use with the Delay Timer.) The dough will be batterlike.

2 Meanwhile make the soaking syrup. Combine the sugar and water in a small pan and heat until sugar is dissolved, about 5 minutes. Cool until warm. Add the champagne; set aside.

3 When the baking cycle ends, place the pan on a rack; pierce the top of the baba in a few places with

1½-POUND LOAF

For the dough:

⅓ cup water
3 large eggs
6 tablespoons unsalted butter, melted

2 cups bread flour
1½ tablespoons sugar
½ teaspoon grated lemon zest
½ teaspoon salt

1¼ teaspoons SAF yeast or 1¾ teaspoons bread machine yeast

For the soaking syrup:

¾ cup sugar
¾ cup water
½ cup sweet champagne or Asti Spumante

For apricot glaze:

⅓ cup apricot jam

2-POUND LOAF

For the dough:

½ cup water
3 large eggs
½ cup (1 stick) unsalted butter, melted

3 cups bread flour
2 tablespoons sugar
¾ teaspoon grated lemon zest
¾ teaspoon salt

1¾ teaspoons SAF yeast or 2¼ teaspoons bread machine yeast

For the soaking syrup:

¾ cup sugar
¾ cup water
½ cup sweet champagne or Asti Spumante

For apricot glaze:

⅓ cup apricot jam

a bamboo skewer. Turn out of the pan onto a deep plate. Slowly pour the champagne soaking syrup all over the cake and let it stand to absorb the puddle that collects at the base. Cover with plastic wrap.

4 To prepare the apricot glaze, place the jam in a small saucepan and boil for 2 minutes to liquify. Drain off any extra soaking syrup from the plate. Brush the cake all over with hot glaze to seal in moisture. Cool and transfer to a clean serving plate before serving, turning the baba on its side to cut into round slices. Store the baba in the refrigerator.

VENETIAN PANETTONE

*Makes 1 large
or 2 small loaves*

P anettone is a Christmas bread that is made all over Italy.
It has a traditional Italian combination of orange peel,
citron, and raisins in an airy egg bread dough. While
panettone was known and eaten in the Middle Ages, it had a different shape than it does now. It looked like an Irish soda bread, a
round freeform loaf with a cross on top. It was first baked in a tall
cylindrical mold by a Milanese baker in 1921, and it is this shape
that is common today.

Fiori di Sicilia, *available from The Baker's Catalogue, is a
combination of vanilla and citrus
flavors, a traditional Sicilian touch
to panettone that gives an aroma of
vanilla and flowers. Vanilla extract
will also do nicely here.*

*This bread is perfect for brunch
with cappucino or tea. Day-old
panettone is good sliced into thick
fingers and baked in a single layer
on an ungreased baking sheet at
300°F for 45 minutes, or until
pale golden and crisp. Similar to
biscotti, these dry toasts can be
served as an accompaniment to
fresh fruits, sorbets, and gelatos.*

❶ Place the dried and candied
fruit in a small bowl and
toss with 2 tablespoons of
the flour. Set aside.

❷ Place the ingredients, except the fruit, in the pan
according to the order
in the manufacturer's in-
structions. Program for

1½-POUND LOAF	2-POUND LOAF
½ cup golden raisins	⅔ cup golden raisins
⅓ cup orange confit (page 481) or minced dried apricots	½ cup orange confit (page 481) or minced dried apricots
2 tablespoons minced dried pineapple or candied citron	3 tablespoons minced dried pineapple or candied citron
1 cup water	1⅓ cups water
2 tablespoons honey	3 tablespoons honey
5 tablespoons unsalted butter, melted	6 tablespoons unsalted butter, melted
3 large egg yolks	4 large egg yolks
2½ teaspoons vanilla extract or *Fiori di Sicilia*	3 teaspoons vanilla extract or *Fiori di Sicilia*
3 cups bread flour	4 cups bread flour
3 tablespoons vanilla sugar	¼ cup vanilla sugar
1½ teaspoons salt	2 teaspoons salt
2 teaspoons SAF yeast or 2½ teaspoons bread machine yeast	2½ teaspoons SAF yeast or 1 tablespoon bread machine yeast
Sifted confectioners' sugar, for dusting	Sifted confectioners' sugar, for dusting

the Dough cycle; press Start. Set a kitchen timer for 10 minutes. When the timer rings, press Stop and unplug the machine. The dough ball will be very delicate, yet smooth and springy. Let the dough rise in the machine until the dough almost reaches the top of the pan. This takes 1 hour to 1 hour and 15 minutes.

3 If you will be making one large loaf, grease a metal panettone tube mold, 5-inch diameter paper panettone pan, 7-inch (#18) charlotte mold, or a 2-pound coffee can. If you will be making two small loaves, line a baking sheet with parchment paper. When the dough has risen to the top of the bread pan, turn the dough out onto a lightly floured work surface. Pat the dough into a large rectangle and sprinkle with the fruit. Fold the dough over and knead lightly to distribute the fruit.

4 *To make one large loaf:* Shape the whole amount of dough into an oval. If you are using the tube mold, place your fingers in the center of the dough and pull open a hole. Set the dough into the pan. If you are using the charlotte mold, paper mold, or 2-pound coffee can, place the oval of dough in it. With kitchen shears, cut an X ½ inch deep into the top of the loaf.

5 *To make two small loaves:* Divide the dough into 2 equal pieces. Form the pieces into tight round balls and place on the baking sheet, at least 3 inches apart. With kitchen shears, cut an X ½ inch deep into the top of each loaf.

6 Cover loosely with plastic wrap and let rise again at room temperature until doubled in bulk, about 1 hour.

7 Twenty minutes before baking, preheat the oven to 375°F.

8 For any loaf other than one made in the panettone mold, gently redefine the X with the kitchen shears, and insert a small nut–sized piece of butter into the cut; it will bake into the loaf. Bake the large loaf for 40 to 45 minutes or the small loaves for 30 to 35 minutes, until the panettone is golden brown and sounds hollow when tapped with your finger. Remove from the baking sheet or slide out of the mold to cool on a rack. Dust with confectioners' sugar before serving.

Panettone: A Traditional Dessert

While panettone is perfect fresh or toasted with morning coffee or afternoon tea, it is also a great dessert. Place slices of panettone on a baking sheet. Butter or dust with ¼ cup of powdered sugar sifted through a mesh strainer. Bake in a preheated 400°F oven until nicely browned and toasted, about 8 to 10 minutes. Remove each slice to an individual serving plate and place a scoop of vanilla ice cream on each slice. Spoon over some Orange Confit (page 481) in its syrup. Or else, do as the Italians do: stand a wedge of panettone on the dessert plate with some Mascarpone Cream on the side.

Mascarpone Cream

Makes about 1¼ cups

⅓ cup cold heavy cream
4 ounces mascarpone cheese
¼ cup sifted confectioners' sugar
1 egg yolk or commercial egg substitute equivalent
2 tablespoons liqueur, such as Grand Marnier, Frangelico, amaretto, or cognac

Using a hand-held electric mixer, whip the cream in a bowl. Combine the remaining ingredients in another bowl and beat until smooth. Fold in the whipped cream. Store, covered, in the refrigerator.

STOLLE DE NÖEL

Makes 2 flat loaves

W hen forming this dough into a loaf to bake in the oven, please note that the traditional flat shape given here is the best for the density of this bread. The dough is rich in butter and dried fruits with a rather firm, dry texture. It is very easy to shape. Think of it as a great big Parker House roll. Stollen keeps perfectly for two weeks at room temperature well wrapped in plastic. Cut the loaf into thin slices to serve with hot coffee spiked with a liqueur, eggnog, or hot mulled cider.

1½- OR 2-POUND-LOAF MACHINES

For the dough:

About ¾ cup milk
1 large egg plus 1 egg yolk
½ teaspoon almond extract
Grated zest of 1 lemon

2¾ cups unbleached
   all-purpose flour
1 cup almond flour
⅓ cup sugar
1 teaspoon salt

2 teaspoons SAF yeast
   or 2½ teaspoons bread
   machine yeast

½ cup (1 stick) unsalted
   butter, at room temperature, cut into 16 pieces

3 tablespoons unsalted
   butter, melted, for
   brushing
2 tablespoons sugar mixed
   with ½ teaspoon ground
   nutmeg, for sprinkling
¾ cup sifted confectioners'
   sugar, for dredging

For the fruit:

¾ cup dried tart cherries
½ cup minced dried apricots
¼ cup dried currants
¼ cup golden raisins
3 tablespoons amber rum
3 tablespoons boiling water
2 tablespoons unbleached
   all-purpose flour

❶ To prepare the fruit, place the dried fruit in a small bowl and cover with the rum and boiling water. Set aside overnight to cool and plump.

Drain the plumped dried fruit (catch any extra liquid in a measuring cup), pat dry with paper towels, and toss with the 2 tablespoons of flour. Add enough milk to the fruit juice to make ¾ cup.

❷ To make the dough, place all the dough ingredients except the butter in the pan according to the order in the manufacturer's instructions. Program for the Dough cycle; press Start. Set a kitchen timer for 7 minutes. The dough ball will be soft.

❸ When the timer rings (you will be in Knead 2), open the lid and, while the machine is running, add a piece or two of the butter at a time, allowing it to be incorporated before adding more pieces. It will take a full minute or two to add all the butter. Close the lid.

4 A few minutes after the butter has been added (still during kneading), open the lid and sprinkle in the fruit a little at a time. Close the lid and let the machine complete the Dough cycle. When the machine beeps at the end of the cycle, press Stop and unplug the machine. Set a timer for 1 hour and let the dough continue to rise in the warm environment of the machine.

5 Line a baking sheet with parchment paper. Turn the dough out onto a lightly floured work surface. Without working the dough further, divide it into 2 equal portions. Using your hands, pat each portion into a 12-by-7-by-¾ inch thick, long oval. Use only enough flour on the work surface table to keep the dough from sticking. Brush the surface of each oval with melted butter and sprinkle each with half of the nutmeg sugar. Make a crease down the center of the oval and, without stretching, fold from the long edge over to within ¾ inch of the opposite side (it will be slightly off center), forming a long, narrow loaf. Taper the ends by pinching and rounding the points slightly. Press the top edge lightly to seal. Repeat to form the second stollen. Transfer the stollens to the baking sheet and place about 4 inches apart. Cover loosely with plastic wrap. Let rise again at room temperature until puffy, 30 to 45 minutes.

6 Twenty minutes before baking, preheat the oven to 350°F.

7 Brush the tops of the stollen with melted butter. Bake for 30 to 35 minutes, or until lightly browned. If the tops are browning too quickly, cover loosely with a tent of aluminum foil. Take care not to overbake. Remove from the baking sheet and place on a wire rack. Place the confectioners' sugar on a large flat plate. Dredge the warm loaf on all sides in the powdered sugar and let it cool completely. Stollen is best if left to age for a few days before serving.

V A R I A T I O N

Stolle de Nöel mit Marzipan

1 cup (one 8-ounce can) almond paste

Prepare the stollen as directed. In Step 5, after brushing with butter and sprinkling with nutmeg sugar, crumble the almond paste and sprinkle half down the center of each loaf. Fold over as directed, completely covering the almond paste. Rise and bake as directed.

Holiday Breads for Entertaining

Aside from serving holiday breads toasted in the morning for breakfast or with tea in the afternoon, you can incorporate them beautifully into elegant, yet personal, family meals and entertaining. This is where your freezer will come in handy—the breads can be baked up to a month ahead, frozen, and then decorated and glazed just before serving.

Here are some ideas for how to serve holiday breads: Place Easter loaves on a buffet table covered with a vibrantly colored tablecloth, and surround the loaves with potted spring flowers (daffodils, crocus,

narcissus) and decorated eggs. Use lemon leaves to garnish. Decorate a Christmas buffet table with pine boughs, twinkling white lights, bowls of glossy red apples, a basket of nuts for cracking, and giant bayberry-scented candles. Breads can be displayed whole (with a gold ribbon tied around) or sliced and arranged on silver trays with candied flowers and marzipan fruits.

You may have some of your own traditions for serving holiday breads. Here are some of my menu suggestions.

Easter Sunday Brunch

Fresh Orange Juice & Cranberry Juice
with Lime Wedges

Spiral-Cut Glazed Ham
Maple Mustard & Horseradish Cream
Spring Asparagus Tart
Creamy Cole Slaw
Bibb Lettuce with Oranges, Red Onions & Olives

A Variety of Easter Breads:
Kulich (page 510)
Sweet Babka with Chocolate Swirl (page 462)
Cardamom Easter Braid (page 504)
Maritozzi Romani (page 480)

Pasqua Cheese (page 601) & Butter Curls
Coffee, Tea, Milk

•••

Christmas Open House

Hot Mulled Red Wine & Hot Spiced Apple Juice
Eggnog with Brandy & Rum on the Side
Champagne, White Wine & Asti Spumante
Mineral Water

Seasonal Crudité Basket with Hot Artichoke Dip
(page 606)
Elegant & Rustic Cheeses with Seasonal Fresh Fruit
Savory Appetizer Cheesecake (page 602)

Mushrooms Stuffed with
Pancetta and Herbs (page 316)
Teriyaki Sesame Chicken Wings
Side of Smoked Salmon with
Flavored Cream Cheeses & Bagels (page 88)
Capers & Lemon
Cold Crab Pâté
Eggplant Caponata on French Bread

Prosciutto-Wrapped Asparagus

Spinach & Feta Filo Triangles

Rosemary Pecans

A Variety of Christmas Breads:
Spicy Pear Bread (page 456)
Stolle de Nöel (page 526)
Venetian Panettone (page 523)
Anise Christmas Bread (page 520)
Apple Challah (page 466)

Christmas Cookies & Gingerbread Men
Chocolate Truffles
Coffee

BOLO REI

1½- OR 2-POUND-LOAF MACHINES

½ cup milk
½ cup water
2 tablespoons amber rum
2 large eggs
6 tablespoons unsalted butter or margarine, partially melted

4 cups unbleached all-purpose flour
½ cup sugar
Grated zest of 1 orange
1½ teaspoons salt

2½ teaspoons SAF yeast or 1 tablespoon bread machine yeast

1 egg yolk beaten with 2 teaspoons rum, for glaze
Whole blanched almonds, whole glacéed dried fruit, candied citrus peel, or candied angelica, for decorating

S panish and Mexican holiday breads are always sweet like this one, shaped into an oversized donut-like ring. Called bolo rei *in Portuguese, and* rosca *in Mexico and the Iberian peninsula, it even shows up in Italy as* aciambella. *The shape comes from when breads were designed as circular objects to symbolize spiral or coiled serpents. If you would like this to be a more festive bread, sprinkle the dough with 1 cup of chopped Holiday Glacéed Dried Fruit (page 505) before rolling it up, but I like it plain as it is given here, with the flavors of rum and orange. (Traditionally a coin or small porcelain doll would also be rolled up in the dough, and it was considered good luck for the diner who got the prize.) This bread is made from Christmas to Epiphany, the feast of the three kings (or the Twelfth Day of Christmas).*

1 Place all the dough ingredients in the pan according to the order in the manufacturer's instructions. Program for the Dough cycle; press Start. The dough ball will be firm and pliable.

2 Line a baking sheet with parchment paper. When the machine beeps at the end of the cycle, press Stop and unplug the machine. Turn the dough out onto a lightly floured work surface. Without working the dough further, roll out with a rolling pin to a 9-by-18-inch rectangle. Roll up jelly-roll fashion, from a long edge. Pinch the seams to seal, leaving the ends open. Place on the baking sheet and form into a round circle by connecting the two open ends. Seal by dipping your fingers in water and pinching closed. Place a greased ovenproof bowl about the same size as the center hole upside down in the space to keep the hole from closing during baking. Cover loosely with plastic wrap and let rise at room temperature for 30 minutes.

3 Twenty minutes before baking, preheat the oven to 350°F.

4 Brush the ring with the egg glaze. Make designs by pressing in the dried fruit and nut pieces (I like a daisy effect). Let rest for another 15 minutes, uncovered.

5 Bake for 30 to 35 minutes, or until golden brown and a cake tester inserted into the center comes out clean. Remove from the baking pan and place on a wire rack. Let cool completely before serving.

GREEK SWEET BREAD

Makes 1 round loaf

T hose of the Greek Orthodox faith have a sweet bread for every major holiday. At Easter there is Lambropsomo, for Christmas, Christopsomo, and for New Year's Day Vasilopita, or St. Basil's Bread. The same basic dough is used for each bread, but the flavoring and shape vary. I shape this loaf into a simple large round. But do vary the flavorings—two variations are given here. I use apple pie spice in the bread. This combination of cinnamon, allspice, and cloves gives a hint of the traditional flavors of the more exotic ground mastic, a resiny spice, and mahlepi seeds, from the pits of St. Lucy's cherries. Use a strong, dark honey if you can. Greek Sweet Bread should be served with honey as a sweet, never with butter.

1½-POUND LOAF

For the dough:
¾ cup fat-free milk
¼ cup fruity olive oil
1 large egg plus 1 egg yolk

3 cups bread flour
¼ cup honey
Grated zest of 1 orange or lemon
1 tablespoon gluten
1½ teaspoons salt
1 teaspoon apple pie spice

2½ teaspoons SAF yeast or 1 tablespoon bread machine yeast

For the glaze:
2 tablespoons corn syrup
2 tablespoons honey
2 tablespoons orange juice

2 tablespoons white or black sesame seeds (nigella)

2-POUND LOAF

For the dough:
⅞ cup fat-free milk
¼ cup plus 1 tablespoon fruity olive oil
1 large egg plus 1 egg yolk

3¾ cups bread flour
⅓ cup honey
Grated zest of 1 orange or lemon
1 tablespoon plus 2 teaspoons gluten
2 teaspoons salt
1¼ teaspoons apple pie spice

1 tablespoon SAF yeast or 1 tablespoon plus ½ teaspoon bread machine yeast

For the glaze:
2 tablespoons corn syrup
2 tablespoons honey
2 tablespoons orange juice

2 tablespoons white or black sesame seeds (nigella)

1 To make the dough, place all the dough ingredients in the pan according to the order in the manufacturer's instructions. Program for the Dough cycle; press Start. (This recipe is not suitable for use with the Delay Timer.)

2 Line a baking sheet with parchment paper. When the machine beeps at the end of the cycle, press Stop and unplug the machine. Turn the dough out onto a lightly floured work surface.

If you are making one of the variations, pat the dough into a fat rectangle and sprinkle with the desired additional ingredients; then fold the dough over, kneading it gently to distribute the additions evenly. Knead the dough into a tight round and place it on the prepared pan. Cover loosely with greased plastic wrap and let rise until doubled in bulk, about 1 hour.

3 Twenty minutes before baking, set the oven rack on the lower third position and preheat the oven to 350°F.

4 Bake for 40 to 45 minutes or until golden brown and the loaf sounds hollow when tapped on the bottom with your finger. Remove the bread from the pan to cool on a rack for a few minutes before glazing.

5 To make the glaze, combine the corn syrup, honey, and orange juice in a small saucepan. Bring to a boil; boil 1 minute. Brush the top of the warm loaf with the glaze and sprinkle with sesame seeds. Cool completely before slicing.

V A R I A T I O N S

Greek Christmas Bread

For 1½-pound loaf:
¼ cup golden raisins
¼ cup dark raisins
¼ cup dried figs, stemmed and chopped
¼ cup chopped toasted walnuts

For 2-pound loaf:
⅓ cup golden raisins
⅓ cup dark raisins
⅓ cup dried figs, stemmed and chopped
⅓ cup chopped toasted walnuts

Soak the dried figs in boiling water for an hour to soften them, or use canned figs. Add the raisins, figs, and nuts as instructed in Step 2.

Greek Easter Bread

For 1½-pound loaf:
½ cup golden raisins

For 2-pound loaf:
⅔ cup golden raisins

Add the raisins as instructed in Step 2.

GOLDEN PANDOLCE

Makes 2 round loaves

F rom the north of Italy, the original home of the early Etruscans, comes this delicate fruit and nut bread that is good for Easter or Christmas. Pandolce *simply means "sweet bread" in Italian. I love the rustic shape of its decorative top; it reminds me of a court jester's cap. Serve this for brunch with some fresh goat cheese and honey.*

1½-POUND LOAF	2-POUND LOAF
½ cup golden raisins	¾ cups golden raisins
2 tablespoons Marsala	3 tablespoons Marsala
1 tablespoon flour	1 tablespoon flour
½ cup milk	⅔ cup milk
½ cup water	⅔ cup water
2 tablespoons Marsala	3 tablespoons Marsala
¼ cup olive oil	⅓ cup olive oil
1 tablespoon orange-flower water	1½ tablespoons orange-flower water
1 teaspoon vanilla extract	1½ teaspoons vanilla extract
3 cups bread flour	4 cups bread flour
¼ cup sugar	⅓ cup sugar
3 tablespoons chopped pine nuts	¼ cup chopped pine nuts
1 tablespoon gluten	1 tablespoon plus 2 teaspoons gluten
1 teaspoon salt	1½ teaspoons salt
½ teaspoon aniseed, crushed	¾ teaspoon aniseed, crushed
2¼ teaspoons SAF yeast or 2¾ teaspoons bread machine yeast	2½ teaspoons SAF yeast or 2¾ teaspoons bread machine yeast
1½ tablespoons butter, cut into 8 pieces, for topping	1½ tablespoons butter, cut into 8 pieces, for topping
1 tablespoon sugar, for sprinkling	1 tablespoon sugar, for sprinkling

1 Combine the raisins and Marsala in a small bowl. Let stand for 30 minutes at room temperature to macerate.

2 Place the ingredients, except the raisins and the tablespoon of flour, in the pan according to the order in the manufacturer's instructions. Program for the Dough cycle; press Start. The dough ball will be slightly soft.

3 Line a baking sheet with parchment paper. When the machine beeps at the end of the cycle, press Stop and unplug the machine. Turn the dough out onto a lightly floured work surface and pat into a fat rectangle. Lift the raisins out of their liquid with a slotted spoon and toss them with the tablespoon of flour.

Reserve the liquid. Sprinkle the dough with the raisins. Fold the dough over and knead gently to evenly distribute. Knead into a tight round and divide into 2 equal portions. Shape each portion into a round loaf. Place the rounds on the prepared pan. Cover loosely with a clean tea towel and let rise until doubled in bulk, about 1 hour and 15 minutes.

4 Twenty minutes before baking, preheat the oven to 350°F, with a rack set in the middle position.

5 With a lamé or small, very sharp knife, cut an X on top of each loaf. With your fingers, pull on the point of one triangular piece of one loaf. You will have a slight skin that has dried during rising. Pull up and back, using the knife to cut just under the skin, like skinning a chicken breast, cutting and pulling back to the rim of the loaf. Peel the triangular piece back and lay it over the side of the loaf. Continue with the other 3 sections of the X. Then repeat with the other loaf. You will have an opened area, or "ear," on top of each. Place a piece of butter just inside the base of each ear. Flip a small portion of each point back over the butter piece. Drizzle the tops with the reserved raisin-soaking liquid, and sprinkle with sugar.

6 Bake for 35 to 40 minutes, until golden brown and the loaves sound hollow when tapped on the bottom with your finger. Remove the loaves from the pan and place on a rack. Let cool completely before slicing.

MARZIPAN KRINGLE

Makes 1 large loaf

1½- OR 2-POUND-LOAF MACHINES

For the dough:

1¼ cups whole milk or light cream
3 large egg yolks
6 tablespoons unsalted butter, cut into pieces

3½ cups unbleached all-purpose flour
¼ cup sugar
1½ teaspoons salt

2¼ teaspoons SAF yeast or 2¾ teaspoons bread machine yeast

For the marzipan filling:

1¼ cups almond paste
½ cup sugar
1 egg white, beaten
1 teaspoon almond extract
1 teaspoon ground cinnamon
¾ cup chopped almonds

For the glaze and topping:

3 tablespoons raw sugar
1 egg white beaten with 1 tablespoon water
½ cup sliced almonds

I love bread made in the beautiful pretzel shape. Whole loaves shaped into pretzels may be unfamiliar to you, but for centuries this has been the shape of bread made for weddings and holidays. Some bakers prefer to shape this loaf into a thick horseshoe instead. Marzipan, also called massepain in French—simply almond paste—is one of my favorite fillings. It is a combination of ground almonds, sugar, and egg whites beaten into a meringue. It is said to have been invented in Milan by nuns. Serve this kringle for brunch with coffee, or tea, and fresh orange juice, and savor every bite.

❶ Place all the dough ingredients in the pan according to the order in the manufacturer's instructions. Program for the Dough cycle; press Start. When the machine beeps at the end of the cycle, press Stop and unplug the machine. Scrape the dough into a greased 4-quart plastic container (I spray with a butter-flavored cooking spray) and cover. Refrigerate for 12 to 24 hours.

❷ To make the filling, place the almond paste, sugar, egg white, almond extract, and cinnamon in a deep bowl. Beat with an electric mixer until just smooth. Set aside.

❸ Line a baking sheet with parchment paper. Turn the dough out onto a lightly floured work surface, preferably a marble slab, and pat into a fat rectangle. With a rolling pin, roll into a 12-by-20-inch rectangle. Spread with the almond filling, leaving a 1-inch border all the way around. Sprinkle with the ¾ cup chopped almonds. Roll up tightly, jelly-roll fashion, into a long 20-inch log. Sprinkle the raw sugar on the work surface and roll the log in the sugar, coating all surfaces. Roll the log back and forth with your palms to extend it to 30 inches. Place it on the baking sheet and form a circle, crossing the ends and then folding them over to touch the center of the circle on the bottom to make a pretzel. Cover loosely with a clean tea towel and let rise until puffy, about 45 minutes.

4 Twenty minutes before baking, preheat the oven to 375°F.

5 Brush the egg glaze over the sugar and sprinkle with the sliced almonds. Bake the loaf until golden brown and firm to the touch, 25 to 30 minutes. Remove from the baking sheet and cool completely on a rack before serving.

EXPRESS LANE BREAD

No-Yeast Quick Breads

Quick breads are exceptionally popular with bakers, and it was only a matter of time before bread machine manufacturers added a cycle specifically for making them. Even after decades of professional yeast baking experience, when I am baking for myself, I often make this type of loaf. Not only do quick breads allow me to quickly assemble the ingredients from an elementary pantry, but I can include my favorite seasonal ingredients in the loaves. Supermarket shelves carry commercial mixes that I doctor to save time. A stash of quick loaves in the freezer makes last-minute breakfasts or serving tea visitors effortless.

True to their name, quick breads, which rely on the power of chemical leaveners rather than yeast to lighten their batters, require no fermentation time. The loaves are baked immediately after mixing—quick and easy. The texture of a quick bread baked in a conventional oven is created by the effect of the high heat on the baking powder and baking soda in the batter. High heat tends to create large bubbles of CO_2. The lower, consistent heat of the bread machine causes the leavenings to react more slowly, making smaller bubbles, and creating a bread with a tighter texture. Traditional breads like pound cakes and gingerbreads bake up beautifully in the bread machine.

Different quick bread recipes work up into different styles of batter consistency, either astonishingly thick, known as a drop batter, or thin enough to be a pour batter. They bake up to be cakelike or more like dense muffins. I have found that a medium-thick creamy batter works best in the bread machine. The loaves can range in texture from a tender pound cake to a tightly grained loaf, depending on the proportions of flour and liquid to the added embellishment. Older bread machines require the baker to mix the batter by hand outside the machine, but the new ones mix the ingredients beautifully with the action of the paddle alone; all you have to do is layer them in the pan. If yours mixes the ingredients for you, just check to make sure there is no clumping or unmixed flour in the corners of a horizontal pan during mixing. Use a soft plastic spatula to scrape down the sides of the pan before the baking starts. I usually do this about six minutes into the mixing.

Quick breads can be sweet or savory, plain or loaded with chopped fruit and nuts. There are many foods to choose from to imaginatively flavor a loaf: dried fruits; nuts; fresh fruits such as bananas, citrus, cranberries, pineapple, and papaya; fresh dates; carrots and parsnips; creamy cheeses; olives; and wild rice. The only rule to remember when making bread machine quick breads is to keep the total amount of these extra ingredients small, otherwise they will add too much weight to the batter and you will end up with a flat loaf.

Accent flavors include pungent liqueurs and aromatic extracts, coffee, crushed crystallized ginger, and many sweet exotic spices. Quick loaves successfully integrate all kinds of whole-grain flours, from whole wheat and cornmeal to oatmeal and bran. To make a loaf more sophisticated, while the loaf is still hot I will pierce it and drizzle it with a mixture of equal parts sugar and fruit juice or an alcoholic spirit, to form a thin glaze of flavor. Or I dust a cooled loaf with confectioners' sugar. A plain, unadorned loaf is just fine, too.

Quick loaves always call for some type of fat to create texture and to contribute to the overall flavor. This may be oil (I always use a cold-pressed variety when using an olive, seed, or nut oil), a melted solid fat, like butter, margarine, or vegetable shortening (I always use unsalted butter—the flavor is delightfully sweet), or a fat substitute, such as applesauce or prune puree. The bread machine cannot cream sugar and butter, so you must use butter melted or at very soft room temperature. Each fat contributes its own textural qualities to a loaf, depending on what type of fat it is and in what proportion it is used.

For quick breads, I always use unbleached all-purpose flour—rather than the bread flour called for in yeast bread recipes—for the best texture and crumb, as quick loaves need a bit of strength to create these qualities, yet should stay tender. White cake or pastry flour is too delicate in an expanding dough to hold any embellishments in suspension, and a baked loaf made with one of these will be much too tender. Bread flour, on the other hand, is much too strong for quick breads (a batter made with it would look stringy), the high gluten content resists the quick action of the chemical leaveners and bakes up into a tough baked good. When making tender quick breads with whole wheat flour, I often use exclusively whole wheat pastry flour to keep the tender texture and lighten up what would otherwise be a heavy whole-grain batter.

The Quick Bread/Cake cycle on the bread machine mixes and bakes a loaf similar to a 9-by-5-inch oven-baked loaf. Do not confuse this cycle with the Quick Yeast Bread, Rapid, or One Hour cycles designed to make faster yeast breads. On many machines you will have to choose the crust setting, light, medium, or dark, when you use the Quick Bread/Cake cycle.

When the mixing is done, you will have a batter, not a dough ball. If the batter does not look sufficiently mixed, press Pause and mix the batter with a few strokes by hand, using a rubber spatula. Press Start and the cycle will resume. The baking may begin immediately, or there may be a rest period after the mixing. Do not open the lid to peek at how the bread is doing until a full thirty minutes into baking to allow the bread to reach its full volume in the heat of the oven. As much as possible, look through the window instead of opening the lid The bread will rise and dry out around the edges first, and then, during the last twenty minutes of baking, will dome slightly in the center.

The Quick Bread/Cake cycle, more than any other, varies widely among different machines, making it a real challenge to develop recipes that work for all machines. The recipes in this chapter were tested on a variety of machines that all had Quick Bread/Cake cycle times of 69, 79, and 89 minutes, depending on whether a light, medium, or dark crust was chosen. This seems to be the most common type of Quick Bread/Cake cycle among newer machines. These recipes should also work well in machines that have longer Quick Bread/Cake cycles, but begin baking immediately after mixing. If the length of the cycle on your machine is longer, you may have to do some experimenting with baking time to achieve the loaf you want. (See page 547 for more information.)

A quick loaf is finished baking when the top looks dry inside the small crack that runs down the center, and feels firm when gently touched with your finger; when the edges pull away slightly from the sides of the pan; and when the loaf is evenly browned around the edges.

If an indentation remains after you have pressed the top lightly with your finger, it is a sure sign that the loaf needs more baking. Often the top of a bread machine loaf will not be browned as one baked in a conventional oven. The last test for doneness is to insert a cake tester into the center of the loaf; it should come out clean with no crumbs or batter attached.

On some machines, the Quick Bread/Cake cycle has an extra feature that allows you to program additional baking time in one minute intervals, if you need it. On other machines, you

may be able to press Stop/Reset and program the Bake Only cycle for more time to finish baking the loaf. Don't worry if a loaf takes as long as about two hours, or 120 minutes, to fully bake. Remember that the bread machine bakes at approximately half the temperature of a conventional oven. On some of the older machines, you have to set the bake time manually; if so, set it for 70 minutes and go from there. Also, I never make a quick bread on the Delay cycle; there are too many perishable ingredients.

When the bread is done, remove the pan from the machine and let the loaf rest in the pan, on a cooling rack, for ten to fifteen minutes, to firm up slightly so that the loaf won't break as you turn it out. I run a thin plastic spatula around the edges right away to loosen the loaf. (Don't leave the pan in the machine with the lid closed for this ten minutes; the descending heat from the baking will continue to cook the loaf.) Then, using heavy oven mitts to protect your fingers and wrists, turn the loaf out of the hot bread pan and place it right side up on a cooling rack, allowing air to circulate around it. Loaves that are especially delicate in texture can stand for fifteen minutes in the refrigerator to firm up slightly before turning out. A word of caution: If loaves are not turned out of the pan within fifteen minutes of when they are taken out of the machine, expect them to be soggy on the bottom and probably hard to extract from the pan in one piece.

Quick loaves are easiest to slice when they have cooled completely. This also allows their flavors and textures to meld enticingly, especially after a loaf has been standing overnight at room temperature or in the refrigerator. Always use a good serrated knife for even slicing, as regular knives will squash, crumble, or otherwise distort a loaf.

Quick breads are not restricted to breakfast or snack fare, although they are perfect for these purposes. The simple loaves are great plain or gently toasted and dressed up with a layer of butter or tangy cheese spread such as cream cheese, ricotta, goat, or kefir cheeses. I also serve slices alongside fruit or vegetable salads for lunch. Day-old sweet or savory loaves make excellent sandwiches or bases for hand-held hors d'oeuvres with seafood, meat, or poultry fillings or toppings. One of my standard holiday and birthday gifts is a homemade quick loaf accompanied by the recipe. Quick loaves stay fresh for about four days.

BANANA BREAD

I am a banana bread lover, like so many bakers, and so I have recipes for many variations, some smooth and others filled with nuts and dried fruit; this one has the crunch of walnuts. I let this loaf stand, wrapped in plastic in the refrigerator overnight, before serving to meld the flavors and set the luscious texture; the bread is excellent chilled. This banana bread is even good enough to serve with a scoop of vanilla ice cream and lightly drizzled with chocolate sauce for dessert.

1 Combine the sour cream and the bananas in a small bowl and mash together with a fork. The mixture can be used immediately or placed in the refrigerator overnight.

2 Place the banana mixture and the rest of the ingredients in the bread pan according to the order in the manufacturer's instructions. Set the crust for dark, if your machine offers crust control for this setting, and program for the Quick Bread/Cake cycle; press Start. The batter will be thick and smooth. When the machine beeps at the end of the cycle, check the bread for doneness. The bread is done when it shrinks slightly from the sides of the pan, the sides are dark brown, and the top is firm to a gentle pressure when touched with your finger. A toothpick or metal skewer will come out clean when inserted into the center of the bread.

3 When the bread is done, immediately remove the pan from the machine. Let the bread stand in the pan for 10 minutes before turning it out, right side up, to cool completely on a rack. Wrap tightly in plastic wrap and store in the refrigerator.

1½- OR 2-POUND-LOAF MACHINES

1½ cups mashed overripe
   bananas (about 2 large)
¼ cup sour cream (any type)

½ cup vegetable oil
2 large eggs
1 teaspoon vanilla extract
½ cup sugar
⅓ cup light brown sugar
⅓ cup dark brown sugar

2 cups unbleached
   all-purpose flour
1 teaspoon baking soda
½ teaspoon baking powder
½ teaspoon salt
½ cup coarsely chopped
   walnuts

GRANOLA BREAKFAST BREAD

1½- OR 2-POUND-
LOAF MACHINES

¾ cup milk
¼ cup plain yogurt
½ cup vegetable or nut oil
2 large eggs
Grated zest of 1 lemon
1 teaspoon vanilla extract
¾ cup sugar

1 cup whole wheat pastry
   flour
1 cup unbleached
   all-purpose flour
¾ cup granola
½ cup chopped dried pine-
   apple or golden raisins
1 tablespoon baking
   powder
½ teaspoon ground
   cinnamon or apple pie
   spice
½ teaspoon salt

Oats and other rolled grains are an excellent addition to quick breads. They are also the basic ingredients in granola, a very popular cereal blend, usually containing oats, dried fruit, nuts, and sunflower seeds all moistened with some honey and oil and baked in a slow oven. Since granola is called for here, you could call this loaf a dressed-up oatmeal bread. Granola can be lowfat or high-fat, depending on the ingredients. It is a cereal that was invented by the Swiss for rejuvenating breakfasts at their renowned European health spas. It was introduced to the American youth as breakfast at the first Woodstock Music Festival in 1969, and afterwards was associated with the hippie culture as a favorite natural breakfast food. It has evolved into one of America's favorite cereals. Granola's crisp texture and earthy-sweet fragrance make this bread a great breakfast treat. Serve thick slices with fresh fruit and juice.

1 Place the ingredients in the pan according to the order in the manufacturer's instructions. Set the crust for dark, if your machine offers crust control for this setting, and program for the Quick Bread/Cake cycle; press Start. The batter will be thick and lumpy. When the machine beeps at the end of the cycle, check the loaf for doneness. The bread is done when it shrinks slightly from the sides of the pan, the sides are dark brown, and the top is firm to a gentle pressure when touched with your finger. A toothpick or metal skewer will come out clean when inserted into the center of the bread.

2 When the bread is done, immediately remove the pan from the machine. Let the bread stand in the pan for 10 minutes before turning it out, right side up, to cool completely on a rack. Brush the top with some melted butter if you like. Wrap tightly in plastic wrap and store at room temperature or refrigerate.

FIG BREAD

The history of the fig is as old as the history of man. Adam covered himself with a fig leaf in the Garden of Eden, the Romans loved the food of the fig tree, and the fig tree was brought to the New World, along with grapes, by the Spanish. The fig can be eaten fresh in the summer and dried in the winter; its delightful sweet nature makes it a favorite in baking. Use the pale Calimyrna, the top produced variety, or the dark purple Mission fig. The figs will soften in hot apple juice, so there will not be any chewy chunks in this quick bread. Serve this bread for breakfast.

1 Heat the apple juice and butter over medium–low heat in a small saucepan on the stovetop, or in a microwave-proof bowl in the microwave, until the butter is melted. Remove from the heat and add the figs and orange zest. Set aside to cool to room temperature, about 1 hour.

2 Place the ingredients in the pan according to the order in the manufacturer's instructions, adding the apple-fig mixture with the liquid ingredients. Set the crust for dark, if your machine offers crust control for this setting, and program for the Quick Bread/Cake cycle; press Start. The batter will be thick and smooth. When the machine beeps at the end of the cycle, check the loaf for doneness. The bread is done when it shrinks slightly from the sides of the pan, the sides are dark brown, and the top is firm to a gentle pressure when touched with your finger. A toothpick or metal skewer will come out clean when inserted into the center of the bread.

3 When the bread is done, immediately remove the pan from the machine. Let the bread stand in the pan for 10 minutes before turning it out, right side up, to cool completely on a rack. Wrap tightly in plastic wrap and chill overnight or up to 3 days before serving.

1½- OR 2-POUND-LOAF MACHINES

1 cup apple juice
4 tablespoons unsalted butter, cut into pieces
½ pound dried figs, stemmed and cut into quarters (1 cup)
Grated zest of 1 orange

2 large eggs
1 teaspoon vanilla extract
⅓ cup sugar

2 cups unbleached all-purpose flour
2½ teaspoons baking powder
½ teaspoon baking soda
½ teaspoon salt

ORANGE POPPY SEED BREAD WITH ORANGE SYRUP

1½- OR 2-POUND-LOAF MACHINES

For the bread:

3 tablespoons poppy seeds
½ cup milk
2 large eggs
⅓ cup vegetable oil
1 cup sugar

1½ cups unbleached
   all-purpose flour
2 teaspoons baking powder
Grated zest of 2 oranges
½ teaspoon salt

For the orange syrup:

¼ cup sugar
¼ cup fresh orange juice

The aromatic poppy seed is a favorite crunchy addition to quick breads. Soaking the seeds before adding them to the batter accentuates their elusive flavor. Poppy seeds can range from a clear slate blue to blue-black in color, with a corresponding wide range of sweetnesses. Store poppy seeds in the freezer to prevent rancidity because, like nuts, they have a high oil content. Cut this excellent bread into thick slices and serve it with tea.

1 Combine the poppy seeds and milk in a bowl. Cover with plastic wrap and refrigerate for 1 hour to macerate and meld the flavors.

2 Place the bread ingredients in the pan according to the order in the manufacturer's instructions, adding the poppy seeds and milk with the liquid ingredients. Set the crust for dark, if your machine offers crust control for this setting, and program for the Quick Bread/Cake cycle; press Start. The batter will be thick and smooth.

3 While the loaf is baking, make the orange syrup. Combine the sugar and orange juice in a small saucepan and heat over low heat until the sugar just dissolves. Set aside.

4 When the machine beeps at the end of the cycle, check the loaf for doneness. The bread is done when it shrinks slightly from the sides of the pan, the sides are dark brown, and the top is firm to a gentle pressure when touched with your finger. A toothpick or metal skewer will come out clean when inserted into the center of the bread.

5 When the bread is done, immediately remove the pan from the machine. Pierce the hot loaf (in the pan) about ten times to the bottom with a bamboo skewer. Immediately pour all of the hot orange syrup over the loaf. Cool for 30 minutes in the pan before carefully turning out onto a rack to cool completely. Wrap the loaf tightly in plastic wrap and let stand at room temperature overnight before serving.

Bread Machine Baker's Hint: Baking with the Quick Bread Cycle

Quick bread cycles vary widely from one machine to the next in the length and baking temperature of the cycle, and in the way the cycle is divided. In addition to differences among manufacturers, new models and models that are only a couple of years old from the same manufacturer can have very different quick bread cycles. This seems to be an area of ongoing adjustment for the bread machine manufacturers.

Most of the newer machines I used to test these recipes offered the choice of light, medium, or dark crust settings, and the cycles lasted 69, 79, or 89 minutes, depending on which crust setting I chose. Other machines have a 110 minute or a 120 minute quick bread cycle, and some of these do not offer a choice of crust setting. The differences in time are due to different baking temperatures. Most machines begin baking as soon as the batter is mixed, but a few have a long pause between mixing and baking.

The recipes in this chapter have been developed with the right proportions and ingredients to bake nicely in bread machines with the 69, 79, and 89 minute quick bread cycle. If your machine has a longer cycle, but begins baking right after mixing, these recipes should also work well, but you will probably need to do a little experimenting with your machine. Begin by programming it just as the recipe instructs, choosing the crust color given if your machine allows you to choose. If your machine has a shorter cycle, let it go to the end and see how the bread turns out. If your machine has a longer cycle, begin testing the loaf for doneness about 1 hour and 10 minutes into the cycle (it may bake at a lower temperature, though, and need the full time). With all quick breads, as with regular breads, it is a good idea to check for doneness 5 to 10 minutes before the end of the baking time. In every recipe I explain how to tell when the loaf is done.

After you've made a few of the recipes in this chapter, you'll develop a sense for how your machine works. If your bread is consistently overbaked, stop the cycle and remove the bread early next time you make it. If it is underbaked and your machine allows you to do so, program Bake Only for some extra time. Note these changes on your recipes.

WHITE AND DARK CHOCOLATE TEA CAKE

1½- OR 2-POUND-LOAF MACHINES

1 cup plain yogurt
¼ cup buttermilk
2 large eggs
¼ cup vegetable oil
2 teaspoons vanilla extract
⅔ cup light brown sugar

2½ cups unbleached
   all-purpose flour
⅓ cup unsweetened Dutch-
   process cocoa powder
½ teaspoon baking powder
1½ teaspoons baking soda
½ teaspoon instant
   espresso powder
¼ teaspoon salt
1 cup white chocolate chips
   or chunks broken off a
   bar of white chocolate

T his is a deep, dark chocolate bread with some white chocolate chips added to the batter. Vanilla extract and espresso powder act as flavor enhancers for the chocolate, an old professional baker's tip. It is so incredibly good, you'll be glad this recipe makes a large loaf. The loaf is quite delicate, so be sure to let it stand in the pan the full time and turn it out gently. It is good served with coffee or alongside fresh fruit, berries, and shaved fresh coconut for dessert.

1 Place the ingredients in the pan according to the order in the manufacturer's instructions. Set the crust for dark, if your machine offers crust control for this setting, and program for the Quick Bread/Cake cycle; press Start. The batter will be thick. When the machine beeps at the end of the cycle, check the loaf for doneness. The cake is done when it shrinks slightly from the sides of the pan, the sides are dark brown, and the top is firm to a gentle pressure when touched with your finger. A toothpick or metal skewer will come out clean when inserted into the center of the bread.

2 When the bread is done, immediately remove the pan from the machine. Let the bread stand in the pan for 10 minutes before turning it out, right side up, to cool completely on a rack before slicing. Wrap tightly in plastic wrap and store at room temperature.

TOASTED COCONUT BREAD

A whole coconut is just the kernel of the fruit that grows on the most common tree in the tropics. The inside of the coconut starts out gelatinous and firms up into the coconut meat we recognize as shredded coconut. Be sure to use unsweetened coconut, as sweetened coconut is very moist and not right for this bread. I use Cook's Cookie Vanilla extract, a blend of two different types of vanilla. Available in most supermarkets, its floral aroma is perfect for this recipe. This is a luscious bread that is as beautiful as it is delicious. It goes well with tropical fruit salads and with chicken salad.

1 Preheat the oven to 350°F.

2 Sprinkle the coconut on an ungreased baking sheet and toast in the oven until lightly browned, about 3 minutes. Transfer immediately to a small bowl and let cool to room temperature.

3 Place the ingredients in the pan according to the order in the manufacturer's instructions, adding the coconut with the dry ingredients. Set the crust for dark, if your machine offers crust control for this setting, and program for the Quick Bread/Cake cycle; press Start. The batter will be thick and smooth. When the machine beeps at the end of the cycle, check the loaf for doneness. The bread is done when it shrinks slightly from the sides of the pan, the sides are dark brown, and the top is firm to a gentle pressure when touched with your finger. A toothpick or metal skewer will come out clean when inserted into the center of the bread.

4 When the bread is done, immediately remove the pan from the machine. Let the bread stand in the pan for 10 minutes before turning it out, right side up, to cool completely on a rack before slicing. Wrap tightly in plastic wrap and store at room temperature.

1½- OR 2-POUND-LOAF MACHINES

1¼ cups (about 2½ ounces) shredded unsweetened coconut

1⅛ cups half-and-half (regular or fat-free)
2 large eggs
¼ cup canola oil
2 teaspoons coconut extract
1 teaspoon vanilla extract
¾ cup sugar

2 cups unbleached all-purpose flour
1 tablespoon baking powder
½ teaspoon salt

Shortcut Vanilla Pound Cake

While this is a shortcut recipe because it uses pound cake mix as the base and is made in the bread machine, it is by no means lacking in texture or flavor. It has the tight, moist crumb that you envy in commercial pound cakes. Since one package of mix makes a loaf only three inches high, I recommend one and a half packages for a taller loaf. You will have to set the Bake Only cycle for some extra time; this dense loaf takes a total of 149 minutes to bake. (Before modern ovens, pound cakes were baked in wood-burning ovens and took at least 2 hours.) This is an excellent cake.

1½- or 2-pound-loaf machines

3 large eggs
1¼ cups buttermilk
2 teaspoons vanilla powder or 1 teaspoon vanilla
   extract
½ teaspoon ground mace
One and a half 16-ounce boxes commercial pound
   cake mix (a half box is 1⅔ cups)

❶ According to the order in the manufacturer's instructions, place the eggs, buttermilk, vanilla, and mace in the pan and sprinkle in the cake mix. Set the crust for dark, if your machine offers crust control for this setting, and program for the Quick Bread/Cake cycle; press Start. The batter will be smooth.

❷ When the machine beeps at the end of the cycle, press Stop/Reset and program for the Bake Only cycle for an additional 50 minutes. The cake is done when it shrinks slightly from the sides of the pan, the sides are dark brown, and the top is firm to a gentle pressure when touched with your finger. A toothpick will come out clean when inserted into the center of the cake.

❸ When the bread is done, immediately remove the pan from the machine. Let the bread stand in the pan for 5 minutes before turning it out, right side up, to cool completely on a rack. Wrap tightly in plastic wrap and store at room temperature.

V A R I A T I O N S

Pound Cake with Cinnamon and Nuts

½ cup chopped pecans or walnuts
1½ teaspoons ground cinnamon or apple pie spice

Prepare as directed, adding the cinnamon and nuts with the dry ingredients.

Pound Cake with Dried Apricots and Prunes

½ cup minced dried apricots
¼ cup minced pitted moist prunes

Prepare as directed, adding the apricots and prunes with the dry ingredients.

Coffee–Kahlua Pound Cake

1 cup coffee-flavored yogurt
¼ cup Kahlua liqueur

Prepare as directed, substituting the yogurt and Kahlua for the buttermilk.

Ginger Pound Cake

3 tablespoons minced candied ginger

Prepare as directed, adding the ginger with the dry ingredients.

Chocolate Pound Cake

1½ teaspoons almond extract
⅓ cup unsweetened Dutch-process cocoa powder
3 tablespoons sugar

Prepare as directed, adding the almond extract with the wet ingredients, and the cocoa and sugar with the dry ingredients.

BOURBON NUT BREAD

T his bread has a firm texture so it slices perfectly, a moist crumb, and a flavorful, buttery essence of nuts infused into it during baking. I tend to make nut breads most often during the cool fall and winter months, and stash lots of loaves in the freezer for unexpected visitors and for gifts. As with all quick bread loaves, wrap this one tightly in plastic wrap and let it rest overnight before slicing to develop flavor and texture. This loaf is the quintessential quick bread; moist, dense, beautifully shaped, and dotted with pieces of nuts.

❶ Place the ingredients in the pan according to the order in the manufacturer's instructions. Set the crust for dark, if your machine offers crust control for this setting, and program for the Quick Bread/Cake cycle; press Start. The batter will be thick. When the machine beeps at the end of the cycle, check the loaf for doneness. The bread is done when it shrinks slightly from the sides of the pan, the sides are dark brown, and the top is firm to a gentle pressure when touched with your finger. A toothpick or metal skewer will come out clean when inserted into the center of the bread.

❷ When the bread is done, immediately remove the pan from the machine. Let the bread stand in the pan for 10 minutes before turning it out, right side up, to cool completely on a rack. Wrap tightly in plastic wrap and chill overnight, or for up to 3 days, before serving.

1½- OR 2-POUND-LOAF MACHINES

¼ cup nut oil or vegetable oil
2 large eggs
1½ teaspoons almond extract
1½ cups sour cream
½ cup bourbon
1 cup light brown sugar

2¼ cups unbleached all-purpose flour
2½ teaspoons baking powder
½ teaspoon baking soda
½ teaspoon salt
1½ teaspoons ground nutmeg
1 teaspoon instant espresso powder
1¼ cups (6 ounces) coarsely chopped pecans or walnuts

DRIED CRANBERRY TEA BREAD

1½- OR 2-POUND-LOAF MACHINES

1½ cups dried cranberries
Boiling water

2 large eggs
2 teaspoons almond extract
1 teaspoon vanilla extract
¼ cup canola or vegetable oil
¾ cup frozen unsweetened apple juice concentrate, thawed
1 cup sugar

1¼ cups unbleached all-purpose flour
1 cup whole wheat pastry flour
1 tablespoon baking powder
½ teaspoon baking soda
1 teaspoon ground cinnamon
½ teaspoon fresh-ground nutmeg
½ teaspoon salt

R aw cranberries have a definite astringent, yet refreshingly tart taste. Now that Ocean Spray offers dried, sweetened cranberries, commercially called Craisins, you can enjoy their delightfully tangy flavor as a great alternative to raisins. This is a recipe adapted from one of my favorite food writers, Jeanne Jones, known for her development of lowfat spa recipes. The combination of apple juice concentrate and almond extract permeates the entire loaf. It has a most intoxicating aroma while baking. Serve this fantastic bread thinly sliced, with sweet butter or whipped cream cheese.

1 Cover the cranberries with boiling water in a small bowl, and let stand for 20 minutes to soften. Drain and pat dry with paper towels. Set aside.

2 Place the ingredients in the pan according to the order in the manufacturer's instructions, adding the cranberries with the dry ingredients. Set the crust for dark, if your machine offers crust control for this setting, and program for the Quick Bread/Cake cycle; press Start. The batter will be thick. When the machine beeps at the end of the cycle, check the loaf for doneness. The bread is done when it shrinks slightly from the sides of the pan, the sides are dark brown, and the top is firm to a gentle pressure when touched with your finger. A toothpick or metal skewer will come out clean when inserted into the center of the bread.

3 When the bread is done, immediately remove the pan from the machine. Let the bread stand in the pan for 10 minutes before turning it out, right side up, to cool completely on a rack before slicing. Wrap tightly in plastic wrap and store in the refrigerator.

CARDAMOM TEA BREAD

Each slice of this breakfast bread is flecked throughout with bits of cardamom, often an underused sweet spice. Native to the Malabar Coast of India, cardamom is the favorite spice of the chilly Scandinavian countries. The papery pod holds a few hard black seeds that can be crushed with a rolling pin or with a mortar and pestle, although cardamom is available already ground. This is another bread that is good toasted the day after baking and spread with raspberry jam.

1½- OR 2-POUND-LOAF MACHINES

⅓ cup vegetable oil
3 large eggs
¼ cup buttermilk
1 tablespoon vanilla extract
1 cup sour cream
¾ cup sugar

2¼ cups unbleached
    all-purpose flour
2 teaspoons baking powder
1 teaspoon baking soda
2½ teaspoons ground
    cardamom
½ teaspoon salt

❶ Place the ingredients in the pan according to the order in the manufacturer's instructions. Set the crust for dark, if your machine offers crust control for this setting, and program for the Quick Bread/Cake cycle; press Start. The batter will be thick and smooth. When the machine beeps at the end of the cycle, check the loaf for doneness. The bread is done when it shrinks slightly from the sides of the pan, the sides are dark brown, and the top is firm to a gentle pressure when touched with your finger. A toothpick or metal skewer will come out clean when inserted into the center of the bread.

❷ When the bread is done, immediately remove the pan from the machine. Let the bread stand in the pan for 10 minutes before turning it out, right side up, to cool completely on a rack before slicing. Wrap tightly in plastic wrap and store at room temperature.

WELSH BARA BRITH

1¼ cups boiling water
2 Earl Grey tea bags
   (can be decaffeinated)
One 8-ounce bag mixed
   dried fruit, chopped
   (about 1 cup)

1 large egg
½ cup milk
1 tablespoon unsalted
   butter, melted or room
   temperature
3 tablespoons orange
   marmalade, ginger
   marmalade, or apricot
   preserves (you can use a
   sugar-free fruit spread)
1 cup light brown sugar

2¾ cups unbleached
   all-purpose flour
1 cup dark or golden raisins
¼ cup chopped candied
   orange peel (page 516)
   or currants
2¾ teaspoons baking
   powder
2 teaspoons apple pie spice
¾ teaspoon salt

This loaf may sound unusual, but it a favorite tea bread among quick bread lovers and very old-fashioned. While bara brith can also be made with yeast, the main requirement is that the cake be speckled with dried fruit steeped for a few hours in tea, rather like a simple fruitcake the Brits so love. From the land of the bard, a dense, rich loaf to serve sliced and buttered with tea. It is especially good during the holidays.

1 Pour the boiling water into a 4-cup glass measuring cup. Add the tea bags and let steep for 10 minutes; remove and squeeze the tea bags dry. Add the dried fruit and stir well. Let stand at room temperature for 1 to 4 hours to plump the fruit and come to room temperature.

2 Place the ingredients in the pan according to the order in the manufacturer's instructions, adding the fruit and all of the soaking liquid with the liquid ingredients. Set the crust for dark, if your machine offers crust control for this setting, and program for the Quick Bread/Cake cycle; press Start. The batter will be thick, smooth, and full of evenly dispersed fruit. When the machine beeps at the end of the cycle, press Stop/Reset and program for the Bake Only cycle for an additional 20 minutes to finish baking. The *bara brith* is done when it shrinks slightly from the sides of the pan, the sides are dark brown, and the top is firm to a gentle pressure when touched with your finger. A toothpick or metal skewer will come out clean when inserted into the center of the cake.

3 When the bread is done, immediately remove the pan from the machine. Let the bread stand in the pan for 10 minutes before turning it out, right side up, to cool completely on a rack before slicing. Wrap tightly in plastic wrap and store in the refrigerator.

The Right Ingredient: Baking Powder and Baking Soda

Quick bread loaves always use a chemical leavener, such as baking powder or baking soda, besides the mechanical action of creaming or beating in plenty of air, to lighten their batters. When the acid and alkaline proportions are balanced in a batter, these leaveners create a chemical reaction that produces lots of carbon dioxide (CO_2) gas bubbles that expand existing air pockets when they come in contact with liquid and then heat. The trapped bubbles also create steam; the final product of all that swelling in the oven is a nicely rounded, moist loaf.

Baking Powder

Modern baking powders are double acting, which simply means they are a mixture of alkaline and acid ingredients: baking soda (sodium bicarbonate), cornstarch (a stabilizer to keep it dry during storage), and sodium aluminum sulfate (some form of phosphate salt), making it a chemical leavener that is complete within itself no matter what type of liquid or fruit is used. Baking powder reacts twice, once when moistened with liquid and again in the hot oven. The baking powder produces carbon dioxide to leaven the batter and flour, and egg proteins will set with the heat and steam around the bubbles, giving texture to the bread. To avoid a slight bitterness in the baked good, use no more than 1½ teaspoons of baking powder to 1 cup of flour. When doubling or tripling a recipe, cut back the total amount of chemical leavener by one quarter. I prefer a superior brand of nonaluminum baking powder that is commonly available, sold under the commercial name of Rumford, as there is no bitter aftertaste. Ideally, use your open can of commercial baking powder

within 4 months for the best leavening power. Test for freshness by placing a teaspoon in a small amount of hot water. If it is fresh, it will fizzle rapidly.

Homemade Baking Powder

You can make your own single-acting baking powder. Combine 1 teaspoon baking soda (the alkali) and 2 teaspoons cream of tartar (the acid) to substitute for 1 tablespoon baking powder. This mixture must be made fresh each time you use it, as it will not remain active if stored. I prefer the action of this cream of tartar mixture over commercial brands of baking powder, as the batters have a slightly finer texture.

Baking Soda

Bicarbonate of soda (baking soda) is used in addition to baking powder when there are acid ingredients—such as buttermilk, yogurt, sour cream, citrus, molasses, honey, maple syrup, vinegar, chocolate, and fruits—in the batter. The combination of the two neutralizes the acid and forms the desired CO_2. For the best results, batters containing baking soda must be baked immediately after mixing and tend to be slightly more coarse crumbed (yet still delightfully tender) than those using baking powder or a combination of the two. Remember that if you substitute a liquid sweetener (such as molasses, honey, or maple syrup) for the sugar in a recipe, the batter will become acid, so you must have some baking soda in the recipe. Recipes using only baking powder are usually nut or whole-grain quick breads that contain regular milk for the liquid. Store your box of baking soda in a cool, dry place, as it tends to absorb moisture from the air and can clump.

ORANGE GINGERBREAD WITH ORANGE WHIPPED CREAM

O ne of the great pleasures of baking gingerbread is the warm, intoxicating fragrance that pervades your kitchen while baking. Gingerbread is often cited as the oldest baked sweet in the world, because it was baked in ancient Greece, many centuries before Christ. Recipes for it were preserved in monasteries during the Dark Ages, although the loaves were more dense than today's gingerbread. Known to early American bakers as "gyngerbredde," recipes for gingerbread arrived with the Pilgrims. Besides its blend of intensely aromatic spices, the heart of a good gingerbread is its molasses. The combination of ground ginger and molasses gives this loaf of gingerbread its characteristic spicy flavor, dark color, and delightfully moist texture. For the best flavor, buy a new bottle of ginger every six to nine months. Orange gingerbread is best eaten the day it is baked.

1½- OR 2-POUND-LOAF MACHINES

For the gingerbread:

4 tablespoons unsalted butter, melted
½ cup light molasses
2 large eggs
Grated zest of 1 orange
½ cup light brown sugar
¾ cup buttermilk
2 teaspoons baking soda dissolved in ¼ cup hot water

2½ cups unbleached all-purpose flour
½ teaspoon baking powder
2 teaspoons ground ginger
1½ teaspoons apple pie spice or ½ teaspoon ground cinnamon, ½ teaspoon allspice, and ½ teaspoon cloves
¾ teaspoon salt
2 tablespoons chopped candied ginger, optional

For the orange whipped cream:

1 cup heavy cream
2 tablespoons confectioners' sugar
2 tablespoons Grand Marnier orange liqueur or thawed orange juice concentrate
½ teaspoon vanilla extract

1 To make the gingerbread, place the gingerbread ingredients in the pan according to the order in the manufacturer's instructions. Set the crust for dark, if your machine offers crust control for this cycle, and program for the Quick Bread/Cake cycle; press Start. The batter will be thick.

2 To prepare the orange whipped cream, combine all the ingredients in a chilled bowl. Beat with an electric mixer until soft peaks are formed. Cover and chill until needed.

3 When the machine beeps at the end of the cycle, check the loaf for doneness. The gingerbread is done when it shrinks slightly from the sides of the pan, the sides are dark brown, and the top is firm to a gentle pressure when touched with your finger. (If the indentation remains, press Stop/Reset and program for the Bake Only cycle; check at intervals until the loaf is done.) A toothpick or metal skewer will come out clean when inserted into the center of the bread.

4 When the bread is done, immediately remove the pan from the machine. Let the bread stand in the pan for 10 minutes before gently turning it out, right side up, to cool completely on a rack before slicing. Serve warm or at room temperature, with a few tablespoons of Orange Whipped Cream on the side.

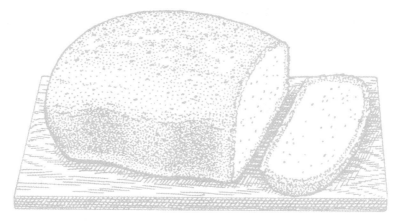

 Bread Machine Baker's Hint: Storing Quick Breads

For short storage, wrap quick breads in plastic for up to one week. The loaves age perfectly at room temperature unless they contain chunks of cheese or other dairy products that can spoil easily, in which case they should be refrigerated. I tend to like most of my loaves chilled, so I store them all in the refrigerator. Quick loaves also keep perfectly for up to three months if frozen in a double layer of self-sealing freezer bags or in a layer of plastic wrap covered by aluminum foil. I find that it is important to label and date the preserved loaves to avoid the inevitable search and all the unwrapping to find a special loaf, as they all tend to look alike after freezing. Let the wrapped loaves thaw to room temperature before serving.

CARROT BREAD

4 large eggs
½ cup nut oil
½ cup vegetable or light olive oil
2 teaspoons vanilla extract
2 cups lightly packed shredded raw carrots
2 cups sugar

3 cups unbleached all-purpose flour
2½ teaspoons baking powder
1½ teaspoons baking soda
2½ teaspoons ground cinnamon or apple pie spice
1 teaspoon salt

C arrots are a commonplace vegetable, but the root rises to new heights in a sweet quick bread. Carrots are often seen in paintings by old European masters, which show carrots in a variety of colors, such as purple and yellow. Sometime in the last two hundred years, an orange variety outgrew all others and became our familiar homey vegetable of today. Carrots grow easily and keep for a long time under refrigeration. The shredded carrots in this beloved quick bread will soften as they bake, adding a definite sweetness and prettiness to this cakelike quick bread that is reminiscent of a steamed pudding.

1 Place the ingredients in the pan according to the order in the manufacturer's instructions. Set the crust for dark, if your machine offers crust control for this setting, and program for the Quick Bread/Cake cycle; press Start. The batter will be thick. When the machine beeps at the end of the cycle, press Stop/Reset and program for the Bake Only cycle for an additional 10 to 15 minutes to finish baking. The bread is done when it shrinks slightly from the sides of the pan, the sides are dark brown, and the top is firm to a gentle pressure when touched with your finger. A toothpick or metal skewer will come out clean when inserted into the center of the bread.

2 When the bread is done, immediately remove the pan from the machine. Let the bread stand in the pan for 10 minutes before turning it out, right side up, to cool completely on a rack. Wrap tightly in plastic wrap and let sit at room temperature overnight, or up to 3 days before serving.

ZUCCHINI BREAD

Zucchini, also known as Italian summer squash, is a vegetable that has made the jump to be a common ingredient in sweet quick breads and cakes with panache. The cylindrical green vegetable is widely available year-round and is also a favorite home gardener's crop. Good ol' zucchini bread is the most requested quick bread recipe I ever get, so I thought it was essential to include it in this collection. I make this as a small loaf, but the recipe can easily be doubled; just be sure to add some extra baking time if it is needed. The loaf is moist and smooth with flecks of zucchini throughout.

1 Place the ingredients in the pan according to the order in the manufacturer's instructions. Set the crust for dark, if your machine offers crust control for this setting, and program for the Quick Bread/Cake cycle; press Start. The batter will be thick and smooth. When the machine beeps at the end of the cycle, check the loaf for doneness. The bread is done when it shrinks slightly from the sides of the pan, the sides are dark brown, and the top is firm to a gentle pressure when touched with your finger. A toothpick or metal skewer will come out clean when inserted into the center of the bread.

2 When the bread is done, immediately remove the pan from the machine. Let the bread stand in the pan for 10 minutes before turning it out, right side up, to cool completely on a rack. Wrap tightly in plastic wrap and store in the refrigerator.

1½- OR 2-POUND-LOAF MACHINES

2 large eggs
½ cup vegetable oil
1½ teaspoons vanilla extract
1 cup sugar
1¼ cups lightly packed shredded zucchini (about 2 medium)

1½ cups unbleached all-purpose flour
1 teaspoon baking soda
¾ teaspoon baking powder
1¼ teaspoons ground cinnamon or apple pie spice
¼ teaspoon salt
½ cup coarsely chopped walnuts

CORNBREAD

1½- OR 2-POUND-LOAF MACHINES

1 large egg
1¼ cups buttermilk
6 tablespoons unsalted butter, melted
⅓ cup sugar

1 cup fine-grind yellow cornmeal, preferably stone-ground
1 cup unbleached all-purpose flour
2 tablespoons toasted wheat germ
1 teaspoon baking soda
½ teaspoon baking powder
½ teaspoon salt

There is something comforting about the grainy texture of cornmeal in a simple homemade cornbread. The Quick Bread cycle's fast mixing is perfect for a cornbread—it comes out dense and moist, great for any meal. I like cornbread for dinner with bean soups and chicken dishes. I also like it reheated for breakfast with butter and maple syrup. While this recipe makes a small loaf similar in quantity to one made in an 8-by-8-inch baking pan, you can double the recipe for a higher loaf. This cornbread yields six thick slices.

❶ Place the ingredients in the pan according to the order in the manufacturer's instructions. Set the crust for medium, if your machine offers crust control for this cycle, and program for the Quick Bread/Cake cycle; press Start. The batter will be thick. When the machine beeps at the end of the cycle, check the loaf for doneness. The cornbread is done when it shrinks slightly from the sides of the pan, the sides are dark brown, and the top is firm to a gentle pressure when touched with your finger. A toothpick or metal skewer will come out clean when inserted into the center of the bread.

❷ When the bread is done baking, immediately remove the pan from the machine. Let the bread stand in the pan for 15 minutes before gently turning it out, right side up, to cool on a rack. Serve warm or at room temperature, the day it is baked, cut into thick slices.

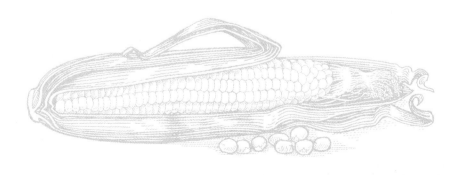

ANADAMA QUICK BREAD

T his traditional *New England bread is usually made with yeast, but combing through old recipes, I found a quick version. Anadama was a staple for the colonial home baker who had cornmeal mush and molasses as daily fare. The melted butter was brushed on with a clean feather, a common tool in the early American baker's kitchen. This bread is a wonderful surprise—one of the best breakfast breads, nutritious, and it tastes ever so good. Eat it fresh or gently toasted.*

1½- OR 2-POUND-LOAF MACHINES
1⅔ cups buttermilk ½ cup light molasses ¼ cup vegetable oil 1 large egg 1¼ cups whole wheat flour 1¼ cups unbleached all-purpose flour ½ cup fine or medium-grind yellow cornmeal, preferably stone-ground 2 teaspoons baking powder 1 teaspoon baking soda 1 teaspoon salt

1 Place the ingredients in the pan according to the order in the manufacturer's instructions. Set the crust for dark, if your machine offers crust control for this setting, and program for the Quick Bread/Cake cycle; press Start. The batter will be thick and smooth. When the machine beeps at the end of the cycle, check the loaf for doneness. The bread is done when it shrinks slightly from the sides of the pan, the sides are dark brown, and the top is firm to a gentle pressure when touched with your finger. A toothpick or metal skewer will come out clean when inserted into the center of the bread.

2 When the bread is done, immediately remove the pan from the machine. Let the bread stand in the pan for 10 minutes before turning it out, right side up, to cool completely on a rack. Brush the top with some melted butter. Wrap tightly in plastic wrap and store at room temperature.

JAMS, PRESERVES, AND CHUTNEYS IN YOUR BREAD MACHINE

Homemade preserves have started to come back into favor during the last decade. They are the best way to deliver the fragrance, flavor, and character of summer's fresh fruit to your table long after the season has passed. Despite the abundance of good commercial jams, making your own homemade jams remains a gratifying and rewarding experience. With a small twist on grandmother's art, making jam in the bread machine is an excellent way to "put up" small-batch jams, fruit butters, and chutneys, without lots of stirring (you don't even have to stir to dissolve the sugar!), fussing with a thermometer, or sterilizing of jars. All you have to do is combine the fruit, sugar, and pectin, and the machine mixes and slowly cooks it. Simply pour the hot jam into clean jars, and store it in the refrigerator for as long as two months, although it will probably get eaten much sooner. Even if you are a first-time preserver, in about an hour and a half you can have two to three cups of exceptional, chunky, fresh-fruit jam, and the chance to partake in the cuisine of nostalgia, rediscovering a taste for this wonderful food.

Jams, preserves, and marmalades are based on ancient techniques for preserving fruit. Every country with abundant fruit has a culinary history of making sweet preserves. The interaction of the fruit, sugar, acid, and pectin in the correct proportions has long been of primary concern. The right balance is what makes the mixture jell. For this reason, working with sugar used to be in the realm of the apothecaries. The prophet and physician Nostradamus made colorful fruit preserves for Catherine de Medici in the Middle Ages. In Greece, jams, known as *glyko*, are eaten by the spoonful from bowls, followed by a drink of water, then a drink of liqueur. They are delicacies that were once considered medicinal preparations.

Old preserve recipes remind us of regional specialties, harking back to the days when home preserving was a necessity, and a practical way to use up all the fruit from a home orchard or garden. There is damson cheese, a thick, concentrated fruit puree rather than an actual cheese, still a specialty in England and Europe today; or a sweet-and-sour pumpkin chutney with vinegar, peppercorns, and gingerroot; green tomato chutney, of course, to save the last tomatoes when the first frost hits; jams like gooseberry and mulberry, if you could get to the fruit before the birds did; or muscadine or scuppernong jam, the Southern alternative to grape jam.

Here I have included recipes for most of the basic jams and preserves, all made using the Jam cycle on your machine. You may substitute fruits of similar character in some of the recipes, for example blackberries or olallieberries in the Fresh Strawberry Jam (but taste these while adding the sugar to adjust for differing tartness), plums in the recipe for apricot jam, and nectarines in the recipes for the peach jam. Do not substitute an entirely different type of fruit in a recipe, as different fruits have different amounts of pectin and acid, and I have added the right proportions of pectin and lemon juice in the recipes to produce jams with substance and proper flavor. I also include recipes for apple butters, ketchup, and various chutneys, which are wonderful as festive condiments, bread or sandwich spreads, accompaniments to grilled or roasted meats, or as flavorful spreads for appetizer toasts. Though the ingredients may vary, all these items are made by the same slow-cooking, constant-stirring process that the bread machine handles so well.

My homemade jams are less sweet than commercial jams, as you may notice. I tend to cut back from the traditional one-to-one sugar-to-fruit proportions that leave the fruit swimming in a clear jelly. These recipes make softer jams. I think they are much more exciting in flavor and color this way, with a balance of fruit flavor and sweetness. As you add the sugar, always do so to your taste, so you can achieve the proper sweetness for your own palate. Taste the fruit before placing it in the pan to get an idea of how sweet it is to begin with. Or, hold back some of the sugar and taste the sugar-fruit mixture after the sugar has dissolved, before you start the machine.

Some sweetening is vital to the process of making jam since sugar attracts the water from the fruit and binds it to the fruit pulp, thereby acting as a preservative. It also helps the thickening process. Pectin, a starch found at least in small amounts in all fruit, forms an "affectionate" network, trapping the sugar and fruit pulp. A bit of acid, usually in the form of lemon juice, encourages the pectin, and the pulp ends up a spreadable paste. The long, chainlike molecules of pectin, naturally occurring in the the cell walls of plants, are especially important for thickening these closed-oven jams, as they cannot be helped along by liquid evaporating during cooking. The lack of evaporation with the bread machine method also results in a greater yield per batch than on the stovetop. Remember that the more sugar you add, the thicker your jam will be, and jams do continue to thicken upon cooling and refrigerating. Never use sugar substitutes, which will not be

effective thickeners. The exception to this rule is powdered fructose. Please note, too, that these recipes may yield a different amount of jam each time you make them, depending on the juiciness and seasonal variations of the fruit. For sophisticated palates, add a light splash of good-quality cognac, Scotch, amaretto, cassis, port, or orange liqueur as the jam finishes cooking.

Pectin comes in 1.75- and 2-ounce packages, depending on the brand. The tiny difference in the quantities is not significant; use half, three-fourths, or whatever portion the recipe calls for when using either size package.

Do not be tempted to double any of the recipes in this chapter. The bread pan has a limited capacity, and can only make small amounts of preserves at one time—the paddle must be able to stir all the jam efficiently. The volume of the ingredients should never exceed 3½ cups total of fruit and sugar, but please check your manufacturer's manual, as the maximum amount varies from model to model. The ingredients will cook down in different degrees depending on the denseness of the fruit used. If you need more jam, make a new batch.

Store your jam in a covered container in the refrigerator up to 2 months. I keep a collection of pretty storage jars such as French *confiture* jars or the tulip-shaped German Weck jars, quilted jelly jars, or glass-topped jars with wire closures (spring-top jars); they look nice set out on the table. Even though sterilizing the jars is not necessary for short-term storage like this, I run them through the dishwasher or wash them well in hot sudsy water and dry them completely before filling them. These preserves can also be frozen in plastic containers or small freezer bags for up to three months.

Bread Machine Baker's Hint: Jams and Preserves Made Easy

Paying attention to the following guidelines will help you get the best results when making jam in the bread machine. Please note that the recipes in this chapter should only be made in machines that have a Jam cycle.

- Prepare the fruit by stemming, peeling (if necessary), seeding, or pitting it. Most of my recipes instruct how to cut the fruit for the jam, and most require that you mash the fruit or crush it into coarse pieces. Soft, small berries can go in whole; the bread machine blade does a lot of mashing. Do not puree the fruit before adding it; you want to recognize bits of the whole fruit when the jam is done.

- Measure fruit *after* crushing, not before. The total volume of crushed fruit with sugar should not exceed 3½ cups, to avoid spillovers onto the electrical element and for efficient and constant mixing by the blade. Check your manufacturer's booklet for your machine's maximum capacity, as some models have a smaller maximum when making jam.

- Make sure the kneading blade is in place before adding the fruit mixture. It must be in place during the Jam cycle, and it is difficult to attach after the bottom of the pan is filled with crushed fruit. The paddle is necessary for stirring, which is crucial to the success of the mixture. You will hear the slow rhythm of the blade stirring through almost the entire cycle.

- Half of a 1¾- or 2-ounce package of powdered pectin is about 2½ tablespoons. Three-fourths of a package is about 3¾ tablespoons. The measurement of the pectin in these recipes does not have to be exact.

- Most of my recipes ask you to add the sugar to taste. Taste the fruit before you add the ingredients to the bread pan, to find out how sweet the fruit is to begin with. To avoid adding too much sugar, hold back some of the sugar called for. Taste the fruit and sugar mixture after it has been sitting in the pan for a few minutes before you start the machine, and adjust the sugar accordingly.

- The jam cycle has a 10-minute preheat, a 60-minute cook cycle, and sometimes a 10-minute cool-down. Make sure the appliance is a few inches away from the wall and any cabinets all the way around its circumference. During the Jam cycle, plenty of heat and steam are released out of the vents in a short period of time. The machine will beep at the end of the full Jam cycle. A jelly or candy thermometer should register about 220°F when inserted into the hot mixture. I remove the pan immediately, and unless I am using heat-resistant jars, such as canning jars, I let it stand for 15 minutes, and then pour the preserves into storage jars.

- I test each batch for doneness as I take it out of the machine by using the cold-saucer test. Spoon a small amount of cooked jam onto a cold plate, or spoon the jam onto a plate at room temperature and then freeze it for 1 minute. Then touch the jam with a spoon or with your finger to see how much it has jelled; if it has the right jam consistency, it is done. Don't forget to taste it, too!

- For the easiest cleanup after pouring the jam out, immediately fill the bread machine pan with warm water and dish soap to soak.

FRESH STRAWBERRY JAM

Makes about 2½ cups jam

U se a combination of overripe and unripe berries. If you have the strawberries on hand, but aren't going to make the jam right away, store the berries, unwashed, wrapped in two layers of paper toweling, in a closed plastic bag in the refrigerator. Because strawberries absorb water quickly, never float berries in water while cleaning them. Just rinse under running water right before using. This is how my mom likes her jam (she makes a few small batches every spring)—not too sweet, kind of runny, with a few whole berries and lots of intense flavor. A basket of strawberries is usually one pint.

1 Coarsely crush the berries with a potato masher, or put them in a food processor and pulse a few times, leaving a few whole berries or chunks. You will have about 2½ cups. Place the fruit in the bread pan. Add the lemon juice and sprinkle with the pectin. Let stand for 10 minutes. Add the sugar.

2 Program the machine for the Jam cycle and press Start. When the machine beeps at the end of the cycle, carefully remove the pan with heavy oven mitts. You can scrape the jam into heat-resistant jars right away, using a rubber spatula. For other jars, let the jam sit in the pan for 15 minutes before transferring. Let stand until cool. Cover and store in the refrigerator for up to 2 months, or spoon into small freezer bags and freeze.

1½- OR 2-POUND-LOAF MACHINES

2 pints (about 1 pound) fresh strawberries, rinsed, drained, and hulled
1 tablespoon fresh lemon juice
Three-fourths of a 1.75- or 2-ounce box powdered fruit pectin
1 cup sugar, or to taste

BLUEBERRY JAM

Makes about 2 cups jam

1½- OR 2-POUND-LOAF MACHINES

1 to 1½ pints (1 pound) fresh blueberries, rinsed
Half of a 1.75- or 2-ounce box powdered fruit pectin
1½ cups sugar, or to taste
3 tablespoons *crème de cassis* liqueur
2 tablespoons fresh lemon juice

B lueberry jam has a loyal following in the jam-lover's community. It is a starling midnight-blue color, and some of the berries remain intact when the jam is done, still evident in every spreading. Crème de cassis *is a tasty fruit liqueur made from black currants, a fruit that contains one of the highest concentrations of vitamin C. It is extremely low proof and very sweet, a nice addition to this jam. I use one bottled in this country by Bonny Doon Vineyards, but there are many types that come from the Burgundy region of France, where it was invented. Crème de cassis is exceptional. Once the bottle is opened, use it within six months for the best flavor.*

❶ Combine all the ingredients in the bread pan. Let stand for 15 minutes to dissolve the sugar.

❷ Program the machine for the Jam cycle and press Start. When the machine beeps at the end of the cycle, carefully remove the pan with heavy oven mitts. You can scrape the jam into heat-resistant jars right away, using a rubber spatula. For other jars, let the jam sit in the pan for 15 minutes before transferring. Let stand until cool. Store, covered, in the refrigerator for up to 2 months, or spoon into small freezer bags and freeze.

RASPBERRY JAM

Makes about 3 cups jam

T he raspberry is an intensely flavored berry. Every berry has lots of little pockets called drupelets, each containing its own seed. Hence, it is characteristic of raspberry jam to be dotted with lots of little seeds. There are red, golden, and black raspberry varieties, all quite tart, so add sugar to this jam to taste. Raspberries are very fragile; be sure to pick over the ones you're using to remove any soft or moldy berries. A box of raspberries is usually half a pint.

1½- OR 2-POUND-LOAF MACHINES

1½ pints (about 3 cups)
 fresh raspberries, rinsed
Half of a 1.75- or 2-ounce
 box powdered fruit pectin
1¾ cups sugar, or to taste
3 tablespoons fresh lemon
 juice

1 Combine all the ingredients in the bread pan. Let stand for 15 minutes to dissolve the sugar.

2 Program the machine for the Jam cycle and press Start. When the machine beeps at the end of the cycle, carefully remove the pan with heavy oven mitts. You can scrape the jam into heat-resistant jars right away, using a rubber spatula. For other jars, let the jam sit in the pan for 15 minutes before transferring. Let stand until cool. Store, covered, in the refrigerator for up to 2 months, or spoon into small freezer bags and freeze.

BOYSENBERRY JAM

Makes about 2 cups jam

1½- OR 2-POUND-LOAF MACHINES

1 pint (about 2½ cups) fresh boysenberries, rinsed

One 1.75- or 2-ounce box powdered fruit pectin

1 cup sugar, or to taste

2 tablespoons fresh lemon juice

Boysenberries, a horticultural cross between raspberries, blackberries, and loganberries, usually do not need any pectin to set up when made on the stovetop, but I add some for the bread machine environment. This is also the recipe to use for blackberry jam. A basket of boysenberries is usually a half pint.

1 Combine all the ingredients in the bread pan. Let stand for 15 minutes to dissolve the sugar.

2 Program the machine for the Jam cycle and press Start. When the machine beeps at the end of the cycle, carefully remove the pan with heavy oven mitts. You can scrape the jam into heat-resistant jars right away, using a rubber spatula. For other jars, let the jam sit in the pan for 15 minutes before transferring. Let stand until cool. Store, covered, in the refrigerator for up to 2 months, or spoon into small freezer bags and freeze.

FRESH BING CHERRY JAM

Makes about 2½ cups jam

T his recipe comes from my local cherry grower, Deborah Olson, of Sunnyvale, California, whose family has tended their orchards of Bing, Burlat, Lorraine, Royal Anne, Tartarian, and Black Republican cherries for over a hundred years. I added the pectin so that the jam would set up properly in the bread machine environment. To pit the cherries, use a cherry pitter, which is an indispensable tool if you are a cherry lover, or use a small paring knife to cut each cherry in half and pick out the pit with the tip of the knife. Some people also use a clean bobby pin to dig the pits out of whole cherries. The little splatters that get on your apron are part of the charm of working with cherries. Use half a lemon to clean the stains off your fingers.

1½- OR 2-POUND-LOAF MACHINES

1 pound (about 2 cups) pitted fresh Bing cherries (you will have both whole cherries and pieces after the pitting)
1 cup sugar, or to taste
1 tablespoon fresh lemon juice
Pinch of salt
1½ tablespoons powdered fruit pectin

1 Combine the cherries, sugar, lemon juice, and salt in the bread pan. Let stand for 15 minutes to dissolve the sugar. Sprinkle with the pectin.

2 Program the machine for the Jam cycle and press Start. When the machine beeps at the end of the cycle, carefully remove the pan with heavy oven mitts. You can scrape the jam into heat-resistant jars right away, using a rubber spatula. For other jars, let the jam sit in the pan for 15 minutes before transferring. Let stand until cool. Store, covered, in the refrigerator for up to 2 months, or spoon into small freezer bags and freeze.

FRESH PEACH JAM

Makes about 2½ cups jam

1½- OR 2-POUND-LOAF MACHINES

3 to 4 large peaches
  (about 1 pound)
1 cup sugar, or to taste
2 tablespoons fresh lemon
  juice
One 1.75- or 2-ounce box
  powdered fruit pectin

P each jam is probably one of the favorites of all time, yet it is difficult to find commercially. Use slightly unripe fruit to get the most pronounced peach flavor. You can also prepare this jam with defrosted frozen, unsweetened peaches. Some peaches are very juicy, in which case the jam will cook up softer.

1 Peel and pit the peaches. Coarsely crush by hand with a potato masher, or pulse a few times in the food processor. You will have about 2½ cups.

2 Combine the peaches, sugar, and lemon juice in the bread pan. Let stand for 30 minutes to dissolve the sugar. Sprinkle with the pectin.

3 Program the machine for the Jam cycle and press Start. When the machine beeps at the end of the cycle, carefully remove the pan with heavy oven mitts. You can scrape the jam into heat-resistant jars right away, using a rubber spatula. For other jars, let the jam sit in the pan for 15 minutes before transferring. Let stand until cool. Store, covered, in the refrigerator for up to 2 months, or spoon into small freezer bags and freeze.

FRESH APRICOT JAM

Makes about 2½ cups jam

I grew up in the Santa Clara Valley in Northern California, where the wonderful climate produces the finest apricots grown in America. Unfortunately, many of the apricot trees were gradually pulled out as houses were built and the Silicon Valley was created, but there are still a few precious apricot trees left, dotted around backyards and vacant lots. Apricot jam is part of the legacy of living here, and for good reason—it is luscious.

1 Place the apricots and the lemon juice in the bread pan. Sprinkle with the pectin. Let stand for 10 minutes. Add the sugar.

2 Program the machine for the Jam cycle and press Start. When the machine beeps at the end of the cycle, carefully remove the pan with heavy oven mitts. You can scrape the jam into heat-resistant jars right away, using a rubber spatula. For other jars, let the jam sit in the pan for 15 minutes before transferring. Let stand until cool. Store, covered, in the refrigerator for up to 6 weeks, or spoon into small freezer bags and freeze.

1½- OR 2-POUND-LOAF MACHINES
2 cups (about 1⅓ pounds) pitted and chopped fresh apricots
1 tablespoon fresh lemon juice
Half of a 1.75- or 2-ounce box powdered fruit pectin
1¼ cups sugar, or to taste

KIWIFRUIT JAM

Makes about 1½ cups jam

**1½- OR 2-POUND-
LOAF MACHINES**

4 large kiwifruit (1 pound),
  peeled, sliced, and
  coarsely chopped
2 tablespoons finely
  julienned lemon zest
3 tablespoons fresh lemon
  juice
1½ tablespoons powdered
  fruit pectin
1½ cups sugar

A California specialty, this extraordinary recipe is from food writer Lou Pappas. She calls this tropical jam with citrus undertones *"dazzling"* for its flavor and pale green color. *The ancient kiwifruit was known as the Chinese gooseberry*, yang tao, *until Freida Caplan, specialty produce maven of Southern California's Freida's Finest, introduced it as the kiwi to the American market in the late 1960s. Kiwifruit is available year-round. This jam is great on all kinds of rye toast.*

1 Combine all the ingredients in the bread pan. Let stand for 20 minutes to dissolve the sugar.

2 Program the machine for the Jam cycle and press Start. When the machine beeps at the end of the cycle, carefully remove the pan with heavy oven mitts. You can scrape the jam into heat-resistant jars right away, using a rubber spatula. For other jars, let the jam sit in the pan for 15 minutes before transferring. Let stand until cool. Store, covered, in the refrigerator for up to 2 months, or spoon into small freezer bags and freeze.

Leftover Jam Cookery

There are a multitude of desserts that use thick jam as an ingredient, including many varieties of cookies. Here are two of the all-time favorites. They are easy and elegant.

Granny's Jammies

Makes about 3½ dozen cookies

Every Christmas my boyfriend's grandmother presented each of us with a tinful of these soft butter cookies made with her homemade jam.

1½ cups (3 sticks) butter, softened
1 cup sugar
3 large egg yolks
1 tablespoon vanilla extract
¼ teaspoon almond extract
3¾ cups unbleached all-purpose flour
¼ teaspoon salt
1 cup raspberry or other jam

1 Preheat the oven to 375°F. Grease or line with parchment paper 2 baking sheets.

2 Using an electric mixer, cream the butter and sugar until fluffy; beat in the egg yolks and extracts. Stir in the flour and salt. Pinch off pieces of dough and roll into 1-inch balls. Place 1½ inches apart on the prepared pans.

3 Using your thumb, press a deep indentation into the center of each ball, spreading out the round of dough. Bake for 8 minutes, just until set. Remove the pan from the oven and fill each indentation with a rounded teaspoon of jam. Continue baking for an additional 5 to 7 minutes, until light golden brown and the jelly is slightly melted. Transfer immediately to a rack to cool completely. Store the cookies in a single layer in an airtight tin.

Cream Cheese Pockets

Makes about 3 dozen cookies

The dough for these pockets is incredibly easy to handle. It can be filled with any flavor of thick jam or preserve you choose.

1 cup (2 sticks) butter, softened
8 ounces cream cheese, softened
¼ cup confectioners' sugar
½ teaspoon salt
2 cups unbleached all-purpose flour
2 cups thick homemade jam or preserves, such as apricot or raspberry
1 cup sifted plain or vanilla confectioners' sugar (page 513)

1 In the workbowl of a food processor, combine the butter, cream cheese, sugar, salt, and flour. Process until the dough just forms a ball. Divide the dough into three equal portions, flatten each portion into a disc, and wrap each disc in plastic wrap. Refrigerate for 1 hour to overnight.

2 Preheat the oven to 350°F. Grease or line with parchment paper 2 baking sheets.

3 On a lightly floured surface, roll the pastry out with a rolling pin until it is ⅛ inch thick. Cut the dough into 2½-inch squares. Place a dab of jam in the center of each. Bring two opposite corners up and pinch to seal them over the center. Place the pockets 1 inch apart on the baking sheets.

4 Bake the cookies until light golden brown, 12 to 15 minutes; they will look a bit underdone, but will crisp as they cool. When cool, dust with confectioners' sugar.

RHUBARB JAM

Makes about 1½ cups jam

1½- OR 2-POUND-LOAF MACHINES

1 pound rhubarb stalks, sliced about ½ inch thick (2 cups)
1½ cups sugar
Half of a 1.75- to 2-ounce box powdered fruit pectin
¼ cup chopped dried apricots

A rhubarb patch is always part of an old-fashioned fruit and vegetable garden. My friend Bob, who grew up in northern Minnesota near the Canadian border, remembers his mother making plenty of rhubarb jam every spring from juicy bundles of stems gathered in a neighbor's yard. The plant has long, red stalks—the edible part—and large leaves, but the leaves are poisonous. This jam is delicious on whole wheat toast or biscuits.

❶ Mix the rhubarb with the sugar in a glass bowl, cover loosely with plastic wrap, and let stand at room temperature for 12 hours.

❷ Combine the rhubarb-sugar mixture, the pectin, and the apricots in the bread pan.

❸ Program the machine for the Jam cycle and press Start. When the machine beeps at the end of the cycle, carefully remove the pan with heavy oven mitts. You can scrape the jam into heat-resistant jars right away, using a rubber spatula. For other jars, let the jam sit in the pan for 15 minutes before transferring. Let stand until cool. Store, covered, in the refrigerator for up to 3 weeks, or spoon into small freezer bags and freeze.

How Much Pectin Is In This Fruit?

Fruits High in Natural Pectin
Tart apples, cranberries, currants, quinces, damson plums, Concord grapes, papayas, blueberries, and blackberries are naturally high in pectin. The peel of lemons and oranges has a lot of natural pectin. Unripe fruit contains more pectin than overripe fruit.

Fruits Low in Natural Pectin
Apricots, nectarines, pineapple, rhubarb, strawberries, raspberries, peaches, cherries, mangoes, bananas, and all overripe fruit are low in pectin. Preserves made from fruits low in natural pectin need some commercial liquid or powdered pectin and a bit more sugar added to jell properly.

APPLE BUTTER

Makes about 2 cups fruit butter

T his is my version of a recipe from Jeanne Jones, who, in my opinion, creates the best spa food recipes this side of the Rockies. No sugar, no fat. The use of dried apples provides a rich thickness that would take hours to achieve if you used fresh ones. Dried apples are easy to find—my grocery store displays them with the packaged nuts and dried apricots. Use fresh, unfiltered apple juice, also known as sweet cider. I like to place half of a split vanilla bean in the jar of apple butter while it is stored in the refrigerator. This spread is culinary magic on fresh bread, toast, or bagels, and pancakes or muffins, too.

1 Combine all the ingredients in the bread pan. Let stand at room temperature for 1 hour to soften the apples.

2 Program the machine for the Jam cycle and press Start. When the machine beeps at the end of the cycle, carefully remove the pan with heavy oven mitts and let cool until warm.

3 Using a rubber spatula, scrape the mixture into a food processor fitted with the metal blade and process until smooth. Scrape the apple butter into a glass jar. Let stand at room temperature until cool. Store, covered, in the refrigerator for up to 2 months.

1½- OR 2-POUND-LOAF MACHINES

¼ pound dried apple rings, chopped (2 cups)
1¼ cups unsweetened, unfiltered apple juice
2 tablespoons apple cider vinegar
1½ teaspoons ground cinnamon
½ teaspoon ground allspice
½ teaspoon ground cloves

PUMPKIN APPLE BUTTER

Makes about 3 cups fruit butter

1½- OR 2-POUND-LOAF MACHINES

One 15-ounce can pumpkin puree
¾ cup (about 1 large) peeled, cored, and coarsely grated fresh Pippin, Granny Smith, or other firm, tart cooking apple
½ cup unsweetened, unfiltered apple juice
½ cup light brown sugar
½ teaspoon ground cinnamon
½ teaspoon ground nutmeg
½ teaspoon ground cloves

3 tablespoons unsalted butter

 his is a recipe from the Libby's pumpkin people, which I've adapted for the machine. It is wonderful on biscuits, toast, or even dabbed on your oatmeal.

1 Combine all the ingredients in the bread pan.

2 Program the machine for the Jam cycle and press Start. When the machine beeps at the end of the cycle, carefully remove the pan with heavy oven mitts. Stir in the butter until it melts. You can scrape the fruit butter into heat-resistant jars right away, using a rubber spatula. For other jars, let the fruit butter sit in the pan for 15 minutes before transferring. Let stand until cool. Store, covered, in the refrigerator for up to 2 months, or spoon into small freezer bags and freeze.

QUICK AND EASY TOMATO KETCHUP

Makes about 3 cups ketchup

T his tangy condiment is a snap when made with canned tomato puree, a great improvement over spending the entire day laboriously peeling and cooking tomatoes that end up reduced to this amount. I make just enough of this ketchup for short-term storage in the refrigerator, saving the fuss of preserving. Bottled commercial ketchup can't compare to your own batch.

1 In a food processor, preferably, or in batches in a blender, combine the tomato puree, onion, shallot, and garlic. Process until just smooth.

2 Pour the tomato mixture into the bread pan. Add the vinegar, water, sugar, and spices.

3 Program the machine for the Jam cycle and press Start. When the machine beeps at the end of the cycle, the ketchup will have reduced slightly and thickened. Add salt and pepper to taste. Carefully remove the pan with heavy oven mitts. You can scrape the ketchup into heat-resistant jars right away, using a rubber spatula. For other jars, let the ketchup sit in the pan for 15 minutes before transferring. Serve warm, room temperature, or chilled. Store covered in the refrigerator for up to 2 months.

1½- OR 2-POUND-LOAF MACHINES

One 28-ounce can tomato puree
1 small yellow onion, cut into chunks
1 large shallot, chopped
1 clove garlic, pressed
½ cup apple cider vinegar
⅓ cup water
¼ cup light brown sugar
1 teaspoon ground allspice
Pinch of ground cinnamon
Pinch of ground cloves
Pinch of ground mace
Pinch of ground ginger
Pinch of Coleman's dry mustard
Pinch of crushed hot red pepper flakes
Fresh-ground black pepper
Sea salt

MANGO CHUTNEY

Makes about 2 cups chutney

1½- OR 2-POUND-LOAF MACHINES

2 fresh firm-ripe mangoes (about 1½ pounds)
¼ cup dark or golden raisins, chopped
1 medium shallot, minced
½ cup dark brown sugar
A scant tablespoon of minced fresh ginger
2 teaspoons hot pepper flakes
Pinch of ground cloves
⅛ teaspoon salt
½ cup apple cider vinegar
2 tablespoons fresh lime juice

Mango is the queen of chutneys. In India there are both fresh mango chutneys, which are like salads to cool the palate, and cooked chutneys, like this one, which are more like preserves. Mangoes are considered an exotic fruit here, but in the Himalayas they have been eaten for over 4,000 years and are known as the "pride of the garden." We get our mangoes from Mexico and the West Indies. The oversized egg-shaped mango, a member of the cashew family, has an addictive flavor reminiscent of a juicy apricot. This chutney is great with Indian food, with Chinese food, or spread with cream cheese on toast.

❶ Peel the mango by standing the fruit stem (wider) end up. Make 4 vertical slices, through the skin, to score the thin tough skin and divide the fruit into quarters lengthwise. Starting at the top, peel the skin back from each quarter, just like a banana. Slice the flesh away from the flat seed in strips. Coarsely chop. You will have about 2 cups.

❷ Combine all the ingredients in the bread pan.

❸ Program the machine for the Jam cycle and press start. When the machine beeps at the end of the cycle, carefully remove the pan with heavy oven mitts. You can scrape the chutney into heat-resistant jars right away, using a rubber spatula. For other jars, let the chutney sit in the pan for 15 minutes before transferring. Let stand until cool. Store, covered, in the refrigerator for up to 2 months. Serve at room temperature.

PEACH CHUTNEY

Makes about 1¾ cups chutney

T here is no better condiment than a stone fruit chutney. It has a great fresh flavor enhanced with pungent spices. Narsai David used to market his own nectarine chutney and I used it so often that when it disappeared from the market, I had to create a recipe of my own. This chutney must be chunky, dark, hot, and sweet all at the same time. It is great with Indian food, barbecued meats, pork chops, or pâtés, and as an ingredient in appetizers. You can use nectarines in place of the peaches.

1½- OR 2-POUND-LOAF MACHINES

3 to 4 fresh peaches (about 1 pound) or 1 pound frozen unsweetened peach slices, defrosted
Piece of fresh gingerroot about 3 inches long
⅓ cup golden raisins, chopped
2 small white boiling onions, minced
1 small clove garlic, minced
¾ cup dark brown sugar
2 teaspoons chili powder
2 teaspoons yellow mustard seeds
¼ teaspoon salt
½ cup apple cider vinegar

❶ Peel the peaches by dipping them briefly into a pan of boiling water to loosen the skins. Immediately cool them by holding them under cold water, and the skins will slip off. Coarsely chop the peaches and place them in the bread pan.

❷ Peel and mince the ginger so you have about 2½ table-spoons. You can use a little more or a little less, depending on how hot you want the chutney. Combine the ginger and all the remaining ingredients with the peaches in the bread pan.

❸ Program the machine for the Jam cycle and press start. When the machine beeps at the end of the cycle, carefully remove the pan with heavy oven mitts. You can scrape the chutney into heat-resistant jars right away, using a rubber spatula. For other jars, let the chutney sit in the pan for 15 minutes before transferring. Let stand until cool. Store, covered, in the refrigerator for up to 2 months. Serve at room temperature.

A Baker's Glossary of Soft, Spreadable Fruits

Preserve has come to be a generic title for any type of fruit spread. It is also the name of a specific type of spreadable fruit, one of the five that can be made in the bread machine. Each type of spreadable fruit calls for a slightly different method of preparation and amount of sugar. Here is a glossary of terms to help you differentiate one type from another. You may notice that jellies are not included here—they are not recommended for the bread machine. Only a bread machine designed for making jams should be used to make preserves. A machine that is not suitable will not cook the preserves properly, and the process will severely damage your machine.

• **Chutney**—Chutney, an Indian word, is a raw or cooked condiment to serve with meals. Cooked chutneys, known as preserved chutneys, are a combination of fruit, sugar, vinegar, and spices with a thick consistency ranging from chunky to smooth. While chutneys can be fiery hot or sweet, the ones with a bit of both are delicious spreads for bread, or as accompaniment to breads, cheeses, and pâtés.

• **Conserve**—Conserves are also made like jam, but contain at least two fruits and often contain raisins and nuts.

• **Fruit Butter**—A butter is made by slow cooking together a fruit puree, sugar, and sometimes spices, to a thick, spreadable consistency.

• **Jam**—A jam is composed of one or more fruits that are chopped or crushed and cooked rapidly with sugar. Jams are gently firm, but do not hold the shape of the jar, and are best made in small batches.

• **Marmalade**—Similar to a jam, marmalades contain small pieces of fruit and peel suspended in a transparent jelly. Orange marmalade is the best known, but marmalade can also be made from lemons or limes.

• **Preserves**—Preserves are whole fruit cooked with sugar so that the fruit retains its shape and becomes tender. The syrup is clear and the consistency of honey. Preserves are also best made in small batches.

APPLE AND DRIED FRUIT CHUTNEY

Makes about 2 cups chutney

T his is a chutney that I have made for years. Although most traditional Indian cookbooks have a similar recipe, I adapted this from a recipe I got from Chef de Cuisine Vincent Brunetto, who had a restaurant called The Campbell House near my home. He served it for an appetizer in a chilled mound next to homemade pâté and fresh bread. Cooking it on the stove always seemed to evaporate too much of the liquid, so using the bread machine is a fine way to make this full-flavored, nicely textured chutney. This chutney is very aromatic while it is cooking. I often use a six-ounce bag of pre-chopped fruit bits—which has raisins, apricots, and dried peaches in it—to save time.

1 Combine all the ingredients in the bread pan.

2 Program the machine for the Jam cycle and press Start. When the machine beeps at the end of the cycle, carefully remove the pan with heavy oven mitts. You can scrape the chutney into heat-resistant jars right away, using a rubber spatula. For other jars, let the chutney sit in the pan for 15 minutes before transferring. Let stand until cool. Store, covered, in the refrigerator, for up to 2 months. Serve at room temperature.

1½- OR 2-POUND-LOAF MACHINES

2 medium tart cooking apples, peeled, cored, and finely chopped
⅔ cup dark brown sugar
⅓ cup finely chopped dried apricots
⅓ cup finely chopped dried pineapple or dried pears
⅓ cup dark or golden raisins
¼ cup finely chopped red bell pepper
Piece of fresh gingerroot about 1 inch long, peeled and grated
1 large shallot, finely chopped
1 clove garlic, pressed
¼ teaspoon ground cayenne pepper
Pinch of hot pepper flakes
Pinch of ground turmeric or curry powder
½ teaspoon salt
⅔ cup apple cider vinegar

Appendix 1

BITS AND PIECES
Crumbs, Croutons, Crostini, and Toasted Appetizers

Breadcrumbs, toasted croutons, and small toasts are practical and delicious uses for day-old bread. Breadcrumbs may be fresh or dried, and are sometimes seasoned. Fresh and dried are not interchangeable in recipes, as the dry crumbs absorb more liquid than the fresh. (Be sure to check your recipe to avoid using the wrong type.)

Croutons, melba toasts, rusks, crostini, and classic plain toasts are all variations on the same toasting process. Any type of sliced homemade bread, from white to wheat to rye, can be given a new life by being slowly dried in an oven, sautéed in a skillet, toasted under a broiler, or even grilled over an open fire. All these toasts are usually a garnish of some type, but do not underestimate the grand roles these humble toasts may play—they can be piled high in a basket to accompany dips or pâtés, or spread with cheeses, herbs, or garlic. Butter croutons may be folded into scrambled eggs. Or they can serve as just the right crisp complement to salads or soups. Who has not enjoyed croutons floating atop a bowl of French onion soup? These toasts can be the basis for myriad toppings, tea sandwiches, and canapés. Bruschetta, an Italian toast, is traditionally topped with a flavorful combination of tomatoes and herbs and may be made as a sweet toast as well. Recipes for toppings and sandwich fillings—in addition to instructions for many different toasts—are given here.

Croutons, melba toasts, rusks, and crostini can be in the form of plain old slices, or they may be cut with a biscuit or cookie cutter, making a pretty assemblage of squares, rectangles, diamonds, or hearts. A famous garnish is *dents de loup*, or wolves' teeth, where a long 4-inch toast has one side cut jagged. You can cut off the crusts, or leave them on. When making tea sandwiches or appetizers, the different shapes help vary the presentation.

Fresh Breadcrumbs

Tear or cut thick slices of bread, with or without crusts, into pieces. Some bakers save bread ends and crusts to make breadcrumbs. Place the bread pieces in a food processor and grind until coarse, even crumbs are formed. When preparing a recipe, measure crumbs using a dry measuring cup, and don't pack them in or you'll lose the fluffy quality. Three ounces of fresh bread will make about 1 cup of crumbs. Keep the crumbs in an airtight container at room temperature and use within 2 days, or freeze the crumbs in plastic freezer bags.

Dry Breadcrumbs

Tear or cut day-old bread, with or without crusts, into pieces. Preheat the oven to 300°F. Line a baking sheet with aluminum foil or parchment paper and spread out the bread pieces on the baking sheet. Bake until they are dry and golden, about 30 minutes. Let them stand at room temperature to cool completely. Grind the bread in a food processor, in small batches, until the desired degree of fineness is reached. Transfer the breadcrumbs to a dry airtight container. Dry breadcrumbs will keep for 1 month, but I use them within a week.

VARIATION

Seasoned Dry Breadcrumbs

For Italian-style seasoned dry breadcrumbs, grind the toasted bread into coarse crumbs; then add 2 tablespoons grated Parmesan cheese and ½ teaspoon *each* dried marjoram and basil for every cup of fine dry bread crumbs. Continue grinding to the desired degree of fineness.

Soup and Salad Croutons

Just about any good homemade bread—egg, pumpernickel, herb, or whole wheat—makes good salad or soup croutons.

Preheat the oven to 375°F. Slice bread into ¾-inch-thick slices, then cut the slices into cubes. Place the cubes on an ungreased baking sheet. Drizzle them with melted butter or olive oil, and bake until dry, about 10 to 15 minutes, stirring about every 5 minutes to keep from burning. Remove the croutons from the oven when just golden, and drizzle with more melted butter or oil. Croutons are best used the day they are made. They can also be frozen for up to 2 months.

VARIATION

Toss the croutons with fresh pressed garlic or sprinkle them with a few tablespoons of grated Parmesan or chopped fresh parsley while they are still hot.

Large Croutons

Float these large croutons in bowls of soup or tuck them in alongside salads. For some recipes you may want to make the croutons as large as half the slice of bread.

Cut day-old bread of any savory type into slices ½ inch to ¾ inch thick, or split day-old rolls in half horizontally. Cut the slices into quarters or eighths. In a sauté pan or skillet, sauté them over medium heat in butter, olive oil, or an equal combination of the two. Turn them as necessary, until the slices are crisp and golden brown. Remove the croutons with tongs, drain them on paper towels, and serve immediately.

These can also be made under a broiler, over a charcoal fire, or in the oven; toss the croutons in oil before preparing them one of these ways.

Herbed Croutons for Soup

These croutons are excellent floated in cream soups such as asparagus, carrot, broccoli, pumpkin, fresh green pea, and zucchini.

Preheat the oven to 400°F. Slice bread into 1-inch-thick slices and cut into cubes. Place the cubes on an ungreased baking sheet. Drizzle them with olive oil and sprinkle with 2 tablespoons minced fresh herbs for every 2 to 3 cups bread cubes. Toast the cubes in the oven until they are dry, stirring often, about every 5 minutes, to keep from burning. Croutons are best used the day they are made.

Melba Toast

In France these are known as sliced croûtes en dentele. *There is a story in one of actress Shirley MacLaine's autobiographies in which she was depressed after the breakup of a relationship. As she sat in her hotel room in Stockholm, she ate an entire box of melba toasts spread with butter, because they were so tasty, while contemplating the ramifications of the breakup. Every time I crunch my way through pieces of melba with butter—a delight everyone should partake of at least once—I remember her story. Melba toast is also a perfect accompaniment to pâté.*

Preheat the oven to 300°F. Cut 1 loaf of firm day-old or frozen bread into ¼-inch-thick slices; then cut them diagonally in half or in quarters, depending on the size you want. Place cut slices in a single layer on an ungreased baking sheet. Bake for 45 minutes to 1 hour, or until they are crisp and evenly golden. Remove the toast from the oven and cool completely. Melba can be made a day ahead and stored in an airtight container at room temperature.

Sweet Rusks

Rusks, like melba toasts, are slices of yeast bread that have been dried in the oven until crisp. If you make your rusks with a sweet bread like panettone or cinnamon bread, they are suitable to serve for breakfast with jam or cream cheese and coffee or tea, or for dessert with puddings or ice cream.

Preheat the oven to 300°F. Cut 1 loaf firm day-old or frozen bread into slices 1 inch thick and lightly spray with a butter-flavored cooking spray. Sprinkle one side of each slice lightly with brown or white sugar. Cut the slices diagonally into halves or quarters, cut out shapes with a biscuit cutter like hearts or half moons, or cut the slices into thick fingers, depending on the size and shape you want. Place the bread in a single layer on an ungreased baking sheet. Bake for 35 to 45 minutes, or until they are crisp and evenly golden. Let the rusks cool completely. These can be made a day ahead and stored in an airtight container at room temperature.

Pita Bread Crisps
Serves 6

Prepare this recipe to serve with Hummus (page 605), Roasted Eggplant Dip (page 605), Hot Artichoke Dip (page 606), or any of the other dips in the following appendix. If you'd like to make a lowfat version of these crisps, brush the smooth side of the pitas with an egg white that has been beaten until foamy instead of with the olive oil; then bake as instructed in the recipe.

6 homemade pitas (page 424)
½ cup olive oil

Preheat the oven to 300°F. Line a baking sheet with parchment paper. Split open each pita horizontally, making 2 thin rounds. Brush the smooth side of each round with olive oil. Place the rounds in a single layer on the baking sheet. Bake until crisp, about 20 minutes. Spread out the crisps on wire racks to cool completely; then break each round into 5 irregularly-shaped pieces. If the pitas lose their crispness before serving, reheat them for a few minutes in the oven.

Garlic Pita Toasts
Makes 48 toast triangles

These toasts are baked for a much longer time than the Pita Bread Crisps, so they turn out more like a melba toast.

4 tablespoons unsalted butter
⅓ cup olive oil or walnut oil
1 to 2 cloves garlic, crushed
6 homemade pitas (page 424)
Kosher or sea salt, for sprinkling

Preheat the oven to 300°F. Combine the butter, oil, and garlic in a small saucepan. Heat until the butter is melted. Line a baking sheet with parchment paper. Cut each pita into quarters, then separate the top and bottom layers so you have 2 triangles from each. Place the triangles on the baking sheet, rough side up, in a single layer. Brush the rough side lightly with the garlic mixture. Sprinkle the triangles with salt. Bake for about 50 minutes, until crisp and lightly golden. Serve at room temperature. Store in an airtight container for up to 5 days.

Focaccia Toasts

Any plain focaccia can be made into crostini and used as you would crackers for an appetizer. The crostini end up looking like oversized rusks. Use Italian Whole Wheat Flatbread (page 410), Schiacciata (page 412), or Wine Focaccia (page 411). Store these toasts in an airtight tin for up to 3 days.

Leftover homemade focaccia, sliced into ⅓-inch-thick slices
Olive oil or olive oil cooking spray
Coarse sea salt, optional

Preheat the oven to 300°F. Line a large baking sheet with parchment paper. The slices of focaccia will be as long as your baking pan was wide. Brush each side of the focaccia with olive oil, or spray with olive oil cooking spray. Sprinkle with coarse sea salt, if desired: I prefer them plain. Arrange the focaccia sticks in a single layer on the baking sheet. Bake for about 30 minutes, or until the toasts are very crisp and lightly browned around the edges. They will be completely dried out and not at all soft. Cool the toasts on racks before serving.

Baguette Crostini
Makes 20 pieces

The baguette shape is perfect for slicing and baking into little toasts to be used in place of crackers. Use fresh or day-old bread.

Twenty ¼- to ½-inch-thick slices Classic Baguette (page 204) or Pain de Paris (page 216)
⅓ cup extra-virgin olive oil or olive oil cooking spray

Preheat the oven to 400°F. Arrange the bread on a baking sheet lined with parchment paper. Brush or spray both sides lightly with olive oil. Bake until lightly toasted, about 5 minutes. Let cool and serve immediately or store in an airtight container.

Lowfat Garlic Crostini
Makes 24 large crostini, serves 8

This is a convenient alternative to brushing oil or butter on the croutons.

6 slices country bread, quartered diagonally, to make 24 pieces
2 cloves garlic, peeled
Olive oil cooking spray

Preheat the oven to 400°F. Place the bread pieces in a single layer on a baking sheet. Bake for 5 minutes, or until lightly toasted. Remove from the oven and rub the toasted side lightly with a clove of garlic; it will be absorbed as you rub. Spray each toast with

some cooking spray. Return to the oven and bake for an additional 3 minutes. Serve immediately or at room temperature within a few hours.

Appetizer Bread Cups
Makes 48 appetizer shells

Bread pressed into small muffin cups and baked until crisp makes the perfect bite-sized containers for fillings like ratatouille, cold chicken liver mousse, goat cheese and fresh herbs, or chopped, marinated, roasted red peppers. You will need four muffin tins with 1½-inch cups to bake these all at once. Or you can bake them in batches.

Twelve ¼-inch-thick slices homemade bread, crusts removed
½ cup olive oil or nut oil

❶ Preheat the oven to 400°F.

❷ Using a rolling pin on a clean work surface, roll and press each slice of bread until flat. Cut each slice into quarters and trim each quarter-slice to make it an even square, or use a 3-inch decorative cutter (scalloped edges look nice) to cut the bread. Using your fingers, press each piece into one cup of a 1½-inch-cup muffin tin. The corners of the squares will extend up out of the cups.

❸ With a small pastry brush, brush the inside of each bread cup with some oil. Bake the bread cups until crisp and golden brown at the edges, 7 to 10 minutes. Turn out the crisp cups onto a rack to cool completely before filling.

Croustades

I love serving food out of an earthy serving vessel like a croustade de pain de mie, an edible bowl made of bread. You remove the top and insides of a stale homemade loaf, such as French Sandwich Pain au Lait (page 51), country bread, or any firm-textured white or wheat loaf. Then you fill the hollow with cheese, dip, creamed chicken, ragout, or sautéed or creamed vegetables. Croustades may be large or small, depending on the size loaf you begin with.

> 1 loaf (rectangular, square, or round) day-old white or whole wheat bread
> Melted butter, margarine, olive oil, or a butter-flavored or olive oil cooking spray

1 Preheat the oven to 350°F.

2 Place the loaf on a baking sheet. With the tip of a knife, cut out a round from the top of the loaf, or turn the loaf on its side and slice a 2- to 4-inch slice off the top. Try to keep the round or slice intact, as it will serve as a lid. Pull out the inside of the bread (use it to make bread crumbs, if you wish), leaving at least a 1-inch-thick wall of bread all around. Brush or spray the inside of the hollowed-out loaf and the lid with the butter, oil, or cooking spray.

3 Bake the hollowed out loaf, with its lid to the side, in the center of the oven until crisp, 20 to 30 minutes, depending on its size. Remove the bread bowl and lid from the oven, and let cool completely before filling. Croustades should be made the day they will be eaten.

Mushroom Ragoût on Croutons
Makes 8 large croutons, serves 4

A ragoût is a thick stew, sometimes containing meat or game. Ragoût comes from the French word ragoûter, "to stimulate the appetite." Somehow a ragoût is the perfect vehicle for using the wonderful bounty of dried mushrooms now offered in most supermarket produce departments. I think of this as the type of food served to the well-fed country folk in a Tolstoy novel, earthy and soul satisfying, in a day when gathering mushrooms for sustenance was a commonplace activity. Serve with cheese, fruit, and a simple salad.

> 1½ cups boiling water
> 1 ounce dried shiitake mushrooms
> 1 ounce dried chanterelle mushrooms
> 1 ounce dried crimini mushrooms
> 2 tablespoons olive oil
> 2 cloves garlic, minced
> 1 yellow onion, chopped
> 2 cups domestic button mushrooms, quartered
> ½ cup dry white wine
> ½ cup cream
> 1 tomato, peeled, seeded, and diced
> 1 tablespoon fresh lemon juice
> 8 large croutons (page 586)
> ¼ cup minced flat-leaf parsley, for garnish
> ¼ cup minced chives, for garnish

1 Place the water in a bowl and add all the dried mushrooms. Let stand at room temperature for 30 minutes to 1 hour. Strain, reserving the liquid.

2 Heat the oil in a large skillet. Add the garlic and onion, and sauté until soft. Add the fresh and reconstituted mushrooms. Sauté for 2 minutes. Add the reserved mushroom liquid and the wine. Turn the heat to medium–high and let the liquid reduce by half.

3 Reduce the heat to low. Add the cream, tomato, and lemon juice. Simmer until thick, about 10 minutes. Season to taste. Place 2 croutons on each plate. Spoon the ragoût over them and sprinkle with parsley and chives. Serve immediately.

Crostini with Red Pepper–Orange Rouille
Makes 4 large crostini, serves 4

Rouille is a Spanish egg-oil sauce similar to mayonnaise, often made by hand using a mortar and pestle. These crostini are very good floating in fish or vegetable soups. If you don't want to use the raw egg yolk, go ahead and use the equivalent of a liquid commercial egg substitute.

One 7-ounce jar roasted red peppers, drained, rinsed, and patted dry
1 clove garlic, minced
Grated zest of 1 orange
½ teaspoon salt
1 egg yolk
½ cup extra-virgin olive oil
Four ½-inch-thick slices homemade country-style bread

1 In a food processor, combine the peppers, garlic, orange zest, and salt. Process just until chopped. Add the egg yolk and puree until the mixture is smooth. With the machine running, gradually add the oil, processing until the mixture is thick. This rouille can be made up to 1 week ahead and refrigerated.

2 Preheat the broiler. Broil the bread on a baking sheet until light brown on both sides. Spread one side of each slice generously with the rouille. Broil again just to heat through, about 30 seconds. Serve immediately.

Artichoke and Mozzarella Crostini
Makes 12 to 16 crostini

Marinated artichoke hearts and mozzarella cheese are a fantastic combination. If you try these once, you will make them again and again.

12 ounces mozzarella cheese, coarsely grated
1 or 2 small cloves garlic, pressed or minced
Two 4-ounce jars marinated artichoke hearts, drained and chopped
3 or 4 slices homemade white bread

1 Preheat the oven to 400°F.

2 In a bowl, combine the cheese, garlic, and artichoke hearts; toss together. Place the bread on a baking sheet, spread some of the cheese and artichoke mixture on each slice, and bake for 8 to 10 minutes, until the topping is melted and golden brown. Cut each crostini into 4 strips. Serve immediately.

Black Olive and Cheese Crostini
Makes 20 crostini, serves 10

Once I made these for a wedding reception with champagne that took place before the guests traveled on to a fancy restaurant for dinner. Despite the promise of an extravagant meal to come, the guests gobbled these up—they were so popular we couldn't keep up with the demand. Don't

continued on next page

pass by this recipe because of the curry powder; it works beautifully here as a flavor accent and is not at all overpowering.

12 ounces medium cheddar cheese, shredded
One 6-ounce can pitted California black olives, chopped by hand or in the food processor, still chunky
½ cup minced fresh chives
1¼ cups mayonnaise
1 tablespoon curry powder
5 slices homemade white bread, cut into quarters

1 Preheat the oven to 400°F.

2 Combine the cheese, olives, and chives in a bowl and toss together. In a separate bowl, stir together the mayonnaise and the curry powder; then add the mayonnaise to the cheese and olive mixture and stir to combine.

3 Place the bread slices on a baking sheet, spread some of the mixture on each, and bake for 8 to 10 minutes, until the topping is melted and golden brown. Serve immediately.

Herb and Goat Cheese Toast
Makes 1 dozen toasts

Fresh goat cheese melds so beautifully with other French cheeses. These toasts are wonderful with tomato soup.

6 slices homemade white, whole wheat, or country bread, cut in half
¼ cup plus 2 tablespoons olive oil
12 ounces Montrachet or domestic chabis goat cheese
12 ounces Swiss cheese, shredded

3 tablespoons minced fresh chives
2 teaspoons minced fresh tarragon
2 cloves garlic, pressed

1 Preheat the oven to 325°F.

2 Brush the bread with ¼ cup of the olive oil and place in a single layer on a baking sheet. Bake the slices for 15 minutes, or until they just begin to brown.

3 In a bowl, combine the cheeses, herbs, 2 tablespoons olive oil, and garlic.

4 Remove the toasts from the oven, pile the cheese mixture on in a thick layer, and return to the oven until melted, about 1 to 2 minutes. Remove from the oven and eat immediately.

Cinnamon Toast Fingers
Makes 24 toast fingers, serves 6 to 8

This is real cinnamon toast, described by poets as disarmingly naive, probably because of its inherent simplicity. But oh the bouquet of warm cinnamon and a good homemade bread. When I make these, I use my delicate Vietnam Extra Fancy cinnamon from Penzeys Spices, and savor every bite. Use a bread with a close texture so that it won't flop around. These are perfect for afternoon tea for two, or more. Darjeeling with milk, please.

1¼ cups sugar
1½ tablespoons ground cinnamon
Eight ½-inch-thick slices homemade white or whole wheat bread, crusts removed
¾ cup (1½ sticks) unsalted butter or margarine, melted, or butter-flavored cooking spray

❶ Preheat the oven to 350°F. Line a large heavy baking sheet with parchment paper.

❷ Combine the sugar and cinnamon on a plate. With a pastry brush, brush both sides, tops, and bottoms of each slice of bread with melted butter or margarine or spray with the cooking spray. Then dip both sides of each slice into the cinnamon sugar. You may need to use your fingers or a spoon to sift sugar all over the bread. Place the slices in a single layer on the baking sheet. Bake until crisp, 10 to 14 minutes, turning the toasts once. Keep an eye on the toasts while they bake to prevent burning. Transfer the toasts from the baking sheet to a cutting board, and cut each slice into 3 wide strips. Serve immediately.

Almond Toasts
Makes 8 toasts

Sweet almond toasts are known in France as bostock. *They are made in bakeries from day-old brioche, and are immensely popular snacks, sort of a flat almond croissant. Some bakeries sprinkle them with kirsch liqueur before baking, but unless you can get a bottle of a top grade brand from France, Germany, or Switzerland, and you are serving adults, the almonds are just fine on their own. Make these open-faced sand-wiches with Brioche Bread (page 77) or Butter Bread (page 75). Serve with café au lait, omelets, and a fruit salad.*

¾ cup (1½ sticks) unsalted butter
¾ cup sugar
5 ounces almonds, finely ground (1½ cups)
1 large egg
1½ teaspoons almond extract

Eight 1-inch-thick slices day-old homemade white bread, sliced from the center of the loaf
1 cup sliced or chopped almonds, for sprinkling
Sifted confectioners' sugar, for dusting

❶ Using an electric mixer, cream the butter and sugar until fluffy. Add the ground almonds, egg, and almond extract. Beat until a smooth paste is formed.

❷ Preheat the oven to 375°F.

❸ Spread each slice of bread almost to the edges with the almond butter. Sprinkle with the sliced almonds. Place the bread in a single layer on an ungreased heavy baking sheet. Bake until the topping begins to brown and puff, and the bottoms of the bread are lightly toasted, about 15 to 20 minutes. Remove from the baking sheet to a serving tray, sprinkle with confectioners' sugar, and serve immediately or at room temperature.

Bruschetta

The original garlic bread, bruschetta are thick slices of chewy day-old bread that are toasted under the broiler or grilled over a wood or charcoal fire. A large clove of garlic is rubbed over the sandpaper-like surface of the toasted slices until the clove disappears completely into the pores of the bread. Then the slices are drizzled with a fruity, flavorful olive oil, the more character the better. There are no exact measurements needed here; one or two slices per person of a bread machine-made loaf would be sufficient. Bruschetta is a great appetizer for guests gathered around the grill sipping red wine, or as an accompaniment to soup or salads.

continued on next page

Homemade Italian, whole wheat Italian, French, or sourdough bread
Whole peeled garlic cloves (1 clove per 2 slices of bread) or a whole head of garlic that has been cut in half horizontally
Extra-virgin olive oil in a small pitcher or cruet

Slice the bread into 2-inch-thick slices. Place the slices in a toaster, under a pre-heated broiler, or on an oiled rack about 4 inches above glowing coals or a gas grill. Toast both sides of the slices until golden brown. Impale the clove of garlic on a fork or hold the cut head by the stem or root end, and while the toast is still hot, rub it with the garlic, using as little or as much as you like. Drizzle the bruschetta with plenty of olive oil. Serve the toast hot.

Summer Tomato Bruschetta
Makes 6 bruschetta

This should be made with vine-ripened tomatoes in the summer and fall.

Six 1-inch-thick slices homemade white or whole wheat country-style bread, preferably sliced from the center of a whole loaf
2 to 3 cloves garlic, peeled, with a thin slice cut from the end of each clove
½ cup extra-virgin olive oil
4 large ripe tomatoes (preferably vine-ripened, just picked, and not refrigerated), cut into ½-inch slices
3 tablespoons sherry wine vinegar
Sea salt and fresh-ground black pepper
1 bunch fresh arugula, leaves only

Lightly toast both sides of the bread over a charcoal or gas grill, under the broiler, or in a toaster oven. Remove the toast from the heat, and rub one side of it with the cut end of a garlic clove. Place the bruschetta on a serving platter. Drizzle with olive oil and top each slice with overlapping slices of tomato. Drizzle with some vinegar and some more olive oil. Sprinkle with salt and a few grinds of black pepper, and scatter with arugula. Serve immediately.

Bruschetta with Cheese and Honey

This recipe comes to America from Italy's Badia a Coltibuono cooking school. A beautiful, very simple dessert, it is best drizzled with a strong honey, such as buckwheat honey, and an assertive, fruity olive oil. In Italy, it was traditionally served with chestnut honey, estate olive oil, and pecorino toscano, a firm sheep's milk cheese. Since pecorino toscano is hard to find here, grill specialist Jay Harlow suggests you substitute Asiago, fontina, or Gruyère. Serve this bruschetta with a dessert wine or coffee.

Homemade Italian, whole wheat Italian, French, or sourdough bread
Extra-virgin olive oil in a small pitcher or cruet
Asiago, fontina, or Gruyère cheese, cut into thick slices
Dark, strong flower or herb honey

Slice the bread into 1-inch-thick slices and place them in a toaster or under a pre-heated broiler or on an oiled grill rack about 4 inches above glowing coals or over a gas grill. Toast one side of the bread until golden brown. Turn them and drizzle with a bit of olive oil, then a layer of cheese. Continue to toast the slices until the cheese is melted, keeping an eye on them so the bread does not burn. Transfer the bruschetta to a dessert plate and serve immediately drizzled with plenty of honey.

Old-Fashioned Tea Sandwiches

Savory little tea sandwiches are a popular and economical style of imaginative entertaining—a rediscovery. Once for a shoestring wedding, I brought Tupperware containers filled with sixteen dozen of my smoked turkey sandwiches as my gift. They almost caused a riot. Tea sandwiches are simply tiny sandwiches, a tasty filling encased by two slices of firm bread. One of the keys to these few-bite wonders is to take special care with the type of bread you use. Bread machine breads of just about any flavor work perfectly because of their tight, firm texture. Some people partially freeze the loaf first, to cut perfect slices by hand or with a home meat slicer. Spread a slice of bread with a topping, place another slice over the top, cut off the crusts, and cut the sandwich in half or quarters, or, if you prefer, into a geometric shape with the aid of a biscuit cutter. You can also leave tea sandwiches open-faced, in which case they are called canapés. You may wish to garnish the tops.

Sandwich fillings can be made a day ahead and the sandwiches assembled in assembly-line fashion the day of the party. This is especially fun if you have a helper. If I am preparing sandwiches for a large number of people, I make the sandwiches a day ahead and refrigerate them overnight in large plastic containers. If you make them a few hours ahead of serving they can also be stored this way, or stack them on a tray, and drape a damp paper towel or a clean damp tea towel over the top, followed by a sheet of plastic wrap, and refrigerate.

Here are some of my favorite tea sandwiches. Be sure the bread is thin and the filling is spread with a light hand. Arrange the sandwiches on a silver tray or platter for an elegant presentation.

Smoked Turkey Sandwiches
Makes about 48 small sandwiches

1½ pounds skinless hickory-smoked turkey breast, cut into chunks
6 scallions, both green and white parts
About ½ cup mayonnaise, just enough to bind
Salt and black pepper
2 loaves bread machine bread, thinly sliced (about 24 slices)

Place the turkey and scallions in the food processor and coarsely grind. Add the mayonnaise and pulse to make a spreadable paste. Season with salt and pepper to taste. Spread the turkey mixture on half of the bread slices. Cover with the remaining slices. Trim the crusts and cut each sandwich into 4 triangles.

Cucumber and Watercress Sandwiches
Makes about 32 small sandwiches

1 bunch watercress, bottom of stems removed, finely chopped
Salt and black pepper
4 tablespoons unsalted butter, softened
About ½ cup mayonnaise, just enough to bind
Grated zest of 1 small lemon
1 long English hothouse cucumber, sliced
1½ loaves bread machine bread, thinly sliced (about 16 slices)

Season the watercress with salt and pepper to taste. Using a food processor, an electric mixer, or by hand, cream the butter and add

continued on next page

the mayonnaise and lemon zest. Spread the mayonnaise butter on all the bread slices, sprinkle half of them with watercress, and cover the watercress with some cucumber slices. Cover with the remaining slices of bread. Trim the crusts and cut each sandwich into 4 triangles.

Avocado and Bacon Sandwiches
Makes about 48 small sandwiches

1½ tablespoons unsalted butter, softened
About ⅔ cup mayonnaise, just enough to bind
¾ teaspoon Worcestershire sauce
Splash of hot red pepper sauce
2 firm-ripe avocados, peeled and halved
2 loaves bread machine bread, thinly sliced (about 24 slices)
8 slices bacon, cooked in a skillet until golden brown, drained on paper towels, and crumbled

Cream the butter and add the mayonnaise, Worcestershire sauce and hot pepper sauce. Spread the mayonnaise butter lightly on half of the bread slices. Slice the avocado halves and place a few slices on each piece of buttered bread before sprinkling with the bacon. Cover with the remaining bread slices. Trim the crusts and cut each sandwich into 4 triangles.

Herb Butter Sandwiches
Makes about 48 small sandwiches

1 bunch flat-leaf parsley
1 bunch fresh basil, leaves only
¼ cup chopped chives
¼ cup mixed fresh aromatic herbs, such as marjoram, savory, and tarragon

¾ cup (1½ sticks) unsalted butter, softened
8 ounces cream cheese, softened
4 ounces goat cheese, softened
2 loaves bread machine bread, thinly sliced (about 24 slices)

Combine the parsley, basil, chives, and mixed herbs in the food processor and pulse to chop. Add the butter, cream cheese, and goat cheese, and pulse to make a spreadable paste. Spread the cheese mixture on half of the bread slices. Cover with the remaining slices. Trim the crusts and cut each sandwich into 4 triangles.

Smoked Salmon Sandwiches
Makes about 32 small sandwiches

½ pound thinly sliced smoked salmon
1 pound cream cheese, softened
Juice of 1 lemon
3 tablespoons chopped fresh dill
8 paper-thin slices of red onion
1½ loaves bread machine bread, thinly sliced (about 16 slices)

Place the smoked salmon in the food processor and pulse to chop. Add the cream cheese, lemon juice, and dill, and pulse to make a spreadable paste. Spread the cheese mixture on half of the bread slices, and top with a slice of red onion. Cover with the remaining slices. Trim the crusts and cut each sandwich into 4 squares or cut out shapes.

Appendix 2

TO EAT WITH YOUR BREAD
Spreads, Butters, Cheeses, and Vegetables

There are just certain types of foods that go perfectly with bread. There is the quintessential bread with butter. Butter is also able to soak up other flavors without their masking its luscious presence—it takes well to honey, fruit, olives, or herbs. Then there is the classic pairing of bread and cheese. The starch in the bread soaks up the excess fat in the cheese, making for a perfect balance. We all have our favorite dip. Dips are great for casual entertaining; in most cases they can, and should, be made a day ahead—giving their flavors a chance to meld. Paired with homemade flatbreads or crisps, dips are at their best. Bread is also good with olives, acting as a foil to their pungent flavor and saltiness. Beyond these, there are a host of bread accompaniments, like roasted vegetables and spreads made of beans or meat, that make bread something special.

In this section, you will find recipes for bread accompaniments that are simple enough for everyday eating and ones to serve to company. There are sweet and savory honeys, butters, cheese spreads, molded cheeses, and fruit curd, something to showcase every type of bread and accompany every occasion.

Whipped Honey Butter
Makes about 1 cup

Whipped honey butter is good served with all kinds of white and wheat toast.

½ cup mild honey
¾ cup (1½ sticks) unsalted butter, at room temperature

In a food processor, process the honey until it is smooth and light, no more than 1 minute, stopping as necessary to scrape down the sides of the workbowl. Cut the butter into pieces, and add it to the workbowl, dropping it in on top of the honey. Process until light in color, about 30 seconds. Scrape the honey butter into a covered container, and store in the refrigerator for up to 1 month. For the best flavor, let stand for 1 hour at room temperature before serving.

Strawberry Butter
Makes about 1 cup

This tart, fresh fruit butter is good spread on Tecate Ranch Whole Wheat (page 126) or Cornmeal and Hominy Bread (page 149).

½ cup fresh strawberries, stemmed
1 tablespoon confectioners' sugar
½ teaspoon balsamic vinegar
½ cup (1 stick) unsalted butter, at room temperature

Sprinkle the berries with the sugar and vinegar and let stand for 5 minutes. In a food processor puree the berry mixture and butter, pulsing until just combined. Do not overprocess. Using plastic wrap to protect your hands, shape the butter mixture into a thick log. Wrap in clean plastic wrap and twist the ends. Refrigerate until firm, and slice to serve. Store for up to 1 week in the refrigerator.

Marmalade Butter
Makes about ½ cup

Serve this with Toasted Walnut Bread (page 322) or Bohemian Black Bread (page 138).

½ cup (1 stick) unsalted butter
3 tablespoons orange marmalade

Using a wooden spoon, an electric mixer, or a food processor, beat the butter and marmalade together, just until blended. Transfer to a serving bowl, cover, and refrigerate for up to 1 month. For the best flavor, let stand at room temperature for 1 hour before serving.

Red Pepper Butter
Makes about 2 cups

Serve thick chilled slices of this alongside French Bread (page 61) or Grissini (page 212).

1 cup (2 sticks) unsalted butter, at room temperature
One 7-ounce jar roasted red peppers, drained and patted dry
1 tablespoon fresh lemon juice
2 tablespoons chopped fresh flat-leaf parsley

In a blender or food processor puree all the ingredients until fluffy and smooth. Using plastic wrap to protect your hands, form the mixture into 2 logs. Wrap in plastic wrap and twist the ends. Store the logs in the refrigerator or freezer for up to 2 weeks. Slice the logs to serve.

Provençal Butter
Makes ½ cup

When you see the word "Provençal," you should be tipped off that one of the ingredients in this recipe will be black olives. Serve this with your homemade dinner rolls.

½ cup (1 stick) unsalted butter, at room temperature
3 tablespoons chopped black olives
2 teaspoons fresh lemon juice
1 small clove garlic, pressed

Combine all the ingredients in the bowl of a food processor or in a mixing bowl. Mix until evenly combined, and the mixture is smooth. Scrape the butter into a small serving bowl. Cover, and refrigerate for up to 2 days. Let stand for 30 minutes before serving.

Spiced Vanilla Honey
Makes 2 cups

This honey is quite addictive. It is a good way to use those old vanilla beans; if they are too shriveled to cut in half, chop them into 2-inch pieces. This honey is really nice in Whipped Honey Butter (page 598).

2 cups mild honey, such as clover or wildflower
1 vanilla bean, cut in half and split lengthwise
1 whole cinnamon stick 4-inches long
2 whole star anise
6 whole cloves

Heat the honey just until warm in a small saucepan on the stovetop, or in a bowl in the microwave. Place the spices in the bottom of a spring-top jar or crock with a lid, and pour the warm honey over the spices. Cover and let sit at room temperature for 1 week to meld the flavors. The honey will keep for 2 months at room temperature.

Sweet Herb Honey
Makes 1½ cups

This is an old British recipe, for spreading on toast or drizzling on bruschetta. Use sweet herbs, such as rosemary, lemon thyme, basil, marjoram, Spanish oregano, or lavender; but use only one type per jar.

1½ cups mild honey
2 teaspoons chopped fresh herb of your choice
1 small whole sprig of same herb

Heat the honey just until warm in a small saucepan on the stovetop, or in a bowl in the microwave. Place the chopped herb in the bottom of a spring-top or clear jelly jar, pour the warm honey over it, and insert the herb sprig (it will look pretty, and will also help identify the type of honey). Tightly cap. Let the honey sit in the refrigerator for about 1 week to meld the flavors, turning the jar every other day (the herbs will float to the top). Scrape off the layer of herbs when the flavor of the honey is strong enough for you. Bring to room temperature before serving. The honey should be eaten within 3 weeks of being made.

Lemon Curd with Fresh Mint
Makes about 2 cups

Lemon curd is a perennial favorite and there is no comparison when it is homemade. I like my lemon curd on the tart side. I mix it in the food processor, which makes an emulsion and cuts down on the vigorous stirring normally required during cooking. The addition of fresh mint is a little surprise. This curd is a must with English Muffins (page 90).

4 tablespoons unsalted butter
1 cup sugar
4 fresh mint leaves
Zest of 2 lemons, cut into strips
¾ cup fresh lemon juice
4 large eggs
2 egg yolks

1 Melt the butter in the top of a double boiler over barely simmering water.

2 Meanwhile, place the sugar and the mint leaves in the bowl of a food processor, and process until the mint leaves are very finely chopped. Add the lemon zest, and process until the ingredients are well combined and the zest is chopped. Add the lemon juice and eggs, and process until a thick emulsion is formed, about 20 seconds.

3 Pour the mixture into the hot butter, stirring constantly with a wire whisk. Cook over simmering water, on medium heat, stirring constantly, until thickened, a full 10 to 15 minutes. Pour the curd into a glass jar and let cool before storing in the refrigerator. Lemon curd should be used within 1 month.

Raspberry Cream Cheese
Makes about 2 cups

The small, plump raspberry is considered the most intensely flavored of all berries. Raspberries are very fragile and mix quickly into room temperature cream cheese to use as an alternative to raspberry jam.

8 ounces light cream cheese, at room temperature

¼ cup fresh raspberries or unsweetened frozen
  raspberries, thawed and drained
1 tablespoon sugar
1 tablespoon framboise or other raspberry liqueur

Using a wooden spoon, an electric mixer, or a food processor, beat the cream cheese until fluffy. Add the berries, sugar, and liqueur. Beat until all the ingredients are just combined. Transfer the mixture to a serving bowl, cover, and refrigerate overnight. Use within 2 days. Let stand at room temperature for 30 minutes to soften before serving.

Pasqua Cheese
Serves about 20

This is a wonderful almond and dried fruit cheese torta for special events, as beautiful as it is delicious. Pasqua or Pashka is from the Greek word pasha, *which means "to pass over." Pasqua cheese is one of the most traditional of Greek Orthodox Easter foods, served with sweet bread like* kulich *or* babka. *This recipe is adapted from one served at Taliesin West, Frank Lloyd Wright's estate near Scottsdale, Arizona, to entertain his staff, students, and guests at Easter. It was a family recipe of his Slavic wife, Olgivanna. I like this version because it does not contain raw egg yolks, a traditional ingredient. The mold that you use is important because the cheese needs to be able to drain properly. I like to use a cone-shaped chinois mesh strainer, since it has a planed tip like the traditional Greek mold, but you can also use a mesh or metal colander, or a new terra-cotta flowerpot lined with plastic wrap beneath the cheesecloth, a hole poked in the bottom of the plastic for drainage.*

⅔ cup sugar
2 ounces (a heaping ⅓ cup) blanched almonds

½ cup (1 stick) unsalted butter
½ cup sour cream
3 pounds large-curd cottage cheese
  (not cream-style)
Grated zest of 2 lemons
1 teaspoon vanilla extract
1 teaspoon almond extract
¼ cup golden raisins or tart dried cherries
¼ cup minced dried apricots
Whole blanched almonds, for decorating

1 Place the sugar and almonds in the workbowl of a food processor, and process until the almonds are finely ground. Transfer the mixture to a small bowl. Place the butter in the workbowl and process until smooth (there is no need to wash the bowl after the almonds). Add the sour cream and 1 pound of the cottage cheese; process until smooth. Add the lemon zest, extracts, and almond mixture; process until well combined. Transfer the mixture to a mixing bowl, add the remaining 2 pounds of cottage cheese, and mix with a wooden spoon to incorporate. Fold in the dried fruits.

2 Line the desired mold with a double layer of cheesecloth moistened with water and rung out, with the excess cloth hanging over the edge. Spoon the cheese mixture into the mold, filling it to the brim. Fold the edges of cloth over the cheese. Cover with plastic wrap and place a heavy object, such as a foil-wrapped brick or large can of stewed tomatoes, on the cheese. Place in a shallow bowl and refrigerate for 24 to 48 hours (can be made 2 days ahead). Drain off the liquid collected in the bowl as often as necessary.

continued on next page

❸ To unmold the cheese, unwrap the top of it, place a serving plate over the mold, and invert. Gently lift off the mold and peel off the cheesecloth. Stud the sides with the whole blanched almonds radiating down. Serve immediately or refrigerate until serving time. Refrigerate any leftovers, tightly wrapped, for up to 4 days.

Cinnamon Date Cheese
Makes about 1½ cups

Cinnamon, the dried inner bark of a tropical evergreen tree, was once considered an important ingredient in ancient love potions. Paired with dates and vanilla in this soft, spreadable breakfast cheese, you will agree that it has a euphoric, as well as delicious, flavor. This is my favorite sweet cheese spread for toast.

4 ounces (about 18) pitted dates
4 ounces cream cheese, at room temperature
4 ounces fresh goat cheese, at room temperature
1½ teaspoons vanilla extract
1 teaspoon ground cinnamon

❶ Cover the dates with water in a small saucepan. Cook, uncovered, over low heat until the dates are soft and the water is absorbed, about 10 minutes. Cool to room temperature.

❷ Place the dates in the work bowl of a food processor and puree them. Add the cream cheese, goat cheese, vanilla extract, and cinnamon. Process just until blended and smooth. Pack the mixture into a decorative crock and refrigerate, covered, until serving, up to 5 days. Serve at room temperature.

Goat Cheese Butter
Makes about 2 cups

The half and half combination of two mild cheeses makes a spread that even people who say they don't like goat cheese will love. Serve with fresh bread or crostini, or use it to dress up your toast drizzled with honey.

6 ounces cream cheese, at room temperature
6 ounces fresh goat cheese, such as domestic chabis or imported Montrachet, at room temperature
2 tablespoons extra-virgin olive oil or domestic nut oil, such as hazelnut or pecan, or honey

Using a wooden spoon, an electric mixer, or a food processor, beat the cheeses together until fluffy and well blended. Scrape the mixture into a small crock or bowl lined with 2 layers of damp cheesecloth. Pack down the cheese, and fold the edges of the cheesecloth over the top to cover completely. Cover with plastic wrap. Store in the refrigerator for up to 2 days. To unmold the cheese, unwrap the top, place a serving plate over it, and invert. Gently lift off the mold, and remove the cheesecloth. Drizzle with the oil and serve.

Savory Appetizer Cheesecake
Makes one 6-inch cheesecake

This cheesecake can be made up to three days ahead and refrigerated until serving. Place on a small pedestal plate and decorate with fresh leaves. Serve at room temperature with plain crostini and any homemade chutney (pages 580 to 583); the cheesecake can be eaten in slices set on the crostini, or it can be treated as a dip.

¼ cup fine dry breadcrumbs
¼ cup finely chopped walnuts
12 ounces cream cheese, at room temperature
4 ounces blue cheese, such as gorgonzola
2 tablespoons sour cream
2 large eggs
2 teaspoons brandy
1¼ tablespoons minced fresh chives
Salt and white pepper

1 Combine the breadcrumbs and the walnuts in a small bowl. Heavily butter a 6-inch round springform pan. Coat the bottom and about 2 inches up the sides of the pan with the crumbs, packing the extra onto the bottom.

2 Wrap the outside bottom and a few inches up the sides of the pan with aluminum foil to prevent leakage.

3 Preheat the oven to 325°.

4 In the workbowl of a food processor, combine the cheeses, sour cream, eggs, and brandy and process until smooth. Add the chives and season with salt and white pepper to taste. Process again to combine. Pour into the prepared pan.

5 Place the foil-wrapped springform pan in a small roasting pan, and pour in warm water until it reaches at least 2 inches up the sides of the pan. Bake for 1 hour and 20 minutes. Turn off the oven and leave the cheesecake in the hot oven with the door ajar for 1 hour, to set. Transfer the cheesecake to a rack to cool completely. Refrigerate overnight. Run a small knife

around the edge before removing the springform sides and serving.

Molded Egg Salad with Lemon Mustard Mayonnaise
Serves 8

I have made this perfectly molded dip dozens of times for parties, with great success. The recipe doubles and triples beautifully. I have used all sizes of heart-shaped cake pans in place of the usual fluted or melon-shaped mold. It is good with Lowfat Garlic Crostini (page 589), Garlic Pita Toasts (page 588), Whole Wheat Pita (page 424), or Naan (page 420).

1 envelope unflavored gelatin
¼ cup cold water
10 large hard-cooked eggs, at room temperature
3 scallions
1 tablespoon chopped fresh chives
¾ cup mayonnaise
2 tablespoons Dijon mustard
3 tablespoons lemon juice
Salt and white pepper

1 Line a decorative 1-quart mold with a layer of plastic wrap. Sprinkle the gelatin over the cold water in a microwave-proof bowl. Let stand for 10 minutes, then heat in the microwave for about 2 minutes to liquify. Peel the hard-cooked eggs.

2 With the food processor running, add the scallions through the feed tube to mince them. Stop the machine and add the eggs, chives, mayonnaise, mustard, lemon juice, and salt and pepper to taste. Process until smooth with bits of green speckled throughout. With the machine

continued on next page

running, slowly pour in the liquid gelatin. Process for a few seconds to evenly combine. Pour into the mold. Cover with plastic wrap and refrigerate overnight.

3 To serve, line a serving platter with kale or nasturtium leaves. Remove the plastic wrap and turn out the egg salad onto the bed of leaves. Serve chilled.

Italian Tuna Pâté
Serves 4

The first time I heard about tuna pâté I couldn't believe there was such a thing. It is a favorite appetizer in Jewish cuisine. It is downright luscious and rather sophisticated for how simple it is. Be sure to make it the day you are going to serve it for the best flavor. While it is best to use imported tuna from Italy packed in olive oil, I also make it with low-salt, water-packed tuna with great results.

1 small shallot
One 7-ounce can solid-pack tuna in olive oil, drained
½ cup (1 stick) unsalted butter, cut into pieces
1 tablespoon fresh lemon juice
Salt and fresh-ground black pepper
1 tablespoon minced fresh parsley or chives, for garnish

With the food processor running, add the shallot through the feed tube to mince it. Stop the machine and add the tuna, butter, and lemon juice. Pulse until smooth. Add salt and pepper to taste. Scrape into a small serving bowl (lined with plastic wrap first if you want to and turn the pâté out onto a serving plate later). Refrigerate until serving. Sprinkle the

top with parsley or chives. The pâté will soften at room temperature. Eat the pâté the day it is made.

Mushroom Pâté
Serves 6

⅔ cup chopped shallots
⅓ cup unsalted butter
1 pound mushrooms, sliced
¼ cup Cognac or brandy
1 tablespoon lemon juice
Salt and fresh-ground black pepper

Place the shallots and butter in a large skillet or sauté pan. Cook over medium heat until the shallots are translucent but not browned, about 3 to 5 minutes. Add the mushrooms and increase the heat to high. Sauté until just slightly browned, about 10 minutes. Remove the mixture from the heat. Add the Cognac and carefully ignite. Stir with a long-handled oversized metal spoon until the flames die out. Puree the mushroom mixture in a food processor. Add the lemon juice, and salt and pepper to taste. Scrape into a covered container and refrigerate overnight to meld the flavors. Eat within 3 days.

Cannellini Bean Spread
Makes about 1¼ cups

For the lowfat lovers, here is a spread that some may prefer over cheese. Cannellini beans are also known as white kidney beans. The combination of mint and parsley is classic Italian; here I add cilantro, another mint-like flavor. Serve with fresh bread or crostini.

1 large clove garlic
¼ cup fresh flat-leaf parsley
2 tablespoons fresh cilantro leaves
1 tablespoon fresh mint
One 15-ounce can cannellini beans, rinsed and drained
3 tablespoons water or liquid drained from the beans
3 tablespoons fresh lemon juice

With the food processor running, add the garlic through the feed tube to chop it. Add the parsley, cilantro, and mint and pulse to chop. Add the beans; process until coarsely chopped. Add the water and lemon juice through the feed tube with the motor running, and process until smooth. Scrape the mixture into a serving bowl and chill until serving. Decorate with a sprig of parsley. This can be made 1 day ahead.

Hummus
Serves 5

Hummus, a must with fresh pita bread (page 424), is the dish that has made Middle Eastern food famous. Every country there has a favorite bean or legume from which they make their creamy, seasoned dips. Tahini, an important ingredient, is a paste made from ground sesame seeds. It tastes a bit more bitter than nut butters, but is the perfect foil to the sweet chickpeas in this hummus. Some people like their hummus real garlicky, others like it milder. Give each person a whole pita and let them tear pieces off and scoop up the dip. I serve hummus with spears of romaine lettuce along with the pita.

2 to 3 cloves garlic, or to taste
Two 15-ounce cans chickpeas

About ⅓ cup hot water
Juice of 1 large lemon
⅓ cup sesame tahini
2 tablespoons extra-virgin olive oil
Pinch of red pepper flakes
Pinch of salt

With the food processor running, add the garlic through the feed tube. Add the chickpeas and while the machine is running, slowly add the hot water until the mixture is a fluffy dipping consistency. Add the remaining ingredients and puree until smooth. Scrape into a serving bowl and refrigerate, covered, until serving. To serve, make a depression in the top of the dip and drizzle with a bit more olive oil, which will pool in the dish. Keeps, refrigerated, for 2 to 3 days.

Roasted Eggplant Dip
Serves 4

This is a variation on baba ghanoush, a wonderful (and lowfat) Mediterranean dish that is good with toasted pita bread, plain or herbed focaccia, or toast. This is nice topped with some sesame seeds that have been lightly toasted in a dry skillet.

2 medium eggplants (about 1¼ pounds)
1 medium shallot
1 whole canned jalapeño pepper
2 tablespoons olive oil
2 teaspoons fresh lemon juice
1 teaspoon fresh lime juice
¼ teaspoon ground cumin
Pinch of salt

❶ Preheat the oven to 400°F.

continued on next page

❷ Cut the eggplants in half lengthwise and place, cut side down, on a lightly greased baking sheet. Bake for 35 to 45 minutes, until tender and the skin is blackened and puckered. Set aside to cool.

❸ Peel the eggplant and discard the skin. With the food processor running, add the shallot through the feed tube. Add the remaining ingredients and process until just combined; this dip is best a bit chunky. Scrape into a serving bowl and refrigerate, covered, until serving. This dip can be made 1 day in advance.

Hot Artichoke Dip
Serves 6

This is the most popular dip I make. It is good hot, warm, or cooled to room temperature. Serve this dip with Pita Bread Crisps (page 588), or with fresh slices of Roman Bread (page 408).

4 scallions
8 ounces cream cheese, at room temperature
1 cup grated Parmesan cheese
One 14-ounce can artichoke hearts or bottoms, drained
½ cup mayonnaise or plain yogurt
Dash of hot red pepper sauce

❶ Preheat the oven to 400°F.

❷ Place the scallions in a food processor and chop. Add the cream cheese and Parmesan cheese and process until smooth. Add the artichokes and process until coarsely chopped. Add the mayonnaise or yogurt and red pepper sauce; process with on and off pulses just until incorporated.

Scrape the mixture into a shallow 4-cup gratin dish or ovenproof dish. (The dip can be made 1 day ahead up to this point and refrigerated.) Bake for 25 minutes, until the dip is bubbly. Serve immediately.

Marinated Fresh Vegetables
Makes 2 quarts, serves about 8

I have been taking these vegetables à la greque to parties for decades. The vegetables do not need cooking; they soften in the vinaigrette as they marinate. I use a wonderful organic apple cider vinegar in the marinade, and store them in big spring-top jars. Prepare the vegetables one to three days before serving. This is a wonderful, crunchy appetizer or salad, especially when accompanied by fresh bread and cheese.

1 cup vegetable oil
½ cup olive oil
½ cup apple cider vinegar
⅓ cup water
1½ tablespoons chopped fresh dill or basil
Grated zest of 1 lemon
Pinch of onion powder
Sea salt and coarse-ground black pepper
½ small head cauliflower, cut into florets
1 to 2 medium carrots, sliced, or 4 ounces baby carrots, halved lengthwise
1 medium yellow crookneck or straight-neck summer squash, cut into ½-inch chunks
2 medium zucchini, cut into ½-inch slices on the diagonal
1 large red pepper, cut into ½-inch strips
⅓ pound large fresh mushrooms, sliced ½ inch thick
One 12-ounce package frozen artichoke hearts, defrosted and drained on paper towels
3 cloves garlic, peeled and halved
1 bay leaf

❶ Combine the oils, vinegar, water, dill or basil, lemon zest, onion powder, salt, and pepper in a bowl. With a whisk or immersion blender, blend until thick.

❷ Layer the vegetables in a tall 2-quart glass jar, and tuck the bay leaf in on top. Pour the vinaigrette over the vegetables. Cover the jar with the lid and turn upside down to moisten all the vegetables. Place the jar right side up in the refrigerator, overnight or up to 3 days. To make sure the marinade is reaching all the vegetables, you may want to let the jar rest on its side occasionally, while it is being refrigerated. Place a paper towel underneath, in case the jar should leak.

❸ To serve, remove the vegetables from the jar with a slotted spoon. The vegetables may be eaten cold or at room temperature. They keep for 4 days.

Lolly's Roasted Red Peppers
Serves 4

Lolly Font is our local Iyengar yoga teacher. She is known by all as an incredible cook, able to go out to the backyard, pluck a few things from the garden, and come up with a fantastic meal in no time. Her way with recipes floats around like gossip in my circle of cooks. These peppers of Lolly's are absolutely famous. You can broil them with cheese, as directed here, and serve them with bread, or just serve the peppers marinated in their own juices with the garlic, parsley, and oil. At one party where I served them, a guest described them as "the caviar of peppers."

4 large red bell peppers, with the thickest flesh you can find
¼ cup olive oil
2 cloves garlic, chopped
2 tablespoons chopped fresh flat-leaf parsley
2 tablespoons chopped fresh basil
2 teaspoons chopped fresh oregano or marjoram
6 ounces whole milk mozzarella, sliced

❶ Place the peppers on a baking sheet and broil them until the skins blister, about 3 minutes. With a pair of metal tongs, turn a quarter turn and broil for 3 minutes. Repeat this until the entire pepper is charred. Immediately place the peppers in a paper or plastic bag. Close the bag and let the peppers sit until they have cooled to room temperature, about 20 minutes. The steam given off by the peppers will loosen their charred skin.

❷ Cut open one side of a pepper and pull out the seeds, ribs, and stem; discard them. Holding the pepper over a small bowl, peel off the skin using a paring knife. The bowl will collect the juices. If some of the skin sticks, rinse the pepper under cold running water. Repeat until all the peppers are seeded and peeled. (You can store the peppers in their juices in a covered container in the refrigerator for up to 3 days, if you wish.)

❸ Cut each pepper into 5 or 6 large pieces and place the pieces in 4 individual gratin dishes. Drizzle each with a tablespoon of oil, some garlic, and any collected juices.

❹ Combine the parsley, basil, and oregano. Distribute the mixture evenly among the 4

continued on next page

dishes. Top the pepper pieces and herbs in each dish with a slice of cheese. Place the dishes under a broiler and broil until the cheese bubbles and begins to brown. Serve immediately.

Basil-Baked Tomatoes
Makes 4 dozen tomato halves, about 1 quart

Use these tomatoes as an ingredient in bread or as an antipasto served with bread, or toss them with pasta or drop them onto pizza or focaccia instead of fresh tomatoes. Once you try these, you will want to have them around all the time. They are, for their sublime flavor and real versatility, a perfect pantry staple. They are especially good with country breads.

> 24 small, ripe Roma tomatoes
> ⅔ cup olive oil
> ¾ cup chopped fresh basil
> 6 cloves garlic, peeled and minced

❶ Preheat the oven to 200°F. Line a large 17-by-11-inch baking sheet with parchment paper.

❷ Cut the tomatoes in half lengthwise, removing the stems, if necessary. Place the tomatoes in a shallow bowl, and toss them with the olive oil so that they are evenly coated. Arrange the tomatoes, cut side up, on the baking sheet. (All the tomatoes should fit on one sheet.) Sprinkle them evenly with the chopped basil and minced garlic.

❸ Bake the tomatoes for 3 to 3½ hours, or until the tomatoes are wrinkled, but still moist. Remove from the oven and let cool to room temperature. Place the tomatoes in a covered container or wide-mouth spring-top jar, and store in the refrigerator for up to 1 month.

Marinated Olives with Herbs and Sun-dried Tomatoes
Makes 1 quart

You can use any type of brine-cured olive for this recipe—Californian, Greek, or any other. These olives will keep for three months in the refrigerator. They look very pretty in the jar, and make a wonderful gift accompanied by a loaf of country bread.

> 4 cups brine-cured black olives, pitted and drained
> 3 cloves garlic, peeled and cut into 4 slices each
> ¼ cup drained oil-packed sun-dried tomato strips, oil reserved if desired, see Note
> 5 julienne strips of orange zest (each about 2 inches long)
> 1 tablespoon chopped fresh basil
> 1 tablespoon chopped fresh marjoram
> ½ cup olive oil

In a bowl, combine all of the ingredients except the oil, and toss to evenly distribute the herbs and the tomatoes. Place the mixture in a springtop quart jar, and pour in the oil. Refrigerate the olives to marinate for at least 3 days before serving. Bring the olives to room temperature to serve.

N O T E :
If you wish, you can use a combination of oil drained from the tomatoes and olive oil to equal the ½ cup olive oil.

Appendix 3

RESOURCES

Bread Machines, Baking Equipment, Flour, Ingredients, and Other Baking Products

The Baker's Catalogue

P.O. Box 876
Norwich, Vermont 05055
800-827-6836
www.kingarthurflour.com

Order Zojirushi and Welbilt bread machines, clay baking pans, mini-loaf pans, baguette pans, pizza pans, thermometers, baking stones, banettons, and just about any other equipment you could possibly need for baking. Brinna Sands has built her King Arthur Flour Company and The Baker's Catalogue mail-order branch to offer a wide variety of the best fresh flours, such as King Arthur Sir Lancelot High-Gluten Flour, Special for Bread Machines Flour (a favorite with all my recipe testers), First Clear Flour, Unbleached All-Purpose Flour (which even works well in the bread machine), Stone Ground Whole Wheat Flour, and White Whole Wheat Flour. Also offers various types of yeast.

K-TEC

1206 South 1680 West
Orem, Utah 84058
800-748-5400
www.k-tecnsa.com

Grain mills, Zojirushi bread machines, bread machine mixes, and other baking supplies.

Williams-Sonoma

P.O. Box 7456
San Francisco, California 94120-7456
800-541-2233
www.williams-sonoma.com

Purveyor of Grande Cuisine bread machines, fine cookware and bakeware, baking stones, baking pans, rolling pins, French bread pans, Kaiser springform pans, decorative pans, bundt pans, and jelly jars. Also bread machine mixes, Scharffen Berger chocolate, Nielsen-Massey vanilla, Australian crystallized ginger, crystallized flowers, mint, and berries, whole roasted chestnuts, Boyajian citrus oils, dried berries, almond extract, Fini balsamic vinegar, and olive oil.

Bread Machines and Baking Equipment

Chef's Catalog

P.O. Box 620048
Dallas, Texas 75262
800-884-2433
www.chefscatalog.com

Sells Breadman bread machines, as well as every other piece of equipment you could want.

Sur La Table Catalog

1765 Sixth Avenue South
Seattle, Washington 98134
800-243-0852
www.surlatable.com

A variety of baking equipment, such as decorative paper loaf pans, pizza pans, 6-inch cake pans, decorative bread tubes, baguette pans, breadstick pans, banettons, baking sheets, Kaiser nonstick loaf pans, and rolling pins. Also sell bread machines and grain mills.

Baking Stones and Clay Pans

Sassafras Enterprises Inc.

1622 West Carroll Avenue
Chicago, Illinois 60612
800-537-4941

Makers of Superstone La Cloche baking dishes, baking stones and tiles, pizza pans, large and small clay loaf pans, rectangular rimmed baking stones, 11-inch wreath bread pans, 4½-inch round bread crocks sold in sets of two, and 6¾-inch round loaf bakers. I use the ceramic baking sheet all the time for focaccia.

Tufty Ceramics, Inc.
47 Main Street
Andover, New York 14806
607-478-5150
Alfred red clay bread pans and pizza pans.

Flours

Bob's Red Mill Natural Foods
5209 SE International Way
Milwaukee, Oregon 97222
503-654-3215

One of my favorite sources for bread flour and stone-ground whole wheat flour. They mill a large variety of fresh flours.

Butte Creek Mill
P.O. Box 561
402 Royal Avenue North
Eagle Point, Oregon 97524
541-826-3531
www.buttecreekmill.com

Wonderful flours stone-ground by an old water-powered mill. I love their stone-ground white flour—it makes fantastic white bread.

Giusto's
344 Littlefield
South San Francisco, California 94080
650-873-6566
www.giustos.com

I have used Giusto's flour both at home and professionally, and find it to be some of the best flour available.

Goldmine Natural Food Company
7805 Arjons Drive
San Diego, California 92126
800-475-3663
www.goldminenaturalfood.com

A full line of premium organic bread and specialty flours and sweeteners.

The Great Valley Mills
1774 County Line Road
Barto, Pennsylvania 19504
800-688-6455

This mill has been operating since 1710 and supplied Washington's troops with flour during the American Revolution. Known for generations for their excellent flours.

Hodgson Mill
1203 Niccum Avenue
Effingham, Illinois 62401
800-525-0177
www.hodgsonmill.com

A full line of stone-ground flours and cornmeals and a flour just for the bread machine. Hodgson's products are staples in Midwest supermarkets. The mill began in the Ozarks 117 years ago.

Walnut Acres Organic Farms
Walnut Acres Road
Penns Creek, Pennsylvania 17862
800-344-9025
www.walnutacres.com

A reliable source for organic bread flour, all-purpose flour, and a full line of specialty flours.

War Eagle Mill
Route 5, P.O. Box 411
11045 War Eagle Road
Rogers, Arkansas 72756
501-789-5343
www.wareaglemill.com

Excellent stone-ground bread flours. I am guessing it must be a great place to visit, too, with a restaurant called the Bean Palace. The mill offers tours and there is a retail store on the premises.

Whole Grains and Specialty Flours (*see also* Flours)

Birkett Mills/The National Buckwheat Institute
P.O. Box 440A
Penn Yan, New York 14527
315-536-3311
www.thebirkettmills.com

This research and information center has its own mill.

The California Press
6200 Washington Street
Yountville, California 94599
707-944-0343
www.californiapress.com

Wonderful virgin nut oils and nut flours (walnut, almond, pistachio, filbert, and pecan).

Gibbs Wild Rice
10400 Billings Road
Live Oak, California 95953
800-824-4932

Gibbs offers a really nice mild-flavored California-grown wild rice.

Gibbs Wild Rice
P.O. Box 277
Dear River, Minnesota 56636
800-344-6378
www.gibbswildrice.com

Order Minnesota-grown wild rice and wild rice flour from this branch of Gibbs.

Grain Millers
315 Madison Street
Eugene, Oregon 97402
800-443-8972
www.grainmillers.com

Organic rolled oats.

Gray's Grist Mill
P.O. Box 422
Adamsville, Rhode Island 02801
508-636-6075
www.burningelectrons.com/GRAYS/

Stone-ground cornmeals; known for using New England strains of corn.

Kamut Association of America
Montana Flour and Grains
P.O. Box 517
Ft. Benton, Montana 59442
800-644-6450
www.kamut.com

This is a source for kamut flour.

Kenyon Cornmeal Company
21 Glenn Rock Road
West Kingston, Rhode Island 02892
800-753-6966
www.kenyongristmill.com

Stone-ground cornmeals.

Lundberg Family Farms
5370 Church Street
P.O. Box 369
Richvale, California 95974
530-882-4551
www.lundberg.com

Wehani rice, American basmati rice, japonica black rice, brown rices, and arborio varieties.

Mountain Ark Trading Company
799 Old Leicester Highway
Asheville, North Carolina 28806
800-643-8909
www.mountainark.com

Specializes in organic flours.

Nu-World Amaranth, Inc.
P.O. Box 2202
Naperville, Illinois 60567
630-369-6819
www.nuworldamaranth.com

This company sells amaranth grain and flour.

Santa Fe School of Cooking

116 West San Francisco Street
Santa Fe, New Mexico 87501
505-983-4511
www.santafeschoolofcooking.com

Blue cornmeals, *harinilla*, *atole*, blue corn masa harina, and the *best* stone-ground masa harina.

Western Trails Cowboy Foods

P.O. Box 460
Bozeman, Montana 59771
406-587-5489
www.cowboyfoods.com

Barley flour, barley flakes, barley grits, and whole grain. The Black Buffalo and Bronze Nugget barleys, either whole or as flour, are especially delicious.

Flours and Specialty Products for Gluten-Free Baking

When you bake for special diets, egg replacers, gluten-free flours, wheat-free bread machine mixes, methocel, xanthan gum, and guar gum are important staples. Here are mail-order sources for those products (*see also* listings for Bob's Red Mill Natural Foods and The Baker's Catalogue):

Ener-G Foods, Inc.

P.O. Box 84487
5960 First Avenue South
Seattle, Washington 98108
800-331-5222
www.ener-g.com

Tadco Niblack Foods

900 Jefferson Road, Building 5
Rochester, New York 14623
800-724-8883

Seeds and Grains for Growing

If you are interested in growing grains in your home garden, here are some resources that offer seeds:

Bountiful Gardens

18001 Shafer Ranch Road
Willits, California 95490
707-459-6410
www.beautifulgardens.org

KUSA Seed Society

P.O. Box 761
Ojai, California 93024

Send $2.50 and a self-addressed stamped envelope to receive their seed and literature catalogue.

Native Seeds/SEARCH

526 North Fourth Avenue
Tucson, Arizona 85705
520-622-5561
www.azstarnet.com/~nss

Redwood City Seed Company

P.O. Box 361
Redwood City, California 94064
650-325-7333
www.ecoseeds.com

Seeds of Change

P.O. Box 15700
Santa Fe, New Mexico 87506
888-762-7333
www.store.yahoo.com/seedsofchange

Preserves, Glacéed and Dried Fruits, Spices, and Other Sweet Bread Ingredients and Bakeware

See also listings for The California Press, The Baker's Catalogue, and Williams-Sonoma.

American Spoon Foods

1668 Clarion Avenue
P.O. Box 566
Petoskey, Michigan 49770
800-222-5886
www.spoonfoods.com

Dried Michigan tart cherries, blueberries, raspberries, and wonderful jamlike spreadable fruit preserves.

Dean & Deluca

560 Broadway
New York, New York 10012
900-999-0306 ext. 268
www.deandeluca.com

New York's famous food purveyor offers, among other things, European bakeware, glacéed fruits, chocolate, cocoa powder, vanilla beans and extracts, *marrons glacés, crème de marrons,* and nuts.

Jaffe Bros.

28560 Lilac Road
Valley Center, California 92082
760-749-1133
www.organicfruitsandnuts.com

Excellent resource for organic dried fruits, raisins, nuts, and seeds.

La Cuisine

323 Cameron Street
Alexandria, Virginia 22314
800-521-1176
www.lacuisineus.com

European bakeware, Silpat baking sheets, hand nut and poppy seed grinder, Valhrona chocolate, cocoa powders, Tahitian vanilla beans and extracts, Swiss glacéed fruits, candied citrus peels, dried berries, shelled pistachios, whole peeled hazelnuts, silver dragées, gold and silver leaf and dust (great for fancy decorating), marzipan decorations, and pearl sugar. I like their India Tree Sugars, especially Dark Muscovado brown sugar (the best brown sugar I have ever tasted), and their sparkling sugars in emerald, ultra violet, hot pink, and other colors great for sprinkling over a powdered sugar icing. Their newsletter *A La Carte* is really fun to read.

Maison Glass

P.O. Box 317H
Scarsdale, New York
800-822-5564

European glacéed fruits, candied chestnuts, and chestnut products for baking; source for my favorite imported chestnut flour.

Miles Kimball

41 West Eighth Avenue
Oshkosh, Wisconsin 54906
920-231-1992
www.mileskimball.com

This catalog offers special bags for storing and giving bread machine breads.

Paradigm Food Works

5775 SW Jean Road, Suite 106A
Lake Oswego, Oregon 97035
800-234-0250

You can order many different chocolates—Guittard, Ghirardelli, Lindt, Merckens, and Peter's—from Paradigm.

Penzeys Spices
582 W19362 Apollo Drive
P.O. Box 993
Muskego, Wisconsin 53150
800-741-7787
www.penzeys.com

Penzeys has exemplary herbs and spices, both whole and ground, extracts, and spice blends. Some of the spices are very specialized, such as ground poppy seeds. They sell true cinnamon from Ceylon and cassia cinnamon from Indonesia (Korintje), China (Tunghing), and Vietnam (my favorite). They also sell cinnamon, rosemary, and saffron oils and single- or double-strength vanilla extracts from Madagascar, Tahiti, and Mexico (especially hard to find). Their catalog has history and stories about the spices, as well as recipes.

Scharffen Berger Chocolate Maker, Inc.
250 South Maple Avenue, Unit C
South San Francisco, California 94080
800-930-4528
www.scharffen-berger.com

This company sells their own extra-bittersweet premium domestic chocolate.

Sweet Celebrations
P.O. Box 39426
Edina, Minnesota 55439
800-328-6722
sweetc.com

This used to be the Maid of Scandinavia catalog; it offers baking resources that no one else does, such as a *lefse* griddle. Order decorating and sanding sugars, vanilla beans and extracts, powdered eggs, cocoa butter, chocolate, almond paste, candied fruits, and nuts.

GENERAL INDEX

C

RECIPE INDEX

C

G

O

P